Fodor's
NORTHERN
CALIFORNIA

Portions of this book appear in *Fodor's California*.

WELCOME TO NORTHERN CALIFORNIA

It's easy to tap into the good life in Northern California. Between rounds of golf at Pebble Beach, winding drives along the breathtaking coast, or scenic treks through Yosemite National Park, you can indulge in a wealth of top-notch outdoor activities. In Napa and Sonoma, eating and drinking are cultivated as high arts. You can sip wine at picturesque vineyards and then dine at stellar locavore restaurants. Urban pleasures await in San Francisco, too, where cable cars zip through vibrant neighborhoods lined with chic boutiques and cutting-edge museums.

TOP REASONS TO GO

★ **San Francisco:** This diverse city beguiles with natural beauty and contagious energy.

★ **Wine Country:** Top-notch whites and reds in Napa, Sonoma, and beyond.

★ **Feasts:** Cutting-edge cuisine, food trucks, fusion flavors, farmers' markets.

★ **Stunning Scenery:** Picture-perfect backdrops from the Golden Gate Bridge to redwoods.

★ **Outdoor Adventures:** National park excursions, hiking, and golfing are all excellent.

★ **Road Trips:** The Pacific Coast Highway offers spectacular views and thrills aplenty.

Fodor's NORTHERN CALIFORNIA

Editorial: Douglas Stallings, *Editorial Director*; Salwa Jabado and Margaret Kelly, *Senior Editors*; Alexis Kelly, Jacinta O'Halloran, and Amanda Sadlowski, *Editors*; Teddy Minford, *Content Editor*; Rachael Roth, *Content Manager*

Design: Tina Malaney, *Art Director*

Photography: Jennifer Arnow, *Senior Photo Editor*

Maps: Rebecca Baer, *Senior Map Editor*; Mark Stroud, *Cartographer*

Production: Jennifer DePrima, *Editorial Production Manager*; Carrie Parker, *Senior Production Editor*; Elyse Rozelle, *Production Editor*; David Satz, *Director of Content Production*

Business & Operations: Chuck Hoover, *Chief Marketing Officer*; Joy Lai, *Vice President and General Manager*; Stephen Horowitz, *Head of Business Development and Partnerships*

Public Relations: Joe Ewaskiw, *Manager*

Writers: Cheryl Crabtree, Amanda Kuehn Carroll, Denise M. Leto, Daniel Mangin, Steve Pastorino, Andrea Powell, Rebecca Flint Marx, and Jerry James Stone, Claire Deeks van der Lee

Editors: Salwa Jabado (lead editor), Margaret Kelly (San Francisco and Napa and Sonoma editor)

Production Editor: Jennifer DePrima

Production Design: Liliana Guia

14th Edition

ISBN 978-1-101-88016-6

ISSN 1543–1045

All details in this book are based on information supplied to us at press time. Always confirm information when it matters, especially if you're making a detour to visit a specific place. Fodor's expressly disclaims any liability, loss, or risk, personal or otherwise, that is incurred as a consequence of the use of any of the contents of this book.

PRINTED IN THE UNITED STATES OF AMERICA

10 9 8 7 6 5 4 3 2 1

CONTENTS

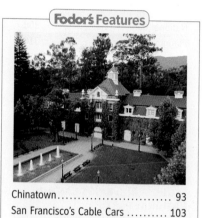

Fodor's Features

MAPS

ABOUT THIS GUIDE

Fodor's Recommendations
Everything in this guide is worth doing—we don't cover what isn't—but exceptional sights, hotels, and restaurants are recognized with additional accolades. Fodor'sChoice★ indicates our top recommendations. Care to nominate a new place? Visit Fodors.com/contact-us.

Trip Costs
We list prices wherever possible to help you budget well. Hotel and restaurant price categories from **$** to **$$$$** are noted alongside each recommendation. For hotels, we include the lowest cost of a standard double room in high season. For restaurants, we cite the average price of a main course at dinner or, if dinner isn't served, at lunch. For attractions, we always list adult admission fees; discounts are usually available for children, students, and senior citizens.

Hotels
Our local writers vet every hotel to recommend the best overnights in each price category, from budget to expensive. Unless otherwise specified, you can expect private bath, phone, and TV in your room. *For expanded hotel reviews and deals, visit Fodors.com.*

Top Picks	Hotels &
★ Fodor'sChoice	Restaurants
	⌂ Hotel
Listings	⤵ Number of
✉ Address	rooms
✉ Branch address	ⵟⵔ Meal plans
☎ Telephone	✕ Restaurant
🖷 Fax	⌂ Reservations
⊕ Website	🏛 Dress code
✉ E-mail	▭ No credit cards
🎟 Admission fee	$ Price
⊙ Open/closed times	**Other**
Ⓜ Subway	⇨ See also
⧋ Directions or Map coordinates	☞ Take note
	🏌 Golf facilities

Restaurants
Unless we state otherwise, restaurants are open for lunch and dinner daily. We mention dress code only when there's a specific requirement and reservations only when they're essential or not accepted.

Credit Cards
The hotels and restaurants in this guide typically accept credit cards. If not, we'll say so.

EUGENE FODOR

Hungarian-born Eugene Fodor (1905–91) began his travel career as an interpreter on a French cruise ship. The experience inspired him to write *On the Continent* (1936), the first guidebook to receive annual updates and discuss a country's way of life as well as its sights. Fodor later joined the U.S. Army and worked for the OSS in World War II. After the war, he kept up his intelligence work while expanding his guidebook series. During the Cold War, many guides were written by fellow agents who understood the value of insider information. Today's guides continue Fodor's legacy by providing travelers with timely coverage, insider tips, and cultural context.

EXPERIENCE
NORTHERN
CALIFORNIA

WHAT'S NEW IN NORTHERN CALIFORNIA

Foodie's Paradise

Great dining is a staple of the California lifestyle, and a new young generation of chefs is challenging old ideas about preparing and presenting great food. The food-truck frenzy continues to fuel movable feasts up and down the state. Esteemed chefs and urban foodies follow the trucks on Twitter as they move around cities 24/7 purveying delicious, cheap, fresh meals. You can find food-laden trucks at sports and entertainment venues, near parks and attractions, and on busy roads and boulevards—and the ensuing lines of hungry patrons.

Diners are also embracing the pop-up concept, where guest chefs offer innovative menus in unconventional settings for a limited time. These pop-up engagements are hosted anywhere from inside a warehouse to outside in a field. Often there is an air of secrecy and anticipation to them, with key details being revealed at the last moment. Visitors can look for local pop-ups listed on foodie websites such as Eater (⊕ *www.eater.com*).

California chefs continue to shop locally for produce and farmer-sourced meat, and many restaurants proudly display their vendors on the menu. Chefs and foodies alike engage in discourse on the ethics and politics of food and farming. Sustainably harvested seafood and "nose to tail" cooking, where as much of the animal as possible is used in an attempt to reduce food waste, are both hot topics these days.

Family Fun

Both kids and adults will be fascinated by the creatures on display in "Tentacles: The Astounding Lives of Octopuses, Squid and Cuttlefishes," the newest exhibit at the Monterey Bay Aquarium.

The supersize and hands-on exhibits at San Francisco's Exploratorium continue to challenge and fascinate visitors of all ages. With trees as tall as they come, the Children's Redwood Forest in Humboldt Redwoods State Park is a great place for kids to romp through some awe-inspiring landscapes.

Wine Discoveries

California offers oenophiles ample opportunities for new discoveries beyond the traditional California Wine Country. Across the state, vineyards are going up in unlikely places.

Venturing just beyond the traditional wine destinations of Napa and Sonoma counties will reward visitors with hidden gems. Areas such as the Petaluma Gap and the Sierra Foothills offer plenty of vineyards to explore. Visitors to Lake Tahoe can even take in some wine tasting at the Truckee River Winery, claiming to be the highest and coldest winery in the nation.

All Aboard

Riding the rails can be a satisfying experience, particularly in California where the distances between destinations sometimes run into the hundreds of miles. You can save money on gas and parking, avoid freeway traffic, and see some of the best the state has to offer. California just broke ground on a high-speed rail project linking San Francisco to Los Angeles. In 2030, when the $68-billion project is complete, the train will make the run between the two cities in less than three hours.

Until then, the best trip is on the luxuriously appointed *Coast Starlight*, a long-distance train with sleeping cars that runs between Seattle and Los Angeles, passing some of California's most beautiful coastline as it hugs the beach. For the best surf-side viewing, get a seat or a room on the left side of the train and ride south to north.

Homegrown Hospitality

Agritourism in California isn't new, but it is on the rise, with farm tours and agricultural festivals sprouting up everywhere.

Wine Country is a particularly fertile area—spurred by the success of vineyards, the area's lavender growers and olive-oil producers have started welcoming visitors. Sonoma County Farm Trail maintains an excellent map and guide to visiting producers in the area.

State of the Arts

California's beauty-obsessed citizens aren't the only ones opting for a fresh look these days: its esteemed art museums are also having a bit of work done.

The San Francisco Museum of Modern Art (SFMOMA) reopened in 2016 after a major expansion project vastly increased the museum's exhibition and support space.

WHAT'S
WHERE

1 Monterey Bay Area.
Postcard-perfect Monterey,
Victorian-flavored Pacific
Grove, and exclusive Carmel
all share this stretch of
California coast. To the north,
Santa Cruz boasts a board-
walk, a UC campus, and
plenty of surfers.

2 San Francisco. To see why
so many have left their hearts
here, you need to visit the
city's iconic neighborhoods—
posh Pacific Heights, the
Hispanic Mission, and
gay-friendly Castro.

3 The Bay Area. The area
that rings San Francisco is
nothing like the city—but it is
home to some of the nation's
great universities, fabulous
bay views, Silicon Valley, and
Alice Waters's Chez Panisse.

4 Napa and Sonoma. With
award-winning vintages, luxe
lodgings, and epicurean eats,
Napa and Sonoma counties
retain their title as *the* California Wine Country.

5 The North Coast. The star
attractions here are natural
ones, from the secluded
beaches and wave-battered
bluffs of Point Reyes National
Seashore to the towering
redwood forests.

**6 Redwood National
Park.** More than 200 miles
of trails, ranging from easy
to strenuous, allow visitors
to see these spectacular
trees in their primitive
environments.

7 Eastern Sierra. In the
Mammoth Lakes region,
sawtooth mountains and
deep powdery snowdrifts
create the state's premier
conditions for skiing and
snowboarding.

**8 Yosemite National
Park.** The views immortalized by photographer Ansel
Adams—towering granite
monoliths, verdant glacial
valleys, and lofty water-
falls—are still camera-ready.

**9 Sequoia and Kings
Canyon National Parks.**
The sight of ancient
redwoods towering above
jagged mountains is
breathtaking.

**10 Sacramento and the
Gold Country.** The 1849
gold rush that built San
Francisco and Sacramento
began here, and the former
mining camps strung along
185 miles of Highway 49
replay their past to the hilt.

11 Lake Tahoe. With miles
of crystalline water reflect-
ing the peaks of the High
Sierra, Lake Tahoe is the
perfect setting for activities
like hiking and golfing in
summer and skiing and
snowmobiling in winter.

12 The Far North. California's far northeast corner is
home to snowcapped Mt.
Shasta and the pristine
Trinity Wilderness.

NORTHERN CALIFORNIA PLANNER

When to Go
Because they offer activities indoors and out, the top California cities rate as all-seasons destinations.

Yosemite is ideal in late spring because roads closed in winter are reopened, and the park's waterfalls—swollen with melting snow—run fast. Autumn is "crush time" in all the wine destinations. Ski resorts typically open around Thanksgiving (they sometimes remain in operation into June).

CLIMATE
It's difficult to generalize about the state's weather beyond saying that precipitation comes in winter and summer is dry in most places. As a rule, inland regions are hotter in summer and colder in winter, compared with coastal areas, which are relatively cool year-round. Fog is a potential hazard any day of the year in coastal regions. As you climb into the mountains, seasonal variations are more apparent: winter brings snow (at elevations above 3,000 feet), autumn is crisp, spring can go either way, and summer is sunny and warm, with an occasional thundershower.

MICROCLIMATES
Mountains separate the California coastline from the state's interior, and the weather can sometimes vary dramatically within a 15-minute drive. On a foggy summer day in San Francisco, you'll be grateful for a sweater—but head 50 miles north inland to Napa Valley, and you'll likely be content in short sleeves. Day and nighttime temperatures can also vary greatly. In Sacramento, the mercury hits the 90s and occasionally exceeds 100°F on August afternoons. Yet as darkness falls, it sometimes plummets to 40°F.

Car Travel
Driving may be a way of life in California, but it isn't cheap (gas prices here are usually among the highest in the nation). It's also not for the fainthearted; you've surely heard horror stories about the Bay Area's freeways, but even the state's scenic highways and byways have their own hassles. For instance, on the dramatic Highway 1 coastal road, twists, turns, and divinely distracting vistas frequently slow traffic; in rainy season, mud slides can close the road altogether. ⚠ Never cross the double line to pass a slower car ahead of you. If you see that cars are backing up behind you, stop at the first available pullout to allow faster drivers to pass.

On California's notorious freeways, other rules apply. Nervous Nellies must resist the urge to stay in the two slow-moving lanes on the far right, used primarily by trucks. To drive at least the speed limit, get yourself in a middle lane. If you're ready to bend the rules a bit, the second lane (lanes are numbered from 1 starting at the center) moves about 5 mph faster. But avoid the far-left lane (the one next to the carpool lane), where speeds range from 75 mph to 90 mph.

Air Travel
Air travelers beginning or ending their vacation in San Francisco have two main airports to choose from: San Francisco International (SFO) or Oakland International (OAK). The former lands you closer to the city core (ground transportation will take about 20 minutes), but the latter is less heavily trafficked and less prone to fog delays. BART, the Bay Area's affordable rapid-transit system, serves both airports. So your decision will probably rest on which one has the best fares and connections for your route.

NORTHERN CALIFORNIA'S TOP EXPERIENCES

Hit the Road

Kings Canyon Highway, Redwood Highway, Tioga Pass, 17-Mile Drive, the Lake Tahoe loop: California has some splendid and challenging roads. You'll drive through a tunnel formed by towering redwood trees on the Redwood Highway. If you venture over the Sierras by way of Tioga Pass (through Yosemite in summer only), you'll see emerald green meadows, gray granite monoliths, and pristine blue lakes—and very few people.

Pan for Gold

Though California's gold rush ended more than a hundred years ago, you can still feel the forty-nine fever on the western face of the Sierra Nevada in Columbia, a well-preserved town populated by costumed interpreters, where you can pan for gold or tour a mine. Or visit Bodie, an eerie ghost town in the eastern Sierra that remains in a state of "arrested decay."

Think Globally, Eat Locally

Over the years California cuisine has evolved from a mere trend into a respected gastronomic tradition: one that pairs local, often organic or sustainable, ingredients with techniques inspired by European, Asian, and, increasingly, Indian and Middle Eastern cookery.

People-Watch

Opportunities for world-class people-watching abound in California. Just saunter the rainbow-flagged streets of San Francisco's Castro neighborhood or the century-old boardwalk in time-warped, resiliently boho Santa Cruz.

Be Transported

San Franciscans take cable cars seriously—and riding on one is a must-do. You may even want to visit the (free!) Cable Car Museum to get a handle on the inner workings or just ring a gripman's bell. But, the city's options for vintage public transport doesn't end there: the lesser known F line streetcars are every bit as photogenic, and they have shorter lines.

Go Wild

California communities host hundreds of annual events, but some of the best are organized by Mother Nature. In Pacific Grove masses of monarch butterflies reliably arrive for their winter vacation every year in October. If you can't make it there, visit the butterfly sanctuary in the California Academy of Sciences in San Francisco.

NORTHERN CALIFORNIA TODAY

The People

California is as much a state of mind as a state in the union—a kind of perpetual promised land that has represented many things to many people. In the 18th century, Spanish missionaries came seeking converts and gold. In the 19th, miners rushed here to search for gold. And, in the years since, a long line of Dust Bowl farmers, land speculators, Haight-Ashbury hippies, migrant workers, dot-commers, real estate speculators, and would-be actors have come chasing their own dreams.

The result is a population that leans toward idealism—without necessarily being as liberal as you might think. (Remember, this is Ronald Reagan's old stomping ground.) And despite the stereotype of the blue-eyed, blond surfer, California's population is not homogeneous either. Ten million people who live here (more than 27% of Californians) are foreign born. Almost half hail from Latin American countries; another third emigrated from Asia, following the waves of Chinese workers who arrived in the 1860s to build the railroads and subsequent waves of Indochinese refugees from the Vietnam War.

The Politics

What's blue and red and green all over? California: a predominantly Democratic state with an aggressive "go green" agenda and policies that make California the greenest state in the nation, supporting more green construction, wind farms, and solar panels.

The Economy

Leading all other states in terms of the income generated by agriculture, tourism, entertainment, and industrial activity, California has the country's most diverse state economy. Moreover, with a gross state product of more than $2 trillion, California would be one of the top 10 economies *in the world* if it were an independent nation.

Despite its wealth ($61,818 median household income) and productivity, California took a large hit in the 2007 recession, but the Golden State's economic history is filled with boom and bust cycles—beginning with the mid-19th-century gold rush that started it all. Optimists already have their eyes on the next potential boom: high-tech and bioresearch, "green companies" focused on alternative energy, renewables, electric cars, and the like.

The Culture

Cultural organizations flourish in California. San Francisco—a city with less than 900,000 residents—has well-regarded ballet, opera, and theater companies, and is home to one of the continent's most noteworthy orchestras. Museums like San Francisco Museum of Modern Art (SFMOMA) and the de Young also represent the city's ongoing commitment to the arts.

The Parks and Preserves

Cloud-spearing redwood groves, snow-tipped mountains, canyon-slashed deserts, primordial lava beds, and a seemingly endless coast: California's natural diversity is staggering—and efforts to protect it started early. Yosemite, the first national park, was established here in 1890, and the National Park Service now oversees 32 sites in California (more than in any other state). When you factor in 280 state parks—which encompass underwater preserves, historic sites, wildlife reserves, dune systems, and other sensitive habitats—the number of acres involved is almost as impressive as the topography itself.

Due to encroaching development and pollution, keeping these natural treasures in pristine condition is an ongoing challenge. For instance, Sequoia and Kings Canyon (which is plagued by pesticides and other agricultural pollutants blown in from the San Joaquin Valley) has been named America's "smoggiest park" by the National Parks Conservation Association, and the Environmental Protection Agency has designated it as an "ozone nonattainment area with levels of ozone pollution that threaten human health."

There is no question that Californians love their 280 state parks. Nearly every park has its grass-roots supporters, who volunteer to raise money, volunteer as rangers, and work other jobs to keep the parks open.

The Cuisine

California gave us McDonald's, Denny's, Carl's Jr., Taco Bell, and, of course, In-N-Out Burger. Fortunately for those of us with fast-clogging arteries, the state also kick-started the health-food movement. Back in the 1970s, California-based chefs put American cuisine on the culinary map by focusing on freshly prepared seasonal ingredients.

Today, this focus has spawned the "locavore" or sustainable food movement—followers try to consume only food produced within a 100-mile radius of where they live, since processing and refining food and transporting goods over long distances is bad for both the body and the environment. This isn't much of a restriction in California, where a huge variety of crops grow year-round. Some 350 cities and towns have certified farmers' markets—and their stalls are bursting with a variety of goods. California has been America's top agricultural producer for the last 50 years, growing more fruits and vegetables than any other state. Dairies and ranches also thrive here, and fishing fleets harvest fish and shellfish from the rich waters offshore.

NORTHERN CALIFORNIA TOP ATTRACTIONS

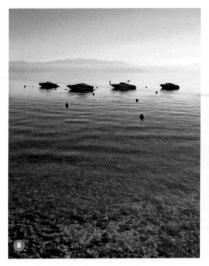

The Golden Gate Bridge

(A) Catching that first glimpse of the iconic Golden Gate Bridge is bound to take your breath away. Completed in 1937, the art deco suspension bridge has become the internationally recognized symbol of San Francisco. While often swathed in an otherworldly fog, on a clear day the city and bay views from the bridge are spectacular.

Lake Tahoe

(B) Deep, clear, and intensely blue, this forest-rimmed body of water straddling the California–Nevada border is one of the continent's prettiest alpine lakes. That environmental controls can keep it that way is something of a miracle, given Tahoe's popularity. Throngs of outdoor adventurers flock to the California side to ski, hike, bike, and boat. On the Nevada side, where casinos are king, gambling often wins out over fresh-air activities—but natural wonders are never far away.

Monterey Bay Aquarium

This aquarium is one of the nation's most spectacular and most respected. A multi-story kelp forest, the million-plus-gallon tank in the Open Seas exhibit, and a dramatically lighted jellyfish experience are just some of the highlights. The aquarium also impresses behind the scenes with its extensive marine research programs and conservation efforts.

Napa Valley

(C) Despite impressive wines being produced throughout the state, the Napa Valley remains California's original and most famous destination for wine. Although the vineyard-blanketed hills are undeniably scenic, the wine itself remains the big draw here. From household names to producers with a cult following, budding oenophiles can educate their palettes on scores of tours and tasting sessions.

Point Reyes National Seashore

(D) Aside from the namesake seashore, this Marin County preserve encompasses ecosystems that range from woodlands and marshlands to heathlike grasslands. The range of wildlife here is equally diverse—depending on when you visit, expect to see gray whales, rare Tule elk, and almost 500 species of birds. December through March you can also see male elephant seals compete for mates.

Redwood National and State Park

A United Nations World Heritage Site, this park along California's north coast is one of the most serene spots on Earth. It holds groves of towering ancient redwood trees, including the world's tallest tree at nearly 380 feet. Drive along the Redwood Highway to experience the majesty of the trees.

San Francisco's Cable Cars

(E) Pricey and touristy for sure, but a chance to ride on one of San Francisco's classic cable cars should not be passed up. Clutching a handrail while riding downhill on one of the exterior running boards can be exhilarating or downright frightening, depending on whom you ask. Sitting inside offers a tamer ride, yet you can watch the gripman at work, listen to the clanging of the bell, and take in the sights as you roll by.

Yosemite National Park

(F) Nature looms large here, both literally and figuratively. In addition to hulking Half Dome, the park is home to El Capitan (the world's largest exposed granite monolith, rising 3,593 feet above the glacier-carved valley floor) and Yosemite Falls (North America's tallest cascade). In Yosemite's signature stand of giant sequoias—the Mariposa Grove—even the trees are Bunyanesque.

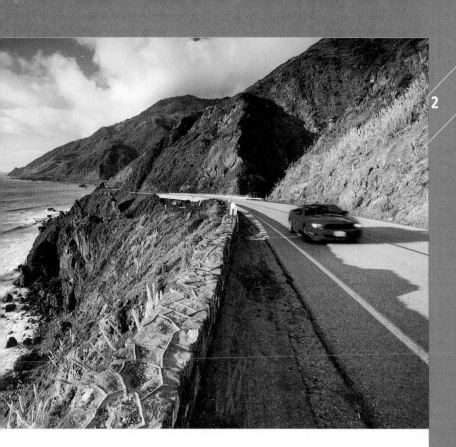

NORTHERN CALIFORNIA'S BEST ROAD TRIPS

GREAT ITINERARIES

No trip to California would be complete without a drive through the state's spectacular scenery. However, adding a road trip to your itinerary is not just a romantic idea: it's often a practical one, too. A road trip is a great way to link together more than one urban area or to venture into some more remote areas of this massive state. Whether you have just a few days or longer to spare, these itineraries will help you hit the road.

THE BEST OF THE NORTHERN COAST, 5 DAYS

Hit the highlights of Northern California in one itinerary: scenic coastal drives, quaint windswept towns, wine tasting, culinary delights, and majestic redwood forests. This route can be done as part of a longer trip north towards the Oregon border, or as part of a loop back down to San Francisco.

Day 1: Marin County and Point Reyes National Seashore
(Without stops, Point Reyes National Seashore is about 1½ hrs by car from San Francisco on Hwy 1. Point Reyes Lighthouse is 45 mins by car from the visitor center.)

As you head out of San Francisco on the Golden Gate Bridge, be sure to pull over at the **scenic lookout** on the north side and take in the spectacular views looking back at the city skyline. If you haven't yet checked out the picturesque harbor community of **Sausalito** just north of the bridge, now is your chance. It will be hard not to linger, but there is much to see today. Bidding San Francisco farewell, you will quickly find yourself in the natural beauty of Marin County. Exit the 101 onto Highway 1 at the chic suburb

Mill Valley, and head towards **Muir Woods National Monument.** Walking among the coastal redwoods, it is hard to imagine San Francisco lies just a few miles away. However, the proximity to the city means that Muir Woods is often crowded, and parking can be difficult if you don't arrive early.

From Muir Woods, continue on Highway 1 past the laid-back beach towns of **Stinson Beach** and **Bolinas** before continuing on to **Point Reyes National Seashore.** Spend the remainder of the day at the park tide pooling, kayaking, hiking one of the many trails, or exploring the **Point Reyes Lighthouse.** In the winter, be on the lookout for migrating gray whales.

The tiny town of **Point Reyes Station** offers a selection of shops and dining options, including **Tomales Bay Foods,** a provisions stop favored by foodies. Spend a quiet evening in town and overnight at one of the small inns nearby.

Day 2: Healdsburg
(Point Reyes Station to Healdsburg, via Jenner, is 2 hrs by car.)

Continue north on Highway 1 past **Bodega Bay,** made famous by the Alfred Hitchcock movie *The Birds.* At Jenner, known for its resident harbor seals, turn on Route 116 and follow the Russian River inland, taking time to stop at a winery or two along the way.

Ditch the car in **Healdsburg** and enjoy strolling through the appealing town square with its excellent selection of tasting rooms and boutiques. The town is home to many acclaimed restaurants and luxurious hotels and is an excellent place to stop for the night. The town's compact layout and quality offerings make Healdsburg a favorite among wine-country destinations.

Eureka
Mackerricher State Park
Ferndale
101

Humboldt
Redwoods State Park

The Avenue of
the Giants

Garberville

PACIFIC
OCEAN

NEVADA

1

Fort Bragg

Mendocino
Little River
Anderson Valley

Philo
Boonville

128

Healdsburg

Lake
Tahoe

Bodega Bay
Point Reyes National Seashore

1

Point Reyes Station
Marin County
Mill Valley
Sausalito
San Francisco

Bolinas
Stinson Beach

Days 3 and 4: Anderson Valley and Mendocino

(Mendocino is 2 hrs by car from Healdsburg. Budget plenty of time for stops in Anderson Valley to ensure the end of this scenic drive is done in the daylight.)

Driving north on the 101 from Healdsburg, pick up Highway 128 at Cloverdale and head into the **Anderson Valley.** This wine region is famous for its excellent Pinot Noir and Gewürztraminer, and the laid-back atmosphere of its tasting rooms can be a refreshing alternative to those in Napa Valley. **Navarro Vineyards, Roederer Estate,** and **Husch Vineyards** are all recommended. The small towns of **Boonville** and **Philo** have several high-quality dining options, and the latter is home to the **Philo Apple Farm's** beloved farm stand.

Continuing on to the coast, Highway 128 follows the Navarro River through several miles of dense and breathtaking redwood forest ending at the ocean. From here you meet up again with Highway 1 as it winds its way along a spectacularly scenic portion of the coast.

With their excellent dining and lodging options, the towns of **Mendocino** and **Little River,** just to the south, are great choices for your overnight stay. Spend the next day and a half exploring the

area. Opportunities for stunning coastal walks abound, including **MacKerricher** and **Van Damme State Parks.** Hike through the unique Pygmy Forest in Van Damme and visit the **Glass Beach** in Fort Bragg. Be sure to save some time to explore the town of Mendocino itself with its quaint New England–style architecture and selection of art galleries and boutiques.

Day 5: Humboldt Redwoods State Park and the Avenue of the Giants

(Mendocino to Eureka via the Avenue of the Giants is 3 hrs by car.)

Driving north on Highway 1, the road eventually curves inland and meets up with U.S. 101 near Leggett. Head north on the 101 to Garberville, a good place to take a break before heading on to the redwoods.

For all the hype, a drive through **The Avenue of the Giants** will still take your breath away. Pick up a copy of the self-guided tour as you enter the 32-mile stretch of road running alongside some of the tallest trees on the planet. The drive weaves through portions of the larger **Humboldt Redwoods State Park.** Take time to get out of the car and take a short hike through Founders Grove or Rockefeller Forest.

Continue on to **Ferndale,** a picturesque town of colorful Victorian buildings that is now largely a tourist destination. You can overnight here, or carry on to the regional city of **Eureka** for a wider variety of dining and accommodation.

From here, you can continue your way up the coast through the **Redwood National Forest** and on to the Oregon border. Alternatively, you can head south on the 101 and either return to **San Francisco,** or easily combine this itinerary with a trip to **Napa Valley** and the rest of **Sonoma.**

ROADS LESS TRAVELED: DISCOVERING THE NORTHERN INTERIOR, 5 DAYS

Mountain peaks, alpine lakes, a lush waterfall, and a striking volcanic landscape are all included on this tour of California's far north. The drive packs a big scenic punch in a short amount of time, and without the crowds found elsewhere in California's national parks. The remote roads and high elevations make parts of this route subject to snow closures well into the spring. Check current road conditions before setting out.

Day 1: Sacramento to Chico
(1½ hrs by car.)

Start your trip with a tour of the highlights of California's capital city, **Sacramento.** Wander the cobblestone streets and historic storefronts of Old Sacramento to get a sense of the city during its gold-rush days. Enjoy a horse-drawn carriage ride through the historic neighborhood or take a cruise along the riverfront. Train enthusiasts of all ages will enjoy the walk-through exhibits at the nearby **California State Railroad Museum.** Finally, don't leave town without taking a guided tour of the magnificent **Capitol** building.

When you have finished your tour of Sacramento, drive north on Highway 99 to **Chico.** Overnighting in Chico gets you a jump-start on the next day's drive, with the added bonus of spending time in this surprisingly bustling agricultural-meets-university town. Stop at the legendary **Sierra Nevada Brewing Company** for a free tour, or enjoy a meal at the brewpub.

Days 2 and 3: Lassen Volcanic National Park
(1½–2 hrs by car from Chico.)

Get an early start on your day, as spectacular scenery awaits you. From Chico, follow Highway 32 towards Chester and branch north at Highway 36 to reach the southern entrance of **Lassen Volcanic National Park.** Spend the next two days exploring the area's geothermal activity and dramatic landscape. Highlights include a hike alongside the bubbling mud pots and hot springs of **Bumpass Hell trail,** views of **Lassen Peak** from Manzanita Lake, or an ascent of the peak itself. The 185-mile **Lassen Scenic Byway** circles the volcanic park and neighboring Lassen National Forest. If you plan ahead, you might score a reservation at **Drakesbad Guest Ranch** or at one of the campgrounds within the park. Otherwise, you will need to bunk in Chester or another neighboring town. Note: in winter, the park is closed to vehicles. Check current road conditions before setting out. If the park is closed, the itinerary can easily be modified to skip it and continue straight to McArthur-Burney Falls from Chico via Highway 299.

Day 4: McArthur-Burney Falls National Park and Mt. Shasta

(McArthur-Burney Falls is about 45 mins by car from Manzanita Lake; the start of the Everitt Memorial Hwy. is approximately 1 hr and 10 mins from the falls.)

Follow Highway 89 north out of Lassen to **McArthur-Burney Falls Memorial State Park.** Arrive early on busy holidays and weekends, as the park entrance will close when filled to capacity. Inside the park, the 129-foot-high falls are a sight to behold as water cascades over the moss-covered rocks. The falls are located near the park visitor center, with a vista point and hiking trail leading down to the bottom.

When you've had your fill of the falls, continue north on Highway 89 to **Mt. Shasta.** Drive up the mountain on the paved Everitt Memorial Highway for incredible views. Time permitting, choose from one of the many day hikes along the route. Alternatively, in winter you can hit the slopes at the nearby **Mt.**

Shasta Board & Ski Park. The charming town of Mount Shasta makes a great place to overnight. Train enthusiasts might prefer to venture 10 miles south to **Dunsmuir** and overnight at the **Railroad Park Resort,** a collection of antique cabooses transformed into a motel.

Day 5: Lake Shasta and Redding

(The exit for Lake Shasta Caverns is approximately 50 mins by car from the town of Mount Shasta. It's another ½ hr by car to reach Redding.)

Drive south on Interstate 5 to Lakehead and take Exit 695 to the **Lake Shasta Caverns.** The two-hour tour of the glittering caverns also includes a boat ride. Tours are offered throughout the day, more frequently in summer.

Back aboveground, anglers and boating enthusiasts should head to one of the marinas dotting the lakeshore to charter the craft of their choice. Houseboats are particularly popular on Lake Shasta, but many rentals come with a two-night minimum. For those more interested in engineering than angling, the hour-long tour of the **Shasta Dam** takes you inside the second-largest concrete dam in the United States. If you are not staying overnight on the lake, drive south and conclude your tour in the nearby city of **Redding** for the best selection of dining and accommodation. Note: this itinerary is designed for those wanting to loop back around to Sacramento and the Bay Area, or to continue on toward either Lake Tahoe or the North Coast. If you plan on driving north into Oregon, visit Shasta Lake prior to Mt. Shasta (take Highway 299 west from Burney) and then continue on Interstate 5 north across the state line.

THE ULTIMATE WINE TRIP: NAPA AND SONOMA, 4 DAYS

On this four-day extravaganza, you'll taste well-known and under-the-radar wines, bed down in plush hotels, and dine at restaurants operated by celebrity chefs. Appointments are required for some of the tastings.

Day 1: Sonoma County
(1½–2 hrs by car from San Francisco, depending on traffic.)

Begin your tour in Geyserville, about 78 miles north of San Francisco on U.S. 101. Visit **Locals Tasting Room,** which pours the wines of special small wineries. Have lunch at nearby **Diavola** or **Catelli's,** then head south on U.S. 101 and Old Redwood Highway to **Healdsburg's J Vineyards and Winery,** known for sparkling wines, Pinot Grigio, and Pinot Noir. After a tasting, backtrack on Old Redwood Highway to Healdsburg. **Hôtel Les Mars** and **h2hotel** are two well-located spots to spend the night. Have dinner at **Chalkboard, Bravas Bar de Tapas,** or **Campo Fina,** all close by.

Day 2: Sonoma Wineries
(1 hr by car from Healdsburg to Glen Ellen.)

Interesting wineries dot the countryside surrounding Healdsburg, among them **Dry Creek Vineyard, Jordan Vineyard & Winery,** and **Unti Vineyards.** Dry Creek produces Zinfandel, Jordan makes Cabernet Sauvignon and Chardonnay, and Unti specializes in Zinfandel, Sangiovese, and obscure Italian and Rhône varietals. In the afternoon, head south on U.S. 101 and east on scenic Highway 12 to **Glen Ellen.** Visit **Jack London State Historic Park,** the memorabilia-filled home of the famous writer. Dine at **Aventine Glen Ellen** or **Glen Ellen Star** and stay at the **Olea Hotel.**

Day 3: Napa Valley
(Glen Ellen to St. Helena is about 30 mins by car without traffic. St. Helena to Yountville is about 15 mins by car, without stops.)

On Day 3, head east from Glen Ellen on Trinity Road, which twists and turns over the Mayacamas Mountains, eventually becoming the Oakville Grade. Unless you're driving, bask in the stupendous **Napa Valley** views. At Highway 29, drive north to **St. Helena.** Focus on history and architecture at **Charles Krug Winery** or let the art and wines at **Hall St. Helena** transport you. Take lunch downtown at **Cindy's Backstreet Kitchen.** Check out St. Helena's shopping, then head south on Highway 29 to Yountville for more shopping. With its mix of gift stores and galleries, **V Marketplace** is a good place to start.

Stay overnight at **Bardessono** or the **North Block Hotel,** both within walking distance of Yountville's famous restaurants. A meal at **The French Laundry** is many visitors' holy grail, but dining at **Bouchon, Bistro Jeanty, Redd,** or Chiarello's **Bottega** will also leave you feeling well served.

Day 4: Oakville to Carneros

(Just over 1 hr by car from Napa to San Francisco, without traffic.)

After breakfast, head north on Highway 29 to **Oakville,** where sipping wine at **Silver Oak Cellars, Nickel & Nickel,** or **B Cellars** will make clear why collectors covet Oakville Cabernet Sauvignons. Nickel & Nickel is on Highway 29; Silver Oak and B Cellars are east of it on Oakville Cross Road. Have a picnic at **Oakville Grocery,** in business on Highway 29 since 1881. Afterward, head south to Highway 121 and turn west to reach the Carneros District. Tour the **di Rosa** arts center (appointment required), then repair across the street to **Domaine Carneros,** which makes French-style sparkling wines. There's hardly a more elegant way to bid a Wine Country adieu than on the Domaine château's vineyard-view terrace before heading back to San Francisco. Give yourself plenty of time to get to your departure airport; traffic is generally heavy as you close in on the Bay Area.

Modifying the Route from San Francisco

The above itinerary is useful if traveling to Wine Country from points farther north. If you prefer to make a loop beginning and ending in San Francisco, the itinerary can be easily modified as follows: Day 1: Head north from San Francisco to the town of Sonoma (1 to 1½ hours by car, depending on traffic) and spend some time exploring the restaurants, shops, and tasting rooms lining the downtown plaza. Several excellent wineries operate nearby, including **Walt Wines** and **Patz & Hall.** From Sonoma, head north to Glen Ellen (20 minutes by car) and pick up the Glen Ellen itinerary described above. Day 2: Continue north to Healdsburg, following the above itinerary in reverse. Overnight in Healdsburg as described. Day 3: Head south on Highway 101 to River Road and then east on Mark Springs Road toward Calistoga (45 minutes by car), a town made famous by its hot springs and mud baths. If time permits, overnight at one of Calistoga's luxury retreats, such as the **Calistoga Ranch,** or enjoy a day of pampering at **Spa Solage.** Otherwise, head south to St. Helena (15 minutes by car) and complete the remainder of the road trip as outlined above.

SIERRA RICHES: YOSEMITE, GOLD COUNTRY, AND TAHOE, 10 DAYS

This tour will show you why Tony Bennett left his heart in San Francisco. It also includes some of the most beautiful places in a very scenic state, plus gold-rush-era history, and a chance to hike a trail or two.

Day 1: San Francisco

Straight from the airport, drop your bags at the lighthearted **Hotel Monaco** near **Union Square** and request a goldfish for your room. A Union Square stroll packs a wallop of people-watching, window-shopping, and architecture viewing. **Chinatown,** chock-full of dim sum shops, storefront temples, and open-air markets, promises authentic bites for lunch. Catch a Powell Street **cable car** to the end of the line and get off to see the bay views and the antique arcade games at **Musée Mécanique,** the hidden gem of otherwise mindless **Fisherman's Wharf.** No need to go any farther than cosmopolitan North Beach for cocktail hour, dinner, and live music.

Day 2: Golden Gate Park
(15 mins by car or taxi, 45 mins by public transport from Union Square.)

In **Golden Gate Park,** linger amid the flora of the **Conservatory of Flowers** and the **San Francisco Botanical Garden at Strybing Arboretum,** soak up some art at the **de Young Museum,** and find serene refreshment at the **San Francisco Japanese Tea Garden.** The Pacific surf pounds the cliffs below the **Legion of Honor** art museum, which has an exquisite view of the **Golden Gate Bridge**—when the fog stays away. Sunset cocktails at the circa-1909 **Cliff House** include a prospect over Seal Rock (actually occupied by sea lions). Eat dinner elsewhere: Pacific Heights, the Mission, and SoMa teem with excellent restaurants.

Day 3: Into the High Sierra
(4–5 hrs by car from San Francisco.)

First thing in the morning, pick up your rental car and head for the hills. Arriving in **Yosemite National Park, Bridalveil Fall,** and **El Capitan,** the 350-story granite monolith, greet you on your way to **Yosemite Village.** Ditch the car and pick up information and refreshment before hopping on the year-round shuttle to explore. Justly famous sights cram Yosemite Valley: massive **Half Dome** and **Sentinel Dome,** thundering **Yosemite Falls,** and wispy **Ribbon Fall** and **Nevada Fall.** Invigorating short hikes off the shuttle route lead to numerous vantage points. Celebrate your arrival in one of the world's most sublime spots with dinner in the dramatic **Majestic Hotel Dining Room** (formerly the Ahwahnee) and stay the night there (reserve well in advance).

Day 4: Yosemite National Park
(Yosemite shuttles run every 10–30 mins.)

Ardent hikers consider **John Muir Trail to Half Dome** a must-do, tackling the rigorous 12-hour round-trip to the top of Half Dome in search of life-changing vistas. For a less technical route, hike downhill from Glacier Point on Four-Mile Trail or **Panorama Trail,** the latter an all-day trek past waterfalls. Less demanding still is a drive to Wawona for a stroll in the **Mariposa Grove of Big Trees** and lunch at the 19th-century **Big Trees Lodge Dining Room** (formerly the Wawona). In bad weather, take shelter in the **Ansel Adams Gallery** and **Yosemite Museum;** in fair conditions, drive up to **Glacier Point** for a breathtaking sunset view.

Day 5: Gold Country South
(2½–3 hrs by car from Yosemite.)

Highway 49 traces the mother lode that yielded many fortunes in gold in the 1850s and 1860s. Step into a living gold-rush town at **Columbia State Historic Park,** where you can ride a stagecoach and pan for riches. **Sutter Creek's** well-preserved downtown bursts with shopping opportunities, but the vintage goods displayed at **Monteverde Store Museum** are not for sale. A different sort of vintage powers the present-day bonanza of **Shenandoah Valley,** heart of the Sierra Foothills Wine Country. Taste your way through Rhône-style blended Zinfandels and Syrahs at boutique wineries such as **Shenandoah Vineyards** and **Sobon Estate.** Amador City's 1879 **Imperial Hotel** places you firmly in the past for the night.

Emerald Bay State Park · Lake Tahoe · Zephyr Cove · South Lake Tahoe · Lake Tahoe-Nevada State Park · NEVADA · Nevada City · Grass Valley · Auburn · Gold Country North · Coloma · Placerville · Sacramento · GOLD COUNTRY · Shenandoah Valley · Amador City · Sutter Creek · SIERRA NEVADA · Gold Country South · Columbia State Historic Park · Stockton · Into the High Sierra · San Francisco · PACIFIC OCEAN · Yosemite National Park

Day 6: Gold Country North
(2 hrs by car from Amador City to Nevada City.)

In **Placerville**, a mine shaft invites investigation at **Hangtown's Gold Bug Mine,** while **Marshall Gold Discovery State Historic Park** encompasses most of **Coloma** and preserves the spot where James Marshall's 1849 find set off the California gold rush. Old Town **Auburn**, with its museums and courthouse, makes a good lunch stop, but if you hold out until you reach Grass Valley you can try authentic miners' pasties. A tour of **Empire Mine State Historic Park** takes you into a mine, and a few miles away horse-drawn carriages ply the narrow, shop-lined streets of downtown **Nevada City.** Both Nevada City and **Grass Valley** hold a collection of bed-and-breakfast inns that date back to gold-rush days. For more contemporary accommodations backtrack to Auburn or Placerville.

Day 7: Lake Tahoe
(1 hr by car from Nevada City, 2 hrs from Placerville.)

Jewel-like **Lake Tahoe** is a straight shot east of Placerville on Highway 50; stop for picnic provisions in commercial **South Lake Tahoe.** A stroll past the three magnificent estates in **Pope-Baldwin Recreation Area** hints at the sumptuous lakefront summers once enjoyed by the elite. High above a glittering cove, **Emerald Bay State Park** offers one of the best lake views as well as a steep hike down to (and back up from) **Vikingsholm,** a replica 9th-century Scandinavian castle. Another fine, old mansion—plus a nature preserve and many hiking trails—lies in **Sugar Pine Point State Park.** Tahoe City offers more history and ample dining and lodging choices.

Day 8: Exploring Lake Tahoe
(Sightseeing cruise lasts 2 hrs.)

The picture-perfect beaches and bays of **Lake Tahoe–Nevada State Park** line the Nevada shoreline, a great place to bask in the sun or go mountain biking. For a different perspective of the lake, get out on the azure water aboard the sternwheeler MS *Dixie II* from **Zephyr Cove.** In South Lake Tahoe, another view unfurls as the **Heavenly Gondola** travels 2½ miles up a mountain. Keep your adrenaline pumping into the evening with some action at the massive casinos clustered in Stateline, Nevada.

Day 9: Return to San Francisco
(About 4 hrs by car from Tahoe City.)

After a long morning of driving, return your rental car in San Francisco and soak up some more urban excitement. Good options include a late lunch at the **Ferry Building,** followed by a visit to the **San Francisco Museum of Modern Art,** or lunch in **Japantown** followed by shopping in **Pacific Heights.** There is excellent people-watching in the **Castro** and the **Haight.** Say good-bye to Northern California at one of the plush lounges or trendy bars in the downtown hotels.

Day 10: Departure
(SFO is 30 mins from downtown both by BART public transport and by car, without traffic.)

Check the weather and your flight information before you start out for the airport: fog sometimes causes delays at SFO. On a clear day, your flight path might give you one last fabulous glimpse of the City by the Bay.

THE INLAND ROUTE: SAN FRANCISCO TO LOS ANGELES VIA THE SIERRAS, 5 DAYS

This itinerary provides an alternate to the more frequented coastal route between San Francisco and Los Angeles and takes in the splendid scenery of the Sierras. This trip just touches the surface of all that Yosemite, Kings Canyon, and Sequoia national parks have to offer. Avid naturalists might want to extend their time in the parks. Either way, plan on spending a few days on either end of the road trip to explore California's two most popular cities.

Day 1: San Francisco to Yosemite
(Yosemite is about 4 hrs from San Francisco by car, depending on traffic.)

Hit the road early for the day's long drive to **Yosemite National Park.** As you approach from Route 120, be sure to top up the tank as there are only a few gas stations within the park. Drive straight to the **Valley Visitor Center** to get an overview of the park. Stretch your legs on the easy loop trail to **Lower Yosemite Falls.** If daylight permits and you are looking for something a bit more strenuous, tackle the **Mist Trail** leading to **Bridalveil and Vernal Falls.** Reserve lodging early at the central valley lodges or campgrounds. Even if you aren't staying there, treat yourself to dinner at the renowned **Majestic Hotel Dining Room** (formerly the Ahwahnee).

Day 2: Exploring Yosemite
Spend today tackling some of the sights in the northern and central areas of the park. Options include the 8½-mile **Panorama Trail** from **Glacier Point** back down to the valley or a drive along the impossibly scenic Tioga Road to **Tuolumne Meadows.** Alternatively, consider a horseback or photography tour. Hikers looking to tackle the strenuous ascent of **Half Dome** should plan on spending an additional day in the park. While some do attempt to complete the trail in one very long day, many consider camping overnight in Little Yosemite Valley to be preferable. If attempting Half Dome, don't forget to secure your wilderness permit in advance. Spend a second night in Yosemite Valley.

Day 3: Yosemite to Kings Canyon
(The Wawona area of the park is about 1 hr by car from Yosemite Valley. From Wawona, Grants Grove Village in Kings Canyon is about 3 hrs by car.)

Make your way south to the **Wawona** section of Yosemite and don't miss the **Mariposa Grove of Big Trees** to see the famous Grizzly Giant before leaving the park. From here, drive south out of Yosemite and link up with Route 180 heading into **Kings Canyon National Park.** Again, remember to get gas along the route. Once inside Kings Canyon, continue along Route 180 for the 30-mile stretch known as the **Kings Canyon Scenic Byway** as it winds between Grant Grove Village and Zumwalt Meadow. There are several vista points or opportunities to stretch your legs en route. Towards the end, enjoy an easy 1½-mile hike along the **Zumwalt Meadows Trail.** Drive back (allow about an hour without stops) and overnight in the Grant Grove area of the park.

Days 4 and 5: Kings Canyon to Sequoia

(Allow ample time to drive Generals Hwy. as parts are steep and winding, and there are many stops to make on the way. Los Angeles is about 3½–4 hrs by car from the Foothills Visitor Center.

Spend the next two days exploring **Generals Highway,** the 43-mile scenic route connecting Kings Canyon and Sequoia national parks. Warm up with a hike into Redwood Canyon Grove, one of the largest sequoia groves in the world. You can choose between a shorter hike

to an overlook point or longer 6- and 10-mile trails that lead deep into the grove. From there, continue the drive into **Sequoia National Park** and spend the rest of the day and the majority of the next exploring its highlights with an overnight at the **Wuksachi Lodge.**

Don't miss the 2-mile **Congress Trail,** an excellent opportunity to walk among the big trees, and the nearby **General Sherman Tree,** a massive specimen. If you want to tour the marble interior of **Crystal Cave,** be sure to reserve tour tickets in advance online or purchase them at the **Lodgepole visitor center.** Challenge your calves on the 350 stone steps of **Moro Rock** and reward your efforts with views over the Middle Fork Canyon. Don't leave the park without making the requisite photo stop at **Tunnel Log,** which, as its name suggests, is a drive-through tunnel carved out of the trunk of a fallen tree. It might take some discipline to pull away from the spectacular scenery, but a 3½-hour drive to Los Angeles awaits. With any luck, an evening arrival will mean you miss much of the city's notorious traffic. However, if you linger a bit longer than expected or simply don't feel up to the drive, Bakersfield is a closer alternative to stop for the night. Note: for the particularly intrepid traveler, this itinerary can be modified to take in **Yosemite and Death Valley national parks** via the **Tioga Pass** and **Mono Lake.** However, travelers should be aware that Tioga Pass is only open in the summer and early fall. By the time the pass opens (usually late May or June), temperatures in Death Valley are already searing hot and the extreme conditions should not be taken lightly. Always travel with an ample supply of drinking water and food, take precautions against the burning sun, limit physical activity, and time outings for early or late in the day.

3

MONTEREY BAY AREA

from Carmel to Santa Cruz

Visit Fodors.com for advice, updates, and bookings

WELCOME TO MONTEREY BAY AREA

TOP REASONS TO GO

★ **Marine life:** Monterey Bay is the location of the world's third-largest marine sanctuary, home to whales, otters, and other underwater creatures.

★ **Getaway central:** For more than a century, urbanites have come to the Monterey Bay area to unwind, relax, and have fun. It's a great place to browse unique shops and galleries, ride a giant roller coaster, or play a round of golf on a world-class course.

★ **Nature preserves:** More than the sea is protected here: the region boasts nearly 30 state parks, beaches, and preserves—fantastic places for walking, jogging, hiking, and biking.

★ **Wine and dine:** The area's rich agricultural bounty translates into abundant fresh produce, great wines, and fabulous dining. It's no wonder more than 300 culinary events take place here every year.

★ **Small-town vibes:** Even the cities here are friendly, walkable places where you'll feel like a local.

0 [____|____] 5 mi
0 [____|____] 5 km

Santa Cruz

17
9
1
4

1 Carmel and Pacific Grove. Exclusive Carmel-by-the-Sea and Carmel Valley Village burst with historic charm, fine dining, and unusual boutiques that cater to celebrity residents and well-heeled visitors. Nearby 17-Mile Drive—quite possibly the prettiest stretch of road you'll ever travel—runs between Carmel-by-the-Sea and Victorian-studded Pacific Grove, home to thousands of migrating monarch butterflies between October and February.

2 Monterey. A former Spanish military outpost, Monterey's well-preserved historic district is a hands-on history lesson. Cannery Row, the center of Monterey's once-thriving sardine industry, has been reborn as a tourist attraction with shops, restaurants, hotels, and the Monterey Bay Aquarium.

3 Around Monterey Bay. Much of California's lettuce, berries, artichokes, and brussels sprouts is grown in Salinas and other towns. Salinas is also home to the National Steinbeck Center, and Moss Landing encompasses pristine wildlife wetlands. Aptos, Capitola, and Soquel are former lumber towns that became popular seaside resorts more than a century ago. Today they're filled with antiques shops, restaurants, and wine-tasting rooms; you'll also find some of the bay's best beaches along the shore here.

4 Santa Cruz. Santa Cruz shows its colors along an old-time beach boardwalk and municipal wharf. A University of California campus imbues the town with arts and culture and a liberal mind-set.

GETTING ORIENTED

3

North of Big Sur the coastline softens into lower bluffs, windswept dunes, pristine estuaries, and long, sandy beaches, bordering one of the world's most amazing marine environments—Monterey Bay. On the Monterey Peninsula, at the southern end of the bay, are Carmel-by-the-Sea, Pacific Grove, and Monterey; Santa Cruz sits at the northern tip of the crescent. In between, Highway 1 cruises along the coastline, passing windswept beaches piled high with sand dunes. Along the route are wetlands and artichoke and strawberry fields.

Updated
by Cheryl
Crabtree

Natural beauty is at the heart of the Monterey Bay area's enormous appeal—it's everywhere, from the redwood-studded hillsides to the pristine shoreline with miles of walking paths and bluff-top vistas. Nature even takes center stage indoors at the world-famous Monterey Bay Aquarium, but history also draws visitors, most notably to Monterey's well-preserved waterfront district. Quaint, walkable towns and villages such as Carmel-by-the-Sea and Carmel Valley Village lure with smart restaurants and galleries, while sunny Aptos, Capitola, Soquel, and Santa Cruz, with miles of sand and surf, attract surfers and beach lovers.

Monterey Bay life centers on the ocean. The bay itself is protected by the Monterey Bay National Marine Sanctuary, the nation's largest undersea canyon—bigger and deeper than the Grand Canyon. On-the-water activities abound, from whale-watching and kayaking to sailing and surfing. Bay cruises from Monterey and Moss Landing almost always encounter other enchanting sea creatures, among them sea otters, sea lions, and porpoises.

Land-based activities include hiking, zip-lining in the redwood canopy, and wine tasting along urban and rural trails. Golf has been an integral part of the Monterey Peninsula's social and recreational scene since the Del Monte Golf Course opened in 1897. Pebble Beach's championship courses host prestigious tournaments, and though the greens fees at these courses can run up to $500, elsewhere on the peninsula you'll find less expensive options. And, of course, whatever activity you pursue, natural splendor appears at every turn.

PLANNING

WHEN TO GO

Summer is peak season; mild weather brings in big crowds. In this coastal region a cool breeze generally blows and fog often rolls in from offshore; you will frequently need a sweater or windbreaker. Off-season, from November through April, fewer people visit and the mood is mellower. Rainfall is heaviest in January and February. Fall and spring days are often clearer than those in summer.

GETTING HERE AND AROUND

AIR TRAVEL

Monterey Regional Airport, 3 miles east of downtown Monterey off Highway 68, is served by Alaska, Allegiant, American, and United. Taxi service costs from $20 to $22 to downtown, and from $28 to $37 to Carmel. Monterey Airbus service between the region and the San Jose and San Francisco airports starts at $40; the Early Bird Airport Shuttle costs from $85 to $195 ($205 from Oakland).

Airport Contacts Monterey Regional Airport (MRY). ⊠ 200 Fred Kane Dr., at Olmsted Rd., off Hwy. 68, Monterey ☎ 831/648–7000 ⊕ www.montereyairport.com.

Ground Transportation Central Coast Cab Company. ☎ 831/626–3333 ⊕ www.centralcoastcab.com. **Early Bird Airport Shuttle.** ☎ 831/462–3933 ⊕ www.earlybirdairportshuttle.com. **Monterey Airbus.** ☎ 831/373–7777 ⊕ www.montereyairbus.com. **Yellow Cab.** ☎ 831/333–1234.

BUS TRAVEL

Greyhound serves Santa Cruz and Salinas from San Francisco and San Jose. The trips take about 3 and 4½ hours, respectively. Monterey-Salinas Transit (MST) provides frequent service in Monterey County (from $1.75 to $3.50; day pass $10), and Santa Cruz METRO ($2; day pass from $6 to $10) buses operate throughout Santa Cruz County. You can switch between the lines in Watsonville.

Bus Contacts Greyhound. ☎ 800/231–2222 ⊕ www.greyhound.com. **Monterey-Salinas Transit.** ☎ 888/678–2871 ⊕ mst.org. **Santa Cruz METRO.** ☎ 831/425–8600 ⊕ scmtd.com.

CAR TRAVEL

Highway 1 runs south–north along the coast, linking the towns of Carmel-by-the-Sea, Monterey, and Santa Cruz; some sections have only two lanes. The freeway, U.S. 101, lies to the east, roughly parallel to Highway 1. The two roads are connected by Highway 68 from Pacific Grove to Salinas; Highway 156 from Castroville to Prunedale; Highway 152 from Watsonville to Gilroy; and Highway 17 from Santa Cruz to San Jose. ■TIP→ Traffic near Santa Cruz can crawl to a standstill during commuter hours. In the morning, avoid traveling between 7 and 9; in the afternoon avoid traveling between 4 and 7.

The drive south from San Francisco to Monterey can be made comfortably in three hours or less. The most scenic way is to follow Highway 1 down the coast. A generally faster route is Interstate 280 south to Highway 85 to Highway 17 to Highway 1. The drive from the Los

Angeles area takes five or six hours. Take U.S. 101 to Salinas and head west on Highway 68. You can also follow Highway 1 up the coast.

TRAIN TRAVEL

Amtrak's *Coast Starlight* runs between Los Angeles, Oakland, and Seattle. You can also take the *Pacific Surfliner* to San Luis Obispo and connect to Amtrak buses to Salinas or San Jose. From the train station in Salinas you can connect with buses serving Carmel and Monterey, and from the train station in San Jose with buses to Santa Cruz.

Train Contacts Amtrak. ☎ 800/872-7245 ⊕ pacificsurfliner.com.

RESTAURANTS

The Monterey Bay area is a culinary paradise. The surrounding waters are full of fish, wild game roams the foothills, and the inland valleys are some of the most fertile in the country—local chefs draw on this bounty for their fresh, truly Californian cuisine. Except at beachside stands and inexpensive eateries, where anything goes, casual but neat dress is the norm. *Restaurant reviews have been shortened. For full information, visit Fodors.com.*

HOTELS

Accommodations in the Monterey area range from no-frills motels to luxurious hotels. Pacific Grove, amply endowed with ornate Victorian houses, is the region's bed-and-breakfast capital; Carmel also has charming inns. Lavish resorts cluster in exclusive Pebble Beach and pastoral Carmel Valley.

High season runs from May through October. Rates in winter, especially at the larger hotels, may drop by 50% or more, and smaller inns often offer midweek specials. Whatever the month, some properties require a two-night stay on weekends. *Hotel reviews have been shortened. For full information, visit Fodors.com.* ■TIP→ Many of the fancier accommodations aren't suitable for children; if you're traveling with kids, ask before you book.

WHAT IT COSTS			
$	**$$**	**$$$**	**$$$$**
Restaurants	under $16	$16–$22	$23–$30	over $30
Hotels	under $120	$120–$175	$176–$250	over $250

Restaurant prices are the average cost of a main course at dinner or, if dinner is not served, at lunch, excluding sales tax of 8¼%–9½% (depending on location). Hotel prices are the lowest cost of a standard double room in high season, excluding service charges and 10%–10½% tax.

TOUR OPTIONS

Ag Venture Tours & Consulting. Crowd-pleasing half- and full-day wine tasting, sightseeing, and agricultural tours are Ag Venture's specialty. Tastings are at Monterey and Santa Cruz Mountains wineries; sightseeing opportunities include the Monterey Peninsula, Big Sur, and Santa Cruz; and the agricultural forays take in the Salinas and Pajaro valleys. Customized itineraries can be arranged. ☎ 831/761-8463 ⊕ agventure-tours.com ✉ From $85 (day) and $363 (overnight).

California Parlor Car Tours. This outfit operates motor-coach tours from San Francisco that include one or two days in Monterey and Carmel. The company's three-day San Francisco–Los Angeles tours include stops in Monterey and Carmel. ☎ *415/474–7500, 800/227–4250* ⊕ *www.californiaparlorcar.com* ✉ *From $80 (day) and $267 (overnight).*

Monterey Guided Wine Tours. The company's guides lead customized wine tours in Monterey, Carmel, and Carmel Valley, along with the Santa Lucia Highlands, the Santa Cruz Mountains, and the Paso Robles area. Tours, which typically last from four to six hours, take place in a town car, a stretch limo, or a party bus. ☎ *831/920–2792* ⊕ *montereyguidedwinetours.com* ✉ *From $85.*

VISITOR INFORMATION

Contacts Monterey County Convention & Visitors Bureau. ☎ *888/221–1010* ⊕ *www.seemonterey.com.* **Monterey Wine Country.** ☎ *831/375–9400* ⊕ *www.montereywines.org.* **Santa Cruz County Conference & Visitors Council.** ✉ *303 Water St., No. 100, Santa Cruz* ☎ *831/425–1234, 800/833–3494* ⊕ *santacruz.org.* **Santa Cruz Mountains Winegrowers Association.** ✉ *725 Front St., No. 112, Santa Cruz* ☎ *831/685–8463* ⊕ *www.scmwa.com.*

CARMEL AND PACIFIC GROVE

As Highway 1 swings inland about 30 miles north of Big Sur, historic Carmel-by-the-Sea anchors the southern entry to the Monterey Peninsula—a gorgeous promontory at the southern tip of Monterey Bay. Just north of Carmel along the coast, the legendary 17-Mile Drive wends its way through private Pebble Beach and the town of Pacific Grove. Highway 1 skirts the peninsula to the east with more direct access to Pebble Beach and Pacific Grove.

CARMEL-BY-THE-SEA

26 miles north of Big Sur.

Even when its population quadruples with tourists on weekends and in summer, Carmel-by-the-Sea, commonly referred to as Carmel, retains its identity as a quaint village. Self-consciously charming, the town is populated by many celebrities, major and minor, and has its share of quirky ordinances. For instance, women wearing high heels do not have the right to pursue legal action if they trip and fall on the cobblestone streets, and drivers who hit a tree and leave the scene are charged with hit-and-run.

Buildings have no street numbers—street names are written on discreet white posts—and consequently no mail delivery. One way to commune with the locals: head to the post office. Artists started this community, and their legacy is evident in the numerous galleries.

GETTING HERE AND AROUND

From north or south follow Highway 1 to Carmel. Head west at Ocean Avenue to reach the main village hub.

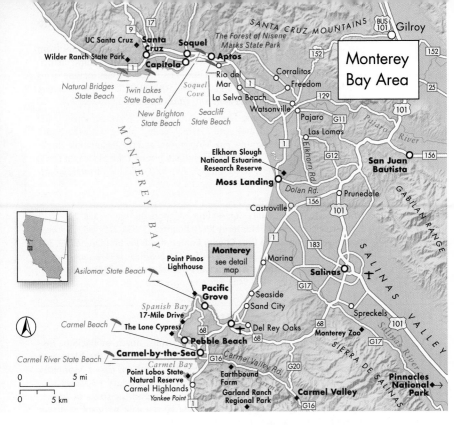

TOURS

Carmel Walks. For insight into Carmel's history and culture, join one of these guided two-hour ambles through hidden courtyards, gardens, and pathways. Tours depart from the Pine Inn courtyard, on Lincoln Street. Call to reserve a spot. ✉ *Lincoln St. at 6th Ave., Carmel* 🕾 *888/284–8405 reservations, 831/373–2813 group reservations* ⊕ *carmelwalks. com* 💷 *From $30.*

ESSENTIALS

Visitor Information Carmel Chamber of Commerce. ✉ *Visitor Center, in Carmel Plaza, Ocean Ave. between Junipero and Mission Sts., Carmel* 🕾 *831/624–2522, 800/550–4333* ⊕ *carmelchamber.org.*

EXPLORING
TOP ATTRACTIONS

Carmel Mission. Long before it became a shopping and browsing destination, Carmel was an important religious center during the establishment of Spanish California. That heritage is preserved in the Mission San Carlos Borroméo del Rio Carmelo, more commonly known as the Carmel Mission. Founded in 1771, it served as headquarters for the mission system in California under Father Junípero Serra. Adjoining the stone church is a tranquil garden planted with California poppies. Museum rooms at the mission include an early kitchen, Serra's spartan sleeping quarters and burial shrine, and the first college library in California. ✉ *3080 Rio Rd., at Lasuen Dr., Carmel* ☎ *831/624–1271* ⊕ *carmelmission.org* 💲 *$6.50.*

Fodor'sChoice ★ **Ocean Avenue.** Downtown Carmel's chief lure is shopping, especially along its main street, Ocean Avenue, between Junipero Avenue and Camino Real. The architecture here is a mishmash of ersatz Tudor, Mediterranean, and other styles. ✉ *Carmel.*

Fodor'sChoice ★ **Point Lobos State Natural Reserve.** A 350-acre headland harboring a wealth of marine life, the reserve lies a few miles south of Carmel. The best way to explore here is to walk along one of the many trails. The Cypress Grove Trail leads through a forest of Monterey cypress (one of only two natural groves remaining) that clings to the rocks above an emerald-green cove. Sea Lion Point Trail is a good place to view sea lions. From those and other trails, you might also spot otters, harbor seals, and (in winter and spring) migrating whales. An additional 750 acres of the reserve is an undersea marine park open to qualified scuba divers. No pets are allowed. ■ TIP→ **Arrive early (or in late afternoon) to avoid crowds; the parking lots fill up.** ✉ *Hwy. 1, Carmel* ☎ *831/624–4909, 831/624–8413 water sports reservations* ⊕ *www.pointlobos.org* 💲 *$10 per vehicle.*

WORTH NOTING

Carmel Wine Walk By-the-Sea. If you purchase a Wine Walk Passport, you can park the car and sample local wines at any 10 of 14 tasting rooms, all within a few blocks of each other in downtown Carmel. Individual passports can be used by two or more people at the same tasting room, and they entitle holders to free corkage at some local restaurants. ✉ *Carmel Chamber of Commerce Visitor Center, San Carlos St., between 5th and 6th Aves., Carmel* ☎ *831/624–2522, 800/550–4333* ⊕ *www.carmelchamber.org/store/wine-walk-by-the-sea* 💲 *$100.*

Dawson Cole Fine Art. Amazing images of dancers, athletes, and other humans in motion come to life in this gallery that is devoted to the artworks of Monterey Bay resident Richard MacDonald, one of the most famed figurative sculptors of our time. ✉ *Lincoln St., at 6th Ave., Carmel* ☎ *800/972–5528* ⊕ *dawsoncolefineart.com* 💲 *Free.*

Tor House. Scattered throughout the pines of Carmel-by-the-Sea are houses and cottages originally built for the writers, artists, and photographers who discovered the area decades ago. Among the most impressive dwellings is Tor House, a stone cottage built in 1919 by poet Robinson Jeffers on a craggy knoll overlooking the sea. Portraits, books, and unusual art objects fill the low-ceilinged rooms. The highlight of the small estate is Hawk Tower, a detached edifice set with stones from the Carmel coastline—as well as one from the Great Wall of China. The docents who lead tours (six people maximum) are well informed about the poet's work and life. Reservations are required. Call the reservation line or click on the reservation link on the website. ✉ *26304 Ocean View Ave., Carmel* ☎ *844/285–0244, 831/624–1840 direct docent office line, Fri. and Sat. only* ⊕ *www.torhouse.org* 💲 *$12* ☞ *No children under 12.*

BEACHES

Carmel Beach. Carmel-by-the-Sea's greatest attraction is its rugged coastline, with pine and cypress forests and countless inlets. Carmel Beach, an easy walk from downtown shops, has sparkling white sands and magnificent sunsets. ■ TIP→ Dogs are allowed to romp off-leash here. **Amenities:** parking (no fee); toilets. **Best for:** sunset; surfing; walking. ⊠ *End of Ocean Ave., Carmel.*

Carmel River State Beach. This sugar-white beach, stretching 106 acres along Carmel Bay, is adjacent to a bird sanctuary, where you might spot pelicans, kingfishers, hawks, and sandpipers. Dogs are allowed on leash. **Amenities:** parking (no fee); toilets. **Best for:** sunrise; sunset; walking. ⊠ *Off Scenic Rd., south of Carmel Beach, Carmel* ☎ *831/649–2836* ⊕ *www.parks.ca.gov* ⊠ *Free.*

WHERE TO EAT

$$$$
EUROPEAN

✕ **Anton and Michel.** Carefully prepared European cuisine is the draw at this airy restaurant. The rack of lamb is carved at the table, the grilled halloumi cheese and tomatoes are meticulously stacked and served with basil and Kalamata olive tapenade, and the desserts are set aflame before your eyes. **Known for:** romantic courtyard with fountain; elegant interior with fireplace lounge; flambé desserts. $ *Average main: $32* ⊠ *Mission St. and 7th Ave., Carmel* ☎ *831/624–2406* ⊕ *antonandmichel.com.*

$$$$
AMERICAN
Fodor'sChoice
★

✕ **Aubergine.** To eat and sleep at luxe L'Auberge Carmel is an experience in itself, but even those staying elsewhere can splurge at the inn's intimate restaurant. Chef Justin Cogley's eight-course prix-fixe tasting menu (your only option at dinner, $150 per person) is a gastronomical experience unrivaled in the region. **Known for:** exceptional chef's choice tasting menu; expert wine pairings; intimate 12-table dining room. $ *Average main: $150* ⊠ *Monte Verde at 7th Ave., Carmel* ☎ *831/624–8578* ⊕ *auberginecarmel.com* ⊗ *No lunch.*

$$$
MODERN
AMERICAN
Fodor'sChoice
★

✕ **Basil.** Eco-friendly Basil was Monterey County's first restaurant to achieve a green dining certification, recognition of chef-owner Soerke Peters's commitment to using organic, sustainably cultivated ingredients in his cuisine. Peters grows many of his own herbs, which find their way into creative dishes such as black squid linguine with sea urchin sauce, creamy duck liver–pear pâté, and smoked venison and other housemade charcuterie. **Known for:** organic ingredients; creative cocktails; year-round patio dining. $ *Average main: $25* ⊠ *Paseo Square, San Carlos St., between Ocean Ave. and 7th Ave., Carmel* ☎ *831/636–8226* ⊕ *basilcarmel.com.*

$$$$
MEDITERRANEAN

✕ **Casanova.** This restaurant inspires European-style celebration and romance: accordions hang from the walls, and tiny party lights flicker along the low ceilings. Dishes from southern France and northern Italy—osso buco, Wagyu beef tartare—predominate. **Known for:** housemade pastas and gnocchi; private dining at antique Van Gogh's table; romantic candlelight dining room. $ *Average main: $32* ⊠ *5th Ave., between San Carlos and Mission Sts., Carmel* ☎ *831/625–0501* ⊕ *www.casanovarestaurant.com.*

$
AMERICAN

✕ **The Cottage Restaurant.** This family-friendly spot serves sandwiches, pizzas, and homemade soups at lunch, but the best meal is breakfast (good thing it's served all day). The menu offers six variations on eggs

Point Lobos State Natural Reserve offers stunning vistas of sea and sky.

Benedict, and all kinds of sweet and savory crepes. **Known for:** artichoke soup; eggs Benedict and crepes; daily specials. ⑤ *Average main: $15* ✉ *Lincoln St. between Ocean and 7th Aves., Carmel* ☎ *831/625–6260* ⊕ *cottagerestaurant.com* ☽ *No dinner.*

$$$$
AMERICAN

✕ **Grasing's Coastal Cuisine.** Chef Kurt Grasing draws from fresh Carmel Coast and Central Valley ingredients to whip up contemporary adaptations of European-provincial and American cooking. Longtime menu favorites include artichoke lasagna in a roasted tomato sauce, duck with fresh cherries in a red wine sauce, a savory paella, and grilled steaks and chops. **Known for:** artichoke heart lasagne; grilled steaks; sophisticated setting. ⑤ *Average main: $39* ✉ *6th Ave. and Mission St., Carmel* ☎ *831/612–0082* ⊕ *grasings.com.*

$$
TAPAS

✕ **Mundaka.** The traditional Spanish-style tapas, made with fresh local ingredients, and the full bar attract legions of locals to this downtown spot. Longtime favorites include the chorizo slider with truffle fries, the authentic Valencian paella, and a charcuterie platter made in-house. **Known for:** Spanish-style tapas; live music; Valencian paella. ⑤ *Average main: $22* ✉ *San Carlos St., between Ocean and 7th Aves., Carmel* ☎ *831/624–7400* ⊕ *www.mundakacarmel.com.*

$$$
ITALIAN

✕ **Vesuvio.** Chef and restaurateur Rich Pèpe heats up the night with this lively trattoria downstairs and swinging rooftop terrace, the Starlight Lounge 65°. Pèpe's elegant take on traditional Italian cuisine yields dishes such as wild-boar Bolognese pappardelle, lobster ravioli, and velvety limoncello mousse cake. **Known for:** traditional cuisine of Campania, Italy; popular gathering spot; live music on rooftop terrace in summer. ⑤ *Average main: $28* ✉ *6th and Junipero Aves., Carmel* ☎ *831/625–1766* ⊕ *vesuviocarmel.com* ☽ *No lunch.*

WHERE TO STAY

$$$$
B&B/INN

☷ **Cypress Inn.** This luxurious inn has a fresh Mediterranean ambience with Moroccan touches. **Pros:** luxury without snobbery; popular lounge and restaurant; British-style afternoon tea on weekends. **Cons:** not for the pet-phobic. ⑤ *Rooms from: $279* ⊠ *Lincoln St. and 7th Ave., Carmel* ☎ *831/624–3871, 800/443–7443* ⊕ *cypress-inn.com* ⌧ *44 rooms* ⦿*Breakfast.*

$$$$
HOTEL

☷ **The Hideaway.** On a quiet street with a residential vibe, The Hideway is a peaceful haven for those seeking stylish comfort in the heart of town. **Pros:** easy walk to shops, restaurants, galleries; recently refurbished; short walk to Carmel Beach; pet-friendly amenities. **Cons:** street parking only; no pool or hot tub. ⑤ *Rooms from: $295* ⊠ *Junipero St. at 8th Ave., Carmel* ☎ *831/625–5222* ⊕ *hideawaycarmel.com* ⌧ *24 rooms* ⦿*Breakfast.*

$$$$
HOTEL

☷ **Hyatt Carmel Highlands.** High on a hill overlooking the Pacific, this place has superb views; accommodations include king rooms with fireplaces, suites with personal Jacuzzis, and full town houses with many perks. **Pros:** killer views; romantic getaway; great food. **Cons:** thin walls; must drive to Carmel. ⑤ *Rooms from: $399* ⊠ *120 Highlands Dr., Carmel* ☎ *831/620–1234, 800/233–1234* ⊕ *carmelhighlands.hyatt. com* ⌧ *48 rooms.*

$$$$
B&B/INN
Fodor'sChoice
★

☷ **L'Auberge Carmel.** Stepping through the doors of this elegant inn is like being transported to a little European village. **Pros:** in town but off the main drag; four blocks from the beach; full-service luxury. **Cons:** touristy area; not a good choice for families. ⑤ *Rooms from: $465* ⊠ *Monte Verde at 7th Ave., Carmel* ☎ *831/624–8578* ⊕ *www.laubergecarmel. com* ⌧ *20 rooms* ⦿*Breakfast.*

$$$$
HOTEL

☷ **La Playa Carmel.** A historic complex of lush gardens and Mediterranean-style buildings, La Playa has light and airy interiors done in Carmel Bay beach-cottage style. **Pros:** residential neighborhood; manicured gardens; two blocks from the beach. **Cons:** four stories (no elevator); busy lobby; some rooms are on the small side. ⑤ *Rooms from: $458* ⊠ *Camino Real at 8th Ave., Carmel* ☎ *831/293–6100, 800/582–8900* ⊕ *laplayahotel.com* ⌧ *75 rooms* ⦿*Breakfast.*

$$
HOTEL

☷ **Mission Ranch.** Movie star Clint Eastwood owns this sprawling property whose accommodations include rooms in a converted barn, and several cottages, some with fireplaces. **Pros:** farm setting; pastoral views; great for tennis buffs. **Cons:** busy parking lot; must drive to the heart of town. ⑤ *Rooms from: $175* ⊠ *26270 Dolores St., Carmel* ☎ *831/624–6436, 800/538–8221, 831/625–9040 restaurant* ⊕ *www. missionranchcarmel.com* ⌧ *31 rooms* ⦿*Breakfast.*

$$$$
B&B/INN

☷ **Tickle Pink Inn.** Atop a towering cliff, this inn has views of the Big Sur coastline, which you can contemplate from your private balcony. **Pros:** close to great hiking; intimate; dramatic views. **Cons:** close to a big hotel; lots of traffic during the day. ⑤ *Rooms from: $309* ⊠ *155 Highland Dr., Carmel* ☎ *831/624–1244, 800/635–4774* ⊕ *ticklepink. com* ⌧ *33 rooms, 1 cottage* ⦿*Breakfast.*

$$$
B&B/INN

☷ **Tradewinds Carmel.** This converted motel with sleek decor inspired by the South Seas encircles a courtyard with waterfalls, a meditation garden, and a fire pit. **Pros:** serene; within walking distance of restaurants;

friendly service. **Cons:** no pool; long walk to the beach. ⑤ *Rooms from: $250* ⊠ *Mission St. at 3rd Ave., Carmel* ☎ *831/624–2776* ⊕ *tradewinds-carmel.com* ⌐⊃ *28 rooms* ⦿⎮ *Breakfast*.

NIGHTLIFE
BARS AND PUBS
Barmel. Al Capone and other Prohibition-era legends once sidled up to this hip nightspot's carved wooden bar. Rock to DJ music and sit indoors, or head out to the pet-friendly patio. Some menu items pay homage to California's early days, and you can order Spanish tapas and wines from the adjacent Mundaka restaurant, which is under the same ownership. ⊠ *San Carlos St., between Ocean and 7th Aves., Carmel* ☎ *831/626–2095* ⊕ *www.mundakacarmel.com*.

Mulligan Public House. A sports bar with seven TV screens, 12 beers on tap, and extensive menu packed with hearty American pub food, Mulligan usually stays open until midnight. ⊠ *5 Dolores St., at Ocean* ☎ *831/250–5910* ⊕ *mulliganspublichouse.com*.

SHOPPING
ART GALLERIES
Carmel Art Association. Carmel's oldest gallery, established in 1927, exhibits original paintings and sculptures by local artists. ⊠ *Dolores St., between 5th and 6th Aves., Carmel* ☎ *831/624–6176* ⊕ *carmelart.org*.

Galerie Plein Aire. The gallery showcases the oil paintings of a group of local artists. ⊠ *Dolores St., between Ocean and 6th Aves., Carmel* ☎ *831/277–6165* ⊕ *galeriepleinaire.com* ⊘ *Closed Tues*.

Gallery Sur. Fine art photography of the Big Sur Coast and the Monterey Peninsula, including scenic shots and golf images, is the focus here. ⊠ *6th Ave., between Dolores and Lincoln Sts., Carmel* ☎ *831/626–2615* ⊕ *gallerysur.com*.

Fodor's Choice ★ **Weston Gallery.** Run by the family of the late Edward Weston, this is hands down the best photography gallery around, with contemporary color photography and classic black-and-whites. ⊠ *6th Ave., between Dolores and Lincoln Sts., Carmel* ☎ *831/624–4453* ⊕ *westongallery.com* ⊘ *Closed Mon*.

MALLS
Carmel Plaza. Tiffany & Co. and J. Crew are among the name brands doing business at this mall on Carmel's east side, but what makes it worth a stop are homegrown enterprises such as Blue Lemon, for artsy, handcrafted clothing and jewelry; Madrigal for women's fashion; and J. Lawrence Khaki's for debonair menswear. Flying Fish Grill and several other restaurants are here, along with the Wrath Wines tasting room (Chardonnay and Pinot Noir). The Carmel Chamber of Commerce Visitor Center (open daily) is on the second floor. ⊠ *Ocean Ave. and Mission St., Carmel* ☎ *831/624–1385* ⊕ *carmelplaza.com*.

SPECIALTY SHOPS
Bittner. The shop carries collectible and vintage pens from around the world. ⊠ *Ocean Ave., between Mission and San Carlos Sts., Carmel* ☎ *831/626–8828* ⊕ *bittner.com*.

elizabethW. Named after the designer and owner's pioneering great-grandmother, elizabethW handcrafts fragrances, essential oils, candles, silk eye pillows, and other soul-soothing goods for bath, body, and home. ⊠ *Ocean Ave., between Monte Verde and Lincoln, Carmel* ☎ *831/626–3892* ⊕ *elizabethw.com.*

Foxy Couture. Shop for one-of-a-kind treasures at this curated collection of gently used luxury couture and vintage clothes and accessories—think Chanel, Hermes, and Gucci—without paying a hefty price tag. ⊠ *San Carlos St., in Vanervort Court, between Ocean and 7th Aves., Carmel* ☎ *831/625–9995* ⊕ *foxycouturecarmel.com.*

Jan de Luz. This shop monograms and embroiders fine linens (including bathrobes) while you wait. ⊠ *Dolores St., between Ocean and 7th Aves., Carmel* ☎ *831/622–7621* ⊕ *www.jandeluz.com.*

CARMEL VALLEY

10 miles east of Carmel.

Carmel Valley Road, which heads inland from Highway 1 south of Carmel, is the main thoroughfare through this valley, a secluded enclave of horse ranchers and other well-heeled residents who prefer the area's sunny climate to coastal fog and wind. Once thick with dairy farms, the valley has evolved into an esteemed wine appellation. Carmel Valley Village has crafts shops, art galleries, and the tasting rooms of numerous local wineries.

GETTING HERE AND AROUND

From U.S. 101 north or south, exit at Highway 68 and head west toward the coast. Scenic, two-lane Laureles Grade winds west over the mountains to Carmel Valley Road north of the village.

TOURS

Carmel Valley Grapevine Express. An incredible bargain, the express—aka MST's Bus 24—travels between downtown Monterey and Carmel Valley Village, with stops near wineries, restaurants, and shopping centers. ☎ *888/678–2871* ⊕ *mst.org* 🚌 *$10 all-day pass.*

EXPLORING
TOP ATTRACTIONS

Bernardus Tasting Room. At the tasting room of Bernardus, known for its Bordeaux-style red blend, called Marinus, and Chardonnays, you can sample current releases and library and reserve wines. ⊠ *5 W. Carmel Valley Rd., at El Caminito Rd.* ☎ *831/298–8021, 800/223–2533* ⊕ *bernardus.com* 🍷 *Tastings $12–$20.*

Cowgirl Winery. Cowgirl chic prevails in the main tasting building here, and it's just plain rustic at the outdoor tables, set amid chickens, a tractor, and a flatbed truck. The wines include Chardonnay, Cabernet Sauvignon, Rosé, and some blends. You can order a wood-fired pizza from sister business Corkscrew Café, and play boccie ball, horseshoes, or corn hole until your food arrives. ⊠ *25 Pilot Rd., off W. Carmel Valley Rd.* ☎ *831/298–7030* ⊕ *cowgirlwinery.com* 🍷 *Tasting $15.*

Fodor's Choice **Folktale Winery & Vineyards.** The expansive winery on a 15-acre estate
★ (formerly Chateau Julienne) offers daily tastings, live music on weekends (plus Friday in summer and fall), and special events and programs

such as Saturday yoga in the vineyard. Best-known wines include the estate Pinot Noir, Sparkling Rosé, and Le Mistral Joseph's Blend. Celebrity chef Todd Fisher cooks up small plates with wine pairing suggestions at the on-site restaurant. Tours of the winery and organically farmed vineyards are available by appointment. ⊠ *8940 Carmel Valley Rd.* ✢ *At Schetter Rd.* ☎ *831/293–7500* ⊕ *folktalewinery.com* 🍷 *Tastings $20–$25.*

Holman Ranch Vineyards Tasting Room. Estate-grown Pinot Gris and Pinot Noir are among the standout wines made by Holman Ranch, which operates a tasting room in Carmel Valley village. If the Heather's Hill Pinot is being poured, be sure to try it. The ranch itself occupies rolling hills once part of the Carmel mission's land grant. You can book winery and vineyard tours by appointment, and the ranch welcomes overnight guests at its 10-room hacienda. ⊠ *19 E. Carmel Valley Rd., Suite C* ☎ *831/659–2640* ⊕ *holmanranch.com* 🍷 *Tastings $8–$12.*

WORTH NOTING

FAMILY **Earthbound Farm.** Pick up fresh vegetables, ready-to-eat meals, gourmet groceries, flowers, and gifts at Earthbound Farm, the world's largest grower of organic produce. You can also take a romp in the kids' garden, cut your own herbs, and stroll through the chamomile aromatherapy labyrinth. Special events, on Saturday from April through December, include bug walks and garlic-braiding workshops. ⊠ *7250 Carmel Valley Rd., Carmel* ☎ *831/625–6219* ⊕ *www.ebfarm.com* 🍷 *Free.*

Garland Ranch Regional Park. Hiking trails stretch across much of this park's 4,500 acres of meadows, forested hillsides, and creeks. ⊠ *Carmel Valley Rd., 9 miles east of Carmel-by-the-Sea* ☎ *831/659–4488* ⊕ *www.mprpd.org.*

WHERE TO EAT

$$$ ✕ **Café Rustica.** European country cooking is the focus at this lively roadEUROPEAN house. Specialties include roasted meats, seafood, pastas, and thin-crust pizzas from the wood-fired oven. **Known for:** Tuscan-flavored dishes from Alsace; open kitchen with wood-fired oven; outdoor patio seating. $ *Average main: $24* ⊠ *10 Delfino Pl., at Pilot Rd., off Carmel Valley Rd.* ☎ *831/659–4444* ⊕ *caferusticavillage.com* ☽ *Closed Mon.*

$$ ✕ **Corkscrew Café.** Farm-fresh food is the specialty of this casual, Old MODERN Monterey–style bistro. Herbs and seasonal produce come from the AMERICAN Corkscrew's own organic gardens; the catch of the day comes from local waters; and the meats are hormone-free. **Known for:** woodfired pizzas; fish tacos; antique corkscrew collection. $ *Average main: $22* ⊠ *55 W. Carmel Valley Rd., at Pilot Rd.* ☎ *831/659–8888* ⊕ *corkscrewcafe.com.*

WHERE TO STAY

$$$$ 🛏 **Bernardus Lodge & Spa.** The spacious guest rooms at this luxury spa RESORT resort have vaulted ceilings, French oak floors, featherbeds, fireplaces, Fodor's Choice patios, and bathrooms with heated-tile floors and soaking tubs for ★ two. **Pros:** exceptional personal service; outstanding food and wine. **Cons:** pricey; some guests can seem snooty. $ *Rooms from: $475* ⊠ *415 W. Carmel Valley Rd.* ☎ *831/658–3400* ⊕ *bernarduslodge.com* ↩ *73 rooms and villas.*

$$$$ 🛏 **Carmel Valley Ranch.** The activity options at this luxury ranch are so
RESORT varied that the resort provides a program director to guide you through
Fodor's Choice them. **Pros:** stunning natural setting; tons of activities; state-of-the-art
★ amenities. **Cons:** must drive several miles to shops and nightlife; pricey.
⑤ *Rooms from: $400* ✉ *1 Old Ranch Rd., Carmel* ☎ *831/625–9500,*
855/687–7262 toll free reservations ⊕ *carmelvalleyranch.com* ⌁ *181*
suites ❍ *No meals.*

$$$ 🛏 **Quail Lodge & Golf Club.** A sprawling collection of ranch-style build-
HOTEL ings on 850 acres of meadows, fairways, and lakes, Quail Lodge offers
FAMILY luxury rooms and outdoor activities at surprisingly affordable rates.
Pros: on the golf course; on-site restaurant. **Cons:** extra fees for athletic
passes and some services; 5 miles from the beach and Carmel Val-
ley Village. ⑤ *Rooms from: $195* ✉ *8205 Valley Greens Dr., Carmel*
☎ *866/675–1101 reservations, 831/624–2888* ⊕ *www.quaillodge.com*
⌁ *93 rooms* ❍ *No meals.*

$$$$ 🛏 **Stonepine Estate Resort.** Set on 330 pastoral acres, the former estate of
RESORT the Crocker banking family has been converted to a luxurious inn. **Pros:**
Fodor's Choice supremely exclusive. **Cons:** difficult to get a reservation; far from the
★ coast. ⑤ *Rooms from: $300* ✉ *150 E. Carmel Valley Rd.* ☎ *831/659–*
2245 ⊕ *www.stonepineestate.com* ⌁ *12 rooms, 3 cottages.*

SPORTS AND THE OUTDOORS
GOLF
Quail Lodge & Golf Club. Robert Muir Graves designed this championship
semiprivate 18-hole course next to Quail Lodge that provides challeng-
ing play for golfers of all skill levels. The scenic course, which incorpo-
rates five lakes and edges the Carmel River, was completely renovated
in 2015 by golf architect Todd Eckenrode to add extra challenge to the
golf experience, white sand bunkers, and other enhancements. For the
most part flat, the walkable course is well maintained, with stunning
views, lush fairways, and ultrasmooth greens. ✉ *8000 Valley Greens
Dr., Carmel* ☎ *831/620–8808 golf shop, 831/620–8866 club concierge*
⊕ *www.quaillodge.com* ⌁ *$185* ⚑ *18 holes, 6500 yards, par 71.*

SPAS
Fodor's Choice **Refuge.** At this co-ed, European-style center on 2 serene acres you can
★ recharge without breaking the bank. Heat up in the eucalyptus steam
room or cedar sauna, plunge into cold pools, and relax indoors in zero-
gravity chairs or outdoors in Adirondack chairs around fire pits. Repeat
the cycle a few times, then lounge around the thermal waterfall pools.
Talk is not allowed, and bathing suits are required. ✉ *27300 Rancho
San Carlos Rd., south off Carmel Valley Rd., Carmel* ☎ *831/620–7360*
⊕ *refuge.com* ⌁ *$44* ☞ *$46 admission; $125 50-min massage (includes
Refuge admission), $12 robe rental, hot tubs (outdoor), sauna, steam
room. Services: Aromatherapy, hydrotherapy, massage.*

PEBBLE BEACH

Off North San Antonio Ave. in Carmel-by-the-Sea or off Sunset Dr. in Pacific Grove.

Fodor's Choice ★ In 1919 the Pacific Improvement Company acquired 18,000 acres of prime land on the Monterey Peninsula, including the entire Pebble Beach coastal region and much of Pacific Grove. Pebble Beach Golf Links and The Lodge at Pebble Beach opened the same year, and the private enclave evolved into a world-class golf destination with three posh lodges, five golf courses, hiking and riding trails, and some of the West Coast's ritziest homes. Pebble Beach has hosted major international golf tournaments and will host the U.S. Open in 2019. The annual Pebble Beach Food & Wine, a four-day event in late April with 100 celebrity chefs, is one of the West Coast's premier culinary festivals.

GETTING HERE AND AROUND

If you drive south from Monterey on Highway 1, exit at 17-Mile Drive/Sunset Drive in Pacific Grove to find the northern entrance gate. Coming from Carmel, exit at Ocean Avenue and follow the road almost to the beach; turn right on North San Antonio Avenue to the Carmel Gate. You can also enter through the Highway 1 Gate off Highway 68. Monterey–Salinas Transit buses provide regular service in and around Pebble Beach.

EXPLORING

Fodor's Choice ★ **The Lone Cypress.** The most-photographed tree along 17-Mile Drive is the weather-sculpted Lone Cypress, which grows out of a precipitous outcropping above the waves about 1½ miles up the road from Pebble Beach Golf Links. You can't walk out to the tree, but you can stop for a view of it at a small parking area off the road.

Fodor's Choice ★ **17-Mile Drive.** Primordial nature resides in quiet harmony with palatial, mostly Spanish Mission–style estates along 17-Mile Drive, which winds through an 8,400-acre microcosm of the Pebble Beach coastal landscape. Dotting the drive are rare Monterey cypresses, trees so gnarled and twisted that Robert Louis Stevenson described them as "ghosts fleeing before the wind." The most famous of these is the **Lone Cypress**. Other highlights include **Bird Rock** and **Seal Rock,** home to harbor seals, sea lions, cormorants, and pelicans and other sea creatures and birds, and the **Crocker Marble Palace,** inspired by a Byzantine castle and easily identifiable by its dozens of marble arches.

Enter 17-Mile Drive at the Highway 1 Gate, at Highway 68; the Carmel Gate, off North San Antonio Avenue; the Pacific Grove Gate, off Sunset Drive; S.F.B. Morse Gate, Morse Drive off Highway 68; and Country Club Gate, at Congress Avenue and Forest Lodge Road. ■ TIP→ If you spend $30 or more on dining or shopping in Pebble Beach and show a receipt upon exiting, you'll receive a refund off the drive's $10 per car fee. ⊠ *Hwy. 1 Gate, 17-Mile Dr., west of Hwy. 1 and Hwy. 68 intersection* 🖻 *$10 per car, free for bicyclists.*

WHERE TO STAY

$$$$
RESORT
Fodor's Choice
★

🏨 **Casa Palmero.** This exclusive boutique hotel evokes a stately Mediterranean villa. **Pros:** ultimate in pampering; sumptuous decor; more private than sister resorts; right on the golf course. **Cons:** pricey; may be *too* posh for some. $ *Rooms from: $975* ✉ *1518 Cypress Dr.* ☎ *831/622–6650, 866/508–9268 reservations* ⊕ *www.pebblebeach. com* 🛏 *24 rooms* ⦿ *Breakfast.*

$$$$
RESORT

🏨 **The Inn at Spanish Bay.** This resort sprawls across a breathtaking stretch of shoreline, and has lush, 600-square-foot rooms. **Pros:** attentive service; many amenities; spectacular views. **Cons:** huge hotel; 4 miles from other Pebble Beach Resorts facilities. $ *Rooms from: $720* ✉ *2700 17-Mile Dr.* ☎ *831/647–7500, 866/508–9268* ⊕ *www.pebblebeach.com* 🛏 *269 rooms.*

$$$$
RESORT

🏨 **The Lodge at Pebble Beach.** Most rooms have wood-burning fireplaces and many have wonderful ocean views at this circa-1919 resort, which expanded to include Fairway One, an additional 38-room complex, in August 2017. **Pros:** world-class golf; borders the ocean and fairways; fabulous facilities. **Cons:** some rooms are on the small side; very pricey. $ *Rooms from: $840* ✉ *1700 17-Mile Dr.* ☎ *831/624–3811, 866/508–9268* ⊕ *www.pebblebeach.com* 🛏 *199 rooms* ⦿ *No meals.*

SPORTS AND THE OUTDOORS

GOLF

Links at Spanish Bay. This course, which hugs a choice stretch of shoreline, was designed by Robert Trent Jones Jr., Tom Watson, and Sandy Tatum in the rugged manner of traditional Scottish links, with sand dunes and coastal marshes interspersed among the greens. A bagpiper signals the course's closing each day. ■TIP➔ **Nonguests of the Pebble Beach Resorts can reserve tee times up to two months in advance.** ✉ *17-Mile Dr., north end* ☎ *866/508–9268* ⊕ *www.pebblebeach.com* 🏌 *$280* ⛳ *18 holes, 6821 yards, par 72.*

Fodor's Choice
★

Pebble Beach Golf Links. Each February, show-business celebrities and golf pros team up at this course, the main site of the glamorous AT&T Pebble Beach National Pro-Am tournament. On most days the rest of the year, tee times are available to guests of the Pebble Beach Resorts who book a minimum two-night stay. Nonguests can reserve a tee time only one day in advance on a space-available basis; resort guests can reserve up to 18 months in advance. ✉ *17-Mile Dr., near The Lodge at Pebble Beach* ☎ *866/508–9268* ⊕ *www.pebblebeach.com* 🏌 *$525* ⛳ *18 holes, 6828 yards, par 72.*

Peter Hay. The only 9-hole, par-3 course on the Monterey Peninsula open to the public, Peter Hay attracts golfers of all skill levels. It's an ideal place for warm ups, practicing short games, and for those who don't have time to play 18 holes. ✉ *17-Mile Dr. and Portola Rd.* ☎ *866/508–9268* ⊕ *www.pebblebeach.com* 🏌 *$30* ⛳ *9 holes, 725 yards, par 27.*

Poppy Hills. An 18-hole course designed in 1986 by Robert Trent Jones Jr., Poppy Hills reopened in 2014 after a yearlong renovation that Jones supervised. Each hole has been restored to its natural elevation along the forest floor, and all 18 greens have been rebuilt with bent grass. Individuals may reserve up to a month in advance. Chef Johnny De Vivo grows

and sources organic ingredients that inspire the menus at the course's restaurant. ■ TIP→ Poppy Hills, owned by a golfing nonprofit, represents good value for this area. ⊠ *3200 Lopez Rd., at 17-Mile Dr.* ☎ *831/250–1819* ⊕ *poppyhillsgolf.com* ✉ *$225* ⚑ *18 holes, 7002 yards, par 73.5.*

Spyglass Hill. With three holes rated among the toughest on the PGA tour, Spyglass Hill, designed by Robert Trent Jones Sr. and Jr., challenges golfers with its varied terrain but rewards them with glorious views. The first five holes border the Pacific, and the other 13 reach deep into the Del Monte Forest. Reservations are essential and may be made up to one month in advance (18 months for resort guests). ⊠ *Stevenson Dr. and Spyglass Hill Rd.* ☎ *866/508–9268* ⊕ *www.pebblebeach.com* ✉ *$395* ⚑ *18 holes, 6960 yards, par 72.*

PACIFIC GROVE

3 miles north of Carmel-by-the-Sea.

This picturesque town, which began as a summer retreat for church groups more than a century ago, recalls its prim and proper Victorian heritage in its host of tiny board-and-batten cottages and stately mansions. However, long before the church groups flocked here the area received thousands of annual pilgrims—in the form of bright orange-and-black monarch butterflies. They still come, migrating south from Canada and the Pacific Northwest to take residence in pine and eucalyptus groves from October through March. In Butterfly Town USA, as Pacific Grove is known, the sight of a mass of butterflies hanging from the branches like a long, fluttering veil is unforgettable.

A prime way to enjoy Pacific Grove is to walk or bicycle the 3 miles of city-owned shoreline along Ocean View Boulevard, a cliff-top area landscaped with native plants and dotted with benches meant for sitting and gazing at the sea. You can spot many types of birds here, including the web-footed cormorants that crowd the massive rocks rising out of the surf. Two Victorians of note along Ocean View are the Queen Anne–style Green Gables, at No. 301—erected in 1888, it's now an inn—and the 1909 Pryor House, at No. 429, a massive, shingled, private residence with a leaded- and beveled-glass doorway.

GETTING HERE AND AROUND

Reach Pacific Grove via Highway 68 off Highway 1, just south of Monterey. From Cannery Row in Monterey, head north until the road merges with Ocean Boulevard and follow it along the coast. MST buses travel within Pacific Grove and surrounding towns.

EXPLORING

FAMILY **Lovers Point Park.** The coastal views are gorgeous from this waterfront park whose sheltered beach has a children's pool and a picnic area. The main lawn has a volleyball court and a snack bar. ⊠ *Ocean View Blvd. northwest of Forest Ave.* ☎ *831/648–5730.*

FAMILY **Monarch Grove Sanctuary.** The sanctuary is a reliable spot for viewing monarch butterflies between November and February. ■ TIP→ The best time to visit is between noon and 3 pm. ⊠ *250 Ridge Rd., off Lighthouse Ave.* ⊕ *www.pgmuseum.org/monarch-viewing.*

Pacific Grove Museum of Natural History. The museum, a good source for the latest information about monarch butterflies, has permanent exhibitions about the butterflies, birds of Monterey County, biodiversity, and plants. There's a native plant garden, and a display documents life in Pacific Grove's 19th-century Chinese fishing village. ⊠ *165 Forest Ave., at Central Ave.* ☎ *831/648–5716* ⊕ *pgmuseum.org* ✉ *$9, free last Sat. of month* ☉ *Closed Mon.*

FAMILY **Point Pinos Lighthouse.** At this 1855 structure, the West Coast's oldest continuously operating lighthouse, you can learn about the lighting and foghorn operations and wander through a small museum containing U.S. Coast Guard memorabilia. ⊠ *Asilomar Ave., between Lighthouse Ave. and Del Monte Blvd.* ☎ *831/648–3176* ⊕ *pointpinoslighthouse. org* ✉ *$2* ☉ *Closed Tues. and Wed.*

BEACHES

Asilomar State Beach. A beautiful coastal area, Asilomar State Beach stretches between Point Pinos and the Del Monte Forest. The 100 acres of dunes, tidal pools, and pocket-size beaches form one of the region's richest areas for marine life—including surfers, who migrate here most winter mornings. Leashed dogs are allowed on the beach. **Amenities:** none. **Best for:** sunrise; sunset; surfing; walking. ⊠ *Sunset Dr. and Asilomar Ave.* ☎ *831/646–6440* ⊕ *www.parks.ca.gov.*

WHERE TO EAT

$$ ✗ **Beach House.** Patrons of this blufftop perch sip classic cocktails, sample California fare, and watch the otters frolic on Lovers Point Beach below. Standout dishes include the crispy shrimp appetizer—tossed in a creamy, spicy sauce—entrées such as bacon-wrapped meat loaf, and crab-stuffed sole topped with citrus beurre blanc. **Known for:** sweeping blufftop views; sunset discounts; heated outdoor patio. ⑤ *Average main: $22* ⊠ *620 Ocean View Blvd.* ☎ *831/375–2345* ⊕ *beachhousepg. com* ☉ *No lunch.*

MODERN
AMERICAN

$$$$ ✗ **Fandango.** The menu here is mostly Mediterranean and southern French, with such dishes as osso buco and paella. The decor follows suit: stone walls and country furniture lend the restaurant the earthy feel of a European farmhouse. **Known for:** wood-fire-grilled rack of lamb, seafood, and beef; convivial residential vibe; traditional European flavors. ⑤ *Average main: $32* ⊠ *223 17th St., south of Lighthouse Ave.* ☎ *831/372–3456* ⊕ *fandangorestaurant.com.*

MEDITERRANEAN
Fodor'sChoice
★

$$$ ✗ **Joe Rombi's La Mia Cucina.** Pasta, fish, steaks, and veal dishes are the specialties at this modern trattoria, the best in town for Italian food. The look is spare and clean, with colorful antique wine posters decorating the white walls. **Known for:** house-made gnocchi, ravioli, and sausage; festive dining room. ⑤ *Average main: $25* ⊠ *208 17th St., at Lighthouse Ave.* ☎ *831/373–2416* ⊕ *lamiacucinaristorante.com* ☉ *Closed Mon. and Tues. No lunch.*

ITALIAN

$$$ ✗ **Passionfish.** South American artwork and artifacts decorate Passionfish, and Latin and Asian flavors infuse the dishes. The chef shops at local farmers' markets several times a week to find the best produce, fish, and meat available, then pairs it with creative sauces like a caper, raisin, and walnut relish. **Known for:** sustainably sourced seafood and organic ingredients; reasonably priced wine list that supports small

MODERN
AMERICAN
Fodor'sChoice
★

producers; slow-cooked meats. $ *Average main: $24* ⊠ *701 Lighthouse Ave., at Congress Ave.* ☎ *831/655–3311* ⊕ *passionfish.net* ☾ *No lunch.*

$$
AMERICAN

✕ **Red House Café.** When it's nice out, sun pours through the big windows of this cozy restaurant and across tables on the porch; when fog rolls in, the fireplace is lit. The American menu changes with the seasons but grilled lamb chops atop mashed potatoes are often on offer for dinner, and a grilled calamari steak might be served for lunch, either in a salad or as part of a sandwich. **Known for:** cozy homelike dining areas; comfort food; stellar breakfast and brunch. $ *Average main: $21* ⊠ *662 Lighthouse Ave., at 19th St.* ☎ *831/643–1060* ⊕ *redhousecafe.com* ☾ *No dinner Mon.*

$$
AMERICAN
FAMILY

✕ **Taste Café and Bistro.** Grilled marinated rabbit, roasted half chicken, filet mignon, and other meats are the focus at Taste, which serves hearty European-inspired food in a casual, open-kitchen setting. **Known for:** grilled meats; house-made desserts; kids' menu. $ *Average main: $22* ⊠ *1199 Forest Ave., at Prescott La.* ☎ *831/655–0324* ⊕ *tastecafebistro.com* ☾ *Closed Sun. and Mon.*

WHERE TO STAY

$$
B&B/INN
Fodor'sChoice
★

⌂ **Green Gables Inn.** Stained-glass windows and ornate interior details compete with spectacular ocean views at this Queen Anne–style mansion. **Pros:** exceptional views; impeccable attention to historic detail. **Cons:** some rooms are small; thin walls. $ *Rooms from: $169* ⊠ *301 Ocean View Blvd.* ☎ *831/375–2095* ⊕ *www.greengablesinnpg.com* ⤸ *11 rooms, 8 with bath* ⦿| *Breakfast.*

$$$
B&B/INN

⌂ **Martine Inn.** The glassed-in parlor and many guest rooms at this 1899 Mediterranean-style villa have stunning ocean views. **Pros:** romantic; exquisite antiques; fancy breakfast; ocean views. **Cons:** not child-friendly; sits on a busy thoroughfare. $ *Rooms from: $219* ⊠ *255 Ocean View Blvd.* ☎ *831/373–3388, 800/852–5588* ⊕ *martineinn.com* ⤸ *25 rooms* ⦿| *Breakfast.*

MONTEREY

2 miles southeast of Pacific Grove, 2 miles north of Carmel.

Monterey is a scenic city filled with early California history: adobe buildings from the 1700s, Colton Hall, where California's first constitution was drafted in 1849, and Cannery Row, made famous by author John Steinbeck. Thousands of visitors come each year to mingle with otters and other sea creatures at the world-famous Monterey Bay Aquarium and in the protected waters of the national marine sanctuary that hugs the shoreline.

GETTING HERE AND AROUND

From San Jose or San Francisco, take U.S. 101 south to Highway 156 West at Prunedale. Head west about 8 miles to Highway 1 and follow it about 15 miles south. From San Luis Obispo, take U.S. 101 north to Salinas and drive west on Highway 68 about 20 miles.

Many MST bus lines connect at the Monterey Transit Center, at Pearl Street and Munras Avenue. In summer (daily from 10 until at least 7) and on weekends and holidays the rest of the year, the free MST Monterey Trolley travels from downtown Monterey along Cannery Row to the Aquarium and back.

TOURS

Monterey Movie Tours. Board a customized motorcoach and relax while a film-savvy local takes you on a scenic tour of the Monterey Peninsula enhanced by film clips from the more than 200 movies shot in the area. The three-hour adventure travels a 32-mile loop through Monterey, Pacific Grove, and Carmel. ☒ *Departs from Monterey Conference Center, 1 Portola Plaza* ☎ *831/372–6278, 800/343–6437* ⊕ *montereymovietours.com* ☒ *$55.*

Old Monterey Walking Tour. Learn all about Monterey's storied past by joining a guided walking tour through the historic district. Tours begin at the Pacific House Museum in Custom House Plaza, across from Fisherman's Wharf and are offered Thursday through Sunday at 10:30, 12:30, and 2. ☒ *Monterey* ⊕ *www.parks.ca.gov/?page_id=951.*

The Original Monterey Walking Tours. Learn more about Monterey's storied past, primarily the Mexican period until California statehood, on a guided tour through downtown Monterey. You can also join a guided walking tour of Cannery Row in the afternoon. Tours last 1½ to 2 hours and are offered Thursday–Sunday at 10 am and 2. Reservations are essential. ☒ *Monterey* ☎ *831/521–4884* ⊕ *www.walkmonterey.com* ☒ *From $25.*

ESSENTIALS

Visitor Information Monterey County Convention & Visitors Bureau. ☎ *888/221–1010* ⊕ *seemonterey.com.*

EXPLORING

TOP ATTRACTIONS

Cannery Row. When John Steinbeck published the novel *Cannery Row* in 1945, he immortalized a place of rough-edged working people. The waterfront street, edging a mile of gorgeous coastline, once was crowded with sardine canneries processing, at their peak, nearly 200,000 tons of the smelly silver fish a year. During the mid-1940s, however, the sardines disappeared from the bay, causing the canneries to close. Through the years the old tin-roof canneries have been converted into restaurants, art galleries, and malls with shops selling T-shirts, fudge, and plastic sea otters. Recent tourist development along the row has been more tasteful, however, and includes stylish inns and hotels, wine tasting rooms, and upscale specialty shops. ☒ *Cannery Row, between Reeside and David Aves.* ⊕ *canneryrow.com.*

Colton Hall. A convention of delegates met here in 1849 to draft the first state constitution. The stone building, which has served as a school, a courthouse, and the county seat, is a city-run museum furnished as it was during the constitutional convention. The extensive grounds outside the hall surround the Old Monterey Jail. ☒ *570 Pacific St., between Madison and Jefferson Sts.* ☎ *831/646–5640* ⊕ *www.monterey.org/museums* ☒ *Free.*

Dali17 at the Museum of Monterey. Whether you're a fan of surrealist art or not, come to Dali17 to gain rare insight into the life and work of famed Spanish artist Salvador Dali, who lived in Monterey in the 1940s. The permanent exhibition houses nearly 600 artworks in various media, including 300 Dali originals. The museum's name reflects Dali's ties to nearby 17 Mile Drive, where he lived, worked, and hosted parties that included Andy Warhol, Walt Disney, Bob Hope, and other celebrities, ⌂ *5 Custom House Plaza* ☎ *831/372–2608* ⊕ *dali17.com* 💲*$20.*

FAMILY   **Fisherman's Wharf.** The mournful barking of sea lions provides a steady soundtrack all along Monterey's waterfront, but the best way to actually view the whiskered marine mammals is to walk along one of the two piers across from Custom House Plaza. Lined with souvenir shops, the wharf is undeniably touristy, but it's lively and entertaining. At Wharf No. 2, a working municipal pier, you can see the day's catch being unloaded from fishing boats on one side and fishermen casting their lines into the water on the other. The pier has a couple of low-key restaurants, from whose seats lucky customers might spot otters and harbor seals. ⌂ *At end of Calle Principal* ⊕ *www.montereywharf.com.*

FAMILY   **Monterey Bay Aquarium.** Sea creatures surround you the minute you hand
Fodor'sChoice   over your ticket at this extraordinary facility: right at the entrance dozens
★   of them swim in a three-story-tall, sunlit kelp-forest tank. All the exhibits here provide a sense of what it's like to be in the water with the animals—sardines swim around your head in a circular tank, and jellyfish drift in and out of view in dramatically lighted spaces that suggest the ocean

depths. A petting pool puts you literally in touch with bat rays, and the million-gallon Open Seas tank illustrates the variety of creatures, from sharks to placid-looking turtles, that live in the eastern Pacific. At the Splash Zone, which has 45 interactive bilingual exhibits, kids can commune with African black-footed penguins, potbellied seahorses, and other creatures. The only drawback to the aquarium experience is that it must be shared with the throngs that congregate daily, but most visitors think it's worth it. The ¡Viva Baja! Life on the Edge exhibit explores the delicate balance of life where the sea meets the sand in Baja, Mexico. Another must-see is *Tentacles: The Astounding Lives of Octopuses, Squid, and Cuttlefishes*, a huge and fascinating display of marine mollusks. ⊠ *886 Cannery Row, at David Ave.* ☎ *831/648–4800 info, 866/963–9645 for advance tickets* ⊕ *montereybayaquarium.org* ⊠ *$50.*

> JOHN STEINBECK'S
> CANNERY ROW
>
> "Cannery Row in Monterey in California is a poem, a stink, a grating noise, a quality of light, a tone, a habit, a nostalgia, a dream. Cannery Row is the gathered and scattered, tin and iron and rust and splintered wood, chipped pavement and weedy lots and junk heaps, sardine canneries of corrugated iron, honky tonks, restaurants and whore houses, and little crowded groceries, and laboratories and flophouses." — John Steinbeck, *Cannery Row*

Fodor's Choice ★ **Monterey State Historic Park.** You can glimpse Monterey's early history in several well-preserved adobe buildings downtown. Some of the structures have gardens that are themselves worthy sights, and they're visitable even if the buildings—among them **Casa Soberanes,** the **Larkin House,** and the **Stevenson House**—are closed.

A good place to start is the **Pacific House Museum.** Once a hotel and saloon, this facility, also a visitor center, commemorates life in pioneer-era California with gold-rush relics and photographs of old Monterey. On the upper floor are Native American artifacts, including gorgeous baskets and pottery. In the same plaza is the **Custom House.** Built by the Mexican government in 1827, it's California's oldest standing public building.

■ TIP➔ If buildings are closed when you visit you can access a cell phone tour 24/7 at 831/998-9458. ⊠ *Pacific House Museum visitor center, 10 Custom House Plaza* ☎ *831/649–7118* ⊕ *www.parks.ca.gov/mshp* ⊠ *Free–$5.*

WORTH NOTING

A Taste of Monterey. Without driving the back roads, you can taste the wines of nearly 100 area vintners (craft beers, too) while taking in fantastic bay views. Bottles are available for purchase, and food is served from noon until closing. ⊠ *700 Cannery Row, Suite KK* ☎ *831/646–5446* ⊕ *atasteofmonterey.com* ⊠ *Tastings $10–$20.*

FAMILY **Dennis the Menace Playground.** The late cartoonist Hank Ketcham designed this play area. Its equipment is on a grand scale and made for Dennis-like daredevils: kid favorites include the roller slide, rock-climbing area, and clanking suspension bridge. You can rent a rowboat

California sea lions are intelligent, social animals that live (and sleep) close together in groups.

or a paddleboat for cruising around U-shaped Lake El Estero, populated with an assortment of ducks, mud hens, and geese. ⊠ *El Estero Park, Pearl St. and Camino El Estero* ☎ *831/646–3866* ⊕ *www.monterey.org/ parks* ☉ *Closed Tues., Sept.–May.*

Presidio of Monterey Museum. This spot has been significant for centuries. Its first incarnation was as a Native American village for the Rumsien tribe. The Spanish explorer Sebastián Vizcaíno landed here in 1602, and Father Junípero Serra arrived in 1770. Notable battles fought here include the 1818 skirmish in which the corsair Hipólito Bruchard conquered the Spanish garrison that stood on this site and claimed part of California for Argentina. The indoor museum tells the stories; plaques mark the outdoor sites. ⊠ *Presidio of Monterey, Corporal Ewing Rd., off Lighthouse Ave.* ☎ *831/646–3456* ⊕ *www.monterey.org/museums* ⊠ *Free* ☉ *Closed Tues. and Wed.*

WHERE TO EAT

$$ ✕ **Monterey's Fish House.** Casual yet stylish and always packed, this sea-
SEAFOOD food restaurant is removed from the hubbub of the wharf. If the dining room is full, you can wait at the bar and savor plump oysters on the half shell. **Known for:** seafood, steaks, house-made pasta; festive atmosphere. $ *Average main: $22* ⊠ *2114 Del Monte Ave., at Dela Vina Ave.* ☎ *831/373–4647* ⊕ *montereyfishhouse.com* ☉ *No lunch weekends.*

$$$ ✕ **Montrio Bistro.** This quirky converted firehouse, with its rawhide walls
AMERICAN and iron indoor trellises, has a wonderfully sophisticated menu. Organic
Fodor's Choice produce and meats and sustainably sourced seafood are used in imagi-
★ native dishes that reflect the area's agriculture—crispy artichoke hearts

with Mediterranean baba ganoush, for instance, and scallop crudo with avocado-jalapeño panna cotta. **Known for:** green-certified restaurant; historic firehouse setting; inventive cocktails. $ *Average main: $30* ⊠ *414 Calle Principal, at W. Franklin St.* ☎ *831/648–8880* ⊕ *montrio.com* ⊗ *No lunch.*

$$$ ✕ **Old Fisherman's Grotto.** Otters and
SEAFOOD seals frolic in the water just below this nautical-theme Fisherman's Wharf restaurant famous for its creamy clam chowder. Seafood paella, sand dabs, filet mignon, teriyaki chicken, and several pastas are among the many entrée options. **Known for:** Monterey-style clam chowder and calamari; Monterey Bay views. $ *Average main: $29* ⊠ *39 Fisherman's Wharf* ☎ *831/375–4604* ⊕ *oldfishermansgrotto.com.*

$ ✕ **Old Monterey Café.** Breakfast here gets constant local raves. The café's
AMERICAN fame rests on familiar favorites: a dozen kinds of omelets, and pancakes from blueberry to cinnamon-raisin-pecan. $ *Average main: $15* ⊠ *489 Alvarado St., at Munras Ave.* ☎ *831/646–1021* ⊗ *No dinner.*

$$$$ ✕ **Restaurant 1833.** Inside the two-story Stokes Adobe, built in 1833,
MODERN this popular restaurant and bar showcases the region's colorful his-
AMERICAN tory and local bounty. Each of the seven dining rooms honors an era
Fodor's Choice and characters from the adobe's past, which includes an early stint as
★ an apothecary. **Known for:** tree-shaded courtyard with fire pits; craft cocktails; extensive wine list. $ *Average main: $32* ⊠ *500 Hartnell St., at Polk St.* ☎ *831/643–1833* ⊕ *www.restaurant1833.com* ⊗ *No lunch. Closed Mon.*

$$$ ✕ **Tarpy's Roadhouse.** Fun, dressed-up American favorites—a little some-
AMERICAN thing for everyone—are served in this renovated early-1900s stone farmhouse several miles east of town. The kitchen cranks out everything from Cajun-spiced prawns to meat loaf with marsala–mushroom gravy to grilled ribs and steaks. **Known for:** American comfort food with a California twist; rustic dining: indoor fireplace or garden courtyard. $ *Average main: $28* ⊠ *2999 Monterey–Salinas Hwy., Hwy. 68* ☎ *831/647–1444* ⊕ *tarpys.com.*

WHERE TO STAY

$$$ 🛏 **InterContinental The Clement Monterey.** Spectacular bay views, upscale
HOTEL amenities, assiduous service, and a superb location next to the aquar-
FAMILY ium propelled this luxury hotel to immediate stardom. **Pros:** a block from the aquarium; fantastic waterfront views from some rooms; great for families. **Cons:** a tad formal; pricey. $ *Rooms from: $229* ⊠ *750 Cannery Row* ☎ *831/375–4500, 866/781–2406 toll free* ⊕ *www.icthe-clementmonterey.com* ⇆ *208 rooms* ⭘ *No meals.*

$$ 🛏 **Monterey Bay Lodge.** Its superior amenities and location bordering El
HOTEL Estero Park give this cheerful facility the edge over other area motels.
FAMILY **Pros:** within walking distance of the beach and a playground; quiet

at night; good family choice. **Cons:** near a busy boulevard. Ⓢ *Rooms from: $150* ⊠ *55 Camino Aguajito* ☎ *831/372–8057, 800/558–1900* ⊕ *montereybaylodge.com* ⇄ *46 rooms* �PO *No meals.*

$$$$
HOTEL

🏨 **Monterey Plaza Hotel & Spa.** Guests at this waterfront Cannery Row hotel can see frolicking sea otters from its wide outdoor patio and many room balconies. **Pros:** on the ocean; many amenities; attentive service. **Cons:** touristy area; heavy traffic. Ⓢ *Rooms from: $269* ⊠ *400 Cannery Row* ☎ *831/920–6710, 855/421–0264* ⊕ *www.montereyplazahotel. com* ⇄ *290 rooms.*

$$$$
B&B/INN
Fodor's Choice
★

🏨 **Old Monterey Inn.** This three-story manor house was the home of Monterey's first mayor, and today it remains a private enclave within walking distance of downtown, set off by lush gardens shaded by huge old trees and bordered by a creek. **Pros:** gorgeous gardens; refined luxury; serene. **Cons:** must drive to attractions and sights; fills quickly. Ⓢ *Rooms from: $289* ⊠ *500 Martin St.* ☎ *831/652–8999, 800/350–2344* ⊕ *www.oldmontereyinn.com* ⇄ *9 rooms, 1 cottage* �PO *Breakfast.*

$$$
HOTEL

🏨 **Spindrift Inn.** This boutique hotel on Cannery Row has beach access and a rooftop garden that overlooks the water. **Pros:** close to aquarium; steps from the beach; friendly staff. **Cons:** throngs of visitors outside; can be noisy; not good for families. Ⓢ *Rooms from: $209* ⊠ *652 Cannery Row* ☎ *831/646–8900, 800/841–1879* ⊕ *spindriftinn.com* ⇄ *45 rooms* �PO *Breakfast.*

NIGHTLIFE AND PERFORMING ARTS

NIGHTLIFE

BARS

Peter B's Brewpub. House-made beers, 15 HDTVs, a decent pub menu, and a pet-friendly patio ensure lively crowds at this craft brewery in back of the Portola Plaza Hotel. ⊠ *2 Portola Plaza* ☎ *831/649–2699* ⊕ *www.peterbsbrewpub.com.*

Turn 12 Bar & Grill. The motorcycles and vintage photographs at this downtown watering hole pay homage to nearby 11-turn Laguna Seca Raceway. The large-screen TVs, heated outdoor patio, happy-hour specials, and live entertainment keep the place jumpin' into the wee hours. ⊠ *400 Tyler St., at E. Franklin St.* ☎ *831/372–8876* ⊕ *turn12barandgrill.com.*

MUSIC FESTIVALS

Monterey Jazz Festival. The world's oldest jazz festival attracts top-name performers to the Monterey Fairgrounds on the third full weekend of September. ☎ *888/248–6499 ticket office, 831/373–3366* ⊕ *montereyjazzfestival.org.*

PERFORMING ARTS

THEATER

Bruce Ariss Wharf Theater (*The New Wharf Theatre*). American musicals past and present are the focus here, with dramas and comedies also in the mix. ⊠ *One Fisherman's Wharf* ☎ *831/649–2332.*

The Monterey Bay National Marine Sanctuary

Although Monterey's coastal landscapes are stunning, their beauty is more than equaled by the wonders that lie offshore. The Monterey Bay National Marine Sanctuary—which stretches 276 miles, from north of San Francisco almost down to Santa Barbara—teems with abundant life, and has topography as diverse as that aboveground.

The preserve's 5,322 square miles include vast submarine canyons, which reach down 10,663 feet at their deepest point. They also encompass dense forests of giant kelp—a kind of seaweed that can grow more than a hundred feet from its roots on the ocean floor. These kelp forests are especially robust off Monterey.

The sanctuary was established in 1992 to protect the habitat of the many species that thrive in the bay. Some animals can be seen quite easily from land. In summer and winter you might glimpse the offshore spray of gray whales as they migrate between their summer feeding grounds in Alaska and their breeding grounds in Baja. Clouds of marine birds—including white-faced ibis, three types of albatross, and more than 15 types of gull—skim the waves, or roost in the rock islands along 17-Mile Drive. Sea otters dart and gambol in the calmer waters of the bay; and of course, you can watch the sea lions—and hear their round-the-clock barking—on the wharves in Santa Cruz and Monterey.

The sanctuary supports many other creatures, however, that remain unseen by most on-land visitors. Some of these are enormous, such as the giant blue whales that arrive to feed on plankton in summer; others, like the more than 22 species of red algae in these waters, are microscopic. So whether you choose to visit the Monterey Bay Aquarium, take a whale-watch trip, or look out to sea with your binoculars, remember you're seeing just a small part of a vibrant underwater kingdom.

SPORTS AND THE OUTDOORS

Monterey Bay waters never warm to the temperatures of their Southern California counterparts—the warmest they get is the low 60s. That's one reason why the marine life here is so diverse, which in turn brings out the fishers, kayakers, and whale-watchers. During the rainy winter, the waves grow larger, and surfers flock to the water. On land pretty much year-round, bikers find opportunities to ride, and walkers have plenty of waterfront to stroll.

BIKING

Adventures by the Sea. You can rent surreys plus tandem, standard, and electric bicycles from this outfit that also conducts bike and kayak tours, and rents kayaks and stand-up paddleboards. There are multiple locations along Cannery Row and Custom House Plaza as well as branches at Lovers Point in Pacific Grove and 17-Mile Drive in Pebble Beach. ✉ *299 Cannery Row* ☎ *831/372–1807, 800/979–3370 reservations* ⊕ *adventuresbythesea.com.*

Bay Bikes. For bicycle and surrey rentals, visit Bay Bikes at here or at 486 Washington Street. ∎TIP→ You can rent a bike on Cannery Row and drop it off at the company's Carmel location at 3600 The Barnyard. ✉ *585 Cannery Row* ☎ *831/655–2453* ⊕ *www.baybikes.com.*

FISHING

Randy's Fishing and Whale Watching Trips. In business since 1949, Randy's takes beginning and experienced fishers out to sea. ✉ *66 Fisherman's Wharf* ☎ *831/372–7440, 800/251–7440* ⊕ *randysfishingtrips.com.*

KAYAKING

Fodor'sChoice **Monterey Bay Kayaks.** For many visitors the best way to see the bay is
★   by kayak. This company rents equipment and conducts classes and natural-history tours. ✉ *693 Del Monte Ave.* ☎ *831/373–5357* ⊕ *www.montereybaykayaks.com.*

WALKING

Monterey Bay Coastal Recreation Trail. From Custom House Plaza, you can walk along the coast in either direction on this 29-mile-long trail and take in spectacular views of the sea. The trail runs from north of Monterey in Castroville south to Pacific Grove, with sections continuing around Pebble Beach. Much of the path follows an old Southern Pacific Railroad route. ☎ *888/221–1010* ⊕ *seemonterey.com/ things-to-do/parks/coastal-trail/.*

WHALE-WATCHING

Thousands of gray whales pass close by the Monterey Coast on their annual migration between the Bering Sea and Baja California, and a whale-watching cruise is the best way to see these magnificent mammals close up. The migration south takes place from December through March; January is prime viewing time. The whales migrate north from March through June. Blue whales and humpbacks also pass the coast; they're most easily spotted in late summer and early fall.

Fast Raft Ocean Safaris. Naturalists lead whale-watching and sightseeing tours of Monterey Bay aboard the 33-foot *Ranger,* a six-passenger, rigid-hull inflatable boat. The speedy craft slips into coves inaccessible to larger vessels; its quiet engines enable intimate marine experiences without disturbing wildlife. Children ages eight and older are welcome to participate. ✉ *32 Cannery Row, Suite F2* ☎ *408/659–3900* ⊕ *www. fastraft.com* ▭ *$150.*

Monterey Bay Whale Watch. The marine biologists here lead three- to five-hour whale-watching tours. ✉ *84 Fisherman's Wharf* ☎ *831/375–4658* ⊕ *montereybaywhalewatch.com.*

Princess Monterey Whale Watching. Tours are offered daily on a 100-passenger high-speed cruiser and a large 100-foot boat. ✉ *96 Fisherman's Wharf* ☎ *831/372–2203, 831/205–2370 reservations* ⊕ *montereywhalewatching.com.*

SHOPPING

Alvarado and nearby downtown streets are good places to start a Monterey shopping spree, especially if you're interested in antiques and collectibles.

Cannery Row Antique Mall. Bargain hunters can sometimes find little treasures at the mall, which houses more than 100 local vendors under one roof. ⊠ *471 Wave St.* ☎ *831/655–0264* ⊕ *canneryrowantiquemall.com.*

Old Monterey Book Co. Antiquarian books and prints are this shop's specialties. ⊠ *136 Bonifacio Pl., off Alvarado St.* ☎ *831/372–3111* ⊗ *Closed Sun. and Mon.*

AROUND MONTEREY BAY

North and east of Monterey is what many call Steinbeck country—the rich agricultural setting for many of famed author John Steinbeck's novels—and it's home to California's newest national park, Pinnacles. North of Monterey, Highway 1 follows the curve of the bay between Monterey and Santa Cruz: passing through a protected national marine estuary at Moss Landing, where otters and seals play alongside humans in kayaks; up to some of the bay's best beaches, including Seacliff and New Brighton state beach parks; to classic California seaside villages Aptos, Soquel, and Capitola; to Santa Cruz, home of surf legends, an historic boardwalk, and UC Santa Cruz. Salinas and Moss Landing are in Monterey County; the other cities and towns covered here are in Santa Cruz County.

GETTING HERE AND AROUND

All the towns in this area are on or just off Highway 1. MST buses serve Monterey County destinations, connecting in Watsonville with Santa Cruz METRO buses, which operate throughout Santa Cruz County.

SALINAS

17 miles east of Monterey on Hwy. 68.

Salinas, a hardworking city surrounded by vineyards and fruit and vegetable fields, honors the memory and literary legacy of John Steinbeck, its most famous native, with the National Steinbeck Center. The facility is in Old Town Salinas, where renovated turn-of-the-20th-century stone buildings house shops and restaurants.

ESSENTIALS

Train Information Salinas Amtrak Station. ⊠ *11 Station Pl., at W. Market St.* ☎ *800/872–7245* ⊕ *www.amtrak.com.*

Visitor Information California Welcome Center. ⊠ *1213 N. Davis Rd., west of U.S. 101, exit 330* ☎ *831/757–8687* ⊕ *visitcalifornia.com/attraction/california-welcome-center-salinas.*

EXPLORING

FAMILY **Monterey Zoo.** Exotic animals, many of them retired from film, television, and live production work or rescued from less than ideal environments, find sanctuary here. The zoo offers daily tours, but for an in-depth experience, stay in a safari bungalow on-site at Vision Quest Safari B&B, where breakfast is delivered in a basket by an elephant. The inn's room rate includes a complimentary zoo tour. ⊠ *400 River Rd., off Hwy. 68* ☎ *831/455–1901, 800/228–7382* ⊕ *www.montereyzoo.com* ⊠ *Tours $12; posttour elephant feeding $5.*

National Steinbeck Center. The center's exhibits document the life of Pulitzer- and Nobel-prize winner John Steinbeck and the history of the nearby communities that inspired novels such as *East of Eden.* Highlights include reproductions of the green pickup-camper from *Travels with Charley* and the bunk room from *Of Mice and Men.* **Steinbeck House,** the author's Victorian birthplace, at 132 Central Avenue, is two blocks from the center. Now a decent restaurant (only open for lunch) and gift shop with docent-led tours, it displays memorabilia. ⊠ *1 Main St., at Central Ave.* ☎ *831/775–4721* ⊕ *steinbeck.org* ⊠ *$13.*

PINNACLES NATIONAL PARK

38 miles southeast of Salinas.

Pinnacles may be the nation's newest national park, but Teddy Roosevelt recognized the uniqueness of this ancient volcano—its jagged spires and monoliths thrusting upward from chaparral-covered mountains—when he made it a national monument in 1908. Though only about two hours from the bustling Bay Area, the outside world seems to recede even before you reach the park's gates.

GETTING HERE AND AROUND

One of the first things you need to decide when visiting Pinnacles is which entrance—east or west—you'll use, because there's no road connecting the two rugged peaks separating them. Entering from Highway 25 on the east is straightforward. The gate is only a mile or so from the turnoff. From the west, once you head east out of Soledad on Highway 146, the road quickly becomes narrow and hilly, with many blind curves. Drive slowly and cautiously along the 10 miles or so before you reach the west entrance.

ESSENTIALS

Pinnacles Visitor Center. At the park's main visitor center, located at the eastern entrance, you can purchase admission passes, get maps, browse books, and buy gifts. The adjacent campground store sells snacks and drinks. ⊠ *Hwy. 146, 2 miles west of Hwy. 25, Paicines* ☎ *831/389–4485* ⊕ *www.nps.gov/pinn.*

West Pinnacles Visitor Contact Station. This station is just past the park's western entrance, about 10 miles east of Soledad. Here you can get maps and information, watch a 13-minute film about Pinnacles, and view some displays. Food and drink aren't available here. ⊠ *Hwy. 146, off U.S. 101, Soledad* ☎ *831/389–4427* ⊕ *www.nps.gov/pinn.*

EXPLORING

FAMILY **Pinnacles National Park.** The many attractions at Pinnacles include talus caves, 30 miles of hiking trails, and hundreds of rock-climbing routes. A mosaic of diverse habitats supports an amazing variety of wildlife species: 185 birds, 49 mammals, 70 butterflies, and nearly 400 bees.

The park is also home to some of the world's remaining few hundred condors in captivity and release areas. Fourteen of California's 25 bat species live in caves and other habitats in the park. President Theodore Roosevelt declared this remarkable 26,000-acre geologic and wildlife preserve a national monument in 1908. President Barack Obama officially designated it a national park in 2013.

The pinnacles are believed to have been created when two major tectonic plates collided and pushed a smaller plate down beneath the earth's crust, spawning volcanoes in what's now called the Gabilan Mountains, southeast of Salinas and Monterey. After the eruptions ceased, the San Andreas Fault split the volcanic field in two, carrying part of it northward to what is now Pinnacles National Park. Millions of years of erosion left a rugged landscape of rocky spires and crags, or pinnacles. Boulders fell into canyons and valleys, creating talus caves and a paradise for modern-day rock climbers. Spring is the most popular time to visit, when colorful wildflowers blanket the meadows; the light and scenery can be striking in fall and winter; the summer heat is often brutal. The park has two entrances—east and west—but they are not connected. The Pinnacles Visitor Center, Bear Gulch Nature Center, Park Headquarters, the Pinnacles Campground, and the Bear Gulch Cave and Reservoir are on the east side. The Chaparral Parking Area is on the west side, where you can feast on fantastic views of the Pinnacles High Peaks from the parking area. Dogs are not allowed on hiking trails. ■TIP➔ The east entrance is 32 miles southeast of Hollister via Highway 25. The west entrance is about 12 miles east of Soledad via Highway 146. ⊠ 5000 Hwy. 146, Paicines ☎ 831/389–4486, 831/389–4427 Westside ⊕ www.nps.gov/pinn ⊞ $10 per vehicle, $5 per visitor if biking or walking.

SPORTS AND THE OUTDOORS
HIKING

Hiking is the most popular activity at Pinnacles, with more than 30 miles of trails for every interest and level of fitness. Because there isn't a road through the park, hiking is also the only way to experience its interior, including the High Peaks, the talus caves, and the reservoir.

Balconies Cliffs-Cave Loop. Grab your flashlight before heading out from the Chaparral Trailhead parking lot for this 2.4-mile loop that takes you through the Balconies Caves. This trail is especially beautiful in spring, when wildflowers carpet the canyon floor. About 0.6 mile from the start of the trail, turn left to begin ascending the Balconies Cliffs Trail, where you'll be rewarded with close-up views of Machete Ridge and other steep, vertical formations; you may run across rock climbers testing their skills. *Easy.* ⊠ *West side of park* ✛ *Trailhead: from West Pinnacles Visitor Contact Station, drive about 2 miles to Chaparral Trailhead parking lot. Trail picks up on west side of lot.*

FAMILY **Moses Spring-Rim Trail Loop.** Perhaps the most popular hike at Pinnacles, this relatively short (2.2 miles) trail is fun for kids and adults. It leads to the Bear Gulch cave system, and if your timing is right, you'll pass by several seasonal waterfalls inside the caves. If it has been raining, check with a ranger, as the caves could be flooded. The upper side of the cave is usually closed in spring and early summer to protect the Townsend's big-ear bats and their pups. *Easy.* ⊠ *East side of park* ⊹ *Trailhead: just past Bear Gulch Nature Center, on south side of overflow parking lot.*

SAN JUAN BAUTISTA

20 miles northeast of Salinas.

Much of the small town that grew up around Mission San Juan Bautista, still a working church, has been protected from development since 1933, when a state park was established here. Small antiques shops and restaurants occupy the Old West and art deco buildings that line 3rd Street.

GETTING HERE AND AROUND

From Highway 1 north or south, exit east onto Highway 156. MST buses do not serve San Juan Bautista.

EXPLORING

San Juan Bautista State Historic Park. With the low-slung, colonnaded **Mission San Juan Bautista** as its drawing card, this park 20 miles northeast of Salinas is about as close to early-19th-century California as you can get. Historic buildings ring the wide green plaza, among them an adobe home furnished with Spanish-colonial antiques, a hotel frozen in the 1860s, a blacksmith shop, a pioneer cabin, and a jailhouse. The mission's cemetery contains the unmarked graves of more than 4,300 Native American converts. ■ TIP➜ On the first Saturday of the month, costumed volunteers engage in quilting bees, tortilla making, and other frontier activities; and sarsaparilla and other nonalcoholic drinks are served in the saloon. ⊠ *19 Franklin St., off Hwy. 156, east of U.S. 101* ☎ *831/623–4881* ⊕ *www.parks.ca.gov* 🖅 *$3 park, $4 mission.*

MOSS LANDING

17 miles north of Monterey, 12 miles north of Salinas.

Moss Landing is not much more than a couple of blocks of cafés and restaurants, art galleries, and studios, plus a busy fishing port, but therein lies its charm. It's a fine place to overnight or stop for a meal and get a dose of nature.

GETTING HERE AND AROUND

From Highway 1 north or south, exit at Moss Landing Road on the ocean side. MST buses serve Moss Landing.

TOURS

Elkhorn Slough Safari Nature Boat Tours. This outfit's naturalists lead two-hour tours of Elkhorn Sough aboard a 27-foot pontoon boat. Reservations are required. ⊠ *Moss Landing Harbor* ☎ *831/633–5555* ⊕ *elkhornslough.com* 🖅 *$38.*

ESSENTIALS

Visitor Information Moss Landing Chamber of Commerce. ☎ *831/633–4501* ⊕ *mosslandingchamber.com.*

EXPLORING

Elkhorn Slough National Estuarine Research Reserve. The reserve's 1,400 acres of tidal flats and salt marshes form a complex environment that supports some 300 species of birds. A walk along the meandering waterways and wetlands can reveal hawks, white-tailed kites, owls, herons, and egrets. Also living or visiting here are sea otters, sharks, rays, and many other animals. ■ TIP→ On weekends, guided walks from the visitor center begin at 10 and 1. On the first Saturday of the month, an early-bird tour departs at 8:30. ⊠ *1700 Elkhorn Rd., Watsonville* ☎ *831–728–2822* ⊕ *elkhornslough.org* 🗃 *$4 day use fee (credit card only)* ☉ *Closed Mon.–Tues.*

WHERE TO EAT AND STAY

$$$
SOUTH
AMERICAN
✕ **Haute Enchilada.** Part of a complex that includes art galleries and an events venue, the Haute adds bohemian character to the seafaring village of Moss Landing. The inventive Latin American–inspired dishes include shrimp and black corn enchiladas topped with a citrus cilantro cream sauce, and roasted *pasilla* chilies stuffed with mashed plantains and caramelized onions. **Known for:** extensive cocktail and wine list; many vegan and gluten-free options; artsy atmosphere. ⑤ *Average main: $24* ⊠ *7902 Moss Landing Rd.* ☎ *831–633–5843* ⊕ *hauteenchilada.com.*

$$
SEAFOOD
✕ **Phil's Fish Market & Eatery.** Exquisitely fresh, simply prepared seafood (try the cioppino) is on the menu at this warehouselike restaurant on the harbor; all kinds of glistening fish are for sale at the market in the front. **Known for:** cioppino; clam chowder; myriad artichoke dishes. ⑤ *Average main: $21* ⊠ *7600 Sandholdt Rd.* ☎ *831–633–2152* ⊕ *philsfishmarket.com.*

$$
B&B/INN
🏠 **Captain's Inn.** Commune with nature and pamper yourself with upscale creature comforts at this green-certified complex in the heart of town. **Pros:** walk to restaurants and shops; tranquil natural setting; free Wi-Fi and parking. **Cons:** rooms in historic building don't have water views; far from urban amenities; not appropriate for young children. ⑤ *Rooms from: $170* ⊠ *8122 Moss Landing Rd.* ☎ *831–633–5550* ⊕ *www.captainsinn.com* ⇗ *10 rooms* 🍽 *Breakfast.*

SPORTS AND THE OUTDOORS
KAYAKING

Monterey Bay Kayaks. Rent a kayak to paddle out into Elkhorn Slough for up-close wildlife encounters. ⊠ *2390 Hwy. 1, at North Harbor* ☎ *831/373–5357* ⊕ *montereybaykayaks.com.*

APTOS

17 miles north of Moss Landing.

Backed by a redwood forest and facing the sea, downtown Aptos— known as Aptos Village—is a place of wooden walkways and false-fronted shops. Antiques dealers cluster along Trout Gulch Road, off Soquel Drive east of Highway 1.

GETTING HERE AND AROUND

Use Highway 1 to reach Aptos from Santa Cruz or Monterey. Exit at State Park Drive to reach the main shopping hub and Aptos Village. You can also exit at Freedom Boulevard or Rio del Mar. Soquel Drive is the main artery through town.

ESSENTIALS

Visitor Information Aptos Chamber of Commerce. ⊠ *7605-A Old Dominion Ct.* ☎ *831/688–1467* ⊕ *aptoschamber.com.*

BEACHES

FAMILY

Fodor'sChoice

★

Seacliff State Beach. Sandstone bluffs tower above popular Seacliff State Beach. The 1.5 mile walk north to adjacent New Brighton State Beach in Capitola is one of the nicest on the bay. Leashed dogs are allowed on the beach. **Amenities:** food and drink; lifeguards; parking (fee); showers; toilets. **Best for:** sunset; swimming; walking. ⊠ *201 State Park Dr., off Hwy. 1* ☎ *831/685–6500* ⊕ *www.parks.ca.gov* 🚗 *$10 per vehicle.*

WHERE TO EAT AND STAY

$$$

MEDITERRANEAN

✕ **Bittersweet Bistro.** A large old tavern with cathedral ceilings houses this popular bistro, where chef-owner Thomas Vinolus draws culinary inspiration from the Mediterranean. The menu changes seasonally, but regular highlights include paella, seafood puttanesca, and pepper-crusted rib-eye steak with Cabernet demi-glace. **Known for:** value-laden happy hour; seafood specials; house-made desserts. ⑤ *Average main: $28* ⊠ *787 Rio Del Mar Blvd., off Hwy. 1* ☎ *831/662–9799* ⊕ *www. bittersweetbistro.com* ⊘ *Closed Mon.*

$$$

HOTEL

FAMILY

🛏 **Best Western Seacliff Inn.** Families and business travelers like this 6-acre property near Seacliff State Beach that's more resort than hotel. **Pros:** walking distance to the beach; family-friendly; hot breakfast buffet. **Cons:** close to freeway; occasional nighttime bar noise. ⑤ *Rooms from: $180* ⊠ *7500 Old Dominion Ct.* ☎ *831/688–7300, 800/780–7234* ⊕ *seacliffinn.com* 🛏 *149 rooms* ⍵ *Breakfast.*

$$$

HOTEL

🛏 **Rio Sands Hotel.** A property-wide makeover completed in 2015 has made this casual two-building complex near the beach an even more exceptional value. **Pros:** two-minute walk to Rio Del Mar Beach (Seacliff State Beach is also nearby); free parking and Wi-Fi; close to a deli and restaurants. **Cons:** some rooms and suites are small; neighborhood becomes congested in summer. ⑤ *Rooms from: $179* ⊠ *116 Aptos Beach Dr.* ☎ *831/688–3207, 800/826–2077* ⊕ *riosands.com* 🛏 *50 rooms* ⍵ *Breakfast.*

$$$$

RESORT

FAMILY

🛏 **Seascape Beach Resort.** It's easy to unwind at this full-fledged resort on a bluff overlooking Monterey Bay. The spacious suites sleep from two to eight people. **Pros:** time share–style apartments; access to miles of beachfront; superb views. **Cons:** far from city life; most bathrooms are small. ⑤ *Rooms from: $300* ⊠ *1 Seascape Resort Dr.* ☎ *831/688–6800, 800/929–7727* ⊕ *seascaperesort.com* 🛏 *285 suites* ⍵ *No meals.*

CAPITOLA AND SOQUEL

4 miles northwest of Aptos.

On the National Register of Historic places as California's first seaside resort town, the village of Capitola has been in a holiday mood since the late 1800s. Casual eateries, surf shops, and ice cream parlors pack its walkable downtown. Inland, across Highway 1, antiques shops line Soquel Drive in the town of Soquel. Wineries dot the Santa Cruz Mountains beyond.

GETTING HERE AND AROUND

From Santa Cruz or Monterey, follow Highway 1 to the Capitola/Soquel (Bay Avenue) exit about 7 miles south of Santa Cruz and head west to reach Capitola and east to access Soquel Village. On summer weekends, park for free in the lot behind the Crossroads Center, a block west of the freeway, and hop aboard the free Capitola Shuttle to the village.

ESSENTIALS

Visitor Information Capitola-Soquel Chamber of Commerce. ⊠ *716-G Capitola Ave., Capitola* ☎ *831/475–6522* ⊕ *capitolachamber.com.*

BEACHES

FAMILY
Fodor'sChoice
★

New Brighton State Beach. Once the site of a Chinese fishing village, New Brighton is now a popular surfing and camping spot. Its Pacific Migrations Visitor Center traces the history of the Chinese and other peoples who settled around Monterey Bay. It also documents the migratory patterns of the area's wildlife, such as monarch butterflies and gray whales. Leashed dogs are allowed in the park. New Brighton connects with Seacliff Beach, and at low tide you can walk or run along this scenic stretch of sand for nearly 16 miles south (though you might have to wade through a few creeks). ■TIP➜ The 1½-mile stroll from New Brighton to Seacliff's concrete ship is a local favorite. **Amenities:** parking (fee); showers; toilets. **Best for:** sunset; swimming; walking. ⊠ *1500 State Park Dr., off Hwy. 1, Capitola* ☎ *831/464–6329* ⊕ *www.parks.ca.gov* ⊠ *$10 per vehicle.*

WHERE TO EAT

$
SEAFOOD
FAMILY

✕ Carpo's. Locals love this casual counter where seafood predominates, but you can also order burgers, salads, and steaks. Baskets of battered snapper are among the favorites, along with calamari, prawns, seafood kebabs, fish and chips, and homemade olallieberry pie. **Known for:** large portions of healthy comfort food; lots of options under $10; soup and salad bar. Ⓢ *Average main: $13* ⊠ *2400 Porter St., at Hwy. 1, Soquel* ☎ *831/476–6260* ⊕ *carposrestaurant.com.*

$$
CAFÉ
FAMILY

✕ Gayle's Bakery & Rosticceria. Whether you're in the mood for an orange-olallieberry muffin, a wild rice and chicken salad, or tri-tip on garlic toast, this bakery-deli's varied menu is likely to satisfy. Munch on your lemon meringue tartlet or chocolate brownie on the shady patio, or dig into the daily blue-plate dinner—teriyaki grilled skirt steak with edamame-shiitake sticky rice, perhaps, or roast turkey breast with Chardonnay gravy—amid the whirl of activity inside. **Known for:** prepared meals to go; on-site bakery and rosticceria; deli and espresso bar. Ⓢ *Average main: $16* ⊠ *504 Bay Ave., at Capitola Ave., Capitola* ☎ *831/462–1200* ⊕ *gaylesbakery.com.*

CALIFORNIA'S OLDEST RESORT TOWN

As far as anyone knows for certain, Capitola is the oldest seaside resort town on the Pacific Coast. In 1856 a pioneer acquired Soquel Landing, the picturesque lagoon and beach where Soquel Creek empties into the bay, and built a wharf. Another man opened a campground along the shore, and his daughter named it Capitola after a heroine in a novel series. After the train came to town in the 1870s, thousands of vacationers began arriving to bask in the sun on the glorious beach.

3

$$$ ✕ **Michael's on Main.** Creative variations on classic comfort food and
AMERICAN live music five nights a week draw lively crowds to this upscale but
casual creekside eatery. Cordon Bleu-trained chef Peter Henry's
menu changes seasonally, but might include skirt steak with pickled
strawberry chimichurri or chargrilled prawns with a Thai chili glaze.
Known for: locally sourced, usually within 50 miles; excellent wine
list; romantic patio overlooking Soquel Creek. ⑤ *Average main: $28*
✉ *2591 Main St., at Porter St., Soquel* ☎ *831/479–9777* ⊕ *michael-sonmain.net* ⊗ *Closed Mon.*

$$$$ ✕ **Shadowbrook.** To get to this romantic spot overlooking Soquel Creek,
EUROPEAN you can take a cable car or walk the stairs down a steep, fern-lined bank
beside a running waterfall. Dining room options include the rooftop
Redwood Room, the wood-paneled Wine Cellar, the creekside, glass-enclosed Greenhouse, the Fireplace Room, and the airy Garden Room.
Known for: romantic creekside setting; prime rib and grilled seafood;
local special-occasion favorite for nearly 70 years. ⑤ *Average main: $32*
✉ *1750 Wharf Rd., at Lincoln Ave., Capitola* ☎ *831/475–1511* ⊕ *www.shadowbrook-capitola.com* ⊗ *No lunch.*

WHERE TO STAY

$$$$ ⛫ **Inn at Depot Hill.** This inventively designed bed-and-breakfast in a
B&B/INN former rail depot views itself as a link to the era of luxury train
travel. **Pros:** short walk to beach and village; historic charm; excellent service. **Cons:** fills quickly; hot-tub conversation audible in
some rooms. ⑤ *Rooms from: $299* ✉ *250 Monterey Ave., Capitola*
☎ *831/462–3376, 800/572–2632* ⊕ *www.innatdepothill.com* ⌑ *12
rooms* ⑩ *Breakfast.*

SANTA CRUZ

5 miles west of Capitola, 48 miles north of Monterey.

The big city on this stretch of the California coast, Santa Cruz (pop.
63,364) is less manicured than Carmel or Monterey. Long known
for its surfing and its amusement-filled beach boardwalk, the town
is a mix of grand Victorian-era homes and rinky-dink motels. The
opening of the University of California campus in the 1960s swung
the town sharply to the left politically, and the counterculture more
or less lives on here. At the same time, the revitalized downtown and
an insane real-estate market reflect the city's proximity to Silicon
Valley and to a growing wine country in the surrounding moun-tains. Amble around the downtown Santa Cruz Farmer's Market
(Wednesday afternoons year-round) to experience the local culture,
which derives much of its character from close connections to food
and farming. The market covers a city block and includes not just
the expected organic produce, but also live music and booths with
local crafts and prepared food.

GETTING HERE AND AROUND

From the San Francisco Bay Area, take Highway 17 south over the
mountains to Santa Cruz, where it merges with Highway 1. Use High-way 1 to get around the area. The Santa Cruz Transit Center is at 920

Pacific Avenue, at Front Street, a short walk from the Wharf and Board-walk, with connections to public transit throughout the Monterey Bay and San Francisco Bay areas. You can purchase day passes for Santa Cruz METRO buses (*Bus Travel, in Planner*) here.

ESSENTIALS

Visitor Information Visit Santa Cruz County. ✉ *303 Water St., No. 100* ☎ *831/425–1234, 800/833–3494* ⊕ *visitsantacruz.org.*

EXPLORING

TOP ATTRACTIONS

Pacific Avenue. When you've had your fill of the city's beaches and waters, take a stroll in downtown Santa Cruz, especially on Pacific Avenue between Laurel and Water streets. Vintage boutiques and moun-tain-sports stores, sushi bars, and Mexican restaurants, day spas, and nightclubs keep the main drag and the surrounding streets hopping from midmorning until late evening.

FAMILY Fodor'sChoice ★ **Santa Cruz Beach Boardwalk.** Santa Cruz has been a seaside resort since the mid-19th century. Along one end of the broad, south-facing beach, the Boardwalk has entertained holidaymakers for more than a century. Its Looff carousel and classic wooden Giant Dipper roller coaster, both dating from the early 1900s, are surrounded by high-tech thrill rides and easygoing kiddie rides with ocean views. Video and arcade games, a minigolf course, and a laser-tag arena pack one gigantic building, which is open daily even if the rides aren't running. You have to pay to play, but you can wander the entire boardwalk for free while sampling carnival fare such as corn dogs and garlic fries. ✉ *Along Beach St.* ☎ *831/423–5590 info line* ⊕ *beachboardwalk.com* 🎟 *$37 day pass for unlimited rides, or pay per ride* ☉ *Some rides closed Sept.–May.*

FAMILY **Santa Cruz Municipal Wharf.** Jutting half a mile into the ocean near one end of the boardwalk, the century-old Municipal Wharf is lined with seafood restaurants, a wine bar, souvenir shops, and outfitters offering bay cruises, fishing trips, and boat rentals. A salty soundtrack drifts up from under the wharf, where barking sea lions lounge in heaps on the crossbeams. Docents from the Seymour Marine Discovery Center lead free 30-minute tours on spring and summer weekends at 1 and 3; meet at the stage on the west side of the wharf between Olitas Cantina and Marini's Candies. ✉ *Beach St. and Pacific Ave.* ☎ *831/459–3800 tour information.*

Santa Cruz Surfing Museum. This museum inside the Mark Abbott Memo-rial Lighthouse chronicles local surfing history. Photographs show old-time surfers, and a display of boards includes rarities such as a heavy redwood plank predating the fiberglass era and the remains of a modern board chomped by a great white shark. Surfer docents reminisce about the good old days. ✉ *Lighthouse Point Park, 701 W. Cliff Dr. near Pelton Ave.* ☎ *831/420–6289* ⊕ *santacruzsurfingmuseum.org* 🎟 *$2 suggested donation* ☉ *Closed Tues. and Wed.*

Fodor'sChoice **West Cliff Drive.** The road that winds along an oceanfront bluff from the
★ municipal wharf to Natural Bridges State Beach makes for a spectacular
drive, but it's even more fun to walk or bike the paved path that paral-
lels the road. Surfers bob and swoosh in Monterey Bay at several points
near the foot of the bluff, especially at a break known as **Steamer Lane.**
Named for a surfer who died here in 1965, the nearby Mark Abbott
Memorial Lighthouse stands at Point Santa Cruz, the cliff's major promontory. From here you can watch pinnipeds hang out, sunbathe, and
frolic on Seal Rock. ⊠ *Santa Cruz.*

WORTH NOTING

FAMILY **Monterey Bay National Marine Sanctuary Exploration Center.** The interactive
and multimedia exhibits at this fascinating interpretive center reveal
and explain the treasures of the nation's largest marine sanctuary. The
two-story building, across from the main beach and municipal wharf,
has films and exhibits about migratory species, watersheds, underwater canyons, kelp forests, and intertidal zones. The second-floor
deck has stellar ocean views and an interactive station that provides
real-time weather, surf, and buoy reports. ⊠ *35 Pacific Ave., near
Beach St.* ☎ *831/421–9993* ⊕ *montereybay.noaa.gov/vc/sec* ⊠ *Free*
☉ *Closed Mon. and Tues.*

Mystery Spot. Hokey tourist trap or genuine scientific enigma? Since
1940, curious throngs baffled by the Mystery Spot have made it one of
the most visited attractions in Santa Cruz. The laws of gravity and phys-
ics don't appear to apply in this tiny patch of redwood forest, where
balls roll uphill and people stand on a slant. ■ TIP➔ **On weekends and
holidays, it's wise to purchase tickets online in advance.** ⊠ *465 Mystery Spot Rd., off Branciforte Dr. (north off Hwy. 1)* ☎ *831/423–8897*
⊕ *mysteryspot.com* ⊠ *$8, parking $5.*

OFF THE
BEATEN
PATH
Surf City Vintners. A dozen tasting rooms of limited-production wineries
occupy renovated warehouse spaces west of the beach. MJA, Sones
Cellars, and Equinox are good places to start. Also here are the Santa
Cruz Mountain Brewing Company and El Salchicheroa, popular for its
homemade sausages, jams, and pickled and candied vegetables. ⊠ *Swift
Street Courtyard, 334 Ingalls St., at Swift St., off Hwy. 1 (Mission St.)*
⊕ *surfcityvintners.com.*

OFF THE
BEATEN
PATH
UC Santa Cruz. The 2,000-acre University of California Santa Cruz campus nestles in the forested hills above town. Its sylvan setting, ocean
vistas, and redwood architecture make the university worth a visit, as
does its **arboretum** ($5, open daily from 9 to 5), whose walking path
leads through areas dedicated to the plants of California, Australia,
New Zealand, and South Africa. ■ TIP➔ **Free shuttles help students
and visitors get around campus, and you can join a guided tour (online
reservation required).** ⊠ *Main entrance at Bay and High Sts. (turn left
on High for arboretum)* ☎ *831/459–0111* ⊕ *www.ucsc.edu/visit.*

OFF THE
BEATEN
PATH
Wilder Ranch State Park. In this park's Cultural Preserve you can visit
the homes, barns, workshops, and bunk house of a 19th-century dairy
farm. Nature has reclaimed most of the ranch land, and native plants
and wildlife have returned to the 7,000 acres of forest, grassland, canyons, estuaries, and beaches. Hike, bike, or ride horseback on miles

of ocean-view trails. Dogs aren't allowed at Wilder Ranch. ⊠ *Hwy. 1, 1 mile north of Santa Cruz* ☎ *831/426–0505 Interpretive Center, 831/423–9703 trail information* ⊕ *www.parks.ca.gov* ⌫ *$10 per car* ⊙ *Interpretive center closed Mon.–Wed.*

BEACHES

FAMILY **Natural Bridges State Beach.** At the end of West Cliff Drive lies this stretch of soft sand edged with tide pools and sea-sculpted rock bridges. ■ TIP→ From September to early January a colony of monarch butterflies roosts in the eucalyptus grove. **Amenities:** lifeguards; parking (fee); toilets. **Best for:** sunrise; sunset; surfing; swimming. ⊠ *2531 W. Cliff Dr.* ☎ *831/423–4609* ⊕ *www.parks.ca.gov* ⌫ *Beach free, parking $10.*

FAMILY **Twin Lakes State Beach.** Stretching a half-mile along the coast on both sides of the small-craft jetties, Twin Lakes is one of Monterey Bay's sunniest beaches. It encompasses Seabright State Beach (with access in a residential neighborhood on the upcoast side) and Black's Beach on the downcoast side. Families often come here to sunbathe, picnic, and hike the nature trail around adjacent Schwann Lake. Parking is tricky on weekends from April through September—you need to pay for an $8 day use permit at a kiosk and the lot fills quickly—but you can park all day in the harbor pay lot and walk here. Leashed dogs are allowed. **Amenities:** food and drink; lifeguards (seasonal); parking; showers; toilets; water sports (seasonal). **Best for:** sunset; surfing; swimming; walking. ⊠ *7th Ave., at East Cliff Dr.* ☎ *831/427–4868* ⊕ *www.parks.ca.gov.*

WHERE TO EAT

$$ ╳ **Assembly.** Seasonal, sustainably farmed local ingredients inspire this MODERN downtown eatery's rustic California cuisine. An adjacent pop-up space AMERICAN temporarily hosts rising chefs who create dishes with ingredients sourced from local purveyors before moving on. **Known for:** rustic locavore fare and seasonal menus; live music Thursday. ⑤ *Average main: $19* ⊠ *1108 Pacific Ave., at Cathcart St.* ☎ *831/824–6100* ⊕ *assembly.restaurant* ⊙ *Closed Mon. and Tues. during off-season; call to verify hrs.*

$$ ╳ **Crow's Nest.** A classic California beachside restaurant, the Crow's SEAFOOD Nest sits right on the water in Santa Cruz Harbor. Vintage surfboards FAMILY and local surf photography line the walls in the main dining room, and nearly every table overlooks sand and surf. **Known for:** house-smoked salmon and calamari apps; crab-cake eggs Benedict and olallieberry pancakes; ocean views. ⑤ *Average main: $21* ⊠ *2218 E. Cliff Dr., west of 7th Ave.* ☎ *831/476–4560* ⊕ *crowsnest-santacruz.com.*

$$ ╳ **Laili Restaurant.** Exotic Mediterranean flavors with an Afghan twist MEDITERRANEAN take center stage at this artsy, stylish space with soaring ceilings. Eve-Fodor's Choice nings are especially lively, when locals come to relax over wine and soft ★ jazz at the blue-concrete bar, the heated patio with twinkly lights, or at a communal table near the open kitchen. **Known for:** house-made pastas and numerous vegetarian and vegan options; fresh naan, chutneys and dips with every meal. ⑤ *Average main: $20* ⊠ *101–B Cooper St., near Pacific Ave.* ☎ *831/423–4545* ⊕ *lailirestaurant.com* ⊙ *Closed Mon.*

$$$
ITALIAN

✕**La Posta.** Authentic Italian fare made with fresh local produce lures diners into cozy, modern-rustic La Posta. Nearly everything is made in-house, from the pizzas and breads baked in the brick oven to the pasta and the vanilla-bean gelato. **Known for:** seasonal wild-nettle lasagne; braised lamb shank. $ *Average main: $24* ⊠ *538 Seabright Ave., at Logan St.* ☎ *831/457–2782* ⊕ *lapostarestaurant.com* ⊙ *Closed Mon. No lunch.*

$$$
EUROPEAN

✕**Oswald.** Sophisticated yet unpretentious European-inspired California cooking is the order of the day at this intimate and stylish bistro. The menu changes seasonally, but might include such items as seafood risotto or crispy duck breast in a pomegranate reduction sauce. **Known for:** classic American burger; craft cocktails. $ *Average main: $30* ⊠ *121 Soquel Ave., at Front St.* ☎ *831/423–7427* ⊕ *oswaldrestaurant.com* ⊙ *Closed Mon. No lunch Sun.–Tues.*

$$$
MEDITERRANEAN
Fodor'sChoice
★

✕**Soif.** Wine reigns at this sleek bistro and wineshop that takes its name from the French word for thirst. The selections come from near and far, and you can order many of them by the taste or glass. **Known for:** Mediterranean-style dishes; well-stocked wine shop. $ *Average main: $25* ⊠ *105 Walnut Ave., at Pacific Ave.* ☎ *831/423–2020* ⊕ *soifwine.com* ⊙ *No lunch.*

WHERE TO STAY

$$$
B&B/INN

Babbling Brook Inn. Though it's in the middle of Santa Cruz, this bed-and-breakfast has lush gardens, a running stream, and tall trees that make you feel like you're in a secluded wood. **Pros:** close to UCSC; within walking distance of downtown shops; woodsy feel. **Cons:** near a high school; some rooms close to a busy street. $ *Rooms from: $249* ⊠ *1025 Laurel St.* ☎ *831/427–2437, 800/866–1131* ⊕ *babblingbrookinn.com* ⇥ *13 rooms* ❑ *Breakfast.*

$$
HOTEL

Carousel Beach Inn. This basic but comfy motel, decorated in bold, retro seaside style and across the street from the Boardwalk is ideal for travelers who want easy access to the sand and the amusement park rides without spending a fortune. **Pros:** steps from Santa Cruz Main Beach; affordable lodging rates and ride packages; free parking and Wi-Fi. **Cons:** no pool or spa; no exercise room; not pet-friendly. $ *Rooms from: $159* ⊠ *110 Riverside Ave.* ☎ *831/425–7090* ⊕ *santacruzmotels.com/carousel.html* ⇥ *34 rooms* ❑ *Breakfast.*

$$$$
RESORT

Chaminade Resort & Spa. Secluded on 300 hilltop acres of redwood and eucalyptus forest with hiking trails, this Mission-style complex commands expansive views of Monterey Bay. Guest rooms were completely remodeled in 2016 and are furnished in an eclectic, bohemian style that pays homage to the artsy local community and the city's industrial past, while incorporating vintage game elements throughout. **Pros:** far from city life; spectacular property; ideal spot for romance and rejuvenation. **Cons:** must drive to attractions and sights; near a major hospital. $ *Rooms from: $269* ⊠ *1 Chaminade La.* ☎ *800/283–6569 reservations, 831/475–5600* ⊕ *www.chaminade.com* ⇥ *156 rooms* ❑ *No meals.*

$$$
HOTEL

Fairfield Inn & Suites by Marriott Santa Cruz. Built from scratch in 2016, this four-story hotel sits at the far northwestern end of Santa Cruz just off Highway 1 and is a good choice for families and business travelers who want to be close to the beach or UC Santa Cruz, but not in the thick of the boardwalk action. **Pros:** convenient location near UC Santa Cruz and Highway 1; great sunset views from some rooms; biking trails near property. **Cons:** no on-site restaurant; open parking lot (not locked). [$] *Rooms from: $179* ⊠ *2956 Mission St.* ✛ *At Western Dr.* ☎ *831/420–0777* ⊕ *marriott.com/sjccr* ⇴ *82 rooms* ⦿| *Breakfast.*

$$$$
HOTEL
☲ **Hotel Paradox.** About a mile from the ocean and two blocks from Pacific Avenue, this stylish, forest-theme complex (part of the Marriott Autograph Collection) is among the few full-service hotels in town. **Pros:** close to downtown and main beach; alternative to beach-oriented lodgings; contemporary feel. **Cons:** pool area can get crowded on warm-weather days; some rooms on the small side. [$] *Rooms from: $279* ⊠ *611 Ocean St.* ☎ *831/425–7100, 855/425–7200* ⊕ *hotelparadox.com* ⇴ *172 rooms* ⦿| *No meals.*

$$$
B&B/INN
☲ **Pacific Blue Inn.** Green themes predominate in this three-story, eco-friendly bed-and-breakfast, on a sliver of prime downtown property. **Pros:** free parking; free bicycles; downtown location. **Cons:** tiny property; not suitable for children. [$] *Rooms from: $189* ⊠ *636 Pacific Ave.* ☎ *831/600–8880* ⊕ *pacificblueinn.com* ⇴ *9 rooms* ⦿| *No meals.*

$$$$
HOTEL
Fodor'sChoice
★
☲ **Santa Cruz Dream Inn.** A short stroll from the boardwalk and wharf, this full-service luxury hotel is the only lodging in Santa Cruz directly on the beach. **Pros:** directly on the beach; easy parking; walk to boardwalk and downtown. **Cons:** expensive; area gets congested on summer weekends. [$] *Rooms from: $369* ⊠ *175 W. Cliff Dr.* ☎ *831/426–4330* ⊕ *dreaminnsantacruz.com* ⇴ *165 rooms* ⦿| *No meals.*

$$$
B&B/INN
Fodor'sChoice
★
☲ **West Cliff Inn.** With views of the boardwalk and Monterey Bay, the West Cliff perches on the bluffs across from Cowell Beach. **Pros:** killer views; walking distance of the beach; close to downtown. **Cons:** boardwalk noise; street traffic. [$] *Rooms from: $249* ⊠ *174 West Cliff Dr.* ☎ *800/979–0910 toll free, 831/457–2200* ⊕ *www.westcliffinn.com* ⇴ *9 rooms, 1 cottage* ⦿| *Breakfast.*

NIGHTLIFE AND PERFORMING ARTS

NIGHTLIFE

Catalyst. This huge, grimy, and fun club books rock, indie rock, punk, death-metal, reggae, and other acts. ⊠ *1011 Pacific Ave.* ☎ *877/987–6487 tickets* ⊕ *catalystclub.com.*

Kuumbwa Jazz Center. The center draws top performers such as the Lee Ritenour and Dave Grusin, Chris Potter, and the Dave Holland Trio; the café serves meals an hour before most shows. ⊠ *320–2 Cedar St.* ☎ *831/427–2227* ⊕ *kuumbwajazz.org.*

Moe's Alley. Blues, salsa, reggae, funk: delightfully casual Moe's presents it all (and more). ⊠ *1535 Commercial Way* ☎ *831/479–1854* ⊕ *moesalley.com* ☉ *Closed Mon.*

PERFORMING ARTS

Tannery Arts Center. The former Salz Tannery now contains nearly 30 studios and live-work spaces for artists whose disciplines range from ceramics and glass to film and digital media; most have public hours of business. The social center is the **Artbar & Cafe,** which in the late afternoons and evenings hosts poets, all types of performers, and live music. Performances also take place at the on-site Colligan Theater. The center also hosts assorted arts events on weekends and occasionally on weekdays. ✉ *1060 River St., at intersection of Hwys. 1 and 9* ⊕ *tanneryartscenter.org/.*

SPORTS AND THE OUTDOORS

ADVENTURE TOURS

Mount Hermon Adventures. Zip-line through the redwoods at this adventure center in the Santa Cruz Mountains. On some summer weekends there's an aerial adventure course with obstacles and challenges in the redwoods. ■TIP➔ To join a tour (reservations essential), you must be at least 10 years old and weigh between 75 and 250 pounds. ✉ *17 Conference Dr., 9 miles north of downtown Santa Cruz near Felton, Mount Hermon* ☎ *831/430–4357* ⊕ *mounthermonadventures.com* ✉ *From $65.*

BICYCLING

Another Bike Shop. Mountain bikers should head here for tips on the best area trails and to browse cutting-edge gear made and tested locally. ✉ *2361 Mission St., at King St.* ☎ *831/427–2232* ⊕ *www.anotherbikeshop.com.*

BOATS AND CHARTERS

Chardonnay II Sailing Charters. The 70-foot *Chardonnay II* departs year-round from Santa Cruz yacht harbor on whale-watching, sunset, and other cruises around Monterey Bay. Most regularly scheduled excursions cost $64; food and drink are served on many of them. Reservations are essential. ✉ *Santa Cruz West Harbor, 790 Mariner Park Way* ☎ *831/423–1213* ⊕ *chardonnay.com.*

Stagnaro Sport Fishing, Charters & Whale Watching Cruises. Stagnaro operates salmon, albacore, and rock-cod fishing expeditions; the fees include bait. The company (aka Santa Cruz Whale Watching) also runs whale-watching, dolphin, and sea-life cruises year-round. ✉ *1718 Brommer St., near Santa Cruz Harbor* ☎ *831/427–0230 whale watching, 888/237–7084 tickets, 831/427–2334 fishing* ⊕ *stagnaros.com* ✉ *From $50.*

GOLF

Pasatiempo Golf Club. Designed by famed golf architect Dr. Alister MacKenzie in 1929, this semiprivate course, set amid undulating hills just above the city, is among the nation's top championship courses. Golfers rave about the spectacular views and challenging terrain. According to the club, MacKenzie, who designed Pebble Beach's exclusive Cypress Point course and Augusta National in Georgia, the home of the Masters Golf Tournament, declared this his favorite layout. ✉ *20 Clubhouse Rd.* ☎ *831/459–9155* ⊕ *www.pasatiempo.com* ✉ *From $260* ⚑ *18 holes, 6125 yards, par 72.*

KAYAKING

Kayak Connection. From March through May, participants in this outfit's tours mingle with gray whales and their calves on their northward journey to Alaska. Throughout the year, the company rents kayaks and paddleboards and conducts tours of Natural Bridges State Beach, Capitola, and Elkhorn Slough. ✉ *Santa Cruz Harbor, 413 Lake Ave., No. 3* ☎ *831/479–1121* ⊕ *kayakconnection.com* ✉ *From $60 for scheduled tours.*

O'Neill: A Santa Cruz Icon

O'Neill wet suits and beachwear weren't exactly born in Santa Cruz, but as far as most of the world is concerned, the O'Neill brand is synonymous with Santa Cruz and surfing legend.

The O'Neill wet-suit story began in 1952, when Jack O'Neill and his brother Robert opened their first Surf Shop in a garage across from San Francisco's Ocean Beach. While shaping balsa surfboards and selling accessories, the O'Neills experimented with solutions to a common surfer problem: frigid waters. Tired of being forced back to shore, blue-lipped and shivering, after just 20 or 30 minutes riding the waves, they played with various materials and eventually designed a neoprene vest.

In 1959 Jack moved his Surf Shop 90 miles south to Cowell's Beach in Santa Cruz. It quickly became a popular surf hangout, and O'Neill's new wet suits began to sell like hotcakes. In the early 1960s, the company opened a warehouse for manufacturing on a larger scale. Santa Cruz soon became a major surf city, attracting wave riders to prime breaks at Steamer Lane, Pleasure Point, and the Hook. In 1965 O'Neill pioneered the first wet-suit boots, and in 1971 Jack's son invented the surf leash. By 1980, O'Neill stood at the top of the world wet-suit market. On June 2, 2017, Jack O'Neill passed away at the age of 94, in his longtime Pleasure Point residence overlooking the surf.

Venture Quest Kayaking. Explore hidden coves and kelp forests on guided two-hour kayak tours that depart from Santa Cruz Wharf. The tours include a kayaking lesson. Venture Quest also rents kayaks (and wet suits and gear), and arranges tours at other Monterey Bay destinations, including Elkhorn Slough. ⊠ *2 Santa Cruz Wharf* ☎ *831/427–2267 kayak hotline, 831/425–8445 rental office* ⊕ *kayaksantacruz.com* 💲 *From $35 for rentals, $60 for tours.*

SURFING
EQUIPMENT AND LESSONS
Club-Ed Surf School and Camps. Find out what all the fun is about at Club-Ed. Your first private or group lesson ($90 and up) includes all equipment. ⊠ *Cowell's Beach, at Santa Cruz Dream Inn* ☎ *831/464–0177* ⊕ *club-ed.com.*

Cowell's Beach Surf Shop. This shop sells gear, clothing, and swimwear; rents surfboards, stand-up paddle boards, and wet suits; and offers lessons. ⊠ *30 Front St.* ☎ *831/427–2355* ⊕ *cowellssurfshop.com.*

Richard Schmidt Surf School. Since 1978 Richard Schmidt has shared the stoke of surfing and the importance of ocean awareness and conservation with legions of students of all ages. Today the outfit offers surfing and standup paddleboard lessons (equipment provided) and marine adventure tours in Santa Cruz and elsewhere on the bay. Locations depend on where the waves are breaking or the wind's a'blowing, but typically convene at Cowell's Beach or Pleasure Point. ⊠ *Santa Cruz* ☎ *831/423–0928* ⊕ *www.richardschmidt.com* 💲 *From $90.*

SHOPPING

Bookshop Santa Cruz. In 2016 the town's best and most beloved independent bookstore celebrated its 50th anniversary of selling new, used, and remaindered titles. The children's section is especially comprehensive, and the shop's special events calendar is packed with readings, social mixers, book signings, and discussions. ✉ *1520 Pacific Ave.* ☎ *831/423–0900* ⊕ *bookshopsantacruz.com.*

O'Neill Surf Shop. Local surfers get their wetties (wet suits) and other gear at this O'Neill store or the one in Capitola, at 1115 41st Avenue. There's also a satellite shop on the Santa Cruz Boardwalk. ✉ *110 Cooper St.* ☎ *831/469–4377* ⊕ *www.oneill.com.*

FAMILY **Santa Cruz Downtown Farmers' Market.** Santa Cruz is famous for its long tradition of organic growing and sustainable living, and its downtown market (one of five countywide) especially reflects the incredible diversity and quality of local agriculture and synergistic daily life of community-minded residents. The busy market, which always has live music, happens every Wednesday from 1:30 to 5:30 (6:30 in summer), rain or shine. The stalls cover much of an entire city block near Pacific Avenue and include fresh produce plus everything from oysters, beer, bread, and charcuterie, to arts and crafts and hot prepared foods made from ingredients sourced from on-site vendors. ✉ *Cedar Street at Lincoln Street* ☎ *831/454–0566* ⊕ *www.santacruzfarmersmarket.org.*

The True Olive Connection. Taste your way through boutique extra-virgin olive oils and balsamic vinegars from around the world at this family-run shop. You can also pick up gourmet food products and olive-oil-based gift items. There's another location in Aptos. ✉ *106 Lincoln St., at. Pacific Ave.* ☎ *831/458–6457* ⊕ *trueoliveconnection.com.*

SAN FRANCISCO

WELCOME TO SAN FRANCISCO

TOP REASONS TO GO

★ **The bay:** It's hard not to gasp as you catch sight of sunlight dancing on the water when you crest a hill, or watch the Golden Gate Bridge vanish and reemerge in the summer fog.

★ **The food:** San Franciscans are serious about what they eat, and with good reason. Home to some of the nation's best chefs, top restaurants, and finest local produce, it's hard not to eat well here.

★ **The shopping:** Shopaholics visiting the city will not be disappointed— San Francisco is packed with browsing destinations, everything from quirky boutiques to massive malls.

★ **The good life:** A laidback atmosphere, beautiful surroundings, and oodles of cultural, culinary, and aesthetic pleasures ... if you spend too much time here, you might not leave.

★ **The great outdoors:** From Golden Gate Park to sidewalk cafés in North Beach, San Franciscans relish their outdoor spaces.

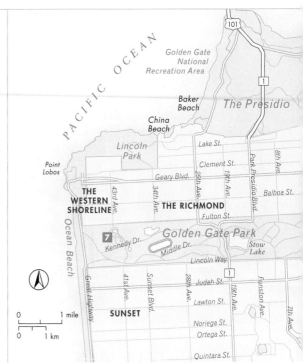

1 **Union Square and Chinatown.** Union Square has hotels, public transportation, and shopping; walking through Chinatown is like visiting a bustling street in Beijing.

2 **SoMa and Civic Center.** SoMa is anchored by SFMOMA and Yerba Buena Gardens; the city's performing arts venues are in Civic Center.

3 **Nob Hill and Russian Hill.** Nob Hill is old-money San Francisco; Russian Hill's steep streets have excellent eateries and shopping.

4 **North Beach.** The city's small Italian neighborhood makes even locals feel as if they're on holiday.

5 **On the Waterfront.** Wandering the shops and attractions of Fisherman's Wharf, Pier 39, and Ghirardelli Square, the only locals you'll meet will be the ones with visitors in tow.

6 **The Marina and the Presidio.** The Marina has trendy boutiques, restaurants, and cafés; the wooded Presidio offers great views of the Golden Gate Bridge.

7 Golden Gate Park and the Western Shoreline. San Francisco's 1,000-acre backyard has sports fields, windmills, museums, and gardens; the windswept Western Shoreline stretches for miles.

8 The Haight, the Castro, and Noe Valley. After you've seen the blockbuster sights, come to these neighborhoods to see where the city's heart beats.

9 The Mission. When the sun sets, people descend on the Mission for

destination restaurants, excellent bargain-price ethnic eateries, and the hippest bar scene around.

10 Pacific Heights and Japantown. Pacific Heights has some of the city's most opulent real estate; Japantown is packed with authentic Japanese shops and restaurants.

GETTING ORIENTED

San Francisco is a compact city; just 46.7 square miles. Essentially a tightly packed cluster of extremely diverse neighborhoods, the city dearly rewards walking. The areas that most visitors cover are easy (and safe) to reach on foot, but many have steep—make that *steep*—hills.

Updated
by Amanda
Kuehn Carroll,
Rebecca Flint
Marx, Denise
Leto, Daniel
Mangin,
Andrea Pow-
ell, and Jerry
James Stone

On a 46½-square-mile strip of land between San Francisco Bay and the Pacific Ocean, San Francisco has charms great and small. Residents cherish their city for the same reasons visitors do: the proximity to the bay, rows of Victorian homes clinging precariously to the hillsides, the sun setting behind the Golden Gate Bridge, the world-class cuisine. Locals and visitors alike spend hours exploring downtown, Chinatown, North Beach, the northern and western waterfronts, and Golden Gate Park, along with colorful neighborhoods like the Haight, the Mission murals, and the Castro.

The city's attraction, though, goes much deeper than its alluring physical space, from the diversity of its neighborhoods to its free-spirited tolerance. Take all these things together and you'll understand why many San Franciscans—despite the dizzying cost of living and the chilly summers—can't imagine calling any place else home.

You won't want to miss the City by the Bay's highlights, whether it's a cable car ride over Nob Hill; a walk down the Filbert Street Steps; gazing at the thundering Pacific from the cliffs of Lincoln Park; cheering the San Francisco Giants to *beat L.A.* in lively AT&T Park; or eating freshly shucked oysters at the Ferry Building. San Francisco is a beautiful metropolis packed with diverse wonders that inspire at every turn.

PLANNING

WHEN TO GO

You can visit San Francisco comfortably any time of year. Possibly the best time is September and October, when the city's summerlike weather brings outdoor concerts and festivals. The climate here always feels Mediterranean and moderate - with a foggy, sometimes chilly bite. The temperature rarely drops below 40°F, and anything warmer than 80°F is considered a heat wave. Be prepared for rain in winter, especially December and January. Winds off the ocean can add to the chill factor. That old joke about summer in San Francisco feeling like winter is true at heart, but once you move inland, it gets warmer. (And some locals swear that the thermostat has inched up in recent years.)

GETTING HERE AND AROUND
AIR TRAVEL

The major gateway to San Francisco is San Francisco International Airport (SFO), 15 miles south of the city. It's off U.S. 101 near Millbrae and San Bruno. Oakland International Airport (OAK) is across the bay, not much farther away from downtown San Francisco (via I-80 east and I-880 south), but rush-hour traffic on the Bay Bridge may lengthen travel times considerably. San Jose International Airport (SJC) is about 40 miles south of San Francisco; travel time depends largely on traffic flow, but plan on an hour and a half with moderate traffic.

Airports San Francisco International Airport (*SFO*). ⊠ *McDonnell and Link Rds., San Francisco* ☎ *800/435–9736, 650/821–8211* ⊕ *www.flysfo.com.* **Oakland International Airport** (*OAK*). ⊠ *1 Airport Dr., Oakland* ⊹ *2 miles west of I–880* ☎ *510/563–3300* ⊕ *www.flyoakland.com.*

Airport Transfers American Airporter. ☎ *415/202–0733* ⊕ *www.americanairporter.com.* **Caltrain.** ☎ *800/660–4287* ⊕ *www.caltrain.com.* **East Bay Shuttle.** ☎ *925/800–4500* ⊕ *www.eastbayshuttle.net.* **GO Lorrie's Airport Shuttle.** ☎ *415/334–9000* ⊕ *www.gosfovan.com.* **Marin Airporter.** ☎ *415/461–4222* ⊕ *www.marinairporter.com.* **Marin Door to Door.** ☎ *415/457–2717* ⊕ *www.marindoortodoor.com.* **SamTrans.** ☎ *800/660–4287* ⊕ *www.samtrans.com.* **SuperShuttle.** ☎ *800/258–3826* ⊕ *www.supershuttle.com.*

BART TRAVEL

BART (Bay Area Rapid Transit) trains, which run until midnight, travel under the bay via tunnel to connect San Francisco with Oakland, Berkeley, and other cities and towns beyond. Within San Francisco, stations are limited to downtown, the Mission, and a couple of outlying neighborhoods.

Trains travel frequently from early morning until evening on weekdays. After 8 pm weekdays and on weekends there's often a 20-minute wait between trains on the same line. Trains also travel south from San Francisco as far as Millbrae. BART trains connect downtown San Francisco to San Francisco International Airport; the ride costs $8.95.

Intracity San Francisco fares are $1.95; intercity fares are $3.20 to $11.45. BART bases its ticket prices on miles traveled and doesn't offer price breaks by zone. The easy-to-read maps posted in BART stations list fares based on destination, radiating out from your starting point of the current station.

During morning and evening rush hour, trains within the city are crowded—even standing room can be hard to come by. Cars at the far front and back of the train are less likely to be filled to capacity. Smoking, eating, and drinking are prohibited on trains and in stations.

Contacts Bay Area Rapid Transit (*BART*). ☎ *415/989–2278* ⊕ *www.bart.gov.*

BOAT TRAVEL

Several ferry lines run out of San Francisco. Blue & Gold Fleet operates a number of routes, including service to Sausalito ($11.50 one-way) and Tiburon ($11.50 one-way). Tickets are sold at Pier 39; boats depart from Pier 41 nearby. Alcatraz Cruises, owned by Hornblower Cruises and Events, operates the ferries to Alcatraz Island ($35.50 including audio tour and National Park Service ranger-led programs) from Pier 33, about a half-mile east of Fisherman's Wharf. Boats leave 14 times a day (more in summer), and the journey itself takes 30 minutes. Allow at least 2½ hours for a round-trip jaunt. Golden Gate Ferry runs daily to and from Sausalito and Larkspur ($11.75 and $11 one-way), leaving from Pier 1, behind the San Francisco Ferry Building. The Alameda/Oakland Ferry operates daily between Alameda's Main Street Terminal, Oakland's Jack London Square, and San Francisco's Pier 41 and the Ferry Building ($6.60 one-way); some ferries go only to Pier 41 or the Ferry Building, so ask when you board. Purchase tickets on board.

Information Alameda/Oakland Ferry. ☎ *877/643–3779* ⊕ *sanfranciscobayferry.com.* **Alcatraz Cruises.** ☎ *415/981–7625* ⊕ *www.alcatrazcruises.com.* **Blue & Gold Fleet.** ☎ *415/705–8200* ⊕ *www.blueandgoldfleet.com.* **Ferry Building Marketplace.** ⊠ *1 Ferry Bldg., at foot of Market St. on Embarcadero, San Francisco* ☎ *415/983–8030* ⊕ *www.ferrybuildingmarketplace.com.* **Golden Gate Ferry.** ☎ *415/923–2000* ⊕ *www.goldengateferry.org.*

CABLE-CAR TRAVEL

Don't miss the sensation of moving up and down some of San Francisco's steepest hills in a clattering cable car. Jump aboard as it pauses at a designated stop, and wedge yourself into any available space. Then just hold on.

The fare (for one direction) is $7. You can buy tickets on board (exact change isn't required but operators can only make change up to $20) or at the kiosks at the cable-car turnarounds at Hyde and Beach Streets and at Powell and Market Streets.

The heavily traveled Powell–Mason and Powell–Hyde lines begin at Powell and Market Streets near Union Square and terminate at Fisherman's Wharf; lines for these routes can be long, especially in summer. The California Street line runs east and west from Market and California Streets to Van Ness Avenue; there's often no wait to board this route.

CAR TRAVEL

Driving in San Francisco can be a challenge because of the one-way streets, snarly traffic, and steep hills. The first two elements can be frustrating enough, but those hills are tough for unfamiliar drivers. ■**TIP→** Remember to curb your wheels when parking on hills—turn wheels away from the curb when facing uphill, toward the curb when facing downhill. You can get a ticket if you don't do this.

MUNI TRAVEL

The San Francisco Municipal Railway, or Muni, operates light-rail vehicles, the historic F-line streetcars along Fisherman's Wharf and Market Street, buses, and the world-famous cable cars. Light rail travels along Market Street to the Mission District and Noe Valley (J line), the Ingleside District (K line), and the Sunset District (L, M, and N lines) while also passing through the West Portal, Glen Park, and Castro neighborhoods.

The N line continues around the Embarcadero to the Caltrain station at 4th and King Streets; the T-line light rail runs from the Castro, down Market Street, around the Embarcadero, and south past Mission Bay and Hunters Point to Sunnydale Avenue and Bayshore Boulevard. Muni provides 24-hour service on select lines to all areas of the city.

On buses and streetcars the fare is $2.50. Exact change is required, and dollar bills are accepted in the fare boxes. For all Muni vehicles other than cable cars, 90-minute transfers are issued free upon request at the time the fare is paid. These are valid for unlimited transfers in any direction until they expire (time is indicated on the ticket). Cable cars cost $7 and include no transfers *(see Cable-Car Travel)*.

One-day ($21), three-day ($32), and seven-day ($42) Passports valid on the entire Muni system can be purchased at several outlets, including the cable-car ticket booth at Powell and Market Streets and the visitor information center downstairs in Hallidie Plaza. A monthly ticket is available for $80, and can be used on all Muni lines (including cable cars) and on BART within city limits. The San Francisco CityPass ($86), a discount ticket booklet to several major city attractions, also covers all Muni travel for seven consecutive days.

The San Francisco Municipal Transit and Street Map ($5) is a useful guide to the extensive transportation system. You can buy the map at most bookstores and at the San Francisco Visitor Information Center, on the lower level of Hallidie Plaza at Powell and Market Streets.

BUS OPERATORS Outside the city, AC Transit serves the East Bay, and Golden Gate Transit serves Marin County and a few cities in southern Sonoma County.

Bus and Muni Information San Francisco Municipal Transportation Agency (*Muni*). ☎ *311, 415/701–3000* ⊕ *www.sfmta.com.*

TAXI TRAVEL

Taxi service is notoriously bad in San Francisco, and finding a cab can be frustratingly difficult. Popular nightspots such as the Mission, SoMa, North Beach, and the Castro are the easiest places to hail a cab off the street; hotel taxi stands are also an option. If you're going to the airport, make a reservation or book a shuttle instead. Taxis in San Francisco charge $3.50 for the first 0.5 mile (one of the highest base rates in the United States), 55¢ for each additional 0.2 mile, and 55¢ per minute in stalled traffic; a $4 surcharge is added for trips from the airport. There's no charge for additional passengers; there's no surcharge for luggage. For trips further than 15 miles outside city limits, multiply the metered rate by 1.5; tolls and tip are extra.

That said, San Francisco's poor taxi service was a direct factor in the creation of ride-sharing services such as Uber and Lyft, which are easy to use and prominent throughout the city and its surrounding areas. San Franciscans generally regard taxis as a thing of the past and use ride-sharing on a day-to-day basis. If you're willing to share a car with strangers, a trip within the city can run as low as $4; rates go up for private rides and during peak demand times. These services are especially economical when going to or from the airport, where a shared ride will run you about $25—half the cost of a cab.

Taxi Companies **Flywheel Taxi.** ☎ *415/970–1303* ⊕ *flywheeltaxi.com.*
Luxor Cab. ☎ *415/282–4141* ⊕ *www.luxorcab.com.* **National Veterans Cab.**
☎ *415/321–8294* ⊕ *sfnationalcab.sftaxischool.com/index.html.* **Yellow Cab.**
☎ *415/333–3333* ⊕ *yellowcabsf.com.*

Complaints **San Francisco Police Department Taxi Complaints.**
☎ *415/701–4400.*

TRAIN TRAVEL

Amtrak trains travel to the Bay Area from some cities in California and
the United States. The *Coast Starlight* travels north from Los Angeles to
Seattle, passing the Bay Area along the way, but contrary to its name,
the train runs inland through the Central Valley for much of its route
through Northern California; the most scenic stretch is in Southern
California, between San Luis Obispo and Los Angeles. Amtrak also
has several routes between San Jose, Oakland, and Sacramento. The
California Zephyr travels from Chicago to the Bay Area, and has spectacular alpine vistas as it crosses the Sierra Nevada range. San Francisco
doesn't have an Amtrak train station but does have an Amtrak bus stop
at the Ferry Building, from which shuttle buses transport passengers to
trains in Emeryville, just over the Bay Bridge. Shuttle buses also connect
the Emeryville train station with BART and other points in downtown
San Francisco. You can buy a California Rail Pass, which gives you 7
days of travel in a 21-day period for $159.

Caltrain connects San Francisco to Palo Alto, San Jose, Santa Clara,
and many smaller cities en route. In San Francisco, trains leave from
the main depot, at 4th and Townsend Streets, and a rail-side stop at
22nd and Pennsylvania Streets. One-way fares are $3.75 to $13.75,
depending on the number of zones through which you travel; tickets
are valid for four hours after purchase time. A ticket is $7.75 from San
Francisco to Palo Alto, at least $9.75 to San Jose. You can also buy
a day pass ($7.50–$27.50) for unlimited travel in a 24-hour period.
It's worth waiting for an express train for trips that last from 1 to 1¾
hours. On weekdays, trains depart three or four times per hour during
the morning and evening, only once or twice per hour during daytime
non-commute hours and late night. Weekend trains run once per hour,
though there are two bullet trains per day, one in late morning and one
in early evening. The system shuts down after midnight. There are no
onboard ticket sales. You must buy tickets before boarding the train or
risk paying up to $250 for fare evasion.

Information **Amtrak.** ☎ *800/872–7245* ⊕ *www.amtrak.com.* **Caltrain.**
☎ *800/660–4287* ⊕ *www.caltrain.com.* **San Francisco Caltrain station.** ✉ *700
4th St., near Townsend St., San Francisco* ☎ *800/660–4287.*

VISITOR INFORMATION

The San Francisco Convention and Visitors Bureau can mail you brochures, maps, and events listings. Once in town, you can stop by the
bureau's info center near Union Square.

Contacts **San Francisco Visitor Information Center.** ✉ *Hallidie Plaza,
lower level, 900 Market St., at Powell St., Union Sq.* ☎ *415/391–2000*
⊕ *www.sftravel.com.*

EXPLORING SAN FRANCISCO

UNION SQUARE AND CHINATOWN

The Union Square area bristles with big-city bravado, while just a stone's throw away is a place that feels like a city unto itself, Chinatown. The two areas share a strong commercial streak, although manifested very differently. In Union Square—a plaza but also the neighborhood around it—the crowds zigzag among international brands, trailing glossy shopping bags. A few blocks north, people dash between small neighborhood stores, their arms draped with plastic totes filled with groceries or souvenirs.

UNION SQUARE

TOP ATTRACTIONS

Union Square. Ground zero for big-name shopping in the city and within walking distance of many hotels, Union Square is home base for many visitors. The Westin St. Francis Hotel and Macy's line two of the square's sides, and Saks, Neiman-Marcus, and Tiffany & Co. edge the other two. Four globular lamp sculptures by the artist R. M. Fischer preside over the landscaped, 2½-acre park, which has a café with outdoor seating, an open-air stage, and a visitor-information booth—along with a familiar kaleidoscope of characters: office workers sunning and brown-bagging, street musicians, shoppers taking a rest, kids chasing pigeons, and a fair number of homeless people. The constant clang of cable cars traveling up and down Powell Street helps maintain a festive mood.

The heart of San Francisco's downtown since 1850, the square takes its name from the violent pro-Union demonstrations staged here before the Civil War. At center stage, Robert Ingersoll Aitken's *Victory Monument* commemorates Commodore George Dewey's victory over the Spanish fleet at Manila in 1898. The 97-foot Corinthian column, topped by a bronze figure symbolizing naval conquest, was dedicated by Theodore Roosevelt in 1903 and withstood the 1906 earthquake. After the earthquake and fire of 1906, the square was dubbed "Little St. Francis" because of the temporary shelter erected for residents of the St. Francis Hotel. Actor John Barrymore (grandfather of actress Drew Barrymore and a notorious carouser) was among the guests pressed into volunteering to stack bricks in the square. His uncle, thespian John Drew, remarked, "It took an act of God to get John out of bed and the United States Army to get him to work." ⊠ *Bordered by Powell, Stockton, Post, and Geary Sts., Union Sq.*

WORTH NOTING

Maiden Lane. Known as Morton Street in the raffish Barbary Coast era, this former red-light district reported at least one murder a week during the late 19th century. Things cooled down after the 1906 fire destroyed the brothels, and these days Maiden Lane is a chic, boutique-lined pedestrian mall (favored by brides-to-be) stretching two blocks, between Stockton and Kearny Streets. Wrought-iron gates close the street to traffic most days between 11 and 5, when the lane becomes a patchwork of umbrella-shaded tables. At **140 Maiden Lane** is the only

The epicenter of high-end shopping, Union Square is lined with department stores.

Frank Lloyd Wright building in San Francisco, fronted by a large brick archway. The graceful, curving ramp and skylights of the interior are said to have been his model for the Guggenheim Museum in New York. ✉ *Between Stockton and Kearny Sts., Union Sq.*

San Francisco Visitor Information Center. Head downstairs from the cable-car terminus to the visitor center, where multilingual staffers answer questions and provide maps and pamphlets. Muni Passports are sold here, and you can pick up discount coupons—the savings can be significant, especially for families. If you're planning to hit the big-ticket stops like the California Academy of Sciences and the Exploratorium and ride the cable cars, consider purchasing a CityPass (*www.citypass.com/san-francisco*) here. ■TIP➔ **The CityPass ($94, $69 ages 5–11), good for nine days, including seven days of transit, will save you 50%.** The pass is also available at the attractions it covers, though if you choose the pass that includes Alcatraz—an excellent deal—you'll have to buy it directly from Alcatraz Cruises. ✉ *Hallidie Plaza, lower level, 900 Market St., at Market and Powell Sts., Union Sq.* ☎ *415/391–2000,* ⊕ *www.sftravel.com* ☾ *Closed Sun. Nov.–Apr.*

Westin St. Francis Hotel. Built in 1904 and barely established as the most sumptuous hotel in town before it was ravaged by fire following the 1906 earthquake, this grande-dame hotel designed by Walter Danforth Bliss and William Baker Faville reopened in 1907 with the addition of a luxurious Italian Renaissance–style residence designed to attract loyal clients from among the world's rich and powerful. The hotel's checkered past includes the ill-fated 1921 bash in the suite of the silent-film superstar Fatty Arbuckle, at which a woman became ill and later died.

Arbuckle endured three sensational trials for rape and murder before being acquitted, by which time his career was kaput. In 1975, Sara Jane Moore, standing among a crowd outside the hotel, attempted to shoot then-President Gerald Ford. Of course the grand lobby contains no plaques commemorating these events. ■ TIP➔ Some visitors make the St. Francis a stop whenever they're in town, soaking up the lobby ambience or enjoying a cocktail in Clock Bar or a meal at the Oak Room Restaurant. ⊠ *335 Powell St., at Geary St., Union Sq.* ☎ *415/397–7000* ⊕ *westinstfrancis.com.*

CHINATOWN
TOP ATTRACTIONS
Chinatown Gate. This is the official entrance to Chinatown. Stone lions flank the base of the pagoda-topped gate; the lions, dragons, and fish up top symbolize wealth, prosperity, and other good things. The four Chinese characters immediately beneath the pagoda represent the philosophy of Sun Yat-sen (1866–1925), the leader who unified China in the early 20th century. Sun Yat-sen, who lived in exile in San Francisco for a few years, promoted the notion of friendship and peace among all nations based on equality, justice, and goodwill. The vertical characters under the left pagoda read "peace" and "trust," the ones under the right pagoda "respect" and "love." The whole shebang telegraphs the internationally understood message of "photo op." Immediately beyond the gate, dive into souvenir shopping on Grant Avenue, Chinatown's tourist strip. ⊠ *Grant Ave. at Bush St., Chinatown.*

Fodor'sChoice   **Tin How Temple.** Duck into the inconspicuous doorway, climb three flights
★   of stairs, and be assaulted by the aroma of incense in this tiny, altar-filled room. In 1852, Day Ju, one of the first three Chinese to arrive in San Francisco, dedicated this temple to the Queen of the Heavens and the Goddess of the Seven Seas, and the temple looks largely the same today as it did more than a century ago. In the entryway, elderly ladies can often be seen preparing "money" to be burned as offerings to various Buddhist gods or as funds for ancestors to use in the afterlife. Hundreds of red-and-gold lanterns cover the ceiling; the larger the lamp, the larger its donor's contribution to the temple. Gifts of oranges, dim sum, and money left by the faithful, who kneel mumbling prayers, rest on altars to different gods. Tin How presides over the middle back of the temple, flanked by one red and one green lesser god. Take a good look around, since taking photographs is not allowed. ⊠ *125 Waverly Pl., between Clay and Washington Sts., Chinatown* ☎ *Free, donations accepted.*

WORTH NOTING
Chinese Historical Society of America Museum and Learning Center. The displays at this small, light-filled gallery document the Chinese-American experience—from 19th-century agriculture to 21st-century food and fashion trends—and include a thought-provoking collection of racist games and toys. The facility also has temporary exhibits of works by contemporary Chinese-American artists. ⊠ *965 Clay St., between Stockton and Powell Sts., Chinatown* ☎ *415/391–1188* ⊕ *www.chsa. org* ☎ *$15, free 1st Sun. of month* ☉ *Closed Mon.*

Union Square
and Chinatown

KEY

b *Bart Stop*

······· *Cable Car*

FAMILY **Golden Gate Fortune Cookie Factory.** Follow your nose down Ross Alley to this tiny but fragrant cookie factory. Two workers sit at circular motorized griddles and wait for dollops of batter to drop onto a tiny metal plate, which rotates into an oven. A few moments later out comes a cookie that's pliable and ready for folding. It's easy to peek in for a moment, and hard to leave without a few free samples. A bagful of cookies—with mildly racy "adult" fortunes or more benign ones—costs under $5. ⊠ *56 Ross Alley, off Washington or Jackson St. west of Grant Ave., Chinatown* 🕾 *415/781–3956* 🕾 *Free.*

Portsmouth Square. Chinatown's living room buzzes with activity. The square, with its pagoda-shape structures, is a favorite spot for morning tai chi; by noon dozens of men huddle around Chinese chess tables, engaged in competition. Kids scamper about the square's two grungy playgrounds (warning: the bathrooms are sketchy). Back in the late 19th century this land was near the waterfront. The square is named for the USS *Portsmouth*, the ship helmed by Captain John Montgomery, who in 1846 raised the American flag here and claimed the then-Mexican land for the United States. A couple of years later, Sam Brannan kicked off the gold rush at the square when he waved his loot and proclaimed, "Gold from the American River!" Robert Louis Stevenson, the author of *Treasure Island,* often dropped by, chatting up the sailors who hung out here. Some of the information he gleaned about life at sea found its way into his fiction. A bronze galleon sculpture, a tribute to Stevenson, anchors the square's northwest corner. A plaque marks the site of California's first public school, built in 1847. ⊠ *Bordered by Walter Lum Pl. and Kearny, Washington, and Clay Sts., Chinatown.*

SOMA, CIVIC CENTER, AND HAYES VALLEY

To a newcomer, SoMa (short for "south of Market") and the Civic Center may look like cheek-by-jowl neighbors—they're divided by Market Street. To locals, though, these areas are separate entities, especially since Market Street itself is considered such a strong demarcation line. Both neighborhoods have a core of cultural sights but more than their share of sketchy blocks. North of the Civic Center lies the western section of the frisky Tenderloin neighborhood, while to the east is hip Hayes Valley.

SOMA
TOP ATTRACTIONS
Contemporary Jewish Museum. Daniel Liebeskind designed the postmodern CJM, whose impossible-to-ignore diagonal blue cube juts out of a painstakingly restored power substation. A physical manifestation of the Hebrew phrase *l'chaim* (to life), the cube may have obscure philosophical origins, but Liebeskind created a unique, light-filled space that merits a stroll through the lobby even if current exhibits don't entice you into the galleries. ■**TIP➔** San Francisco's best Jewish deli, Wise Sons, recently opened a counter in the museum, giving you a chance to sample the company's wildly popular smoked trout. ⊠ *736 Mission St., between 3rd and 4th Sts., SoMa* 🕾 *415/655–7800* ⊕ *www.thecjm.org* 🕾 *$14; $5 Thurs. after 5 pm, free 1st Tues. of month* ⊙ *Closed Wed.*

Museum of the African Diaspora (MoAD). Dedicated to the influence that people of African descent have had all over the world, MoAD focuses on temporary exhibits in its three galleries over two upper floors. With floor-to-ceiling windows onto Mission Street, the museum fits perfectly into the cultural scene of Yerba Buena and is well worth a 30-minute foray. Most striking is its front-window exhibit: a three-story mosaic, made from thousands of photographs, that forms the image of a young girl's face. ■TIP➜ **Walk up the stairs inside the museum to view the photographs up close—Malcolm X is there, Muhammad Ali, too, along with everyday folks—but the best view is from across the street.** ✉ *685 Mission St., SoMa* ☎ *415/358–7200* ⊕ *www.moadsf.org* 🎟 *$10* ⊗ *Closed Mon. and Tues.*

Fodor's Choice
★

San Francisco Museum of Modern Art. Founded in 1935, the San Francisco Museum of Modern Art was the first museum on the West Coast dedicated to modern and contemporary art. In 2016, after a major three-year building expansion designed by Snøhetta, SFMOMA emerged as the largest modern art museum in the country and the revitalized anchor of the Yerba Buena arts district. Nearly tripling its gallery space over seven floors, the museum displays 1,900 of its 33,000-work collection, including a daunting 20-plus temporary exhibits. It can be overwhelming—you could easily spend a day taking it all in, but allow at least two hours; three is better. The original 3rd Street entrance remains, but use the new entrance on Howard Street to experience Richard Serra's gigantic *Sequence*, a gorgeous 15-foot-tall metal walk-through spiral. The museum's expanded collection, showcased on floors three through seven, includes a heavy dose of new art from the Doris and Donald Fisher Collection, one of the greatest private collections of modern and contemporary art in the world. Highlights include a deep collection of German abstract expressionist Gerhard Richter, American painter Ellsworth Kelly, and a tranquil gallery of Agnes Martin. Photography has long been one of the museum's strong suits, and the third floor is dedicated to it. Also look for seminal works by Diego Rivera, Alexander Calder, Chuck Close, Matisse, and Picasso. More than one visitor has been fooled by Duane Hanson's lifelike *Policeman*. Don't miss the new second-floor sculpture terrace with its striking living wall. The first floor is free to the public and contains four large works, as well as the museum's wonderful shop and expensive restaurant. If you don't have hours, save the steep entrance fee and take a spin through here. Ticketing, information, and one gallery are on the second floor; save time and reserve timed tickets online. Take advantage of the variety of well-done audio tours, which focus on specific exhibits or subjects and use positioning technology to locate you in the museum and talk about what you're seeing. Daily guided tours—a quick 25 minutes or 45 minutes—are an excellent way to get a foothold in this expansive space. And if you start to fade, grab a cup of Sightglass coffee at the café on the third floor; another café/restaurant is located by the fifth-floor sculpture garden. The monochromatic bathrooms—a different color on each floor—are surprising and fun. ✉ *151 3rd St., SoMa* ☎ *415/357–4000* ⊕ *www.sfmoma.org* 🎟 *$25.*

Continued on page 97

CHINATOWN

Chinatown's streets flood the senses. Incense and cigarette smoke mingle with the scents of briny fish and sweet vanilla. Rooflines flare outward, pagoda-style. Loud Cantonese bargaining and honking car horns rise above the sharp clack of mah-jongg tiles and the eternally humming cables beneath the street.

Most Chinatown visitors march down Grant Avenue, buy a few trinkets, and call it a day. Do yourself a favor and dig deeper. This is one of the largest Chinese communities outside Asia, and there is far more to it than buying a back-scratcher near Chinatown Gate. To get a real feel for the neighborhood, wander off the main drag. Step into a temple or an herb shop and wander down a flag-draped alley. And don't be shy: residents welcome guests warmly, though rarely in English.

Whatever you do, don't leave without eating something. Noodle houses, bakeries, tea houses, and dim sum shops seem to occupy every other storefront. There's a feast for your eyes as well: in the market windows on Stockton and Grant, you'll see hanging whole roast ducks, fish, and shellfish swimming in tanks, and strips of shiny, pink-glazed Chinese-style barbecued pork.

CHINATOWN'S HISTORY

The Street of Gamblers (Ross Alley), 1898 (top). The first Chinese telephone operator in Chinatown (bottom).

Sam Brannan's 1848 cry of "Gold!" didn't take long to reach across the world to China. Struggling with famine, drought, and political upheaval at home, thousands of Chinese jumped at the chance to try their luck in California. Most came from the Pearl River Delta region, in the Guangdong province, and spoke Cantonese dialects. From the start, Chinese businesses circled around Portsmouth Square, which was conveniently central. Bachelor rooming houses sprang up, since the vast majority of new arrivals were men. By 1853, the area was called Chinatown.

COLD WELCOME

The Chinese faced discrimination from the get-go. Harrassment became outright hostility as first the gold rush, then the work on the Transcontinental Railroad petered out. Special taxes were imposed to shoulder aside competing "coolie labor." Laws forbidding the Chinese from moving outside Chinatown kept the residents packed in like sardines, with nowhere to go but up and down—thus the many basement establishments in the neighborhood. State and federal laws passed in the 1870s deterred Chinese women from immigrating, deeming them prostitutes. In the late 1870s, looting and arson attacks on Chinatown businesses soared.

The coup de grace, though, was the Chinese Exclusion Act, passed by the U.S.

Chinatown's Grant Avenue.

Women and children flooded into the neighborhood after the Great Quake.

Congress in 1882, which slammed the doors to America for "Asiatics." This was the country's first significant restriction on immigration. The law also prevented the existing Chinese residents, including American-born children, from becoming naturalized citizens. With a society of mostly men (forbidden, of course, from marrying white women), San Francisco hoped that Chinatown would simply die out.

OUT OF THE ASHES

When the devastating 1906 earthquake and fire hit, city fathers thought they'd seize the opportunity to kick the Chinese out of Chinatown and get their hands on that desirable piece of downtown real estate. Then Chinatown businessman Look Tin Eli had a brainstorm of Disneyesque proportions.

He proposed that Chinatown be rebuilt, but in a tourist-friendly, stylized, "Oriental" way. Anglo-American architects would design new buildings with pagoda roofs and dragon-covered columns. Chinatown would attract more tourists—the curious had been visiting

on the sly for decades—and add more tax money to the city's coffers. Ka-ching: the sales pitch worked.

PAPER SONS

For the Chinese, the 1906 earthquake turned the virtual "no entry" sign into a flashing neon "welcome!" All the city's immigration records went up in smoke, and the Chinese quickly began to apply for passports as U.S. citizens, claiming their old ones were lost in the fire. Not only did thousands of Chinese become legal overnight, but so did their sons in China, or "sons," if they weren't really related. Whole families in Chinatown had passports in names that weren't their own; these "paper sons" were not only a windfall but also an uncomfortable neighborhood conspiracy. The city caught on eventually and set up an immigration center on Angel Island in 1910. Immigrants spent weeks or months being inspected and interrogated while their papers were checked. Roughly 250,000 people made it through. With this influx, including women and children, Chinatown finally became a more complete community.

A GREAT WALK THROUGH CHINATOWN

■ Start at the Chinatown Gate and walk ahead on Grant Avenue, entering the souvenir gauntlet. (You'll also pass Old St. Mary's Cathedral.)

■ Make a right on Clay Street and walk to Portsmouth Square. Sometimes it feels like the whole neighborhood's here, playing chess and exercising.

■ Head up Washington Street to the Old Chinese Telephone Exchange building, now the EastWest Bank. Across Grant, look left for Waverly Place. Here Free Republic of China (Taiwanese) flags flap over some of the neighborhood's most striking buildings, including Tin How Temple.

■ At the Sacramento Street end of Waverly Place stands the First Chinese Baptist Church of 1908. Just across the way, the Clarion Music Center is full of unusual instruments, as well as exquisite lion-dance sets.

■ Head back to Washington Street and check out the many herb shops.

■ Follow the scent of vanilla down Ross Alley (entrance across from Superior Trading Company) to the Golden Gate Fortune Cookie Factory. Then head across the alley to Sam Bo Trading Co., where religious

items are stacked in the narrow space. Tell the owners your troubles and they'll prepare a package of joss papers, joss sticks, and candles, and tell you how and when to offer them up.

■ Turn left on Jackson Street; ahead is the real Chinatown's main artery, Stockton Street, where most residents do their

grocery shopping. Vegetarians will want to avoid Luen Fat Market (No. 1135), with tanks of live frogs, turtles, and lobster as well as chickens and ducks. Look toward the back of stores for Buddhist altars with offerings of oranges and grapefruit. From here you can loop one block east back to Grant.

FAMILY
Fodor's Choice
★

Yerba Buena Gardens. There's not much south of Market Street that encourages lingering outdoors— or indeed walking at all—with this notable exception. These two blocks encompass the Center for the Arts, the Metreon, and Moscone Convention Center, but the gardens themselves are the everyday draw. Office workers escape to the green swath of the East Garden, the focal point of which is the memorial to Martin

> **LOOK UP!**
>
> When wandering around China-town, don't forget to look up! Above the chintziest souvenir shop might loom an ornate balcony or a curly pagoda roof. The best examples are on the 900 block of Grant Avenue (at Washington Street) and at Waverly Place.

4

Luther King Jr. Powerful streams of water surge over large, jagged stone columns, mirroring the enduring force of King's words that are carved on the stone walls and on glass blocks behind the waterfall. Moscone North is behind the memorial, and an overhead walkway leads to Moscone South and its rooftop attractions. ■TIP→ **The gardens are liveliest during the week and especially during the Yerba Buena Gardens Festival, from May through October (www.ybgfestival.org), with free performances of everything from Latin music to Balinese dance.**

Atop the Moscone Convention Center perch a few lures for kids. The historic Looff carousel (*$4 for two rides*) twirls daily 10–5. South of the carousel is the Children's Creativity Museum (*415/820–3320 creativity.org*), a high-tech, interactive arts-and-technology center (*$12*) geared to children ages 3–12. Just outside, kids adore the excellent slides, including a 25-foot tube slide, at the play circle. Also part of the rooftop complex are gardens, an ice-skating rink, and a bowling alley. ⊠ *Bordered by 3rd, 4th, Mission, and Folsom Sts., SoMa* ⊕ *yerbabuenagardens.com* ☞ *Free.*

WORTH NOTING

Yerba Buena Center for the Arts. You never know what's going to be on display at this facility in Yerba Buena Gardens, but whether it's an exhibit of Mexican street art (graffiti to laypeople), innovative modern dance, or a baffling video installation, it's likely to be memorable. The productions here, which lean toward the cutting edge, tend to draw a young, energetic crowd. ■TIP→ **Present any public library card or public transit ticket to receive a 10% discount.** ⊠ *701 Mission St., SoMa* ☎ *415/978–2787* ⊕ *www.ybca.org* ☞ *Galleries $10, free 1st Tues. of month* ☽ *Closed Mon.*

CIVIC CENTER

Fodor's Choice
★

Asian Art Museum. You don't have to be a connoisseur of Asian art to appreciate a visit to this museum whose monumental exterior conceals a light, open, and welcoming space. The fraction of the Asian's collection on display (about 2,500 pieces out of 15,000-plus total) is laid out thematically and by region, making it easy to follow historical developments.

SoMa and Civic Center

KEY
🚇 Bart Stop

Asian Art Museum **6**
City Hall **7**
Contemporary Jewish
Museum **1**
Museum of the
African Diaspora (MoAD) ...**4**
San Francisco
Museum of Modern Art **5**
Yerba Buena Center
for the Arts **3**
Yerba Buena Gardens **2**

Begin on the third floor, where highlights of Buddhist art in Southeast Asia and early China include a large, jewel-encrusted, exquisitely painted 19th-century Burmese Buddha, and clothed rod puppets from Java. On the second floor you can find later Chinese works, as well as pieces from Korea and Japan. The joy here is all in the details: on a whimsical Korean jar, look for a cobalt tiger jauntily smoking a pipe, or admire the delicacy of the Japanese tea implements. The ground floor is devoted to temporary exhibits and the museum's wonderful gift shop. During spring and summer, visit the museum the first Thursday evening of the month for extended programs and sip drinks while a DJ spins tunes. ⊠ *200 Larkin St., between McAllister and Fulton Sts., Civic Center* ☎ *415/581–3500* ⊕ *www.asianart.org* ⊠ *$20 weekdays, $25 weekends, free 1st Sun. of month; $10 Thurs. 5–9* ⊙ *Closed Mon.*

City Hall. This imposing 1915 structure with its massive gold-leaf dome— higher than the U.S. Capitol's—is about as close to a palace as you're going to get in San Francisco. The classic granite-and-marble behemoth was modeled after St. Peter's Basilica in Rome. Architect Arthur Brown Jr., who also designed Coit Tower and the War Memorial Opera House, designed an interior with grand columns and a sweeping central staircase. San Franciscans were thrilled, and probably a bit surprised, when his firm built City Hall in just a few years. The 1899 structure it replaced had taken 27 years to erect, as corrupt builders and politicians lined their pockets with funds earmarked for it. That building collapsed in about 27 seconds during the 1906 earthquake, revealing trash and newspapers mixed into the construction materials.

City Hall was spruced up and seismically retrofitted in the late 1990s, but the sense of history remains palpable. Some noteworthy events that have taken place here include the marriage of Marilyn Monroe and Joe DiMaggio (1954); the hosing—down the central staircase— of civil-rights and freedom-of-speech protesters (1960); the murders of Mayor George Moscone and openly gay supervisor Harvey Milk (1978); the torching of the lobby by angry members of the gay community in response to the light sentence given to the former supervisor who killed both men (1979); and the registrations of scores of gay couples in celebration of the passage of San Francisco's Domestic Partners Act (1991). In 2004, Mayor Gavin Newsom took a stand against then-current state law by issuing marriage licenses to same-sex partners.

On display in the South Light Court are city artifacts including maps, documents, and photographs. That enormous, 700-pound iron head once crowned the *Goddess of Progress* statue, which topped the old City Hall building until it crumbled during the 1906 earthquake.

Across Polk Street from City Hall is **Civic Center Plaza,** with lawns, walkways, seasonal flower beds, a playground, and an underground parking garage. This sprawling space is generally clean but somewhat grim. Many homeless people hang out here, so the plaza can feel dodgy. ⊠ *Bordered by Van Ness Ave. and Polk, Grove, and McAllister Sts., Civic Center* ☎ *415/554–6023 recorded tour info, 415/554–6139 tour reservations* ⊕ *sfgov.org/cityhall/city-hall-tours* ⊠ *Free* ⊙ *Closed weekends.*

HAYES VALLEY

SFJAZZ Center. Devoted entirely to jazz, the center hosts performances by jazz greats such as McCoy Tyner, Joshua Redman, Regina Carter, and Chick Corea. Walk by and the street-level glass walls will make you feel as if you're inside; head indoors and the acoustics will knock your socks off. ✉ *201 Franklin St., at Fell St., Hayes Valley* ☎ *866/920–5299* ⊕ *www.sfjazz.org.*

NOB HILL AND RUSSIAN HILL

In place of the quirky charm and cultural diversity that mark other San Francisco neighborhoods, Nob Hill exudes history and good breeding. Topped with some of the city's most elegant hotels, Gothic Grace Cathedral, and private blue-blood clubs, it's the pinnacle of privilege. One hill over, across Pacific Avenue, is another old-family bastion, Russian Hill. It may not be quite as wealthy as Nob Hill, but it's no slouch—and it's got jaw-dropping views.

NOB HILL

FAMILY **Cable Car Museum.** One of the city's best free offerings, this museum is an absolute must for kids. You can even ride a cable car here—all three lines stop between Russian Hill and Nob Hill. The facility, which is inside the city's last cable-car barn, takes the top off the system to let you see how it all works. Eternally humming and squealing, the massive powerhouse cable wheels steal the show. You can also climb aboard a vintage car and take the grip, let the kids ring a cable-car bell (briefly), and check out vintage gear dating from 1873. ✉ *1201 Mason St., at Washington St., Nob Hill* ☎ *415/474–1887* ⊕ *www. cablecarmuseum.org* ✉ *Free.*

Grace Cathedral. Not many churches can boast an altarpiece by Keith Haring and not one but two labyrinths. The seat of the Episcopal Church in San Francisco, this soaring Gothic-style structure, erected on the site of the 19th-century railroad baron Charles Crocker's mansion, took 53 years to build, wrapping up in 1964. The gilded bronze doors at the east entrance were taken from casts of Lorenzo Ghiberti's incredible Gates of Paradise, which are on the Baptistery in Florence, Italy. A black-and-bronze stone sculpture of St. Francis by Beniamino Bufano greets you as you enter.

The 35-foot-wide limestone labyrinth is a replica of the 13th-century stone maze on the floor of Chartres Cathedral. All are encouraged to walk the ¼-mile-long labyrinth, a ritual based on the tradition of meditative walking. There's also a terrazzo outdoor labyrinth on the church's north side. The AIDS Interfaith Chapel, to the right as you enter Grace, contains a metal triptych by the late artist Keith Haring and panels from the AIDS Memorial Quilt. ■TIP➜ **Especially dramatic times to view the cathedral are during Thursday-night evensong (5:15 pm) and during special holiday programs.** ✉ *1100 California St., at Taylor St., Nob Hill* ☎ *415/749–6300* ⊕ *www.gracecathedral.org* ✉ *Free; tours $25.*

RUSSIAN HILL
TOP ATTRACTIONS

Lombard Street. The block-long "Crookedest Street in the World" makes eight switchbacks down the east face of Russian Hill between Hyde and Leavenworth Streets. Residents bemoan the traffic jam outside their front doors, but the throngs continue. Join the line of cars waiting to drive down the steep hill, or avoid the whole mess and walk down the steps on either side of Lombard. You take in super views of North Beach and Coit Tower whether you walk or drive—though if you're the one behind the wheel, you'd better keep your eye on the road lest you become yet another of the many folks who ram the garden barriers. ■ TIP→ Can't stand the traffic? Thrill seekers of a different stripe may want to head two blocks south of Lombard to Filbert Street. At a gradient of 31.5%, the hair-raising descent between Hyde and Leavenworth Streets is the city's steepest. Go slowly! ⊠ *Lombard St. between Hyde and Leavenworth Sts., Russian Hill.*

WORTH NOTING

San Francisco Art Institute. The number-one reason for a visit is Mexican master Diego Rivera's *The Making of a Fresco Showing the Building of a City* (1931), in the student gallery to your immediate left inside the entrance. Rivera himself is in the fresco—his broad behind is to the viewer—and he's surrounded by his assistants. They in turn are surrounded by a construction scene, laborers, and city notables such as sculptor Robert Stackpole and architect Timothy Pfleuger. *Making* is one of three San Francisco murals painted by Rivera. The number-two reason to come here is the café, or more precisely the eye-popping, panoramic view from the café, which serves surprisingly decent food for a song.

The **Walter & McBean Galleries** *(415/749–4563; Tues. 11–7, Wed.–Sat. 11–6)* exhibit the often provocative works of established artists. ⊠ *800 Chestnut St., Russian Hill* ☎ *415/771–7020* ⊕ *www.sfai.edu* 🎫 *Galleries free.*

NORTH BEACH

San Francisco novelist Herbert Gold calls North Beach "the longest-running, most glorious, American bohemian operetta outside Greenwich Village." Indeed, to anyone who's spent some time in its eccentric old bars and cafés, North Beach evokes everything from the Barbary Coast days to the no-less-rowdy Beatnik era.

TOP ATTRACTIONS

Fodor'sChoice
★
City Lights Bookstore. Take a look at the exterior of the store: the replica of a revolutionary mural destroyed in Chiapas, Mexico, by military forces; the art banners hanging above the windows; and the sign that says "Turn your sell [sic] phone off. Be here now." This place isn't just doling out best sellers. Designated a city landmark, the hangout of Beat-era writers—Allen Ginsberg and store founder Lawrence Ferlinghetti among them—and independent publishers remains a vital part of San Francisco's literary scene. Browse the three levels of poetry, philosophy, politics, fiction, history, and local zines, to the tune of creaking wood floors. ■TIP➔ Be sure to check the calendar of literary events.

Back in the day, the basement was a kind of literary living room, where writers like Ginsberg and Jack Kerouac would read and even receive mail. Ferlinghetti cemented City Lights' place in history by publishing Ginsberg's *Howl and Other Poems* in 1956. The small volume was ignored in the mainstream … until Ferlinghetti and the bookstore manager were arrested for obscenity and corruption of youth. In the landmark First Amendment trial that followed, the judge exonerated both men, declaring that a work that has "redeeming social significance" can't be obscene. *Howl* went on to become a classic.

Stroll Kerouac Alley, branching off Columbus Avenue next to City Lights, to read the quotes from Ferlinghetti, Maya Angelou, Confucius, John Steinbeck, and the street's namesake embedded in the pavement. ⊠ *261 Columbus Ave., North Beach* ☎ *415/362–8193* ⊕ *www.citylights.com.*

Coit Tower. Whether or not you agree that it resembles a fire-hose nozzle, this 210-foot tower is among San Francisco's most distinctive skyline sights. Although the monument wasn't intended as a tribute to firemen, it's often considered as such because of the donor's special attachment

Continued on page 107

SAN FRANCISCO'S CABLE CARS

The moment it dawns on you that you severely underestimated the steepness of the San Francisco hills will likely be the same moment you look down and realize those tracks aren't just for show—or just for tourists.

Sure, locals rarely use the cable cars for commuting these days. (That's partially due to the $7 fare—hear that, Muni?) So you'll likely be packed in with plenty of fellow sightseers. You may even be approaching cable-car fatigue after seeing its image on so many souvenirs. But if you fear the magic is gone, simply climb on board, and those jaded thoughts will dissolve. Grab the pole and gawk at the view as the car clanks down an insanely steep grade toward the bay. Listen to the humming cable, the clang of the bell, and the occasional quip from the gripman. It's an experience you shouldn't pass up, whether on your first trip or your fiftieth.

HOW CABLE CARS WORK

The mechanics are pretty simple: cable cars grab a moving subterranean cable with a "grip" to go. To stop, they release the grip and apply one or more types of brakes. Four cables, totaling 9 miles, power the city's three lines. If the gripman doesn't adjust the grip just right when going up a steep hill, the cable will start to slip and the car will have to back down the hill and try again. This is an extremely rare occurrence—imagine the ribbing the gripman gets back at the cable car barn!

Gripman: Stands in front and operates the grip, brakes, and bell. Favorite joke, especially at the peak of a steep hill: "This is my first day on the job folks…"

Conductor: Moves around the car, deals with tickets, alerts the grip about what's coming up, and operates the rear wheel brakes.

1 Cable: Steel wrapped around flexible sisal core; 2 inches thick; runs at a constant 9½ mph.

2 Bells: Used for crew communication; alerts other drivers and pedestrians.

3 Grip: Vice-like lever extends through the center slot in the track to grab or release the cable.

4 Grip Lever: Left-hand lever; operates grip.

5 Car: Entire car weighs 8 tons.

6 Wheel Brake: Steel brake pads on each wheel.

7 Wheel Brake Lever: Foot pedal; operates wheel brakes.

8 Rear Wheel Brake Lever: Applied for extra traction on hills.

9 Track Brake: 2-foot-long sections of Monterey pine push down against the track to help stop the car.

10 Track Brake Lever: Middle lever; operates track brakes.

11 Emergency Brake: 18-inch steel wedge, jams into street slot to bring car to an immediate stop.

12 Emergency Brake Lever: Right-hand lever, red; operates emergency brake.

ROUTES

Cars run at least every 15 minutes, from around 6 AM to about 1 AM.

Powell–Hyde line: Most scenic, with classic Bay views. Begins at Powell and Market streets, then crosses Nob Hill and Russian Hill before a white-knuckle descent down Hyde Street, ending near the Hyde Street Pier.

Powell–Mason line: Also begins at Powell and Market streets, but winds through North Beach to Bay and Taylor streets, a few blocks from Fisherman's Wharf.

California line: Runs from the foot of Market Street, at Drumm Street, up Nob Hill and back. Great views (and aromas and sounds) of Chinatown on the way up. Sit in back to catch glimpses of the Bay. ■TIP→ Take the California line if it's just the cable-car experience you're after—the lines are shorter, and the grips and conductors say it's friendlier and has a slower pace.

RULES OF THE RIDE

Tickets. There are ticket booths at all three turnarounds, or you can pay the conductor after you board (they can make change). Try not to grumble about the price—they're embarrassed enough as it is.

■TIP→ If you're planning to use public transit a few times, or if you'd like to ride back and forth on the cable car without worrying about the price, consider a one-day Muni passport. You can get passports online, at the Powell Street turnaround, the TIX booth on Union Square, or the Fisherman's Wharf cable-car ticket booth at Beach and Hyde streets.

All Aboard. You can board on either side of the cable car. It's legal to stand on the running boards and hang on to the pole, but keep your ears open for the grip-man's warnings. ■TIP→ Grab a seat on the outside bench for the best views.

Most people wait (and wait) in line at one of the cable car turnarounds, but you can also hop on along the route. Board wherever you see a white sign showing a figure climbing aboard a brown cable car; wave to the approaching driver, and wait until the car stops.

Riding on the running boards can be part of the thrill.

CABLE CAR HISTORY

HALLIDIE FREES THE HORSES

In the 1850s and '60s, San Francisco's streetcars were drawn by horses. Legend has it that the horrible sight of a car dragging a team of horses downhill to their deaths roused Andrew Smith Hallidie to action. The English immigrant had invented the "Hallidie Ropeway," essentially a cable car for mined ore, and he was convinced that his invention could also move people. In 1873, Hallidie and his intrepid crew prepared to test the first cable car high on Russian Hill. The anxious engineer peered down into the foggy darkness, failed to see the bottom of the hill, and promptly turned the controls over to Hallidie. Needless to say, the thing worked . . . but rides were free for the first two days because people were afraid to get on.

SEE IT FOR YOURSELF

The **Cable Car Museum** is one of the city's best free offerings and an absolute must for kids. (You can even ride a cable car there, since all three lines stop between Russian Hill and Nob Hill.) The museum, which is inside the city's last cable-car barn, takes the top off the system to let you see how it all works.

Eternally humming and squealing, the massive powerhouse cable wheels steal the show. You can also climb aboard a vintage car and take the grip, let the kids ring a cable-car bell (briefly, please!), and check out vintage gear dating from 1873.

■TIP→ The gift shop sells cable car paraphernalia, including an authentic gripman's bell for $600 (it'll sound like Powell Street in your house every day). For significantly less, you can pick up a key chain made from a piece of worn-out cable.

CHAMPION OF THE CABLE CAR BELL

Each September the city's best and brightest come together to crown a bell-ringing champion at Union Square. The crowd cheers gripmen and conductors as they stomp, shake, and riff with the rope. But it's not a popularity contest; the ringers are judged by former bell-ringing champions who take each ping and gong very seriously.

to the local fire company. As the story goes, a young gold rush–era girl, Lillie Hitchcock Coit (known as Miss Lil), was a fervent admirer of her local fire company—so much so that she once deserted a wedding party and chased down the street after her favorite engine, Knickerbocker No. 5, while clad in her bridesmaid finery. She became the Knickerbocker Company's mascot and always signed her name "Lillie Coit 5." When Lillie died in 1929 she left the city $125,000 to "expend in an appropriate manner … to the beauty of San Francisco."

You can ride the elevator to the top of the tower—the only thing you have to pay for here—to enjoy the view of the Bay Bridge and the Golden Gate Bridge; due north is Alcatraz Island. Most visitors saunter right past the 19 fabulous Depression-era murals inside the tower that depict California's economic and political life, but take the time to appreciate the first New Deal art project supported by taxpayer money. The federal government commissioned the paintings from 25 local artists, and ended up funding a controversy. The radical Mexican painter Diego Rivera inspired the murals' socialist-realist style, with its biting cultural commentary, particularly about the exploitation of workers. At the time the murals were painted, clashes between management and labor along the waterfront and elsewhere in San Francisco were widespread. ⊠ *Telegraph Hill Blvd. at Greenwich St. or Lombard St., North Beach* ☎ *415/362–0808* ⊕ *sfrecpark.org* 🎟 *Free; elevator to top $8.*

Grant Avenue. Originally called Calle de la Fundación, Grant Avenue is the oldest street in the city, but it's got plenty of young blood. Here dusty bars such as the Saloon and perennial favorites like the Savoy Tivoli mix with hotshot boutiques, odd curio shops like the antique jumble that is Aria, atmospheric cafés such as the boho haven Caffè Trieste, and authentic Italian delis. While the street runs from Union Square through Chinatown, North Beach, and beyond, the fun stuff in this neighborhood is crowded into the four blocks between Columbus Avenue and Filbert Street. ⊠ *North Beach.*

Fodor'sChoice
★

Telegraph Hill. Residents here have some of the city's best views, as well as the most difficult ascents to their aeries. The hill rises from the east end of Lombard Street to a height of 284 feet and is capped by Coit Tower. Imagine lugging your groceries up that! If you brave the slope, though, you can be rewarded with a "secret treasure" San Francisco moment. Filbert Street starts up the hill, then becomes the **Filbert Steps** when the going gets too steep. You can cut between the Filbert Steps and another flight, the **Greenwich Steps**, on up to the hilltop. As you climb, you can pass some of the city's oldest houses and be surrounded by beautiful, flowering private gardens. In some places the trees grow over the stairs so it feels like you're walking through a green tunnel; elsewhere, you'll have wide-open views of the bay. The cypress trees that grow on the hill are a favorite roost of local avian celebrities, the wild parrots of Telegraph Hill; you'll hear the cries of the cherry-headed conures if they're nearby. And the telegraphic name? It comes from the hill's status as the first Morse code signal station back in 1853. ⊠ *Bordered by Lombard, Filbert, Kearny, and Sansome Sts., North Beach.*

CLOSE UP

The Birds

While on Telegraph Hill, you might be startled by a chorus of piercing squawks and a rushing sound of wings. No, you're not about to have a Hitchcock bird-attack moment. These small, vivid green parrots with cherry red heads number in the hundreds; they're descendants of former pets that escaped or were released by their owners. (The birds dislike cages, and they bite if bothered—must've been some disillusioned owners along the way.)

The parrots like to roost high in the aging cypress trees on the hill, chattering and fluttering, sometimes taking wing en masse. They're not popular with some residents, but they did find a champion in local bohemian Mark Bittner, a former street musician. Bittner began chronicling their habits, publishing a book and battling the homeowners who wanted to cut down the cypresses. A documentary, *The Wild Parrots of Telegraph Hill*, made the issue a cause célèbre. In 2007 City Hall, which recognizes a golden goose when it sees one, stepped in and brokered a solution to keep the celebrity birds in town. The city would cover the homeowners' insurance worries and plant new trees for the next generation of wild parrots.

Washington Square. Once the daytime social heart of Little Italy, this grassy patch has changed character numerous times over the years. The Beats hung out here in the 1950s, hippies camped out in the 1960s and early '70s, and nowadays you're more likely to see elderly Asians doing tai chi than Italian folks reminiscing about the old country. You might also see homeless people hanging out on the benches and young locals sunbathing or running their dogs. Lillie Hitchcock Coit, in yet another show of affection for San Francisco's firefighters, donated the statue of two firemen with a child they rescued. ⊠ *Bordered by Columbus Ave. and Stockton, Filbert, and Union Sts., North Beach.*

WORTH NOTING

Beat Museum. "Museum" might be a stretch for this tiny storefront that's half bookstore, half memorabilia collection. You can see the 1949 Hudson from the movie version of *On the Road* and the shirt Neal Cassady wore while driving Ken Kesey's Merry Prankster bus, "Further." There are also manuscripts, letters, and early editions by Jack Kerouac, Allen Ginsberg, and Lawrence Ferlinghetti; but the true treasure here is the passionate and well-informed staff, which often includes the museum's founder, Jerry Cimino: your short visit may turn into an hours-long trip through the Beat era. ■TIP➔ The excellent Saturday walking tour goes beyond the museum to take in favorite Beat watering holes and hangouts in North Beach. ⊠ *540 Broadway, North Beach* ☎ *415/399–9626* ⊕ *www.thebeatmuseum.org* ⊠ *$8; walking tours $25.*

ON THE WATERFRONT

San Francisco's waterfront neighborhoods have fabulous views and utterly different personalities. Kitschy, overpriced Fisherman's Wharf struggles to maintain the last shreds of its existence as a working wharf, while Pier 39 is a full-fledged consumer circus. The Ferry Building draws well-heeled locals with its culinary pleasures, firmly connecting the Embarcadero and downtown. Between the Ferry Building and Pier 39 a former maritime no-man's-land is filling in with the recently relocated Exploratorium, a new $90-million cruise-ship terminal, Alcatraz Landing, fashionable waterfront restaurants, and restored, pedestrian-friendly piers.

TOP ATTRACTIONS

FAMILY **Alcatraz.** Thousands of visitors come every day to walk in the footsteps of Alcatraz's notorious criminals. The stories of life and death on "the Rock" may sometimes be exaggerated, but it's almost impossible to resist the chance to wander the cell block that tamed the country's toughest gangsters and saw daring escape attempts of tremendous desperation. Fewer than 2,000 inmates ever did time on the Rock, and though they weren't the worst criminals, they were definitely the worst prisoners, including Al "Scarface" Capone, Robert "The Birdman" Stroud, and George "Machine Gun" Kelly.

Some tips for escaping to Alcatraz: 1) Buy your ticket in advance. Visit the website for Alcatraz Cruises (*www.alcatrazcruises.com*) to scout out available departure times for the ferry. Prepay by credit card and keep a receipt record; the ticket price covers the boat ride and the audio tour. Pick up your ticket at the "will call" window at Pier 33 up to an hour before sailing. 2) Dress smart. Bring a jacket to ward off the chill from the boat ride and wear comfortable shoes. 3) Go for the evening tour. You'll get even more out of your Alcatraz experience at night. The evening tour has programs not offered during the day, the bridge-to-bridge view of the city twinkles at night, and your "prison experience" will be amplified as darkness falls. 4) Be mindful of scheduled and limited-capacity talks. Some programs are given only once a day (the schedule is posted in the cell house) and have limited seating, so keep an eye out for a cell-house staffer handing out passes shortly before the start time.

The boat ride to the island is brief (15 minutes), but affords beautiful views of the city, Marin County, and the East Bay. The audio tour, highly recommended, includes observations by guards and prisoners about life in one of America's most notorious penal colonies. Plan your schedule to allow at least three hours for the visit and boat rides combined. Not inspired by the prison? Wander around the lovely native plant gardens and (if the tide is cooperating) the tide pools on the north side of the island. ⊠ *Pier 33, Embarcadero* ☎ *415/981–7625* ⊕ *www.nps.gov/alca* ✉ *$35.50, including audio tour; $42.50 evening tour, including audio.*

FAMILY **Exploratorium.** Walking into this fascinating "museum of science, art, Fodor's Choice and human perception" is like visiting a mad-scientist's laboratory. ★ Most of the exhibits are supersize, and you can play with everything. Signature experiential exhibits include the Tinkering Studio and a glass Bay Observatory building, where the exhibits inside help visitors better understand what they see outside.

Get an *Alice in Wonderland* feeling in the distortion room, where you seem to shrink and grow as you walk across the slanted, checkered floor. In the shadow room, a powerful flash freezes an image of your shadow on the wall; jumping is a favorite pose. "Pushover" demonstrates cow-tipping, but for people: stand on one foot and try to keep your balance while a friend swings a striped panel in front of you (trust us, you're going to fall).

More than 650 other exhibits focus on sea and insect life, computers, electricity, patterns and light, language, the weather, and more. "Explainers"—usually high-school students on their days off—demonstrate cool scientific tools and procedures, like DNA-sample collection and cow-eye dissection. One surefire hit is the pitch-black, touchy-feely Tactile Dome ($8–$15 extra; reservations required). In this geodesic dome strewn with textured objects, you crawl through a course of ladders, slides, and tunnels, relying solely on your sense of touch. Lovey-dovey couples sometimes linger in the "grope dome," but be forewarned: the staff will turn on the lights if necessary. ■TIP➔ Patrons must be at least seven years old to enter the Tactile Dome, and the space is not for the claustrophobic. ✉ *Piers 15–17, Embarcadero* ☎ *415/561–0360 general information, 415/561–0362 Tactile Dome reservations* ⊕ *www.exploratorium.edu* 💲 *$30.*

F-line. The city's system of vintage electric trolleys, the F-line, gives the cable cars a run for their money as a beloved mode of transportation. The beautifully restored streetcars—some dating from the 19th century—run from the Castro District down Market Street to the Embarcadero, then north to Fisherman's Wharf. Each car is unique, restored to the colors of its city of origin, from New Orleans and Philadelphia to Moscow and Milan. ■TIP➔ Purchase tickets on board; exact change is required. ✉ *San Francisco* ⊕ *www.streetcar.org* 💲 *$2.50.*

Fodor's Choice
★ **Ferry Building.** The jewel of the Embarcadero, erected in 1896, is topped by a 230-foot clock tower modeled after the campanile of the cathedral in Seville, Spain. On the morning of April 18, 1906, the tower's four clock faces, powered by the swinging of a 14-foot pendulum, stopped at 5:17—the moment the great earthquake struck—and stayed still for 12 months.

Today San Franciscans flock to the street-level marketplace, stocking up on supplies from local favorites such as Acme Bread, Scharffen Berger Chocolate, Cowgirl Creamery, Blue Bottle Coffee, and Humphry Slocombe ice cream. Slanted Door, the city's beloved high-end Vietnamese restaurant, is here, along with highly regarded Bouli Bar. The seafood bar at Hog Island Oyster Company has fantastic bay view panoramas. On the plaza side, the outdoor tables at Gott's Roadside offer great people-watching with their famous burgers. On Saturday morning the plazas outside the building buzz with an upscale farmers' market where you can buy exotic sandwiches and other munchables. Extending south from the piers north of the building all the way to the Bay Bridge, the waterfront promenade out front is a favorite among joggers and picnickers, with a front-row view of sailboats plying the bay. True to its name, the Ferry Building still serves actual ferries: from its eastern flank

Thousands of visitors take ferries to Alcatraz each day to walk in the footsteps of the notorious criminals who were held on "The Rock."

they sail to Sausalito, Larkspur, Tiburon, and the East Bay. ✉ *Embarcadero at foot of Market St., Embarcadero* ☎ *415/983–8030* ⊕ *www.ferrybuildingmarketplace.com.*

QUICK
BITES
Buena Vista Café. At the end of the Hyde Street cable-car line, the Buena Vista packs 'em in for its famous Irish coffee—which, according to owners, was the first served stateside (in 1952). The place oozes nostalgia, drawing devoted locals as well as out-of-towners relaxing after a day of sightseeing. It's narrow and can get crowded, but this spot provides a fine alternative to the overpriced tourist joints nearby. ✉ *2765 Hyde St., at Beach St., Fisherman's Wharf* ☎ *415/474-5044* ⊕ *www.thebuenavista.com.*

FAMILY
Fodor'sChoice
★
Hyde Street Pier. Cotton candy and souvenirs are all well and good, but if you want to get to the heart of the Wharf—boats—there's no better place to do it than at this pier, one of the Wharf area's best bargains. Depending on the time of day, you might see boatbuilders at work or children pretending to man an early-1900s ship.

Don't pass up the centerpiece collection of historic vessels, part of the **San Francisco Maritime National Historic Park,** almost all of which can be boarded. The *Balclutha,* an 1886 full-rigged three-masted sailing vessel that's more than 250 feet long, sailed around Cape Horn 17 times. Kids especially love the *Eureka,* a side-wheel passenger and car ferry, for her onboard collection of vintage cars. The *Hercules* is a steam-powered tugboat, and the *C.A. Thayer* is a beautifully restored three-masted schooner.

North Beach and On the Waterfront

East
Harbor

Fort
Mason

Aquatic Park

15

Ghirardelli
Sq.

14

Pier 45

Pier 47

13

Fisherman's
Wharf

San Francisco Bay

Russian
Hill Park

Bay St.

Francisco St.

Chestnut St.

North Point St.

Francisco St.

Chestnut St.

Lombard St.

Greenwich St.

Filbert St.

Union St.

Green St.

Broadway

**NORTH
BEACH**

Jefferson St.

Beach St.

North Point St.

Bay St.

Chestnut St.

Pier 41

12

Pier 35

Pier 33

Pier 31

Pier 29

Pier 27

Van Ness Ave.

Polk St.

Larkin St.

Hyde St.

Leavenworth St.

Jones St.

Taylor St.

Mason St.

Powell St.

Stockton St.

Powell St.

**RUSSIAN
HILL**

Pacific Ave.

Jackson St.

Washington St.

Pleasant St.

Huntington
Park

NOB HILL

Tunnel

Green St.

Vallejo St.

Broadway

Stockton St.

Mason St.

Taylor St.

John St.

Washington
Square

9

Columbus Ave.

Grant Ave.

8

11

10

Kearny St.

Chestnut St.

Lombard St.

Bellair St.

Child St.

6

7

Montgomery St.

Sansome St.

Battery St.

Front St.

Davis St.

The Embarcadero

Union St.

Green St.

Pier 23

Pier 19

5

Pier 17

Pier 15

Pier 9

Taylor St.

Mason St.

Powell St.

Tunnel

Bush St.

Sutter St.

Post St.

Union St.

**Transamerica
Pyramid**

4

St. Marys
Sq.

Clay St.

Washington St.

Jackson St.

Pacific Ave.

Sacramento St.

California St.

Pine St.

Sutter St.

Gum St.

Pier 7

Pier 5

Pier 3

Pier 1

Union
Square

DOWNTOWN

Market St.

EMBARCADERO

Justin
Herman
Plaza

3

2

1

Jessie St.

Mission St.

Annie St.

New Montgomery St.

Ecker St.

Elim
Al.

Fremont St.

Mission St.

Audiffred
Building

Minna St.

Natoma St.

Natoma St.

Tehama St.

Clementina St.

Fehama St.

Howard St.

Beale St.

Main St.

Spear St.

Steuart St.

Hawthorne St.

Folsom St.

Essex St.

1st St.

2nd St.

Harrison St.

80

San Francisco - Oakland Bay Bridge

Taber Pl.

Bryant St.

Pier 26

0   350 meters

0   1,000 ft

Across the street from the pier and a museum in itself is the maritime park's **Visitor Center** (*499 Jefferson St., 415/447–5000; June–Aug., daily 9:30–5:30; Sept.–May, daily 9:30–5*), whose fun, large-scale exhibits make it an engaging stop. See a huge First Order Fresnel lighthouse lens and a shipwrecked boat. Then stroll through time in the exhibit "The Waterfront," where you can touch the timber from a gold rush–era ship recovered from below the Financial District; peek into 19th-century storefronts, and see the sails of an Italian fishing vessel. ⊠ *Hyde and Jefferson Sts., Fisherman's Wharf* ☎*415/561–7100* ⊕ *www.nps. gov/safr* ⊠ *Ships $10 (ticket good for 7 days).*

Jackson Square Historic District. This was the heart of the Barbary Coast of the Gay '90s—the 1890s, that is. Although most of the red-light district was destroyed in the fire that followed the 1906 earthquake, the remaining old redbrick buildings, many of them now occupied by advertising agencies, law offices, and antiques firms, retain hints of the romance and rowdiness of San Francisco's early days.

With its gentrified gold rush–era buildings, the 700 block of **Montgomery Street** just barely evokes the Barbary Coast days, but this was a colorful block in the 19th century and on into the 20th. Writers Mark Twain and Bret Harte were among the contributors to the spunky *Golden Era* newspaper, which occupied No. 732 (now part of the building at No. 744). From 1959 to 1996, the late ambulance-chaser extraordinaire, lawyer Melvin Belli, had his headquarters at Nos. 722 and 728–730. There was never a dull moment in Belli's world; he represented clients from the actress Mae West to Gloria Sykes (who in 1964 claimed that a cable-car accident turned her into a nymphomaniac) to the disgraced televangelists Jim and Tammy Faye Bakker. Whenever he won a case, he fired a cannon and raised the Jolly Roger. Belli was also known for receiving a letter from the never-caught Zodiac killer.

Restored 19th-century brick buildings line Hotaling Place, which connects Washington and Jackson Streets. The lane is named for the **A.P. Hotaling Company whiskey distillery** (*451 Jackson St., at Hotaling Pl.*), the largest liquor repository on the West Coast in its day. The exceptional City Guides (*415/557–4266, www.sfcityguides.org*) Gold Rush City walking tour covers this area and brings its history to life. ⊠ *Bordered by Columbus Ave., Broadway, and Washington and Sansome Sts., San Francisco.*

FAMILY
Fodor'sChoice
★
Musée Mécanique. Once a staple at Playland-at-the-Beach, San Francisco's early 20th-century amusement park, the antique mechanical contrivances at this time-warped arcade—including peep shows and nickelodeons—make it one of the most worthwhile attractions at the Wharf. Some favorites are the giant and rather creepy "Laffing Sal," an arm-wrestling machine, the world's only steam-powered motorcycle, and mechanical fortune-telling figures that speak from their curtained boxes. Note the depictions of race that betray the prejudices of the time: stoned Chinese figures in the "Opium-Den" and clown-faced African Americans eating watermelon in the "Mechanical Farm." ■TIP➔Admission is free, but you'll need quarters to bring the machines to life. ⊠ *Pier 45, Shed A, Fisherman's Wharf* ☎ *415/346–2000* ⊕ *museemecaniquesf.com* ⊠ *Free.*

FAMILY **Pier 39.** The city's most popular waterfront attraction draws millions of visitors each year, who come to browse through its shops and concessions hawking every conceivable form of souvenir. The pier can be quite crowded, and the numerous street performers may leave you feeling more harassed than entertained. Arriving early in the morning ensures you a front-row view of the sea lions that bask here, but if you're here to shop—and make no mistake about it, Pier 39 wants your money—be aware that most stores don't open until 9:30 or 10 (later in winter).

Brilliant colors enliven the double-decker **San Francisco Carousel** (*$5 per ride*), decorated with images of such city landmarks as the Golden Gate Bridge and Lombard Street.

Follow the sound of barking to the northwest side of the pier to view the **sea lions** that flop about the floating docks. During the summer, orange-clad naturalists answer questions and offer fascinating facts about the playful pinnipeds—for example, that most of the animals here are males.

At the **Aquarium of the Bay** (*415/623–5300 or 888/732–3483, www. aquariumofthebay.org; $19.95, hrs vary but at least 10–6 daily*) moving walkways transport you through a space surrounded on three sides by water filled with indigenous San Francisco Bay marine life, from fish and plankton to sharks. Many find the aquarium overpriced; if you can, take advantage of the family rate (*$70 for 2 adults and 2 kids under 12*). ⊠ *Beach St. at Embarcadero, Fisherman's Wharf* ⊕ *www.pier39.com.*

WORTH NOTING

FAMILY **San Francisco Railway Museum.** A labor of love brought to you by the same vintage-transit enthusiasts responsible for the F-line's revival, this one-room museum and store celebrates the city's streetcars and cable cars with photographs, models, and artifacts. The permanent exhibit includes the replicated end of a streetcar with a working cab—complete with controls and a bell—for kids to explore; the cool, antique Wiley birdcage traffic signal; and models and display cases to view. Right on the F-line track, just across from the Ferry Building, this is a great quick stop. ⊠ *77 Steuart St., Embarcadero* ☎ *415/974–1948* ⊕ *www. streetcar.org* ⊠ *Free.*

THE MARINA, COW HOLLOW, AND THE PRESIDIO

Yachts bob at their moorings, satisfied-looking folks jog along the Marina Green, and multimillion-dollar homes overlook the bay in the picturesque, if somewhat sterile, Marina neighborhood. Does it all seem a bit too perfect? Well, it got this way after the hard knock of Loma Prieta—the current pretty face was put on after hundreds of homes collapsed in the 1989 earthquake. Just west of this waterfront area is a more natural beauty: the Presidio. Once a military base, this beautiful, sprawling park is mostly green space, with hills, woods, and the marshlands of Crissy Field. Between old-money Pacific Heights and the well-heeled, postcollegiate Marina lies comfortably upscale Cow Hollow.

THE MARINA

Fodor'sChoice **Palace of Fine Arts.** At first glance this stunning, rosy rococo palace seems
★ to be from another world, and indeed, it's the sole survivor of the many
tinted-plaster structures (a temporary classical city of sorts) built for the
1915 Panama-Pacific International Exposition, the world's fair that celebrated San Francisco's recovery from the 1906 earthquake and fire. The
expo buildings originally extended about a mile along the shore. Bernard
Maybeck designed this faux-Roman classic beauty, which was reconstructed in concrete and reopened in 1967. A victim of the elements, the
Palace required a piece-by-piece renovation that was completed in 2008.

The pseudo-Latin language adorning the Palace's exterior urns continues to stump scholars. The massive columns (each topped with four
"weeping maidens"), great rotunda, and swan-filled lagoon have been
used in countless fashion layouts, films, and wedding photo shoots.
After admiring the lagoon, look across the street to the house at 3460
Baker St. If the maidens out front look familiar, they should—they're
original casts of the "garland ladies" you can see in the Palace's colon-
nade. ⊠ *3301 Lyon St., at Beach St., Marina* ☎ 🖥 *Free.*

COW HOLLOW

Octagon House. This eight-sided home sits across the street from its original
site on Gough Street; it's one of two remaining octagonal houses in the city
(the other is on Russian Hill), and the only one open to the public. White
quoins accent each of the eight corners of the pretty blue-gray exterior, and
a colonial-style garden completes the picture. The house is full of antique
American furniture, decorative arts (paintings, silver, rugs), and documents
from the 18th and 19th centuries, including the contents of a time capsule
left by the original owners in 1861 that was discovered during a 1950s renovation. A deck of Revolutionary-era hand-painted playing cards takes an
anti-monarchist position: in place of kings, queens, and jacks, the American
upstarts substituted American statesmen, Roman goddesses, and Indian
chiefs. ⊠ *2645 Gough St., near Union St., Cow Hollow* ☎ *415/441–7512*
⊕ *nscda-ca.org/octagon-house/* 🖥 *Free, donations encouraged.*

THE PRESIDIO
TOP ATTRACTIONS

Fodor'sChoice **Golden Gate Bridge.** With its simple but powerful Art Deco design,
★ the 1.7-mile suspension span that connects San Francisco and Marin
County was built to withstand winds of more than 100 mph. It's also
not a bad place to be in an earthquake: designed to sway almost 28
feet, the Golden Gate Bridge (unlike the Bay Bridge) was undamaged
by the 1989 Loma Prieta quake. If you're walking on the bridge when
it's windy, stand still and you can feel it swaying a bit.

Crossing the Golden Gate Bridge under your own power is exhilarating—a little scary, and definitely chilly. From the bridge's eastern-side
walkway, the only side pedestrians are allowed on, you can take in the
San Francisco skyline and the bay islands; look west for the wild hills
of the Marin Headlands, the curving coast south to Lands End, and
the Pacific Ocean. On sunny days, sailboats dot the water, and brave
windsurfers test the often-treacherous tides beneath the bridge. A vista
point on the Marin County side provides a spectacular city panorama.

A structural engineer, dreamer, and poet named Joseph Strauss worked tirelessly for 20 years to make the bridge a reality, first promoting the idea of it and then overseeing design and construction. Though the final structure bore little resemblance to his original plan, Strauss guarded his legacy jealously, refusing to recognize the seminal contributions of engineer Charles A. Ellis. In 2007, the Golden Gate Bridge district finally recognized Ellis's role, though Strauss, who died less than a year after opening day in 1937, would doubtless be pleased with the inscription on his statue, which stands sentry in the southern parking lot: "The Man Who Built the Bridge."

You won't see it on a T-shirt, but the bridge is perhaps the world's most publicized suicide platform, with an average of one jumper about every 10 days. Signs on the bridge refer the disconsolate to special telephones, and officers patrol the walkway and watch by security camera to spot potential jumpers. A suicide barrier, an unobtrusive net not unlike the one that saved 19 workers during the bridge's construction, is expected to be completed in 2020.

While at the bridge, you can grab a healthy snack at the art deco–style Bridge Café. The Bridge Pavilion sells attractive, high-quality souvenirs and has a small display of historical artifacts. At the outdoor exhibits, you can see the bridge rise before your eyes on hologram panels, learn about the features that make it art deco, and read about the personalities behind its design and construction. City Guides offers free walking tours of the bridge every Thursday and Sunday at 11 am. ⊠ *Lincoln Blvd. near Doyle Dr. and Fort Point, Presidio* 🖀 *415/921–5858* ⊕ *www. goldengatebridge.org* ✉ *Free.*

Fodor's Choice **Presidio.** When San Franciscans want to spend a day in the woods, they
★ come here. The Presidio has 1,400 acres of hills and majestic woods, two small beaches, and stunning views of the bay, the Golden Gate Bridge, and Marin County. Famed environmental artist Andy Goldsworthy's work greets visitors at the Arguello Gate entrance. The 100-plus-foot *Spire,* made of 37 cypress logs reclaimed from the Presidio, looks like a rough, natural version of a church spire. ■ TIP→ The Presidio's best lookout points lie along Washington Boulevard, which meanders through the park.

Part of the **Golden Gate National Recreation Area,** the Presidio was a military post for more than 200 years. Don Juan Bautista de Anza and a band of Spanish settlers first claimed the area in 1776. It became a Mexican garrison in 1822, when Mexico gained its independence from Spain; U.S. troops forcibly occupied the Presidio in 1846. The U.S. Sixth Army was stationed here until 1994.

The Presidio is now a thriving community of residential and nonresidential tenants, who help to fund its operations by rehabilitating and leasing its more than 700 buildings. Bay Area filmmaker George Lucas's 23-acre **Letterman Digital Arts Center,** a digital studio "campus," along the eastern edge of the land, is exquisitely landscaped and largely open to the public. If you have kids in tow or are a *Star Wars* fan yourself, sidle over to the **Yoda Fountain** (Letterman Drive at Dewitt Road), between two of the arts-center buildings, then take your picture with the life-size Darth Vader statue in the lobby, open to the public on weekdays.

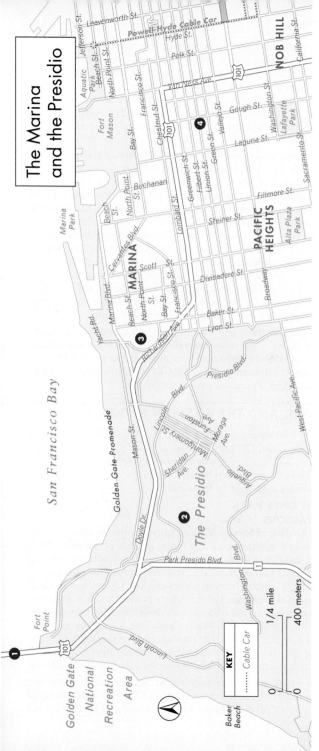

The Marina and the Presidio

San Francisco Bay

Golden Gate National Recreation Area

Fort Point

The Presidio

Golden Gate Promenade

Marina Park

MARINA

Fort Mason

Aquatic Park

NOB HILL

PACIFIC HEIGHTS

Lafayette Park

Alta Plaza Park

Baker Beach

KEY

...... Cable Car

0 — 1/4 mile

0 — 400 meters

Golden Gate Bridge **1**
Octagon House **4**
Palace of Fine Arts **3**
Presidio **2**

Streets labeled:
Leavenworth St., Jefferson St., Powell-Hyde Cable Car, Hyde St., Beach St., North Point St., Polk St., Francisco St., Van Ness Ave., Gough St., Vallejo St., Green St., Union St., Filbert St., Greenwich St., Chestnut St., Bay St., Buchanan, North Point St., Beach St., Cervantes Blvd., Scott St., Lombard St., Fillmore St., Steiner St., Divisadero St., Baker St., Lyon St., Richardson Ave., Marina Blvd., Yacht Rd., Mason St., Doyle Dr., Lincoln Blvd., Presidio Blvd., Funston Ave., Moraga Ave., Montgomery St., Sheridan Ave., Arguello Blvd., West Pacific Ave., Park Presidio Blvd., Washington St., Broadway, Sacramento St., Washington St., Laguna St., California St.

The Presidio Trust, created to manage the Presidio and guide its transformation from military post to national park, has now turned its focus to rolling out the welcome mat to the public. The Presidio's visitor-serving tenants, such as the Asian-theme SenSpa, the House of Air Trampoline Park, Planet Granite climbing gym, the Walt Disney museum, and a fabulous lodge at the Main Post, have helped with this goal. The rental of old military houses and apartments helps too, with top rents pushing $20,000 a month.

Especially popular is **Crissy Field**, a stretch of restored marshland along the sand of the bay. Kids on bikes, folks walking dogs, and joggers share the paved path along the shore, often winding up at the Warming Hut, a combination café and fun gift store at the end of the path, for a hot chocolate in the shadow of the Golden Gate Bridge. Midway along the Golden Gate Promenade that winds along the shore is the Gulf of the Farallones National Marine Sanctuary Visitor Center, where kids can get a close-up view of small sea creatures and learn about the rich ecosystem offshore. Just across from the Palace of Fine Arts, Crissy Field Center offers great children's programs and has cool science displays. West of the Golden Gate Bridge is sandy **Baker Beach,** beloved for its spectacular views and laid-back vibe (read: you'll see naked people here). This is one of those places that inspires local pride.

The Presidio also has a golf course, picnic sites, and the only campground in the city; the views from the many overlooks are sublime. For background and to help plan your time here, stop at the high-tech **Visitor Center** *(210 Lincoln Blvd., 415/561–4323).* ⊠ *Between Marina and Lincoln Park, Presidio* ⊕ *www.presidio.gov.*

GOLDEN GATE PARK AND THE WESTERN SHORELINE

More than 1,000 acres, stretching from the Haight all the way to the windy Pacific coast, Golden Gate Park is a vast patchwork of woods, trails, lakes, lush gardens, sports facilities, museums—even a herd of buffalo. There's more natural beauty beyond the park's borders, along San Francisco's wild Western Shoreline.

GOLDEN GATE PARK
TOP ATTRACTIONS

FAMILY
Fodor's Choice
★

California Academy of Sciences. With its native plant–covered living roof, retractable ceiling, three-story rain forest, gigantic planetarium, living coral reef, and frolicking penguins, the California Academy of Sciences is one of the city's most spectacular treasures. Dramatically designed by Renzo Piano, it's an eco-friendly, energy-efficient adventure in biodiversity and green architecture. The roof's large mounds and hills mirror the local topography, and Piano's audacious design completes the dramatic transformation of the park's Music Concourse. Moving away from a restrictive role as a museum that catalogued natural history, the academy these days is all about sustainability and the future. The locally beloved dioramas in African Hall have survived the transition, however.

By the time you arrive, hopefully you've decided which shows and programs to attend, looked at the academy's floor plan, and designed a plan to cover it all in the time you have. And if not, here's the quick

Armed with only helmets, safety harnesses, and painting equipment, a full-time crew of 38 painters keeps the Golden Gate Bridge clad in International Orange.

version: Head left from the entrance to the wooden walkway over otherworldly rays in the Philippine Coral Reef, then continue to the Swamp to see Claude, the famous albino alligator. Swing through African Hall and gander at the penguins, take the elevator up to the living roof, then return to the main floor and get in line to explore the Rainforests of the World, ducking free-flying butterflies and watching for other live surprises. You'll end up below ground in the Amazonian Flooded Rainforest, where you can explore the academy's other aquarium exhibits. Phew.

■TIP➜ Considering the hefty price of admission here, start out early and take advantage of in-and-out privileges to take a break. ⊠ 55 Music Concourse Dr., Golden Gate Park ☎ 415/379–8000 ⊕ www.calacademy.org ⬤ $34.95, save $3 if you bike, walk, or take public transit here; free 1 Sun. per quarter.

Conservatory of Flowers. Whatever you do, be sure to at least drive by the Conservatory of Flowers—it's too darn pretty to miss. The gorgeous, white-framed 1878 glass structure is topped with a 14-ton glass dome. Stepping inside the giant greenhouse is like taking a quick trip to the rain forest, with its earthy smell and humid warmth. The undeniable highlight is the Aquatic Plants section, where lily pads float and carnivorous plants dine on bugs to the sounds of rushing water. On the east side of the conservatory (to the right as you face the building), cypress, pine, and redwood trees surround the Dahlia Garden, which blooms in summer and fall. Adding to the allure are temporary exhibits such as a past one devoted to prehistoric plants; an annual model-train display punctuated with mini buildings, found objects, and dwarf plants; and a butterfly garden that returns periodically. To the west is the **Rhodo-dendron Dell**, which contains 850 varieties, more than any other garden in the country. It's a favorite local Mother's Day picnic spot. ⊠ *John F. Kennedy Dr. at Conservatory Dr., Golden Gate Park* ☎ *415/666–7001* ⊕ *www.conservatoryofflowers.org* ⊆ *$8, free 1st Tues. of month* ☞ *No strollers allowed inside.*

de Young Museum. It seems that everyone in town has a strong opinion about the de Young Museum: some adore its striking copper facade, while others just hope that the green patina of age will mellow the effect. Most maligned is the 144-foot tower, but the view from its ninth-story observation room, ringed by floor-to-ceiling windows and free to the public, is worth a trip here by itself. The building almost overshadows the de Young's respected collection of American, African, and Oceanic art. The museum also plays host to major international exhibits, such as 100 works from Paris's Musée National Picasso and a collection of the work of Jean Paul Gaultier from the Montreal Museum of Fine Arts; there's often an extra admission charge for these. The annual Bouquets to Art is a fanciful tribute to the museum's collection by notable Bay Area floral designers. On many Friday evenings, the museum hosts fun, free, family-centered events, with live music, art projects for children, and a wine and beer bar (the café stays open late, too). ⊠ *50 Hagiwara Tea Garden Dr., Golden Gate Park* ☎ *415/750–3600* ⊕ *deyoung.famsf. org* ⊆ *$15, good for same-day admittance to the Legion of Honor; free 1st Tues. of month.*

THE WESTERN SHORELINE
TOP ATTRACTIONS

Cliff House. A meal at the Cliff House isn't just about the food—the spectacular ocean view is what brings folks here—but the cuisine won't leave you wanting. The vistas, which include offshore Seal Rock (the barking marine mammals who reside there are actually sea lions), can be 30 miles or more on a clear day—or less than a mile on foggy days. ■TIP➔ Come for drinks just before sunset; then head back into town for dinner.

Three buildings have occupied this site since 1863. The current building dates from 1909; a 2004 renovation has left a strikingly attractive restaurant and a squat concrete viewing platform out back. The complex, owned by the National Park Service, includes a gift shop.

Sitting on the observation deck is the **Giant Camera,** a camera obscura with its lens pointing skyward housed in a cute yellow-painted wooden shack. Built in the 1940s and threatened many times with demolition, it's now on the National Register of Historic Places. Step into the dark, tiny room inside (for a $3 fee); a fascinating 360-degree image of the surrounding area—which rotates as the "lens" on the roof rotates—is projected on a large, circular table. ■TIP➔ In winter and spring you may also glimpse migrating gray whales from the observation deck.

To the north of the Cliff House lie the ruins of the once grand glass-roof **Sutro Baths,** which you can explore on your own (they look a bit like water-storage receptacles). Adolph Sutro, eccentric onetime San Francisco mayor and Cliff House owner, built the bath complex,

Golden Gate Park and the Western Shoreline

California Academy
of Sciences **2**

Cliff House **4**

Conservatory
of Flowers **1**

de Young Museum **3**

Legion of Honor **5**

Lincoln Park **6**

including a train out to the site, in 1896, so that everyday folks could enjoy the benefits of swimming. Six enormous baths (some freshwater and some seawater), more than 500 dressing rooms, and several restaurants covered 3 acres north of the Cliff House and accommodated 25,000 bathers. Likened to Roman baths in a European glass palace, the baths were for decades the favorite destination of San Franciscans in search of entertainment. The complex fell into disuse after World War II, was closed in 1952, and burned down (under questionable circumstances) during demolition in 1966. ⊠ *1090 Point Lobos Ave., Richmond* ☎ *415/386–3330* ⊕ *www.cliffhouse.com* ⌦ *Free.*

Legion of Honor. The old adage of real estate—location, location, location—is at full force here. You can't beat the site of this museum of European art atop cliffs overlooking the ocean, the Golden Gate Bridge, and the Marin Headlands. A pyramidal glass skylight in the entrance court illuminates the lower-level galleries, which exhibit prints and drawings, English and European porcelain, and ancient Assyrian, Greek, Roman, and Egyptian art. The 20-plus galleries on the upper level display the permanent collection of European art (paintings, sculpture, decorative arts, and tapestries) from the 14th century to the present day.

The noteworthy Auguste Rodin collection includes two galleries devoted to the master and a third with works by Rodin and other 19th-century sculptors. An original cast of Rodin's *The Thinker* welcomes you as you walk through the courtyard. As fine as the museum is, the setting and view outshine the collection and also make a trip here worthwhile.

⊠ *34th Ave. at Clement St., Richmond* ☎ *415/750–3600* ⊕ *legionof-honor.famsf.org* ⌦ *$15, free 1st Tues. of month.*

Fodor'sChoice
★

Lincoln Park. Although many of the city's green spaces are gentle and welcoming, Lincoln Park is a wild, 275-acre park in the Outer Richmond with windswept cliffs and panoramic views. The Coastal Trail, the park's most dramatic one, leads out to **Lands End**; pick it up west of the Legion of Honor (at the end of El Camino del Mar) or from the parking lot at Point Lobos and El Camino del Mar. Time your hike to hit Mile Rock at low tide, and you might catch a glimpse of two wrecked ships peeking up from their watery graves. ⚠ Be careful if you hike here; landslides are frequent, and people have fallen into the sea by standing too close to the edge of a crumbling bluff top.

On the tamer side, large Monterey cypresses line the fairways at Lincoln Park's 18-hole golf course, near the Legion of Honor. At one time this land was the Golden Gate Cemetery, where the dead were segregated by nationality; most were indigent and interred without ceremony in the potter's field. In 1900 the Board of Supervisors voted to ban burials within city limits, and all but two city cemeteries (at Mission Dolores and the Presidio) were moved to Colma, a small town just south of San Francisco. When digging has to be done in the park, bones occasionally surface again. ⊠ *Entrance at 34th Ave. at Clement St., Richmond.*

THE HAIGHT, THE CASTRO, AND NOE VALLEY

These distinct neighborhoods wear their personalities large and proud, and all are perfect for just strolling around. Like a slide show of San Franciscan history, you can move from the Haight's residue of 1960s counterculture to the Castro's connection to 1970s and '80s gay life to 1990s gentrification in Noe Valley. Although historic events thrust the Haight and the Castro onto the international stage, both are anything but stagnant—they're still dynamic areas well worth exploring.

THE HAIGHT

Haight-Ashbury Intersection. On October 6, 1967, hippies took over the intersection of Haight and Ashbury Streets to proclaim the "Death of Hip." If they thought hip was dead then, they'd find absolute confirmation of it today, what with the only tie-dye in sight on the famed corner being Ben & Jerry's storefront. ⊠ *Haight.*

4

THE CASTRO

Fodor's Choice
★
Castro Theatre. Here's a classic way to join in the Castro community: grab some popcorn and catch a flick at this 1,500-seat art-deco theater; opened in 1922, it's the grandest of San Francisco's few remaining movie palaces. The neon marquee, which stands at the top of the Castro strip, is the neighborhood's great landmark. The Castro was the fitting host of 2008's red-carpet preview of Gus Van Sant's film *Milk*, starring Sean Penn as openly gay San Francisco supervisor Harvey Milk. The theater's elaborate Spanish baroque interior is fairly well preserved. Before many shows the theater's pipe organ rises from the orchestra pit and an organist plays pop and movie tunes, usually ending with the Jeanette McDonald standard "San Francisco" (go ahead, sing along). The crowd can be enthusiastic and vocal, talking back to the screen as loudly as it talks to them. Classics such as *Who's Afraid of Virginia Woolf?* take on a whole new life, with the assembled beating the actors to the punch and fashioning even snappier comebacks for Elizabeth Taylor. Head here to catch sing-along classics like *Mary Poppins*, a Fellini film retrospective, or the latest take on same-sex love. ⊠ *429 Castro St., Castro* ☎ *415/621–6120* ⊕ *www.castrotheatre.com.*

Harvey Milk Plaza. An 18-foot-long rainbow flag, the symbol of gay pride, flies above this plaza named for the man who electrified the city in 1977 by being elected to its Board of Supervisors as an openly gay candidate. In the early 1970s Milk had opened a camera store on the block of Castro Street between 18th and 19th Streets. The store became the center for his campaign to open San Francisco's social and political life to gays and lesbians.

The liberal Milk hadn't served a full year of his term before he and Mayor George Moscone, also a liberal, were shot in November 1978 at City Hall. The murderer was a conservative ex-supervisor named Dan White, who had recently resigned his post and then became enraged when Moscone wouldn't reinstate him. Milk and White had often been at odds on the board, and White thought Milk had been part of a cabal to keep him from returning to his post. Milk's assassination shocked the gay community, which became infuriated when the infamous "Twinkie defense"—that junk food had led to diminished mental capacity—resulted in a manslaughter verdict for White. During the so-called White Night Riot of May 21, 1979, gays and their allies stormed City Hall, torching its lobby and several police cars.

Milk, who had feared assassination, left behind a tape recording in which he urged the community to continue the work he had begun. His legacy is the high visibility of gay people throughout city government; a bust of him was unveiled at City Hall on his birthday in 2008, and the 2008 film *Milk* gives insight into his life. A plaque at the base of the flagpole lists the names of past and present openly gay and lesbian state and local officials. ⊠ *Southwest corner of Castro and Market Sts., Castro.*

NOE VALLEY

Golden fire hydrant. When all the other fire hydrants went dry during the fire that followed the 1906 earthquake, this one kept pumping. Noe Valley and the Mission District were thus spared the devastation wrought elsewhere in the city, which explains the large number of pre-quake homes here. Every year on April 18 (the anniversary of the quake), folks gather here to share stories about the earthquake, and the famous hydrant gets a fresh coat of gold paint. ⊠ *Church and 20th Sts., southeastern corner, across from Dolores Park, Noe Valley.*

CASTRO AND NOE WALK

The Castro and Noe Valley are both neighborhoods that beg to be walked—or ambled through, really, without time pressure or an absolute destination. Hit the Castro first, beginning at **Harvey Milk Plaza** under the gigantic rainbow flag. If you're going on to Noe Valley, first head east down **Market Street** for the cafés, bistros, and shops, then go back to **Castro Street** and head south, past the glorious art-deco **Castro Theatre**, checking out boutiques and cafés along the way (Cliff's Variety, at 479 Castro Street, is a must). To tour Noe Valley, go east down **18th Street** to Church (at Dolores Park), and then either strap on your hiking boots and head south over the hill or hop the J–Church to **24th Street**, the center of this rambling neighborhood.

MISSION DISTRICT

The Mission has a number of distinct personalities: it's the Latino neighborhood, where working-class folks raise their families and where gangs occasionally clash; it's the hipster hood, where tattooed and pierced twenty- and thirtysomethings hold court in the coolest cafés and bars in town; it's a culinary epicenter, with the strongest concentration of destination restaurants and affordable ethnic cuisine; it's the face of gentrification, where high-tech money prices out longtime commercial and residential renters; and it's the artists' quarter, where murals adorn literally blocks of walls long after the artists have moved to cheaper digs. It's also the city's equivalent of the Sunshine State—this neighborhood's always the last to succumb to fog.

A colorful mosaic mural in the Castro

TOP ATTRACTIONS

Balmy Alley murals. Mission District artists have transformed the walls of their neighborhood with paintings, and Balmy Alley is one of the best-executed examples. Many murals adorn the one-block alley, with newer ones continually filling in the blank spaces. In 1971, artists began teaming with local children to create a space to promote peace in Central America, community spirit, and (later) AIDS awareness; since then dozens of artists have added their vibrant works. ⚠ Be alert here: the 25th Street end of the alley adjoins a somewhat dangerous area. ⊠ *24th St. between and parallel to Harrison and Treat Sts., alley runs south to 25th St., Mission District.*

Fodor's Choice **Dolores Park.** A two-square-block microcosm of life in the Mission, ★ Dolores Park is one of San Francisco's liveliest green spaces: dog lovers and their pampered pups congregate, kids play at the extravagant, recently reconstructed playground, and hipsters hold court, drinking beer on sunny days. During the summer, the park hosts movie nights; performances by Shakespeare in the Park, the San Francisco Mime Troupe, and the San Francisco Symphony; and any number of pop-up events and impromptu parties. Spend a warm day here—maybe sitting at the top of the park with a view of the city and the Bay Bridge—surrounded by locals and that laid-back San Francisco energy, and you may well find yourself plotting your move to the city. ⊠ *Between 18th and 20th Sts. and Dolores and Church Sts., Mission District.*

Mission Dolores. Two churches stand side by side here, including the small adobe **Mission San Francisco de Asís,** which, along with the Presidio's Officers' Club, is the oldest standing structure in San Francisco. Completed in 1791, it's the sixth of the 21 California missions founded by Franciscan friars in the 18th and early 19th centuries. Its ceiling depicts original Ohlone Indian basket designs, executed in vegetable dyes. The tiny chapel includes frescoes and a hand-painted wooden altar.

There's a hidden treasure here, too. In 2004 an archaeologist and an artist crawling along the ceiling's rafters opened a trapdoor behind the altar and rediscovered the mission's original mural, painted with natural dyes by Native Americans in 1791. The centuries have taken their toll, so the team photographed the 20-by-22-foot mural and began digitally restoring the photographic version. Among the images is a dagger-pierced Sacred Heart of Jesus.

The small museum here covers the mission's founding and history, and the pretty little cemetery—which appears in Alfred Hitchcock's film *Vertigo*—contains the graves of mid-19th-century European immigrants. The remains of an estimated 5,000 Native Americans lie in unmarked graves. Services are held in both the old mission and next door in the handsome multidome basilica. ⊠ *Dolores and 16th Sts., Mission District* ☎ *415/621–8203* ⊕ *www.missiondolores.org* ✉ *Suggested donation $7.*

OFF THE BEATEN PATH
Museum of Craft and Design. Right at home in this once-industrial neighborhood now bursting with creative energy, this small, four-room space—definitely a quick view—mounts temporary art and design exhibitions. The focus might be sculpture, metalwork, furniture, or jewelry—or industrial design, architecture, or other topics. The MakeArt Lab gives kids the opportunity to create their own exhibit-inspired work, and the beautifully curated shop sells tempting textiles, housewares, jewelry, and other well-crafted items. ⊠ *2569 3rd St., near 22nd St., Dogpatch* ☎ *415/773–0303* ⊕ *sfmcd.org* ✉ *$8, free 1st Tues. of month.*

WORTH NOTING

Galería de la Raza. San Francisco's premier showcase for contemporary Latino art, the gallery exhibits the works of mostly local artists. Events include readings and spoken word by local poets and writers, screenings of Latin American and Spanish films, and theater works by local minority theater troupes. The gallery may close between exhibits, so call ahead. Just across the street, murals and mosaics festoon the 24th Street/York Street Minipark, a tiny urban playground. A mosaic-covered Quetzalcoatl serpent plunges into the ground and rises, creating hills for little ones to clamber over, and mural-covered walls surround the space. ⊠ *2857 24th St., at Bryant St., Mission District* ☎ *415/826–8009* ⊕ *www.galeriadelaraza.org.*

The Haight, the Castro, Noe Valley, and the Mission District

HAIGHT ASHBURY

CASTRO

NOE VALLEY

POTRERO

MISSION

U.S. Mint

Museum of Craft and Design

Corona Heights Playground

Buena Vista Park

Mission Dolores Park

Sunset Tunnel Pk.

Streets labeled:
Hampshire St.
York St.
Bryant St.
Florida St.
Alabama St.
Mariposa St.
Harrison St.
Folsom St.
Shotwell St.
South Van Ness Ave.
Capp St.
Mission St.
Valencia St.
Guerrero St.
Dolores St.
Landers St.
Church St.
Belcher St.
Steiner St.
Market St.
Noe St.
Castro St.
Collingwood St.
Diamond St.
Eureka St.
Douglass St.
Reservoir St.
Germania St.
Herman St.
Duboce Ave.
Potomac St.
Duboce Park
Walter St.
Carmelita St.
Lloyd St.
Waller St.
Alpine Ter.
Buena Vista Ter.
Buena Vista Ave. East
Roosevelt Way
Delmar St.
Ashbury St.
Frederick St.
Claytony St.
Belvedere St.
Cole St.
Shrader St.
Stanyan St.
Haight St.
Noe St.
16th St.
17th St.
18th St.
19th St.
20th St.
21st St.
22nd St.
14th St.
15th St.
Ford St.
Hancock St.
Gasett St.

16th St Mission
24th St Mission

350 M
1,000 ft
0

Balmy Alley murals **7**
Castro Theatre **2**
Dolores Park **6**
Galeria de la Raza **8**
Golden fire hydrant **5**
Haight-Ashbury intersection **1**
Harvey Milk Plaza **3**
Mission Dolores **4**

PACIFIC HEIGHTS AND JAPANTOWN

Pacific Heights and Japantown are something of an odd couple: privileged, old-school San Francisco and the workaday commercial center of Japanese American life in the city, stacked virtually on top of each other. The sprawling, extravagant mansions of Pacific Heights gradually give way to the more modest Victorians and unassuming housing tracts of Japantown. The most interesting spots in Japantown huddle in the Japan Center, the neighborhood's two-block centerpiece, and along Post Street. You can find plenty of authentic Japanese treats in the shops and restaurants.

PACIFIC HEIGHTS
TOP ATTRACTIONS

Haas-Lilienthal House. A small display of photographs on the bottom floor of this elaborate, gray 1886 Queen Anne house makes clear that despite its lofty stature and striking, round third-story tower, the house was modest compared with some of the giants that fell victim to the 1906 earthquake and fire. The Foundation for San Francisco's Architectural Heritage operates the home, whose carefully kept rooms provide a glimpse into late-19th-century life through period furniture, authentic details (antique dishes in the kitchen built-in), and photos of the family that occupied the house until 1972. ■TIP➔ You can admire hundreds of gorgeous San Francisco Victorians from the outside, but this is the only one that's open to the public, and it's worth a visit. Volunteers conduct one-hour house tours three days a week, and informative two-hour walking tours of Pacific Heights on Sunday afternoon (call or check website for schedule). ⊠ *2007 Franklin St., between Washington and Jackson Sts., Pacific Heights* ☎ *415/441–3004* ⊕ *www.sfheritage.org* ⛿ *Tours $8.*

Spreckels Mansion. Shrouded behind tall juniper hedges at the corner of winding, redbrick Octavia Street, overlooking Lafayette Park, the estate was built for sugar heir Adolph Spreckels and his wife, Alma. Mrs. Spreckels was so pleased with her house that she commissioned George Applegarth to design another building in a similar vein: the Legion of Honor. One of the city's great iconoclasts, Alma Spreckels was the model for the bronze figure atop the Victory Monument in Union Square. These days an iconoclast of another sort owns the mansion: romance novelist Danielle Steel, whose dustup with local columnists over the size of those hedges entertained aficionados of local gossip in 2014. ⊠ *2080 Washington St., at Octavia St., Pacific Heights.*

JAPANTOWN

Japan Center. Cool and curious trinkets, noodle houses and sushi joints, a destination bookstore, and a peek at Japanese culture high and low await at this 5-acre complex designed in 1968 by noted American architect Minoru Yamasaki. The Japan Center includes the shop- and restaurant-filled Kintetsu and Kinokuniya buildings; the excellent Kabuki Springs & Spa; the Hotel Kabuki; and the Sundance Kabuki, Robert Redford's fancy, reserved-seating cinema/restaurant complex.

DID YOU KNOW?

These pastel Victorian homes in Pacific Heights are closer to the original hues sported back in the 1900s. It wasn't until the 1960s that the bold, electric colors now seen around San Francisco gained popularity. Before that, the most typical house paint color was a standard gray.

Pacific Heights and Japantown

The Kinokuniya Bookstore, in the Kinokuniya Building, has an extensive selection of Japanese-language books, *manga* (graphic novels), books on design, English-language translations, and books on Japanese topics. Just outside, follow the Japanese teenagers to Pika Pika, where you and your friends can step into a photo booth and then use special effects and stickers to decorate your creation. On the bridge connecting the center's two buildings, check out Shige Antiques for *yukata* (lightweight cotton kimonos) for kids and lovely silk kimonos, and Asakichi and its tiny incense shop for tinkling wind chimes and display-worthy teakettles. Continue into the Kintetsu Building for a selection of Japanese restaurants.

Between the Miyako Mall and the Kintetsu Building are the five-tier, 100-foot-tall **Peace Pagoda** and the Peace Plaza, where seasonal festivals are held. The pagoda, which draws on the 1,200-year-old tradition of miniature round pagodas dedicated to eternal peace, was designed in the late 1960s by Yoshiro Taniguchi to convey the "friendship and goodwill" of the Japanese people to the people of the United States. The plaza itself is a shadeless, unwelcoming space with little seating. Continue into the Miyako Mall to Ichiban Kan, a Japanese dollar store where you can pick up fun Japanese kitchenware, tote bags decorated with hedgehogs, and erasers shaped like food. ⊠ *Bordered by Geary Blvd. and Fillmore, Post, and Laguna Sts., Japantown.*

Fodor's Choice **Kabuki Springs & Spa.** This serene spa is one Japantown destination that
★ draws locals from all over town, from hipster to grandma, Japanese-
American or not. Balinese urns decorate the communal bath area of
this house of tranquility.

The extensive service menu includes facials, salt scrubs, and mud and
seaweed wraps, in addition to massage. You can take your massage in
a private room with a bath or in a curtained-off area.

The communal baths ($25) contain hot and cold tubs, a large Japanese-
style bath, a sauna, a steam room, and showers. Bang the gong for quiet
if your fellow bathers are speaking too loudly. The clothing-optional
baths are open for men only on Monday, Thursday, and Saturday;
women bathe on Wednesday, Friday, and Sunday. Bathing suits are
required on Tuesday, when the baths are coed.

Men and women can reserve private rooms daily. ⊠ *1750 Geary Blvd.,
Japantown* ☎ *415/922–6000* ⊕ *www.kabukisprings.com.*

WHERE TO EAT

Make no mistake, San Francisco is one of America's top food cities.
Some of the biggest landmarks are restaurants; and for some visitors, chefs like Daniel Patterson are just as big a draw as Alcatraz.
In fact, on a Saturday, the Ferry Building—a temple to local eating—may attract more visitors than the Golden Gate Bridge: cheeses,
breads, "salty pig parts," homemade delicacies, and sensory-perfect
vegetables and fruits attract rabidly dedicated aficionados. You see,
San Franciscans are a little loco about their edibles. If you ask them
what their favorite season is, don't be surprised if they respond,
"tomato season."

Some renowned restaurants are booked weeks or even months in
advance. But you can get lucky at the last minute if you're flexible—and
friendly. Most restaurants keep a few tables open for walk-ins and VIPs.
Show up for dinner early (5:30 pm) or late (after 9 pm) and politely
inquire about any last-minute vacancies or cancellations.

*Use the coordinate (✛ A1) at the end of each listing to locate a site on
the corresponding map. Restaurant reviews have been shortened. For
full information, visit Fodors.com.*

WHAT IT COSTS			
$	$$	$$$	$$$$
Restaurants	under $16	$16–$22	$23–$30	over $30

Restaurant prices are the average cost of a main course at dinner or, if dinner is not
served, at lunch.

UNION SQUARE AND CHINATOWN

$$$$
MODERN
AMERICAN
Fodor'sChoice
★
✕**Liholiho Yacht Club.** Big-hearted, high-spirited cooking has made Chef Ravi Kapur's lively restaurant one of the toughest reservations in town. The menu is inspired but not defined by the chef's native Hawaii. **Known for:** poke; Hawaiian-inspired food; lively buzz. $ *Average main: $35* ✉ *871 Sutter St., Union Sq.* ☎ *415/440–5446* ⊕ *www.lycf.com* ⊘ *Closed Sun. No lunch.* ✛ *D4.*

$$$
CHINESE
✕**Mister Jiu's.** Brandon Jew's ambitious, graceful restaurant offers the chef's contemporary, farm-to-table interpretation of Chinese cuisine. This is the place for hot-and-sour soup garnished with nasturtiums and pot stickers made with Swiss chard and local chicken. **Known for:** modern Chinese food; cocktails. $ *Average main: $30* ✉ *28 Waverly Pl., Chinatown* ☎ *415/857–9688* ⊕ *www.misterjius.com* ⊘ *Closed Sun. and Mon. No lunch.* ✛ *F3.*

$$
CHINESE
FAMILY
✕**R&G Lounge.** Salt-and-pepper Dungeness crab is a delicious draw at this bright, three-level Cantonese eatery that excels in the crustacean. A menu with photographs will help you sort through other HK specialties, including Peking duck and shrimp-stuffed bean curd. **Known for:** crab; Cantonese specialties; extensive menu. $ *Average main: $19* ✉ *631 Kearny St., Chinatown* ☎ *415/982–7877* ⊕ *www.rnglounge.com* ✛ *F3.*

SOMA

$$$$
MODERN
AMERICAN
Fodor'sChoice
★
✕**Benu.** Chef Corey Lee's three-Michelin-star fine-dining mecca is a must-stop for those who hop from city to city, collecting memorable meals. Each of the tasting menu's 15-plus courses is impossibly meticulous, a marvel of textures and flavors. **Known for:** high-end dining; tasting menu; good service. $ *Average main: $285* ✉ *22 Hawthorne St., SoMa* ☎ *415/685–4860* ⊕ *www.benusf.com* ⊘ *Closed Sun. and Mon. No lunch* ✛ *G5.*

$$$
CONTEMPORARY
Fodor'sChoice
★
✕**In Situ.** Benu chef Corey Lee's restaurant at SFMOMA is an exhibition of its own, with a rotating menu comprised of dishes from 80 famous chefs around the world. You might taste David Chang's sausage and rice cakes, Rene Redzepi's wood sorrel granita, or Wylie Dufresne's shrimp grits. **Known for:** global influences; originality; museum location. $ *Average main: $30* ✉ *151 3rd St., SoMa* ☎ *415/941–6050* ⊕ *insitu.sfmoma.org* ⊘ *Closed Wed. No dinner Mon. and Tues.* ✛ *F5.*

$$$
AMERICAN
Fodor'sChoice
★
✕**Marlowe.** Hearty American bistro fare and hip design draw crowds to this Anna Weinberg–Jennifer Puccio production. The menu boasts one of the city's best burgers, and the dining room gleams with white penny tile floors and marble countertops. **Known for:** burgers; strong drinks; festive atmosphere. $ *Average main: $27* ✉ *500 Brannan St., SoMa* ☎ *415/777–1413* ⊕ *www.marlowesf.com* ⊘ *No lunch weekends* ✛ *G6.*

$$$
MODERN
AMERICAN
Fodor'sChoice
★
✕**Trou Normand.** Thad Vogler's second endeavor (Bar Agricole was the first) delivers a fun boozy evening in stunning surroundings. Located off the lobby of the art deco–era Pacific Telephone building, it excels at house-cured salami and charcuterie and classic brandy-based cocktails. **Known for:** house-made charcuterie; brandy-based cocktails. $ *Average main: $26* ✉ *140 New Montgomery St., SoMa* ☎ *415/975–0876* ⊕ *www.trounormandsf.com* ✛ *G4.*

$$$ ✕ **Una Pizza Napoletana.** Inside this bare-bones SoMa spot you'll find
PIZZA one of the best Neapolitan-style pizzas outside of Italy. Chef-owner
and Manhattan transplant Anthony Mangieri is an obsessive artisan,
carefully making each and every pizza by hand. **Known for:** Neapolitan-
style pizza; brief menu. $ *Average main: $25* ✉ *210 11th St., SoMa*
☎ *415/861–3444* ⊕ *www.unapizza.com* ⊗ *Closed Sun.–Tues.* ✛ *D6.*

HAYES VALLEY

$$ ✕ **Nojo Ramen.** For a little bonhomie before the symphony, it's hard to go
JAPANESE wrong with this buzzy (and typically crowded) ramen spot. Noodles are
the star of the menu, and deservedly so, but you'll also find izakaya-style
small plates and comfort food like chicken teriyaki. **Known for:** ramen
with chicken-based (paitan) broth; Japanese comfort foods; long lines.
$ *Average main: $17* ✉ *231 Franklin St., Hayes Valley* ☎ *415/896–
4587* ⊕ *www.nojosf.com* ⊗ *Closed Mon. No lunch.* ✛ *C6.*

$$$$ ✕ **Rich Table.** Sardine potato chips and porcini doughnuts are the most
MODERN popular bites at co-chefs Evan and Sarah Rich's lively restaurant—and
AMERICAN the most indicative of its creativity. The mains are also clever stun-
Fodor's Choice ners: try one of the proteins or pastas, like the Douglas fir gnocchi.
★ **Known for:** creative food; freshly baked bread. $ *Average main: $34*
✉ *199 Gough St., Hayes Valley* ☎ *415/355–9085* ⊕ *www.richtablesf.
com* ⊗ *No lunch* ✛ *C6.*

$$$ ✕ **Zuni Café.** After one bite of Zuni's succulent brick-oven-roasted whole
MEDITERRANEAN chicken with Tuscan bread salad, you'll understand why the two-floor
Fodor's Choice café is a perennial star. Its long copper bar is a hub for a disparate mix of
★ patrons who commune over oysters on the half shell and cocktails and
wine. **Known for:** famous roast chicken; classic San Francisco dining.
$ *Average main: $30* ✉ *1658 Market St., Hayes Valley* ☎ *415/552–
2522* ⊕ *www.zunicafe.com* ⊗ *Closed Mon.* ✛ *C6.*

FINANCIAL DISTRICT

$$$ ✕ **Cotogna.** This urban trattoria is just as in demand as its fancier big
ITALIAN sister, Quince, next door. The draw here is Chef Michael Tusk's flavor-
ful, rustic, seasonally driven Italian cooking. **Known for:** rustic Italian;
fantastic wine list. $ *Average main: $25* ✉ *490 Pacific Ave., Financial
District* ☎ *415/775–8508* ⊕ *www.cotognasf.com* ✛ *F2.*

$$$ ✕ **Perbacco.** Chef Staffan Terje understands the cuisine of northern Italy.
ITALIAN From the complimentary basket of skinny, brittle breadsticks to the
pappardelle with short rib ragu, his entire menu is a delectable paean
to the region. **Known for:** pasta stuffed with meat and cabbage; house-
made cured meats; authentic Northern Italian cuisine. $ *Average main:
$30* ✉ *230 California St., Financial District* ☎ *415/955–0663* ⊕ *www.
perbaccosf.com* ⊗ *Closed Sun. No lunch Sat.* ✛ *G3.*

$$ ✕ **Yank Sing.** This bustling teahouse serves some of San Francisco's best
CHINESE dim sum to office workers on weekdays and boisterous families on
FAMILY weekends. The several dozen varieties prepared daily include both the
classic and the creative. **Known for:** classic dim sum; Shanghai soup
dumplings. $ *Average main: $16* ✉ *49 Stevenson St., Financial District*
☎ *415/541–4949* ⊕ *www.yanksing.com* ⊗ *No dinner* ✛ *F4.*

HOW TO EAT LIKE A LOCAL

San Francisco may well be the most piping-red-hot dining scene in the nation now. After all, with a booming tech industry, there are mouths to feed. Freedom to do what you want. Innovation. Eccentricity. These words define the culture, the food, and the cuisine of the city by the bay. Get in on what locals know by enjoying their favorite foods.

FOOD TRUCKS

This is where experimentation begins, where the overhead is low, and risk-taking is fun. From these mobile kitchens careers are launched. A food meet-up called "Off the Grid" happens in season at Fort Mason where you can have a progressive dinner among the 25 or so trucks. Year-round the convoy roams to different locations, selling things like Korean poutine, Indian burritos, and Vietnamese burgers. Each dish seems to reflect a refusal to follow the norm.

DIM SUM

The tradition of dim sum took hold in San Francisco when Chinese immigrants from Guangdong Province arrived with Cantonese cuisine. These earlier settlers eventually established teahouses and bakeries that sold dim sum, like the steamed dumplings stuffed with shrimp (*har gow*) or pork (*shao mai*). Now carts roll from table to table in Chinatown restaurants—and other parts of the city. Try the grilled and fried bite-size savories but also the sweets like *dan tat*, an egg custard tart.

BARBECUE

Whaaa? San Francisco barbecue? And what would that be? You can bet it's meat from top purveyors nearby. The city is surrounded by grazing lands, where the animals and their minders, the ranchers, are king. Until now, meats came simply plated. Now it's messy, with smokiness, charred crusts, and gorgeous marbling. But you may never hear of a San-Fran-style barbecue because, in the words of one chef, we're "nondenominational." You'll see it all: Memphis, Texas, Carolina, and Kansas City.

ICE CREAM

How ice cream became so popular in a place that spends many of its 365 days below the 75 degree mark is a mystery. But the lines attest to the popularity of the frozen dessert that gets its own San Francisco twist. This is the vanilla-bean vanilla and Tcho chocolate crowd. Bourbon and cornflakes? Reposado tequila? Cheers to that. Diversity and local produce is blended into flavors like ube (purple yam), yuzu, and Thai latte. Vegans, we got you covered, too.

BURRITOS

This stuffed tortilla got its Bay Area start in the 1960s in the Mission District. Because the size and fillings distinguish it from other styles, it became known as the Mission burrito. Look for rice (Southern Californians are cringing), beans, salsa, and enough meat in the

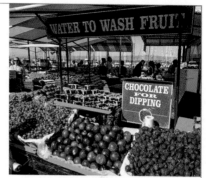

burrito for two meals. The aluminum foil keeps the interior neat, in theory. Popular choices are *carne asada* (beef) and *carnitas* (pork). But then there's *lengua* (beef tongue) and *birria* (goat). This is a hands-on meal. No utensils, please.

COFFEE

Coffee roasters here are like sports teams in other cities. You pick one of the big five or six to be loyal to, and defend it tirelessly. San Francisco favorites source impeccably and blend different beans as if they were wine making. In addition, a few of the big names—Four Barrel, Sightglass, Ritual, Blue Bottle—roast their own to control what they grind and pour at their outlets across the city—and now nationally and internationally.

FARMERS' MARKETS

These are our new grocery stores. They're the places to discover the latest in fruits, vegetables, and dried beans—much of it grown within a 60-mile radius. Cheeses, cured salami, breads, and nuts are sampled. Then there are the local ready-to-eat snacks, like pizza and *huevos rancheros*. The most popular market is the one on Saturday at the Ferry Plaza.

Left: Several farmers' markets occupy the Ferry Building; top right: One of the many farmers' markets in the city; bottom right: Dim sum being served at a local restaurant.

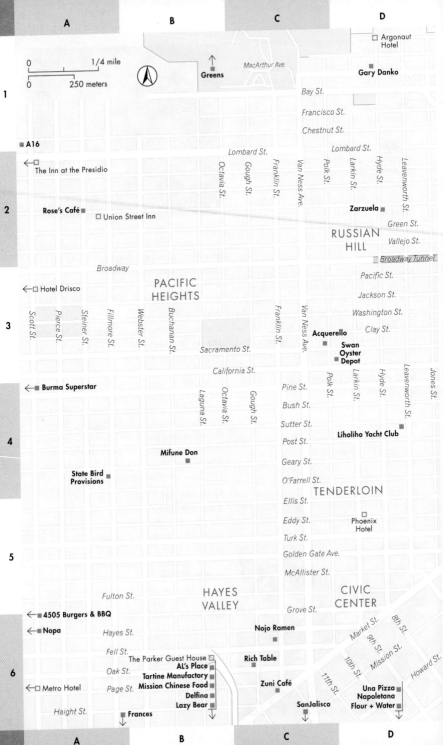

A

0 |—————|—————| **1/4 mile**
0 |—————|—————| **250 meters**

1

■ A16

← □ The Inn at the Presidio

2

Rose's Café ■
□ Union Street Inn

Broadway

← □ Hotel Drisco

PACIFIC HEIGHTS

3

Scott St.
Pierce St.
Steiner St.
Fillmore St.
Webster St.
Buchanan St.

Sacramento St.

California St.

← ■ Burma Superstar

4

Mifune Don ■

State Bird
Provisions ■

5

Fulton St.

HAYES VALLEY

← ■ 4505 Burgers & BBQ

← ■ Nopa

Hayes St.

Fell St.   The Parker Guest House □

Oak St.   AL's Place ■

6

□ Metro Hotel   Page St.   Tartine Manufactory ■
                                 Mission Chinese Food ■
                                 Delfina ■
            Haight St.   Lazy Bear ■
                          ■ Frances
                              ↓   ↓

B

MacArthur Ave.

↑
Greens ■

Lombard St.   Lombard St.

Octavia St.
Gough St.
Franklin St.

Laguna St.
Octavia St.
Gough St.

Nojo Ramen ■

Rich Table ■

Zuni Café ■

SanJalisco
↓

C

Van Ness Ave.
Polk St.
Larkin St.
Hyde St.
Leavenworth St.

Green St.

RUSSIAN HILL

Vallejo St.

░ *Broadway Tunnel*

Pacific St.

Jackson St.

Washington St.

Franklin St.
Van Ness Ave.

Clay St.

Acquerello ■

Swan
Oyster
Depot ■

Pine St.

Bush St.

Sutter St.

Polk St.
Larkin St.
Hyde St.
Leavenworth St.
Jones St.

Post St.

Geary St.

O'Farrell St.

TENDERLOIN

Ellis St.

Eddy St.   Phoenix
                Hotel □

Turk St.

Golden Gate Ave.

McAllister St.

CIVIC CENTER

Grove St.

D

□ Argonaut
  Hotel

Gary Danko ■

Bay St.

Francisco St.

Chestnut St.

Zarzuela ■

Liholiho Yacht Club ■

Market St.
8th St.
9th St.
Mission St.
10th St.
11th St.
Howard St.

Una Pizza
Napoletana ■
Flour + Water ■
↓

Where to Eat and Stay in San Francisco

E **F** **G** **H**

Jefferson St.
Beach St.
North Point St.
Hotel Zoe
Fisherman's Wharf
Francisco St.
San Remo Hotel
Chestnut St.
Columbus Ave.
Bay St.
The Embarcadero
Pier 35
Pier 33
Pier 31
Pier 29
Pier 27

1

Lombard St.
Greenwich St.
Filbert St.
Union St.
Tony's Pizza
Napoletana
NORTH
BEACH
TELEGRAPH
HILL
Fog City
Front St.
The Embarcadero
Pier 23
Pier 19
Pier 17
Pier 15
Pier 9
San Francisco Bay

2

Cotogna
Tosca
Cafe
Columbus Ave.
Montgomery St.
Sansome St.
Battery St.
Davis St.
Clay St.
Pier 7
Pier 5
Pier 3
Pier 1

Taylor St.
Mason St.
Powell St.
Stockton St.
Grant Ave.
NOB
HILL
CHINATOWN
R+G Lounge
Mister Jiu's
Fairmont
San Francisco
Ritz-Carlton,
San Francisco
FINANCIAL
DISTRICT
Perbacco
Front St.
Davis St.
Drumm St.
Hog Island
Oyster Company
Slanted
Door
Hotel Vitale

3

Golden Gate Hotel
Kearny St.
Hotel
Triton
Market St.
Steuart St.
Spear St.

UNION SQUARE
Hotel G
Hotel Diva
Westin
St. Francis
Yank Sing
Stevenson St.
New Montgomery St.
Main St.
Beale St.
Fremont St.
1st St.
80

4

The St. Regis
San Francisco
Four Seasons Hotel
San Francisco
Trou Normand
2nd St.
Hawthorne St.
Hotel Zetta
San Francisco
In Situ
Benu
Howard St.
3rd St.

5

Mission St.
4th St.
5th St.
SOMA
6th St.
Folsom St.
7th St.
Bryant St.
Brannan St.
Townsend St.
King St.
Harrison St.
Marlowe

6

KEY	
□	Hotels
■	Restaurants
■	Restaurants in Hotels
⊕	following reviews indicates map-grid coordinates

E **F** **G** **H**

Eating with Kids

Kids can be fussy eaters, and parents can be, too. Fortunately, there are plenty of excellent options in the city that will satisfy both.

Barney's Gourmet Burgers. With locations all over the Bay Area, including this one not far from Fort Mason, this chain caters to older kids and their parents with mile-high burgers and giant salads. But Barney's doesn't forget "kids under 8," who have their own menu featuring a burger, an all-beef frank, and chicken strips. And they don't forget parents, offering a nice selection of wines by the glass and beer on tap. ⊠ *3344 Steiner St., near Union St.* ☎ *415/563–0307* ⊕ *www. barneyshamburgers.com 3:C6.*

City View Restaurant. Nearby in Chinatown, City View Restaurant serves a varied selection of dim sum, with tasty pork buns for kids and more-exotic fare for adults. ⊠ *662 Commercial St., near Kearny St.* ☎ *415/398–2838 1:E4.*

The Ferry Building *(1:G4)*on the Embarcadero has plenty of kid-friendly options, from **Mijita Cocina Mexicana,** which has its own kids' menu, to **Gott's Roadside,** for burgers, shakes, and more. (And the outdoor access can help keep the little ones entertained.)

Park Chalet. Finally, both kids and adults love to be by the ocean, and the Park Chalet, hidden behind the two-story Beach Chalet, offers pizza, mac and cheese, sticky ribs, and a big banana split. ⊠ *1000 Great Hwy., at Fulton St.* ☎ *415/386–8439 3:A3.*

Rosamunde Sausage Grill. In Lower Haight, the small Rosamunde Sausage Grill serves just that—a slew of different sausages, from Polish to duck to *Weisswurst* (Bavarian veal). You get your choice of two toppings, like grilled onions, sauerkraut, and chili, and since there are only six stools, plan on take-out. ■TIP→ Head to nearby Duboce Park, with its cute playground. ⊠ *545 Haight St., between Steiner and Fillmore Sts.* ☎ *415/437–6851 3:D3.*

NOB HILL AND RUSSIAN HILL

$$
SEAFOOD
Fodor'sChoice
★

✕ **Swan Oyster Depot.** Half fish market and half diner, this small, slim, family-run seafood operation, open since 1912, has no tables, just a narrow marble counter with about 18 stools. Most people come in to buy perfectly fresh salmon, halibut, crabs, and other seafood to take home. **Known for:** fresh seafood; long lines. $ *Average main: $18* ⊠ *1517 Polk St., Polk Gulch* ☎ *415/673–1101* ▬ *No credit cards* ☾ *Closed Sun. No dinner* ✛ *D3.*

$$
TAPAS

✕ **Zarzuela.** Full-blooded Spaniards swear by the paella at this tiny old-world-style bistro, complete with matador posters on the wall. Also not to be missed is the homemade sangria—or any of the impressive roster of tapas prepared by Madrid-bred chef Lucas Gasco. **Known for:** authentic tapas; not-to-be-missed sangria. $ *Average main: $21* ⊠ *2000 Hyde St., Russian Hill* ☎ *415/346–0800* ☾ *Closed Sun. and Mon. No lunch* ✛ *D2.*

VAN NESS/POLK

$$$$ ✕ **Acquerello.** Chef-co-owner Suzette Gresham has elicited plenty of
ITALIAN swoons over the years with her high-end but soulful Italian cooking.
Fodor's Choice Her Parmesan *budino* (pudding) is a star of the menu, which features
★ both classic and cutting-edge dishes. **Known for:** prix-fixe dining; Par-
mesan budino; extensive Italian wine list. $ *Average main: $95* ⊠ *1722
Sacramento St., Polk Gulch* ☎ *415/567–5432* ⊕ *www.acquerello.com*
⊗ *Closed Sun. and Mon. No lunch* ✛ *C3.*

NORTH BEACH

$$$ ✕ **Tony's Pizza Napoletana.** Locals hotly debate who makes the city's best
PIZZA pizza, and for many Tony Gemignani takes the prize. Repeatedly crowned
FAMILY the World Champion Pizza Maker at the World Pizza Cup in Naples, he's
renowned here for his flavorful dough and impressive range. **Known for:**
World Champion Pizza chef; multiple pizza ovens and pie styles; family din-
ing. $ *Average main: $27* ⊠ *1570 Stockton St., North Beach* ☎ *415/835–
9888* ⊕ *www.tonyspizzanapoletana.com* ⊗ *Closed Tues.* ✛ *E2.*

$$$ ✕ **Tosca Cafe.** Following a much-heralded revamp, this 1919 boho classic
ITALIAN continues to attract both celebs and local scenesters. The room is dark
and clubby, and the food skews Italian, with a raft of pastas and antipasti. **Known for:** Italian-American comfort food; tasty cocktails; signature roast chicken for two. $ *Average main: $28* ⊠ *242 Columbus Ave.,
North Beach* ☎ *415/986–9651* ⊕ *www.toscacafesf.com* ⊗ *No lunch* ✛ *F3.*

ON THE WATERFRONT

FISHERMAN'S WHARF

$$$$ ✕ **Gary Danko.** This San Francisco classic has earned a legion of fans—and
AMERICAN a Michelin star—for its namesake chef's refined and creative cooking.
The cost of a meal is pegged to the number of courses, from three to five,
and the menu spans a classic yet Californian style that changes seasonally. **Known for:** prix-fixe menu; fine dining; extensive wine list. $ *Aver-
age main: $87* ⊠ *800 N. Point St., Fisherman's Wharf* ☎ *415/749–2060*
⊕ *www.garydanko.com* ⊗ *No lunch* 🏛 *Jacket required* ✛ *D1.*

EMBARCADERO

$$ ✕ **Fog City.** All but hidden on a far-flung stretch of the Embarcadero, this
AMERICAN 21st-century diner is well worth the hike. It's best known for its updated
FAMILY classics, like a short-rib BLT with kimchi mayo and corn bread that
emerges hot from the wood-fired oven. **Known for:** updated diner food;
excellent cocktails; views of Battery St. and the Embarcadero. $ *Av-
erage main: $21* ⊠ *1300 Battery St., Embarcadero* ☎ *415/982–2000*
⊕ *www.fogcitysf.com* ✛ *G2.*

$$ ✕ **Hog Island Oyster Company.** A thriving oyster farm north of San Fran-
SEAFOOD cisco in Tomales Bay serves up its harvest at this raw bar and restaurant
in the Ferry Building. Devotees come here for impeccably fresh oysters
and clams on the half shell. **Known for:** fresh oysters; first-rate seafood
stew; busy raw bar. $ *Average main: $17* ⊠ *Ferry Bldg., Embarcadero
at Market St., Embarcadero* ☎ *415/391–7117* ⊕ *www.hogislandoysters.
com* ✛ *H3.*

4

$$$ ✕ **Slanted Door.** If you're looking for homey Vietnamese food served
VIETNAMESE in a down-to-earth dining room at a bargain-basement price, *don't*
stop here. Celebrated chef-owner Charles Phan has mastered the
upmarket, Western-accented Vietnamese menu. **Known for:** upscale
Vietnamese food; great cocktails. ⑤ *Average main: $30* ⌧ *Ferry Bldg.,
Embarcadero at Market St., Embarcadero* ☎ *415/861–8032* ⊕ *www.
slanteddoor.com* ⊹ *H3.*

THE MARINA

$$$ ✕ **A16.** Named after a highway that runs through Southern Italy, this
ITALIAN trattoria specializes in the food from that region, done very, very well.
The menu is stocked with pizza and rustic pastas like *maccaronara* with
ragu napoletana and house-made salted ricotta, as well as entrées like
roasted chicken with sage salsa verde. **Known for:** excellent Southern
Italian food; mostly Southern Italian wine list; lively bar. ⑤ *Average
main: $25* ⌧ *2355 Chestnut St., Marina* ☎ *415/771–2216* ⊕ *www.
a16pizza.com* ☉ *No lunch Mon. and Tues.* ⊹ *A1.*

$$$ ✕ **Greens.** Owned and operated by the San Francisco Zen Center, this
VEGETARIAN legendary vegetarian restaurant gets some of its fresh produce from
the center's organic Green Gulch Farm. Despite the lack of meat,
hearty dishes from chef Annie Somerville—such as green curry and
wild-mushroom-leek pizza—really satisfy. **Known for:** sweeping views;
hearty vegetarian food. ⑤ *Average main: $24* ⌧ *Bldg. A, Fort Mason, 2
Marina Blvd., Marina* ☎ *415/771–6222* ⊕ *www.greensrestaurant.com*
☉ *No lunch Mon.* ⊹ *B1.*

COW HOLLOW

$$$ ✕ **Rose's Café.** Although it's open morning until night, this cozy café
ITALIAN is most synonymous with brunch. Sleepy-headed locals turn up for
FAMILY delights like the breakfast pizza of smoked ham, eggs, and fontina and
the French toast with caramelized apples. **Known for:** popular Sunday
brunch; breakfast pizza; top-notch ingredients. ⑤ *Average main: $28*
⌧ *2298 Union St., Cow Hollow* ☎ *415/775–2200* ⊕ *www.rosescafesf.
com* ⊹ *A2.*

THE CASTRO

$$$ ✕ **Frances.** Still one of the hottest tickets in town, chef Melissa Perello's
MODERN simple, sublime restaurant is a consummate date-night destination.
AMERICAN Perello's seasonal California-French cooking is its own enduring love
affair. **Known for:** seasonal menu; neighborhood gem; tough reserva-
tion. ⑤ *Average main: $30* ⌧ *3870 17th St., Castro* ☎ *415/621–3870*
⊕ *www.frances-sf.com* ☉ *Closed Mon. No lunch* ⊹ *A6.*

THE MISSION

$$ ✕ **AL's Place.** AL is Chef Aaron London, and his place is a sunny, white-
MODERN washed corner spot that serves inventive, Michelin-starred vegetable-
AMERICAN forward cooking. London's menu changes frequently, but some dishes,

like lightly cured trout and grits with seasonal produce, stick around. **Known for:** seasonal cooking; inventive vegetable-heavy menu; fries with cult following. ⑤ *Average main: $17* ✉ *1499 Valencia St., Mission* ☎ *415/416–6136* ⊕ *www.alsplacesf.com* ⊙ *Closed Mon. and Tues. No lunch.* ✛ *B6.*

$$$
ITALIAN
Fodor'sChoice
★

✕ **Delfina.** To find Craig and Annie Stoll's cultishly adored Northern Italian spot, just look for the crowds. They're a constant fixture here, as are deceptively simple, exquisitely flavored dishes like the signature spaghetti with plum tomatoes. **Known for:** signature spaghetti with plum tomatoes; long waits; much-lauded panna cotta. ⑤ *Average main: $27* ✉ *3621 18th St., Mission District* ☎ *415/552–4055* ⊕ *www.delfinasf.com* ⊙ *No lunch* ✛ *B6.*

$$$
ITALIAN

✕ **Flour + Water.** This hot spot is synonymous with pasta, though its blistery thin-crust Neapolitan pizzas are also top notch. The grand experience here is the seven-course pasta-tasting menu (extra for wine pairings). **Known for:** difficult to get a reservation; delicious pizzas and pastas; noisy scene. ⑤ *Average main: $26* ✉ *2401 Harrison St., Mission District* ☎ *415/826–7000* ⊕ *www.flourandwater.com* ⊙ *No lunch* ✛ *D6.*

$$$$
MODERN
AMERICAN

✕ **Lazy Bear.** There's no end to the buzz of chef David Barzelay's pop-up turned permanent, or the quest for a ticket to one of his modern American dinners. A reservation for the 14-plus-course prix-fixe menu that changes monthly is required. **Known for:** hot-ticket often resold; communal dining; dinner party setup. ⑤ *Average main: $160* ✉ *3416 19th St., Mission District* ☎ *415/874–9921* ⊕ *www.lazybearsf.com* ⊙ *Closed Sun. and Mon. No lunch.* ✛ *B6.*

$
CHINESE

✕ **Mission Chinese Food.** While the setting is somewhat one-star, the food draws throngs for its bold, cheerfully inauthentic riffs on Chinese cuisine. The kitchen pumps out some fine and super-fiery kung pao pastrami as well as other dishes made with quality meats and ingredients, like salt cod fried rice with mackerel confit, and sour chili chicken. **Known for:** kung pao pastrami; salt cod fried rice; to-go spot due to long waits. ⑤ *Average main: $14* ✉ *2234 Mission St., Mission District* ☎ *415/863–2800* ⊕ *www.missionchinesefood.com* ⊙ *Closed Wed.* ✛ *B6.*

$
MEXICAN
FAMILY

✕ **SanJalisco.** This colorful old-time, sun-filled, family-run restaurant is a neighborhood favorite, and not only because it serves breakfast all day—though the hearty *chilaquiles* hit the spot. On weekends, adventurous eaters may opt for *birria*, a spicy barbecued goat stew, or *menudo*, a tongue-searing soup made from beef tripe. **Known for:** breakfast all day; beef-tripe menudo; delicious sangria. ⑤ *Average main: $11* ✉ *901 S. Van Ness Ave., Mission District* ☎ *415/648–8383* ⊕ *www.sanjalisco.com* ✛ *C6.*

$$$$
MODERN
AMERICAN
FAMILY

✕ **Tartine Manufactory.** Little Tartine bakery has expanded big time, with this sunny, cathedral-like space in the Heath Ceramics building. This is where you come for Chad Robertson's bread and Liz Prueitt's pastries, but also for breakfast, lunch, and dinner. **Known for:** Chad Robertson's bread; Liz Prueitt's pastries; seasonal salads. ⑤ *Average main: $32* ✉ *595 Alabama St., Mission District* ☎ *415/757–0007* ⊕ *www.tartinemanufactory.com* ⊙ *No dinner Mon. and Tues.* ✛ *B6.*

JAPANTOWN

$ ✕**Mifune Don.** Thin brown soba and thick white udon are the stars at this
JAPANESE long-popular outpost of a celebrated Osaka restaurant. There's usually
FAMILY a line, but the house-made noodles, served both hot and cold and with
a score of toppings, are worth the wait (and the line moves quickly).
Known for: house-made soba and udon; savory Japanese pancakes; long
lines. ⑤ *Average main: $12* ✉ *22 Peace Plaza, Suite 560, Japantown*
☎ *415/346–1993* ◷ *Closed Tues.* ✛ *B4.*

WESTERN ADDITION

$$ ✕**4505 Burgers & BBQ.** Noted butcher Ryan Farr is behind the tender,
BARBECUE deliciously charred brisket at this hipster-chic barbecue shack. The
smoker here works overtime, churning out an array of meats that
can be had by the plate and pound. **Known for:** smoked meats; deli-
cious sides; juicy burgers. ⑤ *Average main: $17* ✉ *705 Divisadero, at
Grove St., Western Addition* ☎ *415/231–6993* ⊕ *www.4505meats.
com* ✛ *A6.*

$$$ ✕**Nopa.** This is the good-food granddaddy of the hot corridor of the
AMERICAN same name (NoPa equals North of the Panhandle). The Cali-rustic fare
here draws dependable crowds, especially on the weekends. **Known
for:** California cooking; flatbread topped with bacon and Treviso
cheese; lively crowd. ⑤ *Average main: $24* ✉ *560 Divisadero St.,
Western Addition* ☎ *415/864–8643* ⊕ *www.nopasf.com* ◷ *No lunch
weekdays* ✛ *A6.*

$$$ ✕**State Bird Provisions.** It's more or less impossible to nab a reservation at
MODERN Stuart Brioza and Nicole Krasinski's game-changing, Michelin-starred
AMERICAN restaurant. But if you do walk in and brave the 90-plus-minute wait,
Fodor'sChoice you'll eventually be rewarded with inventive bites served from dim
★ sum–style carts. **Known for:** dim sum–style dining; long waits. ⑤ *Aver-
age main: $30* ✉ *1529 Fillmore St., Western Addition* ☎ *415/795–1272*
⊕ *www.statebirdsf.com* ◷ *No lunch* ✛ *A4.*

THE RICHMOND

$ ✕**Burma Superstar.** Locals make the trek to the "Avenues" for this
ASIAN perennially crowded spot's flavorful, well-prepared Burmese food. Its
signature dish is the extraordinary tea leaf salad, a combo of spicy,
salty, crunchy, and sour that is mixed table-side. **Known for:** tea leaf
salad; samusa soup; long lines. ⑤ *Average main: $15* ✉ *309 Clement
St., Richmond* ☎ *415/387–2147* ⊕ *www.burmasuperstar.com* ✛ *A4.*

WHERE TO STAY

San Francisco accommodations are diverse, ranging from cozy inns and kitschy motels, to chic little inns and true grande dames, housed in century-old structures and sleek high-rises. While the tech boom has skyrocketed the prices of even some of the most dependable low-cost options, luckily, some Fodor's faves still offer fine accommodations without the jaw-dropping prices to match those steep hills. In fact, the number of reasonably priced accommodations is impressive.

Hotel reviews have been shortened. For full information, visit Fodors. com. Use the coordinate (✛ A1) at the end of each listing to locate a site on the corresponding map.

WHAT IT COSTS			
$	$$	$$$	$$$$
Hotels	under $150	$150–$249	$250–$350	over $350

Hotel prices are the lowest cost of a standard double room in high season.

UNION SQUARE

$
B&B/INN
FAMILY
Fodor's Choice
★

Golden Gate Hotel. Budget seekers looking for accommodations around Union Square will enjoy this four-story Edwardian with bay windows, an original birdcage elevator, hallways lined with historical photographs, and rooms decorated with antiques, wicker pieces, and Laura Ashley bedding and curtains. **Pros:** friendly staff; free Wi-Fi; spotless rooms; comfortable bedding; good location if you're a walker. **Cons:** some rooms share a bath; resident cat and dog, so not good for guests with allergies; some rooms on small side. ⑤ *Rooms from: $145* ✉ *775 Bush St., Union Sq.* ☎ *415/392–3702, 800/835–1118* ⊕ *www. goldengatehotel.com* ⟿ *23 rooms* ❦ *Breakfast* ✛ *E4.*

$$
HOTEL
FAMILY

Hotel Diva. Entering this magnet for urbanites craving modern decor requires stepping over footprints, handprints, and autographs embedded in the sidewalk by visiting stars; in the rooms, designer carpets complement mid-century-modern chairs and brushed-steel headboards whose shape mimics that of ocean waves. **Pros:** punchy design; in the heart of the theater district; accommodating staff. **Cons:** few frills; tiny bathrooms (but equipped with eco-friendly bath products); many rooms are small. ⑤ *Rooms from: $189* ✉ *440 Geary St., Union Sq.* ☎ *415/885–0200, 800/553–1900* ⊕ *www.hoteldiva.com* ⟿ *130 rooms* ❦ *No meals* ✛ *E4.*

$$
HOTEL

Hotel Triton. One of San Francisco's early concept boutique hotels, the Triton may have been eclipsed by newcomers in both style and substance, but its staff remains attentive and the hotel's location at the convergence of Chinatown, the Financial District, and Union Square keeps it worthy of consideration. **Pros:** attentive service; arty environs; good location. **Cons:** rooms and baths are on the small side; hallways feel cramped; needs a reboot. ⑤ *Rooms from: $219* ✉ *342 Grant Ave., Union Sq.* ☎ *415/394–0500, 877/793–9931* ⊕ *www.hoteltriton.com* ⟿ *140 rooms* ❦ *No meals* ✛ *F4.*

$$$$ 🏨 **Westin St. Francis.** The survivor of two major earthquakes, some
HOTEL headline-grabbing scandals, and even an attempted presidential assassination, this grande dame that dates to 1904 remains ever above the
fray. **Pros:** prime Union Square location; great views from some rooms;
special weekend rates part of year. **Cons:** rooms in original building
can be small; public spaces lack the panache of days gone by. ⑤ *Rooms
from: $356* ✉ *335 Powell St., Union Sq.* ☎ *415/397–7000, 800/917–
7458* ⊕ *www.westinstfrancis.com* ➵ *1,195 rooms* ¡⊙¡ *No meals* ✛ *E4.*

SOMA

$$$$ 🏨 **Four Seasons Hotel San Francisco.** Occupying floors 5 through 17 of a
HOTEL skyscraper, the Four Seasons delivers subdued elegance in rooms with
contemporary artwork, fine linens, floor-to-ceiling windows that overlook Yerba Buena Gardens or downtown, and bathrooms with deep
soaking tubs and glass-enclosed showers. **Pros:** near museums, galleries, restaurants, shopping, and clubs; terrific fitness facilities; luxurious
rooms and amenities. **Cons:** pricey; rooms can feel sterile. ⑤ *Rooms
from: $525* ✉ *757 Market St., SoMa* ☎ *415/633–3000, 800/332–3442,
800/819–5053* ⊕ *www.fourseasons.com/sanfrancisco* ➵ *277 rooms*
¡⊙¡ *No meals* ✛ *F4.*

$$$ 🏨 **Hotel Zetta San Francisco.** With a playful lobby lounge, the London-
HOTEL style Cavalier brasserie, and slick-yet-homey tech-friendly rooms, this
Fodor'sChoice trendy redo behind a stately 1913 neoclassical facade is a leader in the
★ SoMa hotel scene. **Pros:** tech amenities and arty design; fine restaurant
and lounge; noteworthy fitness center. **Cons:** lots of hubbub and traffic;
no bathtubs; aesthetic mildly too frenetic for some guests. ⑤ *Rooms
from: $289* ✉ *55 5th St., SoMa* ☎ *415/543–8555* ⊕ *hotelzetta.com*
➵ *116 rooms* ¡⊙¡ *No meals* ✛ *E5.*

$$$$ 🏨 **The St. Regis San Francisco.** Across from Yerba Buena Gardens and
HOTEL SFMOMA, the luxurious and modern St. Regis is favored by celebri-
Fodor'sChoice ties such as Lady Gaga and Al Gore. **Pros:** excellent views; stunning lap
★ pool; luxe spa. **Cons:** expensive rates; small front-desk area; cramped
space for passenger unloading. ⑤ *Rooms from: $358* ✉ *125 3rd St.,
SoMa* ☎ *415/284–4000* ⊕ *www.stregis.com/sanfrancisco* ➵ *260 rooms*
¡⊙¡ *No meals* ✛ *F4.*

THE TENDERLOIN

$$ 🏨 **Phoenix Hotel.** A magnet for the boho crowd, the Phoenix is retro and
HOTEL low-key, with bamboo furniture, white bedspreads, and original pieces
by local artists, as well as modern amenities like iHome docking stations. **Pros:** mellow staffers set boho tone; cheeky design, hip restaurant/
bar; free parking. **Cons:** somewhat seedy location; no elevators; can be
loud in the evenings. ⑤ *Rooms from: $249* ✉ *601 Eddy St., Tenderloin*
☎ *415/776–1380, 800/248–9466* ⊕ *www.thephoenixhotel.com* ➵ *44
rooms* ¡⊙¡ *Breakfast* ✛ *D5.*

HAYES VALLEY

$ Metro Hotel. These tiny rooms, with simple yet modern decor and
HOTEL   equipped with private, if small, bathrooms, are within walking distance
Fodor'sChoice   to the lively Haight, Hayes Valley, Panhandle, NoPa, and Castro neigh-
★   borhoods. **Pros:** can't beat the price; out-of-downtown location; friendly
staffers. **Cons:** small rooms and bathrooms; street noise; only difficult
street parking available. $ Rooms from: $107 ⊠ 319 Divisadero St.,
Hayes Valley ☎ 415/861–5364 ⊕ www.metrohotelsf.com ⤳ 24 rooms
❚❂❙ No meals ✛ A6.

NOB HILL

4

$$$$ Fairmont San Francisco. Dominating the top of Nob Hill like a Euro-
HOTEL   pean palace, the Fairmont indulges guests in luxury—rooms in the main
building, adorned in sapphire blues with platinum and pewter accents,
have high ceilings, decadent beds, and marble bathrooms; rooms in
the newer Tower, many with fine views, have a neutral color palette
with bright-silver notes. **Pros:** huge bathrooms; stunning lobby; great
location. **Cons:** some older rooms are small; hills can be challenging
for those on foot. $ Rooms from: $459 ⊠ 950 Mason St., Nob Hill
☎ 415/772–5000, 800/257–7544 ⊕ www.fairmont.com/san-francisco
⤳ 592 rooms ❚❂❙ No meals ✛ E3.

$$$$ Ritz-Carlton, San Francisco. A tribute to beauty and attentive, profes-
HOTEL   sional service, the Ritz-Carlton emphasizes luxury and elegance, which
Fodor'sChoice   is evident in the Ionic columns that grace the neoclassical facade and
★   the crystal chandeliers that illuminate marble floors and walls in the
lobby. **Pros:** terrific service; beautiful surroundings; Parallel 37 restaurant and Lobby Lounge. **Cons:** expensive; hilly location; no pool.
$ Rooms from: $570 ⊠ 600 Stockton St., at California St., Nob Hill
☎ 415/296–7465, 800/542–8680 ⊕ www.ritzcarlton.com/sanfrancisco
⤳ 336 rooms ❚❂❙ No meals ✛ E3.

NORTH BEACH

$ San Remo Hotel. A few blocks from Fisherman's Wharf, this three-
HOTEL   story 1906 Italianate Victorian—once home to longshoremen and Beat
Fodor'sChoice   poets—has a narrow stairway from the street leading to the front desk
★   and labyrinthine hallways. **Pros:** inexpensive rates; free Wi-Fi; rooftop
penthouse (reserve way ahead) has private deck with Coit Tower views.
Cons: some rooms are dark; only the penthouse suite has a private
bath; parking (discounted fee) is off-site. $ Rooms from: $119 ⊠ 2237
Mason St., North Beach ☎ 415/776–8688, 800/352–7366 ⊕ www.san-
remohotel.com ▭ No credit cards ✆ 64 rooms ❚❂❙ No meals ✛ E1.

FISHERMAN'S WHARF

$$$ Argonaut Hotel. The Argonaut's spacious guest rooms have exposed-
HOTEL   brick walls, wood-beam ceilings, and best of all, windows that open to
FAMILY   the sea air and the sounds of the waterfront; many rooms enjoy Alca-
Fodor'sChoice   traz and Golden Gate Bridge views. **Pros:** bay views; near Hyde Street
★   cable car; toys for the kids. **Cons:** nautical theme isn't for everyone;

cramped public areas; far from crosstown attractions. $\boxed{S}$ *Rooms from: $269* ✉ *495 Jefferson St., at Hyde St., Fisherman's Wharf* ☎ *415/563–0800, 866/415–0704* ⊕ *www.argonauthotel.com* ⇨ *252 rooms* ⊙*No meals* ✛ *D1.*

$$$
HOTEL

☒ **Hotel Zoe Fisherman's Wharf.** Multimillion-dollar renovations in 2017 transformed the dowdy former Best Western Tuscan into a smart-looking boutique hotel with guest-room interiors inspired by luxury Mediterranean yachts. **Pros:** cozy feeling; steps from Fisherman's Wharf; smart-looking contemporary design. **Cons:** congested touristy area; small rooms. $\boxed{S}$ *Rooms from: $279* ✉ *425 N. Point St., at Mason St., Fisherman's Wharf* ☎ *415/561–1100, 800/648–4626* ⊕ *www.hotelzoesf.com* ▭ *No credit cards* ⇨ *221 rooms* ⊙*No meals* ✛ *E1.*

EMBARCADERO

$$$$
HOTEL
FAMILY
Fodor's Choice
★

☒ **Hotel Vitale.** The emphasis on luxury and upscale relaxation at this eight-story bay-front property is apparent in every thoughtful detail: little vases of lavender mounted outside each room; limestone-lined baths stocked with top-of-the-line products; the penthouse-level day spa with soaking tubs set in a rooftop bamboo forest. **Pros:** family-friendly studios; great waterfront views; penthouse spa. **Cons:** some rooms feel cramped; "urban fee" adds further expense to an already pricey property; only partial bay views from some rooms. $\boxed{S}$ *Rooms from: $385* ✉ *8 Mission St., Embarcadero* ☎ *415/278–3700, 888/890–8688* ⊕ *www. hotelvitale.com* ⇨ *200 rooms* ⊙*No meals* ✛ *H3.*

THE MARINA, COW HOLLOW, AND THE PRESIDIO

$$$
B&B/INN
Fodor's Choice
★

☒ **The Inn at the Presidio.** Built in 1903 and opened as a hotel in 2012, this two-story, Georgian Revival–style structure once served as officers' quarters but now has 26 guest rooms—most of them suites—complete with gas fireplaces and modern-meets-salvage-store finds such as wrought-iron beds, historic black-and-white photos, and Pendleton blankets. **Pros:** Golden Gate Bridge views; away-from-it-all feeling yet still in the city; Presidio's hiking and biking trails, Disney museum, and other attractions. **Cons:** no on-site restaurant; no elevator; challenging to get a taxi; far from downtown attractions. $\boxed{S}$ *Rooms from: $295* ✉ *42 Moraga Ave., Presidio* ☎ *415/800–7356* ⊕ *www.innatthepresidio. com* ⇨ *26 rooms* ⊙*Breakfast* ✛ *A2.*

$$
B&B/INN
Fodor's Choice
★

☒ **Union Street Inn.** Antiques, unique artwork, and such touches as candles, fresh flowers, wineglasses, and fine linens make rooms in this green-and-cream 1902 Edwardian popular with honeymooners and those looking for a romantic getaway with an English countryside ambience. **Pros:** personal service; excellent full breakfast; romantic setting. **Cons:** parking is difficult; no air-conditioning; no elevator. $\boxed{S}$ *Rooms from: $249* ✉ *2229 Union St., Cow Hollow* ☎ *415/346–0424* ⊕ *www. unionstreetinn.com* ⇨ *6 rooms* ⊙*Breakfast* ✛ *A2.*

THE MISSION

$$
B&B/INN
Fodor's Choice
★

The Parker Guest House. Two yellow 1909 Edwardian houses enchant travelers wanting an authentic San Francisco experience; dark hallways and steep staircases lead to bright earth-toned rooms with private tiled baths (most with tubs), comfortable sitting areas, and cozy linens. **Pros:** handsome affordable rooms; just steps from Dolores Park and the vibrant Castro District on a Muni line; elaborate gardens. **Cons:** stairs can be challenging for those with limited mobility. $ *Rooms from: $179* ⊠ *520 Church St., Mission District* ☏ *415/621–4139* ⊕ *parkerguesthouse.com* ☞ *21 rooms* |○| *Breakfast* ✛ *B6.*

PACIFIC HEIGHTS AND JAPANTOWN

$$$$
HOTEL
Fodor's Choice
★

Hotel Drisco. Pretend you're a denizen of one of San Francisco's wealthiest residential neighborhoods while you stay at this understated, elegant 1903 Edwardian hotel. **Pros:** full renovation of property in 2017; great service and many amenities; quiet residential retreat. **Cons:** far from downtown (but free weekday-morning chauffeur service); room-rate uptick since renovation; on a steep hill. $ *Rooms from: $499* ⊠ *2901 Pacific Ave., Pacific Heights* ☏ *415/346–2880, 800/634–7277* ⊕ *www.hoteldrisco.com* ☞ *48 rooms* |○| *Breakfast* ✛ *A3.*

NIGHTLIFE

After hours, business folk and the working class give way to costume-clad partygoers, hippies and hipsters, downtown divas, frat boys, and those who prefer something a little more clothing-optional.

Entertainment information is printed in the "Datebook" section and the more calendar-based "96 Hours" section of the *San Francisco Chronicle* (⊕ *www.sfgate.com*). Also consult any of the free alternative weeklies, notably the *SF Weekly* (⊕ *www.sfweekly.com*), which blurbs nightclubs and music, and the *San Francisco Bay Guardian* (⊕ *www.sfbg.com*), which lists neighborhood, avant-garde, and budget events. SF Station (⊕ *www.sfstation.com*; online only) has an up-to-date calendar of entertainment goings-on.

You're better off taking public transportation or taxis on weekend nights, unless you're heading downtown (Financial District or Union Square) and are willing to park in a lot. There's only street parking in North Beach, the Mission, Castro, and the Haight, and finding a spot can be practically impossible. Muni stops running between 1 am and 5 am but has its limited Owl Service on a few lines—including the K, N, L, 90, 91, 14, 24, 38, and 22—every 30 minutes. Service cuts have put a dent in frequency; check ⊕ *www.sfmuni.com* for current details. You can sometimes hail a taxi on the street in well-trodden nightlife locations like North Beach or the Mission, but you can also call for one (*415/626–2345 Yellow Cab, 415/648–3181 Arrow*). The best option by far is booking a taxi with a smartphone-based app (*www.uber.com, www.lyft.com*). ■TIP➜ Cabs in San Francisco are more expensive than in other areas of the United States; expect to pay at least $15 to get anywhere within the city. Keep in mind that BART service across the bay stops shortly after midnight.

UNION SQUARE

BARS

Harry Denton's Starlight Room. Forget low-key drinks—the only way to experience Harry Denton's is to go for a show. Cough up the cover charge and enjoy the opulent, over-the-top decor and entertainment (some of the best cover bands in the business, usually playing Top 40 hits from the '60s, '70s, and '80s). Velvet booths and romantic lighting help re-create the 1950s high life on the 21st floor of the Sir Francis Drake Hotel, and the small dance floor is packed on Friday and Saturday nights. Jackets are preferred for men. Call ahead—the room is sometimes closed for private events on weekdays. ⊠ *Sir Francis Drake Hotel, 450 Powell St., between Post and Sutter Sts., Union Sq.* ☎ *415/395–8595* ⊕ *www.starlightroomsf.com.*

Pacific Cocktail Haven. PCH for short, this neighborhood hangout has taken over the space that once belonged to the Latin sensation Cantina. Having a convivial aura and industrial-chic decor, PCH hits all the right notes. Plus the well-chosen and unique ingredients mean there's a little something for everyone. And the glassware is as dazzling as the elixirs inside. ■TIP➔ The must-try cocktail is the Oh Snap!, a concoction of gin, sugar snap peas, citrus, and absinthe. ⊠ *580 Sutter St., at Mason St., Union Sq.* ☎ *415/398–0195* ⊕ *www.pacificcock-tailsf.com* ⊗ *Closed Sun.*

SOMA

BARS

City Beer Store. Called CBS by locals, this friendly tasting room cum liquor mart has a wine-bar's sensibility. Perfect for connoisseurs and the merely beer curious, CBS stocks more than 300 different bottled beers, and more than a dozen are on tap. The indecisive can mix and match six-packs to go. ■TIP➔ Come early: The small space fills up quickly on event nights. ⊠ *1168 Folsom St., at 8th St., SoMa* ☎ *415/503–1033* ⊕ *www.citybeerstore.com.*

21st Amendment Brewery. This popular brewery is known for its range of beer types, with multiple taps going at all times. In the spring, the Hell or High Watermelon—a wheat beer—gets rave reviews. ■TIP➔ Serious beer drinkers should try the Back in Black, a black IPA-style beer this brewpub helped pioneer. The space has an upmarket warehouse feel, though exposed wooden ceiling beams, framed photos, whitewashed brick walls, and hardwood floors make it feel cozy. It's a good spot to warm up before a Giants game and an even better place to party after they win. ⊠ *563 2nd St., between Federal and Brannan Sts., SoMa* ☎ *415/369–0900* ⊕ *www.21st-amendment.com.*

GAY NIGHTLIFE

The Stud. Glam trans women, gay bears, tight-teed pretty boys, ladies and their ladies, and a handful of straight onlookers congregate here to dance to live DJ sounds and watch world-class drag performers on the small stage. The entertainment is often campy, pee-your-pants funny, and downright fantastic. Each night's music is different—from funk, soul, and hip-hop to '80s tunes and disco favorites. ■TIP→ At Frolic, the Stud's most outrageous party (second Saturday of the month), club goers dance the night away dressed as bunnies, kittens, and even stranger creatures. ⊠ *399 9th St., at Harrison St., SoMa* ☎ *415/863–6623* ⊕ *www.studsf.com* ⊗ *Closed Mon.*

THE TENDERLOIN

BARS

Fodor'sChoice **Bourbon & Branch.** Bourbon & Branch reeks of Prohibition-era speak-
★ easy cool. It's not exclusive, though: everyone is granted a password. The place has sex appeal, with tin ceilings, bordello-red silk wallpaper, intimate booths, and low lighting; loud conversations and cell phones are not allowed. The menu of expertly mixed cocktails and quality bourbon and whiskey is substantial, though the servers aren't always authorities. ■TIP→ Your reservation dictates your exit time, which is strictly enforced. There's also a speakeasy within the speakeasy called Wilson & Wilson, which is more exclusive, but just as funky. ⊠ *501 Jones St., at O'Farrell St., Tenderloin* ☎ *415/346-1735* ⊕ *www.bourbonandbranch.com.*

MUSIC CLUBS

Fodor'sChoice **Great American Music Hall.** You can find top-drawer entertainment at
★ this eclectic nightclub. Acts range from the best in blues, folk, and jazz to up-and-coming college-radio and American-roots artists to indie rockers such as OK Go, Mates of State, and Cowboy Junkies. The colorful marble-pillared emporium (built in 1907 as a bordello) also accommodates dancing at some shows. Pub grub is available on most nights. ⊠ *859 O'Farrell St., between Polk and Larkin Sts., Tenderloin* ☎ *415/885–0750* ⊕ *www.slimspresents.com.*

HAYES VALLEY

BARS

Fodor'sChoice **Smuggler's Cove.** With the decor of a pirate ship and a slew of rum-
★ based cocktails, you half expect Captain Jack Sparrow to sidle up next to you at this offbeat, Disney-esque hangout. But don't let the kitschy ambience fool you. The folks at Smuggler's Cove take rum so seriously they even make their own, which you can sample along with more than 200 other offerings, some of them vintage and very hard to find. A punch card is provided so you can try all 70 cocktails and remember where you left off without getting shipwrecked. The small space fills up quickly, so arrive early. ⊠ *650 Gough St., at McAllister St., Hayes Valley* ☎ *415/869–1900* ⊕ *www.smugglerscovesf.com.*

NORTH BEACH

BARS

Fodor'sChoice **Vesuvio Cafe.** If you're hitting only one bar in North Beach, it should be
★ this one. The low-ceilinged second floor of this raucous boho hangout, little altered since its 1960s heyday (when Jack Kerouac frequented the place), is a fine vantage point for watching the colorful Broadway Street

and Columbus Avenue intersection. Another part of Vesuvio's appeal is its diverse clientele, from older neighborhood regulars and young couples to Bacchanalian posses. ⊠ *255 Columbus Ave., at Broadway St., North Beach* ☎ *415/362–3370* ⊕ *www.vesuvio.com.*

CABARET

Club Fugazi. The claim to fame here is *Beach Blanket Babylon,* a wacky musical send-up of San Francisco moods and mores that has been going strong since 1974, making it the longest-running musical revue anywhere. Although the choreography is colorful, the singers brassy, and the satirical songs witty, the real stars are the comically exotic costumes and famous ceiling-high "hats"—which are worth the price of admission alone. The revue sells out as early as a month in advance, so order tickets as far ahead as possible. Those under 21 are admitted only to the Sunday matinee. ■TIP→ If you don't shell out the extra money for reserved seating, you won't have an assigned seat—so get your cannoli to go and arrive at least 30 minutes prior to showtime to get in line. ⊠ *678 Green St., at Powell St., North Beach* ☎ *415/421–4222* ⊕ *www. beachblanketbabylon.com.*

MUSIC CLUBS

Bimbo's 365 Club. The plush main room and adjacent lounge of this club, here since 1951, retain a retro vibe perfect for the "Cocktail Nation" programming that keeps the crowds entertained. For a taste of the old-school San Francisco nightclub scene, you can't beat it. Indie low-fi and pop bands such as Stephen Malkmus and the Jicks and Camera Obscura play here. ⊠ *1025 Columbus Ave., at Chestnut St., North Beach* ☎ *415/474–0365* ⊕ *www.bimbos365club.com.*

EMBARCADERO

BARS

Hard Water. This waterfront restaurant and bar with stunning bay views pays homage to America's most iconic spirit—bourbon—with a wall of whiskeys and a lineup of specialty cocktails. The menu, crafted by Charles Phan of Slanted Door fame, includes spicy pork-belly cracklings, corn-bread-crusted alligator, and other fun snacks. ⊠ *Pier 3, Suite 3–102, at Embarcadero, Embarcadero* ☎ *415/392–3021* ⊕ *www.hardwaterbar.com.*

THE WESTERN SHORELINE

BARS

The Riptide. A cozy cabin bar that's the perfect finale for beachgoers, Riptide is a surfer favorite, but you don't have to own a board to feel at home. You'll find classic beers, good food, and all at wallet-friendly prices. There's live music most nights, which swings somewhere between bluegrass to karaoke. Many tourists fooled by San Francisco's definition of summer end up warming their popsicle toes at the bar's fireplace. Sunday's feature a bacon Bloody Mary, great for hangovers. ⊠ *3639 Taraval St, Sunset* ☎ *415/681–8433* ⊕ *www.riptidesf.com.*

THE MISSION

BARS

Fodor's Choice ★ **El Rio.** A dive bar in the best sense has a calendar chock-full of events, from free bands and films to Salsa Sunday (seasonal), all of which keep Mission kids coming back. Bands play several nights a week, and there are plenty of other events. No matter what day you attend, expect to find a diverse gay-straight crowd. When the weather's warm, the large patio out back is especially popular, and the midday dance parties are *the* place to be. ⊠ *3158 Mission St., between César Chavez and Valencia Sts., Mission District* ☎ *415/282–3325* ⊕ *www.elriosf.com.*

Zeitgeist. It's a bit divey, a bit rock and roll, but a good place to relax with a cold one or an ever-popular (and ever-strong) Bloody Mary in the large beer "garden" (there's not much greenery) on a sunny day. Grill food is available, and if you're lucky. one of the city's most famous food-cart operators, the Tamale Lady, will drop by. If you own a trucker hat, a pair of Vans, and a Pabst Blue Ribbon T-shirt, you'll fit right in. ⊠ *199 Valencia St., at Duboce Ave., Mission District* ☎ *415/255–7505* ⊕ *www.zeitgeistsf.com.*

GAY NIGHTLIFE

Martuni's. A mixed crowd enjoys cocktails in the semi-refined environment of this bar where the Castro, the Mission, and Hayes Valley intersect; variations on the martini are a specialty. In the intimate back room a pianist plays nightly, and patrons take turns boisterously singing show tunes. Martuni's often gets busy after symphony and opera performances—Davies Hall and the Opera House are both within walking distance. ■ TIP➔ **The Godiva Chocolate Martini is a crowd favorite.** ⊠ *4 Valencia St., at Market St., Mission District* ☎ *415/241–0205.*

POTRERO HILL

MUSIC CLUBS

Bottom of the Hill. This is a great live-music dive—in the best sense of the word—and truly the epicenter for Bay Area indie rock. The club has hosted some great acts over the years, including the Strokes and the Throwing Muses. Rap and hip-hop acts occasionally make it to the stage. ⊠ *1233 17th St., at Texas St., Potrero Hill* ☎ *415/621–4455* ⊕ *www.bottomofthehill.com.*

WESTERN ADDITION

MUSIC CLUBS

The Fillmore. This is *the* club that all the big names, from Coldplay to Clapton, want to play. San Francisco's most famous rock-music hall presents national and local acts: rock, reggae, grunge, jazz, folk, acid house, and more. Go upstairs to view the amazing collection of rock posters lining the walls. At the end of each show, free apples are set near the door, and staffers hand out collectible posters. ■ TIP➔ **Avoid steep service charges by purchasing tickets at the club's box office on Sunday from 10 to 4.** ⊠ *1805 Geary Blvd., at Fillmore St., Western Addition* ☎ *415/346–6000* ⊕ *www.thefillmore.com.*

PERFORMING ARTS

Sophisticated, offbeat, and often ahead of the curve, San Francisco's performing arts scene supports world-class opera, ballet, and theater productions, along with alternative-dance events, avant-garde plays, groundbreaking documentaries, and a slew of spoken-word and other literary happenings.

The best guide to the arts is printed in the "Datebook" section and the "96 Hours" section of the *San Francisco Chronicle* (⊕ *www.sfgate.com*). Also check out the city's free alternative weeklies, including *SF Weekly* (⊕ *www.sfweekly.com*) and the *San Francisco Bay Guardian* (⊕ *www.sfbg.com*).

Online, SF Station (⊕ *www.sfstation.com*) has a frequently updated arts and nightlife calendar. *San Francisco Arts Monthly* (⊕ *www.sfarts.org*), which is published at the end of the month, has arts features and events listings, plus a helpful "Visiting San Francisco?" section. For offbeat, emerging-artist performances, consult CounterPULSE (⊕ *www.counterpulse.org*).

TICKETS

City Box Office. This charge-by-phone service sells tickets for many performances and lectures. You can also buy tickets online, or in person on weekdays from 9:30 to 5:30. ⊠ *180 Redwood St., Suite 100, off Van Ness Ave., between Golden Gate Ave. and McAllister St., Civic Center* ☎ *415/392–4400* ⊕ *www.cityboxoffice.com.*

San Francisco Performances. SFP brings an eclectic array of top-flight global music and dance talents to various venues—mostly the Yerba Buena Center for the Arts, Davies Symphony Hall, and Herbst Theatre. Artists have included Yo-Yo Ma, Edgar Meyer, the Paul Taylor Dance Company, and Midori. Tickets can be purchased in person through City Box Office, online, or by phone. ⊠ *500 Sutter St., Suite 710, Financial District* ☎ *415/392–2545* ⊕ *www.sfperformances.org.*

TIX Bay Area. Half-price, same-day tickets for many local and touring shows go on sale (cash only) at the TIX booth in Union Square, which is open daily from 10 to 6. Discount purchases can also be made online. ⊠ *350 Powell St., at Geary St., Union Sq.* ☎ *415/433–7827* ⊕ *www.tixbayarea.org.*

DANCE

Fodor'sChoice
★

San Francisco Ballet. For ballet lovers, the nation's oldest professional company is reason alone to visit the Bay Area. SFB's performances, for the past three decades under the direction of Helgi Tomasson, have won critical raves. The primary season runs from February through May. The repertoire includes full-length ballets such as *Don Quixote* and *Sleeping Beauty*; the December presentation of *The Nutcracker* is truly spectacular. The company also performs bold new dances from star choreographers such as William Forsythe and Mark Morris, alongside modern classics by George Balanchine and Jerome Robbins. Tickets are available at the **War Memorial Opera House.** ⊠ *War Memorial Opera House, 301 Van Ness Ave., at Grove St., Civic Center* ☎ *415/865–2000* ⊕ *www.sfballet.org.*

FILM

Fodor's Choice ★ **Castro Theatre.** A large neon sign marks the exterior of this 1,400-plus-seat Art Deco movie palace whose exotic interior transports you back to 1922, when the theater first opened. High-profile festivals present films here, along with classic revivals and foreign flicks. There are a few cult-themed drag shows every month. ■ TIP➔ Lines for the Castro's popular sing-along movie musicals often trail down the block. ✉ *429 Castro St., near Market St., Castro* ☎ *415/621–6120* ⊕ *www.castrotheatre.com.*

MUSIC

Fodor's Choice ★ **San Francisco Symphony.** One of America's top orchestras performs from September through May, with additional summer performances of light classical music and show tunes. The orchestra and its charismatic music director, Michael Tilson Thomas, known for his daring programming of 20th-century American works, often perform with soloists of the caliber of Andre Watts, Gil Shaham, and Renée Fleming. The symphony's adventurous projects include its collaboration with the heavy-metal band Metallica. ■ TIP➔ Deep discounts on tickets are often available through Travelzoo, Groupon, and other vendors. ✉ *Davies Symphony Hall, 201 Van Ness Ave., at Grove St., Civic Center* ☎ *415/864–6000* ⊕ *www.sfsymphony.org.*

SFJAZZ Center. Jazz legends Branford Marsalis and Herbie Hancock have performed at the snazzy center, as have Rosanne Cash and world-music favorite Esperanza Spaulding. The sight lines and acoustics here impress. Shows often sell out quickly. ✉ *201 Franklin St., Hayes Valley* ☎ *866/920–5299* ⊕ *www.sfjazz.org.*

MUSIC FESTIVALS

Fodor's Choice ★ **Stern Grove Festival.** The nation's oldest continual free summer music festival hosts Sunday-afternoon performances of symphony, opera, jazz, pop music, and dance. The amphitheater is in a beautiful eucalyptus grove, perfect for picnicking before the show. World-music favorites such as Ojos de Brujas, Seu Jorge, and Shuggie Otis get the massive crowds dancing. ■ TIP➔ Shows generally start at 2 pm, but arrive hours earlier if you want to see the performances up close—and dress for cool weather, as the fog often rolls in. ✉ *Sigmund Stern Grove, Sloat Blvd. at 19th Ave., Sunset* ☎ *415/252–6252* ⊕ *www.sterngrove.org.*

OPERA

Fodor's Choice ★ **San Francisco Opera.** Founded in 1923, this internationally recognized organization has occupied the War Memorial Opera House since the building's completion in 1932. From September through January and June through July, the company presents a dozen or so operas. SF opera frequently collaborates with European companies and presents unconventional, sometimes edgy projects designed to attract younger audiences. Translations are projected above the stage during most non-English productions. ✉ *War Memorial Opera House, 301 Van Ness Ave., at Grove St., Civic Center* ☎ *415/864–3330 tickets* ⊕ *www.sfopera.com* ✆ *Box office: 199 Grove St., at Van Ness Ave.; open Mon. 10–5, Tues.–Fri. 10–6.*

PERFORMING ARTS CENTERS

Fodor's Choice
★
War Memorial Opera House. With its soaring vaulted ceilings and marble foyer, this elegant 3,146-seat venue, built in 1932, rivals the Old World theaters of Europe. Part of the San Francisco War Memorial and Performing Arts Center, which also includes Davies Symphony Hall and Herbst Theatre, this is the home of the San Francisco Opera and the San Francisco Ballet. ⊠ *301 Van Ness Ave., at Grove St., Civic Center* ☎ *415/621–6600* ⊕ *www.sfwmpac.org.*

Fodor's Choice
★
Yerba Buena Center for the Arts. Across the street from the San Francisco Museum of Modern Art and abutting a lovely urban garden, this performing arts complex schedules interdisciplinary art exhibitions, touring and local dance troupes, music, film programs, and contemporary theater events. You can depend on the quality of the productions at Yerba Buena. Film buffs often come here to check out the San Francisco Cinematheque (*www.sfcinematheque.org*), which showcases experimental film and digital media. And dance enthusiasts can attend concerts by a roster of city companies that perform here, including Smuin Ballet/SF (*www.smuinballet.org*), ODC/San Francisco (*www.odcdance.org*), the Margaret Jenkins Dance Company (*www.mjdc.org*), and Alonzo King's Lines Ballet (*www.linesballet.org*). The Lamplighters (*www.lamplighters.org*), an alternative opera that specializes in Gilbert and Sullivan, also performs here. ⊠ *3rd and Howard Sts., SoMa* ☎ *415/978–2787* ⊕ *www.ybca.org.*

THEATER

American Conservatory Theater. One of the nation's leading regional theater companies presents about eight plays a year, from classics to contemporary works, often in repertory. The season runs from early fall to late spring. In December ACT stages a beloved version of Charles Dickens's *A Christmas Carol.* ⊠ *415 Geary St., Union Sq.* ☎ *415/749–2228* ⊕ *www.act-sf.org.*

SHOPPING

With its grand department stores and funky secondhand boutiques, San Francisco summons a full range of shopping experiences. From the anarchist bookstore to the mouthwatering specialty-food purveyors at the gleaming Ferry Building, the local shopping opportunities reflect the city's various personalities. Visitors with limited time often focus their energies on the high-density Union Square area, where several major department stores tower over big-name boutiques. But if you're keen to find unique local shops, consider moving beyond the square's radius.

Each neighborhood has its own distinctive finds, whether it's 1960s housewares, cheeky stationery, or vintage Levi's. If shopping in San Francisco has a downside, it's that real bargains can be few and far between. Sure, neighborhoods such as the Lower Haight and the Mission have thrift shops and other inexpensive stores, but you won't find many discount outlets in the city, where rents are sky-high and space is at a premium.

UNION SQUARE

ART GALLERIES

Fodor's Choice
★
Berggruen Gallery. Twentieth-century American and European paintings are displayed throughout three airy floors. Some recent exhibitions have included the works of Robert Kelly and Isca Greenfield-Sanders. Look for thematic shows here, too; past exhibits have had titles such as Summer Highlights and Four Decades. ⊠ *10 Hawthorne St., at Howard St., Union Sq.* ☎ *415/781–4629* ⊕ *www.berggruen.com.*

Fodor's Choice
★
Fraenkel Gallery. This renowned gallery represents museum-caliber photographers or their estates, including Nicholas Nixon, Nan Goldin, Richard Misrach, and Garry Winogrand. Recent shows have included work by Robert Adams, Idris Khan, and Hiroshi Sugimoto. Most shows feature one or two artists, but the annual Several Exceptionally Good Recently Acquired Pictures showcases the range of works the gallery exhibits. ⊠ *49 Geary St., 4th fl., between Kearny St. and Grant Ave., Union Sq.* ☎ *415/981–2661* ⊕ *fraenkelgallery.com* ⊘ *Closed Sun. and Mon.*

CLOTHING: MEN AND WOMEN

Fodor's Choice
★
Margaret O'Leary. If you can only buy one piece of clothing in San Francisco, make it a hand-loomed cashmere sweater by this Irish-born local legend. The perfect antidote to the city's wind and fog, the sweaters are so beloved by San Franciscans that some of them never wear anything else. Pick up an airplane wrap for your trip home, or a media cozy to keep your tech toasty. Another store is in Pacific Heights, at 2400 Fillmore Street. ⊠ *1 Claude La., at Sutter St., just west of Kearny St., Union Sq.* ☎ *415/391–1010* ⊕ *www.margaretoleary.com.*

Scotch & Soda. With clean, tailored lines and deep solid colors, there is something elegant yet cutting-edge for every age here. Based on Amsterdam couture, and carrying European labels, this hive of a shop is cool but friendly; it also has an old but new feel to it. The Bodycon Peplum dress is a classic, as is the men's stretch wool blazer. This is a good place to visit if you're looking for a new pair of denims, or a cool shirt for a night out. ⊠ *59 Grant Ave., between Geary and O'Farrell Sts., Union Sq.* ☎ *415/644–8334* ⊕ *www.scotch-soda.com.*

DEPARTMENT STORES

Fodor's Choice
★
Gump's. It's a San Francisco institution, dating to the 19th century, and it's a strikingly luxurious one. The airy store exudes a museumlike vibe, with its large decorative vases, sumptuous housewares, and Tahitian-pearl display. It's a great place to pick up gifts, such as the Golden Gate Bridge note cards or silver-plated butter spreaders in a signature Gump's box. ⊠ *135 Post St., near Kearny St., Union Sq.* ☎ *415/982–1616* ⊕ *www.gumps.com.*

FURNITURE, HOUSEWARES, AND GIFTS

Fodor's Choice
★
Diptyque. The original Diptyque boutique in Paris has attracted a long line of celebrities. You can find the full array of scented candles and fragrances in this chic shop that would be at home on the boulevard St-Germain. Trademark black-and-white labels adorn the popular L'eau toilet water, scented with geranium and sandalwood. Candles come in traditional and esoteric scents, including lavender, basil, leather, and fig tree. Also available are Mariage Frères teas. ⊠ *73 Geary St., at Grant Ave., Union Sq.* ☎ *415/402–0600* ⊕ *www.diptyqueparis.com.*

CHINATOWN

TOYS AND GADGETS

Chinatown Kite Shop. The kites sold here range from basic diamond shapes to box- and animal-shaped configurations. ■TIP→ Colorful dragon kites make great souvenirs. ⊠ 717 Grant Ave., near Sacramento St., Chinatown ☎ 415/989–5182 ⊕ www.chinatownkite.com.

SOMA

BOOKS

Fodor'sChoice **Chronicle Books.** This local beacon of publishing produces inventively
★ designed fiction, cookbooks, art books, and other titles, as well as diaries, planners, and address books—all of which you can purchase at three airy and attractive spaces. The other stores are at 680 2nd Street, near AT&T Park, and 1846 Union Street, in Cow Hollow. ⊠ Metreon Westfield Shopping Center, 165 4th St., near Howard St., SoMa ☎ 415/369–6271 ⊕ www.chroniclebooks.com.

FOOD AND DRINK

K&L Wine Merchants. More than any other wine store, this one has an ardent cult following around town. The friendly staffers promise not to sell what they don't taste themselves, and weekly events—on Thursday from 5 pm to 6:30 pm and Saturday from noon to 3 pm—open the tastings to customers. The best-seller list for varietals and regions for both the under- and over-$30 categories appeals to the wine lover in everyone. ⊠ 855 Harrison St., at 4th St., SoMa ☎ 415/896–1734 ⊕ www.klwines.com.

HAYES VALLEY

FOOD AND DRINK

Arlequin Wine Merchant. If you like the wine list at Absinthe Brasserie, you can walk next door and pick up a few bottles from its highly regarded sister establishment. This small, unintimidating shop carries hard-to-find wines from small producers. Why wait to taste? Crack open a bottle on the patio out back. ⊠ 384 Hayes St., at Gough St., Hayes Valley ☎ 415/863–1104 ⊕ www.arlequinwinemerchant.com.

Miette Confiserie. There is truly nothing sweeter than a cellophane bag tied with blue-and-white twine and filled with malt balls or chocolate sardines from this European-style apothecary. Grab a gingerbread cupcake or a tantalizing macaron or some shortbread. The pastel-color cake stands make even window-shopping a treat. ⊠ 449 Octavia Blvd., between Hayes and Fell Sts., Hayes Valley ☎ 415/626–6221 ⊕ www.miette.com.

NORTH BEACH

FOOD AND DRINK

Fodor'sChoice **Molinari Delicatessen.** This store has been making its own salami, sau-
★ sages, and cold cuts since 1896. Other homemade specialties include meat and cheese ravioli, tomato sauces, and fresh pastas. ■TIP→ Do like the locals: grab a made-to-order sandwich for lunch and eat it at

one of the sidewalk tables or over at Washington Square Park. ⊠ *373 Columbus Ave., at Vallejo St., North Beach* ☎ *415/421–2337* ⊕ *www. molinarisalame.com.*

EMBARCADERO

FARMERS' MARKETS

Fodor's Choice
★
Ferry Plaza Farmers' Market. The partylike Saturday edition of the city's most upscale and expensive farmers' market places baked goods, gourmet cheeses, smoked fish, and fancy pots of jam alongside organic basil, specialty mushrooms, heirloom tomatoes, handcrafted jams, and juicy-ripe locally grown fruit. On Saturday about 100 vendors pack in along three sides of the building, and sandwiches and other prepared foods are for sale in addition to fruit, vegetable, and other samples free for the nibbling. Smaller markets take place on Tuesday and Thursday. (The Thursday one doesn't operate from about late December through March.) ⊠ *Ferry Plaza, at Market St., Embarcadero* ☎ *415/291–3276* ⊕ *www.ferrybuildingmarketplace.com.*

THE HAIGHT

MUSIC

Fodor's Choice
★
Amoeba Music. With more than 2.5 million new and used CDs, DVDs, and records at bargain prices, this warehouselike offshoot of the Berkeley original carries titles you can't find on Amazon. No niche is ignored—from electronica and hip-hop to jazz and classical—and the stock changes daily. ■ TIP→ Weekly in-store performances attract large crowds. ⊠ *1855 Haight St., between Stanyan and Shrader Sts., Haight* ☎ *415/831–1200* ⊕ *www.amoeba.com.*

THE MISSION

ART GALLERIES

Southern Exposure. An artist-run, nonprofit gallery, this is an established venue for cutting-edge art. In addition to exhibitions, lectures, performances, and film, video screenings take place. ⊠ *3030 20th St., at Alabama St., Mission District* ☎ *415/863–2141* ⊕ *soex.org* ⊗ *Closed Sun. and Mon.*

FURNITURE, HOUSEWARES, AND GIFTS

Fodor's Choice
★
Paxton Gate. Elevating gardening to an art, this serene shop offers beautiful earthenware pots, amaryllis and narcissus bulbs, decorative garden items, and coffee-table books such as *An Inordinate Fondness for Beetles.* The collection of taxidermy and preserved bugs provides more unusual gift ideas. A couple of storefronts away is too-cute Paxton Gate Curiosities for Kids, jam-packed with retro toys, books, and other stellar finds. ⊠ *824 Valencia St., between 19th and 20th Sts., Mission District* ☎ *415/824–1872* ⊕ *www.paxtongate.com.*

PACIFIC HEIGHTS

BEAUTY

BeneFit Cosmetics. You can find this locally based line of cosmetics and skin-care products at Macy's and Sephora, but it's much more fun to come to one of the eponymous boutiques. No-pressure salespeople dab you with whimsical makeup such as Ooh La Lift concealer and Tinted Love, a stain for lips and cheeks. ✉ *2117 Fillmore St., between California and Sacramento Sts., Pacific Heights* ☎ *415/567–0242* ⊕ *www.benefitcosmetics.com.*

JAPANTOWN

BOOKS

Kinokuniya Bookstore. The selection of English-language books about Japanese culture—everything from medieval history to origami instructions—is one of the finest in the country. Kinokuniya is the city's biggest seller of Japanese-language books. Dozens of glossy Asian fashion magazines attract the young and trendy; the manga and anime books and magazines are wildly popular, too. ✉ *Kinokuniya Bldg., 1581 Webster St., at Geary Blvd., Japantown* ☎ *415/567–7625* ⊕ *www.kinokuniya.com/us.*

THE BAY AREA

WELCOME TO THE BAY AREA

TOP REASONS TO GO

★ **Bite into the "Gourmet Ghetto":** Eat your way through this area of North Berkeley, starting with a slice of perfect pizza from Cheese Board Pizza (just look for the line).

★ **Find solitude at Point Reyes National Seashore:** Hike beautifully rugged—and often deserted—beaches at one of the most beautiful places on Earth, period.

★ **Sit on a dock by the bay:** Admire the beauty of the Bay Area from the rocky, picturesque shores of Sausalito or Tiburon.

★ **Go barhopping in Oakland's hippest hood:** Spend an evening swinging through the watering holes of Uptown, Oakland's artsy-hip and fast-rising corner of downtown.

★ **Walk among giants:** Walking into Muir Woods, a mere 12 miles north of the Golden Gate Bridge, is like entering a cathedral built by God.

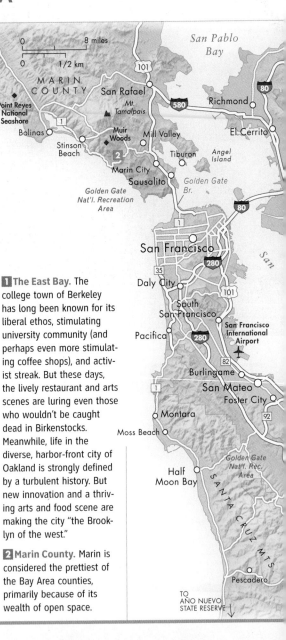

1 **The East Bay.** The college town of Berkeley has long been known for its liberal ethos, stimulating university community (and perhaps even more stimulating coffee shops), and activist streak. But these days, the lively restaurant and arts scenes are luring even those who wouldn't be caught dead in Birkenstocks. Meanwhile, life in the diverse, harbor-front city of Oakland is strongly defined by a turbulent history. But new innovation and a thriving arts and food scene are making the city "the Brooklyn of the west."

2 **Marin County.** Marin is considered the prettiest of the Bay Area counties, primarily because of its wealth of open space.

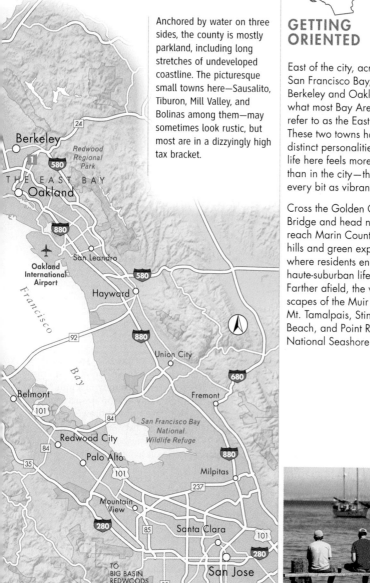

Anchored by water on three sides, the county is mostly parkland, including long stretches of undeveloped coastline. The picturesque small towns here—Sausalito, Tiburon, Mill Valley, and Bolinas among them—may sometimes look rustic, but most are in a dizzyingly high tax bracket.

GETTING ORIENTED

East of the city, across the San Francisco Bay, lie Berkeley and Oakland, in what most Bay Area residents refer to as the East Bay. These two towns have distinct personalities, but life here feels more relaxed than in the city—though every bit as vibrant.

Cross the Golden Gate Bridge and head north to reach Marin County's rolling hills and green expanses, where residents enjoy an haute-suburban lifestyle. Farther afield, the wild land-scapes of the Muir Woods, Mt. Tamalpais, Stinson Beach, and Point Reyes National Seashore await.

5

Updated by
A. K. Carroll

It's rare for a metropolis to compete with its suburbs for visitors, but the view from any of San Francisco's hilltops shows that the Bay Area's temptations extend far beyond the city limits. East of the city are the energetic urban centers of Berkeley and Oakland. Famously radical Berkeley is also comfortably sophisticated, while Oakland has an arts and restaurant scene so hip that it pulls San Franciscans across the bay. To the north is Marin County with its dramatic coastal beauty and chic, affluent villages.

PLANNING

WHEN TO GO

As with San Francisco, you can visit the rest of the Bay Area any time of year, and it's especially nice in late spring and fall. Unlike San Francisco, though, the surrounding areas are reliably sunny in summer—it gets hotter as you head inland. Even the rainy season has its charms, as otherwise golden hills turn a rich green and wildflowers become plentiful. Precipitation is usually the heaviest between November and March. Berkeley is a university town, so it's easier to navigate the streets and find parking near the university between semesters, but there's also less buzz around town.

GETTING HERE AND AROUND

BART TRAVEL

Using public transportation to reach Berkeley or Oakland is ideal. The under- and aboveground BART (Bay Area Rapid Transit) trains make stops in both towns. Trips to either take about a half hour one-way from the center of San Francisco. BART does not serve Marin County.

Contacts BART. ☎ 510/465–2278 ⊕ www.bart.gov.

BOAT AND FERRY TRAVEL

For sheer romance, nothing beats the ferry; there's service from San Francisco to Sausalito, Tiburon, and Larkspur in Marin County, and to Alameda and Oakland in the East Bay.

The Golden Gate Ferry crosses the bay to Larkspur and Sausalito from San Francisco's Ferry Building (⊠ *Market St. and the Embarcadero*). Blue & Gold Fleet ferries depart daily for Sausalito and Tiburon from Pier 41 at Fisherman's Wharf; weekday commuter ferries leave from the Ferry Building for Tiburon. The trip to either Sausalito or Tiburon takes from 25 minutes to an hour. Purchase tickets from terminal vending machines.

The Angel Island–Tiburon Ferry sails to the island daily from April through October and on weekends the rest of the year.

The San Francisco Bay Ferry runs several times daily between San Francisco's Ferry Building or Pier 41 and Oakland's Jack London Square by way of Alameda. The trip lasts from 25 to 45 minutes, and leads to Oakland's waterfront shopping and restaurant district. Purchase tickets on board.

Boat and Ferry Lines Angel Island–Tiburon Ferry. ☎ 415/435–2131 ⊕ www.angelislandferry.com. **Blue & Gold Fleet.** ☎ 415/705–8200 ⊕ www.blueandgoldfleet.com. **Golden Gate Ferry.** ☎ 415/921–5858 ⊕ www.goldengateferry.org. **San Francisco Bay Ferry.** ☎ 707/643–3779, 800/643–3779 ⊕ sanfranciscobayferry.com.

BUS TRAVEL

Golden Gate Transit buses travel north to Sausalito, Tiburon, and elsewhere in Marin County from the Transbay Temporary Terminal (located at Howard and Main, two blocks south of Market) and other points in San Francisco. For Mt. Tamalpais State Park and West Marin (Stinson Beach, Bolinas, and Point Reyes Station), take any route to Marin City and then transfer to the West Marin Stagecoach. San Francisco Muni buses primarily serve the city, though the 76X does cross the Golden Gate and end at the Marin Headlands Visitors Center on weekends.

Though less speedy than BART, over 30 AC Transit bus lines provide service to and from the Transbay Temporary Terminal and throughout the East Bay, even after BART shuts down. The F and FS lines will get you to Berkeley, while lines C, P, B, and O take you to Oakland and Piedmont.

Bus Lines AC Transit. ☎ 510/891–4777 ⊕ www.actransit.org. **Golden Gate Transit.** ☎ 511 ⊕ www.goldengatetransit.org. **San Francisco Muni.** ☎ 311 ⊕ www.sfmta.com. **West Marin Stagecoach.** ☎ 511 ⊕ www.marintransit.org.

CAR TRAVEL

To reach the East Bay from San Francisco, take Interstate 80 East across the San Francisco–Oakland Bay Bridge. For U.C. Berkeley, merge onto Interstate 580 West and take exit 11 for University Avenue. For Oakland, merge onto Interstate 580 East. To reach downtown, take Interstate 980 West from Interstate 580 East and exit at 14th Street. Travel time varies depending on traffic, but should take about 30 minutes (or an hour if it's rush hour).

For all points in Marin, head north on U.S. 101 and cross the Golden Gate Bridge. Sausalito, Tiburon, the Marin Headlands, and Point Reyes National Seashore are all accessed off U.S. 101. The scenic coastal route, Highway 1, also called Shoreline Highway and Panoramic for certain stretches, can be accessed off U.S. 101 as well. Follow this road to Muir Woods, Mt. Tamalpais State Park, Muir Beach, Stinson Beach, and Bolinas. From Bolinas, you can continue north on Highway 1 to Point Reyes.

RESTAURANTS

The Bay Area is home to many popular and innovative restaurants, such as Chez Panisse in Berkeley and Commis in Oakland—for which reservations must be made well in advance. There are also countless casual but equally tasty eateries to test out; expect an emphasis on organic seasonal produce, locally raised meats, craft cocktails, and curated wine menus. Marin's dining scene trends toward the sleepy side, so be sure to check hours ahead of time. *Restaurant reviews have been shortened. For full information, visit Fodors.com.*

HOTELS

With a few exceptions, hotels in Berkeley and Oakland tend to be standard-issue, but many Marin hotels package themselves as cozy retreats. Summer in Marin is often booked well in advance, despite weather that can be downright chilly. Check for special packages during this season. *Hotel reviews have been shortened. For full information, visit Fodors.com.*

WHAT IT COSTS			
	$	$$	$$$	$$$$
Restaurants	under $16	$16–$22	$23–$30	over $30
Hotels	under $150	$150–$199	$200–$250	over $250

Restaurant prices are the average cost of a main course at dinner or, if dinner is not served, at lunch. Hotel prices are the lowest cost of a standard double room in high season.

TOURS

Fodor'sChoice
★
Best Bay Area Tours. Morning and afternoon tours of Muir Woods and Sausalito include at least 90 minutes in the redwoods before heading on to Sausalito. On returning to the city, tours make a scenic stop in the Marin Headlands to enjoy fantastic views. Knowledgeable guides lead small tours in comfortable vans, and hotel pickup is included, though park entrance is not. Another tour option includes a visit to Muir Woods and Wine Country exploration. ☎ *877/705–8687* ⊕ *bestbayareatours.com* ✉ *From $60.*

THE EAST BAY

To many San Franciscans, the East Bay is a world away. But don't fall into that trap, because there's much to see on the other side of the Bay Bridge—industrial-chic Emeryville, the rolling hills of Orinda, and the upscale shopping suburb of Walnut Creek to name a few. Add on Berkeley, with its world-class university, and edgy Oakland, with its booming arts culture, nightlife, and restaurant scenes, and you've got plenty of reasons to venture east.

BERKELEY

2 miles northeast of Bay Bridge.

Berkeley is the birthplace of the Free Speech Movement, the radical hub of the 1960s, the home of arguably the nation's top public university, and a frequent site of protests and political movements. The city of 115,000 is also a culturally diverse breeding ground for social trends, a bastion of the counterculture, and an important center for Bay Area writers, artists, and musicians. Berkeley residents, students, and faculty spend hours nursing coffee concoctions while they read, discuss, and debate at the dozens of cafés that surround campus. It's the quintessential university town, with numerous independent bookstores, countless casual eateries, myriad meetups, and thousands of cyclists.

Oakland may have Berkeley beat when it comes to ethnic diversity and cutting-edge arts, but unless you're accustomed to sipping hemp milk lattes while planning a protest prior to yoga, you'll likely find Berkeley charmingly offbeat.

GETTING HERE AND AROUND

BART is the easiest way to get to Berkeley from San Francisco. Exit at the Downtown Berkeley station, and walk a block up Center Street to get to the western edge of campus. AC Transit buses F and FS lines stop near the university and 4th Street shopping. By car, take Interstate 80 East across the Bay Bridge, merge onto Interstate 580 West, and take the University Avenue exit through downtown Berkeley or take the Ashby Avenue exit and turn left on Telegraph Avenue. Once you arrive, explore on foot. Berkeley is very pedestrian-friendly.

ESSENTIALS

Visitor Information Koret Visitor Center. ⊠ *2227 Piedmont Ave., at California Memorial Stadium* ☎ *510/642–5215* ⊕ *visit.berkeley.edu.* **Visit Berkeley.** ⊠ *2030 Addison St., Suite 102* ☎ *510/549–7040, 800/847–4823* ⊕ *www.visitberkeley.com.*

EXPLORING

TOP ATTRACTIONS

4th Street. Several blocks centering on 4th Street north of University Avenue have evolved from light industrial uses into an upscale shopping and dining district. The compact area is busiest on bright weekend afternoons. The Stained Glass Garden, Builders Booksource, and the Apple Store are among shoppers' favorites, along with a slew of boutiques, a fascinating reptile-filled Vivarium, and several wonderful paper stores. ⊠ *4th St. between University Ave. and Cedar St.* ⊕ *www.fourthstreet.com.*

QUICK
BITES

Cheese Board Pizza. A jazz combo entertains the line that usually snakes down the block outside Cheese Board Pizza; it's that good. The cooperatively owned takeout spot and restaurant draws devoted customers with the smell of just-baked garlic on the pie of the day. **Known for:** vegetarian pizza by the slice or slab; live music performances. ⊠ *1504–1512 Shattuck Ave., at Vine St.* ☎ *510/549-3183* ⊕ *cheeseboardcollective.coop/pizza.*

Fodor's Choice
★

Gourmet Ghetto. The success of Alice Water's Chez Panisse defined California cuisine and attracted countless other food-related enterprises to a stretch of Shattuck Avenue now known as the Gourmet Ghetto. Foodies will do well to spend a couple of hours here poking around the shops, grabbing a quick bite, or indulging in a full meal.

The line stretches down the block in front of **Cheese Board Pizza** (*1512 Shattuck*), where live jazz bands serenade diners who spill out onto the sidewalk and median. Next door is the **Cheese Board Collective** and its fabulous bakery and cheese counter. Nearby, **César** (*1515 Shattuck*) wine bar and tapas house provides afternoon quaffs and late-night drinks, while the food stands of the **Epicurious Garden** (*1509–1513 Shattuck*) sell everything from sushi to gelato. In the back of the upscale food court, a small terraced garden winds up four levels to the **Imperial Tea Court**, a zenlike teahouse rife with imports and tea ware.

Across Vine, the **Vintage Berkeley** (*2113 Vine*) wineshop offers regular tastings and a great selection of reasonably priced bottles within the walls of a historic former pump house. Coffee lovers can head to the original **Peet's Coffee & Tea** at the corner of Walnut and Vine (*2124 Vine*) or venture to No. 1600 for a cup of Philz custom-blend coffee.

South of Cedar Street is the art-filled **Guerilla Cafe** (No. 1620), a breakfast and lunch spot beloved for its waffles (and Blue Bottle Coffee). Also look for the **Local Butcher Shop** (No. 1600), which sells locally sourced meat and hearty made-to-order sandwiches. For high-end food at takeout prices, try the salads, sandwiches, and signature potato puffs at **Grégoire**, around the corner on Cedar Street (No. 2109) or pastrami, latkes, and other Jewish deli fare at local favorite **Saul's Restaurant and Delicatessen** (No. 1475). **Masse's Pastries** with its delicate tortes, dainty eclairs, and decadent desserts (No. 1469) is a museum of edible artwork. We could go on, but you get the idea. ⊠ *Shattuck Ave. between Delaware and Rose Sts., North Berkeley* ⊕ *www.gourmetghetto.org.*

FAMILY
Fodor'sChoice
★

Tilden Regional Park. Stunning bay views, a scaled-down steam train, and a botanic garden that boasts the nation's most complete collection of California plant life are the hallmarks of this 2,000-acre park in the hills just east of the U.C. Berkeley campus. The garden's visitors center offers tours, as well as information about Tilden's other attractions, including its picnic spots, Lake Anza swimming site, golf course, and hiking trails (the paved **Nimitz Way,** at Inspiration Point, is a popular hike with wonderful sunset views). ■TIP➔ Children love Tilden's interactive Little Farm and vintage carousel. ⊠ *Tilden Regional Park, 2501 Grizzly Peak Blvd., Tilden Park* ☎ *510/544–2747 Park Office* ⊕ *www. ebparks.org/parks/tilden* ▭ *Free to park and botanic garden.*

University of California. Known simply as "Cal," the founding campus of California's university system is one of the leading intellectual centers in the United States and a major site for scientific research. Chartered in 1868, the university sits on 178 oak-covered acres split by Strawberry Creek; it's bound by Bancroft Way to the south, Hearst Avenue to the north, Oxford Street to the west, and Gayley Road to the east. Campus highlights include bustling and historic **Sproul Plaza** (*Bancroft Way and Sather Rd.*), the seven floors and 61-bell carillon of **Sather Tower** (*Campanile Esplanade*), the nearly 3 million artifacts in the **Phoebe A. Hearst Museum of Anthropology** (Kroeber Hall), hands-on **Lawrence Hall of Science** (*1 Centennial Dr.*), the vibrant 34-acre **Botanical Gardens** (*200 Centennial Dr.*), and the eclectic and extensive collections housed in the **Art Museum & Pacific Film Archive** (*2155 Center*). ⊠ *Berkeley* ☎ *510/642–6000* ⊕ *www.berkeley.edu.*

The University of California is the epicenter of Berkeley's energy and activism.

University of California Botanical Garden. Thanks to Berkeley's temperate climate, over 10,000 types of plants from all corners of the world flourish in the 34-acre University of California Botanical Garden. Free garden tours are given regularly. Benches and shady picnic tables make this a relaxing place for a snack with a breathtaking view. ⊠ *200 Centennial Dr.* ☎ *510/643–2755* ⊕ *botanicalgarden.berkeley.edu* 🎫 *$10.*

WHERE TO EAT

Dining in Berkeley may be low-key when it comes to dress, but it's top-of-class in quality, even in less-refined spaces. Late diners beware: Berkeley is an "early to bed" kind of town.

$

DINER

FAMILY

✕ **Bette's Oceanview Diner.** Checkered floors, vintage burgundy booths, and an old-time jukebox set the scene at this retro-chic diner. The wait for a seat at breakfast can be quite long; luckily Bette's To Go is always an option. **Known for:** soufflé pancakes; spicy scrambles; meatloaf and gravy. ⑤ *Average main: $13* ⊠ *1807 4th St., near Delaware St., 4th Street* ☎ *510/644–3230* ⊕ *www.bettesdiner.com* ☉ *No dinner.*

$$$$

MODERN

AMERICAN

Fodor'sChoice

★

✕ **Chez Panisse Café & Restaurant.** Alice Waters's legendary eatery is known for its locally sourced ingredients, formal prix-fixe menus, and personal service, while its upstairs café offers simpler fare in a more casual setting. Both menus change daily and legions of loyal fans insist that Chez Panisse lives up to its reputation. **Known for:** sustainably sourced meats; inventive use of seasonal ingredients. ⑤ *Average main: $125* ⊠ *1517 Shattuck Ave., at Vine St., North Berkeley* ☎ *510/548–5525 restaurant, 510/548–5049 café* ⊕ *www.chezpanisse.com* ☉ *Closed Sun. No lunch in the restaurant.*

$$
MODERN
MEXICAN
Fodor'sChoice
★

✕**Comal.** Relaxed yet trendy, Comal's cavernous indoor dining space and intimate back patio and fire pit draw a diverse, decidedly casual crowd for creative Mexican-influenced fare and well-crafted cocktails. The menu centers on small dishes that lend themselves to sharing and are offered alongside more than 100 tequilas and mezcals. **Known for:** margaritas and mezcal; fresh fish tacos; wood-fired entrées. ⑤ *Average main: $16* ⊠ *2020 Shattuck Ave., near University Ave., Downtown* ☎ *510/926–6300* ⊕ *www.comalberkeley.com* ⊗ *No lunch.*

$$$
MODERN ITALIAN

✕**Corso.** This lively spot serves up a seasonal menu of excellent Florentine cuisine and Italian wines in a sparse but snazzy space. The open kitchen dominates a room, which includes closely spaced tables and festive flickering candles. **Known for:** handcrafted pasta; housemade salumi; Northern Italian specialties; extensive wine list. ⑤ *Average main: $24* ⊠ *1788 Shattuck Ave., at Delaware St., North Berkeley* ☎ *510/704–8004* ⊕ *www.corsoberkeley.com* ⊗ *No lunch.*

$$
MODERN
AMERICAN

✕**Gather.** All things local, organic, seasonal, and sustainable reside harmoniously under one roof at Gather. This haven for vegans, vegetarians, and carnivores alike is a vibrant, well-lit space that boasts funky light fixtures, shiny wood furnishings, and banquettes made of recycled leather belts. **Known for:** sustainable Californian cuisine; wood-fired pizzas; crispy brussels sprouts. ⑤ *Average main: $22* ⊠ *2200 Oxford St., at Allston Way* ☎ *510/809–0400* ⊕ *www.gatherrestaurant.com.*

$$$
JAPANESE
Fodor'sChoice
★

✕**Ippuku.** More Tokyo street chic than standard sushi house, this *izakaya*—the Japanese equivalent of a bar with appetizers—is decked with bamboo-screen booths. Servers pour an impressive array of sakes and *shōchū* and serve up surprising fare. **Known for:** shōchū selection; charcoal-grilled yakitori skewers. ⑤ *Average main: $25* ⊠ *2130 Center St., Downtown* ☎ *510/665–1969* ⊕ *www.ippukuberkeley.com* ⊗ *Closed Mon. No lunch.*

$
CAFÉ

✕**1951 Coffee.** The first java spot of its kind, 1951 Coffee Company is a nonprofit coffee shop inspired and powered by refugees. In addition to crafting high-caliber coffee drinks and dishing out local pastries and sandwiches, this colorful café also serves as an inspiring advocacy space for refugees. Just three blocks south of campus, it's a favorite meet-up spot for locals and students alike. **Known for:** Verve coffee; Starter Bakery pastries; chai latte. ⑤ *Average main: $7* ⊠ *2410 Channing Way, at Dana St.* ☎ *510/848–6252 ext. 270* ⊕ *1951coffee.com.*

$$$
MODERN
AMERICAN

✕**Rivoli.** Italian-inspired dishes using fresh California ingredients star on a menu that changes regularly. Inventive offerings are served in a tight modern dining room with captivating views of the lovely back garden. **Known for:** line-caught fish and sustainably sourced meats; curated wine list. ⑤ *Average main: $28* ⊠ *1539 Solano Ave., at Neilson St.* ☎ *510/526–2542* ⊕ *www.rivolirestaurant.com* ⊗ *No lunch.*

$
AMERICAN
FAMILY
Fodor'sChoice
★

✕**Saul's.** High ceilings and red-leather booths add to the friendly, retro atmosphere of Saul's deli, a Berkeley institution that is well known for its homemade sodas and enormous sandwiches. Locals swear by its pastrami sandwiches, stuffed-cabbage rolls, and challah French toast. **Known for:** pastrami sandwich; deli hash. ⑤ *Average main: $15* ⊠ *1475 Shattuck Ave., near Vine St., North Berkeley* ☎ *510/848–3354* ⊕ *www. saulsdeli.com* ⊗ *Closed Thanksgiving and Yom Kippur.*

5

Famed Berkeley restaurant Chez Panisse focuses on seasonal local ingredients.

WHERE TO STAY

For inexpensive lodging, investigate University Avenue, west of campus. The area can be noisy, congested, and somewhat dilapidated, but it does include a few decent motels and chain properties. All Berkeley lodgings, except for the swanky Claremont, are strictly mid-range.

$$
HOTEL

The Bancroft Hotel. Renovated in 2012, this eco-friendly boutique hotel—across from the U.C. campus—is quaint, charming, and completely green. **Pros:** closest hotel in Berkeley to U.C. campus; friendly staff; many rooms have good views. **Cons:** some rooms are quite small; despite renovation, the building shows its age with thin walls; no elevator. $ *Rooms from: $160* ⊠ *2680 Bancroft Way* ☎ *510/549–1000, 800/549–1002 toll-free* ⊕ *bancrofthotel.com* ↝ *22 rooms* ❙○❙ *Breakfast.*

$$$$
HOTEL
FAMILY
Fodor'sChoice
★

Claremont Resort and Spa. Straddling the Oakland–Berkeley border, this amenities-rich Fairmont property—which celebrated its centennial in 2015—beckons like a gleaming white castle in the hills. **Pros:** amazing spa; supervised child care; solid business amenities; excellent dining and bar options; nearby hiking trails. **Cons:** parking is pricey; mandatory facilities charge. $ *Rooms from: $299* ⊠ *41 Tunnel Rd., at Ashby and Domingo Aves., Claremont* ☎ *510/843–3000, 800/257–7544 reservations* ⊕ *www.fairmont.com/claremont-berkeley* ↝ *276 rooms* ❙○❙ *No meals.*

$$$
HOTEL
Fodor'sChoice
★

Hotel Shattuck Plaza. This historic boutique hotel sits amid Berkeley's downtown arts district, just steps from the U.C. campus and a short walk from the Gourmet Ghetto. **Pros:** central location near public transit; special date night and B&B packages; modern facilities; good views;

great restaurant; pet friendly; free pass to nearby YMCA. **Cons:** public and street parking only; limited on-site fitness center. 🔄 *Rooms from: $209* ✉ *2086 Allston Way, at Shattuck Ave., Downtown* ☎ *510/845–7300* ⊕ *www.hotelshattuckplaza.com* ⤵ *199 rooms* ❐ *No meals.*

NIGHTLIFE AND PERFORMING ARTS
NIGHTLIFE

Fodor's Choice ★ **Freight & Salvage Coffeehouse.** Some of the most talented practitioners of folk, jazz, gospel, blues, world-beat, and bluegrass perform in this nonprofit coffeehouse, one of the country's finest folk music and story-telling venues. Most tickets cost less than $30. ✉ *2020 Addison St., between Shattuck Ave. and Milvia St.* ☎ *510/644–2020* ⊕ *www.thefreight.org.*

Fodor's Choice ★ **Tupper & Reed.** Housed in the former music shop of John C. Tupper and Lawrence Reed, this music-inspired cocktail haven features a symphony of carefully crafted libations, which are mixed with live music performed by local musicians. The historic 1925 building features a reservations-only balcony bar, cozy nooks, antique fixtures, a pool table, and romantic fireplaces. ✉ *2271 Shattuck Ave., at Kitteredge St., Downtown* ☎ *510/859–4472* ⊕ *www.tupperandreed.com.*

PERFORMING ARTS

Berkeley Repertory Theatre. One of the region's most highly respected and innovative repertory theaters, Berkeley Rep performs the work of classic and contemporary playwrights. Well-known pieces such as *Tartuffe* and *Macbeth* mix with world premieres and edgier fare like Green Day's *American Idiot* and Lemony Snicket's *The Composer Is Dead.* The theater's complex is in the heart of downtown Berkeley's arts district, near BART's Downtown Berkeley station. ✉ *2025 Addison St., near Shattuck Ave.* ☎ *510/647–2949* ⊕ *www.berkeleyrep.org.*

Cal Performances. Based out of U.C. Berkeley, this series runs from September through May. It features a varied bill of internationally acclaimed artists ranging from classical soloists to the latest jazz, world-music, theater, and dance ensembles. Past performers include Alvin Ailey American Dance Theatre, the National Ballet of China, Peter Sellars, and Yo-Yo Ma. ✉ *101 Zellerbach Hall, Suite 4800, Dana Str. and Bancroft Way* ☎ *510/642–9988* ⊕ *calperformances.org.*

SHOPPING

Fodor's Choice ★ **Amoeba Music.** Heaven for audiophiles and movie collectors, this legendary Berkeley favorite is *the* place to head for new and used CDs, vinyl, cassettes, VHS tapes, Blu-ray discs, and DVDs. The massive and ever-changing stock includes thousands of titles for all music tastes, as well as plenty of Amoeba merch. There are branches in San Francisco and Hollywood, but this is the original. ✉ *2455 Telegraph Ave., at Haste St.* ☎ *510/549–1125* ⊕ *www.amoeba.com.*

Kermit Lynch Wine Merchant. Credited with taking American appreciation of Old World wines to a higher level, this small shop is a great place to peruse as you educate your palate. The friendly salespeople will happily direct you to the latest French and Italian bargains. ✉ *1605 San Pablo Ave., at Cedar St.* ☎ *510/524–1524* ⊕ *www.kermitlynch.com* ☟ *Closed Sun. and Mon.*

Moe's Books. The spirit of Moe—the creative, cantankerous, cigar-smoking late proprietor—lives on in this world-famous four-story house of new and used books. Students and professors come here to browse the large selection, which includes literary and cultural criticism, art titles, and literature in foreign languages. ⊠ *2476 Telegraph Ave., near Haste St.* ☎ *510/849–2087* ⊕ *www.moesbooks.com.*

OAKLAND

East of Bay Bridge.

In contrast to San Francisco's buzz and beauty and Berkeley's storied counterculture, Oakland's allure lies in its amazing diversity. Here you can find a Nigerian clothing store, a Gothic revival skyscraper, a Buddhist meditation center, and a lively salsa club, all within the same block.

Oakland's multifaceted nature reflects its colorful and tumultuous history. Once a cluster of Mediterranean-style homes and gardens that served as a bedroom community for San Francisco, the town had a major rail terminal and port city by the turn of the 20th century. Already a hub of manufacturing, Oakland became a center for shipbuilding and industry when the United States entered World War II. New jobs in the city's shipyards, railroads, and factories attracted thousands of laborers from across the country, including sharecroppers from the Deep South, Mexican Americans from the southwest, and some of the nation's first female welders. Neighborhoods were imbued with a proud but gritty spirit, along with heightened racial tension. In the wake of the civil rights movement, racial pride gave rise to militant groups like the Black Panther Party, but they were little match for the economic hardships and racial tensions that plagued Oakland. In many neighborhoods the reality was widespread poverty and gang violence—subjects that dominated the songs of such Oakland-bred rappers as the late Tupac Shakur. The highly publicized protests of the Occupy Oakland movement in 2011 and 2012 and the #BlackLivesMatter movement of 2014 and 2015 illustrate just how much Oakland remains a mosaic of its past.

Oakland's affluent reside in the city's hillside homes and wooded enclaves like Claremont, Piedmont and Montclair, which provide a warmer, more spacious alternative to San Francisco, while a constant flow of newcomers ensures continued diversity, vitality, and growing pains. Many neighborhoods to the west and south of the city center have yet to be touched by gentrification, but a renovated downtown and vibrant arts scene has injected new energy into the city. Even San Franciscans, often loath to cross the Bay Bridge, come to Uptown and Temescal for the nightlife, arts, and restaurants.

Everyday life here revolves around the neighborhood. In some areas, such as Piedmont and Rockridge, you'd swear you were in Berkeley or San Francisco's Noe Valley. Along Telegraph Avenue just south of 51st Street, Temescal is littered with hipsters and pulsing with creative culinary and design energy. These are perfect places for browsing, eating, or relaxing between sightseeing trips to Oakland's architectural gems, rejuvenated waterfront, and numerous green spaces.

GETTING HERE AND AROUND

Driving from San Francisco, take Interstate 80 East across the Bay Bridge, then take Interstate 580 East to the Grand Avenue exit for Lake Merritt. To reach downtown and the waterfront, take Interstate 980 West from Interstate 580 East and exit at 12th Street; exit at 18th Street for Uptown. For Temescal, take Interstate 580 East to Highway 24 and exit at 51st Street.

By BART, use the Lake Merritt Station for the Oakland Museum and southern Lake Merritt; the Oakland City Center–12th Street Station for downtown, Chinatown, and Old Oakland; and the 19th Street Station for Uptown, the Paramount Theatre, and the north side of Lake Merritt.

By bus, take the AC Transit's C and P lines to get to Piedmont in Oakland. The O bus stops at the edge of Chinatown near downtown Oakland.

Oakland's Jack London Square is an easy hop on the ferry from San Francisco. Those without cars can take advantage of the free Broadway Shuttle, which runs from the Jack London Square to 27th Street via downtown on weekdays and Friday and Saturday nights.

Be aware of how quickly neighborhoods can change. Walking is generally safe downtown and in the Piedmont and Rockridge areas, but avoid walking west and southeast of downtown, especially at night.

Shuttle Contact Broadway Shuttle. ⊕ *www.meetdowntownoak.com.*

ESSENTIALS

Visitor Information Visit Oakland. ⊠ *481 Water St., near Broadway, Jack London Square* ☎ *510/839–9000* ⊕ *www.visitoakland.org.*

EXPLORING
TOP ATTRACTIONS

FAMILY **Oakland Museum of California.** This museum surveys the state's art, history, and natural wonders in three galleries of absorbing, interactive exhibits. Travel through myriad ecosystems, from the sand dunes of the Pacific to the volcanic Mt. Shasta, and discover over 2,000 species in the expansive Gallery of California Natural Sciences. Explore disparate integrated stories in the rambling Gallery of California History, which includes everything from Ohlone baskets to Gold Rush era artifacts. Of particular interest in the Gallery of California Art are photographs by Dorothea Lange and paintings by members of the Bay Area figurative school. Stop by the Blue Oak café for a snack or relax for a minute in the flower gardens, which are open to the public at no charge during hours of operation. ■TIP→ On Friday evenings the museum gets lively, with live music, food trucks, and half-price admission. ⊠ *1000 Oak St., at 10th St., Downtown* ☎ *510/318–8400, 888/625–6873 toll-free* ⊕ *museumca.org* 🎟 *$16, free 1st Sun. of month* ☉ *Closed Mon. and Tues.*

Fodor'sChoice ★ **Paramount Theatre.** A glorious Art Deco specimen, the Paramount operates as a venue for concerts and performances of all kinds, from the Oakland Symphony to Jerry Seinfeld and Elvis Costello. The popular classic movie nights start off with a 30-minute Wurlitzer concert. ■TIP→ Docent-led tours, offered the first and third Saturday of the month, are fun and informative. ⊠ *2025 Broadway, at 20th St., Uptown* ☎ *510/465–6400* ⊕ *www.paramounttheatre.com* 🎟 *Tour $5.*

FAMILY
Fodor's Choice
★

Rockridge. This fashionable upscale neighborhood is one of Oakland's most desirable places to live. Explore the tree-lined streets that radiate out from **College Avenue** just north and south of the Rockridge BART station for a look at California Craftsman bungalows at their finest. By day College Avenue between Broadway and Alcatraz Avenue is crowded with shoppers buying fresh flowers, used books, and clothing; by night the same folks are back for handcrafted meals, artisan wines, and locally brewed ales. With its specialty-food shops and quick bites to go, **Market Hall,** an airy European-style marketplace at Shafter Avenue, is a hub of culinary activity. ⊠ *College Ave., between Alcatraz Ave. and Broadway, Rockridge* ⊕ *www.rockridgedistrict.com.*

Fodor's Choice
★

Temescal. Centering on Telegraph Avenue between 40th and 51st Streets, Temescal (the Aztec term for "sweat house") is a low-pretension, moneyed-hipster hood with young families and middle-aged folks thrown into the mix. A critical mass of excellent eateries draws folks from around the Bay Area; there's veteran **Doña Tomás** (*5004 Telegraph Ave.*) and favorites **Pizzaiola** (*5008 Telegraph Ave.*) and **Aunt Mary's** (*4640 Telegraph Ave.*) as well as **Bakesale Betty** (*5098 Telegraph Ave.*), where folks line up for the fried-chicken sandwich. Old-time dive bars and smog-check stations share space with the trendy children's clothing shop **Ruby's Garden** (*5026 Telegraph Ave.*) and the stalwart **East**

Bay Depot for Creative Reuse (*4695 Telegraph Ave.*), where you might find a bucket of buttons or 1,000 muffin wrappers among birdcages, furniture, lunch boxes, and ribbon.

Around the corner, **Temescal Alley** (*49th St.*), a tucked-away lane of tiny storefronts, crackles with the creative energy of local makers. Surprising finds can be had at **Crimson Horticultural Rarities** (*No. 470*) or at the home-decor shop at **Bounty and Feast** (*No. 482*). Don't miss grabbing a sweet scoop at **Curbside Creamery** (*No. 482*). ⊠ *Telegraph Ave., between 40th and 51st Sts., Temescal* ⊕ *www.temescaldistrict.org.*

Fodor's Choice ★ **Uptown.** This is where nightlife and cutting-edge art happens in Oakland, along the Telegraph Avenue/Broadway corridor north of downtown. Dozens of galleries cluster around Telegraph, showing everything from photography and site-specific installations to glasswork and fiber arts. The first Friday of each month, thousands descend for **Art Murmur** (*oaklandartmurmur.org*), a late-night gallery event that has expanded into **First Friday** (*oaklandfirstfridays.org*), a veritable neighborhood festival featuring food trucks, street vendors, and live music along Telegraph Avenue.

Lively restaurants with a distinctly urban vibe make Uptown a dining destination every night of the week. Favorites include craft cocktails and eclectic Japanese-inspired fare at **Hopscotch** (*1915 San Pablo Ave.*), beautiful beverages and stylish cuisine at Art Deco **Flora** (*1900 Telegraph Ave.*), tasty tapas and modern Spanish fare at trendy **Duende** (*468 19th*), upscale Southern comfort food at elegant **Picán** (*2295 Broadway*), and innovative Oaxacan fare and mezcal magic at **Calavera** (*2337 Broadway*) just to name a few.

Toss in the bevy of bars and there's plenty within walking distance to keep you busy for an entire evening: **Cafe Van Kleef** (*1621 Telegraph Ave.*), the friendly jumble that started it all Uptown; **Bar Three Fifty-Five** (*355 19th St.*), a house of great cocktails; strikingly beautiful but low-key **Dogwood** (*1644 Telegraph Ave.*), which has tasty nibbles; **Drake's Dealership** (*2325 Broadway*), with its spacious hipster-friendly beer garden; **Lost and Found** (*2040 Telegraph Ave.*), home of draft brews and cornhole boards; and **Somar** (*1727 Telegraph Ave.*), a bar, music lounge, and gallery in one. Uptown's shopping is exploding as well, with local goods at the fore; be sure to stop by **Oaklandish** (*1444 Broadway*) for T-shirts, jeans, and everything Oaktown. The **Paramount Theatre** (*2025 Broadway*), **Fox Theater** (*1807 Telegraph Ave.*), and other art-deco architectural gems distinguish this neighborhood. ⊠ *Oakland* ✛ *Telegraph Ave. and Broadway from 14th to 27th Sts.*

WHERE TO EAT

$$
MEDITERRANEAN
✕ **À Côté.** This Mediterranean hot spot is all about seasonal small plates, cozy tables, family-style eating, and excellent wine. Heavy wooden tables, intimate dining nooks, natural light, and a heated patio make this an ideal destination for couples, families, and the after-work crowd. **Known for:** Pernod mussels; exquisite small plates; global and regional wine list. ⑤ *Average main: $22* ⊠ *5478 College Ave., at Taft Ave., Rockridge* ☎ *510/655–6469* ⊕ *acoterestaurant.com* ⊗ *No lunch.*

$
SOUTHERN
FAMILY
Fodor's Choice
★

✕ **Brown Sugar Kitchen.** Influenced by Tanya Holland's African American heritage and French culinary education, the menu at this bustling little West Oakland dining destination features local, organic ingredients and sweet and savory dishes paired with sumptuous wines. The dining room is small, but inviting with a long, sleek counter, red-leather stools, and spacious booths and tables. **Known for:** fried chicken and cornmeal waffles; bacon-cheddar-scallion biscuits; smoked chicken and shrimp gumbo. ⑤ *Average main: $15* ✉ *2534 Mandela Pkwy., at 26th St., West Oakland* ☎ *510/839–7685* ⊕ *www.brownsugarkitchen.com* ⊘ *Closed Mon. No dinner.*

$$$
MODERN
MEXICAN

✕ **Calavera.** This Oaxacan-inspired hot spot offers inventive and elevated plates in an industrial-chic space with lofty ceilings, warm wooden tables, exposed brick walls, and heated outdoor dining. Innovative cocktails like the salted-air margarita come from a beautiful bar with a library of over 100 agaves. **Known for:** innovative and beautiful cocktails; wide selection of tequilas and mezcal; carnitas tacos served in nixtamal heirloom corn tortillas; fresh ceviche. ⑤ *Average main: $25* ✉ *2337 Broadway, at 24th St., Uptown* ☎ *510/338–3273* ⊕ *calaveraoakland.com* ⊘ *Closed Mon.*

$$$$
AMERICAN

✕ **Camino.** Russell Moore cooked at Chez Panisse for two decades before he and Allison Hopelain opened this restaurant, which focuses on simple, seasonal, straightforward dishes that are cooked in an enormous, crackling *camino* (Italian for "fireplace"). Served on redwood tables in a Craftsman-meets-refectory-style dining room, the ever-changing menu has only three entrées—each cooked over its own open fire—that feature top-notch ingredients and pair perfectly with creative craft cocktails. **Known for:** wood-fired dishes; craft cocktails. ⑤ *Average main: $32* ✉ *3917 Grand Ave., at Boulevard Way, Grand Lake* ☎ *510/547–5035* ⊕ *www.caminorestaurant.com* ⊘ *Closed Tues. No lunch* ⌔ *No tipping.*

$$$$
AMERICAN
Fodor's Choice
★

✕ **Commis.** A slender, unassuming storefront houses the only East Bay restaurant with a Michelin star (two of them, in fact). The room is minimalist and polished: nothing distracts from the artistry of chef James Syhabout, who creates a multicourse dining experience based on the season and his distinctive vision. **Known for:** inventive multicourse tasting menu; Michelin-winning execution. ⑤ *Average main: $149* ✉ *3859 Piedmont Ave., at Rio Vista Ave., Piedmont* ☎ *510/653–3902* ⊕ *commisrestaurant.com* ⊘ *Closed Mon. and Tues. No lunch.*

$$
INDIAN

✕ **Juhu Beach Club.** All the color, flavor, and fun of Mumbai's Juhu Beach is contained within the brightly colored walls of this festive funky Temescal eatery. Childhood memories, Indian street food, and family recipes have inspired Preeti Mistry's menu of spicy starters, savory sliders, inventive drinks, and edgy modern main courses. **Known for:** pav slider sandwiches; modern takes on traditional street food; refreshing drinks (both boozy and booze-free). ⑤ *Average main: $22* ✉ *5179 Telegraph Ave., at 51st St., Temescal* ☎ *510/652–7350* ⊕ *juhubeachclub.com.*

$$
ITALIAN
FAMILY

✕ **Pizzaiolo.** Chez Panisse alum Charlie Hallowell helms the kitchen of this rustic-chic Oakland institution. Diners of all ages perch on wooden chairs with red-leather backs and nosh on farm-to-table Italian fare from a daily changing menu. **Known for:** seasonal wood-fired pizza; delicious daily breakfast pastries; rustic California-Italian entrées. ⑤ *Average main: $22* ✉ *5008 Telegraph Ave., at 51st St., Temescal* ☎ *510/652–4888* ⊕ *www.pizzaiolooakland.com* �》 *Closed Sun. No lunch.*

$$$
MEDITERRANEAN
Fodor'sChoice
★

✕ **Shakewell.** Two *Top Chef* vets opened this stylish Lakeshore restaurant, which serves creative and memorable Mediterranean small plates in a lively setting that features an open kitchen, wood-fired oven, communal tables, and snug seating. As the name implies, well-crafted cocktails are shaken (or stirred) and poured with panache. **Known for:** wood-oven paella; Spanish and Mediterranean small plates; craft cocktails. ⑤ *Average main: $25* ✉ *3407 Lakeshore Ave., near Mandana Blvd.* ☎ *510/251–0329* ⊕ *www.shakewelloakland.com* ☽ *Closed Mon. No lunch Tues.*

WHERE TO STAY

$$
HOTEL

🛏 **Best Western Plus Bayside Hotel.** Sandwiched between the serene Oakland Estuary and an eight-lane freeway, this all-suites property has handsome accommodations with balconies or patios, many overlooking the water. **Pros:** attractive, budget-conscious choice; free parking; free shuttle to and from airport, Jack London Square, and downtown; scenic water views. **Cons:** not within walking distance of anything of interest; freeway-side rooms can be loud. ⑤ *Rooms from: $159* ✉ *1717 Embarcadero, off I–880, at 16th St. exit* ☎ *510/356–2450* ⊕ *hotelsinoaklandca.h.bestwestern.com* ⤶ *81 rooms* ❍❘ *Breakfast.*

$$
HOTEL
FAMILY

🛏 **Waterfront Hotel.** This thoroughly modern, pleasantly appointed Joie de Vivre property sits among the many high-caliber restaurants of Jack London Square. **Pros:** great location; lovely views; dog-friendly; excellent hotel restaurant, Lungomare; complimentary wine-and-cheese hour during the week; free shuttle service to downtown (limited hours); easy access to the ferry. **Cons:** passing trains can be noisy on city side; parking is pricey. ⑤ *Rooms from: $180* ✉ *10 Washington St., Jack London Square* ☎ *510/836–3800 front desk, 888/842–5333 reservations* ⊕ *www.jdvhotels.com* ⤶ *145 rooms* ❍❘ *No meals.*

NIGHTLIFE

Back when rent was still relatively cheap, artists flocked to Oakland, giving rise to a cultural scene—visual arts, indie music, spoken word, film—that's still buzzing, especially in Uptown. Trendy new spaces pop up regularly and the beer-garden renaissance is already well-established. Whether you're a self-proclaimed beer snob or just someone who enjoys a cold drink on a sunny day, there's something for everyone. Oakland's nightlife scene is less crowded and more intimate than what you'll find in San Francisco. Music is just about everywhere, though the most popular venues are downtown.

BARS

Fodor'sChoice
★

Café Van Kleef. Long before Uptown got hot, the late Peter Van Kleef was serving stiff fresh-squeezed greyhounds, telling tales about his collection of pop culture mementos, and booking live music at Café Van Kleef, a funky café-bar that crackles with creative energy—there's still live music every weekend. This local favorite still serves some of the stiffest drinks in town. ✉ *1621 Telegraph Ave., between 16th and 17th Sts., Uptown* ☎ *510/763–7711* ⊕ *cafevankleef.com.*

The Layover Music Bar and Lounge. Bright, bold, and unabashedly bohemian, this hangout filled with recycled furniture is constantly evolving because everything is for sale, from the artwork to the pillows, rugs, and lamps. The busy bar serves up signature organic cocktails, and live entertainment includes comedy shows, storytelling, and local DJs. ⊠ *1517 Franklin St., near 15th St., Uptown* ☎ *510/834–1517* ⊕ *www.oaklandlayover.com.*

Make Westing. This sprawling industrial-chic space is always abuzz with hipsters playing bocce, the post-work crowd sipping old-fashioneds, or pretheater couples passing mason jars of Dungeness crab dip. The patio's your best bet for a conversation on a busy evening. ⊠ *1741 Telegraph Ave., at 18th St., Uptown* ☎ *510/251–1400* ⊕ *makewesting.com.*

BREWPUBS AND BEER GARDENS

Beer Revolution. Hard-core beer geeks: with hundreds of bottled beers and 50 taps, this craft beer and bottle shop is for you. Tear yourself away from the beer lists and grab a table on the patio. ⊠ *464 3rd St., at Broadway, Jack London Square* ☎ *510/452–2337* ⊕ *www.beer-revolution.com.*

FAMILY
Fodor's Choice
★
Lost & Found. The diversions on the spacious, succulent-filled patio include Ping-Pong, cornhole, and community tables full of chilled-out locals. The beer selection ranges from blue collar to Belgian and a seasonal menu focuses on internationally inspired small bites. ⊠ *2040 Telegraph Ave., at 21st St., Uptown* ☎ *510/763–2040* ⊕ *www.lostand-found510.com* ⊗ *Closed Mon.*

The Trappist. Brick walls, dark wood, soft lighting, and a buzz of conversation set a warm and mellow tone inside this old Victorian space that's been renovated to resemble a traditional Belgian pub. The setting (which includes two bars and a back patio) is definitely a draw, but the real stars are the artisan beers—more than a hundred Belgian, Dutch, and North American brews. Light fare includes bar snacks and meat and cheese boards. ⊠ *460 8th St., near Broadway, Old Oakland* ☎ *510/238–8900* ⊕ *www.thetrappist.com.*

ROCK, POP, HIP-HOP, FOLK, AND BLUES CLUBS

Fox Theater. This renovated 1928 theater, Oakland's favorite performance venue, is a remarkable feat of Mediterranean Moorish architecture and has seen the likes of Willie Nelson, Counting Crows, Rebelution, and B.B. King, to name a few. The venue boasts good sight lines, a state-of-the-art sound system, brilliant acoustics, and a restaurant and bar, among other amenities. ⊠ *1807 Telegraph Ave., between 18th and 19th Sts., Uptown* ☎ *510/302–2250* ⊕ *thefoxoakland.com.*

Fodor's Choice
★
Yoshi's. Opened in 1972 as a sushi bar, Yoshi's has evolved into one of the area's best jazz and live music venues. The full Yoshi's experience includes traditional Japanese and Asian fusion cuisine in the adjacent restaurant. ⊠ *510 Embarcadero W, between Washington and Clay Sts., Jack London Square* ☎ *510/238–9200* ⊕ *www.yoshis.com* ⊑ *$20–$80.*

SHOPPING

Pop-up shops and stylish, locally focused stores are scattered throughout the funky alleys of Old Oakland, Uptown, Rockridge, and Temescal, while the streets around Lake Merritt and Grand Lake offer more modest boutiques.

Maison d'Etre. Close to the Rockridge BART station, this store epitomizes the Rockridge neighborhood's funky-chic shopping scene. Look for high-end housewares and impulse buys like whimsical watches, imported fruit-tea blends, and funky slippers. ✉ *5640 College Ave., at Keith Ave., Rockridge* ☎ *510/658–2801* ⊕ *maisondetre.com.*

Fodor'sChoice **Oaklandish.** This is the place for Oaktown swag. What started in 2000 ★ as a public art project of local pride has become a celebrated brand around the bay, and a portion of the proceeds from hip Oaklandish brand T-shirts and accessories supports grassroots nonprofits committed to bettering the local community. It's good-looking stuff for a good cause. ✉ *1444 Broadway, near 15th St., Uptown* ☎ *510/251–9500* ⊕ *oaklandish.com.*

MARIN COUNTY

Marin is, quite simply, a knockout—its abundance of protected parkland, open-space preserves, and rugged coastline are some of the most breathtaking and ecologically diverse in the world. The territory ranges from chaparral, grassland, and coastal scrub to broadleaf, redwood, and evergreen forest. It's well worth the drive over the Golden Gate Bridge to explore the stunning Marin Headlands and the sprawling beauty of Point Reyes National Seashore and its 80 miles of shoreline.

While Cyra McFadden's literary soap opera, *The Serial,* depicted Marin County as a bastion of hot-tubbing and "open" marriages, increasingly jet-set Marinites spend more time on outdoor activities, including surfing, cycling, kayaking, and hiking. Adrenaline junkies mountain bike down Mt. Tamalpais, while solitary folk wander along Point Reyes's empty beaches. Artists and musicians who arrived in the 1960s set a boho tone for mellow country towns, but much of Marin is undeniably chic, with high-tech companies making their mark in the local economy; this *is* one of the wealthiest counties in the nation.

After exploring Marin's natural beauty, consider a stop in one of its lovely villages. Most cosmopolitan is Sausalito, the town just over the Golden Gate Bridge from San Francisco. Across the inlet from Sausalito, Tiburon and Belvedere are lined with grand homes that regularly appear on fund-raising circuits, and to the north, landlocked Mill Valley is a hub of wining and dining and tony boutiques. Book Passage, a noted bookseller in the next town, Corte Madera, hosts regular readings by top-notch authors, and Larkspur, San Anselmo, and Fairfax beyond have walkable downtown areas, each a bit folksier than the next but all with good restaurants and shops and a distinct sense of place.

In general, the farther west you go, the more rural things become. Separated from the inland county by the slopes and ridges of giant Mt. Tamalpais, West Marin beckons to mavericks, artists, ocean lovers, and free spirits. Stinson Beach has tempered its isolationist attitude to accommodate out-of-towners, as have Inverness and Point Reyes Station. Bolinas, on the other hand, would prefer to keep to itself.

VISITOR INFORMATION

Contact Marin Convention & Visitors Bureau. ⊠ *1 Mitchell Blvd., Suite B, San Rafael* ☎ *415/925–2060* ⊕ *www.visitmarin.org.*

THE MARIN HEADLANDS

Due west of the Golden Gate Bridge's northern end.

The term *Golden Gate* has become synonymous with the world-famous bridge, but it was first given to the narrow waterway that connects the Pacific and the San Francisco Bay. To the north of the Golden Gate Strait lies the Marin Headlands, part of the Golden Gate National Recreation Area (GGNRA), which boasts some of the area's most dramatic scenery.

GETTING HERE AND AROUND

Driving from San Francisco, head north on U.S. 101. Just after you cross the Golden Gate Bridge, take exit 442 for Alexander Avenue. Keep left at the fork and follow signs for "San Francisco/U.S. 101 South", go through the tunnel under the freeway, and turn right up the hill. Muni bus 76X runs hourly from Sutter and Sansome Streets to the Marin Headlands Visitor Center on weekends and major holidays only.

EXPLORING

TOP ATTRACTIONS

FAMILY
Fodor's Choice
★

Marin Headlands. The headlands stretch from the Golden Gate Bridge to Muir Beach. Photographers perch on the southern headlands for spectacular shots of the city and bridge. Equally remarkable are the views north along the coast and out to the ocean, where the Farallon Islands are visible on clear days.

The headlands' strategic position at the mouth of San Francisco Bay made them a logical site for military installations from 1890 through the Cold War. Today you can explore the crumbling concrete batteries where naval guns once protected the area. The headlands' main attractions are centered on Fts. Barry and Cronkhite, which are separated by Rodeo Lagoon and Rodeo Beach, a dark stretch of sand that attracts sand-castle builders and dog owners.

The visitor center is a worthwhile stop for its exhibits on the area's history and ecology, and kids enjoy the "please touch" educational sites and small play area inside. You can pick up guides to historic sites and wildlife, and get information about programming and guided walks. ⊠ *Golden Gate National Recreation Area, Visitors Center, Fort Barry Chapel, Ft. Barry, Bldg. 948, Field and Bunker Rds., Sausalito* ☎ *415/331–1540* ⊕ *www.nps.gov/goga/marin-headlands.htm.*

FAMILY
Point Bonita Lighthouse. A restored beauty that still guides ships to safety with its original 1855 refractory lens, the lighthouse anchors

the southern headlands. Half the fun of a visit is the steep half-mile walk from the parking area through a rock tunnel, across a suspension bridge, and down to the lighthouse. Signposts along the way detail the bravado of surfmen, as the early lifeguards were called, and the tenacity of the "wickies," the first keepers of the light. ■ TIP→ Call about 90-minute full-moon tours. ⊠ *End of Conzelman Rd., Ft. Barry, Bldg. 948, Sausalito* ☎ *415/331–1540* ⊕ *www.nps.gov/goga/pobo.htm* ⊗ *Closed Tues.–Fri.*

SAUSALITO

2 miles north of Golden Gate Bridge.

Bougainvillea-covered hillsides and an expansive yacht harbor give Sausalito the feel of an Adriatic resort. The town sits on the northwestern edge of San Francisco Bay, where it's sheltered from the ocean by the Marin Headlands; the mostly mild weather here is perfect for strolling and outdoor dining. Nevertheless, morning fog and afternoon winds can roll over the hills without warning, funneling through the central part of Sausalito once known as Hurricane Gulch.

South of Bridgeway, which snakes between the bay and the hills, a waterside esplanade is lined with restaurants on piers that lure diners with good seafood and even better views. Stairs along the west side of Bridgeway and throughout town climb into wooded hillside neighborhoods filled with both rustic and opulent homes, while back on the northern portion of the shoreline, harbors shelter a community of over 400 houseboats. As you amble along Bridgeway past shops and galleries, you'll notice the absence of basic services. Find them and more on Caledonia Street, which runs parallel to Bridgeway and inland a couple of blocks. While ferry-side shops flaunt kitschy souvenirs, smaller side streets and narrow alleyways offer eccentric jewelry and handmade crafts.

■ TIP→ The ferry is the best way to get to Sausalito from San Francisco; you get more romance (and less traffic) and disembark in the heart of downtown.

Sausalito developed its bohemian flair in the 1950s and '60s, when creative types, including artist Jean Varda, poet Shel Silverstein, and madam Sally Stanford, established an artists' colony and a houseboat community here (this is Otis Redding's "Dock of the Bay"). Both the spirit of the artists and the neighborhood of floating homes persist. For a close-up view of the quirky community, head north on Bridgeway, turn right on Gate Six Road, park where it dead-ends, and enter through the unlocked gates.

GETTING HERE AND AROUND

From San Francisco by car or bike, follow U.S. 101 north across the Golden Gate Bridge and take exit 442 for Alexander Avenue, just past Vista Point; continue down the winding hill to the water to where the road becomes Bridgeway. Golden Gate Transit buses will drop you off in downtown Sausalito, and the ferries dock downtown as well. The center of town is flat, with plenty of sidewalks and bay views. It's a pleasure and a must to explore on foot.

Marin County

0   5 mi

0   5 km

ESSENTIALS

Visitor Information Sausalito Chamber of Commerce. ✉ 1913 Bridgeway ☎ 415/331–7262 ext. 10 ⊕ www.sausalito.org. **Sausalito Information Kiosk.** ✉ El Portal St. ⚓ At the foot of El Portal St. at the Ferry Pier ☎ 415/331–1093 ⊕ www.oursausalito.com.

EXPLORING

Sally Stanford Drinking Fountain. There's an unusual historic landmark on the Sausalito Ferry Pier—a drinking fountain inscribed "Have a drink on Sally" in remembrance of Sally Stanford, the former San Francisco brothel madam who became Sausalito's mayor in the 1970s. Sassy Sally would have appreciated the fountain's eccentric attachment: a knee-level basin with the inscription "Have a drink on Leland," in memory of her beloved dog. ✉ *Sausalito Ferry Pier, Anchor St. at Humboldt St., off the southwest corner of Gabrielson Park* ⊕ *www.oursausalito.com/sausalito-ferry-1.html.*

QUICK BITES

Hamburgers Sausalito. Patrons queue up daily outside this tiny street-side shop for organic Angus beef patties that are made to order on a wheel-shaped grill. Brave the line (it moves fast) and take your food to the esplanade to enjoy fresh air and bay-side views. **Known for:** legendary burgers. ✉ 737 Bridgeway, at Anchor St. ☎ 415/332–9471 ⊘ No dinner.

Sausalito Ice House Visitors Center and Museum. The local historical society operates this dual educational exhibit and visitor center, where you can get your bearings, learn some history, and find out what's happening in town. ⊠ *780 Bridgeway, at Bay St.* ☏ *415/332–0505* ⊕ *www.sausalito-historicalsociety.com* ⊗ *Closed Mon.*

Viña del Mar Plaza and Park. The landmark Plaza Viña del Mar, named for Sausalito's sister city in Chile, marks the center of town. Adjacent to the parking lot and ferry pier, the plaza is flanked by two 14-foot-tall elephant statues, which were created for the San Francisco Panama–Pacific International Exposition in 1915. It also features a picture-perfect fountain that's great for people-watching. ⊠ *Bridgeway and El Portal St.* ⊕ *www.oursausalito.com/parks-in-sausalito/vina-del-mar-park.html.*

WHERE TO EAT

$$
SEAFOOD
FAMILY
Fodor'sChoice
★

✕**Fish.** If you're looking for fresh sustainably caught seafood, head to this gleaming dockside fish house a mile north of downtown. Order at the counter—cash only—and then grab a seat by the floor-to-ceiling windows or at a picnic table on the pier, overlooking the yachts and fishing boats. **Known for:** fish of the day; barbecued oysters; sustainably caught, fire-grilled entrées. ⑤ *Average main: $20* ⊠ *350 Harbor Dr., at Gate 5 Rd., off Bridgeway* ☏ *415/331–3474* ⊕ *www.331fish.com* ▭ *No credit cards* ⌖ *Cash only.*

$$$
FRENCH

✕**Le Garage.** Brittany-born Olivier Souvestre serves traditional French bistro fare in a relaxed, bay-side setting that feels more sidewalk café than the converted garage that it is. The restaurant seats only 35 inside and 15 outside, so make reservations or arrive early. **Known for:** PEI mussels and house-cut fries; weekend brunch. ⑤ *Average main: $26* ⊠ *85 Liberty Ship Way, Suite 109* ☏ *415/332–5625* ⊕ *www.legaragebistrosausalito.com* ⌖ *No reservations for weekend brunch.*

$$$
ITALIAN

✕**Poggio.** A hillside dining destination, Poggio serves modern Tuscan-style comfort food in a handsome, Old World–inspired space whose charm spills onto the sidewalks. An extensive and ever-changing menu of antipasti, pasta, hearty entrées, and pizzas emerges from the open kitchen's wood-fired oven. **Known for:** fresh local ingredients and traditional Northern Italian dishes; rotisserie chicken with property-grown organic herbs and vegetables; polpettini meatballs. ⑤ *Average main: $30* ⊠ *777 Bridgeway, at Bay St.* ☏ *415/332–7771* ⊕ *www.poggiotrattoria.com.*

$$$
JAPANESE
Fodor'sChoice
★

✕**Sushi Ran.** Sushi aficionados swear that this tiny, stylish restaurant—in business for more than three decades—is the Bay Area's best option for raw fish, but don't overlook the excellent Pacific Rim fusions, a melding of Japanese ingredients and French cooking techniques. Book in advance or expect a wait, which you can soften by sipping one of the bar's 45 by-the-glass sakes. **Known for:** fish imported from Tokyo's famous Tsukiji market; local miso glazed black cod. ⑤ *Average main: $30* ⊠ *107 Caledonia St., at Pine St.* ☏ *415/332–3620* ⊕ *www.sushiran.com* ⊗ *No lunch weekends.*

5

WHERE TO STAY

$$
B&B/INN
🏨 **Hotel Sausalito.** Handcrafted furniture and tasteful original art and reproductions give this Mission Revival-style inn the feel of a small European hotel. **Pros:** great staff; central location; solid mid-range hotel; vouchers to nearby Cafe Tutti provided. **Cons:** no room service; some rooms are small; daily public parking fee. ⑤ *Rooms from: $175* ✉ *16 El Portal, at Bridgeway* ☎ *415/332–0700* ⊕ *www.hotelsausalito.com* ➷ *16 rooms* ¹⁰¹ *No meals.*

$$$$
B&B/INN
🏨 **The Inn Above Tide.** The balconies at the Inn Above Tide literally hang over the water, and each of its rooms has a perfect 10 view that takes in wild Angel Island as well as the city lights across the bay. **Pros:** great complimentary breakfast; minutes from restaurants and attractions; central but tranquil setting. **Cons:** costly daily parking; some rooms are on the small side; five rooms have no balcony. ⑤ *Rooms from: $380* ✉ *30 El Portal* ☎ *415/332–9535, 800/893–8433* ⊕ *www.innabovetide.com* ➷ *31 rooms* ¹⁰¹ *Breakfast.*

TIBURON

7 miles north of Sausalito, 11 miles north of Golden Gate Bridge.

On a peninsula that was named Punta de Tiburon (Shark Point) by 18th-century Spanish explorers, this beautiful Marin County community retains the feel of a village—it's more low-key than Sausalito—despite the encroachment of commercial establishments from the downtown area. The harbor faces Angel Island across Raccoon Strait, and San Francisco is directly south across the bay—which means the views from the decks of harbor restaurants are major attractions. Since 1884, when the San Francisco and North Pacific Railroad relocated their ferry terminal facilities to the harbor town, Tiburon has centered on the waterfront. ■ **TIP→ The ferry is the most relaxing (and fastest) way to get here, and allows you to skip traffic and parking problems.**

GETTING HERE AND AROUND

Blue & Gold Fleet ferries travel between San Francisco and Tiburon daily. By car, head north from San Francisco on U.S. 101 and get off at CA 131/Tiburon Boulevard/East Blithedale Avenue (Exit 447). Turn right onto Tiburon Boulevard and drive just over 4 miles to downtown. Golden Gate Transit serves downtown Tiburon from San Francisco; watch for changes during evening rush hour. Tiburon's Main Street is made for wandering, as are the footpaths that frame the water's edge.

ESSENTIALS

Visitor Information Tiburon. ✉ *Town Hall, 1505 Tiburon Blvd.* ☎ *415/435–7373* ⊕ *www.destinationtiburon.org.*

EXPLORING

FAMILY **Ark Row.** The second block of Main Street is known as Ark Row and has a tree-shaded walk lined with antiques and specialty stores. Some of the buildings are actually old 19th-century ark houseboats that floated in Belvedere Cove before being beached and transformed into stores.

■TIP→ If you're curious about architectural history, the Tiburon Heritage & Arts Commission has a self-guided walking-tour map, available online and at local businesses. ⊠ *Ark Row, Main St., south of Juanita La.* ⊕ *tiburonheritageandarts.org.*

Old St. Hilary's Landmark and John Thomas Howell Wildflower Preserve. The architectural centerpiece of this attraction is a stark-white 1888 Carpenter Gothic church that overlooks the town and the bay from its hillside perch. Surrounding the church, which was dedicated as a historical monument in 1959, is a wildflower preserve that's spectacular in May and June, when the rare black or Tiburon jewel flower blooms. Expect a steep walk uphill to reach the preserve. The Landmarks Society will arrange guided tours by appointment. ■TIP→ The hiking trails behind the landmark wind up to a peak that has views of the entire Bay Area. ⊠ *201 Esperanza St., off Mar West St. or Beach Rd.* ☎ *415/435–1853* ⊕ *landmarkssociety.com/landmarks/st-hilarys/* ⊗ *Church closed Mon.– Sat. and Nov.–Mar.*

WHERE TO EAT

$$$
AMERICAN
✕ **The Caprice.** For more than 50 years this Tiburon landmark that overlooks the bay has been the place to come to mark special occasions with local wines and European-American comfort food. The views are spectacular, and soft-yellow walls and starched white tablecloths help to make the space bright and light. **Known for:** seared sea scallops; shellfish risotto; rack of lamb; California wines. $ *Average main: $28* ⊠ *2000 Paradise Dr.* ☎ *415/435–3400* ⊕ *www.thecaprice.com* ⊗ *No lunch.*

$$$
SICILIAN
✕ **Luna Blu.** Friendly, informative staff serve Sicilian-inspired seafood in this lively sliver of an Italian restaurant just a stone's throw from the ferry. Take a seat on the heated patio overlooking the bay, or cozy up with friends on one of the high-sided booths near the bar. **Known for:** sustainably caught seafood and local, organic ingredients; weekend English tea service. $ *Average main: $25* ⊠ *35 Main St.* ☎ *415/789–5844* ⊕ *lunablurestaurant.com* ⊗ *Closed Tues. No lunch weekdays.*

$
AMERICAN
FAMILY
✕ **New Morning Cafe.** Omelets and scrambles are served all day long at this homey triangular bay-side café with sunny outdoor seating. If you're past morning treats, choose from the many soups, salads, and sandwiches, best enjoyed at picnic tables. **Known for:** hearty American breakfast fare. $ *Average main: $13* ⊠ *1696 Tiburon Blvd., near Juanita Ln.* ☎ *415/435–4315* ⊗ *No dinner.*

$$$
AMERICAN
✕ **Sam's Anchor Cafe.** Open since 1920, this casual dockside restaurant, rife with plastic chairs and blue-checked oilcloths, is the town's most famous eatery. Most people flock to the deck for beers, views, sunsets, and exceptionally tasty seafood. **Known for:** cioppino; Painted Hills natural beef burgers; patio beverages. $ *Average main: $24* ⊠ *27 Main St.* ☎ *415/435–4527* ⊕ *www.samscafe.com.*

WHERE TO STAY

$$$$
B&B/INN
🛏 **Waters Edge Hotel.** Checking into this stylish downtown hotel feels like tucking away into an inviting retreat by the water—the views are stunning and the lighting is perfect. **Pros:** complimentary wine and cheese for guests every evening; restaurants/sights are minutes away; free bike rentals for guests; pet-friendly; free Wi-Fi. **Cons:** downstairs rooms

lack privacy and balconies; paid self-parking; fitness center is off-site. ⑤ *Rooms from: $279* ✉ *25 Main St., off Tiburon Blvd.* ☎ *415/789–5999, 877/789–5999* ⊕ *www.marinhotels.com* ⤴ *23 rooms* ❖| *Breakfast.*

MILL VALLEY

2 miles north of Sausalito, 4 miles north of Golden Gate Bridge.

Chic and woodsy Mill Valley has a dual personality. Here, as elsewhere in the county, the foundation is a superb natural setting. Virtually surrounded by parkland, the town lies at the base of Mt. Tamalpais and contains dense redwood groves traversed by countless creeks. But this is no lumber camp. Smart restaurants and chichi boutiques line streets that have been traversed by more rock stars than one might suspect.

The rustic village flavor isn't a modern conceit, but a holdover from the town's early days as a center for the lumber industry. In 1896, the Mt. Tamalpais Scenic Railroad—dubbed "The Crookedest Railroad in the World" because of its curvy tracks—began transporting visitors from Mill Valley to the top of Mt. Tam and down to Muir Woods, and the town soon became a vacation retreat for city slickers. The trains stopped running in the 1930s, as cars became more popular, but the old railway depot still serves as the center of town: the 1929 building has been transformed into the popular Depot Bookstore & Cafe, at 87 Throckmorton Avenue.

The small downtown area has the constant bustle of a leisure community; even at noon on a Tuesday, people are out shopping for fancy cookware, eco-friendly home furnishings, and boutique clothing.

GETTING HERE AND AROUND
By car from San Francisco, head north on U.S. 101 and get off at CA 131/Tiburon Boulevard/East Blithedale Avenue (Exit 447). Turn left onto East Blithedale Avenue and continue west to Throckmorton Avenue; turn left to reach Lytton Square, then park. Golden Gate Transit buses serve Mill Valley from San Francisco. Once here, explore the town on foot.

ESSENTIALS
Visitor Information Mill Valley Chamber of Commerce and Visitor Center. ✉ *85 Throckmorton Ave.* ☎ *415/388–9700* ⊕ *www.millvalley.org.*

EXPLORING
FAMILY **Lytton Square.** Mill Valley locals congregate on weekends to socialize in the coffeehouses and cafés near the town's central square, but it bustles most of the day. Shops, restaurants, and cultural venues line the nearby streets. ✉ *Miller and Throckmorton Aves.*

OFF THE
BEATEN
PATH

Marin County Civic Center. A wonder of arches, circles, and skylights just 10 miles north of Mill Valley, the Civic Center was Frank Lloyd Wright's largest public project and has been designated a national and state historic landmark, as well as a UNESCO World Heritage Site. One-hour docent-led tours leave from the café on the second floor Wednesday mornings at 10:30. Or grab a self-guided tour map from the center's gift shop or website. ✉ *3501 Civic Center Dr., off N. San Pedro Rd., San Rafael* ☎ *415/473–3762 Visitor Services Office* ⊕ *www.marincounty. org/depts/cu/tours* 🎟 *Free admission; $10 tour fee.*

WHERE TO EAT

$$$ ✕ **Balboa Café.** With intimate lighting, rich wood accents, and fresh-
AMERICAN pressed white linens, this modern California café offers an upscale
dining experience complete with classic cocktails, an extensive wine
list, and beautiful bistro-inspired dishes that feature locally sourced
ingredients. The bar is always bustling, with a daily happy hour
that extends into dinner; brunch is served on the weekends. **Known
for:** Balboa burger; local wines; huevos rancheros; Dungeness crab
risotto; Japanese himachi crudo. $ *Average main: $24* ✉ *38 Miller
Ave., at Sunnyside Ave.* ☎ *415/381–7321* ⊕ *balboacafemv.com* ⊗ *No
lunch Mon.*

$$$ ✕ **Buckeye Roadhouse.** House-smoked meats and fish, grilled steaks, clas-
AMERICAN sic salads, and decadent desserts bring locals and visitors back again
and again to this 1937 lodge-style roadhouse. Enjoy a Marin martini
at the cozy mahogany bar or sip local wine beside the river-rock fireplace. **Known for:** oysters dingo; chili-lime "brick" chicken; smoked
beef brisket. $ *Average main: $30* ✉ *15 Shoreline Hwy., off U.S. 101*
☎ *415/331–2600* ⊕ *www.buckeyeroadhouse.com.*

$$$$ ✕ **El Paseo.** Rock & Roll Hall of Famer Sammy Hagar helped to restore
CONTEMPORARY this 1947 California Mission–style restaurant, which reopened in
2011 with a Spanish-influenced California cuisine menu. The secluded
brick walkway, bougainvillea-framed courtyard, and candlelit dining
room provide the perfect setting for a romantic night out. **Known
for:** deviled eggs with crispy chorizo; Akaushi steak frites; patio-side
paella; daily happy hour. $ *Average main: $32* ✉ *17 Throckmorton
Ave., at E. Blithedale Ave.* ☎ *415/388–0741* ⊕ *www.elpaseomillvalley.
com* ⊗ *No lunch.*

$$$$ ✕ **Molina.** A cozy and clean aesthetic, a convivial vibe, and impeccable
CONTEMPORARY cuisine have turned this snug neighborhood spot into a destination
Fodor's Choice restaurant. Owner-chef (and DJ) Todd Shoberg creates a modest nightly
★ menu of small plates, entrées, and desserts that focus on wood-fired
offerings and the freshest local ingredients. **Known for:** California
coastal dishes; curated wine menu. $ *Average main: $32* ✉ *17 Madrona
St., between Lovell and Throckmorton Aves.* ☎ *415/383–4200* ⊕ *www.
molinarestaurant.com* ⊗ *No lunch.*

WHERE TO STAY

$$$$ 🏨 **Mill Valley Inn.** The only hotel in downtown Mill Valley is comprised
B&B/INN of a main building, the Creek House, with smart-looking European-
inspired rooms, and two small cottages tucked among the trees. **Pros:**
minutes from local shops and restaurants; some rooms have balconies,
soaking tubs, and fireplaces; free parking; free mountain bikes. **Cons:**
limited room service; dark in winter because of surrounding trees; some
rooms are not accessible via elevator. $ *Rooms from: $289* ✉ *165
Throckmorton Ave., near Miller Ave.* ☎ *415/389–6608, 855/334–7946*
⊕ *www.marinhotels.com* ⇆ *25 rooms* ⦿*Breakfast.*

$$ 🏨 **Mountain Home Inn.** Abutting 40,000 acres of state and national parks,
B&B/INN this airy wooden inn sits on the skirt of Mt. Tamalpais, where you
can follow hiking trails all the way to Stinson Beach. **Pros:** amazing
terrace and views; peaceful, remote setting; in-room massage avail-
able; cooked-to-order breakfast. **Cons:** nearest town is a 12-minute

drive away; restaurant can get crowded on sunny weekend days; no on-site fitness option. ⑤ *Rooms from: $199* ✉ *810 Panoramic Hwy., at Edgewood Ave.* ☎ *415/381–9000* ⊕ *www.mtnhomeinn.com* ⇨ *10 rooms* ⦿ *Breakfast.*

NIGHTLIFE

BREWPUS AND BEERGARDENS
Mill Valley Beerworks. A great place to rest your feet after shopping or hiking, this neighborhood taproom serves a rotating selection of local and imported drafts and bottles. A simple menu of small plates and mains includes locally sourced cheeses, brussels sprouts, and burgers. ✉ *173 Throckmorton Ave.* ☎ *415/888–8218* ⊕ *millvalleybeerworks.com.*

MUSIC VENUES
Sweetwater Music Hall. With the help of part-owner Bob Weir of the Grateful Dead, this renowned nightclub and café reopened in a historic Masonic Hall in 2012. Famous as well as up-and-coming bands play on most nights, and local stars such as Bonnie Raitt and Huey Lewis have been known to stop in for a pickup session. ✉ *19 Corte Madera Ave., between Throckmorton and Lovell Aves.* ☎ *415/388–3850, 877/987–6487 tickets* ⊕ *www.sweetwatermusichall.com.*

MUIR WOODS NATIONAL MONUMENT

12 miles northwest of the Golden Gate Bridge.

Climbing hundreds of feet into the sky, *Sequoia sempervirens* are the tallest living things on Earth—some are more than 1,800 years old. One of the last remaining old-growth stands of these redwood behemoths, Muir Woods is nature's cathedral: imposing, awe-inspiring, reverence-inducing, and not to be missed.

GETTING HERE AND AROUND
If you drive to Muir Woods on a weekend or during peak season, expect to find epic traffic jams around the tiny parking areas and adjacent roads. Do yourself a favor and take a shuttle if you can. Marin Transit's Route 66 Muir Woods shuttle (*$5 round-trip* ⊕ *www.marintransit.org*) provides regular transport from the Sausalito ferry landing, as well as Marin City, on a seasonal schedule. Private bus tours run year-round. To drive directly from San Francisco by car, take U.S. 101 north across the Golden Gate Bridge to exit 445B for Mill Valley/Stinson Beach, then follow signs for Highway 1 north and Muir Woods.

EXPLORING
FAMILY

Fodor's Choice

★

Muir Woods National Monument. Nothing gives perspective like walking among some of the world's last old-growth redwoods. The 550 acres of Muir Woods National Monument contain some of the most majestic redwoods in the world—some more than 250 feet tall. Though much of California's 2 million acres of redwood forest were lost to the logging industry, this stand was saved from destruction by William and Elizabeth Kent, who purchased the land in 1905, and later gifted it to the federal government. Theodore Roosevelt declared the space a national monument in 1908 and Kent named it after naturalist John Muir, whose environmental campaigns helped to establish the national park system.

The gorgeous old-growth redwood trees in Muir Woods are often enveloped in fog, which provides the moisture to help them survive the dry summers.

Part of the Golden Gate National Recreation Area, Muir Woods is a pedestrian's park. The popular 2-mile main trail, which begins at the park headquarters, has been covered by a wooden boardwalk, and provides easy access to streams, ferns, azaleas, and redwood groves. Summer weekends can prove busy, so if you prefer a little serenity, consider taking a more challenging route, such as the **Dipsea Trail** which climbs west from the forest floor to soothing views of the ocean and the Golden Gate Bridge. For a complete list of trails, which vary in difficulty and distance, check with rangers.

Picnicking and camping aren't allowed, and neither are pets. Crowds can be large, especially from May through October, so try to come early in the morning or late in the afternoon. The **Muir Woods Visitor Center** has books and exhibits about redwood trees and the woods' history; the **Muir Woods Trading Company** serves hot food, organic pastries, and other tasty snacks, and the gift shop offers plenty of souvenirs.

◼TIP➜ Cell service in the park is limited, so plan directions and communication ahead of time. ⊠ *1 Muir Woods Rd., off Panoramic Hwy., Mill Valley* ☎ *415/388–2595 park information, 511 Marin transit* ⊕ *www.nps.gov/muwo* ⊠ *$10; free on government holidays.*

MT. TAMALPAIS STATE PARK

13 miles northwest of Golden Gate Bridge.

The view of Mt. Tamalpais from all around the bay can be a beauty, but that's nothing compared to the views *from* the mountain, which range from jaw-dropping to spectacular and take in San Francisco, the East Bay, the coast, and beyond—on a clear day, all the way to the Farallon Islands, 25 miles away.

GETTING HERE AND AROUND

By car, take U.S. 101 north across the Golden Gate Bridge and exit 445B for Mill Valley/Stinson Beach. Continue north on Highway 1, which will turn into Panoramic Highway. By bus, take Golden Gate Transit to Marin City; in Marin City transfer to the West Marin Stagecoach, Route 61, and get off at Pantoll Ranger Station (*415/226–0855* ⊕ *www.marintransit. org/stage.html*). Once here, the only way to explore is on foot or by bike.

EXPLORING

FAMILY

Fodor's Choice

★

Mt. Tamalpais State Park. Although the summit of Mt. Tamalpais is only 2,571 feet high, the mountain rises practically from sea level, dominating the topography of Marin County. Adjacent to Muir Woods National Monument, Mt. Tamalpais State Park affords views of the entire Bay Area and the Pacific Ocean to the west. The name for the sacred mount comes from the Coast Miwok tribe and means "west hill," though some have tied it to a folktale about the "sleeping maiden" in the mountain's profile. For years the 6,300-acre park has been a favorite destination for hikers. There are more than 200 miles of trails, some rugged but many developed for easy walking through meadows, grasslands, and forests and along creeks. Mt. Tam, as it's called by locals, is also the birthplace (in the 1970s) of mountain biking, and today many spandex-clad bikers whiz down the park's winding roads.

The park's major thoroughfare, Panoramic Highway, snakes its way up from U.S. 101 to the **Pantoll Ranger Station** and then drops down to the town of Stinson Beach. Pantoll Road branches off the highway at the station, connecting up with Ridgecrest Boulevard. Along these roads are numerous parking areas, picnic spots, scenic overlooks, and trailheads. Parking is free along the roadside, but there's an $8 fee (cash or check only) at the ranger station and additional charges for walk-in campsites and group use.

The **Mountain Theater,** also known as the Cushing Memorial Amphitheatre, is a natural 4,000-seat amphitheater that was reconstructed with stone by the Civilian Conservation Corps in the 1930s. It has showcased summer "Mountain Plays" since 1913.

The **Rock Spring Trail** starts at the Mountain Theater and gently climbs for 1½ miles to the **West Point Inn,** which was once a stop on the Mt. Tam railroad route. Relax at a picnic table and stock up on water before forging ahead, via Old Railroad Grade Fire Road and the Miller Trail, to Mt. Tam's Middle Peak, which is another 1½–2 miles depending on route.

Starting from the Pantoll Ranger Station, the precipitous **Steep Ravine Trail** brings you past stands of coastal redwoods and, in the springtime, small waterfalls. Take the connecting **Dipsea Trail** to reach the town of Stinson Beach and its swath of golden sand. ■ TIP➜ If you're too weary to make the 3½-mile trek back up, Marin Transit Bus 61 takes you from Stinson Beach back to the ranger station. ⊠ *Pantoll Ranger Station, 3801 Panoramic Hwy., at Pantoll Rd.* ☎ *415/388–2070* ⊕ *www.parks.ca.gov.*

BEACH TOWNS

The winds whip wildly around Marin County's miles of coastline. The unruly waves and cool breeze make it more of an adventure than your typical day at the beach. Still, the natural beauty, rocky shores, and stunning views are nothing to balk at.

GETTING HERE AND AROUND

If you're driving, take U.S. 101 north to exit 445B (Highway 1 toward Mill Valley/Stinson Beach) and follow signs. Public transit serves Stinson Beach and Bolinas, but not Muir Beach.

MUIR BEACH

12 miles northwest of Golden Gate Bridge, 6 miles southwest of Mill Valley.

Except on the sunniest of weekends, Muir Beach is relatively quiet, but the drive here can be quite the scenic adventure.

GETTING HERE AND AROUND

A car is the best way to reach Muir Beach. From Highway 1, follow Pacific Way southwest ¼ mile.

EXPLORING

Green Gulch Farm Zen Center. Giant eucalyptus trees frame the long and winding road that leads to this tranquil Buddhist practice center. Meditation programs, tea instruction, gardening classes, and various other workshops and events take place here; there's also an extensive organic garden. Visitors are welcome to roam the property and walk through the gardens that reach down toward Muir Beach. Public Sunday programs are especially geared toward visitors. ⊠ *1601 Shoreline Hwy., at Green Gulch Rd.* ☎ *415/383–3134 welcome center* ⊕ *www.sfzc.org* ⊠ *free.*

BEACHES

FAMILY **Muir Beach.** Small but scenic, this beach—a rocky patch of shoreline off Highway 1 in the northern Marin Headlands—is a good place to stretch your legs and gaze out at the Pacific. Locals often walk their dogs here; families and cuddling couples come for picnicking and sunbathing. At one end of the sand are waterfront homes (and occasional nude sunbathers) and at the other are the bluffs of the Golden Gate National Recreation Area. A land bridge connects directly from the parking lot to the beach, as well as a short trail that leads to a scenic overlook and connects to other coastal paths. **Amenities:** parking (free); toilets. **Best for:** solitude; sunsets; walking. ⊠ *100 Pacific Way, off Shoreline Hwy.* ⊕ *www.nps.gov/goga/planyourvisit/muirbeach.htm.*

WHERE TO STAY

$$$ **Pelican Inn.** From its slate roof to its whitewashed plaster walls, this
B&B/INN inn looks so Tudor that it's hard to believe it was built in the 1970s, but the Pelican is English to the core, with its cozy upstairs guest rooms (no elevator), draped half-tester beds, a sun-filled solarium, and bangers and grilled tomatoes for breakfast. **Pros:** five-minute walk to beach; great bar and restaurant; peaceful setting. **Cons:** 20-minute drive to nearby attractions; rooms are quite small and rustic; remote location; limited amenities. ⑤ *Rooms from: $222* ⊠ *10 Pacific Way, off Hwy. 1* ☎ *415/383–6000* ⊕ *www.pelicaninn.com* ⤺ *7 rooms* ⊠ *Breakfast.*

STINSON BEACH

20 miles northwest of Golden Gate Bridge.

This laid-back hamlet is all about the beach, and folks come from all over the Bay Area to walk its sandy, often windswept shore. Ideal day trip: a morning hike at Mt. Tam followed by lunch at one of Stinson's unassuming eateries and a leisurely beach stroll.

GETTING HERE AND AROUND

If you're driving, take U.S. 101 to the Mill Valley/Stinson Beach/Highway 1 exit and follow the road west and then north. By bus, take Golden Gate Transit to Marin City and then transfer to the West Marin Stagecoach (61) for Bolinas.

BEACHES

FAMILY **Stinson Beach.** When the fog hasn't rolled in, this expansive stretch of sand is about as close as you can get in Marin to the stereotypical feel of a Southern California beach. There are several clothing-optional areas, among them a section called Red Rock Beach. ⚠ **Swimming at Stinson Beach can be dangerous; the undertow is strong and sharks sightings, though infrequent, have occurred; lifeguards are on duty May–September.** On any hot summer weekend, roads to Stinson are packed and the parking lot fills, so factor this into your plans. The town itself—population 600, give or take—has a nonchalant surfer vibe, with a few good eating options and pleasant hippie-craftsy browsing. **Amenities:** food and drink; lifeguards; parking (free); showers; toilets. **Best for:** nudists; sunset; surfing; swimming; walking. ⊠ *Hwy. 1, 1 Calle Del Sierra* ☏ *415/868–0942 lifeguard tower* ⊕ *www.stinsonbeachonline. com* ☞ *No pets allowed on the beach.*

WHERE TO EAT AND STAY

$$ ✕ **Parkside Cafe.** The Parkside is popular for its 1950s beachfront snack bar, but the adjoining café, coffee bar, marketplace, and bakery shouldn't be missed either. A full menu featuring fresh ingredients, local seafood, wood-fired pizzas, and just-baked breads is served. **Known for:** local seafood; clam chowder; rustic house-made breads. ⑤ *Average main: $21* ⊠ *43 Arenal Ave., off Shoreline Hwy.* ☏ *415/868–1272* ⊕ *www.parksidecafe.com.*

AMERICAN
FAMILY

$$ ✕ **Sand Dollar Restaurant.** Constructed from three barges that were floated over from Tiburon in the 1920s, this family-owned restaurant still attracts wayfarers from Muir Beach to Bolinas. Sip whiskey at the bar or nosh on local seafood and down a beer on the deck, preferably on warm summer weekends, when live jazz and blue grass draw a vibrant crowd. **Known for:** fresh seafood; local oysters; sunny patio for dining and drinking. ⑤ *Average main: $20* ⊠ *3458 Shoreline Hwy.* ☏ *415/868–0434* ⊕ *www.stinsonbeachrestaurant.com.*

AMERICAN
Fodor's Choice
★

$$ ⊞ **Sandpiper Lodging.** Recharge, rest, and enjoy the local scenery at this ultrapopular lodging that books up months, even years, in advance. **Pros:** beach chairs, towels, and toys provided; lush gardens with BBQ; minutes from the beach and town; free resident car parking. **Cons:** walls are thin; limited amenities. ⑤ *Rooms from: $165* ⊠ *1 Marine Way, off Arenal Ave.* ☏ *415/868–1632* ⊕ *www.sandpiperstinsonbeach.com* ☞ *11 rooms* ❏ *No meals.*

B&B/INN
FAMILY

$ ⊞ **Stinson Beach Motel.** Built in the 1930s, this motel is surrounded by flowering greenery, and rooms are clean, simple, and summery. **Pros:** minutes from the beach; cozy, unpretentious rooms; kitchenettes in cottages. **Cons:** smaller rooms are cramped. ⑤ *Rooms from: $140* ⊠ *3416 Shoreline Hwy.* ☏ *415/868–1712* ⊕ *www.stinsonbeachmotel.com* ☞ *8 rooms* ❏ *No meals.*

B&B/INN

POINT REYES NATIONAL SEASHORE

Bear Valley Visitor Center is 12 miles north of Bolinas.

With sandy beaches stretching for miles, a dramatic rocky coastline, a gem of a lighthouse, and idyllic, century-old dairy farms, Point Reyes National Seashore is one of the most varied and strikingly beautiful corners of the Bay Area.

GETTING HERE AND AROUND

From San Francisco, take U.S. 101 north, head west at Sir Francis Drake Boulevard (Exit 450B) toward San Anselmo, and follow the road just under 20 miles to Bear Valley Road. From Stinson Beach or Bolinas, drive north on Highway 1 and turn left on Bear Valley Road. If you're going by bus, take one of several Golden Gate Transit buses to Marin City; in Marin City transfer to the West Marin Stagecoach (you'll switch buses in Olema). Once at the visitor center, the best way to get around is on foot.

EXPLORING

FAMILY **Bear Valley Visitor Center.** A life-size orca model hovers over the center's engaging exhibits about the wildlife and history of the Point Reyes National Seashore. The rangers at the barnlike facility are fonts of information about beaches, whale-watching, hiking trails, and camping. Restrooms are available, as well as trailhead parking and a picnic area with barbecue grills. Winter hours may be shorter and summer weekend hours may be longer; call or check the website for details. ⊠ *Bear Valley Visitor Center, 1 Bear Valley Visitor Center Access Rd., west of Hwy. 1, off Bear Valley Rd., Point Reyes Station* ☎ *415/464–5100* ⊕ *www.nps.gov/pore/planyourvisit.*

FAMILY
Fodor's Choice
★
Duxbury Reef. Excellent tide pooling can be had along the 3-mile shoreline of Duxbury Reef; it's the most extensive tide pool area near Point Reyes National Seashore, as well as one of the largest shale intertidal reefs in North America. Look for sea stars, barnacles, sea anemones, purple urchins, limpets, sea mussels, and the occasional abalone. But check a tide table (*tidesandcurrents.noaa.gov*) or the local papers if you plan to explore the reef—it's accessible only at low tide. The reef is a 30-minute drive from the Bear Valley Visitor Center. Take Highway 1 south from the center, turn right at Olema–Bolinas Road (keep an eye peeled; the road is easy to miss), left on Horseshoe Hill Road, right on Mesa Road, left on Overlook Drive, and then right on Elm Road, which dead-ends at the Agate Beach County Park parking lot. ⊹ *At Duxbury Point, 1 mile west of Bolinas* ⊕ *www.ptreyes.org/activities/tidepools.*

FAMILY **Palomarin Field Station & Point Reyes Bird Observatory.** Birders adore Point Blue Conservation Science, which maintains the Palomarin Field Station and the Point Reyes Bird Observatory (PRBO) that are located in the southernmost part of Point Reyes National Seashore. The Field Station, open daily from sunrise to sunset, has excellent interpretive exhibits, including a comparative display of real birds' talons. The surrounding woods harbor some 200 bird species. As you hike the quiet trails through forest and along ocean cliffs, you're likely to see biologists banding birds to aid in the study of their life cycles. ■ TIP→ Visit Point Blue's website for

detailed directions and to find out when banding will occur. ✉ *999 Mesa Rd., Bolinas* ☎ *415/868–0655 field station, use ext. 395 to check conditions, 707/781–2555 headquarters* ⊕ *www.pointblue.org.*

FAMILY
Fodor's Choice
★ **Point Reyes Lighthouse & Visitor Center.** In operation since December 1, 1870, this lighthouse—which was decommissioned in 1975—is one of the premier attractions of the Point Reyes National Seashore. It occupies the tip of Point Reyes, 21 miles from the Bear Valley Visitor Center, a scenic 40-minute drive over hills scattered with longtime dairy farms. The lighthouse originally cast a rotating beam lighted by four concentric wicks that burned lard oil. Keeping the wicks lighted and the 6,000-pound Fresnel lens soot-free in Point Reyes's perpetually foggy climate was a constant struggle that reputedly drove a few early attendants to alcoholism and insanity.

■TIP➔ The lighthouse is one of the best spots on the coast for watching gray whales. On both legs of their annual migration, the magnificent animals pass close enough to see with the naked eye. Southern migration peaks in mid-January, and the whales head back north in March; see the slower mothers and calves in late April and early May. Humpback whales can be spotted feeding in the summer months.

On busy whale-watching weekends (from late December through mid-April), buses shuttle visitors from the Drakes Beach parking lot to the top of the stairs leading down to the lighthouse and the road is closed to private vehicles. However you've arrived, consider whether you have it in you to walk down—and up—the 308 steps to the lighthouse. The view from the bottom is worth the effort, but the whales are also visible from the cliffs above the lighthouse. Keep in mind that the parking lot is a quarter-mile trek from the visitor center and the lighthouse steps are open only during visitor center hours. ■TIP➔ Winds can be chilly, and food, water, gas, and other resources are scarce, so be sure to come prepared. ✉ *Lighthouse Visitor Center, 27000 Sir Francis Drake Blvd., western end of Sir Francis Drake Blvd., Inverness* ☎ *415/669–1534 visitor center* ⊕ *www.nps.gov/pore/planyourvisit/lighthouse.htm* ☾ *Closed Tues.–Thurs.* ☞ *Fee for weekend shuttle.*

FAMILY
Fodor's Choice
★ **Point Reyes National Seashore.** One of the Bay Area's most spectacular treasures and the only national seashore on the West Coast, the 71,000-acre Point Reyes National Seashore encompasses hiking trails, secluded beaches, and rugged grasslands as well as Point Reyes itself, a triangular peninsula that juts into the Pacific. The town of **Point Reyes Station** is a one-main-drag affair with some good places to eat and gift shops that sell locally made and imported goods.

When explorer Sir Francis Drake sailed along the California coast in 1579, he allegedly missed the Golden Gate and San Francisco Bay, but he did land at what he described as a convenient harbor. In 2012 the federal government conceded a centuries-long debate and officially recognized Drake's Bay, which flanks the point on the east, as that harbor, designating the spot a National Historic Landmark and silencing competing claims in the 433-year-old controversy. Today Point Reyes's hills and dramatic cliffs attract other kinds of explorers: hikers, whale-watchers, and solitude seekers.

The infamous San Andreas Fault runs along the park's eastern edge and up the center of Tomales Bay; take the short **Earthquake Trail** from the visitor center to see the impact near the epicenter of the 1906 earthquake that devastated San Francisco. A half-mile path from the visitor center leads to **Kule Loklo,** a reconstructed Miwok village that sheds light on the daily lives of the region's first inhabitants. From here, trails also lead to the park's hike-in campgrounds (no car camping).

■ TIP➜ In late winter and spring, take the short walk at Chimney Rock, just before the lighthouse, to the Elephant Seal Overlook. Even from the cliff, the male seals look enormous as they spar, growling and bloodied, for resident females.

You can experience the diversity of Point Reyes's ecosystems on the scenic **Coast Trail,** which starts at the Palomarin Trailhead, just outside Bolinas. From here, it's a 3-mile trek through eucalyptus groves and pine forests and along seaside cliffs to beautiful and tiny Bass Lake. To reach the Palomarin Trailhead, take Olema–Bolinas Road toward Bolinas, turn right on Mesa Road, follow signs to Point Blue Conservation Science, and then continue until the road dead-ends.

The 4.7-mile-long (one-way) **Tomales Point Trail** follows the spine of the park's northernmost finger of land through a Tule Elk Preserve, providing spectacular ocean views from the high bluffs. Expect to see elk, but keep your distance from the animals. To reach the moderately easy hiking trail, take Sir Francis Drake Boulevard through the town of Inverness; when you come to a fork, veer right to stay on Pierce Point Road and continue until you reach the parking lot at Pierce Point Ranch. ⊠ *Bear Valley Visitor Center, 1 Bear Valley Visitor Center Access Rd., west of Hwy. 1, off Bear Valley Rd., Point Reyes Station* ☎ *415/464–5100* ⊕ *www.nps.gov/pore.*

WHERE TO EAT

$$
PIZZA
FAMILY

✕ **Café Reyes.** Sunny patio seating, hand-tossed pizza, and organic local ingredients are the selling points of this laid-back café. The semi-industrial dining room, which is built around a brick oven, features glazed concrete floors, warm-painted walls, and ceilings high enough to accommodate full-size market umbrellas. **Known for:** wood-fired pizza; Drake's Bay fresh oysters; outdoor patio dining. $ *Average main: $16* ⊠ *11101 Hwy. 1, Point Reyes Station* ☎ *415/663–9493* ⊗ *Closed Mon. and Tues.*

$$$
SEAFOOD
FAMILY
Fodor's Choice
★

✕ **Hog Island Oyster Co. Marshall Oyster Farm & the Boat Oyster Bar.** Take a short trek north on Highway 1 to the gritty mecca of Bay Area oysters—the Hog Island Marshall Oyster Farm. For a real culinary adventure, arrange to shuck and barbecue your own oysters on one of the outdoor grills (all tools supplied, reservations required), or for the less adventurous, the Boat Oyster Bar is an informal outdoor café that serves raw and BBQ oysters, local snacks, and tasty beverages. **Known for:** fresh, raw, and BBQ oysters. $ *Average main: $25* ⊠ *20215 Shoreline Hwy.* ☎ *415/663–9218* ⊕ *hogislandoysters.com/locations/marshall* ⊗ *Oyster Bar closed Tues.–Thurs. No dinner.*

$$ ✕ **Osteria Stellina.** Chef-owner Christian Caiazzo's menu of "Point Reyes
ITALIAN   Italian" cuisine puts an emphasis on showcasing hyperlocal ingredients
Fodor's Choice   like Marin-grown kale and Sonoma cheese. Pastas, pizzas, and a hand-
★   ful of entrées are served in a rustic-contemporary space with a raw
bar that serves local oysters all day long. **Known for:** locally sourced
produce and seafood; fresh oysters; inventive pizzas; decadent desserts.
⑤ *Average main: $20 ✉ 11285 Hwy. 1, at 3rd St., Point Reyes Station*
☎ *415/663–9988 ⊕ www.osteriastellina.com.*

$$$$ ✕ **Sir and Star at the Olema.** With lovely garden views, creative and crypti-
AMERICAN   cally named dishes, and upscale-rustic decor that somehow incorporates
taxidermied animals, this historic roadhouse (located within the Olema
Inn) elicits both rants and raves, often from diners sharing the same
table. The locally focused menu of California cuisine changes season-
ally; a special prix fixe is offered by reservation on Saturday evenings.
Known for: inventive presentation of local ingredients; avant-garde
small plates. ⑤ *Average main: $35 ✉ 10000 Sir Francis Drake Blvd.,
at Hwy. 1, Olema ☎ 415/663–1034 ⊕ sirandstar.com ☾ Closed Mon.
and Tues. No lunch.*

$$ ✕ **Station House Cafe.** In good weather, hikers fresh from the park fill
AMERICAN   the Station House's lovely outdoor garden as well as its homey indoor
tables, banquettes, and bar stools, so prepare for a wait. The com-
munity-centric eatery is locally focused and serves a blend of modern
and classic California dishes comprised of organic seasonal ingredients, sustainable hormone-free meats, and wild-caught seafood. **Known
for:** signature popovers; hearty breakfast items; local fresh seafood.
⑤ *Average main: $22 ✉ 11180 Hwy. 1, at 2nd St., Point Reyes Station*
☎ *415/663–1515 ⊕ www.stationhousecafe.com ☾ Closed Wed.*

NAPA AND
SONOMA

WELCOME TO NAPA AND SONOMA

TOP REASONS TO GO

★ **Touring wineries:** Let's face it: this is the reason you're here, and the range of excellent sips to sample would make any oeno-phile (or novice drinker, for that matter) giddy.

★ **Biking:** Gentle hills and vineyard-laced farmland make Napa and Sonoma perfect for combining lei-surely back-roads cycling with winery stops.

★ **Browsing the farmers' markets:** Many towns in Napa and Sonoma have seasonal farmers' markets, each rounding up an amazing variety of local produce.

★ **A meal at The French Laundry:** Chef Thomas Keller's Yountville restau-rant is one of the country's best. The mastery of flavors and attention to detail are subtly remarkable.

★ **Wandering di Rosa:** Though this art and nature preserve is just off the busy Carneros Highway, it's a relatively unknown treasure. The galleries and gardens are filled with hundreds of artworks.

1 Napa Valley. You'll find big names all around, from high-profile wineries to world-renowned chefs. Napa, the valley's oldest town, sweet-life St. Helena, and down-to-earth Calistoga all make good home bases here. Calistoga has the extra draw of local thermal springs. Yountville has become a culinary boomtown, while the tiny communities of Oakville and Rutherford are home to historic wineries such as Robert Mondavi and Ingle-nook. Rutherford in particu-lar is the source for outstanding Cabernet Sauvignon.

2 Sonoma Valley. Historic attractions and an unpreten-tious attitude prevail here. The town of Sonoma, with its picture-perfect central plaza, is rich with 19th-century buildings. Glen Ellen, meanwhile, has a special connection with author Jack London.

GETTING ORIENTED

The Napa and Sonoma valleys run parallel, northwest to southeast , and are separated by the Mayacamas Mountains. Southwest of Sonoma Valley are several other important viticultural areas in Sonoma county, including the Dry Creek, Alexander, and Russian River Valleys. The Carneros, which spans southern Sonoma and Napa counties, is just north of San Pablo Bay.

Updated by
Daniel Mangin

In California's premier wine region, the pleasures of eating and drinking are celebrated daily. It's easy to join in at famous wineries and rising newcomers off country roads, or at trendy in-town tasting rooms. Chefs transform local ingredients into feasts, and gourmet groceries sell perfect picnic fare. Yountville, Healdsburg, and St. Helena have small-town charm as well as luxurious inns, hotels, and spas, yet the natural setting is equally sublime, whether experienced from a canoe on the Russian River or the deck of a winery overlooking endless rows of vines.

The Wine Country is also rich in history. In Sonoma you can explore California's Spanish and Mexican pasts at the Sonoma Mission, and the origins of modern California wine making at Buena Vista Winery. Some wineries, among them St. Helena's Beringer and Rutherford's Inglenook, have cellars or tasting rooms dating to the late 1800s. Calistoga is a flurry of late-19th-century Steamboat Gothic architecture, though the town's oldest-looking building, the medieval-style Castello di Amorosa, is a 21st-century creation.

Tours at the Napa Valley's Beringer, Mondavi, and Inglenook—and at Buena Vista in the Sonoma Valley—provide an entertaining overview of Wine Country history. The tour at the splashy visitor center at St. Helena's Hall winery will introduce you to 21st-century wine-making technology, and over in Glen Ellen's Benziger Family Winery you can see how its vineyard managers apply biodynamic farming principles to grape growing. At numerous facilities you can play winemaker for a day at seminars in the fine art of blending wines. If that strikes you as too much effort, you can always pamper yourself at a luxury spa.

To delve further into the fine art of Wine Country living, pick up a copy of *Fodor's Napa and Sonoma*.

PLANNING

WHEN TO GO

High season extends from April through October. In summer, expect the days to be hot and dry, the roads filled with cars, and traffic heavy at the tasting rooms. Hotel rates are highest during the height of harvest, in September and October. Then and in summer book lodgings well ahead. November, except for Thanksgiving week, and December before Christmas are less busy. The weather in Napa and Sonoma is pleasant nearly year-round. Daytime temperatures average from about 55°F during winter to the 80s in summer, when readings in the 90s and higher are common. April, May, and October are milder but still warm. The rainiest months are usually from December through March.

GETTING HERE AND AROUND

AIR TRAVEL

Wine Country regulars often bypass San Francisco and Oakland and fly into Santa Rosa's Charles M. Schulz Sonoma County Airport (STS) on Alaska, Allegiant, and American, nonstop from several West Coast cities, Las Vegas, and Phoenix. Several major agencies rent cars here. ■ TIP→ Alaska allows passengers flying out of STS to check up to one case of wine for free.

BUS TRAVEL

Bus travel is an inconvenient way to explore the Wine Country, though it is possible. Take Golden Gate Transit from San Francisco to connect with Sonoma County Transit buses. VINE connects with BART commuter trains in the East Bay and the San Francisco Bay Ferry in Vallejo *(see Ferry Travel, below)*. VINE buses serve the Napa Valley and connect the towns of Napa and Sonoma.

CAR TRAVEL

Driving your own car is by far the most convenient way to get to and explore the Wine Country. In light traffic, the trip from San Francisco or Oakland to the southern portion of either Napa or Sonoma should take about an hour. Distances between Wine Country towns are fairly short, and in normal traffic you can drive from one end of the Napa or Sonoma valley to the other in less than an hour. Although this is a mostly rural area, the usual rush hours still apply, and high-season weekend traffic can often be slow.

Five major roads serve the region. U.S. 101 and Highways 12 and 121 travel through Sonoma County. Highway 29 and the parallel, more scenic, and often less crowded Silverado Trail travel north–south between Napa and Calistoga.

The easiest way to travel between the Napa Valley and Sonoma County is along Highway 12/121 to the south, or Highway 128 to the north. Travel between the middle sections of either area requires taking the slow, winding drive over the Mayacamas Mountains on the Oakville Grade, which links Oakville, in Napa, and Glen Ellen, in Sonoma.

■ TIP→ If you're wine tasting, either select a designated driver or be careful of your wine intake—the police keep an eye out for tipsy drivers.

6

From San Francisco to Napa: Cross the Golden Gate Bridge, then go north on U.S. 101. Head east on Highway 37 toward Vallejo, then north on Highway 121, aka the Carneros Highway. Turn left (north) when Highway 121 runs into Highway 29.

From San Francisco to Sonoma: Cross the Golden Gate Bridge, then go north on U.S. 101, east on Highway 37 toward Vallejo, and north on Highway 121. When you reach Highway 12, take it north to the town of Sonoma. For Sonoma County destinations north of Sonoma Valley stay on U.S. 101, which passes through Santa Rosa and Healdsburg.

From Berkeley and Oakland: Take Interstate 80 north to Highway 37 west, then on to Highway 29 north. For the Napa Valley, continue on Highway 29; to reach Sonoma County, head west on Highway 121.

FERRY TRAVEL
The San Francisco Bay Ferry sails from the Ferry Building and Pier 41 in San Francisco to Vallejo, where you can board VINE Bus 11 to the town of Napa. Buses sometimes fill in for the ferries.

RESTAURANTS
Farm-to-table Modern American cuisine is the prevalent style in the Napa Valley and Sonoma County, but this encompasses both the delicate preparations of Thomas Keller's highly praised The French Laundry and the upscale comfort food served throughout the Wine Country. The quality (and hype) often means high prices, but you can also find appealing, inexpensive eateries, especially in the towns of Napa, Calistoga, Sonoma, and Santa Rosa, and many high-end delis prepare superb picnic fare. At pricey restaurants you can save money by having lunch instead of dinner. With a few exceptions (noted in individual restaurant listings), dress is informal. *Restaurant reviews have been shortened. For full information, visit Fodors.com.*

HOTELS
The fanciest accommodations are concentrated in the Napa Valley towns of Yountville, Rutherford, St. Helena, and Calistoga; Sonoma County's poshest lodgings are in Healdsburg. The spas, amenities, and exclusivity of high-end properties attract travelers with the means and desire for luxury living. The cities of Napa and Santa Rosa are the best bets for budget hotels and inns, but even at a lower price point you'll still find a touch of Wine Country glamour. On weekends, two- or even three-night minimum stays are commonly required at smaller lodgings. Book well ahead for stays at such places during the busy summer or fall season. If your party will include travelers under age 16, inquire about policies regarding younger guests; some smaller lodgings discourage (or discreetly forbid) children. *Hotel reviews have been shortened. For full information, visit Fodors.com.*

WHAT IT COSTS				
	$	**$$**	**$$$**	**$$$$**
Restaurants	under $16	$16–$22	$23–$30	over $30
Hotels	under $200	$200–$300	$301–$400	over $400

Restaurant prices are the average cost of a main course at dinner or, if dinner is not served, at lunch. Hotel prices are for the lowest cost of a standard double room in high season.

TASTINGS AND TOURS

Many wineries require reservations for tours, seminars, and tastings, which in most cases are made through booking websites such as CellarPass and VinoVisit. A good scheduling strategy is to book appointment-only wineries in the morning, saving the ones that allow walk-ins until the afternoon. That way, if lunch or other winery visits take longer than expected you won't be stressed about having to arrive at later stops at a precise time.

Many visitors prefer to leave the scheduling and driving to seasoned professionals. Whether you want to tour wineries in a van or bus along with other passengers or spring for a private limo, there are plenty of operators who can accommodate you. Tours generally last from five to seven hours and stop at four or five wineries. Rates vary from $80 per person to $250 or more, depending on the vehicle and whether the tour includes other guests. On most tours, at least one stop includes a behind-the-scenes look at production facilities and the chance to meet winemakers or others involved in the wine-making process. Most tour operators will pick you up at your hotel or a specified meeting place. You can also book a car and driver by the hour for shorter trips. Rates for limo generally run from $50 to $85 per hour, and there's usually a two- or three-hour minimum. ■ TIP→ Some tours include lunch and tasting and other fees, but not all do, so ask.

THE NAPA VALLEY

With more than 500 wineries and many of the biggest brands in the business, the Napa Valley is the Wine Country's star. With a population of about 79,000, Napa, the valley's largest town, lures with its cultural attractions and (relatively) reasonably priced accommodations. A few miles farther north, compact Yountville is densely packed with top-notch restaurants and hotels, and Rutherford and Oakville are renowned for their Cabernet Sauvignon–friendly soils. Beyond them, St. Helena teems with elegant boutiques and restaurants, and casual Calistoga, known for spas and hot springs, has the feel of an Old West frontier town.

Napa Valley

Mount St Helena

Robert Louis Stevenson State Park

THE PALISADES

Aetna Springs

POPE VALLEY

Pope Valley

Lake Berryessa

Lake Berryessa Recreation Area

Dunaweal Ln.

Calistoga

Howell Mtn. Rd.

Angwin
Angwin Airport

Knoxville Rd.

Larkmead Ln.

Chiles Pope Valley Rd.

Petrified Forest Rd.

Diamond Mountain

Bothe-Napa State Park

Bale Grist Mill State Historic Park

Deer Park
Sanitarium Rd.

NAPA COUNTY

Lake Hennessy

Sage Canyon Rd.

Atlas Peak

FOSS VALLEY

SONOMA COUNTY

St. Helena

NAPA

Silverado Trail

Lake Hennessy City Recreation Area

Sugarloaf Ridge State Park

Rutherford

Oakville Cross Rd.

Napa River

Silverado Trail

Hood Mountain Regional Park

Adobe Canyon Rd.

Bald Mountain

Mt St. John

Oakville Grade Rd.

Oakville

Yountville Cross Rd.

Yountville Hills
Yountville

Big Ranch Rd.

Oak Knoll

Sonoma Hwy.

Annadel State Park

Kenwood

Trinity Rd.

Mt Veeder

VALLEY

Monticello Rd.

SONOMA VALLEY

Glen Ellen

Sonoma Mountain

REDWOOD CANYON

Dry Creek Rd.

Traucas St.
Pueblo
Lincoln

Jack London State Park

VALLEY OF THE MOON

Agua Caliente

Boyes Hot Springs

CARNEROS VALLEY

Redwood Rd.

Browns Valley Rd.

Henry Rd.

Napa

SONOMA MOUNTAINS

Arnold Dr.

Sonoma

Napa Rd.

Dealy La.

Old Sonoma Rd.

Imola Ave.

Adobe Rd.

Petaluma

Lakeville Hwy.

Bonness Rd.

Carneros Hwy.

Napa County Airport

0   4 mi
0   4 km

NAPA

46 miles northeast of San Francisco.

After many years as a blue-collar burg detached from the Wine Country scene, the Napa Valley's largest town (population about 80,000) has evolved into one of its shining stars. Masaharu Morimoto and other chefs of note operate restaurants here, swank hotels and inns can be found downtown and beyond, and the nightlife options include the West Coast edition of the famed Blue Note jazz club. A walkway that follows the Napa River has made downtown more pedestrian-friendly, and the Oxbow Public Market, a complex of high-end food purveyors, is popular with locals and tourists. Nearby Copia, operated by the Culinary Institute of America, hosts cooking demonstrations and other activities open to the public and has a shop and a restaurant. If you establish your base in Napa, plan on spending at least a half day strolling the downtown district.

GETTING HERE AND AROUND

Downtown Napa lies a mile east of Highway 29—take the 1st Street exit and follow the signs. Ample parking, much of it free for the first three hours and some for the entire day, is available on or near Main Street. Several VINE buses serve downtown and beyond.

EXPLORING
TOP ATTRACTIONS

Artesa Vineyards & Winery. From a distance the modern, minimalist architecture of Artesa blends harmoniously with the surrounding Carneros landscape, but up close its pools, fountains, and the large outdoor sculptures by resident artist Gordon Huether of Napa make a vivid impression. So, too, do the wines: mostly Chardonnay and Pinot Noir but also Cabernet Sauvignon, Merlot, and other limited releases like Albariño and Tempranillo. You can sample wines by themselves without a reservation or, at tastings for which a reservation is required, paired with chocolate, cheese, or tapas. ■TIP→ The tour, conducted daily, explores wine making and the winery's history. ⊠ *1345 Henry Rd., off Old Sonoma Rd. and Dealy La., Napa* ☎ *707/224–1668* ⊕ *www.artesawinery.com* 🍷 *Tastings $25–$60, tour $40 (includes tasting).*

Fodor's Choice **di Rosa.** A formidable array of artworks from the 1960s to the present ★ by Northern California artists is displayed on this 217-acre property. The works can be found not only in galleries and in the former residence of its late founder, Rene di Rosa, but also throughout the surrounding landscape. Some works were commissioned especially for di Rosa, among them Paul Kos's meditative *Chartres Bleu,* a video installation in a chapel-like setting that replicates a stained-glass window from the cathedral in Chartres, France. ■TIP→ You can view the current temporary exhibition and a few permanent works at the Gatehouse Gallery, but to experience the breadth of the collection you'll need to book a tour. ⊠ *5200 Sonoma Hwy./Hwy. 121, Napa* ☎ *707/226–5991* ⊕ *www.dirosaart.org* 🍷 *Gatehouse Gallery $5, tours $12–$15* ⊗ *Closed Mon. and Tues.*

Continued on page 216

WINE
TASTING *in*
NAPA *and*
SONOMA

VISITING WINERIES

Tasting rooms range from the grand to the humble, offering everything from a few sips of wine to in-depth tours of facilities and vineyards. Many are open for drop-in visits, usually daily from around 10 am to 5 pm. Others require guests to make reservations. First-time visitors frequently enjoy the history-oriented tours at Charles Krug and Inglenook, or ones at Mondavi and J Vineyards that highlight the process as well. The environments at some wineries reflect their founders' other interests: art and architecture at Artesa and Hall St. Helena, movie making at Francis Ford Coppola, and medieval history at the Castello di Amorosa.

Many wineries describe their pourers as "wine educators," and indeed some of them have taken online or other classes and have passed an exam to prove basic knowledge of appellations, grape varietals, vineyards, and wine-making techniques. The one constant, however, is a deep, shared pleasure in the experience of wine tasting. To prepare you for winery visits, we've covered the fundamentals: tasting rooms, fees and what to expect, and the types of tours wineries offer.

Fees. In the past few years, tasting fees have skyrocketed. Most Napa wineries charge $25 or $30 to taste a few wines, though $40, $50, or even $75 fees aren't unheard of. Sonoma wineries are often a bit cheaper, in the $15 to $35 range, and you'll still find the occasional freebie.

Some winery tours are free, in which case you're usually required to pay a separate fee if you want to taste the wine. If you've paid a fee for the tour—generally from $20 to $40—your wine tasting is usually included in that price.

Whether you're a serious wine collector making your annual pilgrimage to Nothern California's Wine Country or a newbie who doesn't know the difference between a Merlot and Mourvèdre but is eager to learn, you can have a great time touring Napa and Sonoma wineries. Your gateway to the wine world is the tasting room, where staff members are happy to chat with curious guests.

(opposite page) Carneros vineyards in autumn, Napa Valley. (top) Pinot Gris grapes. (bottom) Bottles from Far Niente winery.

MAKING THE MOST OF YOUR TIME

■**Call ahead.** Some wineries require reservations to visit or tour. It's wise to check before visiting.

■**Come on weekdays.** Especially between June and October, try to visit on weekdays to avoid traffic-clogged roads and crowded tasting rooms. For more info on the best times of year to visit, see this chapter's Planner.

■**Get an early start.** Tasting rooms are often deserted before 11 am or so, when most visitors are still lingering over a second cup of coffee. If you come early, you'll have the staff's undivided attention. You'll usually encounter the largest crowds between 3 and 5 pm.

■**Schedule strategically.** Visit appointment-only wineries in the morning and ones that allow walk-ins in the afternoon. It'll spare you the stress of being "on time" for later stops.

■**Hit the Trail.** Beringer, Mondavi, and other high-profile wineries line heavily trafficked Highway 29, but the going

(top) Sipping and swirling in the DeLoach tasting room. (bottom) Learning about barrel aging at Robert Mondavi Winery.

is often quicker on the Silverado Trail, which runs parallel to the highway to the east. You'll find famous names here, too, among them the sparkling wine house Mumm Napa Valley, but the traffic is often lighter and sometimes the crowds as well.

Domaine Carneros.

AT THE BAR

In most tasting rooms, you'll be handed a list of the wines available that day. The wines will be listed in a suggested tasting order, starting with the lightest-bodied whites, progressing to the most intense reds, and ending with dessert wines. If you can't decide which wines to choose, tell the server what types of wines you usually like and ask for a recommendation.

The server will pour you an ounce or so of each wine you select. As you taste it, feel free to take notes or ask questions. Don't be shy—the staff are there to educate you about the wine. If you don't like a wine, or you've simply tasted enough, feel free to pour the rest into one of the dump buckets on the bar.

TOURS

Tours tend to be the most exciting (and the most crowded) in September and October, when the harvest and crush-ing are underway. Tours typically last from 30 minutes to an hour and give you a brief overview of the winemaking process. At some of the older wineries, the tour guide might focus on the history of the property.

■ TIP➔ If you plan to take any tours, wear comfortable shoes, since you might be walking on wet floors or dirt or gravel pathways or stepping over hoses or other equipment.

MONEY-SAVING TIPS

■ Many hotels and B&Bs distribute coupons for free or discounted tastings to their guests—don't forget to ask.

■ If you and your travel partner don't mind sharing a glass, servers are happy to let you split a tasting.

■ Some wineries will refund all or part of the tasting fee if you buy a bottle. Usually one fee is waived per bottle purchased, though sometimes you must buy two or three.

■ Almost all wineries will also waive the fee if you join their wine club program. However, this typically commits you to buying a certain number of bottles on a regular basis, so be sure you really like the wines before signing up.

Preston of Dry Creek bottles only estate-grown grapes.

TOP 2-DAY ITINERARIES

First-Timer's Napa Tour

Start: Oxbow Public market, Napa. Get underway by browsing the shops selling wines, spices, locally grown produce, and other fine foods, for a taste of what the Wine Country has to offer.

Inglenook, Rutherford. The tour here is a particularly fun way to learn about the history

of Napa winemaking—and you can see the old, atmospheric, ivy-covered château.

Frog's Leap, Rutherford. Friendly, unpretentious, and knowledgeable staff makes this place great for wine newbies. (Make sure you get that reservation lined up.)

Dinner and Overnight: St. Helena. Splurge at Meadowood Napa Valley and you won't need to leave the property for

Domaine Carneros

di Rosa Preserve

Old Sonoma Rd.

121

12

Oxbow Public Market

Napa

29

N A P A
C O U N T Y

Yountville

Robert Mondavi

Far Niente

Oakville

KEY

First-Timer's Napa Tour
Wine Buff's Tour

Silverado Trail

Stag's Leap Wine Cellars

Wine Buff's Tour

Start: Stag's Leap Wine Cellars, Yountville, Napa. Famed for its Cabernet Sauvignon and Bordeaux blends.

Silver Oak, Oakville. Schedule a tour of this celebrated winery and taste the flagship Cabernet Sauvignon.

Mumm Napa, Rutherford. Come for the bubbly—which is available in a variety of tastings—stay for the photography exhibits.

Dinner and Overnight: Yountville. Have dinner at one of the Thomas Keller restaurants. Splurge at Bardessono; save at Maison Fleurie.

Next Day: Robert Mondavi, Oakville. Spring for the reserve room tasting so you can sip the top-of-the-line wines, especially the Cabernet Sauvignon. Head across Highway 29 to the Oakville Grocery to pick up a picnic lunch.

Far Niente, Oakville. You have to make a reservation and the fee for the tasting an extravagant dinner at its restaurant. Save at El Bonita Motel with dinner at Gott's.

Next Day: Poke around St. Helena's shops, then drive to Yountville for lunch.

di Rosa, Napa. Call ahead to book a one- or two-hour tour of the acres of gardens and galleries, which

are chock-full of thousands of works of art.

Domaine Carneros, Napa. Toast your trip with a glass of outstanding bubbly.

Sonoma Backroads

Start: Iron Horse Vineyards, Russian River Valley.
Soak up a view of vine-covered hills and Mount St. Helena while sipping a sparkling wine or Pinot Noir at this beautifully rustic spot.

Dutton-Goldfield Winery, Russian River Valley.
A terrific source for Pinot Noir and Chardonnay, the stars of this valley.

Dinner and Overnight: Forestville. Go all out with a stay at the Farmhouse Inn, whose award-winning restaurant is one of the best in all of Sonoma.

Next Day: Westside Road, Russian River Valley.
This scenic route, which follows the river, is crowded with worthwhile wineries like Arista and Rochioli—but it's not crowded with visitors. Pinot fans will find a lot to love. Picnic at either winery and enjoy the view.

Balletto Vineyards, Santa Rosa. End on an especially relaxed note with a walk through the vineyards and a patio tasting.

and tour is steep, but the payoff is an especially intimate winery experience. You'll taste excellent Cabernet and

Chardonnay, then end your trip on a sweet note with a dessert wine.

WINE TASTING 101

TAKE A GOOD LOOK.
Hold your glass by the stem, raise it to the light, and take a close look at the wine. Check for clarity and color. (This is easiest to do if you can hold the glass in front of a white background.) Any tinge of brown usually means that the wine is over the hill or has gone bad.

BREATHE DEEP.
1. Sniff the wine once or twice to see if you can identify any smells.

2. Swirl the wine gently in the glass. Aerating the wine this way releases more of its aromas. (It's called "volatilizing the esters," if you're trying to impress someone.)

3. Take another long sniff. You might notice that experienced wine tasters spend more time sniffing the wine than drinking it. This is because this step is where the magic happens. The number of scents you might detect is almost endless, from berries, apricots, honey, and wildflowers to leather, cedar, or even tar. Does the wine smell good to you? Do you detect any "off" flavors, like wet dog or sulfur?

AT LAST! TAKE A SIP.
1. Swirl the wine around your mouth so that it makes contact with all your taste buds and releases more of its aromas. Think about the way the wine feels in your mouth. Is it watery or rich? Is it crisp or silky? Does it have a bold flavor, or is it subtle? The weight and intensity of a wine are called its body.

2. Hold the wine in your mouth for a few seconds and see if you can identify any developing flavors. More complex wines will reveal many different flavors as you drink them.

SPIT OR SWALLOW.
The pros typically spit, since they want to preserve their palate (and sobriety!) for the wines to come, but you'll find that swallowers far outnumber the spitters in the winery tasting rooms. Whether you spit or swallow, notice the flavor that remains after the wine is gone (the finish).

Sniff

Sip

DODGE THE CROWDS

To avoid bumping elbows in the tasting rooms, look for wineries off the main drags of Highway 29 in Napa and Highway 12 in Sonoma. The back roads of the Russian River, Dry Creek, and Alexander valleys, all in Sonoma, are excellent places to explore. In Napa, try the northern end. Also look for wineries that are open by appointment only; they tend to schedule visitors carefully to avoid a big crush at any one time.

HOW WINE IS MADE

1. CRUSHING
Harvested grapes go into a stemmer-crusher, which separates stems from fruit and crushes the grapes to release "free-run" juice.

2. PRESSING
Remaining juice is gently extracted from grapes. Usually done by pressing grapes against the walls of a tank with an inflatable bladder.

3. FERMENTING
Extracted juice (and also grape skins and pulp, when making red wine) goes into stainless-steel tanks or oak barrels to ferment. During fermentation, sugars convert to alcohol.

4. AGING
Wine is stored in stainless-steel or oak casks or barrels, or sometimes in concrete vessels, to develop flavors.

5. RACKING
Wine is transferred to clean barrels; sediment is removed. Wine may be filtered and fined (clarified) to improve its clarity, color, and sometimes flavor.

6. BOTTLING
Wine is bottled either at the winery or at a special facility, then stored again for bottle-aging.

WHAT'S AN APPELLATION?

American Viticultural Area (AVA) or, more commonly, an appellation. What can be confusing is that some appellations encompass smaller subappellations. The Rutherford, Oakville, and Mt. Veeder AVAs, for instance, are among the Napa Valley AVA's 15 subappellations. Wineries often buy grapes from outside their AVA, so their labels might reference different appellations. A winery in the warmer Napa Valley, for instance, might source Pinot Noir grapes from the cooler Russian River Valley, where they grow better. The appellation listed on a label always refers to where a wine's grapes were grown, not to where the wine was made. By law, if a label bears the name of an appellation, 85% of the grapes must come from it.

Wine and contemporary art find a home at di Rosa.

Domaine Carneros. A visit to this majestic château is an opulent way to enjoy the Carneros District—especially in fine weather, when the vineyard views are spectacular. The château was modeled after an 18th-century French mansion owned by the Taittinger family. Carved into the hillside beneath the winery, the cellars produce sparkling wines reminiscent of those made by Taittinger, using only Los Carneros AVA grapes. The winery sells flights and glasses of its sparklers, Chardonnay, Pinot Noir, and other wines. Enjoy them all with cheese and charcuterie plates, caviar, or smoked salmon. Seating is in the Louis XV–inspired salon or on the terrace overlooking the vines. The tour covers traditional methods of making sparkling wines. Both tours and tastings are by appointment only. ✉ *1240 Duhig Rd., at Hwy. 121, Napa* ☎ *707/257–0101, 800/716–2788* ⊕ *www.domainecarneros.com* 🗐 *Tastings $10–$250, tour $50.*

Fodor'sChoice ★ **Oxbow Public Market.** The market's two dozen stands provide an introduction to Northern California's diverse artisanal food products. Swoon over decadent charcuterie at the Fatted Calf (great sandwiches, too), slurp oysters at Hog Island, or chow down on duck or salmon tacos at C Casa. You can sample wine (and cheese) at the Oxbow Cheese & Wine Merchant, ales at Fieldwork Brewery's taproom, and barrel-aged cocktails and handcrafted vodkas at the Napa Valley Distillery. Napa Bookmine is among the few nonfood vendors here. ■ TIP→ If you don't mind eating at the counter, you can select a steak at the Five Dot Ranch meat stand and pay $8 above market price ($12 with two sides) to have it grilled on the spot, a real deal for a quality slab. ✉ *610 and 644 1st St., at McKinstry St., Napa* ⊕ *www.oxbowpublicmarket.com.*

WORTH NOTING

Etude Wines. You're apt to see or hear hawks, egrets, Canada geese, and other wildlife on the grounds of Etude, known for its sophisticated Pinot Noirs. Although the winery and its light-filled tasting room are in Napa County, the grapes for its flagship Carneros Estate Pinot Noir come from the Sonoma portion of Los Carneros, as do those for the rarer Heirloom Carneros Pinot Noir. Chardonnay, Pinot Blanc, Pinot Noir, and other wines are poured daily at the tasting bar and in good weather on the patio. Pinot Noirs from Carneros, the Sonoma Coast, Oregon, and Santa Barbara County are compared at the Study of Pinot Noir sessions ($50), for which reservations are required. ■ TIP→ Single-vineyard Napa Valley Cabernets are another Etude emphasis; those from Rutherford and Oakville are particularly good. ⊠ *1250 Cuttings Wharf Rd., 1 mile south of Hwy. 121, Napa* ☎ *707/257–5782* ⊕ *www.etudewines.com* ☜ *Tastings $20–$50.*

The Hess Collection. About 9 miles northwest of Napa, up a winding road ascending Mt. Veeder, this winery is a delightful discovery. The limestone structure, rustic from the outside but modern and airy within, contains Swiss owner Donald Hess's world-class art collection, including large-scale works by contemporary artists such as Andy Goldsworthy, Anselm Kiefer, and Robert Rauschenberg. Cabernet Sauvignon is a major strength, and the 19 Block Cuvée, Mount Veeder, a Cabernet blend, shows off Malbec and other estate varietals. Tastings outdoors in the garden and the courtyard take place from spring to fall, with cheese or nuts and other nibbles accompanying the wines. ■ TIP→ Among the wine-and-food pairings offered year-round, most of which involve a guided tour of the art collection, is a fun one showcasing locally made artisanal chocolates. ⊠ *4411 Redwood Rd., west off Hwy. 29 at Trancas St./Redwood Rd. exit, Napa* ☎ *707/255–1144* ⊕ *www.hesscollection.com* ☜ *Tastings $25–$175, art gallery free.*

Napa Valley Wine Train. Several centuries-old restored Pullman railroad cars and a two-story 1952 Vista Dome car with a curved glass roof travel a leisurely, scenic route between Napa and St. Helena. All trips include a well-made lunch or dinner. Guests on the Quattro Vino tour enjoy a four-course lunch and tastings at four wineries, with stops at one or two wineries incorporated into other tours. Murder-mystery plays are among the regularly scheduled special events. ■ TIP→ It's best to make this trip during the day, when you can enjoy the vineyard views. ⊠ *1275 McKinstry St., off 1st St., Napa* ☎ *707/253–2111, 800/427–4124* ⊕ *www.winetrain.com* ☜ *From $146.*

Stag's Leap Wine Cellars. A 1973 Stag's Leap Wine Cellars S.L.V. Cabernet Sauvignon put this winery and the Napa Valley on the enological map by placing first in the famous Judgment of Paris tasting of 1976. The grapes for that wine came from a vineyard visible from the stone-and-glass Fay Outlook & Visitor Center, which has broad views of a second fabled Cabernet vineyard (Fay) and the promontory that gives both the winery and the Stags Leap District AVA their names. The top-of-the-line Cabernets from these vineyards are poured at the $45 Estate Collection Tasting. Among the other options are a cave tour and tasting and special wine-and-food pairings. ⊠ *5766 Silverado Trail, at Wappo Hill Rd., Napa* ☎ *707/261–6410* ⊕ *www.cask23.com* ☜ *Tasting $45, tours (with tastings by appointment only) $75 and up.*

6

WHERE TO EAT

$$$

MODERN
AMERICAN

Fodor'sChoice

★

✕ **The Corner Napa.** Equal parts 21st-century gentleman's club and brooding urban loft, this downtown restaurant seduces with a suave palette of marble, leather, bronze, and polished walnut surfaces. Chef Dustin Falcon's cuisine is similarly elegant, with pickled pearl onions, apple, sherry, and candied pecans elevating a garden beets salad, and Sicilian pistachio, Medjool dates, spiced yogurt, and fried naan balls playing well with each other and their dish's centerpiece, pan-seared Spanish octopus. **Known for:** contemporary decor; international wine list; specialty cocktails and rare spirits. Ⓢ *Average main: $28* ⊠ *660 Main St., near 5th St., Napa* ☎ *707/927–5552* ⊕ *www.cornerbarnapa.com* ☾ *Closed Mon. No lunch Tues.–Sat.*

$$$

ECLECTIC

✕ **Grace's Table.** A dependable, varied, three-squares-a-day menu makes this modest corner restaurant occupying a brick-and-glass storefront many Napans' go-to choice for a simple meal. Iron-skillet corn bread with lavender honey and butter shows up at all hours, with chilaquiles scrambled eggs a breakfast favorite, savory fish tacos a lunchtime staple, and cassoulet and pork osso buco risotto popular for dinner. **Known for:** congenial staffers; good beers on tap; eclectic menu focusing on France, Italy, and the Americas. Ⓢ *Average main: $24* ⊠ *1400 2nd St., at Franklin St., Napa* ☎ *707/226–6200* ⊕ *www.gracestable.net.*

$$$$

MODERN
AMERICAN

Fodor'sChoice

★

✕ **La Toque.** Chef Ken Frank's La Toque is the complete package: his imaginative modern American cuisine, served in a formal dining space, is complemented by a wine lineup that earned the restaurant a coveted *Wine Spectator* Grand Award. Built around seasonal local ingredients, the prix-fixe menu, which changes frequently, might include potato rösti with caviar, sole with eggplant and almond-hazelnut *picada* sauce, and five-spice Liberty Farm duck breast with black trumpet mushrooms. **Known for:** elaborate preparations; astute wine pairings. Ⓢ *Average main: $80* ⊠ *Westin Verasa Napa, 1314 McKinstry St., off Soscol Ave., Napa* ☎ *707/257–5157* ⊕ *www.latoque.com* ☾ *No lunch.*

$$$

JAPANESE

Fodor'sChoice

★

✕ **Miminashi.** Japanese *izakaya*—gastropubs that serve appetizers downed with sake or cocktails—provided the inspiration for chef Curtis Di Fede's buzz-worthy downtown Napa restaurant. Ramen, fried rice, and yakitori anchor the menu, whose highlights include smoked-trout potato croquettes, crispy skewered chicken skin, and the ooh-inspiring *okonomiyaki* pancake with bacon and cabbage, topped by dried fermented tuna flakes. **Known for:** soft-serve ice cream for dessert and from to-go window; wines and sakes that elevate the cuisine. Ⓢ *Average main: $28* ⊠ *821 Coombs St., near 3rd St., Napa* ☎ *707/254–9464* ⊕ *miminashi.com* ☾ *No lunch weekends.*

$$$$

JAPANESE

✕ **Morimoto Napa.** *Iron Chef* star Masaharu Morimoto is the big name behind this downtown Napa hot spot where everything is delightfully overdone, right down to the desserts. Organic materials such as twisting grapevines above the bar and rough-hewn wooden tables seem simultaneously earthy and modern, creating a fitting setting for the gorgeously plated Japanese fare, from sashimi served with grated fresh wasabi to elaborate concoctions that include sea-urchin carbonara made with udon noodles. **Known for:** elaborate concoctions; gorgeous plating; omakase menu. Ⓢ *Average main: $36* ⊠ *610 Main St., at 5th St., Napa* ☎ *707/252–1600* ⊕ *www.morimotonapa.com.*

$$$$
MODERN
AMERICAN
Fodor'sChoice
★

✕ **Torc.** *Torc* means "wild boar" in an early Celtic dialect, and owner-chef Sean O'Toole, who formerly helmed kitchens at top Manhattan, San Francisco, and Yountville establishments, occasionally incorporates the restaurant's namesake beast into his eclectic offerings. O'Toole and his team enhance dishes such as roast chicken—recently prepared with Florence fennel, hedgehog mushroom, pickle lily, and bergamot—with style and precision. **Known for:** gracious service; specialty cocktails; Bengali sweet-potato pakora and deviled-egg appetizers. $ *Average main: $33* ✉ *1140 Main St., at Pearl St., Napa* ☎ *707/252–3292* ⊕ *www.torcnapa.com* ☉ *Closed Tues. No lunch weekdays.*

$$$
SPANISH
Fodor'sChoice
★

✕ **ZuZu.** At festive ZuZu the focus is on tapas, paella, the signature suckling pig, and other Spanish favorites often downed with cava or sangria. Regulars revere the paella, made with Spanish *bomba* rice, and small plates that might include white anchovies with sliced egg and rémoulade on grilled bread. **Known for:** singular flavors and spicing; Latin jazz on the stereo; sister restaurant La Taberna for bar bites three doors south. $ *Average main: $29* ✉ *829 Main St., near 3rd St., Napa* ☎ *707/224–8555* ⊕ *www.zuzunapa.com* ☉ *No lunch weekends.*

WHERE TO STAY

$$$
HOTEL
Fodor'sChoice
★

🛏 **Andaz Napa.** Part of the Hyatt family, this boutique hotel with an urban-hip vibe has luxurious rooms with flat-screen TVs, laptop-size safes, and white-marble bathrooms stocked with high-quality bath products. **Pros:** proximity to downtown restaurants, theaters, and tasting rooms; access to modern fitness center; complimentary beverage upon arrival; complimentary snacks and nonalcoholic beverages in rooms. **Cons:** parking can be a challenge on weekends; unremarkable views from some rooms. $ *Rooms from: $359* ✉ *1450 1st St., Napa* ☎ *707/687–1234* ⊕ *andaznapa.com* ⇆ *141 rooms* ⦿ *No meals.*

$$$$
RESORT
Fodor'sChoice
★

🛏 **Carneros Resort & Spa.** Freestanding board-and-batten cottages with rocking chairs on each porch are simultaneously rustic and chic at this luxurious property made even more so by a $6.5 million makeover. **Pros:** cottages have lots of privacy; beautiful views from hilltop pool and hot tub; heaters on private patios. **Cons:** a long drive to destinations up-valley. $ *Rooms from: $600* ✉ *4048 Sonoma Hwy./Hwy. 121, Napa* ☎ *707/299–4900, 888/400–9000* ⊕ *www.thecarnerosinn. com* ⇆ *86 rooms* ⦿ *No meals.*

$$
B&B/INN
Fodor'sChoice
★

🛏 **Inn on Randolph.** A few calm blocks from the downtown action, the restored Inn on Randolph is a sophisticated haven celebrated for its gourmet gluten-free breakfasts and snacks. **Pros:** quiet residential neighborhood; gourmet breakfasts; sophisticated decor; romantic setting. **Cons:** a bit of a walk from downtown. $ *Rooms from: $299* ✉ *411 Randolph St., Napa* ☎ *707/257–2886* ⊕ *www.innonrandolph.com* ⇆ *10 rooms* ⦿ *Breakfast.*

$$
B&B/INN

🛏 **Napa River Inn.** Part of a complex of restaurants, shops, a nightclub, and a spa, this waterfront inn is within easy walking distance of downtown hot spots. **Pros:** wide range of room sizes and prices; near downtown action; pet friendly. **Cons:** river views could be more scenic; some rooms get noise from nearby restaurants. $ *Rooms from: $299* ✉ *500 Main St., Napa* ☎ *707/251–8500, 877/251–8500* ⊕ *www.napariverinn. com* ⇆ *66 rooms* ⦿ *Breakfast.*

6

NIGHTLIFE AND PERFORMING ARTS

Fodor's Choice ★ **Blue Note Napa.** The famed New York jazz room's West Coast club hosts national headliners such as Chris Botti, Dee Dee Bridgewater, and Coco Montoya, along with local talents such as Lavay Smith & Her Red Hot Skillet Lickers. Chef Jessica Sedlacek, formerly of The French Laundry and Bouchon in Yountville, supplies the culinary pizzazz—hearty entrées such as boneless crispy chicken and a massive pork chop, and lighter fare that includes raw oysters, chicken wings, and bacon-inflected potato fritters (an instant hit). ⊠ *Napa Valley Opera House, 1030 Main St., at 1st St., Napa* ☎ *707/603–1258* ⊕ *www.bluenotenapa.com.*

Cadet Wine + Beer Bar. Cadet plays things urban-style cool with a long bar, high-top tables, an all-vinyl soundtrack, and a low-lit, generally loungelike feel. The two owners describe their outlook as "unabashedly pro-California," but their lineup of 150-plus wines and beers circles the globe. The crowd here is youngish, the vibe festive. ⊠ *930 Franklin St., at end of pedestrian alley between 1st and 2nd Sts., Napa* ☎ *707/224–4400* ⊕ *www.cadetbeerandwinebar.com.*

YOUNTVILLE

9 miles north of the town of Napa.

These days Yountville is something like Disneyland for food lovers. You could stay here for a week and not exhaust all the options—several of them owned by The French Laundry's Thomas Keller—and the tiny town is full of small inns and high-end hotels that cater to those who prefer to walk (not drive) after an extravagant meal. It's also well located for excursions to many big-name Napa wineries, especially those in the Stags Leap District, from which big, bold Cabernet Sauvignons helped make the Napa Valley's wine-making reputation.

GETTING HERE AND AROUND

Downtown Yountville sits just off Highway 29. Approaching from the south take the Yountville exit—from the north take Madison—and proceed to Washington Street, home to the major shops and restaurants. Yountville Cross Road connects downtown to the Silverado Trail, along which many noted wineries do business. The free Yountville Trolley serves the town daily from 10 am to 7 pm (on-call service until 11 except on Sunday).

EXPLORING

TOP ATTRACTIONS

Fodor's Choice ★ **Cliff Lede Vineyards.** Inspired by his passion for classic rock, owner and construction magnate Cliff Lede named the blocks in his Stags Leap District vineyard after hits by the Grateful Dead and other bands. The vibe at his efficient, high-tech winery is anything but laid-back, however. Cutting-edge agricultural and enological science informs the vineyard management and wine making here. Architect Howard Backen designed the winery and its tasting room, where Lede's Sauvignon Blanc, Cabernet Sauvignons, and other wines, along with some from sister winery FEL, which produces much-lauded Anderson Valley Pinot Noirs, are poured. ■ TIP➔ **Walk-ins are welcome at the tasting bar, but appointments are required for the veranda outside and a nearby gallery that often displays rock-related art.** ⊠ *1473 Yountville Cross Rd., off*

Silverado Trail, Yountville ☎ *707/944–8642* ⊕ *cliffledevineyards.com* ▭ *Tastings $30–$50.*

Fodor'sChoice ★ **Ma(i)sonry Napa Valley.** An art-and-design gallery that also pours the wines of about two dozen limited-production wineries, Ma(i)sonry occupies a manor house constructed in 1904 from Napa River stone. Tasting flights of wines by distinguished winemakers such as Heidi Barrett, Philippe Melka, and Thomas Rivers Brown can be sampled in fair weather in the sculpture garden, in a private nook, or at the communal redwood table, and in any weather indoors among the contemporary artworks and well-chosen *objets*—which might include 17th-century furnishings, industrial lamps, or slabs of petrified wood. ■TIP➔ **Walk-ins are welcome, space permitting, but during summer, at harvest, and on weekends and holidays it's best to book in advance.** ✉ *6711 Washington St., at Pedroni St., Yountville* ☎ *707/944–0889* ⊕ *www. maisonry.com* ▭ *Tasting $35–$55.*

Fodor'sChoice ★ **Stewart Cellars.** Three stone structures meant to mimic Scottish ruins coaxed into modernity form this complex that includes public and private tasting spaces, a bright outdoor patio, and a café with accessible vegan- and carnivore-friendly cuisine. The attention to detail in the ensemble's design mirrors that of the wines, whose grapes come from Stagecoach, Beckstoffer Las Piedras (for the intense Nomad Cabernet), and other coveted vineyards. Although Cabernet is the focus, winemaker Blair Guthrie, with input from consulting winemaker Paul Hobbs, also makes Chardonnay, Pinot Noir, and Merlot. ■TIP➔ **On sunny days this is a good stop around lunchtime, when you can order a meal from the café and a glass of wine from the tasting room—for permit reasons this must be done separately—and enjoy them on the patio.** ✉ *6752 Washington St., near Pedroni St., Yountville* ☎ *707/963–9160* ⊕ *www.stewartcellars.com* ▭ *Tastings $35–$85.*

WHERE TO EAT

$$$$
MODERN
AMERICAN
Fodor'sChoice ★
✕ **Ad Hoc.** At this low-key dining room with zinc-top tables and wine served in tumblers, superstar chef Thomas Keller offers a single, fixed-price menu nightly, with a small but decadent Sunday brunch. The dinner selection might include smoked beef short ribs with creamy herb rice and charred broccolini, or sesame chicken with radish kimchi and fried rice. **Known for:** casual cuisine; great price for a Thomas Keller meal; don't-miss buttermilk-fried-chicken night. ⑤ *Average main: $55* ✉ *6476 Washington St., at Oak Circle, Yountville* ☎ *707/944–2487* ⊕ *www.adhocrestaurant.com* ⊙ *No lunch Mon.–Sat.; no dinner Tues. and Wed.* ☞ *Call a day ahead to find out the next day's menu.*

$$$
FRENCH
Fodor'sChoice ★
✕ **Bistro Jeanty.** Escargots, cassoulet, *daube de boeuf* (beef stewed in red wine), and other French classics are prepared with the utmost precision at this country bistro whose lamb tongue and other obscure delicacies delight daring diners. Regulars often start with the rich tomato soup in a flaky puff pastry before proceeding to sole meunière or coq au vin, completing the French sojourn with warm apple tarte tatin and other authentic desserts. **Known for:** traditional preparations; oh-so-French ambience. ⑤ *Average main: $27* ✉ *6510 Washington St., at Mulberry St., Yountville* ☎ *707/944–0103* ⊕ *www.bistrojeanty.com.*

$$$ ✕ **Bouchon.** The team that created The French Laundry is also behind
FRENCH   this place, where everything—the lively and crowded zinc-topped bar,
Fodor'sChoice   the elbow-to-elbow seating, the traditional French onion soup—could
★   have come straight from a Parisian bistro. Roasted chicken with leeks
and oyster mushrooms and steamed mussels served with crispy, addic-
tive *frites* (french fries) are among the perfectly executed entrées. **Known
for:** bistro classics; rabbit and salmon rillettes. ⑤ *Average main: $27*
⊠ *6534 Washington St., near Humboldt St., Yountville* ☎ *707/944–
8037* ⊕ *www.bouchonbistro.com.*

$$$$ ✕ **The French Laundry.** An old stone building laced with ivy houses chef
AMERICAN   Thomas Keller's destination restaurant. Some courses on the two prix-
Fodor'sChoice   fixe menus, one of which highlights vegetables, rely on luxe ingredi-
★   ents such as *calotte* (cap of the rib eye); other courses take humble
elements like fava beans and elevate them to art. **Known for:** signa-
ture starter "oysters and pearls"; intricate flavors; superior wine list.
⑤ *Average main: $310* ⊠ *6640 Washington St., at Creek St., Yountville*
☎ *707/944–2380* ⊕ *www.frenchlaundry.com* ⊗ *No lunch Mon.–Thurs.*
⋒ *Jacket required* ☞ *Reservations essential weeks ahead (call or check
website for precise instructions).*

$$$ ✕ **Mustards Grill.** Cindy Pawlcyn's Mustards fills day and night with
AMERICAN   fans of her hearty cuisine, equal parts updated renditions of traditional
American dishes—what Pawlcyn dubs "deluxe truck stop classics"—
and fanciful contemporary fare. Barbecued baby back pork ribs and a
lemon-lime tart piled high with brown-sugar meringue fall squarely in
the first category, with sweet corn tamales with tomatillo-avocado salsa
and wild mushrooms representing the latter. **Known for:** roadhouse setting; convivial mood; hoppin' bar. ⑤ *Average main: $27* ⊠ *7399 St. Hel-
ena Hwy./Hwy. 29, 1 mile north of Yountville, Napa* ☎ *707/944–2424*
⊕ *www.mustardsgrill.com.*

$ ✕ **Protéa Restaurant.** A meal at Yountville's The French Laundry moti-
LATIN AMERICAN   vated Puerto Rico–born Anita Cartagena to pursue a career as a chef,
Fodor'sChoice   which she did for several years at nearby Ciccio and elsewhere before
★   opening this perky storefront serving Latin-inspired multi-culti fast-
food cuisine. What's in season and the chef's whims determine the
order-at-the-counter fare, but Puerto Rican rice bowls (often with pork),
empanadas, and sweet-and-sour ramen stir-fries make regular appear-
ances. **Known for:** patio and rooftop seating; beer and wine lineup;
eager-to-please staff. ⑤ *Average main: $13* ⊠ *6488 Washington St., at
Oak Circle, Yountville* ☎ *707/415–5035* ⊕ *www.proteayv.com.*

$$$ ✕ **Redd.** Chef Richard Reddington's culinary influences include Califor-
MODERN   nia, Mexico, Europe, and Asia, but his dishes, like his minimalist dining
AMERICAN   room, feel modern and unfussy. The glazed pork belly with apple puree,
Fodor'sChoice   set amid a pool of soy caramel, is an example of the East-meets-West
★   style, and the seafood preparations—among them petrale sole, clams,
and chorizo poached in a saffron-curry broth—exhibit a similar trans-
continental dexterity. **Known for:** five-course tasting menu; street-side
outdoor patio; cocktails and small plates at the bar. ⑤ *Average main:
$30* ⊠ *6480 Washington St., at Oak Circle, Yountville* ☎ *707/944–2222*
⊕ *www.reddnapavalley.com.*

$$ × **Redd Wood.** Chef Richard Reddington's casual restaurant special-
ITALIAN izes in thin-crust wood-fired pizzas and contemporary variations on
rustic Italian classics. With sausage soup laced with cabbage and tur-
nip, pizzas such as the white anchovy with herb sauce and mozza-
rella, and the pork-chop entrée enlivened by persimmon, Redd Wood
does for Italian comfort food what nearby Mustards Grill does for
the American version: it spruces it up but retains its innate pleasures.
Known for: industrial decor; easygoing service. $ *Average main: $21*
⊠ *North Block Hotel, 6755 Washington St., at Madison St., Yountville*
☎ *707/299–5030* ⊕ *www.redd-wood.com.*

WHERE TO STAY

$$$$ 📷 **Bardessono.** Although Bardessono bills itself as the "greenest luxury
RESORT hotel in America," there's nothing spartan about its accommodations;
Fodor's Choice arranged around four landscaped courtyards, the rooms have luxurious
★ organic bedding, gas fireplaces, and huge bathrooms with walnut floors.
Pros: large rooftop lap pool; excellent spa, with in-room treatments
available. **Cons:** expensive; limited view from some rooms. $ *Rooms
from: $700* ⊠ *6526 Yount St., Yountville* ☎ *707/204–6000* ⊕ *www.
bardessono.com* ⟿ *62 rooms* ⦿❙ *No meals.*

$$ 📷 **Maison Fleurie.** A stay at this comfortable inn places you within easy
B&B/INN walking distance of Yountville's fine restaurants. **Pros:** smallest rooms a
bargain; outdoor hot tub; pool (open in season); free bike rental. **Cons:**
breakfast room can be crowded at peak times. $ *Rooms from: $219*
⊠ *6529 Yount St., Yountville* ☎ *707/944–2056, 800/788–0369* ⊕ *www.
maisonfleurienapa.com* ⟿ *13 rooms* ⦿❙ *Breakfast.*

$$$ 📷 **Napa Valley Lodge.** Clean rooms in a convenient motel-style setting
HOTEL draw travelers willing to pay more than at comparable lodgings in the
city of Napa to be within walking distance of Yountville's tasting rooms,
restaurants, and shops. **Pros:** clean rooms; filling continental breakfast;
large pool area. **Cons:** no elevator; lacks amenities of other Yount-
ville properties. $ *Rooms from: $350* ⊠ *2230 Madison St., Yountville*
☎ *707/944–2468, 888/944–3545* ⊕ *www.napavalleylodge.com* ⟿ *55
rooms* ⦿❙ *Breakfast.*

$$$$ 📷 **North Block Hotel.** With chic Tuscan style, this 20-room hotel has
HOTEL dark-wood furniture and a brown-and-sage decor. **Pros:** extremely
comfortable beds; attentive service; room service by Redd Wood res-
taurant. **Cons:** outdoor areas get some traffic noise. $ *Rooms from:
$420* ⊠ *6757 Washington St., Yountville* ☎ *707/944–8080* ⊕ *north-
blockhotel.com* ⟿ *20 rooms* ⦿❙ *No meals.*

SPORTS AND THE OUTDOORS
BALLOONING
Napa Valley Aloft. Between 8 and 12 passengers soar over the Napa
Valley in balloons that launch from downtown Yountville. Rates
include preflight refreshments and a huge breakfast. ⊠ *V Marketplace,
6525 Washington St., near Mulberry St., Yountville* ☎ *707/944–4400,
855/944–4408* ⊕ *www.nvaloft.com* ⊴ *From $220.*

6

BIKING

Fodor'sChoice ★ **Napa Valley Bike Tours.** With dozens of wineries within 5 miles, this shop makes a fine starting point for guided and self-guided vineyard and wine-tasting excursions. The outfit also rents bikes. ✉ *6500 Washington St., at Mulberry St., Yountville* ☎ *707/944–2953* ⊕ *www.napavalleybik-etours.com* ⬚ *From $124 (½-day guided tour).*

SPAS

Fodor'sChoice ★ **The Spa at Bardessono.** Many of this spa's patrons are hotel guests who take their treatments in their rooms' large, customized bathrooms—all of them equipped with concealed massage tables—but the main facility is open to guests and nonguests alike. An in-room treatment popular with couples starts with massages in front of the fireplace and ends with a whirlpool bath and a split of sparkling wine. For the two-hour Yountville Signature treatment, which can be enjoyed in-room or at the spa, a shea-butter-enriched sugar scrub is applied, followed by a massage with antioxidant Chardonnay grape-seed oil and a hydrating hair-and-scalp treatment. The spa engages massage therapists skilled in Swedish, Thai, and several other techniques. In addition to massages, the services include facials, waxing, and other skin-care treatments, as well as manicures and pedicures. ✉ *Bardessono Hotel, 6526 Yount St., at Mulberry St., Yountville* ☎ *707/204–6050* ⊕ *www.bardessono.com/ spa* ⬚ *Treatments $60–$630.*

SHOPPING

V Marketplace. This two-story redbrick market, which once housed a winery, a livery stable, and a brandy distillery, now contains clothing boutiques, art galleries, a chocolatier, and food, wine, and gift shops. Celebrity chef Michael Chiarello operates a restaurant (Bottega), a tasting room for his wines, and Ottimo, with pizza, fresh mozzarella, and other stands plus retail items. Show some love to the shops upstairs, especially Knickers and Pearls (lingerie and loungewear), Montecristi Panama Hats (Johnny Depp found one he liked), and Lemondrops (kids' clothing and toys). ✉ *6525 Washington St., near Mulberry St., Yountville* ☎ *707/944–2451* ⊕ *www.vmarketplace.com.*

OAKVILLE

2 miles northwest of Yountville.

A large butte that runs east–west just north of Yountville blocks the cooling fogs from the south, facilitating the myriad microclimates of the Oakville AVA, home to several high-profile wineries.

GETTING HERE AND AROUND

Driving along Highway 29, you'll know you've reached Oakville when you see the Oakville Grocery on the east side of the road. You can reach Oakville from the Sonoma County town of Glen Ellen by heading east on Trinity Road from Highway 12. The twisting route, along the mountain range that divides Napa and Sonoma, eventually becomes the Oakville Grade. The views on this drive are breathtaking, though the continual curves make it unsuitable for those who suffer from motion sickness.

EXPLORING

TOP ATTRACTIONS

B Cellars. The chefs take center stage in the open-hearth kitchen of this boutique winery's hospitality house, and with good reason: creating food-friendly wines is B Cellars's raison d'être. Visits to the Oakville facility—all steel beams, corrugated metal, and plate glass yet remarkably cozy—begin with a tour of the winery's culinary garden and caves. Most guests return to the house to sample wines paired with small bites, with some visitors remaining in the caves for exclusive tastings of Cabernet Sauvignons from several historic vineyards of Andy Beckstoffer, a prominent grower. Kirk Venge, whose fruit-forward style well suits the winery's food-oriented approach, crafts these and other wines, among them red and white blends and single-vineyard Cabernets from other noteworthy vineyards. ■TIP→ The B Cellars wine-and-food pairings, all strictly by appointment, are outstanding. ⊠ *703 Oakville Cross Rd., west of Silverado Trail, Oakville* ☎ *707/709–8787* ⊕ *www.bcellars.com* ☜ *Tastings $37–$135.*

Fodor's Choice ★ **Far Niente.** Guests arriving at Far Niente are welcomed by name and treated to a glimpse of one of the Napa Valley's most beautiful properties. By appointment only, small groups are escorted through the historic 1885 stone winery, including some of the 40,000 square feet of aging caves, for a lesson on the labor-intensive method of making Far Niente's flagship wines: a Cabernet Sauvignon blend and a Chardonnay. Next on the agenda is a peek at the Carriage House, which holds a gleaming collection of classic cars. The seated tasting of wines and cheeses that follows concludes on a sweet note with Dolce, a late-harvest wine made from Semillon and Sauvignon Blanc grapes. ⊠ *1350 Acacia Dr., off Oakville Grade Rd., Oakville* ☎ *707/944–2861* ⊕ *www.farniente.com* ☜ *Tasting and tour $75.*

Fodor's Choice ★ **Silver Oak.** The first review of this winery's Napa Valley Cabernet Sauvignon declared the debut 1972 vintage not all that good and, at $6 a bottle, overpriced. Oops. The celebrated Bordeaux-style Cabernet blend, still the only Napa Valley wine bearing its winery's label each year, evolved into a cult favorite, and Silver Oak founders Ray Duncan and Justin Meyer received worldwide recognition for their signature use of exclusively American oak to age the wines. At the Oakville tasting room, constructed out of reclaimed stone and other materials from a 19th-century Kansas flour mill, you can sip the current Napa Valley vintage, its counterpart from Silver Oak's Alexander Valley operation, and a library wine without an appointment. One is required for tours, private tastings, and food-wine pairings. ⊠ *915 Oakville Cross Rd., off Hwy. 29, Oakville* ☎ *707/942-7022* ⊕ *www.silveroak. com* ☜ *Tastings $30–$75, tour $50 (includes tasting).*

6

RUTHERFORD

2 miles northwest of Oakville.

With its singular microclimate and soil, Rutherford is an important viticultural center, with more big-name wineries than you can shake a corkscrew at. Cabernet Sauvignon is king here. The well-drained, loamy soil is ideal for those vines, and since this part of the valley gets plenty of sun, the grapes develop exceptionally intense flavors.

GETTING HERE AND AROUND

Wineries around Rutherford are dotted along Highway 29 and the parallel Silverado Trail north and south of Rutherford Road/Conn Creek Road, on which wineries can also be found.

EXPLORING

TOP ATTRACTIONS

FAMILY

Fodor's Choice

★

Frog's Leap. John Williams, owner of Frog's Leap, maintains a sense of humor about wine that translates into an entertaining yet informative experience—if you're a novice, the tour here is a fun way to begin your education. You'll taste wines that might include Zinfandel, Merlot, Chardonnay, Sauvignon Blanc, and an estate-grown Cabernet Sauvignon. The winery includes a barn built in 1884, 5 acres of organic gardens, an eco-friendly visitor center, and a frog pond topped with lily pads. Reservations are required for all visits here. ■TIP➔ The tour is recommended, but you can also just sample wines either inside or on a porch overlooking the garden. ⊠ *8815 Conn Creek Rd., Rutherford* ☎ *707/963–4704, 800/959–4704* ⊕ *www.frogsleap.com* 🍷 *Tastings $20–$25; tour $25.*

Inglenook. Filmmaker Francis Ford Coppola began his wine-making career in 1975, when he bought part of the historic Inglenook estate. Over the decades he reunited the original property acquired by Inglenook founder Gustave Niebaum, remodeled Niebaum's ivy-covered 1880s château, and purchased the rights to the Inglenook name. The Inglenook Experience ($50), an escorted tour of the château, vineyards, and caves, ends with a seated tasting of wines paired with artisanal cheeses. Among the topics discussed are the winery's history and the evolution of Coppola's signature wine, Rubicon, a Cabernet Sauvignon–based blend. The Heritage Tasting ($45), which also includes a Rubicon pour, is held in the opulent Pennino Salon. Reservations are required for some tastings and tours, and are recommended for all. ■TIP➔ Walk-ins can sip wines by the glass or bottle at The Bistro, a wine bar with a picturesque courtyard. ⊠ *1991 St. Helena Hwy./Hwy. 29, at Hwy.128, Rutherford* ☎ *707/968–1100, 800/782–4266* ⊕ *www.inglenook.com* 🍷 *Tastings $45–$50, private experiences from $75.*

Mumm Napa. In Mumm's light-filled tasting room or adjacent outdoor patio you can enjoy bubbly by the flight, but the sophisticated sparkling wines, elegant setting, and vineyard views aren't the only reasons to visit. An excellent gallery displays original Ansel Adams prints and presents temporary exhibitions by premier photographers. Winery tours cover the major steps in making sparklers. For a leisurely tasting of several vintages of the top-of-the-line DVX wines, book an

Frog's Leap's picturesque country charm extends all the way to the white picket fence.

Oak Terrace tasting ($50; reservations recommended Friday through Sunday). ■TIP→ **Carlos Santana fans may want to taste the sparklers the musician makes in collaboration with Mumm's winemaker, Ludovic Dervin.** ⊠ *8445 Silverado Trail, 1 mile south of Rutherford Cross Rd., Rutherford* ☎ *707/967–7700, 800/686–6272* ⊕ *www.mummnapa.com* ⊟ *Tastings $20–$50, tour $40 (includes tasting).*

WHERE TO EAT AND STAY

$$$$
MODERN
AMERICAN
Fodor's Choice
★

✕ **Restaurant at Auberge du Soleil.** Possibly the most romantic roost for a dinner in all the Wine Country is a terrace seat at the Auberge du Soleil resort's illustrious restaurant, and the Mediterranean-inflected cuisine more than matches the dramatic vineyard views. The prix-fixe dinner menu, which relies largely on local produce, might include veal sweetbreads and chanterelles in a caramelized shallot sauce or prime beef pavé with hearts of palm, lobster mushrooms, and bok choy. **Known for:** polished service; comprehensive wine list; over-the-top weekend brunch. ⑤ *Average main: $115* ⊠ *Auberge du Soleil, 180 Rutherford Hill Rd., off Silverado Trail, Rutherford* ☎ *707/963–1211, 800/348–5406* ⊕ *www.aubergedusoleil.com.*

$$$
AMERICAN
Fodor's Choice
★

✕ **Rutherford Grill.** Dark-wood walls, subdued lighting, and red leather banquettes make for a perpetually clubby mood at this trusty Rutherford hangout. Many entrées—steaks, burgers, fish, succulent rotisserie chicken, and barbecued pork ribs—emerge from an oak-fired grill operated by master technicians. **Known for:** French dip sandwich; reasonably priced wine list. ⑤ *Average main: $29* ⊠ *1180 Rutherford Rd., at Hwy. 29, Rutherford* ☎ *707/963–1792* ⊕ *www.rutherfordgrill.com.*

$$$$
RESORT
Fodor'sChoice
★

☆ **Auberge du Soleil.** Taking a cue from the olive-tree-studded landscape, this hotel with a renowned restaurant and spa cultivates a luxurious look that blends French and California style. **Pros:** stunning views over the valley; spectacular pool and spa areas; the most expensive suites are fit for a superstar. **Cons:** stratospheric prices; least expensive rooms get some noise from the bar and restaurant. ⑤ *Rooms from: $875* ✉ *180 Rutherford Hill Rd., Rutherford* ☎ *707/963–1211, 800/348–5406* ⊕ *www.aubergedusoleil.com* ⤴ *50 rooms* ❍❘ *Breakfast.*

ST. HELENA

2 miles northwest of Oakville.

Downtown St. Helena is a symbol of how well life can be lived in the Wine Country. Sycamore trees arch over Main Street (Highway 29), a funnel of outstanding restaurants and tempting boutiques. At the north end of town looms the hulking stone building of the Culinary Institute of America at Greystone. Weathered stone and brick buildings from the late 1800s give off that gratifying whiff of history.

The town got its start in 1854, when Henry Still built a store. Still wanted company, so he donated land lots on his town site to anyone who wanted to erect a business. Soon he was joined by a wagon shop, a shoe shop, hotels, and churches. Dr. George Crane planted a vineyard in 1858, and was the first to produce wine in commercially viable quantities. A German winemaker named Charles Krug followed suit a couple of years later, and other wineries soon followed.

GETTING HERE AND AROUND

Downtown stretches along Highway 29, called Main Street here. Many wineries lie north and south of downtown along Highway 29. More can be found off Silverado Trail, and some of the most scenic spots are on Spring Mountain, which rises southwest of town.

EXPLORING

TOP ATTRACTIONS

Charles Krug Winery. A historically sensitive renovation of its 1874 Redwood Cellar Building transformed the former production facility of the Napa Valley's oldest winery into an epic hospitality center. Charles Krug, a Prussian immigrant, established the winery in 1861 and ran it until his death in 1892. Italian immigrants Cesare Mondavi and his wife, Rosa, purchased Krug in 1943, and operated it with their sons Peter and Robert (who later opened his own winery). Krug, still run by Peter's family, specializes in small-lot Yountville and Howell Mountain Cabernet Sauvignons and makes Chardonnay, Merlot, Pinot Noir, Sauvignon Blanc, Zinfandel, and a Zinfandel port. The tour is by appointment only. ■ **TIP→ To sample the small-lot Cabernets, book a Family Reserve & Limited Release Tasting ($40).** ✉ *2800 Main St./Hwy. 29, across from the Culinary Institute of America, St. Helena* ☎ *707/967–2229* ⊕ *www.charleskrug.com* ✉ *Tastings $20–$40, tour $60 (includes tasting).*

Fodor'sChoice
★

Hall St. Helena. The Cabernet Sauvignons produced here are works of art and the latest in organic-farming science and wine-making technology. A glass-walled tasting room allows guests to see in action some of the high-tech equipment winemaker Steve Leveque employs to craft wines that also include Merlot, Cabernet Franc, and Sauvignon Blanc. Westward from the second-floor tasting area, rows of neatly spaced Cabernet vines capture the eye, and beyond them the tree-studded Mayacamas Mountains. The main guided tour takes in the facility, the grounds, and a restored 19th-century winery, passing by artworks—inside and out—by John Baldessari, Jaume Plensa, Jesús Moroles, and other contemporary talents. ■TIP➔ **Among the engaging seminars here is the Ultimate Cabernet Experience ($125), the winery's flagship tasting of current and library releases, as well as wines still aging in barrel.** ✉ *401 St. Helena Hwy./Hwy. 29, near White La., St. Helena* 🕾 *707/967–2626* ⊕ *www.hallwines.com* 🥂 *Tastings $40–$250, tours $40–$50.*

Fodor's Choice
★

Joseph Phelps Vineyards. An appointment is required for tastings at the winery started by the late Joseph Phelps, but it's well worth the effort—all the more so after an inspired renovation of the main redwood structure, a classic of 1970s Northern California architecture. Known for wines crafted with grace and precision, Phelps does produce fine whites, but the blockbusters are red, particularly the Cabernet Sauvignon and the luscious-yet-subtle Bordeaux-style blend called Insignia. In good weather, one-hour seated tastings take place on a terrace overlooking vineyards and oaks. At 90-minute tastings as thoughtfully conceived as the wines, guests explore such topics as wine-and-cheese pairing, wine blending, and the role oak barrels play in wine making. Participants in the blending seminar mix the various varietals that go into the Insignia blend. ✉ *200 Taplin Rd., off Silverado Trail, St. Helena* 🕾 *707/963–2745, 800/707–5789* ⊕ *www.josephphelps.com* 🥂 *Tastings and seminars $75–$200.*

Pride Mountain Vineyards. This winery 2,200 feet up Spring Mountain straddles Napa and Sonoma counties, confusing enough for visitors but even more complicated for the wine-making staff: government regulations require separate wineries and paperwork for each side of the property. It's one of several amusing Pride Mountain quirks, but winemaker Sally Johnson's "big red wines," including a Cabernet Sauvignon that earned 100-point scores from a major wine critic two years in a row, are serious business. At tastings and on tours you can learn about the farming and cellar strategies behind Pride's acclaimed Cabs (the winery also produces Syrah, a Cab-like Merlot, Viognier, and Chardonnay among others). The tour, which takes in vineyards and caves, also includes tastings of wine still in barrel. ■TIP➔ **The views here are knock-your-socks-off gorgeous.** ✉ *4026 Spring Mountain Rd., off St. Helena Rd. (extension of Spring Mountain Rd. in Sonoma County), St. Helena* 🕾 *707/963–4949* ⊕ *www.pridewines.com* 🥂 *Tastings $20–$75.*

WORTH NOTING

Beringer Vineyards. Brothers Frederick and Jacob Beringer opened the winery that still bears their name in 1876. One of California's earliest bonded wineries, it is the oldest one in the Napa Valley never to have missed a vintage—no mean feat, given Prohibition. Frederick's grand Rhine House Mansion, built in 1884, serves as the reserve tasting room. Here, surrounded by Belgian art-nouveau hand-carved oak and walnut furniture and stained-glass windows, you can sample wines that include a limited-release Chardonnay, a few big Cabernets, and a Sauterne-style dessert wine. A less expensive tasting takes place in the original stone winery. Reservations are required for some tastings and recommended for tours. ■TIP➔ The one-hour Taste of Beringer ($50) tour of the property and sensory gardens surveys the winery's history and wine making and concludes with a seated wine-and-food pairing. ✉ *2000 Main St./ Hwy. 29, near Pratt Ave., St. Helena* ☎ *707/963–8989, 866/708–9463* ⊕ *www.beringer.com* 🍷 *Tastings $25–$125, tours $30–$50.*

Culinary Institute of America at Greystone. The West Coast headquarters of the country's leading school for chefs is in the 1889 Greystone Cellars, an imposing building once the world's largest stone winery. On the ground floor you can check out the quirky Corkscrew Museum and browse the Spice Islands Marketplace shop, stocked with gleaming gadgets and many cookbooks. The Bakery Café by illy serves soups, salads, sandwiches, and baked goods. One-day and multiday cooking and beverage classes take place weekly, public cooking demonstrations on weekends. Students run the Gatehouse Restaurant, which serves lunch and dinner except during semester breaks. ✉ *2555 Main St./Hwy. 29, St. Helena* ☎ *707/967–1100* ⊕ *www.ciachef.edu/california* 🍷 *Museum free, cooking demonstrations $25, class prices vary.*

WHERE TO EAT

$$
MODERN
AMERICAN
Fodor's Choice
★

✕ **Cindy's Backstreet Kitchen.** At her up-valley outpost, Cindy Pawlcyn serves variations on the comfort food she made popular at Mustards Grill, but spices things up with dishes influenced by Mexican, Central American, and occasionally Asian cuisines. Along with staples such as meat loaf with garlic mashed potatoes and beef and duck burgers served with impeccable fries, the menu might include a rabbit tostada or curried chicken salad. **Known for:** warm pineapple upside-down cake; ethereal parfait. 💲 *Average main: $22* ✉ *1327 Railroad Ave., at Hunt St., 1 block east of Main St., St. Helena* ☎ *707/963–1200* ⊕ *www. cindysbackstreetkitchen.com.*

$$
ITALIAN
Fodor's Choice
★

✕ **Cook St. Helena.** A curved marble bar spotlit by contemporary art-glass pendants adds a touch of style to this downtown restaurant whose Northern Italian cuisine pleases with similarly understated sophistication. Mussels with house-made sausage in a spicy tomato broth, chopped salad with pancetta and pecorino, and the daily changing risotto are among the dishes regulars revere. **Known for:** top-quality ingredients; reasonably priced local and international wines; Cook Tavern two doors down for beer, wine, and cocktail-friendly small plates. 💲 *Average main: $22* ✉ *1310 Main St., near Hunt Ave., St. Helena* ☎ *707/963–7088* ⊕ *www.cookshelena.com.*

$$$
MODERN
AMERICAN

✕ **Farmstead at Long Meadow Ranch.** Housed in a high-ceilinged former barn, Farmstead revolves around an open kitchen where executive chef Stephen Barber's team prepares meals with grass-fed beef and lamb, fruits and vegetables, eggs, olive oil, wine, honey, and other ingredients from parent company Long Meadow Ranch. Entrées might include wood-grilled trout with fennel, brussels sprouts, pears, and hazelnuts, or a pork chop with broccolini, jalapeño grits, and apple chutney. **Known for:** Tuesday fried-chicken night; house-made charcuterie; seasonal cocktails. 💲 *Average main: $24* ✉ *738 Main St., at Charter Oak Ave., St. Helena* ☎ *707/963–4555* ⊕ *www.longmeadowranch.com/farmstead-restaurant.*

$$$
MODERN
AMERICAN
Fodor'sChoice
★

✕ **Goose & Gander.** The pairing of food and drink at G&G is as likely to involve cool cocktails as wine. Main courses such as grilled sturgeon, pork loin with sweet-potato hash, and Wagyu beef with Bordelaise sauce work well with starters that might include lamb merguez toast and mushroom soup from wild and cultivated fungi. **Known for:** intimate main dining room with fireplace; alfresco dining on patio in good weather; basement bar among Napa's best drinking spots. $ *Average main: $29* ✉ *1245 Spring St., at Oak St., St. Helena* ☎ *707/967–8779* ⊕ *www.goosegander.com.*

$
AMERICAN

✕ **Gott's Roadside.** A 1950s-style outdoor hamburger stand goes upscale at this spot whose customers brave long lines to order breakfast sandwiches, juicy burgers, root-beer floats, and garlic fries. Choices not available a half century ago include the ahi tuna burger and the chili-spice-marinated chicken breast served with Mexican slaw. **Known for:** tasty (if pricey) 21st-century diner cuisine; shaded picnic tables (arrive early or late for lunch to get one); second branch at Napa's Oxbow Public Market. $ *Average main: $13* ✉ *933 Main St./Hwy. 29, St. Helena* ☎ *707/963–3486* ⊕ *www.gotts.com* ☞ *Reservations not accepted.*

$$$$
MODERN
AMERICAN

✕ **Press.** Few taste sensations surpass the combination of a sizzling steak and a Napa Valley red, a union the chef and sommeliers at Press celebrate with a reverence bordering on obsession. Grass-fed beef cooked on the cherry-and-almond-wood-fired grill and rotisserie is the star— especially the rib eye for two—but the cooks also prepare pork chops, free-range chicken, fish, and even vegetarian dishes such as carrot and yellow-eye bean cassoulet. **Known for:** extensive wine cellar; impressive cocktails; casual-chic ambience. $ *Average main: $48* ✉ *587 St. Helena Hwy./Hwy. 29, at White La., St. Helena* ☎ *707/967–0550* ⊕ *www. pressthelena.com* ☽ *Closed Tues. No lunch.*

$$$$
MODERN
AMERICAN
Fodor'sChoice
★

✕ **The Restaurant at Meadowood.** Chef Christopher Kostow has garnered rave reviews—and three Michelin stars for several years running—for creating a unique dining experience. Patrons choosing the Tasting Menu option ($275 per person) enjoy their meals in the dining room, its beautiful finishes aglow with warm lighting, but up to four guests can select the Counter Menu ($500 per person) for the chance to sit in the kitchen and watch Kostow's team prepare the food. **Known for:** complex cuisine; first-class service; romantic setting. $ *Average main: $275* ✉ *900 Meadowood La., off Silverado Trail N, St. Helena* ☎ *707/967–1205, 800/458–8080* ⊕ *www.therestaurantatmeadowood.com* ☽ *Closed Sun. No lunch* ☞ *Jacket suggested but not required.*

$$$$
MEDITERRANEAN
Fodor'sChoice
★

✕ **Terra.** In an 1884 fieldstone building, chef Hiro Sone gives an unexpected twist to Italian and southern French cuisine, though for a few dishes, among them the signature sake-marinated black cod in a shiso broth, he draws on his Japanese background. Homey yet elegant desserts, courtesy of Sone's wife, Lissa Doumani, might include a chocolate mousseline with chocolate–peanut butter crunch and toasted marshmallow. **Known for:** prix-fixe menu; old-school romance and service; Bar Terra for cocktails, lighter fare à la carte. $ *Average main: $85* ✉ *1345 Railroad Ave., off Hunt Ave., St. Helena* ☎ *707/963–8931* ⊕ *www.terrarestaurant.com* ☽ *Closed Tues. No lunch.*

6

WHERE TO STAY

$
HOTEL
🖥 **El Bonita Motel.** The tidy rooms at this roadside motel are nice enough for budget-minded travelers, and the landscaped grounds and picnic tables put this property a cut above similar accommodations. **Pros:** cheerful rooms; hot tub; microwaves and mini-refrigerators. **Cons:** road noise is a problem in some rooms. ⑤ *Rooms from: $196* ✉ *195 Main St./Hwy. 29, St. Helena* ☎ *707/963–3216, 800/541–3284* ⊕ *www.elbonita.com* ⇨ *52 rooms* ⦿ *Breakfast.*

$$$
HOTEL
🖥 **Harvest Inn by Charlie Palmer.** Although this inn sits just off Highway 29, its patrons remain mostly above the fray, strolling 8 acres of landscaped gardens, enjoying views of the vineyards adjoining the property, partaking in spa services, and drifting to sleep in beds adorned with fancy linens and down pillows. **Pros:** garden setting; spacious rooms; well-trained staff. **Cons:** some lower-price rooms lack elegance; high weekend rates. ⑤ *Rooms from: $354* ✉ *1 Main St., St. Helena* ☎ *707/963–9463, 800/950–8466* ⊕ *www.harvestinn.com* ⇨ *78 rooms* ⦿ *Breakfast.*

$$$$
RESORT
Fodor'sChoice
★
🖥 **Meadowood Napa Valley.** Founded in 1964 as a country club, Meadowood has evolved into a five-star resort, a gathering place for Napa's wine-making community, and a celebrated dining destination. **Pros:** superb restaurant; hiking trails; gracious service; all-organic spa. **Cons:** very expensive; far from downtown St. Helena. ⑤ *Rooms from: $650* ✉ *900 Meadowood La., St. Helena* ☎ *707/963–3646, 800/458–8080* ⊕ *www.meadowood.com* ⇨ *85 rooms* ⦿ *No meals.*

CALISTOGA

3 miles northwest of St. Helena.

With false-fronted, Old West–style shops and 19th-century inns and hotels lining its main drag, Lincoln Avenue, Calistoga comes across as more down-to-earth than its more polished neighbors. Don't be fooled, though. On its outskirts lie some of the Wine Country's swankest (and priciest) resorts and its most fanciful piece of architecture, the medieval-style Castello di Amorosa winery.

Calistoga was developed as a spa-oriented getaway from the start. Sam Brannan, a gold rush–era entrepreneur, planned to use the area's natural hot springs as the centerpiece of a resort complex. His venture failed, but old-time hotels and bathhouses—along with some glorious new spas—still operate. You can come for an old-school mud bath, or go completely 21st century and experience lavish treatments based on the latest innovations in skin and body care.

GETTING HERE AND AROUND

Highway 29 heads east (turn right) at Calistoga, where in town it is signed as Lincoln Avenue. If arriving via the Silverado Trail, head west at Highway 29/Lincoln Avenue.

EXPLORING

TOP ATTRACTIONS

Ca' Toga Galleria d'Arte. The boundless wit, whimsy, and creativity of the Venetian-born Carlo Marchiori, this gallery's owner-artist, finds expression in paintings, watercolors, ceramics, sculptures, and other artworks. Marchiori often draws on mythology and folktales for his inspiration. A stop at this magical gallery may inspire you to tour **Villa Ca' Toga,** the artist's fanciful Palladian home, a tromp-l'oeil tour de force open for tours from May through October on Saturday mornings only, by appointment. ⊠ *1206 Cedar St., near Lincoln Ave., Calistoga* ☎ *707/942–3900* ⊕ *www.catoga.com* ☾ *Closed Tues. and Wed.*

Fodor'sChoice **Schramsberg.** On a Diamond Mountain site first planted to grapes in the
★ early 1860s, Schramsberg produces sparkling wines using the *méthode traditionnelle* (aka *méthode champenoise*). A fascinating tour covering Schramberg's history and wine-making techniques precedes the tasting. In addition to glimpsing the winery's historic architecture you'll visit caves, some dug in the 1870s by Chinese laborers, where 2 million–plus bottles are stacked in gravity-defying configurations. Tastings include generous pours of very different bubblies. To learn more about them, consider attending the session at which the wines are paired with cheeses; not held every day, this tasting focuses on the ways wine influences our experience of food and vice versa. All visits here are by appointment. ⊠ *1400 Schramsberg Rd., off Hwy. 29, Calistoga* ☎ *707/942–4558, 800/877–3623* ⊕ *www.schramsberg.com* ✉ *Tastings and tours $65–$120.*

Fodor'sChoice **Venge Vineyards.** As the son of Nils Venge, the first winemaker to earn
★ a 100-point score from the wine critic Robert Parker, Kirk Venge had a hard act to follow. Now a consultant to exclusive wineries himself, Kirk is an acknowledged master of balanced, fruit-forward Bordeaux-style blends. At his casual ranch-house tasting room you can sip wines that might include the estate Bone Ash Cabernet Sauvignon, an Oakville Merlot, a Syrah from the Stagecoach Vineyard in the Vaca hills, and the Silencieux Cabernet, a blend of grapes from several appellations. Tastings are by appointment only. ■**TIP→** With its views of the well-manicured Bone Ash Vineyard and, west across the valley, Diamond Mountain, the ranch house's porch would make for a magical perch even if Venge's wines weren't works of art in themselves. ⊠ *4708 Silverado Trail, 1½ miles south of downtown, near Dunaweal La., Calistoga* ☎ *707/942–9100* ⊕ *www.vengevineyards.com* ✉ *Tasting $25* ☾ *Reservations recommended 3–4 wks in advance for weekend visits.*

WORTH NOTING

Castello di Amorosa. An astounding medieval structure complete with drawbridge and moat, chapel, stables, and secret passageways, the Castello commands Diamond Mountain's lower eastern slope. Some of the 107 rooms contain replicas of 13th-century frescoes (cheekily signed, "[the-artist's-name].com"), and the dungeon has an iron maiden from Nuremberg, Germany. You must pay for a tour to see most of Dario Sattui's extensive eight-level property, though with a basic tasting you'll have access to part of the complex. Bottlings of note include several Italian-style wines, including La Castellana, a robust "super Tuscan" blend of Cabernet Sauvignon, Sangiovese, and Merlot; and Il Barone, a deliberately big Cab made largely from Rutherford grapes. ■**TIP→** The two-hour Royal Food & Wine Pairing Tour by sommelier Mary Davidek ($85, by appointment only) is among the Wine Country's best. ⊠ *4045 N. St. Helena Hwy./Hwy. 29, near Maple La., Calistoga* ☎ *707/967–6272* ⊕ *www.castellodiamorosa.com* ✉ *Tastings $25–$35, tours $40–$85 (include tastings).*

All it needs is a fair maiden: Castello di Amorosa's re-created castle.

Chateau Montelena. Set amid a bucolic northern Calistoga landscape, this winery helped establish the Napa Valley's reputation for high-quality wine making. At the pivotal Paris tasting of 1976, the Chateau Montelena 1973 Chardonnay took first place, beating out four white Burgundies from France and five other California Chardonnays, an event immortalized in the 2008 movie *Bottle Shock*. A 21st-century Napa Valley Chardonnay is always part of a Current Release Tasting ($25)—the winery also makes Sauvignon Blanc, Riesling, a fine estate Zinfandel, and Cabernet Sauvignon—or you can opt for a Limited Release Tasting ($50) focusing more on Cabernets. The walking Estate Tour takes in the grounds and covers the history of this stately property whose stone winery building was erected in 1888. Guests board a vehicle for the seasonal Vineyard Tour. Tours and some tastings require a reservation. ✉ *1429 Tubbs La., off Hwy. 29, Calistoga* ☎ *707/942-5105* ⊕ *www.montelena.com* ✉ *Tastings $25–$75, tours $40–$78.*

Tamber Bey Vineyards. Endurance riders Barry and Jennifer Waitte share their passion for horses and wine at their glam-rustic winery north of Calistoga. Their 22-acre Sundance Ranch remains a working equestrian facility, but the site has been revamped to include a state-of-the-art winery with separate fermenting tanks for grapes from Tamber Bey's vineyards in Yountville, Oakville, and elsewhere. The winemakers produce three Chardonnays and a Sauvignon Blanc, but the stars are several subtly powerful reds, including the flagship Oakville Cabernet Sauvignon and a Yountville Merlot. A recent vintage of the top-selling wine, the Rabicano blend, contained Cabernet Sauvignon, Merlot, Petit

Verdot, and Cabernet Franc. Visits to taste or tour require an appointment. ✉ *1251 Tubbs La., at Myrtledale Rd., Calistoga* ☎ *707/942–2100* ⊕ *www.tamberbey.com* 🍷 *Tastings $35–$65, tour $10 extra.*

WHERE TO EAT

$$$
MODERN
AMERICAN
Fodor's Choice
★

✕ **Evangeline.** Brandon Sharp, formerly of nearby Solbar, opened this restaurant whose gas-lamp-style lighting fixtures, charcoal-black hues, and bistro cuisine evoke old New Orleans with a California twist. Executive chef Gustavo Rios puts a jaunty spin on dishes that might include shrimp étouffée or grilled salmon with a chicory salad; the elaborate weekend brunch, with everything from buttermilk waffles to shrimp po'boys, is an up-valley favorite. **Known for:** outdoor courtyard; palate-cleansing Sazeracs and signature old-fashioneds; gumbo ya-ya and addictive fried pickles. ⑤ *Average main: $24* ✉ *1226 Washington St., near Lincoln Ave., Calistoga* ☎ *707/341–3131* ⊕ *www.evangelin-enapa.com* 🕐 *No lunch weekdays.*

$$
MODERN
AMERICAN

✕ **Sam's Social Club.** Tourists, locals, and spa guests—some of the latter in bathrobes after treatments—assemble at this resort restaurant for breakfast, lunch, bar snacks, or dinner. Lunch options include pizzas, sandwiches, an aged-cheddar burger, and entrées such as chicken paillard, with the burger reappearing for dinner along with grilled salmon, rib-eye steak frites, and similar fare, perhaps preceded by oysters and other cocktail-friendly starters. **Known for:** casual atmosphere; active patio scene; thin-crust lunch pizzas. ⑤ *Average main: $22* ✉ *Indian Springs Resort and Spa, 1712 Lincoln Ave., at Wappo Ave., Calistoga* ☎ *707/942–4969* ⊕ *www.samssocialclub.com.*

$$$$
MODERN
AMERICAN
Fodor's Choice
★

✕ **Solbar.** As befits a restaurant at a spa resort, the sophisticated menu at Solbar is divided into "healthy, lighter dishes" and "hearty cuisine," with the stellar wine list's many half-bottle selections encouraging moderation, too. On the lighter side, grilled yellowfin tuna might come with charred carrots, mole amarillo, and toasted pumpkin seeds, with heartier options recently including a wood-grilled pork tenderloin with jasmine rice, chili-laced cashews, and mustard greens. **Known for:** stylish dining room; festive outdoor patio; Sunday brunch. ⑤ *Average main: $33* ✉ *Solage Calistoga, 755 Silverado Trail, at Rosedale Rd., Calistoga* ☎ *877/684–9146* ⊕ *www.solagecalistoga.com/solbar.*

WHERE TO STAY

$$$$
RESORT
Fodor's Choice
★

🏨 **Calistoga Ranch.** Spacious cedar-shingle lodges throughout this posh wooded property have outdoor living areas, and even the restaurant, spa, and reception space have outdoor seating and fireplaces. **Pros:** many lodges have private hot tubs on the deck; lovely hiking trails on the property; guests have reciprocal facility privileges at Auberge du Soleil and Solage Calistoga. **Cons:** innovative indoor-outdoor organization works better in fine weather than in rain or cold. ⑤ *Rooms from: $895* ✉ *580 Lommel Rd., Calistoga* ☎ *707/254–2800, 855/942–4220* ⊕ *www.calistogaranch.com* 🛏 *50 guest lodges* ❑ *No meals.*

$$
B&B/INN
Fodor's Choice
★

🏨 **Embrace Calistoga.** Extravagant hospitality defines the Napa Valley's luxury properties, but Embrace Calistoga—the renamed Luxe Calistoga still run by the same attentive owners—takes the prize in the "small lodging" category. **Pros:** attentive owners; marvelous breakfasts; restaurants, tasting rooms, and shopping within walking distance. **Cons:**

the hum of street traffic. $ *Rooms from: $269* ✉ *1139 Lincoln Ave., Calistoga* ☎ *707/942–9797* ⤳ *5 rooms* ⊙ *Breakfast.*

$$ ⬚ **Indian Springs Resort and Spa.** Stylish Indian Springs—operating as a
RESORT spa since 1862—ably splits the difference between laid-back and chic
in accommodations that include lodge rooms, dozens of suites, 14
duplex cottages, three stand-alone bungalows, and two houses. **Pros:**
palm-studded grounds with outdoor seating areas; on-site Sam's Social
Club restaurant; enormous mineral pool. **Cons:** lodge rooms are small.
$ *Rooms from: $239* ✉ *1712 Lincoln Ave., Calistoga* ☎ *707/942–4913*
⊕ *www.indianspringscalistoga.com* ⤳ *113 rooms* ⊙ *No meals.*

$$$$ ⬚ **Solage Calistoga.** The aesthetic at this 22-acre property is Napa Val-
RESORT ley barn meets San Francisco loft: guest rooms have high ceilings, pol-
Fodor's Choice ished concrete floors, recycled walnut furniture, and all-natural fabrics
★ in soothingly muted colors. **Pros:** great service; complimentary bikes;
separate pools for kids and adults. **Cons:** vibe may not suit everyone.
$ *Rooms from: $530* ✉ *755 Silverado Trail, Calistoga* ☎ *855/942–7442,
707/226–0800* ⊕ *www.solagecalistoga.com* ⤳ *89 rooms* ⊙ *No meals.*

SPAS

Fodor's Choice **Spa Solage.** This eco-conscious spa has reinvented the traditional Cal-
★ istoga mud and mineral-water therapies. Case in point: the hour-long
"Mudslide," a three-part treatment that includes a mud body mask (in
a heated lounge), a soak in a thermal bath, and a power nap in a sound-
vibration chair. The mud here is a mix of clay, volcanic ash, and essential
oils. Traditional spa services—combination Shiatsu-Swedish and other
massages, full-body exfoliations, facials, and waxes—are available, as
are fitness and yoga classes. ✉ *755 Silverado Trail, at Rosedale Rd.,
Calistoga* ☎ *707/226–0825, 855/790–6023* ⊕ *www.solagecalistoga.
com/spa* ▭ *Treatments $110–$510.*

SPORTS AND THE OUTDOORS

Calistoga Bikeshop. Options here include regular and fancy bikes that rent
for $28 and up for two hours, and there's a self-guided Cool Wine Tour
($110) that includes tastings at three or four small wineries. ✉ *1318
Lincoln Ave., near Washington St., Calistoga* ☎ *707/942–9687* ⊕ *www.
calistogabikeshop.net.*

THE SONOMA VALLEY

The birthplace of modern California wine making—Count Aragon
Haraszthy opened Buena Vista Winery here in 1857—Sonoma Valley
seduces with its unpretentious attitude and pastoral landscape. Tasting
rooms, restaurants, and historic sites, among the latter the last mission
established in California by Franciscan friars, abound near Sonoma Plaza.
Beyond downtown Sonoma, the wineries and attractions are spread out
along gently winding roads. Sonoma County's half of the Carneros Dis-
trict lies within Sonoma Valley, whose other towns of note include Glen
Ellen and Kenwood. Sonoma Valley tasting rooms are often less crowded
than those in Napa or northern Sonoma County, especially midweek, and
the vibe here, though sophisticated, is definitely less sceney.

SONOMA

14 miles west of Napa, 45 miles northeast of San Francisco.

One of the few towns in the valley with multiple attractions not related to food and wine, Sonoma has plenty to keep you busy for a couple of hours before you head out to tour the wineries. And you needn't leave town to taste wine. There are about three dozen tasting rooms within steps of the tree-filled Sonoma plaza, some of which pour wines from more than one winery. The valley's cultural center, Sonoma was founded in 1835 when California was still part of Mexico.

GETTING HERE AND AROUND

Highway 12 (signed as Broadway near Sonoma Plaza) heads north into Sonoma from Highway 121 and south from Santa Rosa into downtown Sonoma, where (signed as West Spain Street) it travels east to the plaza. Parking is relatively easy to find on or near the plaza, and you can walk to many restaurants, shops, and tasting rooms. Signs point the way to several wineries a mile or more east of the plaza.

EXPLORING

TOP ATTRACTIONS

Gundlach Bundschu. "Gun lock bun shoe" gets you close to pronouncing this winery's name correctly, though everyone here shortens it to Gun Bun. The Bundschu family, which has owned most of this property since 1858, makes reds that include Cabernet Franc, Cabernet Sauvignon, Merlot, and a Bordeaux-style blend of each vintage's best grapes. Gewürztraminer, Chardonnay, and two rosés are also in the mix. Parts of the 1870 stone winery where standard tastings ($20) unfold are still used for wine making. For a more comprehensive experience, book a cave tour ($40), a Pinzgauer vehicle vineyard tour ($60), or a Heritage Reserve ($85) pairing of limited-release wines with small gourmet bites. Some tastings and all tours are by appointment only. ■TIP➔ On some summer days you can enjoy the outdoor Vista Courtyard's broad vineyard views while tasting wines paired with cheese and charcuterie ($30). ⊠ 2000 Denmark St., at Bundschu Rd., off 8th St. E, 3 miles southeast of Sonoma Plaza, Sonoma ☎ 707/938–5277 ⊕ www.gunbun.com ☎ Tastings $20–$30, tours $40–$85 (include tastings).

Fodor's Choice **Patz & Hall.** Sophisticated single-vineyard Chardonnays and Pinot ★ Noirs are the trademark of this respected winery whose tastings take place in a fashionable single-story residence 3 miles southeast of Sonoma Plaza. It's a Wine Country adage that great wines are made in the vineyard—the all-star fields represented here include Hyde, Durell, and Gap's Crown—but winemaker James Hall routinely surpasses peers with access to the same fruit, proof that discernment and expertise (Hall is a master at oak aging) play a role, too. You can sample wines at the bar and on some days on the vineyard-view terrace beyond it, but to learn how food friendly these wines are, consider the Salon Tasting, at which they're paired with gourmet bites crafted with equal finesse. Tastings are by appointment only. ⊠ 21200 8th St. E, near Peru Rd., Sonoma ☎ 707/265–7700 ⊕ www.patzhall.com ☎ Tastings $30–$60.

Ram's Gate Winery. Stunning views, ultrachic architecture, and wines made from grapes grown by acclaimed producers make a visit to Ram's Gate an event. The welcoming interior spaces—think Restoration Hardware with a dash of high-style whimsy—open up to the entire western Carneros. In fine weather you'll experience the cooling breezes that sweep through the area while sipping sophisticated wines, mostly Pinot Noirs and Chardonnays, but also Pinot Blanc, Sauvignon Blanc, Cabernet Sauvignon, and Syrah. With grapes sourced from the Sangiacomo, Hudson, and other illustrious vineyards, winemaker Jeff Gaffner focuses on creating balanced wines that express what occurred in nature that year. All visits are by appointment only. ■ TIP→ You can sip current releases at the tasting bar ($40), take a tour-and-taste ($65), or tour and enjoy wines paired with food ($90). ✉ 28700 Arnold Dr./Hwy. 121, Sonoma ☎ 707/721–8700 ⊕ www.ramsgatewinery.com ✉ Tastings $40–$90; tour $65 (includes tasting) ⊘ Closed Tues. and Wed.

Fodor'sChoice **Scribe.** Andrew and Adam Mariani, sons of California walnut grow-
    ★   ers, established Scribe in 2007 on land first planted to grapes in 1858 by Emil Dresel, a German immigrant. Dresel's claims to fame include cultivating Sonoma's first Riesling and Sylvaner, an achievement the brothers honor by growing both varietals on land he once farmed. Using natural wine-making techniques they craft bright, terroir-driven wines from those grapes, along with Chardonnay, Pinot Noir, Syrah, and Cabernet Sauvignon. In restoring their property's 1915 Mission Revival–style hacienda the brothers preserved various layers of history—original molding and light fixtures, for instance, but also fragments of floral-print wallpaper and 1950s newspapers. Now a tasting space, the hacienda served during Prohibition as a bootleggers' hideout, and its basement harbored a speakeasy: two intriguing tales among many associated with this historic site. Tastings are by appointment only. ✉ 2100 Denmark St., off Napa Rd., Sonoma ☎ 707/939–1858 ⊕ scribewinery.com ✉ Tasting price varies; contact winery.

Sonoma Mission. The northernmost of the 21 missions established by Franciscan friars in California, Sonoma Mission was founded in 1823 as Mission San Francisco Solano. It serves as the centerpiece of **Sonoma State Historic Park,** which includes several other sites in Sonoma and nearby Petaluma. Some early mission structures were destroyed, but all or part of several remaining buildings date to the days of Mexican rule over California. Worth a look are the **Sonoma Barracks,** a half block west of the mission at 20 East Spain Street, which housed troops under the command of General Mariano Guadalupe Vallejo, who controlled vast tracts of land in the region. **General Vallejo's Home,** a Victorian-era structure, is a few blocks west. ✉ 114 E. Spain St., at 1st St. E, Sonoma ☎ 707/938–9560 ⊕ www.parks.ca.gov/?page_id=479 ✉ $3, includes same-day admission to other historic sites.

Fodor'sChoice **Walt Wines.** You could spend a full day sampling wines in the tast-
    ★   ing rooms bordering or near Sonoma Plaza, but be sure not to miss Walt, which specializes in Pinot Noir from Sonoma County, Mendocino County (just to the north), California's Central Coast, and Oregon's Willamette Valley. Walk-ins are welcome to taste several wines inside a mid-1930s Tudor-inspired home or, weather permitting, at backyard

Sonoma County

tables beneath a tall, double-trunk redwood tree. To see how winemaker Megan Gunderson Paredes's wines pair with food—in this case small bites from The Girl & the Fig across the street—make a reservation for the Root 101: A Single Vineyard Exploration. At both tastings you'll learn about the origins of this sister winery to Hall St. Helena. ✉ *380 1st St. W, at W. Spain St., Sonoma* ☎ *707/933–4440* ⊕ *www.waltwines. com* ✉ *Tastings $30–$60.*

WORTH NOTING

Buena Vista Winery. The birthplace of modern California wine making has been transformed into an entertaining homage to the accomplishments of the 19th-century wine pioneer Count Agoston Haraszthy. Tours pass through the original aging caves dug deep into the hillside by Chinese laborers, and banners, photos, and artifacts inside and out convey the history made on this site. Reserve tastings ($40) include library and current releases, plus barrel samples. The rehabilitated former press house (used for pressing grapes into wine), which dates to 1862, hosts the standard tastings. Chardonnay, Pinot Noir, several red blends, and a vibrant Petit Verdot are the strong suits here. Tours are by appointment only. ■ TIP→ The high-tech Historic Wine Tool Museum displays implements, some decidedly low-tech, used to make wine over the years. ✉ *18000 Old Winery Rd., off E. Napa St., Sonoma* ☎ *800/926–1266* ⊕ *www.buenavistawinery.com* ✉ *Tastings $20–$50, tours $25–$40.*

WHERE TO EAT

$$$ ✕ **Cafe La Haye.** The dining room is compact, the open kitchen even
AMERICAN more so, but chef Jeffrey Lloyd turns out understated, sophisticated fare
Fodor'sChoice emphasizing local ingredients. Chicken, beef, pasta, and fish get deluxe
★ treatment without fuss or fanfare—the daily roasted chicken and the risotto specials are always good. **Known for:** Napa-Sonoma wine list with clever French complements; signature butterscotch pudding dessert; owner Saul Gropman on hand to greet diners. ⑤ *Average main: $24* ✉ *140 E. Napa St., at 1st St. E, Sonoma* ☎ *707/935–5994* ⊕ *www. cafelahaye.com* ♡ *Closed Sun. and Mon. No lunch.*

$$$ ✕ **El Dorado Kitchen.** This restaurant owes its visual appeal to its clean lines
MODERN and handsome decor, but the eye inevitably drifts westward to the open
AMERICAN kitchen, where executive chef Armando Navarro's crew crafts dishes full of subtle surprises. The menu might include ahi tuna tartare with wasabi tobiko caviar as a starter, with paella awash with seafood and dry-cured Spanish chorizo sausage among the entrées. **Known for:** subtle tastes and textures; truffle-oil fries with Parmesan; spiced crepes and other desserts. ⑤ *Average main: $26* ✉ *El Dorado Hotel, 405 1st St. W, at W. Spain St., Sonoma* ☎ *707/996–3030* ⊕ *www.eldoradosonoma.com/restaurant.*

$$$ ✕ **The Girl & the Fig.** At this hot spot for inventive French cooking inside
FRENCH the historic Sonoma Hotel bar you can always find a dish with owner
Fodor'sChoice Sondra Bernstein's signature figs on the menu, whether it's a fig-and-
★ arugula salad or an aperitif blending sparkling wine with fig liqueur. Also look for duck confit, a burger with matchstick fries, and wild flounder meunière. **Known for:** wine list emphasis on Rhône varietals; artisanal cheese platters; croques monsieurs and eggs Benedict at Sunday brunch. ⑤ *Average main: $24* ✉ *Sonoma Hotel, 110 W. Spain St., at 1st St. W, Sonoma* ☎ *707/938–3634* ⊕ *www.thegirlandthefig.com.*

$$$ ✕**Harvest Moon Cafe.** Everything at this little restaurant with an odd,
AMERICAN   zigzag layout is so perfectly executed and the vibe is so genuinely warm
Fodor'sChoice   that a visit here is deeply satisfying. The ever-changing menu might
★   include homey dishes such as grilled half chicken with baked polenta
or pan-seared Hawaiian ono with jasmine rice and eggplant. **Known
for:** friendly service; back patio with central fountain. $ *Average main:
$25* ✉ *487 1st St. W, at W. Napa St., Sonoma* ☎ *707/933–8160* ⊕ *www.
harvestmooncafesonoma.com* ⊗ *Closed Tues. No lunch.*

$$$$ ✕**LaSalette Restaurant.** Born in the Azores and raised in Sonoma, chef-
PORTUGUESE   owner Manuel Azevedo serves three- and five-course prix-fixe meals
Fodor'sChoice   inspired by his native Portugal. The wood-oven-roasted fish is always
★   worth trying, and there are usually boldly flavored lamb and pork
dishes, along with soups, stews, salted cod, and other hearty fare.
Known for: authentic Portuguese cuisine; sophisticated spicing; olive-oil
cake with queijo fresco (fresh cheese) ice cream. $ *Average main: $55*
✉ *452 1st St. E, near E. Spain St., Sonoma* ☎ *707/938–1927* ⊕ *www.
lasalette-restaurant.com.*

$$$$ ✕**Oso Sonoma.** Chef David Bush, who achieved national recognition for
MODERN   his food pairings at St. Francis Winery, owns this barlike small-plates
AMERICAN   restaurant whose menu evolves throughout the day. Lunch might see mole
braised pork-shoulder tacos or an achiote chicken sandwich, with din-
ner fare perhaps of steamed mussels, harissa roasted salmon, or roasted
forest mushrooms with baby spinach and polenta. **Known for:** bar menu
between lunch and dinner; Korean soju cocktails; decor of reclaimed
materials. $ *Average main: $32* ✉ *9 E. Napa St., at Broadway, Sonoma*
☎ *707/931–6926* ⊕ *www.ososonoma.com* ⊗ *No lunch Mon.–Wed.*

$ ✕**Sunflower Caffé.** Cheerful art and brightly painted walls set a jolly tone
AMERICAN   at this casual eatery whose assets include sidewalk seating with Sonoma
Plaza views and the verdant patio out back. Omelets and waffles are
the hits at breakfast, with the smoked duck breast sandwich, served on
a baguette and slathered with caramelized onions, a favorite for lunch.
Known for: combination café, gallery, and wine bar; local cheeses and
hearty soups; free Wi-Fi. $ *Average main: $13* ✉ *421 1st St. W, at
W. Spain St., Sonoma* ☎ *707/996–6645* ⊕ *www.sonomasunflower.com*
⊗ *No dinner.*

WHERE TO STAY

$$ ⌂ **Inn at Sonoma.** They don't skimp on the little luxuries here: wine and
B&B/INN   hors d'oeuvres are served every evening in the lobby, and the cheerfully
painted rooms are warmed by gas fireplaces. **Pros:** last-minute specials
are a great deal; free soda available in the lobby. **Cons:** on a busy street
rather than right on the plaza. $ *Rooms from: $220* ✉ *630 Broadway,
Sonoma* ☎ *707/939–1340, 888/568–9818* ⊕ *www.innatsonoma.com*
⏎ *27 rooms* ❘⊙❘ *Breakfast.*

$$$ ⌂ **MacArthur Place Hotel & Spa.** Guests at this 7-acre boutique property
HOTEL   five blocks south of Sonoma Plaza bask in ritzy seclusion in plush accom-
Fodor'sChoice   modations set amid landscaped gardens. **Pros:** secluded garden setting;
★   high-style furnishings; on-site steak house. **Cons:** a bit of a walk from
the plaza; some traffic noise audible in street-side rooms. $ *Rooms from:
$399* ✉ *29 E. MacArthur St., Sonoma* ☎ *707/938–2929, 800/722–1866*
⊕ *www.macarthurplace.com* ⏎ *64 rooms* ❘⊙❘ *Breakfast.*

6

$
B&B/INN
FAMILY

Sonoma Creek Inn. The small but cheerful rooms at this motel-style inn are individually decorated with painted wooden armoires, cozy quilts, and brightly colored contemporary artwork. **Pros:** clean, well-lighted bathrooms; lots of charm for the price; popular with bicyclists. **Cons:** office not staffed 24 hours a day; a 10-minute drive from Sonoma Plaza. $ *Rooms from: $145 ⊠ 239 Boyes Blvd., off Hwy. 12, Sonoma ☎ 707/939–9463, 888/712–1289 ⊕ www.sonomacreekinn.com ↝ 16 rooms ⊙ No meals.*

SPAS

Willow Stream Spa at Fairmont Sonoma Mission Inn & Spa. With 40,000 square feet and 30 treatment rooms, the Wine Country's largest spa provides every amenity you could possibly want, including pools and hot tubs fed by local thermal springs. Although the place fills with patrons in summer and on some weekends, the vibe is always soothing. The signature bathing ritual includes an exfoliating shower, dips in two mineral-water soaking pools, an herbal steam, and a dry-salt sauna and rain tunnel. The regime draws to a close with cool-down showers. Other popular treatments involve alkaline baths, aloe-gel wraps, and massages in styles from Swedish to Thai. For a touch of the exotic designed to leave your skin luminous, try a caviar facial. The most requested room among couples is outfitted with a two-person copper bathtub. ⊠ *100 Boyes Blvd./Hwy. 12, 2½ miles north of Sonoma Plaza, Sonoma ☎ 707/938–9000 ⊕ www. fairmont.com/sonoma/willow-stream ☐ Treatments $65–$528.*

SHOPPING

Sonoma Plaza is a shopping magnet, with tempting boutiques and specialty food purveyors facing the square or within a block or two.

G's General Store. The inventory of this "modern general store" runs the gamut from cute bunny LED nightlights and Euro-suave kitchen utensils to bright-print shirts and a log-and-leather sofa fit for a ski chalet. The owner used to buy for Smith & Hawken and Williams-Sonoma, so expect upscale merch presented with style. ⊠ *19 W. Napa St., near Broadway, Sonoma ☎ 707/933–8082 ⊕ www.ggeneralstore.com.*

Fodor'sChoice
★

Sonoma Valley Certified Farmers Market. To discover just how bountiful the Sonoma landscape is—and how talented its farmers and food artisans are—head to Depot Park, just north of the Sonoma Plaza, on Friday morning. This market is considered Sonoma County's best. ⊠ *Depot Park, 1st St. W, at the Sonoma Bike Path, Sonoma ☎ 707/538–7023 ⊕ www.svcfm.org.*

GLEN ELLEN

7 miles north of Sonoma.

Unlike its flashier Napa Valley counterparts, Glen Ellen eschews well-groomed sidewalks lined with upscale boutiques and restaurants, preferring instead its crooked streets, some with no sidewalks at all, shaded with stands of old oak trees. Jack London, who represents Glen Ellen's rugged spirit, lived in the area for many years; the town commemorates him with place names and nostalgic establishments. Hidden among sometimes-ramshackle buildings abutting Sonoma and Calabasas creeks are low-key shops and galleries worth poking through, and several fine dining establishments.

GETTING HERE AND AROUND

Glen Ellen sits just off Highway 12. From the north or south, take Arnold Drive west and follow it south less than a mile. The walkable downtown straddles a half-mile stretch of Arnold Drive.

EXPLORING

Fodor's Choice ★ **Benziger Family Winery.** One of the best-known Sonoma County wineries sits on a sprawling estate in a bowl with 360-degree sun exposure, the benefits of which are explored on tram tours that depart several times daily. Guides explain Benziger's biodynamic farming practices and provide a glimpse of the extensive cave system. The regular tram tour costs $25; another tour costing $50 concludes with a seated tasting. Known for Chardonnay, Cabernet Sauvignon, Merlot, Pinot Noir, and Sauvignon Blanc, the winery is a beautiful spot for a picnic. ■TIP→ Reserve a seat on the tram tour through the winery's website or arrive early in the day on summer weekends and during harvest season. ✉ *1883 London Ranch Rd., off Arnold Dr., Glen Ellen* ☎ *707/935–3000, 888/490–2739* ⊕ *www.benziger.com* 🍷 *Tastings $20–$40, tours $25–$50.*

Fodor's Choice ★ **Jack London State Historic Park.** The pleasures are pastoral and intellectual at author Jack London's beloved Beauty Ranch. You could easily spend the afternoon hiking some of the 30-plus miles of trails that loop through meadows and stands of oaks, redwoods, and other trees. Manuscripts and personal artifacts depicting London's travels are on view at the House of Happy Walls Museum, which provides an overview of the writer's life and literary passions. A short hike away lie the ruins of Wolf House, which burned down just before London was to move in. Also open to visitors are a few outbuildings and the restored Cottage, a wood-framed building where he penned many of his later works. He's buried on the property. ■TIP→ Well-known performers headline the park's Broadway Under the Stars series, a hot ticket in summer. ✉ *2400 London Ranch Rd., off Arnold Dr., Glen Ellen* ☎ *707/938–5216* ⊕ *www.jacklondonpark.com* 🍷 *Parking $10 ($5 walk-in or bike), includes admission to museum; cottage $4.*

Fodor's Choice ★ **Lasseter Family Winery.** Immaculately groomed grapevines dazzle the eye at John and Nancy Lasseter's secluded winery, and it's no accident: Phil Coturri, Sonoma Valley's premier organic and biodynamic vineyard manager, tends them. Even the landscaping, which includes an insectary to attract beneficial bugs, is meticulously maintained. Come harvesttime, winemaker Julia Lantosca oversees gentle processes that transform the fruit into wines of purity and grace: a Semillon–Sauvignon Blanc blend, two rosés, and Bordeaux and Rhône reds. As might be expected of a storyteller as accomplished as John, whose screenwriting credits include *Toy Story, Cars,* and other Pixar features, evocative labels illustrate the tale behind each wine. These stories are well told on tours that precede tastings of wines, paired with local artisanal cheeses, in an elegant room whose east-facing window frames vineyard and Mayacamas Mountains views. All visits are by appointment only. ✉ *1 Vintage La., off Dunbar Rd., Glen Ellen* ☎ *707/933–2814* ⊕ *www.lasseterfamilywinery.com* 🍷 *Tastings (some with tours) $25–$45.*

6

Hitching a ride on the Benziger Family Winery tram tour

WHERE TO EAT

$$ ✕ **Aventine Glen Ellen.** A Wine Country cousin to chef Adolfo Veronese's
ITALIAN same-named San Francisco and Hollywood establishments, this Ital-
Fodor'sChoice ian restaurant occupies an 1839 sawmill from California's Mexican
★ period. Veronese's varied menu includes several pizzas (the seasonal
one with black truffle honey, béchamel, and wild arugula is a savory
masterpiece), an equal number of pasta dishes, a daily risotto, and sev-
eral meat and fish entrées. **Known for:** chicken parmigiana the envy of
local Sicilian grandmothers; outdoor patio overlooking Sonoma Creek.
⑤ *Average main: $20* ✉ *Jack London Village, 14301 Arnold Dr., ¾ mile
south of downtown, Glen Ellen* ☎ *707/934–8911* ⊕ *www.aventinehos-
pitality.com/glen-ellen* ۩ *Closed Mon. and Tues.*

$$ ✕ **The Fig Cafe.** The compact menu at this cheerful bistro, a Glen Ellen
FRENCH fixture, focuses on California and French comfort food—pot roast and
duck confit, for instance, as well as thin-crust pizza. Steamed mussels are served with crispy fries, which also accompany the sirloin
burger, and weekend brunch brings out locals and tourists for French
toast, corned-beef hash, and pizza with applewood-smoked bacon and
poached eggs. **Known for:** casual ambience; no corkage fee, so good
for enjoying your winery discoveries. ⑤ *Average main: $18* ✉ *13690
Arnold Dr., at O'Donnell La., Glen Ellen* ☎ *707/938–2130* ⊕ *www.
thefigcafe.com* ۩ *No lunch weekdays.*

$$$ ✕ **Glen Ellen Star.** Chef Ari Weiswasser honed his craft at The French
ECLECTIC Laundry, Daniel, and other bastions of culinary finesse, but at his Wine
Fodor'sChoice Country outpost he prepares haute-rustic cuisine, much of it emerg-
★ ing from a wood-fired oven that burns a steady 600°F. Crisp-crusted,
richly sauced Margherita and other pizzas thrive in the torrid heat,

as do tender whole fish entrées and vegetables roasted in small iron skillets. **Known for:** kitchen-view counter for watching chefs cook; enclosed patio; Weiswasser's sauces, emulsions, and spices. $ *Average main: $28* ☒ *13648 Arnold Dr., at Warm Springs Rd., Glen Ellen* ☎ *707/343–1384* ⊕ *glenellenstar.com* ⊗ *No lunch.*

WHERE TO STAY

$$
B&B/INN
Fodor'sChoice
★

Gaige House. Asian objets d'art and leather club chairs cozied up to the lobby fireplace are just a few of the graceful touches in this luxurious but understated bed-and-breakfast. **Pros:** beautiful lounge areas; lots of privacy; excellent service; full breakfasts, afternoon wine and appetizers. **Cons:** sound carries in the main house; the least expensive rooms are on the small side. $ *Rooms from: $275* ☒ *13540 Arnold Dr., Glen Ellen* ☎ *707/935–0237, 800/935–0237* ⊕ *www.gaige.com* ⤳ *23 rooms* ⦿ *Breakfast.*

$$
B&B/INN
Fodor'sChoice
★

Olea Hotel. The husband-and-wife team of Ashish and Sia Patel operate this boutique lodging that's at once sophisticated and down-home country casual. **Pros:** beautiful style; welcoming staff; chef-prepared breakfasts; complimentary wine throughout stay. **Cons:** fills up quickly on weekends; minor road noise in some rooms. $ *Rooms from: $288* ☒ *5131 Warm Springs Rd., west off Arnold Dr., Glen Ellen* ☎ *707/996–5131* ⊕ *www.oleahotel.com* ⤳ *15 rooms* ⦿ *Breakfast.*

KENWOOD

4 miles north of Glen Ellen.

Tiny Kenwood consists of little more than a few restaurants, shops, tasting rooms, and a historic train depot, now used for private events. But hidden in this pretty landscape of meadows and woods at the north end of Sonoma Valley are several good wineries, most just off the Sonoma Highway. Varietals grown here at the foot of the Sugarloaf Mountains include Sauvignon Blanc, Chardonnay, Zinfandel, and Cabernet Sauvignon.

GETTING HERE AND AROUND

To get to Kenwood from Glen Ellen, head northeast on Arnold Drive and north on Highway 12. Sonoma Transit Bus 30 and Bus 38 serve Kenwood from Glen Ellen and Sonoma.

EXPLORING

TOP ATTRACTIONS

Fodor'sChoice
★

B Wise Vineyards Cellar. The stylish roadside tasting room of this producer of small-lot reds sits on the valley floor, but B Wise's winery and vineyards occupy a prime spot high in the Moon Mountain District AVA. B Wise made its name crafting big, bold Cabernets. One comes from owner Brion Wise's mountain estate and another from the nearby Monte Rosso Vineyard, some of whose Cabernet vines are among California's oldest. These hearty mountain-fruit Cabs contrast with a suppler one from the Napa Valley's Coombsville AVA. Mark Herold, known for several cult wines, makes the Cabernets with Massimo Monticelli, who's responsible for the rest of the uniformly excellent lineup: Sonoma Coast Chardonnay; Russian River Valley, Sonoma

Coast, and Willamette Valley (Oregon) Pinot Noir; and estate Syrah, Petite Sirah, Petit Verdot, and Zinfandel. ✉ *9077 Sonoma Hwy., at Shaw Ave., Kenwood* ☎ *707/282-9169* ⊕ *www.bwisevineyards.com* 🍷 *Tasting $20.*

Kunde Estate Winery & Vineyards. On your way into Kunde you pass a terrace flanked by fountains, virtually coaxing you to stay for a picnic with views over the vineyard. Family owned for more than a century, Kunde prides itself on producing 100% estate wines from its 1,850-acre property, which rises 1,400 feet from the valley floor. Kunde's whites include several Chardonnays and a Sauvignon Blanc, with Cabernet Sauvignon, Merlot, and a Zinfandel from 1880s vines among the reds. Two wines of note available only through the winery, both in the Destination Series, are the Red Dirt Red blend of seven varietals and the Dunfillan Cuvée, made from Cabernet and Syrah grapes. ■TIP→ Make a reservation for the Mountain Top Tasting, a tour by luxury van that ends with a sampling of reserve wines. ✉ *9825 Sonoma Hwy./Hwy. 12, Kenwood* ☎ *707/833-5501* ⊕ *www.kunde.com* 🍷 *Tastings $15–$50, Mountain Top Tasting $50, grounds and cave tour free.*

St. Francis Winery. Nestled at the foot of Mt. Hood, St. Francis has earned national acclaim for its wine-and-food pairings. With its red-tile roof and bell tower and views of the Mayacamas Mountains just to the east, the winery's California Mission–style visitor center occupies one of Sonoma County's most scenic locations. The charm of the surroundings is matched by the mostly red wines, including rich, earthy Zinfandels from the Dry Creek, Russian River, and Sonoma valleys. Chef Bryan Jones's five-course small bites-and-wine-pairings ($68)— Liberty duck breast cassoulet with one of the Zins, for example—are offered from Thursday through Monday; pairings with cheeses and charcuterie ($35) are available daily. ✉ *100 Pythian Rd., off Hwy. 12, Kenwood* ☎ *888/675-9463, 707/833-0242* ⊕ *www.stfranciswinery. com* 🍷 *Tastings $15–$68.*

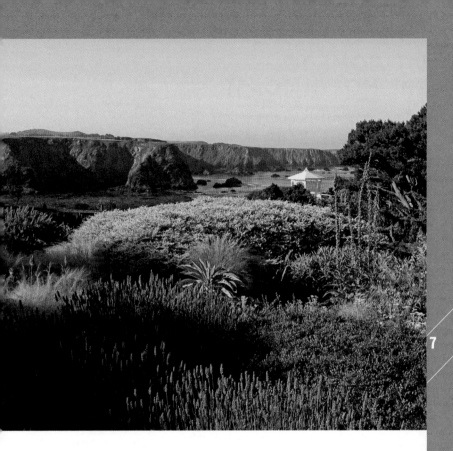

THE NORTH COAST

from the Sonoma Coast to
Redwood State Parks

WELCOME TO THE NORTH COAST

TOP REASONS TO GO

★ **Scenic coastal drives:** There's hardly a road here that *isn't* scenic.

★ **Wild beaches:** This stretch of California is one of nature's masterpieces. Revel in the unbridled, rugged coastline, without a building in sight.

★ **Dinnertime:** When you're done hiking the beach, refuel with delectable food; you'll find everything from fish tacos to foie gras.

★ **Romance:** Here you can end almost every day with a perfect sunset.

★ **Wildlife:** Watch for migrating whales, sunbathing sea lions, and huge Roosevelt elk with majestic antlers.

1 The Sonoma Coast. As you enter Sonoma County from the south on Highway 1, you pass first through gently rolling pastureland. North of Bodega Bay dramatic shoreline scenery takes over. The road snakes up, down, and around sheer cliffs and steep inclines— some without guardrails— where cows seem to cling precariously. Stunning vistas (or cottony fog) and hairpin turns make for an exhilarating drive.

2 The Mendocino Coast. The timber industry gave birth to most of the small towns along this stretch of coastline. Although tourism now drives the economy, the region has retained much of its old-fashioned charm. The beauty of the landscape, of course, has not changed. Inland lies the Anderson Valley, whose wineries mostly grow cool-climate grapes.

3 Redwood Country. There's a different state of mind in Humboldt County. Here, instead of spas, there are old-time hotels. Instead of wineries, there are breweries. The landscape is primarily thick redwood forest; the interior mountains get snow in winter and sizzle in summer while the coast sits covered in fog. Until as late as 1924 there was no road north of Willits; the coastal towns were reachable only by sea. That legacy is apparent in the communities of today: Eureka and Arcata, both former ports, are sizeable, but otherwise towns are tiny and nestled in the woods, and people have an independent spirit that recalls the original homesteaders.

4 Redwood State Parks. For a pristine encounter with giant redwoods, make the trek to these coastal parks where even casual visitors have easy access to the trees.

Smith River
Point St. George
Crescent City
199
SISKIYOU MOUNTAINS
101
96
KLAMATH MOUNTAINS
Klamath
Redwood National
& State Parks **4**
Orick
Patrick's Point
State Park
Trinidad
96
McKinleyville
Willow Creek
Arcata Bay **3** Arcata
Humboldt Bay Eureka
299
Fortuna
COAST
Ferndale Hydesville
Cape
Mendocino Rio 36 Hayfork
Point Dell
Gorda Humboldt
Redwoods
State Park
KING MTN RANGE Garberville
Leggett
Laytonville
R
A
1 101
Fort Bragg
N
Willits
P Mendocino
A Little River 20
C Albion G
I **2** Elk 128 Ukiah 20
F ANDERSON Lucerne E
I VALLEY
C Point Arena Kelseyville Clearlake S
Cloverdale Lower Lake
Gualala
O Pacific Coast Hwy 1
C Stewarts Healdsburg
E Point **1** Calistoga
A Jenner 101 Saint Helena
N Occidental Santa Rosa
Sebastopol 29
Bodega Bay Napa
Petaluma Sonoma
Inverness Novato Vallejo
Point Reyes 1 Concord
National Seashore Richmond **80**
Bolinas Berkeley
San Francisco Oakland
Daly City

0 _____ 30 mi
0 _____ 30 km

7

GETTING ORIENTED

It's all but impossible to explore the Northern California coast without a car. Indeed, you wouldn't want to—driving here is half the fun. The main road is Highway 1, two lanes that twist and turn (sometimes 180 degrees) up cliffs and down through valleys. Towns appear every so often, but this is mostly a land of green pasture, dense forest, and natural, undeveloped coastline. ■TIP➔ Pace yourself: Most drivers stop frequently to appreciate the views, and you can't safely drive faster than 30 or 40 mph on many portions of the highway. Don't plan to drive too far in one day.

Updated by
Daniel Mangin

The spectacular coastline between Marin County and the Oregon border defies expectations. The landscape is defined by the Pacific Ocean, but instead of boardwalks and bikinis there are ragged cliffs and pounding waves— and the sunbathers are mostly sea lions. Instead of strip malls and freeways, you'll find a single-lane road that follows a fickle shoreline. Although the towns along the way vary from deluxe spa retreat to hippie hideaway, all are reliably sleepy—and that's exactly why many Californians escape here to enjoy nature unspoiled.

This stretch of Highway 1 is made up of numerous little worlds, each different from the last. From Point Reyes toward Bodega Bay, the land spreads out into green, rolling pastures and sandy beaches. The road climbs higher and higher as it heads north through Sonoma County, and in Mendocino County the coastline follows the ins and outs of lush valleys where rivers pour down from the forests and into the ocean. At Humboldt County the highway heads inland to the redwoods, and then returns to the shoreline at the tidal flats surrounding the ports of Eureka and Arcata. Heading north to the Oregon border, the coast is increasingly wild and lined with giant redwood trees.

When you travel the North Coast, turn off your phone; you won't have much of a signal anyway. Everything about life here says slow down. If you don't, you might miss a noble Roosevelt elk grazing in a roadside field or a pod of migrating whales cruising along the shore.

PLANNING

WHEN TO GO

The North Coast is a year-round destination, though when you go determines what you will see. The migration of the Pacific gray whales is a wintertime phenomenon, which lasts roughly from mid-December to early April. Wildflowers follow the winter rain, as early as January in southern areas through June and July farther north. Summer is the high season for tourists, but spring, fall, and even winter are arguably better times to visit. The pace is slower, towns are quieter, and lodging is cheaper.

The coastal climate is similar to San Francisco's, although winter nights are colder than in the city. In July and August thick fog can drop temperatures to the high 50s, but fear not. You need only drive inland a few miles to find temperatures that are often 20 degrees higher.

GETTING HERE AND AROUND

AIR TRAVEL

Arcata/Eureka Airport (ACV), 14 miles north of Eureka in McKinleyville, is served by subsidiaries of Alaska and United, and a few other small airlines. Taking City Cab to Eureka costs about $55 and takes roughly 25 minutes. Door-to-door Airporter shuttle rides cost $20 to Arcata and Trinidad, $24 to Eureka, and $50 to Ferndale for the first person, $5 for each additional person.

Airport Contacts Arcata/Eureka Airport. ⊠ *3561 Boeing Ave., McKinleyville* ☎ *707/445–9651* ⊕ *flyhumboldt.org.*

Ground Transportation Contacts City Cab. ☎ *707/442–4551* ⊕ *www. cityambulance.com/CityCab.htm.* **Door-to-Door Airporter.** ☎ *888/338–5497, 707/839–4186* ⊕ *www.doortodoorairporter.com.*

BUS TRAVEL

Greyhound buses travel along U.S. 101 from San Francisco to Garberville, Eureka, and Arcata. Humboldt Transit Authority connects Eureka, Arcata, and Trinidad.

Bus Contacts Greyhound. ☎ *800/231–2222* ⊕ *www.greyhound.com.* **Humboldt Transit Authority.** ☎ *707/443–0826* ⊕ *www.hta.org.*

CAR TRAVEL

U.S. 101 has excellent services, but long stretches separate towns along Highway 1. ■ TIP→ **If you're running low on fuel and see a gas station, stop for a refill.** Twisting Highway 1 is the scenic route to Mendocino from San Francisco, but the fastest one is U.S. 101 north to Highway 128 west (from Cloverdale) to Highway 1 north. The quickest route to the far North Coast is straight up U.S. 101.

Road Conditions Caltrans. ☎ *800/427–7623* ⊕ *www.dot.ca.gov.*

RESTAURANTS

Restaurants here, a few with regional reputations but most off the culinary world's radar, entice diners with dishes fashioned from the abundant fresh seafood and locally grown vegetables and herbs. Attire is usually informal, though at pricier establishments dressy casual is the norm. Most kitchens close at 8 or 8:30 and few places serve past 9:30. Many restaurants close in January or early February. *Restaurant reviews have been shortened. For full information, visit Fodors.com.*

HOTELS

Restored Victorians, rustic lodges, country inns, and vintage motels are among the accommodations available here. Few have air-conditioning (the ocean breezes make it unnecessary), and many have no phones or TVs in the rooms. Budget accommodations are rare, but in winter you're likely to find reduced rates and nearly empty lodgings. In summer and on the weekends, though, make bed-and-breakfast reservations as far ahead as possible—rooms at the best inns often sell out months in advance. *Hotel reviews have been shortened. For full information, visit Fodors.com.*

WHAT IT COSTS			
$	**$$**	**$$$**	**$$$$**
RESTAURANTS under $16	$16–$22	$23–$30	over $30
HOTELS under $120	$120–$175	$176–$250	over $250

Restaurant prices are the average cost of a main course at dinner or, if dinner is not served, at lunch, excluding sales tax of 7.5–8¼%. Hotel prices are the lowest cost of a standard double room in high season, excluding service charges and 8%–11% tax.

VISITOR INFORMATION

Contacts Humboldt County Convention and Visitors Bureau. ⊠ *322 1st St., Eureka* ☎ *707/443–5097, 800/346–3482* ⊕ *redwoods.info.* **Sonoma County Tourism.** ☎ *707/522–5800, 800/576–6662* ⊕ *www.sonomacounty.com.* **Visit Mendocino County.** ⊠ *345 N. Franklin St., Fort Bragg* ☎ *707/964–9010, 866/466–3636* ⊕ *www.visitmendocino.com.*

THE SONOMA COAST

State parks and beaches and small seaside towns line Sonoma County's rugged, photogenic coastline. Highway 1 curves its way more than 55 miles from Marin to Mendocino County. Along the way you can tidepool, walk the beach, and hike redwood-studded trails. From some of the higher perches you might spot a whale in winter.

BODEGA BAY

23 miles west of Santa Rosa.

From this working town's busy harbor west of Highway 1, commercial boats pursue fish and Dungeness crab. In 1962 Alfred Hitchcock shot *The Birds* in the area. The Tides Wharf complex, an important location, is no longer recognizable, but a few miles inland, in Bodega, you can find Potter Schoolhouse, now a private residence.

GETTING HERE AND AROUND

To reach Bodega Bay, exit U.S. 101 at Santa Rosa and take Highway 12 west (called Bodega Highway west of Sebastopol) 23 miles to the coast. A scenic alternative is to take U.S. 101's East Washington Street/Central Petaluma exit and follow signs west to Bodega Bay; just after you merge onto Highway 1, you'll pass through down-home Valley Ford. Mendocino Transit Authority (⊕ *mendocinotransit.org*) Route 95 buses serve Bodega Bay.

EXPLORING

Sonoma Coast Vineyards. This boutique winery with an oceanview tasting room makes cool-climate Chardonnays and Pinot Noirs from grapes grown close to the Pacific. The Antonio Mountain and Balistreri Family Vineyards Pinot Noirs stand out among wines that also include a mildly oaky Sauvignon Blanc, a Syrah, and a well-balanced sparkler. ⊠ *555 Hwy. 1* ☎ *707/921–2860* ⊕ *www.sonomacoastvineyards.com* ⊒ *$20.*

BEACHES

Fodor'sChoice ★ **Sonoma Coast State Park.** The park's gorgeous sandy coves stretch for 17 miles from Bodega Head to 4 miles north of Jenner. **Bodega Head** is a popular whale-watching perch in winter and early spring, and **Rock Point, Duncan's Landing,** and **Wright's Beach**, at about the halfway mark, have good picnic areas. Rogue waves have swept people off the rocks at Duncan's Landing Overlook, so don't stray past signs warning you away. Calmer **Shell Beach**, about 2 miles north, is known for beachcombing, tidepooling, and fishing. Walk the blufftop **Kortum Trail** or drive about 2½ miles north of Shell Beach to **Blind Beach.** Near the mouth of the Russian River just north of here at **Goat Rock Beach**, you'll find harbor seals; pupping season is from March through August. Bring binoculars and walk north from the parking lot to view the seals. During summer, lifeguards are on duty at some beaches, but strong rip currents and heavy surf keep most visitors on shore. **Amenities:** parking; toilets. **Best for:** solitude; sunset; walking. ⊠ *Park Headquarters/Salmon Creek Ranger Station, 3095 Hwy. 1, 2 miles north of Bodega Bay* ☎ *707/875–3483* ⊕ *www.parks.ca.gov* ⊒ *$8 per vehicle.*

WHERE TO EAT AND STAY

$
SEAFOOD
Fodor'sChoice ★ **✕ Spud Point Crab Company.** Crab sandwiches, clam chowder New England or Manhattan style, and house-made crab cakes with roasted red pepper sauce star on the brief menu of this shacklike operation. Place your order inside, and enjoy your meal to go or at one of the marina-view picnic tables outside. **Known for:** family-run operation; opens at 9 am; superb chowder; seafood cocktails. ⑤ *Average main: $9* ⊠ *1910 Westshore Rd.* ☎ *707/875–9472* ⊕ *www.spudpointcrab.com* ☉ *No dinner.*

$$$$
MODERN
AMERICAN
Fodor'sChoice ★ **✕ Terrapin Creek Cafe & Restaurant.** Intricate but not fussy cuisine based on locally farmed ingredients and the fruits de mer has made this restaurant the darling of western Sonoma County. Start with raw Marin Miyagi oysters, rich mushroom soup, or (in-season) Dungeness crabmeat ragout before moving on to halibut or other fish pan-roasted to perfection. **Known for:** intricate cuisine; a top Bay Area "foodies" choice. ⑤ *Average main: $31* ⊠ *1580 Eastshore Rd.* ☎ *707/875–2700* ⊕ *www.terrapincreekcafe.com* ☉ *Closed Tues. and Wed.*

$$$$
HOTEL
Fodor's Choice
★

Bodega Bay Lodge. Looking out to the ocean across a wetland, the lodge's shingle-and-river-rock buildings contain Bodega Bay's finest accommodations. **Pros:** fireplaces and patios or balconies in most rooms; operated by a trusted upscale California brand; ocean views. **Cons:** pricey in-season; parking lot in foreground of some rooms' views; fairly long drive to other fine-dining restaurants. ⑤ *Rooms from: $350* ✉ *103 Coast Hwy. 1* ☎ *707/875–3525, 888/875–2250* ⊕ *www.bodegabaylodge.com* ⌂ *83 rooms* ⦿| *No meals.*

$
HOTEL

Bodega Harbor Inn. As humble as can be, this is one of the few places on this stretch of the coast with rooms for around $100 a night. **Pros:** budget choice; rooms for larger groups; ocean views from public areas and some rooms. **Cons:** an older facility; nondescript rooms; behind a shopping center. ⑤ *Rooms from: $99* ✉ *1345 Bodega Ave.* ☎ *707/875–3594* ⊕ *www.bodegaharborinn.com* ⌂ *16 rooms* ⦿| *No meals.*

SPORTS AND THE OUTDOORS
WHALE-WATCHING

Fodor's Choice
★

Bodega Bay Sailing Adventures. Part salty dog and part jolly entertainer, Captain Rich conducts three-hour Bodega Bay tours on his 33-foot sailboat. Whales are often sighted from winter into early spring, and sea lions and harbor seals commonly appear. The sunset tour is especially fun. ✉ *Meeting place near sport fishing center, 1418 Bay Flat Rd.* ☎ *707/318–2251* ⊕ *www.bodegabaysailing.org* ⌂ *From $95.*

FORT ROSS STATE HISTORIC PARK

22 miles north of Bodega Bay.

With its reconstructed Russian Orthodox chapel, stockade, and officials' quarters, Fort Ross looks much the way it did after the Russians made it their major California coastal outpost in 1812. An excellent museum documents the fort's history.

GETTING HERE AND AROUND

From Bodega Bay, take Highway 1 north to Fort Ross. From Santa Rosa, head west on Highway 116 about 33 miles to Jenner, then north 12 miles on Highway 1. The Mendocino Transit Authority (⊕ *mendocinotransit.org*) Route 95 bus serves the area.

EXPLORING

FAMILY
Fort Ross State Historic Park. Russian settlers established Fort Ross in 1812 on land they leased from the native Kashia people. The Russians hoped to gain a foothold in the Pacific coast's warmer regions and to produce crops and other supplies for their Alaskan fur-trading operations. In 1841, with the local marine mammal population depleted and farming having proven unproductive, the Russians sold their holdings to John Sutter, later of gold-rush fame. The land was privately ranched for decades, and became a state park in 1909. One original Russian-era structure remains, as does a cemetery. The rest of the compound has been reconstructed to look much as it did during Russian times. An excellent small museum documents the history of the fort, the Kashia people, and the ranch and state-park eras. ✉ *19005 Hwy. 1, Jenner* ☎ *707/847–3437* ⊕ *www.fortross.org* ⌂ *$8 per vehicle* ☞ *No dogs allowed past parking lot and picnic area.*

The Sonoma and Mendocino Coasts

Leggett

Laytonville

Westport

Fort Bragg
Noyo
Mendocino Coast
Botanical Gardens
Caspar
Pine Grove
Mendocino
Little River
Albion
Navarro River
Redwoods
State Park

Willits

101

Calpella

20

Navarro
Handley Cellars
Roederer Estate
Navarro Vineyards
Elk
Husch Vineyards
Anderson
Valley
Philo
Boonville

Ukiah

20

Lucerne

Clear
Lake

Manchester
Point Arena
Point Arena Lighthouse
Point Arena

253

Pennyroyal
Farms
128
Maple Creek Winery
Yorkville

Lakeport

Hopland

Kelseyville

Clearlake

Lower Lake

20

29

Anchor Bay
Gualala

Sea Ranch

Stewarts Point
Kruse
Rhododendron
Reserve
Salt Point State Park
Fort Ross State Historic Park

1

Pacific Coast Highway

ALEXANDER VALLEY

Cloverdale
Geyserville
128
Healdsburg

Middletown

29

Calistoga

NAPA VALLEY

Fort Ross

1

Jenner

Guerneville
101
116
Occidental
Freestone

Santa
Rosa

Saint
Helena

Salmon Creek
Bodega Bay

Sebastopol
Valley Ford

SONOMA VALLEY

29

Bodega Bay
Dillon Beach
Tomales Point

Tomales

Sonoma

Tomales
Bay

Marshall

Petaluma

Point Reyes

Inverness

Drakes
Bay

Point Reyes
Station
Olema

Novato

101

San
Rafael

Bolinas
Stinson Beach

Mt. Tamalpais

Marin City

PACIFIC OCEAN

FARALLON ISLANDS

San Francisco

80

Daly City

101

280

0   15 mi

0   15 km

Surfers check out the waves near Bodega Bay on the Sonoma Coast.

WHERE TO EAT AND STAY

$$$
MODERN AMERICAN
× **Coast Kitchen.** On a sunny afternoon or at sunset, glistening ocean views from the Coast Kitchen's outdoor patio and indoor dining space elevate dishes emphasizing seafood and local produce both farmed and foraged. Starters like a baby gem lettuce and chicory salad and buttermilk brined fried quail precede entrées that include seared ahi tuna and aged rib eye. **Known for:** oceanview patio (frequent whale sightings in winter and spring); Sonoma County cheeses, wines, and produce; fresh ingredients. $ *Average main: $25* ⊠ *Timber Cove, 21780 Hwy. 1, 3 miles north of Fort Ross State Historic Park, Jenner* ☎ *707/847–3231* ⊕ *www.coastkitchensonoma.com.*

$$$$
RESORT
Fodor's Choice
★
☷ **Timber Cove Resort.** Restored well beyond its original splendor, this resort anchored to a craggy oceanfront cliff is by far the Sonoma Coast's coolest getaway. **Pros:** dramatic sunsets; grand public spaces; destination restaurant. **Cons:** almost too cool for the laid-back Sonoma Coast; pricey oceanview rooms; occasional hospitality miscues. $ *Rooms from: $290* ⊠ *21780 Hwy. 1, Jenner* ☎ *707/847–3231* ⊕ *www.timbercoveresort.com* ➪ *46 rooms* ⦿ *No meals.*

SALT POINT STATE PARK

6 miles north of Fort Ross.

Enjoy dramatic views, forested acres, and a rocky, rugged shoreline along Highway 1's 5-mile route through this park. With the hiking, picnicking, horseback riding, scuba diving, and fishing opportunities, you'll want to stay a while.

GETTING HERE AND AROUND

Exit U.S. 101 in Santa Rosa and travel west on Highway 116 about 33 miles to Jenner, then north 18 miles on Highway 1 to reach the park. Mendocino Transit Authority (⊕ *mendocinotransit.org*) Route 95 buses serve the area.

EXPLORING

Salt Point State Park. For 5 miles, Highway 1 winds through this park, 6,000 acres of forest, meadows, and rocky shoreline. Heading north, the first park entrance (on the right) leads to forest hiking trails and several campgrounds. The next entrance—the park's main road—winds through meadows and along the wave-splashed coastline. This is also the route to the visitor center and **Gerstle Cove**, a favorite spot for scuba divers and sunbathing seals. Next along the highway is **Stump Beach Cove**, with picnic tables, toilets, and a ¼-mile walk to the sandy beach. The park's final entrance is at **Fisk Mill Cove**, where centuries of wind and rain erosion have carved unusual honeycomb patterns in the sandstone called "tafonis." A five-minute walk uphill from the parking lot leads to a dramatic view of **Sentinel Rock**, an excellent spot for sunsets.

Just up the highway, narrow, unpaved Kruse Ranch Road leads to the **Kruse Rhododendron State Reserve**, where each May thousands of rhododendrons bloom within a quiet forest of redwoods and tan oaks. ⊠ *25050 Hwy. 1* ☎ *707/847–3221, 707/865–2391* ⊕ *www.parks.ca.gov* ⊠ *$8 per vehicle.*

WHERE TO STAY

$$$$
B&B/INN
☆ **Sea Ranch Lodge.** Wide-open oceanview vistas and minimalist design keep the focus on nature at this tranquil lodge 29 miles north of Jenner. **Pros:** all rooms are oceanfront; on-site spa; peaceful experience. **Cons:** remote location; some guests find decor dated; expensive in-season. ⑤ *Rooms from: $274* ⊠ *60 Sea Walk Dr., Sea Ranch* ☎ *707/785–2371, 800/732–7262* ⊕ *www.searanchlodge.com* ⬅ *19 rooms* ⦿ *Breakfast.*

THE MENDOCINO COAST

The rocky coastline north of Sonoma County will take your breath away, and not only because the setting is so much more dramatic than the prototypical sandy So-Cal beach: hairpin turns and abrupt switchbacks are the order of the day from Gualala in the south past Fort Bragg in the north.

GUALALA

16 miles north of Salt Point State Park.

This former lumber port on the Gualala River has become a headquarters for exploring the coast. The busiest town on Highway 1 between Bodega Bay and Mendocino, it has all the basic services plus some galleries and gift shops.

GETTING HERE AND AROUND

To make the 71-mile trip from Santa Rosa to Gualala, head north on U.S. 101 to River Road (Exit 494) and drive west to the Pacific Ocean. At Jenner, turn north on Highway 1. From the town of Mendocino, head south on Highway 1 for 35 miles. Mendocino Transit Authority (⊕ *mendocinotransit.org*). Routes 75 and 95 buses serve the area from Santa Rosa.

EXPLORING

Gualala Arts Center. Stop here to see free exhibits of regional art. The center also runs the Dolphin Gallery behind the post office in town. ✉ *46501 Gualala Rd.* ☎ *707/884–1138* ⊕ *www.gualalaarts.org.*

Gualala Point Regional Park. This 195-acre park with picnic areas and a long, sandy beach is an excellent whale-watching spot from December through April. Birders and hikers head here year-round. Take the Bluff Top Trail for ocean vistas, the River Trail for views of the Gualala River estuary, a wildlife haven. ✉ *42401 Hwy. 1, 1 mile south of Gualala* ☎ *707/785–2377* ⊕ *www.sonoma-county.org/parks/pk_glala.htm* ✐ *$7 per vehicle (day use).*

EN ROUTE

Point Arena Lighthouse. For an outstanding view of the ocean and, in winter, migrating whales, take the marked road off Highway 1 north of town to the 115-foot lighthouse. It's possible to stay out here, in one of four rental units ($$–$$$$), all of which have full kitchens. On weekends there's a two-night minimum. ✉ *45500 Lighthouse Rd., off Hwy. 1, Point Arena* ✚ *15 miles north of Gualala (33 miles south of Mendocino), head northwest on Lighthouse Rd.* ☎ *707/882–2809, 877/725–4448* ⊕ *www.pointarenalighthouse.com* ✐ *Tour $7.50 ($5 if no tour).*

WHERE TO EAT AND STAY

$$$$

AMERICAN

✗ **St. Orres.** Inside one of this lodge's two Russian-style onion-dome towers is a spectacular atrium dining room where locally farmed and foraged ingredients appear in dishes such as garlic flan with black chanterelles and rack of wild boar with apple-pear latkes. The prix-fixe menu includes soup and salad but no appetizer or dessert (available à la carte). **Known for:** elaborate weekend brunch; romantic setting; small-plates à la carte menu in bar. $ *Average main: $50* ✉ *36601 S. Hwy. 1, 3 miles north of Gualala* ☎ *707/884–3335 restaurant* ⊕ *www.saintorres.com* ⊘ *No lunch weekdays. Occasionally closed midweek in winter.*

$$$

HOTEL

Fodor's Choice

★

☷ **Mar Vista Cottages.** Escape to nature and retro-charm at these refurbished, gadget-free 1930s cottages, four of which have two bedrooms and eight with one bedroom. **Pros:** commune-with-nature solitude; peaceful retreat; walking path to beach. **Cons:** no other businesses within walking distance; no TVs or phones in rooms; two-night minimum on weekends. $ *Rooms from: $190* ✉ *35101 S. Hwy 1, 5 miles north of Gualala* ☎ *707/884–3522, 877/855–3522* ⊕ *www.marvista-mendocino.com* ⇱ *12 rooms* ☉ *No meals.*

ANDERSON VALLEY

29 miles north of Point Arena.

At the town of Albion, Highway 128 leads southeast into the Anderson Valley, Mendocino's primary wine-growing region. Most of the first 13 miles wind through redwood forest along the Navarro River, then the road opens up to reveal farms and vineyards. In the towns of Philo, Boonville, and Yorkville you'll find eclectic bed-and-breakfasts, small eateries, and dozens of wineries.

Tasting rooms here are more low-key than their counterparts in Napa, but the wineries here produce world-class wines, particularly Pinot Noirs and Gewürztraminers, whose grapes thrive in the moderate coastal climate. Many wineries straddle Highway 128, mostly in Navarro and Philo with a few east of Boonville, where the Anderson Valley Brewing Company has been producing quality ales for more than three decades.

GETTING HERE AND AROUND

From the coast, pick up Highway 128 at Albion. From inland points south, take Highway 128 northwest from U.S. 101 at Cloverdale. From inland points north, exit U.S. 101 in Ukiah and take Highway 253 southwest 17 miles to Boonville. Mendocino Transit Authority (⊕ *mendocinotransit.org*) Route 75 buses serve the area.

EXPLORING

TOP ATTRACTIONS

Fodor's Choice ★ **Anderson Valley Brewing Company.** Brewery tours, tastings in the Tap Room, and 18 holes of disc golf provide a diversified experience at the home of Boont Amber Ale, double and triple Belgian style ales, and other consistent award-winning brews. Local winemakers clear their palates with the Bourbon Barrel Stout, aged in Wild Turkey barrels. ⊠ *17700 Hwy. 253, Boonville* ☎ *707/895–2337* ⊕ *www.avbc.com* ⊠ *Tastings from $10.*

Goldeneye Winery. The Napa Valley's well-respected Duckhorn Wine Company makes Pinot Noirs here from local grapes, along with a Gewürztraminer, a Pinot Gris, a Chardonnay, and a blush Vin Gris of Pinot Noir. Leisurely tastings take place in either a restored farmhouse or on a patio with vineyard and redwood views. ⊠ *9200 Hwy. 128, Philo* ☎ *800/208–0438, 707/895–3202* ⊕ *www.goldeneyewinery.com* ⊠ *Tastings $15–$45* ⊙ *Closed. Tues. and Wed. in Jan. and Feb.*

Lula Cellars. Seventeen miles inland from Highway 1, the fun, relaxing, and pet-friendly Lula is among the Anderson Valley wineries closest to the coast. Owner-winemaker Jeff Hansen, who started Lula in 2007 after decamping from the Napa Valley, produces Sauvignon Blanc, Gewürztraminer, Zinfandel, and a rosé of Zinfandel and Pinot Noir, but his four Pinot Noirs, each flavorful and with its own personality, are the highlights. ⊠ *2800 Guntley Rd., at Hwy. 128, Philo* ☎ *707/895–3737* ⊕ *www.lulacellars.com* ⊠ *$5.*

Maple Creek Winery. Chardonnay, Pinot Noir, and Zinfandel are the specialties of this winery whose artist owner, Tom Rodrigues, also makes Merlot, two dessert wines, and the intriguing Cowboy Red, a blend of

Zinfandel, Merlot, and Carignane. If the art that adorns Maple Creek labels looks familiar, there's a reason: Tom's also responsible for ones at the Napa Valley's Far Niente and other top wineries. Picnickers are welcome (wines are sold by the glass). ⊠ *20799 Hwy. 128* ☏ *707/895–3001* ⊕ *www.maplecreekwine.com* ⌑ *$10.*

FAMILY **Navarro River Redwoods State Park.** Described by locals as the "11-mile-long redwood tunnel to the sea," this park that straddles Highway 128 is great for walks amid second-growth redwoods and for summer swimming in the gentle Navarro River. In late winter and spring, when the river is higher, you also can fish, canoe, and kayak. ⊠ *Hwy. 128, 2 miles east of Hwy. 1, Navarro* ☏ *707/937–5804* ⊕ *www.parks.ca.gov.*

Navarro Vineyards. A visit to this family-run winery is a classic Anderson Valley experience. Make time if you can for a vineyard tour—the guides draw from years of hands-on experience to explain every aspect of production, from sustainable farming techniques to the choices made in aging and blending. Best known for Alsatian varietals such as Gewürztraminer and Riesling, Navarro also makes Chardonnay, Pinot Noir, and other wines. The tasting room sells cheese and charcuterie for picnickers. ⊠ *5601 Hwy. 128, Philo* ☏ *707/895–3686, 800/537–9463* ⊕ *www.navarrowine.com* ⌑ *Tasting free.*

FAMILY
Fodor's Choice
★
Pennyroyal Farms. At this Boonville ranch with a contempo-barn tasting room you can sample estate Sauvignon Blanc, one of Mendocino's best rosés, and velvety Pinot Noirs, along with cheeses made on the premises from goat and sheep milk. Tours of the farmstead (reservations recommended) take place daily at 10 and 2. The wines, cheeses, pastoral setting, and especially the darlin' goats win most guests' hearts. On weekends, chefs prepare panini, salads, and other meals enjoyed on the patio on sunny days. ⊠ *14930 Hwy. 128, Boonville* ☏ *707/895–2410* ⊕ *www.pennyroyalfarm.com* ⌑ *Tastings $5–$15, tours $20* ⊙ *No tours Tues. and Wed.*

WORTH NOTING

Handley Cellars. International folk art collected by winemaker Milla Handley adorns the tasting room at this Anderson Valley pioneer whose lightly oaked Chardonnays and Pinot Noirs earn high praise from wine critics. The winery, which has a patio picnic area, also makes Gewürztraminer, Pinot Gris, Riesling, Zinfandel, very good sparklers, and several other wines. ⊠ *3151 Hwy. 128, Philo* ☏ *707/895–3876, 800/733–3151* ⊕ *www.handleycellars.com* ⌑ *Tasting free.*

Husch Vineyards. A former pony barn houses the cozy tasting room of the Anderson Valley's oldest winery. Wines of note include Gewürztraminer, Chardonnay, Pinot Noir, and a Zinfandel from old-vine grapes. You can picnic on the deck here or at tables under grape arbors. ⊠ *4400 Hwy. 128, Philo* ☏ *800/554–8724* ⊕ *www.huschvineyards.com* ⌑ *Tasting free.*

Roederer Estate. The Anderson Valley is particularly hospitable to Pinot Noir and Chardonnay grapes, the two varietals used to create Roederer's sparkling wines. The view of vineyards and rolling hills from the patio is splendid. ⊠ *4501 Hwy. 128, Philo* ☏ *707/895–2288* ⊕ *www.roedererestate.com* ⌑ *Tasting $6.*

WHERE TO EAT AND STAY

$$$

MODERN
AMERICAN

Fodor's Choice

★

✕ **Bewildered Pig.** Chef Janelle Weaver cooked for seven years at a prestigious appointment-only Napa Valley winery, perfecting skills that serve her well at her low-key yet polished roadside restaurant. On her Mendo-centric menu, which might include braised English short ribs or herbed gnocchi Parisienne with smoked pork jus, Weaver credits the many local farmers and producers who supply her ingredients. **Known for:** cast-iron Dutch-oven sourdough bread; phenomenally fresh salads; vegan, gluten-free options. ⑤ *Average main: $28* ✉ *1810 Hwy. 128, Philo* ☎ *707/895–2088* ⊕ *www.bewilderedpig.com* ⊗ *Closed Mon. and Tues. No lunch.*

$

AMERICAN

Fodor's Choice

★

✕ **Lauren's.** Boonville locals and frequent visitors love Lauren's for its down-home vibe and healthful comfort food—veggie and ground-beef burgers, pizzas, pot roast, chicken tostadas, meat loaf, and curry noodle bowls—many of whose ingredients are grown or produced nearby. Chocolate brownie sundaes and (seasonally) apple tarts and honey-baked pears are among the desserts worth a trip on their own. **Known for:** down-home vibe; diverse Mendocino wine selection ; trivia nights 2nd and 4th Thursday of the month. ⑤ *Average main: $15* ✉ *14211 Hwy. 128, Boonville* ☎ *707/895–3869* ⊕ *laurensgoodfood. com* ⊗ *Closed Mon. No dinner Sun. (except for occasional pop-ups) and Mon. No lunch Mon.–Wed.*

$

AMERICAN

✕ **Mosswood Market Café and Bakery.** Pastries for breakfast; wraps, salads, hot soup, and sandwiches for lunch; and espresso drinks all day powered by Sonoma County's Flying Goat Coffee make this sweet café in downtown Boonville a fine stop for a quick bite. Order at the counter and enjoy your meal—the oven roasted turkey and chicken mango wraps and Reuben and albacore tuna sandwiches are among the lunch-time choices—at tables inside or out front. **Known for:** empanadas; Danishes and scones; vegan options. ⑤ *Average main: $10* ✉ *14111 Hwy. 128, Boonville* ☎ *707/895–3635.*

$$$$

AMERICAN

Fodor's Choice

★

✕ **Table 128.** Proprietor Johnny Schmitt and his staff prepare one prix-fixe meal per night (reservations essential on summer and fall weekends), with platters of food brought to the table for sharing. Expect an expertly prepared entrée like prosciutto-wrapped halibut or slow-roasted lamb, a sophisticated side dish (radicchio with polenta, perhaps, or curried cauliflower soup), and panna cotta or a fruit tart for dessert. **Known for:** home cooking done at a high level; fresh oysters and paella on summer Sundays; tree-shaded outdoor patio. ⑤ *Average main: $58* ✉ *Boonville Hotel, 14050 Hwy. 128, Boonville* ☎ *707/895–2210* ⊕ *www.boonvillehotel.com* ⊗ *No lunch. Closed Mon.–Thurs. Nov.–Apr., closed Tues. and Wed. May–Oct.*

$$$

HOTEL

🛏 **Boonville Hotel.** From the street this looks like a standard small-town hotel with seven free-standing cottages out back in the garden, but once you cross the threshold you begin to sense the laid-back sophistication that makes the entire Anderson Valley so appealing. **Pros:** stylish but homey; beautiful gardens and grounds; on-site Table 128 restaurant for prix-fixe meals served family style. **Cons:** two-night stay required on most weekends; not great for kids; lacks big-hotel amenities. ⑤ *Rooms from: $195* ✉ *14050 Hwy. 128, Boonville* ☎ *707/895–2210* ⊕ *www. boonvillehotel.com* 🛏 *15 rooms* ⦿ *Breakfast.*

7

You'll find excellent vintages and great places to taste wine in the Anderson Valley—but it's much more laid-back than Napa.

$$$$
HOTEL
Fodor's Choice
★

🛏 **The Philo Apple Farm.** Two founders of the renowned Napa Valley restaurant The French Laundry are among the owners of this farm with three tasteful, inviting cottages and one guest room set in an organic heirloom apple orchard. **Pros:** rustic-contemporary touches in cottages and room; working farm; relaxing back-to-nature experience. **Cons:** occasionally hot in summer; few "activities"; room service only upon request. ⑤ *Rooms from: $300* ✉ *18501 Greenwood Rd., Philo* ☎ *707/895–2333* ⊕ *www.philoapplefarm.com* 🛏 *4 rooms* ⑩ *Breakfast.*

LITTLE RIVER

5 miles north of Anderson Valley.

The town of Little River is not much more than a post office and a convenience store; Albion, its neighbor to the south, is even smaller. Along this winding portion of Highway 1, though, you'll find numerous inns and restaurants, all of them quiet and situated to take advantage of the breathtaking ocean views.

GETTING HERE AND AROUND

From inland points south, exit U.S. 101 at Cloverdale and follow Highway 128 northwest about 56 miles to Highway 1, then head north 7 miles. From points north, exit U.S. 101 in Ukiah at Highway 253 and follow it west 17 miles to Boonville, where you'll pick up Highway 128 and drive northwest to Highway 1. Mendocino Transit Authority (⊕ *mendocinotransit.org*) Route 60 buses serve the area.

EXPLORING

Van Damme State Park. Best known for its beach, this park is a prime abalone diving spot. Upland trails lead through lush riparian habitat and the bizarre **Pygmy Forest**, where acidic soil and poor drainage have produced mature cypress and pine trees that are no taller than a person. The visitor center has displays on ocean life and the historical significance of the redwood lumber industry along the coast. ⊠ *Little River Park Rd., off Hwy. 1* ☎ *707/937–5804* ⊕ *www.parks.ca.gov.*

WHERE TO EAT AND STAY

$$$
FRENCH
Fodor's Choice
★

✕ **Ledford House.** The only thing separating this bluff-top wood-and-glass restaurant from the Pacific Ocean is a great view. Entrées evoke the flavors of southern France and include hearty bistro dishes—stews, cassoulets, and pastas—and large portions of grilled meats and freshly caught fish (though the restaurant also is vegetarian friendly). **Known for:** Mendocino-centric wine list; live jazz nightly; oceanview bar. ⑤ *Average main: $26* ⊠ *3000 N. Hwy. 1, Albion* ☎ *707/937–0282* ⊕ *www.ledfordhouse.com* ⊘ *Closed Mon. and Tues. and late-Feb.– early-Mar. and mid-Oct.–early Nov. No lunch.*

$$$
B&B/INN

🛏 **Albion River Inn.** Contemporary New England–style cottages at this inn overlook the dramatic bridge and seascape where the Albion River empties into the Pacific. **Pros:** marvelous ocean views; great bathtubs; romantic glassed-in restaurant. **Cons:** often foggy in summer; no TV in rooms; could use uptick in style. ⑤ *Rooms from: $195* ⊠ *3790 N. Hwy. 1, Albion* ☎ *707/937–1919, 800/479–7944* ⊕ *albionriverinn.com* ⤳ *22 rooms* ⦿| *Breakfast.*

MENDOCINO

3 miles north of Little River.

A flourishing logging town in the late-19th century, Mendocino seduces 21st-century travelers with windswept cliffs, phenomenal Pacific Ocean views, and boomtown-era New England–style architecture. Following the timber industry's mid-20th-century decline, artists and craftspeople began flocking here, and so did Hollywood: Elia Kazan chose Mendocino as the backdrop for his 1955 film adaptation of John Steinbeck's *East of Eden,* starring James Dean, and the town stood in for fictional Cabot Cove, Maine, in the long-running TV series *Murder, She Wrote.* As the arts community thrived, restaurants, cafés, and inns sprang up. Today, the small downtown area consists almost entirely of places to eat and shop.

GETTING HERE AND AROUND

From U.S. 101, exit at Cloverdale and follow Highway 128 northwest about 56 miles and Highway 1 north 10 miles. Mendocino Transit Authority (⊕ *mendocinotransit.org*) Route 60 buses serve the area.

EXPLORING

Ford House. The restored Ford House, built in 1854, serves as the visitor center for Mendocino Headlands State Park and the town. The house has a scale model of Mendocino as it looked in 1890, when it had 34 water towers and a 12-seat public outhouse. From the museum, you can head out on a 3-mile trail across the spectacular seaside cliffs that border the town. ⊠ *45035 Main St., west of Lansing St.* ☎ *707/937–5397* ⊕ *mendoparks.org/mendocino-headlands-state-park-ford-house-museum* ☑ *$2.*

WHERE TO EAT AND STAY

$$$ ✕ **Cafe Beaujolais.** The yellow Victorian cottage that houses this popular
AMERICAN restaurant is surrounded by a garden of heirloom and exotic plantings. Local ingredients find their way into appetizers such as butter-braised beets and Dungeness crab cakes and entrées like pan-roasted California sturgeon and duck two ways (crispy-skin breast and leg confit). **Known for:** breads from a wood-fired brick oven; Mendocino wines; garden of heirloom and exotic plantings. ⑤ *Average main: $30* ⊠ *961 Ukiah St.* ☎ *707/937–5614* ⊕ *www.cafebeaujolais.com* ⊘ *No lunch Mon. and Tues.*

$$$$ ☷ **Brewery Gulch Inn.** The feel is modern yet tasteful at this smallish inn.
B&B/INN **Pros:** luxury in tune with nature; peaceful ocean views; complimentary
Fodor'sChoice wine hour and light buffet. **Cons:** must drive to town; expensive in-sea-
★ son; two-night minimum on weekends. ⑤ *Rooms from: $350* ⊠ *9401 N. Hwy. 1, 1 mile south of Mendocino* ☎ *707/937–4752, 800/578–4454* ⊕ *www.brewerygulchinn.com* ⤳ *11 rooms* ⑩ *Breakfast.*

$$ ☷ **Glendeven Inn Mendocino.** If Mendocino is the New England village
B&B/INN of the West Coast, then Glendeven is the local country manor with sea
Fodor'sChoice views. **Pros:** great ocean views; elegant; romantic. **Cons:** not within
★ walking distance of town; on the main drag; two-night minimum on weekends. ⑤ *Rooms from: $170* ⊠ *8205 N. Hwy. 1* ☎ *707/937–0083, 800/822–4536* ⊕ *glendeven.com* ⤳ *6 rooms, 4 suites* ⑩ *Breakfast.*

$$$ ☷ **MacCallum House.** Set on two flower-filled acres in the middle of town,
B&B/INN this inn is a perfect mix of Victorian charm and modern luxury. **Pros:** excellent breakfast; central location; outstanding restaurant. **Cons:** luxury suites on a separate property are more modern; some rooms in main house lack charm; some guests find the look dated. ⑤ *Rooms from: $179* ⊠ *45020 Albion St.* ☎ *707/937–0289, 800/609–0492* ⊕ *www.maccallumhouse.com* ⤳ *30 rooms* ⑩ *Breakfast.*

SPORTS AND THE OUTDOORS

Catch-A-Canoe and Bicycles Too. Rent kayaks and regular and outrigger canoes here year-round, as well as mountain and suspension bicycles. The outfit's tours explore Big River and its estuary. ⊠ *Stanford Inn by the Sea, Comptche-Ukiah Rd., east of Hwy. 1* ☎ *707/937–0273* ⊕ *www.catchacanoe.com* ☑ *From $65.*

FORT BRAGG

10 miles north of Mendocino.

Fort Bragg is a working-class town that many feel is the most authentic place on the coast. The city maintains a local feel since most people who work at the area hotels and restaurants also live here, as do many artists. A stroll down Franklin Street, one block east of Highway 1, takes you past bookstores, antiques shops, and boutiques.

The North Coast is famous for its locally caught Dungeness crab; be sure to try some during your visit.

GETTING HERE AND AROUND

From U.S. 101 at Willits follow Highway 20 west about 33 miles to Highway 1. Mendocino Transit Authority (⊕ *mendocinotransit.org*) Route 60 buses serve the town.

EXPLORING

Fodor's Choice
★

Mendocino Coast Botanical Gardens. Something beautiful is always abloom in these marvelous gardens. Along 3½ miles of trails, including pathways with ocean views and observation points for whale-watching, lie a profusion of flowers. The rhododendrons are at their peak from April through June; the dahlias begin their spectacular show in August and last into October. In winter the heather and camellias add more than a splash of color. The main trails are wheelchair accessible. ⊠ *18220 N. Hwy. 1, 2 miles south of Fort Bragg* ☎ *707/964–4352* ⊕ *www.garden-bythesea.org* 🖾 *$15.*

Museum in the Triangle Tattoo Parlor. At the top of a steep staircase, this several-room museum pays homage to Fort Bragg's rough-and-tumble past with memorabilia that includes early 20th-century Burmese tattooing instruments, pictures of astonishing tattoos from around the world, and a small shrine to the late sword-swallowing sideshow king Captain Don Leslie. ⊠ *356–B N. Main St.* ☎ *707/964–8814* ⊕ *www.triangletattoo.com* 🖾 *Free.*

Pacific Star Winery. When the sun's out and you're sipping wine while viewing whales or other sea creatures swimming offshore, this blufftop winery's outdoor tasting spaces feel mystical and magical. Equally beguiling on a brooding stormy day, Pacific Star has still more aces up its sleeve: engaging owners, and cheery staffers pouring a lineup of obscure varietals like Charbono and Brunello, a cousin of Sangiovese. The wines, among them a vibrant Mendocino Zin, are good, and they're reasonably priced. ■TIP→ **A downtown tasting room (401 North Main Street) opens daily each afternoon.** ⊠ *33000 N. Hwy. 1, 12 miles north of downtown* ☎ *707/964–1155* ⊕ *www.pacificstarwinery. com* ⊡ *Tasting $5* ⊘ *Closed Tues. and Wed.*

FAMILY   **The Skunk Train.** A reproduction train travels the route of its 1920s predecessor, a fume-spewing gas-powered motorcar that shuttled passengers along a rail line dating from the 1880s logging days. Nicknamed the Skunk Train, the original traversed redwood forests inaccessible to automobiles. The main round-trip trek between Fort Bragg and the town of Northspur, 21 miles inland, takes a little over four hours. There are also shorter excursions to the town of Willits as well as seasonal and holiday-themed tours. ⊠ *Foot of Laurel St., west of Main St.* ☎ *707/964–6371, 866/457–5865* ⊕ *www.skunktrain. com* ⊡ *From $25.*

BEACHES

Glass Beach. A gravel path on Elm Street three blocks west of Main Street leads to wild coastline with miles of blufftop trails. The sandy coves nearest the road contain dazzling sea glass (from the city dump once in this area) the surf pulverized into beautiful treasures. Some of the glass disappeared after early 2017 storms, but there's still some to see. Don't take any with you, though; it's against the law. There's no swimming at this beach either, for safety's sake. **Amenities:** parking (free); toilets. **Best for:** sunset; walking. ⊠ *Elm St. and Old Haul Rd.* ⊕ *www.parks.ca.gov* ⊡ *Free.*

MacKerricher State Park. This park begins at Glass Beach, known for its sea glass, and stretches north for 9 miles, beginning with rocky headlands that taper into dunes and sandy beaches. The headland is a good place for whale-watching from December to mid-April. Fishing at Lake Cleone (a freshwater lake stocked with trout), canoeing, hiking, tidepooling, jogging, bicycling, beachcombing, camping, and harbor seal watching at Laguna Point are among the popular activities, many of which are accessible to the mobility-impaired. Be vigilant for rogue waves—don't turn your back on the sea. Dogs must be leashed. **Amenities:** parking; toilets. **Best for:** solitude; sunset; walking. ⊠ *24100 MacKerricher Park Rd., off Hwy. 1, 3 miles north of town* ☎ *707/937–5804* ⊕ *www.parks.ca.gov* ⊡ *Free.*

WHERE TO EAT AND STAY

$ ✕ **Cowlick's Ice Cream.** Candy-cap mushroom (tastes like maple syrup)
AMERICAN   and black raspberry chocolate chunk are among this fun ice cream
FAMILY   shop's top-selling flavors. Chocolate, mocha almond fudge, and ginger appear year-round, supplemented by blackberry-cheesecake, pumpkin, eggnog, and other seasonal offerings; the sorbets might include lemon, pear, or strawberry. **Known for:** handmade ice cream; chai, yellow-cake batter, and other wiggy flavors. ⑤ *Average main: $5* ⊠ *250 N. Main St.* ☎ *707/962–9271* ⊕ *www.cowlicksicecream.com.*

$ ╳ **Piaci Pub and Pizzeria.** The seats are stools and your elbows might
ITALIAN bang a neighbor's, but nobody seems to mind at this casual spot for
thin-crust pizzas (more than a dozen types), focaccia, and calzones. The
food—there are several salads, too—is simple, but everything is carefully prepared and comes out tasty. **Known for:** cash-only; well-chosen
beers; dog-friendly outdoor tables. ⑤ *Average main: $15* ⊠ *120 W.
Redwood Ave.* ☎ *707/961–1133* ⊕ *www.piacipizza.com* ═ *No credit
cards* ☾ *No lunch Sun.*

$$$$ ⊓ **Inn at Newport Ranch.** Attention to detail in both design and hospital-
B&B/INN ity make for an incomparable stay at this 2,000-acre working cattle
Fodor'sChoice ranch with 1½ miles of private coastline. **Pros:** over-the-top design;
★ mesmerizing Pacific views; horse riding, oceanside cocktails by a fire
pit, and other diversions. **Cons:** all this design and glamour comes at a
price; lengthy drive back from Mendocino and Fort Bragg restaurants
at night; coast can be foggy in summer. ⑤ *Rooms from: $350* ⊠ *31502
N. Hwy. 1* ☎ *707/962–4818* ⊕ *theinnatnewportranch.com* ⇆ *11 rooms*
⎟◎⎟ *Breakfast.*

$$ ⊓ **Weller House Inn.** It's hard to believe that this house was abandoned
B&B/INN and slated for demolition when it was purchased in 1994 and carefully
Fodor'sChoice restored. **Pros:** handcrafted details; radiant heat in the wood floors;
★ colorful and tasteful rooms. **Cons:** some guests find it too old-fashioned;
pet cleaning fee; no TVs in rooms. ⑤ *Rooms from: $150* ⊠ *524 Stewart
St.* ☎ *707/964–4415* ⊕ *www.wellerhouse.com* ⇆ *9 rooms* ⎟◎⎟ *Breakfast.*

SPORTS AND THE OUTDOORS
WHALE-WATCHING
All Aboard Adventures. Captain Tim of All Aboard operates whale-
watching trips from late December through April. ⊠ *Noyo Harbor,
32410 N. Harbor Dr.* ☎ *707/964–1881* ⊕ *www.allaboardadventures.
com* ⊠ *From $40.*

REDWOOD COUNTRY

North of Mendocino in Humboldt County stand some of California's
tallest and oldest redwoods. Many are easily accessible along or not
too far off U.S. 101.

HUMBOLDT REDWOODS STATE PARK

86 miles northeast of Fort Bragg, 46 miles south of Eureka.

Conservationists banded together a century ago as the Save the Red-
woods League and scored a key victory when a memorial grove was
dedicated in 1921. That grove is now part of Humboldt Redwoods
State Park, which these days has grown to nearly 53,000 acres, about
a third of which are filled with untouched old-growth coast redwoods.

GETTING HERE AND AROUND
Access the park right off U.S. 101. *(See Bus Travel, at the beginning of
this chapter, for Humboldt County public transportation information.)*

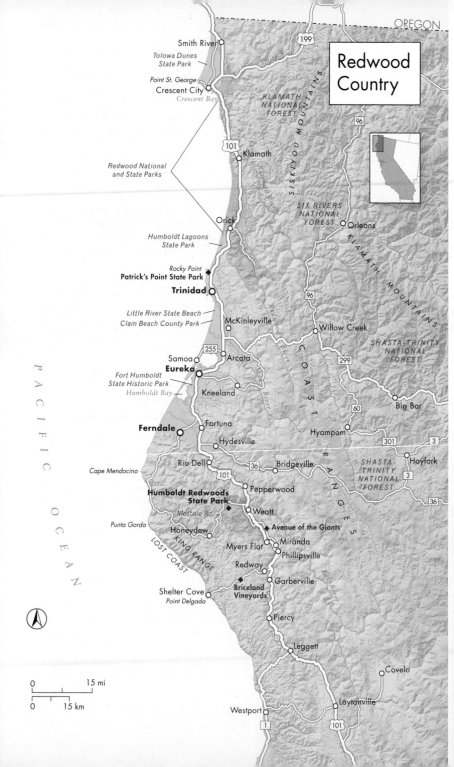

Redwood Country

OREGON

199

96

96

299

60

301

3

36

36

101

255

101

1

101

PACIFIC OCEAN

LOST COAST

KING RANGE

SISKIYOU MOUNTAINS

KLAMATH NATIONAL FOREST

SIX RIVERS NATIONAL FOREST

KLAMATH MOUNTAINS

SHASTA-TRINITY NATIONAL FOREST

COAST RANGES

SHASTA-TRINITY NATIONAL FOREST

Smith River
Tolowa Dunes State Park
Point St. George
Crescent City
Crescent Bay
Klamath
Redwood National and State Parks
Orick
Humboldt Lagoons State Park
Rocky Point
Patrick's Point State Park
Trinidad
Little River State Beach
Clam Beach County Park
McKinleyville
Willow Creek
Orleans
Samoa
Arcata
Eureka
Fort Humboldt State Historic Park
Humboldt Bay
Kneeland
Big Bar
Ferndale
Fortuna
Hydesville
Hyampom
Cape Mendocino
Rio Dell
Bridgeville
Hayfork
Humboldt Redwoods State Park
Pepperwood
Mattole Rd.
Weott
Punta Gorda
Avenue of the Giants
Honeydew
Myers Flat
Miranda
Phillipsville
Redway
Shelter Cove
Point Delgada
Garberville
Briceland Vineyards
Piercy
Leggett
Covelo
Westport
Laytonville

0   15 mi
0   15 km

EXPLORING

FAMILY

Fodor's Choice

★

Avenue of the Giants. Some of the tallest trees on Earth tower over this magnificent 32-mile stretch of two-lane blacktop, also known as Highway 254, that follows the south fork of the Eel River through Humboldt Redwoods State Park. The highway runs more or less parallel to U.S. 101 from Phillipsville in the south to the town of Pepperwood in the north. A brochure available at either end of the highway or the **visitor center,** 2 miles south of Weott, contains a self-guided tour, with short and long hikes through various redwood groves. A trail at **Founders Grove** passes by several impressive trees, among them the fallen 362-foot-long Dyerville Giant, whose root base points skyward 35 feet. The tree can be reached via a short trail that begins 4 miles north of the visitor center. About 6 miles north of the center lies **Rockefeller Forest.** The largest remaining old-growth coast redwood forest, it contains more than a third of the 100 tallest trees in the world. ⊠ *Humboldt Redwoods State Park Visitor Center, Hwy. 254, Weott* ☎ *707/946–2263* ⊕ *www.parks. ca.gov* ☜ *Free; $8 day-use fee for Williams Grove.*

OFF THE
BEATEN
PATH

Briceland Vineyards. Lean yet flavorful Humboldt County Pinot Noirs are the specialty of this three-decades-old winery set amid the trees. In good weather the delightfully low-key tastings take place in front of the weathered original winery building. Guests sip Gewürztraminer (surprisingly dry), Viognier, or other whites before sampling Pinots and perhaps Syrah or Zinfandel. ∎TIP➔ From late May through August drop-ins are welcome 1–5 on weekends, otherwise tastings are by appointment. ⊠ *5959 Briceland Rd., 10½ miles southwest of Avenue of the Giants southern entrance* ✛ *Take Briceland Rd. 5½ miles west from Redwood Dr. in Redway (from north, U.S. 101 Exit 642; from south, Exit 639B)* ☎ *707/923–2429* ⊕ *bricelandvineyards. com* ☜ *Tastings $15.*

7

FERNDALE

35 miles northwest of Weott, 19 miles south of Eureka.

Ferndale, best known for its colorful Victorian architecture, much of it Stick-Eastlake, is well worth the 5-mile detour off U.S. 101. Many shops carry a self-guided tour map that highlights the most interesting historic buildings. Gift shops and ice-cream stores comprise a fair share of the businesses here, but Ferndale remains a fully functioning small town, and descendants of the Portuguese and Scandinavian dairy farmers who settled here continue to raise dairy cows in the surrounding pastures.

GETTING HERE AND AROUND

To get to Ferndale from U.S. 101, follow Highway 211 southwest 5 miles. Public transit doesn't serve the town.

EXPLORING

Ferndale Historic Cemetery. The well-worn gravestones at Ferndale's eastside cemetery provide insight into the hard, often short lives of the European immigrants who cultivated this area in the mid-18th century. At the top of the hill, sweeping (and photogenic) vistas unfold of the town, its farms, and the ocean. ⊠ *Craig St. and Berding St.* ☜ *Free.*

Ferndale Museum. The main building of this museum exhibits Victoriana and historical photographs and has a display of an old-style barbershop and another of Wiyot Indian baskets. In the annex are a horse-drawn buggy, a re-created blacksmith's shop, and antique farming, fishing, and dairy equipment. Don't miss the historic Bosch-Omori seismograph, installed in 1933 in Ferndale; it's still checked daily for recordings of earthquake activity. ⊠ *515 Shaw Ave.* ☎ *707/786–4466* ⊕ *www.ferndale-museum.org* ⌨ *$2* ☉ *Closed Jan., Mon. yr-round, Tues. Oct.–Dec. and Feb.–May.*

Lost Coast Scenic Drive. A loop drive counterclockwise from Ferndale yields amazing ocean views and winds through forests and small towns before heading into Humboldt Redwoods State Park and then back up U.S. 101 toward the starting point. The road has numerous curves and some rugged stretches in need of repair, but driving this 100 or so mile stretch is exhilarating. ■TIP➡ **Allot four hours for this excursion.** ⊠ *Ferndale* ✛ *Head southwest from Ferndale on Wildcat Ave., which soon becomes Mattole Rd. Follow Mattole west to the coast, south to Petrolia, and east to Honeydew and the park. At U.S. 101 head north back toward Ferndale.* ⊕ *redwoods.info/showrecord.asp?id=3870.*

WHERE TO STAY

$$
B&B/INN
Gingerbread Mansion. A dazzler that rivals San Francisco's "painted ladies," this Victorian mansion has detailed exterior spindle work, turrets, and gables. **Pros:** elegant decor; relaxing atmosphere; friendly staff. **Cons:** some may find the place gaudy; two-night minimum on weekends; lacks standard hotel amenities. ⑤ *Rooms from: $165* ⊠ *400 Berding St.* ☎ *707/786–4000* ⊕ *www.gingerbread-mansion.com* ⌨ *11 rooms* ⦿*Breakfast.*

SHOPPING

Blacksmith Shop. With two storefronts in Ferndale, this shop celebrates the survival of traditional blacksmithing arts in the area. The hand-forged works sold here range from flatware to furniture, and especially nice are the rough-handled chef's knives—so sharp there are Band-Aids stuffed in behind the display, just in case. ⊠ *455 and 491 Main St.* ☎ *707/786–4216* ⊕ *www.ferndaleblacksmith.com.*

EUREKA

19 miles north of Ferndale.

With a population of 27,000, Eureka is the North Coast's largest city, a good place to fuel up, buy groceries, and learn a little about the region's mining, timber, and fishing pasts. The chamber of commerce visitor center has maps of self-guided driving tours of the town's nearly 100 Victorians, among them the flamboyant 1886 Queen Anne–style **Carson Mansion**, at 143 M Street. The home can only be viewed from outside, but it's worth a look and a photo or two. Art galleries and antiques stores liven up the district from C to I street between 2nd and 3rd streets, and a walking pier extends into the harbor.

GETTING HERE AND AROUND

U.S. 101 travels through Eureka. Eureka Transit (⊕ *www.eurekatransit. org*) buses serve the town.

VISITOR CENTER
Eureka Chamber of Commerce. ⊠ 2112 Broadway ☎ 707/442–3738 ⊕ www.eurekachamber.com.

EXPLORING
Blue Ox Millworks. This woodshop is among a handful in the country specializing in Victorian-era architecture, but what makes it truly unique is that its craftspeople use antique tools to do the work. Visitors can watch craftsmen use printing presses, lathes, and other equipment to create gingerbread trim, fence pickets, and other signature Victorian embellishments. The shop is less interesting on Saturday, when most craftspeople take the day off. ⊠ 1 X St. ☎ 707/444–3437, 800/248–4259 ⊕ www.blueoxmill.com ☎ $10 ⊗ Closed Sat. Dec.–Mar., Sun. yr-round.

WHERE TO EAT AND STAY

$
AMERICAN
✕ **Lost Coast Brewery and Cafe.** This bustling microbrewery is the best place in town to relax with a pint of ale or porter. Soups and salads, plus burgers, tacos, and light meals are served for lunch and dinner. **Known for:** outstanding beers; happy hour weekdays 4–6; brewery tours. ⑤ *Average main: $12* ⊠ 617 4th St. ☎ 707/445–4480 ⊕ www.lostcoast.com.

$$$
AMERICAN
Fodor'sChoice
★
✕ **Restaurant 301.** The chef at the elegant restaurant inside the Carter House uses ingredients selected from the farmers' market, local cheese makers and ranchers, and the on-site gardens. The dishes (there's always a fresh seafood offering) are prepared with a delicate hand and a sensuous imagination. **Known for:** one of California's best wine lists; à la carte, prix-fixe options; bar menu (weekday happy hour's a deal). ⑤ *Average main: $29* ⊠ 301 L St. ☎ 707/444–8062, 800/404–1390 ⊕ carterhouse.com ⊗ No lunch.

$$$
HOTEL
Fodor'sChoice
★
Carter House Inns. Owner Mark Carter says he trains his staff always to say yes; whether it's breakfast in bed or an in-room massage, someone here will get you what you want. **Pros:** elegant ambience; every detail in place; aim-to-please service. **Cons:** not suitable for children; expensive restaurant; two-night minimum on weekends. ⑤ *Rooms from: $189* ⊠ 301 L St. ☎ 707/444–8062, 800/404–1390 ⊕ www.carterhouse.com ⌂ 32 rooms ⦿ Breakfast.

SPORTS AND THE OUTDOORS
WHALE-WATCHING
Humboats Kayak Adventures. You can rent kayaks and book kayaking tours that from December to June include whale-watching trips. Half-day river kayaking trips pass beneath massive redwoods; the whale-watching outings get you close enough for good photos. ⊠ Woodley Island Marina, 601 Startare Dr., Dock A ☎ 707/443–5157 ⊕ www.humboats.com ☎ From $30 rentals, $55 tours.

TRINIDAD

23 miles north of Eureka.

A mellow base for exploring the southern portion of Redwood National Park, coastal Trinidad got its name from the Spanish mariners who entered the bay on Trinity Sunday, June 9, 1775. Formerly the principal trading post for mining camps along the Klamath and Trinity rivers, these days Trinidad is a quiet and genuinely charming community with several beaches and ample sights and activities to entertain low-key visitors.

GETTING HERE AND AROUND

Trinidad sits right off U.S. 101. From Interstate 5, head west from Redding on Highway 299 and north on U.S. 101 north of Arcata. Redwood Transit System (⊕ *www.redwoodtransit.org*) provides bus service.

EXPLORING

Patrick's Point State Park. On a forested plateau almost 200 feet above the surf, the park has stunning views of the Pacific, great whale- and sea lion–watching spots, campgrounds, picnic areas, bike paths, and hiking trails through old-growth spruce forest. There are also tidal pools at Agate Beach, a re-created Yurok Indian village, and a small visitor center with exhibits. It's uncrowded and sublimely quiet here. Dogs are not allowed on trails or the beach. ⊠ *U.S. 101, 5 miles north of Trinidad* ☎ *707/677–3570* ⊕ *www.parks.ca.gov* ⊠ *$8 per vehicle.*

BEACHES

FAMILY **Clam Beach County Park and Little River State Beach.** These two adjoining oceanfront areas stretch for several miles south of Trinidad. The sandy beach here is exceptionally wide. Beachcombing and savoring fabulous sunsets are favorite activities. The two parks share day-use facilities. **Amenities:** parking; toilets. **Best for:** solitude; sunset; walking. ⊠ *Clam Beach Dr. & U.S. 101, 6 miles south of Trinidad* ☎ *707/445–7651* ⊕ *www. parks.ca.gov* ⊠ *Free (day use).*

WHERE TO EAT AND STAY

$$$ ✕ **Larrupin' Cafe.** Set in a two-story house on a quiet country road north
AMERICAN   of town, this restaurant—one of the best places to eat on the North
Fodor's Choice   Coast—is often thronged with people enjoying fresh seafood, Cornish
★   game hen, mesquite-grilled ribs, and vegetarian dishes. The garden setting and candlelight stir thoughts of romance. **Known for:** garden setting; outside patio; smoked beef brisket. $ *Average main: $29* ⊠ *1658 Patrick's Point Dr.* ☎ *707/677–0230* ⊕ *www.larrupin.com* ⊗ *No lunch.*

$$$$ ☷ **Trinidad Bay Bed and Breakfast Inn.** Staying at this small Cape Cod–
B&B/INN   style inn perched above Trinidad Bay is like spending the weekend at a friend's vacation house. **Pros:** great location above bay; lots of light; tall windows in Tidepool room. **Cons:** main house can feel crowded at full occupancy; expensive in summer; two-night minimum on weekends. $ *Rooms from: $275* ⊠ *560 Edwards St.* ☎ *707/677–0840* ⊕ *www. trinidadbaybnb.com* ⇄ *4 rooms* ⦙⊙⦙ *Breakfast.*

$$$$ ☷ **Turtle Rocks Oceanfront Inn.** This comfortable inn has the best view in
B&B/INN   Trinidad, and the builders have made the most of it, adding private, glassed-in decks to each room so that guests can fully enjoy the ocean and sunning sea lions. **Pros:** great ocean views; comfortable king beds; surrounding landscape left natural and wild. **Cons:** no businesses within walking distance; interiors may be too spare for some guests; can be foggy here in summer. $ *Rooms from: $295* ⊠ *3392 Patrick's Point Dr., 4½ miles north of town* ☎ *707/677–3707* ⊕ *www.turtlerocksinn. com* ⇄ *6 rooms* ⦙⊙⦙ *Breakfast.*

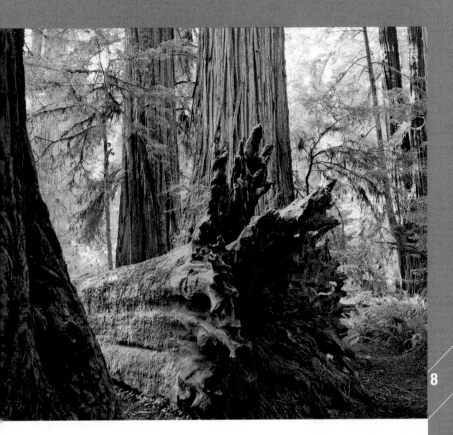

REDWOOD
NATIONAL PARK

WELCOME TO REDWOOD NATIONAL PARK

TOP REASONS TO GO

★ **Giant trees:** These mature coastal redwoods are the tallest trees in the world.

★ **Hiking to the sea:** The park's trails wind through majestic redwood groves, and many connect to the Coastal Trail, which runs along the western edge of the park.

★ **Rare wildlife:** Mighty Roosevelt elk favor the park's flat prairie and open lands; seldom-seen black bears roam the back-country; trout and salmon leap through streams; and Pacific gray whales swim along the coast during their spring and fall migrations.

★ **Stepping back in time:** Hike mossy and mysterious Fern Canyon Trail and explore a prehistoric scene of lush vegetation and giant ferns—a memorable scene in *Jurassic Park 2* was shot here.

★ **Getting off-the-grid:** Amid the majestic redwoods you're out of cell-phone range, offering a rare opportunity to disconnect.

1 Del Norte Coast Redwoods State Park. The rugged terrain of this far northwestern corner of California combines stretches of treacherous surf, steep cliffs, and forested ridges. On a clear day it's postcard-perfect; with fog, it's mysterious and mesmerizing.

2 Jedediah Smith Redwoods State Park. Gargantuan old-growth redwoods dominate the scenery here. The Smith River cuts through canyons and splits across boulders, carrying salmon to the inland creeks where they spawn.

3 Prairie Creek Redwoods State Park. The forests here give way to spacious, grassy plains where abundant wildlife thrives. Roosevelt elk are a common sight in the meadows and down to Gold Bluffs Beach, where a short trail leads to Fern Canyon.

4 Orick Area. The highlight of the southern portion of Redwood National and State Parks is the Tall Trees Grove. It's difficult to reach and requires a special pass, but it's worth the hassle—this section has some of the tallest coast redwood trees. The current world-record holder, a 379-footer named Hyperion, was discovered outside the grove in 2006.

GETTING ORIENTED

U.S. 101 weaves through the southern portion of Redwood National Park, skirts around the center, and then slips back through redwoods in the north and on to Crescent City. The entire park spans about 50 miles north to south. The Kuchel Visitor Center, Prairie Creek Redwoods State Park, Tall Trees Grove, Fern Canyon, and Lady Bird Johnson Grove are in the southern section. In the central section, where the Klamath River Overlook is the dominant feature, the narrow, mostly graveled Coastal Drive loop yields ocean vistas. To the north are Mill Creek Trail, Enderts Beach, and Crescent Beach Overlook in Del Norte Coast Redwoods State Park, as well as Jedediah Smith Redwoods State Park, Stout Grove, Little Bald Hills, and Simpson-Reed Grove.

8

Updated by
Daniel Mangin

Soaring more than 350 feet high, the coastal redwoods that give this park its name are miracles of efficiency—some have survived hundreds of years, a few more than two millennia. These massive trees glean nutrients from the rich alluvial flats at their feet and from the moisture and nitrogen trapped in their uneven canopy. Their huge, thick-bark trunks can hold thousands of gallons of water, reservoirs that have helped them withstand centuries of firestorms.

PLANNING

WHEN TO GO

Campers and hikers flock to the park from mid-June to early September. The crowds disappear in winter, but you'll have to contend with frequent rains and nasty potholes on side roads. Temperatures fluctuate widely: the foggy coastal lowland is much cooler than the higher-altitude interior.

The average annual rainfall is between 90 and 100 inches, most of it falling between November and April. During the dry summer, thick fog rolling in from the Pacific veils the forests, providing the redwoods a large portion of their moisture intake.

PLANNING YOUR TIME
REDWOOD IN ONE DAY

From Crescent City head south on U.S. 101. A mile south of Klamath, detour onto the 8-mile-long, narrow, and mostly unpaved **Coastal Drive** loop. Along the way, you'll pass the old **Douglas Memorial Bridge**, destroyed in the 1964 flood. Coastal Drive turns south above Flint Ridge. In less than a mile you'll reach the **World War II Radar Station**, which looks like a farmhouse, its disguise in the 1940s. Continue south to the intersection with Alder Camp Road, stopping at the **High Bluff Overlook**.

From the Coastal Drive turn left to reconnect with U.S. 101. Head south to reach **Newton B. Drury Scenic Parkway,** a 10-mile drive through an old-growth redwood forest with access to numerous trailheads. This road is open to all noncommercial vehicles. Along the way, stop at **Prairie Creek Visitor Center,** housed in a small redwood lodge. Enjoy a picnic lunch and an engaging tactile walk in a grove behind the lodge on the Revelation Trail, which was designed for vision-impaired visitors. Back on the parkway head north less than a mile and drive out on unpaved **Cal-Barrel Road,** which leads east through redwood forests. Return to the parkway, continue south about 2 miles to reconnect with U.S. 101, and turn west on mostly unpaved **Davison Road** (motorhomes/RVs and trailers are prohibited). In about 30 minutes you'll curve right to **Gold Bluffs Beach.** Continue north to the **Fern Canyon** trailhead. Return to U.S. 101, and drive south to the turnoff for the **Thomas H. Kuchel Visitor Center.** Pick up free permits—only 50 a day are granted—to visit the **Tall Trees Grove** and head north on U.S. 101 to the turnoff for **Bald Hills Road,** a steep route (motorhomes/RVs and trailers are not advised). If you visit the grove, allow at least four hours round-trip from the information center. You could also bypass the turnoff to the grove and continue south on Bald Hills Road to 3,097-foot **Schoolhouse Peak.** For a simpler jaunt, turn onto Bald Hills Road and follow it for 2 miles to the **Lady Bird Johnson Grove Nature Loop Trail.** Take the footbridge to the easy 1-mile loop, which follows an old logging road through a mature redwood forest. ■TIP→ Motorhomes/RVs and trailers are not allowed on Coastal Drive, Cal-Barrel Road, and Davison Road, and are not advised on Bald Hills Road.

GETTING HERE AND AROUND
CAR TRAVEL
U.S. 101 runs north–south the entire length of the park. You can access all the main park roads via U.S. 101 and U.S. 199, which runs east–west through the park's northern portion. Many roads within the park aren't paved, and winter rains can turn them into obstacle courses; sometimes they're closed completely. Motorhomes/RVs and trailers aren't permitted on some routes. The drive from San Francisco to the park's southern end takes about five hours via U.S. 101. From Portland it takes roughly the same amount of time to reach the park's northern section by way of Interstate 5 to U.S. 199. ■TIP→ Don't rely solely on GPS, which is not always accurate; closely consult park maps, available at the visitor information centers.

PARK ESSENTIALS
PARK FEES AND PERMITS
Admission to Redwood National Park and the related state parks is free. To visit the popular Tall Trees Grove, you must get a free permit at the Kuchel Visitor Center in Orick. The fee to camp at the state parks is $35. Free permits, available at the Kuchel, Crescent City, and (summer only) Hiouchi visitor centers, are needed to stay at all designated backcountry camps.

8

Plants and Wildlife in Redwood

Coast redwoods, the world's tallest trees, grow in the moist, temperate climate of California's North Coast. The current record holder, topping out at 379 feet (or 386, depending on who's measuring), was found in the Redwood Creek watershed in 2006. These ancient giants thrive in an environment that exists in only a few hundred coastal miles along the Pacific Ocean. They commonly live 600 years—though some have been around for more than 2,000 years.

DIVERSE, COMPLEX
A healthy redwood forest is diverse and includes Douglas firs, western hemlocks, tan oaks, and madrone trees. The complex soils of the forest floor support a profusion of ferns, mosses, and fungi, along with numerous shrubs and berry bushes. In spring, California rhododendron bloom all over, providing a dazzling purple and pink contrast to the dense greenery.

OLD-GROWTH FORESTS
Redwood National and State Parks hold nearly 50% of California's old-growth redwood forests. Of the original 3,125 square miles (2 million acres) in the Redwoods Historic Range, only 4% survived logging that began in 1850. A quarter of these trees are privately owned and on managed land. The rest are on public tracts.

WILDLIFE SPECIES
In the park's backcountry, you might spot mountain lions, black bears, black-tailed deer, river otters, beavers, and minks. Roosevelt elk roam the flatlands, and the rivers and streams teem with salmon and trout. Gray whales, seals, and sea lions cavort near the coastline. More than 400 species of birds have been recorded in the parks, which are located along the Pacific Flyway.

PARK HOURS
The park is open year-round, 24 hours a day.

VISITOR INFORMATION
Park Contact Information Redwood National and State Parks. ⊠ 1111 2nd St., Crescent City ☎ 707/465-7335 ⊕ www.nps.gov/redw.

VISITOR CENTERS
Hiouchi Information Center. This small center at Jedediah Smith Redwoods State Park has exhibits about the area flora and fauna and screens a park film. A starting point for ranger programs, the center has restrooms and a picnic area. ⊠ U.S. 199, 2 miles west of Hiouchi and 9 miles east of Crescent City ⊹ Southeast of entrance to Jedediah Smith Campground ☎ 707/458-3294 ⊕ www.nps.gov/redw.

Fodor's Choice ★ **Prairie Creek Visitor Center.** In a small redwood lodge, this center has a massive stone fireplace. The wildlife displays include a section of a tree a young elk died beside. Because of the peculiar way the redwood grew around the elk's skull, the tree appears to have antlers. The center has information about summer programs in Prairie Creek Redwoods State Park, and you'll find a gift shop, a picnic area, restrooms, and exhibits on flora and fauna. Roosevelt elk often roam the vast field adjacent to the center, and several trailheads begin nearby. Stretch your legs

Good Reads

■ The *Redwood Official National and State Parks Handbook,* published by the Redwood Parks Association, covers the area's ecology, botany, natural and cultural history, and common wildlife.

■ Richard Preston's spellbinding *The Wild Trees: A Story of Passion and Daring* chronicles the redwood-climbing exploits of several botanists fiercely passionate about California's endangered tall trees and the ecosystem that supports them.

■ If you plan on hiking, stop at one of the visitor centers and purchase the inexpensive *Redwood National Park Trail Guide,* with details about more than 200 miles of trails.

with an easy stroll along **Revelation Trail,** a short loop that starts behind the lodge. ⊠ *Prairie Creek Rd., off U.S. 101 near southern end of Newton B. Drury Scenic Pkwy., Orick* ☎ 707/488–2039 ⊕ *www. parks.ca.gov/prairiecreek.*

Fodor'sChoice
★ **Thomas H. Kuchel Visitor Center.** The park's southern section contains the largest and best of the Redwoods visitor centers. Rangers here dispense brochures, advice, and free permits to drive up the access road to Tall Trees Grove. Whale-watchers find the center's deck an excellent observation point, and bird-watchers enjoy the nearby Freshwater Lagoon, a popular layover for migrating waterfowl. Many of the center's exhibits are hands-on and kid-friendly. ⊠ *Off U.S. 101 beside Redwood Creek Beach County Park, Orick* ☎ 707/465–7765 ⊕ *www.nps.gov/redw.*

EXPLORING

SCENIC DRIVES

Coastal Drive. The 8-mile, narrow, and mostly unpaved Coastal Drive takes about one hour to traverse. Weaving through stands of redwoods, the road yields close-up views of the Klamath River and expansive panoramas of the Pacific. Recurring landslides have closed sections of the original road; this loop, closed to trailers and RVs, is all that remains. Hikers access the Flint Ridge section of the Coastal Trail off the drive. ⊠ *Klamath ✛ 1 mile south of Klamath off U.S. 101; take Klamath Beach Rd. exit and follow signs.*

Fodor'sChoice
★ **Newton B. Drury Scenic Parkway/Big Tree Wayside.** This paved 10-mile route threads through Prairie Creek Redwoods State Park and old-growth redwoods. It's open to all noncommercial vehicles. North of the Prairie Creek Visitor Center you can make the 0.8-mile walk to Big Tree Wayside and observe Roosevelt elk in the prairie. ⊠ *Orick ✛ Entrances off U.S. 101 about 5 miles south of Klamath and 5 miles north of Orick.*

SCENIC STOPS

Crescent Beach Overlook. The scenery here includes ocean views and, in the distance, Crescent City and its working harbor. In balmy weather this is a great place for a picnic. From the overlook you can spot migrating gray whales between November and April. ⊠ *Off Enderts Beach Rd., 4½ miles south of downtown Crescent City.*

Fodor's Choice   **Fern Canyon.** Enter another world and be surrounded by 50-foot canyon
★   walls covered with sword, deer, and five-finger ferns. Allow an hour to explore the ¼-mile-long vertical garden along a 0.7-mile loop. From the northern end of Gold Bluffs Beach it's an easy walk, although you'll have to wade across or scamper along planks that traverse a small stream several times (in addition to driving across a couple of streams on the way to the parking area). But the lush, otherworldly surroundings, which appeared in *Jurassic Park 2*, are a must-see when creeks aren't running too high. Motorhomes/RVs and all trailers are prohibited on the road to Fern Canyon. You can also hike to the canyon from Prairie Creek Visitor Center along the moderately challenging West Ridge–Friendship Ridge–James Irvine Loop, 12½ miles round-trip. ⊠ *North of Gold Bluffs Beach, Orick ✛ 2¾ miles north of Orick, take Davison Rd. northwest off U.S. 101 and follow signs to Gold Bluffs Beach ⊕ www.nps.gov/redw.*

Lady Bird Johnson Grove. One of the park's most accessible spots to view big trees, the grove was dedicated by, and named for, the former first lady. A 1-mile nature loop follows an old logging road through a mature redwood forest. Allow 45 minutes to complete the trail. ⊠ *Bald Hills Rd., Orick ✛ 1 mile north of Orick off U.S. 101, then 2½ miles to trailhead ⊕ www.nps.gov/redw.*

Tall Trees Grove. At the Kuchel and other visitor centers you can obtain a free permit to make the steep 14-mile drive to this redwood grove that once contained the world-record holder for tallest tree. Rangers dispense only 50 permits maximum a day, first come, first served. The hike from the trailhead parking lot is 4 miles round-trip. ⊠ *Tall Trees Access Rd., off Bald Hills Rd., Orick ✛ 1 mile north of Orick, head east and south from U.S. 101 on Bald Hills Rd. for about 7 miles, then southwest on unpaved access road about 6½ miles to trailhead ⌒ Trailers and RVs not allowed in trailhead parking lot.*

SPORTS AND THE OUTDOORS

BICYCLING

Besides the roadways, you can bike on several trails. Best bets include the 11-mile Lost Man Creek Trail, which begins 3 miles north of Orick; the 12-mile round-trip Coastal Trail (Last Chance Section), which starts at the southern end of Enderts Beach Road and becomes steep and narrow as it travels through dense slopes of foggy redwood forests; and the 19-mile, single-track Ossagon Trail Loop, on which you're likely to see elk as you cruise through redwoods before coasting oceanside toward the end.

CLOSE UP

Best Campgrounds in Redwood

Within a 30-minute drive of Redwood National and State Parks are roughly 60 public and private camping facilities. None of the four primitive areas in Redwood—DeMartin, Flint Ridge, Little Bald Hills, and Nickel Creek—is a drive-in site. You will need to get a free permit from any visitor center except Prairie Creek before camping in these campgrounds, and along Redwood Creek in the backcountry. Bring your own water because drinking water isn't available at any of these sites. These campgrounds, plus Gold Bluffs Beach, are first come, first served.

If you'd rather drive than hike in, Redwood has four developed campgrounds—Elk Prairie, Gold Bluffs Beach, Jedediah Smith, and Mill Creek—that are within the state-park boundaries. None has RV hookups, and some length restrictions apply. Fees are $35 in state park campgrounds. For details and reservations, call ☎ 800/444–7275 or check ⊕ www.reserveamerica.com.

Elk Prairie Campground. Roosevelt elk frequent this popular campground adjacent to a prairie and old-growth redwoods. ✉ *On Newton B. Drury Scenic Pkwy., 6 miles north of Orick in Prairie Creek Redwoods State Park* ☎ *800/444–7275.*

Gold Bluffs Beach Campground. You can camp in tents right on the beach at this Prairie Creek Redwoods State Park campground near Fern Canyon. ✉ *At end of Davison Rd., 5 miles south of Prairie Creek Visitor Center off U.S. 101* ☎ *800/444–7275.*

Jedediah Smith Campground. This is one of the few places to camp—in tents or RVs—within groves of old-growth redwood forest. ✉ *10 miles east of Crescent City on U.S. 199* ☎ *800/444–7275.*

Mill Creek Campground. Redwoods tower over large Mill Creek, in Del Norte Coast Redwoods State Park. ✉ *East of U.S. 101, 7 miles southeast of Crescent City* ☎ *800/444–7275.*

Nickel Creek Campground. An easy hike gets you to these five primitive sites in Redwood National Park; near tide pools, they have great ocean views. ✉ *On Coastal Trail ½ mile from end of Enderts Beach Rd.* ☎ *707/465–7335.*

8

HIKING

MODERATE

Coastal Trail. This easy-to-difficult trail runs most of the park's length; smaller sections that vary in difficulty are accessible at frequent, well-marked trailheads. The moderate-to-difficult **DeMartin section** leads past 6 miles of old-growth redwoods and through prairie. If you're up for a real workout, hike the brutally difficult but stunning **Flint Ridge section,** 4½ miles of steep grades and numerous switchbacks past redwoods and Marshall Pond. The moderate 5½-mile-long **Klamath section,** which connects the Wilson Creek Picnic Area and the Klamath River Overlook, with a short detour to Hidden Beach and its tide pools, provides coastal views and whale-watching opportunities. *Moderate.* ✉ *Klamath* ⊹ *Trailheads: DeMartin, U.S. 101 mile markers 12.8 (south) and 15.6 (north); Flint Ridge,*

Douglas Bridge parking area, north end of Coastal Dr. (east), and off Klamath Beach Rd. (west); Klamath, Requa Rd. at Klamath River Overlook (south), Wilson Creek Picnic Area, off U.S. 101 (north) ⊕ *www.nps.gov/redw.*

KAYAKING

With many miles of often shallow rivers, streams, and estuarial lagoons, kayaking is a popular pastime in the park.

OUTFITTERS

Humboats Kayak Adventures. You can rent kayaks and book kayaking tours that from December to June include whale-watching trips. Half-day river kayaking trips pass beneath massive redwoods; the whale-watching outings get you close enough for good photos. ⊠ *Woodley Island Marina, 601 Startare Dr., Dock A, Eureka* ☏ *707/443–5157* ⊕ *www.humboats.com* ✉ *From $30 rentals, $55 tours.*

Fodor's Choice **Kayak Zak's.** This outfit rents kayaks and stand-up paddleboards, good
★ for touring the beautiful estuarial and freshwater lagoons of Humboldt Lagoons State Park. You can also book a guided nature paddle. Rentals at the Stone Lagoon Visitor Center take place year-round, and on most summer weekends Kayak Zak's sets up a trailer at nearby Big Lagoon. The lagoons are stunning. Herds of Roosevelt elk sometimes traipse along the shoreline of Big Lagoon; raptors, herons, and waterfowl abound in both lagoons; and you can paddle across Stone Lagoon to a spectacular secluded Pacific-view beach. ⊠ *Stone Lagoon Visitor Center, 115336 U.S. 101, about 5½ miles south of Orick, Trinidad* ☏ *707/498–1130* ⊕ *www.kayakzak.com* ✉ *From $30.*

WHALE-WATCHING

Good vantage points for whale-watching include Crescent Beach Overlook, the Kuchel Visitor Center in Orick, points along the Coastal Trail, and the Klamath River Overlook. From late November through January is the best time to see their southward migrations; from February through April the whales return, usually passing closer to shore.

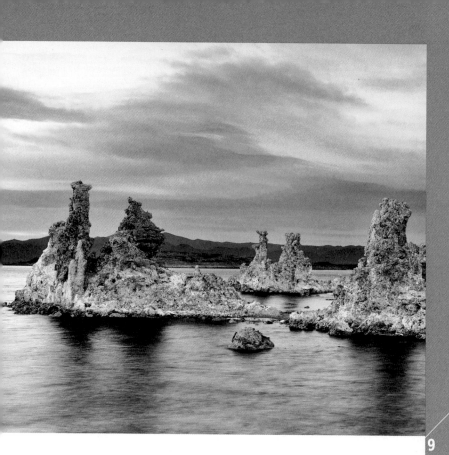

9

EASTERN SIERRA

WELCOME TO THE EASTERN SIERRA

TOP REASONS TO GO

★ **Hiking:** Whether you walk the paved loops in the national parks or head off the beaten path into the backcountry, a hike through groves and meadows or alongside streams and waterfalls will allow you to see, smell, and feel nature up close.

★ **Winter fun:** Famous for its incredible snow-pack—some of the deepest in the North American continent—the Sierra Nevada has something for every winter-sports fan.

★ **Live it up:** Mammoth Lakes is eastern California's most exciting resort area.

★ **Road trip heaven:** Legendary Highway 395 is one of California's most scenic byways, and stops in Independence, Lone Pine, Bishop, and Bodie Ghost Town give you a glimpse of Old West history.

★ **Go with the flow:** Fish, float, raft, and row in the abundant lakes, hot springs, creeks, and rivers.

1 Owens Valley. Lying in the shadow of the Eastern Sierra Nevada and Mount Whitney—the tallest peak in the contiguous USA—the stunningly scenic Owens Valley stretches along U.S. 395 from the town of Olancha, in the south, to the Mono–Inyo county line, in the north. The White Mountains border the valley on the east. This high-desert region, with tiny Old West towns and numerous hiking trails and fishing spots, offers many opportunities for off-the-beaten-track adventures in an uncrowded, pristine setting.

2 Mammoth Lakes. A jewel in the vast Eastern Sierra Nevada, the Mammoth Lakes area lies just east of the Sierra crest, on the backside of Yosemite and the Ansel Adams Wilderness. It's a place of rugged beauty, where giant sawtooth mountains drop into the vast deserts of the Great Basin. In winter, 11,053-foot-high Mammoth Mountain offers the finest skiing and snowboarding in California—sometimes as late as June or even July. Once the snows melt, Mammoth transforms itself into a warm-weather playground, with fishing, mountain biking, golfing, hiking, and horseback riding.

Nine deep-blue lakes are spread throughout the Mammoth Lakes Basin, and another 100 lakes dot the surrounding countryside.

GETTING ORIENTED

The transition between Los Angeles and the Mojave Desert and the rugged Eastern Sierra may be the most dramatic in California sightseeing; as you head into the mountains, your temptation to stop the car and gawk will increase with every foot gained in elevation. U.S. 395 is the main north–south road on the eastern side of the Sierra Nevada, at the western edge of the Great Basin, and a gateway to Death Valley National Park. It's one of California's most beautiful highways; plan to snap pictures at roadside pullouts, and be sure to check out the small towns and attractions along the way. Highway 395 is generally open year-round, which gives you easy access to winter sports, spring wildflower viewing, summer hiking, and fall leaf peeping.

9

3 East of Yosemite National Park. The area to the east of Yosemite National Park includes some ruggedly handsome, albeit desolate, terrain, most notably around Mono Lake, just east of Lee Vining. The June Lake Loop area, between Mammoth Lakes and Lee Vining, is often called the "Switzerland of California" for its series of lakes and creeks bordered by towering peaks. Northeast of Lee Vining is Bodie State Historic Park, a well-preserved ghost town that dates back to California's Gold Rush era.

Updated by Cheryl Crabtree

The Eastern Sierra's granite peaks and giant sequoias bedazzle heart and soul so completely that for many visitors the experience surpasses that at more famous urban attractions. Most of the Sierra's wonders lie within national parks, but outside them deep-blue Mono Lake and its tufa towers never cease to astound. The megaresort Mammoth Lakes, meanwhile, lures skiers and snowboarders in winter and hikers and mountain bikers in summer.

The Eastern Sierra is accessed most easily via Highway 395, which travels the length of the region from the Mojave Desert in the south to Bridgeport in the north. Main towns along the route include Lone Pine, Independence, Bishop, Mammoth Lakes, June Lake, and Lee Vining, a small town at the eastern endpoint of Tioga Road from Yosemite National Park. Pristine lakes and rolling hills outside the parks offer year-round opportunities for rest and relaxation. Or not. In winter the thrill of the slopes—and their relative isolation compared to busy Lake Tahoe—draws a hearty breed of outdoor enthusiasts. In summer a hike through groves and meadows or alongside streams and waterfalls allows you to see, smell, and feel nature up close.

PLANNING

GETTING HERE AND AROUND
AIR TRAVEL
Three main airports provide access to the Eastern Sierra: Fresno Yosemite International (FAT), on the western side, and, on the eastern side, Mammoth–Yosemite (MMH), 6 miles east of Mammoth Lakes, and Reno–Tahoe (RNO), 130 miles north of Mammoth Lakes via U.S. 395. Alaska, Allegiant, American, Delta, Frontier, JetBlue, Southwest, United, and a few other carriers serve Fresno and Reno. Alaska, United, and JetSuiteX serve Mammoth Lakes.

Airports Fresno Yosemite International Airport (*FAT*). ⊠ *5175 E. Clinton Ave., Fresno* ☎ *800/244–2359 automated information, 559/454–2052 terminal info desk* ⊕ *www.flyfresno.com.* **Mammoth Yosemite Airport.** ⊠ *1200 Airport Rd., Mammoth Lakes* ☎ *760/934–2712, 888/466–2666* ⊕ *www.visitmammoth. com/fly.* **Reno–Tahoe International Airport.** ⊠ *2001 E. Plumb La., Reno* ☎ *775/328–6400* ⊕ *www.renoairport.com.*

BUS TRAVEL

Eastern Sierra Transit Authority buses serve Mammoth Lakes, Bishop, and other eastern Sierra towns along Highway 395, from Reno in the north to Lancaster in the south. In summer YARTS (Yosemite Area Regional Transportation System) connects Yosemite National Park with Mammoth Lakes, June Lake, and Lee Vining in the Eastern Sierra, and Central Valley cities and towns in the west, including Fresno and Merced. This is a good option during summer, when parking in Yosemite Valley and elsewhere in the park can be difficult.

Bus Contacts Eastern Sierra Transit Authority. ☎ *760/872–1901 general, 760/924–3184 Mammoth Lakes* ⊕ *www.estransit.com.* **YARTS.** ☎ *877/989–2787, 209/388–9589* ⊕ *www.yarts.com.*

CAR TRAVEL

Interstate 5 and Highway 99 travel north–south along the western side of the Sierra Nevada. U.S. 395 follows a roughly parallel route on the eastern side. In summer, Tioga Pass Road in Yosemite National Park opens to car and bus travel, intersecting with U.S. 395 at Lee Vining.

From San Francisco: Head east on Interstate 80 to Sacramento, then continue on Interstate 80 to U.S. 395, east of Lake Tahoe's north shore, or take U.S. 50 to Lake Tahoe's south shore and continue on 207E to U.S. 305, then head south.

From Los Angeles: Head north on Interstate 5, exiting and continuing north onto Highway 14 and later onto U.S. 395.

■ TIP➔ Gas stations are few and far between in the Sierra, so fill your tank when you can. Between October and May heavy snow may cover mountain roads. Always check road conditions before driving. Carry tire chains, and know how to install them. On Interstate 80 and U.S. 50 chain installers assist travelers (for $40), but elsewhere you're on your own.

Travel Reports Caltrans Current Highway Conditions. ☎ *800/427–7623* ⊕ *www.dot.ca.gov.*

TRAIN TRAVEL

Amtrak's daily *San Joaquin* train stops in Fresno and Merced, where you can connect to YARTS for travel to Yosemite National Park and in summer to smaller gateway towns, including Mammoth Lakes, June Lake, and Lee Vining.

Train Contact Amtrak. ☎ *800/872–7245, 215/856–7952 international* ⊕ *www.amtrak.com.*

RESTAURANTS

Most small towns in the Sierra Nevada have at least one restaurant. Standard American fare is the norm, but you'll also find sophisticated cuisine. With few exceptions, dress is casual. Local grocery stores and delis stock picnic fixings, good to have on hand should the opportunity for an impromptu meal under giant trees emerge. *Restaurant reviews have been shortened. For full information, visit Fodors.com.*

HOTELS

The lodgings in Mammoth Lakes and nearest Yosemite National Park generally fill up the quickest; book hotels everywhere in the Eastern Sierra well in advance in summer. *Hotel reviews have been shortened. For full information, visit Fodors.com.*

Hotel Contacts Mammoth Reservations. ☎ 800/223-3032 ⊕ www.mammothreservations.com.

WHAT IT COSTS			
$	**$$**	**$$$**	**$$$$**
Restaurants	under $16	$16–$22	$23–$30	over $30
Hotels	under $120	$120–$175	$176–$250	over $250

Restaurant prices are the average cost of a main course at dinner or, if dinner is not served, at lunch. Hotel prices are the lowest cost of a standard double room in high season.

TOURS

Mammoth All Weather Shuttle. This outfit operates summer tours from Mammoth Lakes to Yosemite; north to June Lake, Mono Lake, and Bodie Ghost Town; and around the lakes region. The company also transfers passengers from the Mammoth Yosemite Airport into town, drops off and picks up hikers at trailheads, and runs charters to Bishop, Los Angeles, Reno, and Las Vegas airports—useful when inclement weather causes flight cancellations at Mammoth's airport. ⊠ *Mammoth Lakes* ☎ *760/709-2927* ⊕ *www.mawshuttle.com* ⊠ *From $60.*

VISITOR INFORMATION

Eastern Sierra Visitor Center. Pull off the 395 at this one-stop, interagency center for visitor, wilderness, and highway information, plus views of Mount Whitney. You can also pick up wilderness permits, rent or buy bear-resistant food containers, and picnic on the grounds. It's open year-round from 9 to 5 (8 to 5 May–October). ⊹ *2 miles south of Lone Pine, at junctions of U.S. Hwy. 395 and CA Hwy. 136* ☎ *760/876-6200* ⊕ *www.fs.usda.gov/recarea/inyo/recarea/?recid=20698.*

Mammoth Lakes Tourism. ⊠ *Mammoth Lakes* ☎ *760/934-2712, 888/466-2666* ⊕ *www.visitmammoth.com.*

Mono County Tourism. ⊠ *Mammoth Lakes* ☎ *800/845-7922* ⊕ *mono-county.org.*

OWENS VALLEY

Along U.S. 395 east of the Sierra Nevada.

In this undervisited region the snowcapped Sierra Nevada range abruptly and majestically rises to the west, and the high desert whistles to the east. In between are a series of roadside towns full of character, history, and outfits that cater to adventurers and other visitors. The best dining and lodging options can be found along U.S. 395 in Lone Pine and Bishop.

LONE PINE

30 miles west of Panamint Valley.

Mt. Whitney towers majestically over this tiny community, which supplied nearby gold- and silver-mining outposts in the 1860s, and for the past century the town has been touched by Hollywood glamour: several hundred movies, TV episodes, and commercials have been filmed here.

GETTING HERE AND AROUND

Arrive by car via U.S. 395 from the north or south, or Highway 190 or Highway 138 from Death Valley National Park. No train or regularly scheduled bus service is available.

ESSENTIALS

Visitor Information Lone Pine Chamber of Commerce. ⊠ *120 S. Main St., at Whitney Portal Rd.* ☎ *760/876–4444* ⊕ *www.lonepinechamber.org.*

EXPLORING
TOP ATTRACTIONS

Alabama Hills. Drop by the Lone Pine Visitor Center for a map of the Alabama Hills and take a drive up Whitney Portal Road (turn west at the light) to this wonderland of granite boulders. Erosion has worn the rocks smooth; some have been chiseled to leave arches and other formations. The hills have become a popular location for rock climbing. Tuttle Creek Campground sits among the rocks, with a nearby stream for fishing. The area has served as a scenic backdrop for hundreds of films; ask about the self-guided tour of the various movie locations at the visitor center. ⊠ *Whitney Portal Rd., 4½ miles west of Lone Pine.*

Mt. Whitney. Straddling the border of Sequoia National Park and Inyo National Forest–John Muir Wilderness, Mt. Whitney (14,496 feet) is the highest mountain in the contiguous United States. A favorite game for travelers passing through Lone Pine is trying to guess which peak is Mt. Whitney. Almost no one gets it right, because Mt. Whitney is hidden behind other mountains. There is no road that ascends the peak, but you can catch a glimpse of the mountain by driving curvy Whitney Portal Road west from Lone Pine into the mountains. The pavement ends at the trailhead to the top of the mountain, which is also the start of the 211-mile John Muir Trail from Mt. Whitney to Yosemite National Park. Day and overnight permits are required to ascend Mt. Whitney. The highly competitive lottery for these permits opens on February 1st. At the portal, a restaurant (known for its pancakes) and a small store cater to hikers and campers staying at Whitney Portal Campground. You can see a waterfall from the parking lot and go fishing in a small trout pond. The portal area is closed from mid-October to early May; the road closes when snow conditions require. ⊠ *Whitney Portal Rd., west of Lone Pine* ⊕ *www.fs.usda.gov/attmain/inyo.*

WORTH NOTING

Museum of Western Film History. Hopalong Cassidy, Barbara Stanwyck, Roy Rogers, John Wayne—even Robert Downey Jr.—are among the stars who have starred in Westerns and other films shot in the Alabama Hills and surrounding dusty terrain. The marquee-embellished museum relates this Hollywood-in-the-desert tale via exhibits and a rollicking 20-minute documentary. ⊠ *701 S. Main St., U.S. 395* ☎ *760/876–9909* ⊕ *www.museumofwesternfilmhistory.org* ⊠ *$5.*

WHERE TO EAT AND STAY

$
AMERICAN
✕ **Alabama Hills Café & Bakery.** The extensive breakfast and lunch menus at this eatery just off the main drag include many vegetarian items. Portions are huge. **Known for:** many vegetarian and vegan options; convenient refueling stop on the 395; on-site bakery. ⑤ *Average main: $13* ⊠ *111 W. Post St., at S. Main St.* ☎ *760/876–4675.*

$$$
AMERICAN
✕ **Seasons Restaurant.** This inviting, country-style diner serves all kinds of traditional American fare. For a special treat, try the medallions of Cervena elk, smothered in port wine, dried cranberries, and toasted walnuts; finish with the Baileys Irish Cream cheesecake or the lemon crème brûlée for dessert. **Known for:** high-end dining in remote area; steaks and wild game; children's menu. ⑤ *Average main: $27* ⊠ *206 S. Main St.* ☎ *760/876–8927* ⊕ *www.seasonslonepine.com* ⊗ *No lunch. Closed Mon.*

$
HOTEL
🛏 **Dow Villa Motel and Dow Hote.** Built in 1923 to cater to the film industry, the Dow Villa Motel and the historic Dow Hotel sit in the center of Lone Pine. **Pros:** clean rooms; great mountain views; in-room whirlpool tubs in motel. **Cons:** some rooms share bathrooms. ⑤ *Rooms from: $119* ⊠ *310 S. Main St.* ☎ *760/876–5521, 800/824–9317* ⊕ *www. dowvillamotel.com* ⥢ *95 rooms* ¶⊗ *No meals.*

INDEPENDENCE

17 miles north of Lone Pine.

Named for a military outpost that was established near here in 1862, sleepy Independence has some wonderful historic buildings and is worth a stop for two other reasons. The Eastern California Museum provides a marvelous overview of regional history, and 6 miles south of the small downtown lies the Manzanar National Historic Site, one of 10 camps in the West where people of Japanese descent were confined during the Second World War.

GETTING HERE AND AROUND

Greyhound passes through town, but most travelers arrive by car on U.S. 395.

EXPLORING

TOP ATTRACTIONS

FAMILY **Eastern California Museum.** The highlights of this museum dedicated to Inyo County and the Eastern Sierra's history include photos and artifacts from the Manzanar War Relocation Center, Paiute and Shoshone baskets, and a yard full of equipment used by early miners and ranchers. ✉ *155 N. Grant St., at W. Center St.* ☎ *760/878–0258* ⊕ *www. inyocounty.us/ecmsite* ⧉ *Free.*

Fodor's Choice ★ **Manzanar National Historic Site.** A reminder of an ugly episode in U.S. history, the former Manzanar War Relocation Center is where more than 11,000 Japanese-Americans were confined behind barbed-wire fences between 1942 and 1945. A visit here is both deeply moving and inspiring—the former because it's hard to comprehend that the United States was capable of confining its citizens in such a way, the latter because those imprisoned here showed great pluck and perseverance in making the best of a bad situation. Most of the buildings from the 1940s are gone, but two sentry posts, the auditorium, and numerous Japanese rock gardens remain. One of eight guard towers and two barracks have been reconstructed, and a mess hall has been restored. Interactive exhibits inside the barracks include audio and video clips from people who were incarcerated in Manzanar during WWII. You can drive the one-way dirt road on a self-guided tour past various ruins to a small cemetery, where a monument stands. Signs mark where the barracks, a hospital, a school, and the fire station once stood. An outstanding 8,000-square-foot interpretive center has exhibits and documentary photographs and screens a short film. ✉ *Independence* ✛ *West side of U.S. 395 between Independence and Lone Pine* ☎ *760/878–2194* ⊕ *www.nps.gov/manz* ⧉ *Free.*

WORTH NOTING

FAMILY **Mt. Whitney Fish Hatchery.** A delightful place for a family picnic, the hatchery was one of California's first trout farms. The Tudor Revival–style structure, completed in 1917, is an architectural stunner, its walls nearly 3 feet thick with locally quarried granite. Fish production ceased in 2007 after a fire and subsequent mudslide, but dedicated volunteers staff the facility and raise trout for display purposes in a large pond out front. Bring change for the fish-food machines. ✉ *1 Golden Trout Circle, 2 miles north of town* ☎ *760/279-1592* ⊕ *www.wildlife.ca.gov/ Fishing/Hatcheries/Mount-Whitney* ⧉ *Free (donations welcomed)* ⊗ *Closed mid-Dec.–mid-Apr. Closed Tues. and Wed.*

EN ROUTE **Ancient Bristlecone Pine Forest.** About an hour's drive from Independence or Bishop you can view some of the oldest living trees on Earth, some of which date back more than 40 centuries. The world's largest bristlecone pine can be found in Patriarch Grove, while the world's oldest known living tree is along Methusula Trail in Schulman Grove. Getting to Patriarch Grove is slow going along the narrow dirt road, especially for sedans with low clearance. ✉ *Schulman Grove visitor center, White Mountain Rd., Bishop* ✛ *From U.S. 395, turn east onto Hwy. 168 and follow signs for 23 miles* ⊕ *www.fs.usda.gov/main/ inyo/home* ⧉ *$3.*

EN
ROUTE
Schulman Grove Visitor Center. At the Schulman Grove Visitor Center, open late May–October, you can learn about the bristlecone and take a walk to the 4,700-year-old Methuselah tree. ☎ *760/873–2500* ⊕ *www.bishopvisitor.com* �'s *Closed Nov.–mid-May.*

BISHOP

43 miles north of Independence.

One of the biggest towns along U.S. 395, bustling Bishop has views of the Sierra Nevada and the White and Inyo mountains. First settled by the Northern Paiute Indians, the area was named in 1861 for cattle rancher Samuel Bishop, who established a camp here. Paiute and Shoshone people reside on four reservations in the area. Bishop kicks off the summer season with its Mule Days Celebration. Held over Memorial Day weekend, the five-day event includes mule races, a rodeo, an arts-and-crafts show, and country-music concerts.

GETTING HERE AND AROUND

To fully enjoy the many surrounding attractions, you should get here by car. Arrive and depart via U.S. 395 or, from Nevada, U.S. 6. Local transit provides limited service to nearby tourist sites.

ESSENTIALS

Bus Information Eastern Sierra Transit Authority. ☎ *760/872–1901* ⊕ *www.estransit.com.*

Visitor Information Bishop Chamber of Commerce. ⊠ *690 N. Main St., at Park St.* ☎ *760/873–8405, 888/395–3952* ⊕ *www.bishopvisitor.com.*

EXPLORING

FAMILY **Laws Railroad Museum.** The laid-back and wholly nostalgic railroad museum celebrates the Carson and Colorado Railroad Company, which set up a narrow-gauge railroad yard here in 1883. Among the exhibits are a self-propelled car from the Death Valley Railroad, a stamp mill from an area mine, and a full village of rescued buildings, including a post office, the original 1883 train depot, and a restored 1900 ranch house. Many of the buildings are full of "modern amenities" of days gone by. ⊠ *200 Silver Canyon Rd., off U.S. 6, 4.5 miles north of town* ☎ *760/873–5950* ⊕ *www.lawsmuseum.org* 🗲 *$5 suggested donation.*

Mule Days Celebration. For five days around Memorial Day weekend more than 30,000 tourists and locals pack into Bishop to celebrate the humble mule. Activities include what organizers bill as the longest nonmotorized parade in the world, a rodeo, and good old-fashioned country-and-western concerts. ⊠ *1141 N. Main St.* ☎ *760/872–4263* ⊕ *www.muledays.org.*

WHERE TO EAT AND STAY

$ ✕ **Erick Schat's Bakkerÿ.** A bustling stop for motorists traveling to and
BAKERY from Mammoth Lakes, this shop is crammed with delicious pastries, cookies, rolls, and other baked goods. The biggest draw, though, is the sheepherder bread, a hand-shaped and stone hearth–baked sourdough that was introduced during the gold rush by immigrant Basque

sheepherders in 1907. **Known for:** sheepherder bread and pastries; convenient place to stock up; hefty sandwiches. [$] *Average main: $10* ✉ *763 N. Main St., near Park St.* ☎ *760/873–7156* ⊕ *www.erickschatsbakery.com.*

$$
B&B/INN
🛏 **Bishop Creekside Inn.** The nicest spot to stay in Bishop, this clean and comfortable mountain-style hotel is a good base from which to explore the town or go skiing and trout fishing nearby. **Pros:** nice pool; spacious and modern rooms. **Cons:** pets not allowed. [$] *Rooms from: $170* ✉ *725 N. Main St.* ☎ *760/872–3044, 800/273–3550* ⊕ *www.bishopcreeksideinn.com* ⇌ *89 rooms* ❙◉❙ *Breakfast.*

SPORTS AND THE OUTDOORS

The Owens Valley is trout country; its glistening alpine lakes and streams are brimming with feisty rainbow, brown, brook, and golden trout. Good spots include Owens River, the Owens River gorge, and Pleasant Valley Reservoir. Although you can fish year-round here, some fishing is catch-and-release. Bishop is the site of fishing derbies throughout the year, including the Blake Jones Blind Bogey Trout Derby in March. Rock-climbing, mountain biking, and hiking are also popular Owens Valley outdoor activities.

FISHING

Reagan's Sporting Goods. Stop at Reagan's to pick up bait, tackle, and fishing licenses and to find out where the fish are biting. They can also recommend guides. ✉ *963 N. Main St.* ☎ *760/872–3000* ⊕ *www.reagansportinggoods.com.*

TOURS

Sierra Mountain Center. The guided experiences Sierra Mountain offers include hiking, skiing, snowshoeing, rock-climbing, and mountain-biking trips for all levels of expertise. ✉ *200 S. Main St.* ☎ *760/873–8526* ⊕ *www.sierramountaincenter.com* ✉ *From $130.*

Sierra Mountain Guides. Join expert guides on custom and scheduled alpine adventures, from backcountry skiing and mountaineering to backpacking and mountain running. Programs range from half-day forays to treks that last several weeks. ✉ *312 N. Main St.* ☎ *760/648–1122* ⊕ *www.sierramtnguides.com* ✉ *From $150.*

MAMMOTH LAKES

30 miles south of the eastern edge of Yosemite National Park.

International real-estate developers joined forces with Mammoth Mountain Ski Area to transform the once sleepy town of Mammoth Lakes (elevation 7,800 feet) into an upscale ski destination. Relatively sophisticated dining and lodging options can be found at the Village at Mammoth complex, and multimillion-dollar renovations to tired motels and restaurants have revived the "downtown" area of Old Mammoth Road. Also here is the hoppin' Mammoth Rock 'n' Bowl, a two-story activity, dining, and entertainment complex. Winter is high season at Mammoth; in summer, the room rates drop.

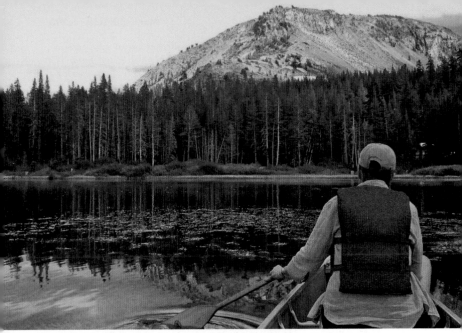
Twin Lakes, in the Mammoth Lakes region, is a great place to unwind.

GETTING HERE AND AROUND

The best way to get to Mammoth Lakes is by car. The town is about 2 miles west of U.S. 395 on Highway 203, signed as Main Street in Mammoth Lakes and Minaret Road west of town. In summer and early fall (until the first big snow) you can drive to Mammoth Lakes east through Yosemite National Park on scenic Tioga Pass Road; signed as Highway 120 outside the park, the road connects to U.S. 395 north of Mammoth. In summer YARTS provides once-a-day public-transit service between Mammoth Lakes and Yosemite Valley. The shuttle buses of Eastern Sierra Transit Authority serve Mammoth Lakes and nearby tourist sites.

ESSENTIALS

Visitor Information Mammoth Lakes Visitor Center. ✉ *Welcome Center, 2510 Main St., near Sawmill Cutoff Rd.* ☎ *760/934–2712, 888/466–2666* ⊕ *www.visitmammoth.com.*

EXPLORING

TOP ATTRACTIONS

Fodor's Choice
★

Devils Postpile National Monument. Volcanic and glacial forces sculpted this formation of smooth, vertical basalt columns. For a bird's-eye view, take the short, steep trail to the top of a 60-foot cliff. To see the monument's second scenic wonder, **Rainbow Falls,** hike 2 miles past Devils Postpile. A branch of the San Joaquin River plunges more than 100 feet over a lava ledge here. When the water hits the pool below, sunlight turns the resulting mist into a spray of color. From mid-June to early September, day-use visitors must ride the shuttle bus from the

Mammoth Mountain Ski Area to the monument. ⊠ *Mammoth Lakes ✛ 13 miles southwest of Mammoth Lakes off Minaret Rd. (Hwy. 203)* ☎ *760/934–2289, 760/872–1901 shuttle* ⊕ *www.nps.gov/depo* 🖃 *$10 per vehicle (allowed when the shuttle isn't running, usually early Sept.– mid-Oct.), $7 per person shuttle.*

Fodor'sChoice
★
Mammoth Lakes Basin. Mammoth's seven main lakes are popular for fishing and boating in summer, and a network of multiuse paths connects them to the North Village. First comes Twin Lakes, at the far end of which is Twin Falls, where water cascades 300 feet over a shelf of volcanic rock. Also popular are Lake Mary, the largest lake in the basin; Lake Mamie; and Lake George. ■ TIP→ Horseshoe Lake is the only lake in which you can swim. ⊠ *Lake Mary Rd., off Hwy. 203, southwest of town.*

Mammoth Rock 'n' Bowl. A sprawling complex with sweeping views of the Sherwin Mountains, Mammoth Rock 'n' Bowl supplies one-stop recreation, entertainment, and dining. Downstairs are 12 bowling lanes, lounge areas, Ping-Pong and foosball tables, dartboards, and a casual bar-restaurant ($$) serving burgers, pizzas, and small plates. The upstairs floor has three golf simulators, a pro shop, and Mammoth Rock Brasserie ($$$), an upscale dining room and lounge. ■ TIP→ If the weather's nice, sit on the outdoor patio or the upstairs deck and enjoy the unobstructed vistas. ⊠ *3029 Chateau Rd., off Old Mammoth Rd.* ☎ *760/934–4200* ⊕ *mammothrocknbowl.com* 🖃 *Bowling: $7 per game per person evenings and weekends, $5 before 5 pm and after 10 pm; $3 shoe rental.*

FAMILY
Fodor'sChoice
★
Panorama Gondola. Even if you don't ski, ride the gondola to see Mammoth Mountain, the aptly named dormant volcano that gives Mammoth Lakes its name. Gondolas serve skiers in winter and mountain bikers and sightseers in summer. The high-speed, eight-passenger gondolas whisk you from the chalet to the summit, where you can learn about the area's volcanic history in the interpretive center, have lunch in the café, and take in top-of-the-world views. Standing high above the tree line, you can look west 150 miles across the state to the Coastal Range; to the east are the highest peaks of Nevada and the Great Basin beyond. You won't find a better view of the Sierra High Country without climbing. ■ TIP→ The air is thin at the 11,053-foot summit; carry water, and don't overexert yourself. ⊠ *Boarding area at Main Lodge, off Minaret Rd. (Hwy. 203), west of village center* ☎ *760/934–0745, 800/626–6684* ⊕ *www.mammothmountain.com* 🖃 *$29.*

WORTH NOTING

Hot Creek Fish Hatchery. This outdoor fish hatchery has the breeding ponds for many of the fish—typically from 3 to 5 million annually— with which the state stocks Eastern Sierra lakes and rivers. In recent years budget cuts have reduced these numbers, but locals have formed foundations to keep the hatchery going. For more details, take the worthwhile self-guided tour. ■ TIP→ Kids enjoy feeding the fish here. ⊠ *121 Hot Creek Hatchery Rd., off U.S. 395 (airport exit), about 10 miles southeast of Mammoth Lakes* ☎ *760/934–2664* 🖃 *Free.*

9

Hot Creek Geological Site. Forged by an ancient volcanic eruption, the geological site is a landscape of boiling hot springs, fumaroles, and occasional geysers. Swimming is prohibited—the water can go from warm to boiling in a short time—but you can look down from the parking area into the canyon to view the steaming volcanic features, a very cool sight indeed. Fly-fishing for trout is popular upstream from the springs. ⊠ *Hot Creek Hatchery Rd., off U.S. 395 (airport exit), about 10 miles southeast of Mammoth Lakes* ☎ *760/924–5501* ⊕ *www. fs.usda.gov/inyo* ⊠ *Free.*

Minaret Vista. The glacier-carved sawtooth spires of the Minarets, the remains of an ancient lava flow, are best viewed from the Minaret Vista. Pull off the road, park your car in the visitors' viewing area, and walk along the path, which has interpretive signs explaining the spectacular peaks, ridges, and valleys beyond. ⊠ *Off Hwy. 203, 1¼ mile west of Mammoth Mountain Ski Area.*

Village at Mammoth. This huge complex of shops, restaurants, and luxury accommodations is the town's tourist center, and the venue for many special events—check the website for the weekly schedule. The complex is also the transfer hub for the free public transit system, with fixed routes throughout the Mammoth Lakes area. The free village gondola starts here and travels up the mountain to Canyon Lodge and back. ■TIP→ Unless you're staying in the village and have access to the on-site lots, parking can be very difficult here. ⊠ *100 Canyon Blvd.* ☎ *760/924–1575* ⊕ *villageatmammoth.com.*

WHERE TO EAT

$$
CAFÉ

✕ **Black Velvet.** Start your day the way scores of locals do—with a stop at the slick Black Velvet espresso bar for Belgian waffles, baked treats, and coffee drinks made from small batches of beans roasted on-site. Then return in the afternoon or evening to hang out with friends in the upstairs wine bar (open 4 to 9), It's also a great place to hang out with a steamy cup of organic tea or a craft beer and log onto the free Wi-Fi. **Known for:** small-batch coffee roasting; small-lot wines by the glass; Belgian waffles. $ *Average main: $16* ⊠ *3343 Main St., Suite F* ☎ ⊕ *www.blackvelvetcoffee.com.*

$
WINE BAR

✕ **Bleu Handcrafted Foods.** Handcrafted artisanal cheeses and meats, wine and beer tastings, bread baked on-site, and specialty meats and seafood draw patrons to Bleu, a combination market and wine bar. Bleu also cooks up savory pub fare at The Eatery at Mammoth Brewing Company. **Known for:** array of meats and cheeses; wine tasting; order-ahead box lunches. $ *Average main: $12* ⊠ *3325 Main St., Unit C* ☎ *760/914–2538* ⊕ *www.bleufoods.com.*

$
AMERICAN

✕ **Burgers.** Don't even think about coming to this bustling restaurant unless you're hungry. Burgers is known, appropriately enough, for its burgers and sandwiches, and everything comes in mountainous portions. **Known for:** great service; hefty portions; burgers and seasoned fries. $ *Average main: $13* ⊠ *6118 Minaret Rd., across from the Village* ☎ *760/934–6622* ⊕ *www.burgersrestaurant.com* ☼ *Closed 2 wks in May and 4–6 wks in Oct. and Nov.*

$$ ✕ **Mammoth Brewing Company.** Steps from the Village gondola and
AMERICAN main bus transfer hub, this brewery lures hungry patrons with about a
dozen craft beers on tap and tasty grub cooked up by Bleu Handcrafted
Foods. Tasting flights, a contemporary vibe at two spacious bar areas,
and a beer garden add to the appeal. **Known for:** craft beer made on-
site; upscale pub food; popular local hangout. ⑤ *Average main: $16*
⊠ *18 Lake Mary Rd.* ✛ *At intersection of Main St. and Minaret Rd.*
☎ *760/934–7141* ⊕ *mammothbrewingco.com.*

$$$ ✕ **The Mogul.** Come here for straightforward steaks—top sirloin, New
STEAKHOUSE York, filet mignon, and T-bone. The only catch is that the waiters cook
FAMILY them, and the results vary depending on their experience. **Known for:**
traditional alpine atmosphere; servers custom-grill your order; all-you-
can-eat salad bar. ⑤ *Average main: $30* ⊠ *1528 Tavern Rd., off Old
Mammoth Rd.* ☎ *760/934–3039* ⊕ *www.themogul.com* ⊘ *No lunch.*

$$$ ✕ **Petra's Bistro & Wine Bar.** The ambience at Petra's—quiet, dark, and
AMERICAN warm (there's a great fireplace)—complements its seductive meat and
seafood entrées and smart selection of mostly California-made wines.
The service is top-notch. **Known for:** romantic atmosphere; attentive
service; lively downstairs bar. ⑤ *Average main: $29* ⊠ *Alpenhof Lodge,
6080 Minaret Rd.* ☎ *760/934–3500* ⊕ *www.petrasbistro.com* ⊘ *Closed
Mon. No lunch.*

$$$$ ✕ **Restaurant at Convict Lake.** The lake is one of the most spectacular
AMERICAN spots in the Eastern Sierra, and the food here lives up to the view. Beef
Fodor'sChoice Wellington, rack of lamb, and pan-seared local trout, all beautifully pre-
★ pared, are among the specialties. ⑤ *Average main: $34* ⊠ *Convict Lake
Rd. off U.S. 395, 4 miles south of Mammoth Lakes* ☎ *760/934–3803*
⊕ *www.convictlake.com* ⊘ *No lunch early Sept.–mid-June.*

$$ ✕ **Toomey's.** A passionate baseball fan, chef Matt Toomey designed this
MODERN casual space near the Village Gondola to resemble a dugout, and deco-
AMERICAN rated it with baseball memorabilia. After a day outdoors, relax over
FAMILY lobster taquitos, giant chicken wings, fish tacos, and Angus beef sliders.
Known for: lobster taquitos and fish tacos; curbside take-out delivery
to your car; homemade organic and gluten-free desserts. ⑤ *Average
main: $20* ⊠ *6085 Minaret Rd., at the Village* ☎ *760/924–4408* ⊕ *www.
toomeyscatering.com.*

WHERE TO STAY

$$ ⌂ **Alpenhof Lodge.** Across from the Village at Mammoth, this mom-and-
B&B/INN pop motel offers basic comforts and a few niceties such as the attractive
pine furniture. **Pros:** convenient for skiers; reasonable rates. **Cons:** some
bathrooms are small; rooms above pub can be noisy. ⑤ *Rooms from:
$159* ⊠ *6080 Minaret Rd., Box 1157* ☎ *760/934–6330, 800/828–0371*
⊕ *www.alpenhof-lodge.com* ⌇ *54 rooms, 3 cabins* ⦿*Breakfast.*

$$$ ⌂ **Double Eagle Resort and Spa.** Lofty pines tower over this very fine
RESORT spa retreat on the June Lake Loop. **Pros:** pretty setting; spectacular
Fodor'sChoice indoor pool; 1½ miles from June Mountain Ski Area. **Cons:** expensive;
★ remote. ⑤ *Rooms from: $249* ⊠ *5587 Hwy. 158, Box 736, June Lake*
☎ *760/648–7004* ⊕ *www.doubleeagle.com* ⌇ *17 2-bedroom cabins, 16
rooms, 1 3-bedroom house* ⦿*No meals.*

9

$$ ▦ **Holiday Haus.** A short walk from the Village, Holiday Haus emerged
HOTEL   from a property-wide renovation as a collection of contemporary moun-
tain-activity-themed rooms and suites—many with full kitchens—at
relatively affordable prices. **Pros:** free parking and Wi-Fi; good option
for groups and families; walk to the Village. **Cons:** showers, no tubs in
most rooms; no 24-hour desk; basic breakfast. ⑤ *Rooms from: $124*
✉ *3905 Main St.* ☏ *760/934–2414* ⊕ *holidayhausmotelandhostel.com*
⤳ *23 rooms,1 cabin, 1 26-bed hostel.*

$$$ ▦ **Juniper Springs Resort.** Tops for slope-side comfort, these condominium-
RESORT   style units have full kitchens and ski-in ski-out access to the mountain.
Pros: bargain during summer; direct access to the slopes; good views. **Cons:**
no nightlife within walking distance; no air-conditioning. ⑤ *Rooms from:*
$199 ✉ *4000 Meridian Blvd.* ☏ *760/924–1102, 800/626–6684* ⊕ *www.*
mammothmountain.com ⤳ *204 studios and apartments* ⑩ *No meals.*

$$ ▦ **Mammoth Mountain Inn.** If you want to be within walking distance of the
RESORT   Mammoth Mountain Main Lodge, this is the place. **Pros:** great location;
big rooms; a traditional place to stay. **Cons:** can be crowded in ski season.
⑤ *Rooms from: $134* ✉ *1 Minaret Rd.* ☏ *760/934–2581, 800/626–6684*
⊕ *www.mammothmountain.com* ⤳ *124 rooms, 91 condos.*

$$$ ▦ **Sierra Nevada Resort & Spa.** A full-service resort in the heart of Old
RESORT   Mammoth, the Sierra Nevada has it all: three restaurants, four bars,
a dedicated spa facility, on-site ski and snowboard rentals, a seasonal
pool and Jacuzzi, seasonal miniature golf, and room and suite options
in three buildings. **Pros:** many on-site amenities; walk to restaurants
on property or downtown; complimentary shuttle service. **Cons:** must
drive or ride a bus or shuttle to the slopes; thin walls in older rooms.
⑤ *Rooms from: $199* ✉ *164 Old Mammoth Rd.* ☏ *760/934–2515,*
800/824–5132, 760/934–7319 ⊕ *thesierranevadaresort.com* ⤳ *143*
rooms, 6 townhomes ⑩ *No meals.*

$$$ ▦ **Tamarack Lodge Resort & Lakefront Restaurant.** On the edge of the John
RESORT   Muir Wilderness Area, where cross-country ski trails lace the woods,
Fodor'sChoice   this 1924 lodge looks like something out of a snow globe. **Pros:** rus-
★   tic; eco-sensitive; many nearby outdoor activities. **Cons:** pricey; shared
bathrooms for some main lodge rooms. ⑤ *Rooms from: $239* ✉ *Lake*
Mary Rd., off Hwy. 203 ☏ *760/934–2442, 800/626–6684* ⊕ *www.*
tamaracklodge.com ⤳ *46 rooms and cabins* ⑩ *No meals.*

$$$ ▦ **The Village Lodge.** With their exposed timbers and peaked roofs, these
RESORT   four-story condo buildings at the epicenter of Mammoth's dining and
nightlife scene pay homage to Alpine style. **Pros:** central location; clean;
big rooms; good restaurants nearby. **Cons:** pricey; can be noisy outside.
⑤ *Rooms from: $239* ✉ *1111 Forest Trail* ☏ *760/934–1982, 800/626–*
6684 ⊕ *www.mammothmountain.com* ⤳ *277 units* ⑩ *No meals.*

$$$$ ▦ **Westin Monache Resort.** On a hill just steps from the Village at Mam-
RESORT   moth, the Westin provides full-service comfort and amenities close to
Fodor'sChoice   restaurants, entertainment, and free public transportation. **Pros:** upscale
★   amenities; prime location; free gondola to the slopes is across the street.
Cons: long, steep stairway down to village; added resort fee. ⑤ *Rooms*
from: $359 ✉ *50 Hillside Dr.* ☏ *760/934–0400, 888/627–8154 reserva-*
tions, 760/934–4686 ⊕ *www.westinmammoth.com* ⤳ *230 rooms and*
suites ⑩ *No meals.*

CLOSE UP

Camping in the Eastern Sierra

Camping in the Sierra Nevada means gazing up at awe-inspiring constellations and awakening to the sights of nearby meadows and streams and the unforgettable landscape of giant granite. Dozens of campgrounds, from remote, tents-only areas to sprawling full-service facilities close to the main attractions, operate in the Eastern Sierra. Be aware that Yosemite National Park's most accessible campgrounds can be jam-packed and claustrophobic in the summer. Luckily, there are many options to the east, including calm and beautiful sites such as Lake Mary Campground in the Mammoth Lakes

area. The following campsites are recommended. Reserve sites at www. recreation.gov.

Convict Lake Campground. A 10-minute drive south of Mammoth, this campground near the Convict Lake Resort is run by the U.S. Forest Service. ⊠ *Convict Lake Rd., 2 miles off U.S. 395* ☎ *760/924–5501* ⊊ *88 campsites.*

Lake Mary Campground. There are few sites as beautiful as this lakeside campground at 8,900 feet, open from June to September. ⊠ *Lake Mary Loop Dr., off Hwy. 203* ☎ *760/924– 5501* ▭ *No credit cards* ⊊ *48 sites (tent or RV)* ▯ *No meals.*

SPORTS AND THE OUTDOORS

BIKING

Fodor'sChoice ★ **Mammoth Mountain Bike Park.** The park opens when the snow melts, usually by July, and has 100-plus miles of single-track trails—from mellow to super-challenging. Chairlifts and shuttles provide trail access, and rentals are available. ⊠ *Mammoth Mountain Ski Area* ☎ *760/934–0677, 800/626-6684* ⊕ *www.mammothmountain.com* ⊠ *$55 day pass.*

FISHING

The main fishing season runs from the last Saturday in April until the end of October; there are opportunities for ice fishing in winter. Crowley Lake is the top trout-fishing spot in the area; Convict Lake, June Lake, and the lakes of the Mammoth Basin are other prime spots. One of the best trout rivers is the San Joaquin, near Devils Postpile. Hot Creek, a designated Wild Trout Stream, is renowned for fly-fishing (catch-and-release only).

Kittredge Sports. This outfit rents rods and reels and conducts guided trips. ⊠ *3218 Main St., at Forest Trail* ☎ *760/934–7566* ⊕ *kittredgesports.com.*

Sierra Drifters Guide Service. To maximize your time on the water, get tips from local anglers, or better yet, book a guided fishing trip, contact Sierra Drifters. ⊠ *Mammoth Lakes* ☎ *760/935–4250* ⊕ *www.sierradrifters.com.*

9

HIKING

Hiking in Mammoth is stellar, especially along the trails that wind through alpine scenery around the Lakes Basin. Carry lots of water; and remember, the air is thin at 8,000-plus feet.

Visit the Mammoth Lakes Trail System website (⊕ *www.mammoth-trails.org*) for descriptions of more than 300 miles of trails, maps, and a wealth of information on recreation in Mammoth Lakes and the Inyo National Forest in all seasons.

U.S. Forest Service Ranger Station. Stop at the ranger station, just east of the town of Mammoth Lakes, for an area trail map and permits for backpacking in wilderness areas. ⊠ *2510 Main St., Hwy. 203* ☎ *760/924–5501* ⊕ *www.fs.usda.gov/main/inyo.*

EASY

Convict Lake Loop. This 2.8-mile trail loops gently around deep blue Convict Lake, a popular site for anglers. Feast your eyes on stunning views of tall peaks, glistening water, and aspen and cottonwood groves while you hike. *Easy.* ⊠ *Trailhead: at Convict Lake, 9 miles south of Mammoth Lakes.*

FAMILY   **Minaret Falls.** Hike along portions of both the Pacific Crest and John Muir trails on this scenic trail (3 miles round-trip) that leads to Devil's Postpile, Minaret Falls, and natural volcanic springs. This is a good family hike, especially in late summer when the water has receded a bit and kids can climb boulders and splash around. *Easy.* ⊠ *Trailhead: At Devil's Postpile National Monument.*

MODERATE

Emerald Lake and Sky Meadows. The first part of this trail travels through shady pine forest along Coldwater Creek to bright-green Emerald Lake (1.8 miles round-trip). Extend the hike by climbing up a trail along an inlet stream up to Gentian Meadow and Sky Meadows (4 miles round-trip), especially beautiful in July and August when various alpine wildflowers, fed by snowmelt, are at their peak splendor. *Moderate.* ⊠ *Trailhead: Coldwater Campground, Mammoth Lakes.*

DIFFICULT

Duck Lake. This popular and busy trail (11 miles round-trip) heads up Coldwater Canyon along Mammoth Creek, past a series of spectacular lakes and wildflower meadows over 10,797-foot Duck Pass to dramatic Duck Lake, which eventually links up with the John Muir Trail. *Difficult.* ⊠ *Trailhead: Coldwater Campground.*

HORSEBACK RIDING

Stables around Mammoth are typically open from June through September.

Mammoth Lakes Pack Outfit. This company runs day and overnight horseback and mule trips and will shuttle you to the high country. ⊠ *Lake Mary Rd., between Twin Lakes and Lake Mary* ☎ *888/475–8747,* ⊕ *www.mammothpack.com.*

McGee Creek Pack Station. These folks customize pack trips or will shuttle you to camp alone. ⊠ *2990 McGee Creek Rd., Crowley Lake* ☎ *760/935–4324 summer, 760/878–2207, 800/854–7407* ⊕ *www. mcgeecreekpackstation.com.*

Why Is There So Much Snow?

The Sierra Nevada receives some of the deepest snow anywhere in North America. In winter, houses literally get buried, and homeowners have to build tunnels to their front doors (though many install enclosed wooden walkways). In the high country, it's not uncommon for a single big storm to bring 10 feet of snow and for 30 feet of snow to accumulate at the height of the season. In the enormous bowls of Mammoth Mountain, you might ski past a tiny pine that looks like a miniature Christmas tree—until you remember that more than 30 feet of tree is under the snow.

To understand the weather, you have to understand the terrain. The Sierra Nevada are marked by a gentle western rise from sea level to the Sierra crest, which tops out at a whopping 14,494 feet at Sequoia National Park's Mt. Whitney, the highest point in the continental United States. On the eastern side of the crest, at the escarpment, the mountains drop sharply—as much as 5,000 feet—giving way to the Great Basin and the high-mountain deserts of Nevada and Utah.

When winter storms blow in off the Pacific, carrying vast stores of water with them, they race across the relatively flat, 100-mile-wide Central Valley. As they ascend the wall of

mountains, though, the decrease in temperature and the increase in pressure on the clouds force them to release their water. Between October and April, that means snow—lots of it. Storms can get hung up on the peaks for days, dumping foot after foot of the stuff. By the time they finally cross over the range and into the Great Basin, there isn't much moisture left for the lower elevations on the eastern side. This is why, if you cross the Sierra eastward on your way to U.S. 395, you'll notice that brightly colored wildflowers and forest-green trees give way to pale-green sagebrush and brown sand as you drop out of the mountains.

The coastal cities and farmlands of the rest of the state depend heavily on the water from the Sierra snowpack. Most of the spring and summer runoff from the melting snows is caught in reservoirs in the foothills and routed to farmlands and cities throughout the state via a complex system of levees and aqueducts, which you'll no doubt see in the foothills and Central Valley, to the west of the range. But much of the water remains in the mountains, forming lakes, most notably giant Lake Tahoe to the north, Mono Lake to the east, and the thousands of little lakes along the Sierra Crest. The lakes are an essential part of the ecosystem, providing water for birds, fish, and plant life.

SKIING

In winter, check the On the Snow website or call the Snow Report for information about Mammoth weather conditions.

FAMILY **June Mountain Ski Area.** Snowboarders especially dig June Mountain, a compact, low-key resort north of Mammoth Mountain. Three beginner-to-intermediate terrain areas—the Surprise Fun Zone, Mambo Playground, and Bucky's Adventure—are for both skiers and boarders. There's rarely a line for the lifts here: if you must ski on a weekend and want to avoid the crowds, this is the place to come, and in a storm it's better protected from wind and blowing snow than Mammoth is. (If it starts to storm, you can use your Mammoth ticket at June.) The services include a rental-and-repair shop, a ski school, and a sports shop. There's food, but the options are better at Mammoth. ■TIP➔ Kids 12 and under ski and ride free. ✉ *3819 Hwy. 158/June Lake Loop, off U.S. 395, 22 miles northwest of Mammoth, June Lake* ☎ *760/648–7733, 888/586–3686* ⊕ *www.junemountain.com* 🖃 *From $99* ⤳ *35 trails on 1,400 acres, rated 35% beginner, 45% intermediate, 20% advanced. Longest run 2 miles, base 7,545 feet, summit 10,190 feet. Lifts: 7.*

Fodor'sChoice
★
Mammoth Mountain Ski Area. One of the West's largest and best ski areas, Mammoth has more than 3,500 acres of skiable terrain and a 3,100-foot vertical drop. The views from the 11,053-foot summit are some of the most stunning in the Sierra. Below, you'll find a 6½-mile-wide swath of groomed boulevards and canyons, as well as pockets of tree-skiing and a dozen vast bowls. Snowboarders are everywhere on the slopes; there are thirteen outstanding freestyle terrain parks of varying difficulty, with jumps, rails, tabletops, and giant super pipes—this is the location of several international snowboarding competitions, and, in summer, mountain-bike meets. Mammoth's season begins in November and often lingers into July. Lessons and equipment are available, and there's a children's ski and snowboard school. Mammoth runs free shuttle-bus routes around town and to the ski area, and the Village Gondola runs from the Village complex to Canyon Lodge. However, only overnight guests are allowed to park at the Village for more than a few hours. ■TIP➔ The main lodge is dark and dated, unsuited in almost every way for the crush of ski season. **Facilities:** 150 trails; 3,500 acres; 3,100-foot vertical drop; 28 lifts. ✉ *Minaret Rd., west of Mammoth Lakes, Rte. 203, off U.S. 395* ☎ *760/934–2571, 800/626–6684, 760/934–0687 shuttle* ⊕ *www.mammothmountain. com* 🖃 *From $135.*

Tamarack Cross Country Ski Center. Trails at the center, adjacent to Tamarack Lodge, meander around several lakes. Rentals are available. ✉ *Lake Mary Rd., off Hwy. 203* ☎ *760/934–5293, 760/934–2442* ⊕ *tamaracklodge.com* 🖃 *$58 all-inclusive day rate.*

SKI RENTALS AND RESOURCES
Fodor'sChoice
★
Black Tie Ski Rentals. Skiers and snowboarders love this rental outfit whose staffers will deliver and custom-fit equipment for free. They also offer slope-side assistance. ✉ *Mammoth Lakes* ☎ *760/934–7009* ⊕ *mammothskis.com.*

Footloose. When the U.S. Ski Team visits Mammoth and needs boot adjustments, everyone heads to Footloose, the best place in town—and possibly all California—for ski-boot rentals and sales, as well as custom insoles. ✉ *3043 Main St., at Mammoth Rd.* ☎ *760/934–2400* ⊕ *www. footloosesports.com.*

Kittredge Sports. Advanced skiers should consider this outfit, which has been around since the 1960s. ✉ *3218 Main St.* ☎ *760/934–7566* ⊕ *kittredgesports.com.*

OntheSnow.com. Get the latest ski and snow reports and weather forecasts for Mammoth Mountain and other resorts, in English and several other languages. ⊕ *www.onthesnow.com/california/mammoth-mountain-ski-area/ski-resort.html.*

Snow Report. For information on winter conditions around Mammoth, call the Snow Report. ⊠ *Mammoth Lakes* ☎ *760/934–7669, 888/766–9778.*

FAMILY **Woolly's Tube Park & Snow Play.** Ride a lift to the top of the hill and whoosh down in a high-speed snow tube as often as you like during a 1¼-hour session. The park has six lanes, a heated deck, and snack shop. Discounts available for a second session if you're not ready to stop riding. Little ones can hang out in the snow play area with sleds and saucers. ⊠ *9000 Minaret Rd.* ☎ *800/626–6684 reservations, 760/934–7533 direct line* ⊕ *www.mammothmountain.com* ☞ *$34–$39 first session (must be 42" tall to ride), play area $15.*

SNOWMOBILING

Mammoth Snowmobile Adventures. Mammoth Snowmobile Adventures conducts guided tours along wooded trails. ⊠ *Mammoth Mountain Main Lodge* ☎ *760/934–9645, 800/626–6684* ⊕ *www.mammothmountain.com* ☞ *From $109.*

EAST OF YOSEMITE NATIONAL PARK

Most people enter Yosemite National Park from the west, having driven out from the Bay Area or Los Angeles. The eastern entrance on Tioga Pass Road (Highway 120 off Highway 395), however, provides stunning, sweeping views of the High Sierra. Gray rocks shine in the bright sun, with scattered, small vegetation sprinkled about the mountainside. To drive from Lee Vining to Tuolumne Meadows is an unforgettable experience, but keep in mind that the road tends to be closed for at least seven months of the year.

9

LEE VINING

20 miles east of Tuolumne Meadows, 30 miles north of Mammoth Lakes.

Tiny Lee Vining is known primarily as the eastern gateway to Yosemite National Park (summer only) and the location of vast and desolate Mono Lake. Pick up supplies at the general store year-round, or stop here for lunch or dinner before or after a drive through the high country. In winter the town is all but deserted, except for the ice climbers who come to scale frozen waterfalls.

GETTING HERE AND AROUND

Lee Vining is on U.S. 395, north of the road's intersection with Highway 120 and on the south side of Mono Lake. In summer YARTS public transit can get you here from Yosemite Valley, but you'll need a car to explore the area.

ESSENTIALS

Visitor Information Lee Vining Chamber of Commerce. ☎ *760/647–6629*
⊕ *www.leevining.com.* **Mono Basin National Forest Scenic Area Visitor
Center.** ✉ *Visitor Center Dr., off U.S. 395, 1 mile north of Hwy. 120* ☎ *760/647–
3044* ⊕ *www.monolake.org/visit/vc.*

EXPLORING

Fodor'sChoice ★   **Mono Lake.** Since the 1940s Los Angeles has diverted water from this lake,
exposing striking towers of tufa, or calcium carbonate. Court victories
by environmentalists have meant fewer diversions, and the lake is rising
again. Although to see the lake from U.S. 395 is stunning, make time to
visit South Tufa, whose parking lot is 5 miles east of U.S. 395 off Highway 120. There in summer you can join the naturalist-guided **South Tufa
Walk,** which lasts about 90 minutes. The **Scenic Area Visitor Center,** off
U.S. 395, is a sensational stop for its interactive exhibits and sweeping
Mono Lake views (closed in winter). In town at U.S. 395 and 3rd Street,
the **Mono Lake Committee Information Center & Bookstore,** open from
9 to 5 daily (extended hours in summer), has more information about
this beautiful area. ✉ *Hwy. 120, east of Lee Vining* ☎ *760/647–3044
visitor center, 760/647–6595 info center* ⊕ *www.monolake.org* ☜ *Free.*

EN
ROUTE   **June Lake Loop.** Heading south from Lee Vining, U.S. 395 intersects the
June Lake Loop. This gorgeous 17-mile drive follows an old glacial
canyon past Grant, June, Gull, and other lakes before reconnecting with
U.S. 395 on its way to Mammoth Lakes. ■TIP→ The loop is especially
colorful in fall. ✉ *Hwy. 158 W.*

WHERE TO EAT AND STAY

$$
AMERICAN   ✕**Tioga Gas Mart & Whoa Nelli Deli.** This might be the only gas station in
the United States serving craft beers and lobster taquitos, but its appeal
goes beyond novelty. Succulent fish tacos with mango salsa and barbe-
cued ribs with a huckleberry glaze are among the many well-executed
dishes. **Known for:** fish tacos; regular live music; convenient location.
⑤ *Average main: $16* ✉ *Hwy. 120 and U.S. 395* ☎ *760/647–1088*
⊕ *www.whoanelliedeli.com* ☉ *Closed early Nov.–late Apr.*

$$
B&B/INN   ⛉ **Lake View Lodge.** Enormous rooms and landscaping that includes sev-
eral shaded sitting areas set this motel apart from its competitors in town.
Pros: attractive; peaceful; clean; friendly staff. **Cons:** could use updating.
⑤ *Rooms from: $129* ✉ *51285 U.S. 395* ☎ *760/647–6543, 800/990–
6614* ⊕ *www.lakeviewlodgeyosemite.com* ☞ *76 rooms, 12 cottages.*

BODIE STATE HISTORIC PARK

31 miles northeast of Lee Vining.

Bodie State Historic Park's scenery is spectacular, with craggy, snowcapped peaks looming over vast prairies. The town of Bridgeport is
the gateway to the park, and the only supply center for miles around.
Bridgeport's claim to fame is that most of the 1947 film-noir classic
Out of the Past, starring Robert Mitchum in his prime as a private eye
whose past catches up with him, was filmed here. In winter, much of
Bridgeport shuts down.

GETTING HERE AND AROUND

A car is the best way to reach this area. Bodie is on Highway 270 about 13 miles east of U.S. 395.

EXPLORING

Fodor's Choice   **Bodie Ghost Town.** The mining village of Rattlesnake Gulch, abandoned
★   mine shafts, and the remains of a small Chinatown are among the sights at this fascinating ghost town. The town boomed from about 1878 to 1881, but by the late 1940s all its residents had departed. A state park was established here in 1962, with a mandate to preserve everything in a state of "arrested decay." Evidence of Bodie's wild past survives at an excellent museum, and you can tour an old stamp mill where ore was crushed into fine powder to extract gold and silver. Bodie lies 13 miles east of U.S. 395 off Highway 270. The last 3 miles are unpaved, and snow may close the highway from late fall through early spring. No food, drink, or lodging is available in Bodie. ⊠ *Bodie Rd., off Hwy. 270, Bodie* ☎ *760/647–6445* ⊕ *www.parks.ca.gov/bodie/* ✉ *$8.*

YOSEMITE
NATIONAL PARK

WELCOME TO YOSEMITE NATIONAL PARK

TOP REASONS TO GO

★ **Wet and wild:** An easy stroll brings you to the base of Lower Yosemite Fall, where roaring springtime waters make for misty lens caps and lasting memories.

★ **Tunnel vision:** Approaching Yosemite Valley, Wawona Road passes through a mountainside and emerges before one of the park's most heart-stopping vistas.

★ **Inhale the beauty:** Pause to smell the light, pristine air as you travel about the High Sierra's Tioga Pass and Tuolumne Meadows, where 10,000-foot granite peaks just might take your breath away.

★ **Walk away:** Leave the crowds behind—but do bring along a buddy—and take a hike somewhere along Yosemite's 800 miles of trails.

★ **Winter wonder:** Winter's hush floats into Yosemite on snowflakes. Lift your face to the sky and listen to the trees.

1 Yosemite Valley. At an elevation of 4,000 feet, in roughly the center of the park, beats Yosemite's heart. This is where you'll find the park's most famous sights and biggest crowds.

2 Wawona and Mariposa Grove. The park's southern tip holds Wawona, with its grand old hotel and pioneer history center, and the Mariposa Grove of Giant Sequoias. These are closest to the south entrance, 35 miles (a one-hour drive) south of Yosemite Village.

3 Tuolumne Meadows. The highlight of east-central Yosemite is this wildflower-strewn valley with hiking trails, nestled among sharp, rocky peaks. It's a 1½-hour drive northeast of Yosemite Valley along Tioga Road (closed mid-October–late May).

4 Hetch Hetchy. The most remote, least visited part of Yosemite accessible by automobile, this glacial valley is dominated by a reservoir and veined with wilderness trails. It's near the park's western boundary, about a half-hour drive north of the Big Oak Flat entrance.

CALIFORNIA

GETTING ORIENTED

Yosemite is so large that you can think of it as five parks. Yosemite Valley, famous for waterfalls and cliffs, and Wawona, where the giant sequoias stand, are open all year. Hetch Hetchy, home of less-used backcountry trails, is most accessible from late spring through early fall. The subalpine high country, Tuolumne Meadows, is open for summer hiking and camping; in winter it's accessible via cross-country skis or snowshoes. Yosemite Ski & Snowboard Area (formerly Badger Pass) is open in winter only. Most visitors spend their time along the park's southwestern border, between Wawona and Big Oak Flat entrance; a bit farther east in Yosemite Valley and Yosemite Ski & Snowboard Area; and along the east–west corridor of Tioga Road, which spans the park north of Yosemite Valley and bisects Tuolumne Meadows.

10

Updated
by Cheryl
Crabtree

By merely standing in Yosemite Valley and turning in a circle, you can see more natural wonders in a minute than you could in a full day pretty much anywhere else. Half Dome, Yosemite Falls, El Capitan, Bridalveil Fall, Sentinel Dome, the Merced River, white-flowering dogwood trees, maybe even bears ripping into the bark of fallen trees or sticking their snouts into beehives — it's all in Yosemite Valley.

In the mid-1800s, when tourists were arriving to the area, the valley's special geologic qualities and the giant sequoias of Mariposa Grove 30 miles to the south so impressed a group of influential Californians that they persuaded President Abraham Lincoln to grant those two areas to the state for protection on June 30, 1864. On October 1, 1890—thanks largely to lobbying efforts by naturalist John Muir and Robert Underwood Johnson, the editor of *Century Magazine*—Congress set aside an additional 1,500 square miles for Yosemite National Park; the valley and Mariposa Grove remained under state control until 1906, when they merged with the national park.

PLANNING

WHEN TO GO

During extremely busy periods—such as weekends and holidays throughout the year—you will experience delays at the entrance gates. For smaller crowds, visit midweek. Or come January through April, when the park is a bit less busy and the days usually are sunny and clear.

Summer rainfall is rare. In winter, heavy snows occasionally cause road closures, and tire chains or four-wheel drive may be required on the roads that remain open. The road to Glacier Point beyond the turnoff for Yosemite Ski & Snowboard Area is closed after the first major snowfall; Tioga Road is closed from late October through May or mid-June. Mariposa Grove Road is typically closed for a shorter period in winter.

PLANNING YOUR TIME
YOSEMITE IN ONE DAY

Begin at the **Valley Visitor Center,** where you can watch the documentary *Spirit of Yosemite* (which inexplicably shows no animals other than one deer). A minute's stroll from there is the **Indian village of the Ahwahnee,** which recalls American Indian life circa 1870. Take another 20 minutes to see the **Yosemite Museum.** Then, hop aboard the free shuttle to Yosemite Falls and hike the **Lower Yosemite Fall Trail** to the base of the falls. Then proceed via shuttle or a 20-minute walk to lunch at **Yosemite Valley Lodge.**

Next choose one of three things: leisurely exploring **Half Dome Village (formerly Curry Village)**—perhaps going for a swim or ice-skating, shopping, renting a bike, or having a beer on the deck; checking out family-friendly **Happy Isles Nature Center** and the adjacent nature trail; or hiking up the **Mist Trail** to the Vernal Fall footbridge to admire the view.

Hop back on the shuttle, then disembark at **The Majestic Yosemite Hotel (formerly The Ahwahnee).** Step into the Great Lounge, which has a magnificent fireplace and Indian artwork, and sneak a peek into the Dining Room, if you're up for a splurge. Get back on the shuttle, and head to **Yosemite Village,** where you can grab some food. Get back in your car and drive to **El Capitan picnic area** and enjoy an outdoor evening meal. At this time of day, "El Cap" should be sun-splashed. (You will have gotten several good looks at world-famous **Half Dome** throughout the day.) Any sunlight left? If so, continue driving on around to take a short hike at the base of **Bridalveil Fall.**

GETTING HERE AND AROUND
AIR TRAVEL

The closest airport to the south and west entrances is Fresno Yosemite International Airport (FAT). Mammoth Yosemite Airport (MMH) is closest to the east entrance.

BUS AND TRAIN TRAVEL

Amtrak's daily San Joaquin train stops in Merced and connects with YARTS buses that travel to Yosemite Valley along Highway 140 from Merced. YARTS buses also travel along Highway 41 from Fresno, and Highway 120 from Sonora, with scheduled stops at towns along the way. Once you're in Yosemite you can take advantage of the free shuttle buses, which operate on low emissions, have 21 stops, and run from 7 am to 10 pm year-round. Buses run about every 10 minutes in summer, a bit less frequently in winter. A separate (but also free) summer-only shuttle runs out to El Capitan. Also in summer, you can take the morning "hikers' bus" from Yosemite Valley to Tuolumne or pay to ride the bus up to Glacier Point. During the snow season, buses run regularly between Yosemite Valley and Yosemite Ski & Snowboard Area.

CAR TRAVEL

Roughly 200 miles from San Francisco, 300 miles from Los Angeles, and 500 miles from Las Vegas, Yosemite takes a while to reach—and its many sites and attractions merit much more time than what rangers say is the average visit: four hours.

10

Of the park's four entrances, Arch Rock is the closest to Yosemite Valley. The road that goes through it, Route 140 from Merced and Mariposa, is a scenic western approach that snakes alongside the boulder-packed Merced River. Route 41, through Wawona, is the way to come from Los Angeles (or Fresno, if you've flown in and rented a car). Route 120, through Crane Flat, is the most direct route from San

> **PLAN YOUR VISIT**
>
> It's wise to visit the Plan Your Visit section of the park website, ⊕ *nps.gov/yose*, for helpful tips and practical information such as water safety, bears and food storage, and how to avoid rare diseases such as plague and hantavirus.

Francisco. The only way in from the east is Tioga Road, which may be the best route in terms of scenery—though due to snow accumulation it's open for a frustratingly short amount of time each year (typically early June through mid-October).

There are few gas stations within Yosemite (Crane Flat and Wawona; none in the valley), so fuel up before you reach the park. From late fall until early spring, the weather is especially unpredictable, and driving can be treacherous. You should carry chains during this period as they are required when roads are icy and when it snows.

PARK ESSENTIALS

PARK FEES AND PERMITS

The admission fee, valid for seven days, is $30 per vehicle, $25 per motorcycle, or $15 per individual.

If you plan to camp in the backcountry or climb Half Dome, you must have a wilderness permit. Availability of permits depends upon trailhead quotas. It's best to make a reservation, especially if you will be visiting May through September. You can reserve two days to 26 weeks in advance by phone, mail, or fax (preferred method) (⊠ *Box 545, Yosemite, CA 95389* ☏ *209/372–0740* 🖷 *209/372–0739*); you'll pay $5 per person plus $5 per reservation if and when your reservations are confirmed. You can download the reservation forms from ⊕ *www.nps.gov/yose/planyourvisit/upload/wildpermitform. pdf*. Without a reservation, you may still get a free permit on a first-come, first-served basis at wilderness permit offices at Big Oak Flat, Hetch Hetchy, Tuolumne Meadows, Wawona, the Wilderness Center in Yosemite Village, and Yosemite Valley in summer. From fall to spring, visit the Valley Visitor Center.

PARK HOURS

The park is open 24/7 year-round. All entrances are open at all hours, except for Hetch Hetchy entrance, which is open roughly dawn to dusk. Yosemite is in the Pacific time zone.

CELL-PHONE RECEPTION

Cell-phone reception depends on the service provider and can be hit or miss everywhere in the park. There are public telephones at park entrance stations, visitor centers, all restaurants and lodging facilities in the park, gas stations, and in Yosemite Village.

EDUCATIONAL OFFERINGS
CLASSES AND SEMINARS

Art Classes. Professional artists conduct workshops in watercolor, etching, drawing, and other mediums. Bring your own materials or purchase the basics at the Yosemite Art Center. Children under 12 must be accompanied by an adult. The center also offers beginner art workshops and children's art and family craft programs ($5–$15 per person). ⊠ *Art Activity Center, Yosemite Village* ☏ *209/372–1442* ⊕ *www.yosemite-conservancy.org* ✉ *$15* ⊘ *No classes Sun. Closed Dec.–Feb.*

Yosemite Outdoor Adventures. Naturalists, scientists, and park rangers lead multihour to multiday educational outings on topics from woodpeckers to fire management to pastel painting. Most sessions take place spring through fall, but a few focus on winter phenomena. ⊠ *Yosemite National Park* ☏ *209/379–2317* ⊕ *www.yosemiteconservancy.org* ✉ *From $99.*

MUSEUMS

Nature Center at Happy Isles. Designed for children, this old-fashioned museum has dioramas with several stuffed animals, including a baby bear. A rotating selection of hands-on, kid-friendly exhibits teaches tykes and their parents about the park's ecosystem. Books, toys, T-shirts, and water bottles are stocked in the small gift shop. ⊠ *Yosemite National Park* ⊹ *Off Southside Dr., about ¾ mile east of Half Dome Village* ✉ *Free* ⊘ *Closed Oct.–Apr.*

Yosemite Museum. This small museum consists of a permanent exhibit that focuses on the history of the area and the people who once lived here. An adjacent gallery promotes contemporary and historic Yosemite art in revolving gallery exhibits. A docent demonstrates traditional Native American basket-weaving techniques a few days a week. ⊠ *Yosemite Village* ☏ *209/372–0299* ✉ *Free.*

RANGER PROGRAMS

Junior Ranger Program. Children ages seven and up can participate in the informal, self-guided Junior Ranger program. A park activity handbook is available at the Valley Visitor Center, the Nature Center at Happy Isles, and the Wawona Visitor Center. Once kids complete the book, rangers present them with a badge and, in some cases, a certificate. ⊠ *Valley Visitor Center or the Nature Center at Happy Isles* ☏ *209/372–0299.*

Ranger-Led Programs. Rangers lead entertaining walks and give informative talks several times a day from spring to fall. The schedule is more limited in winter, but most days you can find a program somewhere in the park. In the evenings at Yosemite Valley Lodge and Half Dome Village, lectures, slide shows, and documentary films present unique perspectives on Yosemite. On summer weekends, campgrounds at Half Dome Village and Tuolumne Meadows host sing-along campfire programs. Schedules and locations are posted on bulletin boards throughout the park as well as in the indispensable *Yosemite Guide*, which is distributed to visitors as they arrive at the park. ⊠ *Yosemite National Park* ⊕ *nps.gov/yose.*

10

RESTAURANTS

Yosemite National Park has a couple of moderately priced restaurants in lovely (which almost goes without saying) settings: the Mountain Room at Yosemite Valley Lodge and Wawona Hotel's dining room. The Majestic Yosemite Hotel (formerly The Ahwahnee) provides one of the finest dining experiences in the country.

Otherwise, food service is geared toward satisfying the masses as efficiently as possible. Yosemite Valley Lodge's food court is the valley's best lower-cost, hot-food option; Half Dome Village Pavilion's offerings are overpriced and usually fairly bland, but you can get decent pizzas on the adjacent outdoor deck. In Yosemite Valley Village, the Village Grill whips up burgers and fries, Degnan's Deli has made-to-order sandwiches, and Loft Pizzeria has a chaletlike open dining area in which you can enjoy pizza, salads, and desserts.

The White Wolf Lodge and Tuolumne Meadows Lodge—both off Tioga Road and therefore guaranteed open only from early June through September—have small restaurants where meals are competently prepared. Tuolumne Meadows also has a grill, and the gift shop at Glacier Point sells premade sandwiches, snacks, and hot dogs. During the ski season you'll also find one at Yosemite Ski & Snowboard Area, off Glacier Point Road.

HOTELS

Indoor lodging options inside the park appear more expensive than initially seems warranted, but that premium pays off big-time in terms of the time you'll save—unless you are bunking within a few miles of a Yosemite entrance, you will face long commutes to the park when you stay outside its borders (though the Yosemite View Lodge, on Route 140, is within a reasonable half-hour's drive of Yosemite Valley).

Because of Yosemite National Park's immense popularity—not just with tourists from around the world but with Northern Californians who make weekend trips here—reservations are all but mandatory. Book up to one year ahead. ■ TIP➔ If you're not set on a specific hotel or camp but just want to stay somewhere inside the park, call the main reservation number to check for availability and reserve (888/413–8869 or 602/278–8888 international). Park lodgings have a seven-day cancellation policy, so you may be able to snag last-minute reservations.

⚠ A trademark dispute with the former park concessioner, Delaware North, has resulted in Yosemite National Park changing the names of several historic park lodges and properties, including the iconic Ahwahnee. This guide uses the new names: Yosemite Lodge at the Falls is now Yosemite Valley Lodge; The Ahwahnee is now The Majestic Yosemite Hotel; Curry Village is now Half Dome Village; Wawona Hotel is now Big Trees Lodge; and Badger Pass Ski Area is now Yosemite Ski & Snowboard Area. For the latest information visit the Yosemite National Park website.

Hotel and restaurant reviews have been shortened. For full information, visit Fodors.com.

WHAT IT COSTS				
	$	$$	$$$	$$$$
Restaurants	under $12	$12–$20	$21–$30	over $30
Hotels	under $100	$100–$150	$151–$200	over $200

Restaurant prices are the average cost of a main course at dinner, or if dinner is not served, at lunch. Hotel prices are the lowest cost of a standard double room in high season.

TOURS

Fodor's Choice ★ **Ansel Adams Camera Walks.** Photography enthusiasts shouldn't miss these 90-minute guided camera walks offered four mornings (Monday, Tuesday, Thursday, and Saturday) each week by professional photographers. All are free, but participation is limited to 15 people. Meeting points vary, and advance reservations are essential. ⊠ *Yosemite National Park* ☎ *209/372–4413* ⊕ *www.anseladams.com* 💲 *Free.*

Discover Yosemite. This outfit operates daily tours to Yosemite Valley, Mariposa Grove, and Glacier Point in 14- and 29-passenger vehicles. The Highway 41 route stops in Bass Lake, Oakhurst, and Fish Camp, and the Highway 140 route departs from Mariposa, Midpines, and El Portal. Rates include lunch. Sunset tours to Sentinel Dome are additional summer options. ☎ *559/642–4400, 800/585–0565* ⊕ *www.discoveryosemite.com* 💲 *From $124.*

VISITOR INFORMATION

Park Contact Information Yosemite National Park. ☎ *209/372–0200* ⊕ *www.nps.gov/yose.*

VISITOR CENTERS

Valley Visitor Center. Learn about Yosemite Valley's geology, vegetation, and human inhabitants at this visitor center, which is also staffed with helpful rangers and contains a bookstore with a wide selection of books and maps. Two films, including one by Ken Burns, alternate on the half hour in the theater behind the visitor center. ⊠ *Yosemite Village* ☎ *209/372–0200* ⊕ *www.nps.gov/yose.*

Yosemite Conservation Heritage Center. This small but striking National Historic Landmark (formerly Le Conte Memorial Lodge), with its granite walls and steeply pitched shingle roof, is Yosemite's first permanent public information center. Step inside to see the cathedral-like interior, which contains a library and environmental exhibits. To find out about evening programs, check the kiosk out front. ⊠ *Southside Dr., about ½ mile west of Half Dome Village* ⊕ *sierraclub.org/yosemite-heritage-center* ⊙ *Closed Mon., Tues., and Oct.–Apr.*

EXPLORING

HISTORIC SITES

Indian Village of Ahwahnee. This solemn smattering of structures, accessed by a short loop trail behind the Yosemite Valley Visitor Center, is a look at what Native American life might have been like in the 1870s. One interpretive sign points out that the Miwok people referred to the 19th-century newcomers as "Yohemite" or "Yohometuk," which have been translated as meaning "some of them are killers." ⊠ *Northside Dr., Yosemite Village* 🖼 *Free.*

Pioneer Yosemite History Center. Some of Yosemite's first structures—those not occupied by Native Americans, that is—were relocated here in the 1950s and 1960s. You can spend a pleasurable and informative half hour walking about them and reading the signs, perhaps springing for a self-guided-tour pamphlet (50¢) to further enhance the history lesson. Weekends and some weekdays in the summer, costumed docents conduct free blacksmithing and "wet-plate" photography demonstrations, and for a small fee you can take a stagecoach ride. ⊠ *Rte. 41, Wawona* 🖀 *209/375–9531* 🖼 *Free* ⊙ *Closed Mon., Tues., and mid-Sept.–early June.*

SCENIC STOPS

El Capitan. Rising 3,593 feet—more than 350 stories—above the valley, El Capitan is the largest exposed-granite monolith in the world. Since 1958, people have been climbing its entire face, including the famous "nose." You can spot adventurers with your binoculars by scanning the smooth and nearly vertical cliff for specks of color. ⊠ *Yosemite National Park* ✛ *Off Northside Dr., about 4 miles west of the Valley Visitor Center.*

Fodor's Choice ★ **Glacier Point.** If you lack the time, desire, or stamina to hike more than 3,200 feet up to Glacier Point from the Yosemite Valley floor, you can drive here—or take a bus from the valley—for a bird's-eye view. You are likely to encounter a lot of day-trippers on the short, paved trail that leads from the parking lot to the main overlook. Take a moment to veer off a few yards to the Geology Hut, which succinctly explains and illustrates what the valley looked like 10 million, 3 million, and 20,000 years ago. ⊠ *Yosemite National Park* ✛ *Glacier Point Rd., 16 miles northeast of Rte. 41* 🖀 *209/372–0200* ⊙ *Closed late Oct.–mid-May.*

Fodor's Choice ★ **Half Dome.** Visitors' eyes are continually drawn to this remarkable granite formation that tops out at more than 4,700 feet above the valley floor. Despite its name, the dome is actually about three-quarters intact. You can hike to the top of Half Dome on an 8.5-mile (one-way) trail whose last 400 feet must be ascended while holding onto a steel cable. Permits are required (and checked on the trail), and available only by lottery. Call *877/444–6777* or visit *www.recreation.gov* well in advance of your trip for details. Back down in the valley, see Half Dome reflected in the Merced River by heading to Sentinel Bridge just before sundown. The brilliant orange light on Half Dome is a stunning sight. ⊠ *Yosemite National Park* ⊕ *www.nps.gov/yose/planyourvisit/halfdome.htm.*

Yosemite's Valley Floor

KEY

- Ranger Station
- Campground
- Picnic Area
- Restaurant
- Lodge
- Trailhead
- Restrooms
- Scenic Viewpoint
- Walking/Hiking Trails
- John Muir Trail
- Bicycle Path
- Valley Floor

Half Dome

Liberty Cap

Mist Trail

Nevada Fall

Footbridge

Emerald Pools

John Muir Trail

Vernal Fall

Mist Trail

Clark Point

Panorama Cliff

Grizzly Peak

Sierra Point

John Muir Trail

Illilouette Gorge

Washington Column

Happy Isles Bridge

Road open only to bicycles and Shuttlebuses

Upper Pines

Clarks Bridge

Nature Center at Happy Isles

bicycle path

North Pines

Royal Arch Cascade

Royal Arches

Lower Pines

Half Dome Village Store

HALF DOME VILLAGE

Road open only to bicycles and Shuttlebuses

Glacier Point

Panorama Trail

bicycle path

Medical Clinic

The Majestic Yosemite Hotel

Village Store

Auto Repair

Housekeeping Camp

Yosemite Conservation Heritage Center

Illilouette Fall

Four Mile Trail

Glacier Point Road

Panono Trail

1/2 mi

1/2 km

Wilderness Office

P.O.

Road open only to bicycles and Shuttlebuses

YOSEMITE VILLAGE

Ahwahneechee Village

Ansel Adams Gallery

Valley Visitor Center

Chapel

Moran Point

Union Point

Sentinel Dome

Yosemite Falls

Yosemite Valley Lodge

Merced River

bicycle path

Sentinel Fall

Four Mile Trail

The Tunnel View viewpoint offers one of the most famous views of Yosemite with Bridalveil Falls, Half Dome, and the Yosemite Valley.

Hetch Hetchy Reservoir. When Congress approved the O'Shaughnessy Dam in 1913, pragmatism triumphed over aestheticism. Some 2.5 million residents of the San Francisco Bay Area continue to get their water from this 117-billion-gallon reservoir. Although spirited efforts are being made to restore the Hetch Hetchy Valley to its former, pristine glory, three-quarters of San Francisco voters in 2012 ultimately opposed a measure to even consider draining the reservoir. Eight miles long, the reservoir is Yosemite's largest body of water, and one that can be seen up close from several trails. ⊠ *Hetch Hetchy Rd., about 15 miles north of the Big Oak Flat entrance station.*

High Country. The above-tree-line, high-alpine region east of the valley— a land of alpenglow and top-of-the-world vistas—is often missed by crowds who come to gawk at the more publicized splendors. Summer wildflowers, which usually pop up mid-July through August, carpet the meadows and mountainsides with pink, purple, blue, red, yellow, and orange. On foot or on horseback are the only ways to get here. For information on trails and backcountry permits, check with the visitor center. ⊠ *Yosemite National Park.*

Mariposa Grove of Giant Sequoias. Of Yosemite's three sequoia groves— the others being Merced and Tuolumne, both near Crane Flat well to the north—Mariposa is by far the largest and easiest to walk around. Grizzly Giant, whose base measures 96 feet around, has been estimated to be one of the largest in the world. Perhaps more astoundingly, it's about 1,800 years old. Up the hill, you'll find more sequoias, a small museum, and fewer people. Summer weekends are usually crowded here.

Plants and Wildlife in Yosemite

Dense stands of incense cedar and Douglas fir—as well as ponderosa, Jeffrey, lodgepole, and sugar pines—cover much of the park, but the stellar standout, quite literally, is the *Sequoiadendron giganteum*, the giant sequoia. Sequoias grow only along the west slope of the Sierra Nevada between 4,500 and 7,000 feet in elevation. Starting from a seed the size of a rolled-oat flake, each of these ancient monuments assumes remarkable proportions in adulthood; you can see them in the Mariposa Grove of Big Trees. In late May the valley's dogwood trees bloom with white, starlike flowers. Wildflowers, such as black-eyed Susan, bull thistle, cow parsnip, lupine, and meadow goldenrod, peak in June in the valley and in July at higher elevations.

The most visible animals in the park—aside from the omnipresent western gray squirrels, which fearlessly attempt to steal your food at every campground and picnic site—are the mule deer. Though sightings of bighorn sheep are infrequent in the park itself, you can sometimes see them on the eastern side of the Sierra Crest, just off Route 120 in Lee Vining Canyon. You may also see the American black bear, which often has a brown, cinnamon, or blond coat. The Sierra Nevada is home to thousands of bears, and you should take all necessary precautions to keep yourself—and the bears—safe. Bears that acquire a taste for human food can become very aggressive and destructive and often must be destroyed by rangers, so store all your food and even scented toiletries in the bear lockers located at many campgrounds and trailheads, or use bear-resistant canisters if you'll be hiking in the backcountry.

Watch for the blue Steller's jay along trails, near public buildings, and in campgrounds, and look for golden eagles soaring over Tioga Road.

Please note that due to major reconstruction the lower grove, which includes Grizzly Giant, Fallen Monarch, and the California Tunnel Tree, will be closed until late fall 2017. Shuttle service will resume when the grove reopens. Check the Yosemite website before visiting this area. ⊠ *Yosemite National Park* ⊹ *Rte. 41, 2 miles north of the south entrance station* ⊕ *www.nps.gov/yose/planyourvisit/mg.htm.*

Sentinel Dome. The view from here is similar to that from Glacier Point, except you can't see the valley floor. A moderately steep 1.1-mile path climbs to the viewpoint from the parking lot. Topping out at an elevation of 8,122 feet, Sentinel is more than 900 feet higher than Glacier Point. ⊠ *Glacier Point Rd., off Rte. 41.*

Tuolumne Meadows. The largest subalpine meadow in the Sierra (at 8,600 feet) is a popular way station for backpack trips along the Pacific Crest and John Muir trails. The setting is not as dramatic as Yosemite Valley, 56 miles away, but the almost perfectly flat basin, about 2½ miles long, is intriguing, and in July it's resplendent with wildflowers. The most popular day hike is up Lembert Dome, atop which you'll have breathtaking views of the basin below. Keep in mind that Tioga Road rarely opens before June and usually closes by mid-October. ⊠ *Tioga Rd. (Rte. 120), about 8 miles west of the Tioga Pass entrance station.*

WATERFALLS

Yosemite's waterfalls are at their most spectacular in May and June. When the snow starts to melt (usually peaking in May), streaming snowmelt spills down to meet the Merced River. By summer's end, some falls, including the mighty Yosemite Falls, trickle or dry up. Their flow increases in late fall, and in winter they may be hung dramatically with ice. Even in drier months, the waterfalls can be breathtaking. If you choose to hike any of the trails to or up the falls, be sure to wear shoes with no-slip soles; the rocks can be extremely slick. Stay on trails at all times.

■ TIP→ Visit the park during a full moon and you can stroll without a flashlight and still make out the ribbons of falling water, as well as silhouettes of the giant granite monoliths.

Bridalveil Fall. This 620-foot waterfall is often diverted dozens of feet one way or the other by the breeze. It is the first marvelous site you will see up close when you drive into Yosemite Valley. ⊠ *Yosemite Valley, access from parking area off Wawona Rd.*

Nevada Fall. Climb Mist Trail from Happy Isles for an up-close view of this 594-foot cascading beauty. If you don't want to hike (the trail's final approach is quite taxing), you can see it—albeit distantly—from Glacier Point. Stay safely on the trail, as there have been fatalities in recent years after visitors have fallen and been swept away by the water. ⊠ *Yosemite Valley, access via Mist Trail from Nature Center at Happy Isles.*

Ribbon Fall. At 1,612 feet, this is the highest single fall in North America. It's also the first waterfall to dry up in summer; the rainwater and melted snow that create the slender fall evaporate quickly at this height. Look just west of El Capitan for the best view of the fall from the base of Bridalveil Fall. ⊠ *Yosemite Valley, west of El Capitan Meadow.*

Vernal Fall. Fern-covered black rocks frame this 317-foot fall, and rainbows play in the spray at its base. You can get a distant view from Glacier Point, or hike to see it close up. You'll get wet, but the view is worth it. ⊠ *Yosemite Valley, access via Mist Trail from Nature Center at Happy Isles.*

Fodor's Choice ★ **Yosemite Falls.** Actually three falls, they together constitute the highest combined waterfall in North America and the fifth highest in the world. The water from the top descends a total of 2,425 feet, and when the falls run hard, you can hear them thunder across the valley. If they dry up—that sometimes happens in late summer—the valley seems naked without the wavering tower of spray. If you hike the mile-long loop trail (partially paved) to the base of the Lower Fall in spring, prepare to get wet. You can get a good full-length view of the falls from the lawn of Yosemite Chapel, off Southside Drive. ⊠ *Yosemite Valley, access from Yosemite Valley Lodge or trail parking area.*

GOOD READS

■ *The Photographer's Guide to Yosemite*, by Michael Frye, is an insider's guide to the park, with maps for shutterbugs looking to capture perfect images.

■ John Muir penned his observations of the park he long advocated for in *The Yosemite*.

■ *Yosemite and the High Sierra*, edited by Andrea G. Stillman and John Szarkowski, features beautiful reproductions of landmark photographs by Ansel Adams, accompanied by excerpts from the photographer's journals written when Adams traveled in Yosemite National Park in the early 20th century.

■ An insightful collection of essays accompanies the museum-quality artworks in *Yosemite: Art of an American Icon*, by Amy Scott.

■ Perfect for budding botanists, *Sierra Nevada Wildflowers*, by Karen Wiese, identifies more than 230 kinds of flora growing in the Sierra Nevada region.

SPORTS AND THE OUTDOORS

BIKING

One enjoyable way to see Yosemite Valley is to ride a bike beneath its lofty granite monoliths. The eastern valley has 12 miles of paved, flat bicycle paths across meadows and through woods, with bike racks at convenient stopping points. For a greater challenge but at no small risk, you can ride on 196 miles of paved park roads—but bicycles are not allowed on hiking trails or in the backcountry. Kids under 18 must wear a helmet.

TOURS AND OUTFITTERS

Yosemite bike rentals. You can arrange for rentals from Yosemite Valley Lodge and Half Dome Village bike stands. Bikes with child trailers, baby-jogger strollers, and wheelchairs are also available. The cost for bikes is $12.50 per hour, or $30.50 a day. ⊠ *Yosemite Valley Lodge or Half Dome Village* ☎ *209/372–4386* ⊕ *www.travelyosemite.com.*

10

BIRD-WATCHING

More than 250 bird species have been spotted in the park, including the sage sparrow, pygmy owl, blue grouse, and mountain bluebird. Park rangers lead free bird-watching walks in Yosemite Valley a few days each week in summer; check at a visitor center or information station for times and locations. Binoculars sometimes are available for loan.

TOURS

Birding seminars. The Yosemite Conservancy organizes day- and weekend-long seminars for beginner and intermediate birders, as well as bird walks a few times a week. They can also arrange private naturalist-led walks any time of year. ⊠ *Yosemite National Park* ☎ *209/379–2321* ⊕ *www.yosemiteconservancy.org* 🔳 *From $99.*

HIKING

TOURS AND OUTFITTERS

Wilderness Center. This facility provides free wilderness permits, which are required for overnight camping (advance reservations are available for $5 per person plus $5 per reservation and are highly recommended for popular trailheads in summer and on weekends). The staff here also provides maps and advice to hikers heading into the backcountry, and rents and sells bear-resistant canisters, which are required if you don't have your own. ⊠ *Between the Ansel Adams Gallery and the post office, Yosemite Village* ☎ *209/372–0308.*

Yosemite Mountaineering School and Guide Service. From April to November, you can learn to climb, hire a guide, or join a two-hour to full-day trek with Yosemite Mountaineering School. They also rent gear and lead backpacking and overnight excursions. Reservations are recommended. In winter, cross-country ski programs are available at Yosemite Ski & Snowboard Area. ⊠ *Yosemite Mountain Shop, Half Dome Village* ☎ *209/372–8344* ⊕ *yosemitemountaineering.com.*

EASY

Fodor'sChoice ★ **Yosemite Falls Trail.** Yosemite Falls is the highest waterfall in North America. The upper fall (1,430 feet), the middle cascades (675 feet), and the lower fall (320 feet) combine for a total of 2,425 feet, and when viewed from the valley appear as a single waterfall. The ¼-mile trail leads from the parking lot to the base of the falls. Upper Yosemite Fall Trail, a strenuous 7.2-mile round-trip climb rising 2,700 feet, takes you above the top of the falls. Lower trail: *Easy.* Upper trail: *Difficult.* ⊠ *Yosemite National Park* ✛ *Trailhead: off Camp 4, north of Northside Dr.*

MODERATE

Mist Trail. Except for Lower Yosemite Fall, more visitors take this trail (or portions of it) than any other in the park. The trek up to and back from Vernal Fall is 3 miles. Add another 4 miles total by continuing up to 594-foot Nevada Fall; the trail becomes quite steep and slippery in its final stages. The elevation gain to Vernal Fall is 1,000 feet, and to Nevada Fall an additional 1,000 feet. The Merced River tumbles down both falls on its way to a tranquil flow through the valley. *Moderate.* ⊠ *Yosemite National Park* ✛ *Trailhead: at Happy Isles.*

Fodor'sChoice ★ **Panorama Trail.** Few hikes come with the visual punch that this 8½-mile trail provides. It starts from Glacier Point and descends to Yosemite Valley. The star attraction is Half Dome, visible from many intriguing angles, but you also see three waterfalls up close and walk through a manzanita grove. If you take the last bus from the valley floor to Glacier Point before starting your hike, you might run out of daylight before you finish. *Moderate.* ⊠ *Yosemite National Park* ✛ *Trailhead: at Glacier Point.*

DIFFICULT

Fodor'sChoice ★ **John Muir Trail to Half Dome.** Ardent and courageous trekkers continue on from Nevada Fall to the top of Half Dome. Some hikers attempt this entire 10- to 12-hour, 16¾-mile round-trip trek in one day; if you're

planning to do this, remember that the 4,800-foot elevation gain and the 8,842-foot altitude will cause shortness of breath. Another option is to hike to a campground in Little Yosemite Valley near the top of Nevada Fall the first day, then climb to the top of Half Dome and hike out the next day. Get your wilderness permit (required for a one-day hike to Half Dome, too) at least a month in advance. Be sure to wear hiking boots and bring gloves. The last pitch up the back of Half Dome is very steep—the only way to climb this sheer rock face is to pull yourself up using the steel cable handrails, which are in place only from late spring to early fall. Those who brave the ascent will be rewarded with an unbeatable view of Yosemite Valley below and the high country beyond. Only 300 hikers per day are allowed atop Half Dome, and they all must have permits, which are distributed by lottery, one in the spring before the season starts and another two days before the climb. Contact *www.recreation.gov* for details. *Difficult.* ⊠ *Yosemite National Park* ✢ *Trailhead: at Happy Isles* ⊕ *www.nps. gov/yose/planyourvisit/halfdome.htm.*

HORSEBACK RIDING

Reservations for guided trail rides must be made in advance at the hotel tour desks or by phone. Scenic trail rides range from two hours to a half day; four- and six-day High Sierra saddle trips are also available.

TOURS AND OUTFITTERS

Big Trees Stable. Two-hour rides at these stables start at $65, and half-day rides are $88.50. Reservations are recommended. ⊠ *Rte. 41, Wawona* ☏ *209/375–6502* ⊕ *www.travelyosemite.com/things-to-do/horseback-mule-riding/* 🖼 *From $65.*

RAFTING

Rafting is permitted only on designated areas of the Middle and South Forks of the Merced River. Check with the Valley Visitor Center for closures and other restrictions.

OUTFITTERS

Half Dome Village Recreation Center. The per-person rental fee ($31) at Half Dome Village Recreation Center covers the four- to six-person raft, two paddles, and life jackets, plus a return shuttle at the end of your trip. ⊠ *South side of Southside Dr., Half Dome Village* ☏ *209/372–4386* ⊕ *www.travelyosemite.com/things-to-do/rafting/* 🖼 *From $31.*

ROCK CLIMBING

The granite canyon walls of Yosemite Valley are world-renowned for rock climbing. El Capitan, with its 3,593-foot vertical face, is the most famous, but there are many other options here for all skill levels.

TOURS AND OUTFITTERS

Yosemite Mountaineering School & Guide Service. The one-day basic lesson at Yosemite Mountaineering School and Guide Service includes some bouldering and rappelling, and three or four 60-foot climbs. Climbers must be at least 10 years old and in reasonably good physical condition. Intermediate and advanced classes include instruction in first aid, anchor building, multipitch climbing, summer snow climbing, and big-wall climbing. There's a Nordic program in the winter. ⊠ *Yosemite Mountain Shop, Half Dome Village* ☎ *209/372–8444* ⊕ *www.travelyosemite.com* ⊠ *From $148.*

WINTER SPORTS

The beauty of Yosemite under a blanket of snow has long inspired poets and artists, as well as ordinary folks. Skiing and snowshoeing activities in the park center on Yosemite Ski & Snowboard Area, California's oldest snow-sports resort, which is about 40 minutes away from the valley on Glacier Point Road. Here you can rent equipment, take a lesson, have lunch, join a guided excursion, and take the free shuttle back to the valley after a drink in the lounge.

ICE-SKATING

Half Dome Village Ice Rink. Winter visitors have skated at this outdoor rink for decades, and there's no mystery why: it's a kick to glide across the ice while soaking up views of Half Dome and Glacier Point. ⊠ *South side of Southside Dr., Half Dome Village* ☎ *209/372–8319* ⊕ *www. travelyosemite.com* ⊠ *$10 per session, $4 skate rental.*

SKIING AND SNOWSHOEING

Yosemite Ski & Snowboard Area. California's first ski resort has five lifts and 10 downhill runs, as well as 90 miles of groomed cross-country trails. Free shuttle buses from Yosemite Valley operate between December and the end of March, weather permitting. Lessons, backcountry guiding, and cross-country and snowshoeing tours are also available. You can rent downhill, telemark, and cross-country skis, plus snowshoes and snowboards. **Facilities:** 10 trails; 90 acres; 800-foot vertical drop; 5 lifts. ⊠ *Yosemite National Park* ⊹ *Badger Pass Rd., off Glacier Point Rd., 18 miles from Yosemite Valley* ☎ *209/372–8430* ⊕ *www.travelyosemite.com/winter/yosemite-ski-snowboard-area/* ⊠ *Lift ticket: from $48.*

Yosemite Cross-Country Ski School. The highlight of Yosemite's cross-country skiing center is a 21-mile loop from Yosemite Ski & Snowboard Area to Glacier Point. You can rent cross-country skis for $25 per day at the Cross-Country Ski School, which also rents snowshoes ($24 per day) and telemarking equipment ($30). ☎ *209/372–8444* ⊕ *www. travelyosemite.com.*

Yosemite Mountaineering School. This branch of the Yosemite Mountaineering School, open at the Yosemite Ski & Snowboard Area during ski season only, conducts snowshoeing, cross-country skiing, telemarking, and skate-skiing classes starting at $35. ⊠ *Badger Pass Ski Area* ☎ *209/372–8444* ⊕ *www.yosemitepark.com.*

Yosemite Ski & Snowboard Area School. The gentle slopes of Yosemite Ski & Snowboard Area make the ski school an ideal spot for children and beginners to learn downhill skiing or snowboarding for as little as $70 for a group lesson. ☎ *209/372–8430* ⊕ *www.travelyosemite.com.*

10

SHOPPING

Ansel Adams Gallery. Framed prints of the famed nature photographer's best works are on sale here, as are affordable posters. New works by contemporary artists are available, along with American Indian jewelry and handicrafts. The gallery's elegant camera shop conducts photography workshops, from free camera walks a few mornings a week to five-day workshops. ⊠ *Northside Dr., Yosemite Village* ☎ *209/372–4413.*

Majestic Hotel Gift Shop. This shop sells more upscale items, such as American Indian crafts, photographic prints, handmade ceramics, and elegant jewelry. For less expensive gift items, browse the small book selection, which includes writings by John Muir. ⊠ *The Majestic Yosemite Hotel, Ahwahnee Rd.* ☎ *209/372–1409.*

Yosemite Mountain Shop. A comprehensive selection of camping, hiking, backpacking, and climbing equipment, along with experts who can answer all your questions, make this store a valuable resource for outdoors enthusiasts. This is the best place to ask about climbing conditions and restrictions around the park, as well as purchase almost any kind of climbing gear. ⊠ *Half Dome Village* ☎ *209/372–8396.*

NEARBY TOWNS

Marking the southern end of the Sierra's gold-bearing mother lode, **Mariposa** is the last town before you enter Yosemite on Route 140 to the west of the park. In addition to a fine mining museum, Mariposa has numerous shops, restaurants, and service stations.

Motels and restaurants dot both sides of Route 41 as it cuts through the town of **Oakhurst**, a boomtown during the Gold Rush that is now an important regional refueling station in every sense of the word, including organic foods and a full range of lodging options. Oakhurst has a population of about 3,000 and sits 15 miles south of the park.

Almost surrounded by the Sierra National Forest, **Bass Lake** is a warm-water reservoir whose waters can reach 80 degrees F in summer. Created by a dam on a tributary of the San Joaquin River, the lake is owned by Pacific Gas and Electric Company and is used to generate electricity as well as for recreation.

As you climb in elevation along Highway 41 northbound, you see nothing but trees until you get to **Fish Camp**, where there's a post office and general store, but no gasoline. (For gas, head 7 miles north to Wawona, in Yosemite, or 14 miles south to Oakhurst.)

Near the park's eastern entrance, the tiny town of **Lee Vining** is home to the eerily beautiful, salty Mono Lake, where millions of migratory birds nest. Visit **Mammoth Lakes**, about 40 miles southeast of Yosemite's Tioga Pass entrance, for excellent skiing and snowboarding in winter, with fishing, mountain biking, hiking, and horseback riding in summer. Nine deep-blue lakes form the Mammoth Lakes Basin, and another hundred dot the surrounding countryside. Devils Postpile National Monument sits at the base of Mammoth Mountain.

Visitor Information Mammoth Lakes Tourism. ⊠ *2510 Main St., Mammoth Lakes* ☎ *760/934-2712, 888/466-2666* ⊕ *www.visitmammoth.com.* **Mono Lake Information Center and Bookstore.** ☎ *760/647-6595* ⊕ *www. leevining.com.* **Tuolumne County Visitors Bureau.** ⊠ *193 S. Washington St., Sonora* ☎ *209/533-4420, 800/446-1333* ⊕ *visittuolumne.com.* **Visit Yosemite/Madera County.** ⊠ *40343 Hwy. 41, Oakhurst* ☎ *559/683-4636* ⊕ *www.yosemitethisyear.com.* **Yosemite Mariposa County Tourism Bureau.** ⊠ *5065 Hwy. 140, Suite E, Mariposa* ☎ *209/742-4567, 866/425-3366* ⊕ *www. yosemite.com.*

NEARBY ATTRACTIONS

FAMILY **California State Mining and Mineral Museum.** A California state park since 1999, the museum has displays on gold-rush history including a replica hard-rock mine shaft to walk through, a miniature stamp mill, and a 13-pound chunk of crystallized gold. ⊠ *5005 Fairground Rd., off Hwy. 49, Mariposa* ☎ *209/742-7625* ⊕ *www.parks.ca.gov* 🎫 *$4.*

Fresno Flats Historical Village and Park. For a dose of colorful foothills history, make a quick stop at this engaging local museum centered around two 1870s houses. ⊠ *School Rd. and Indian Springs Rd., Oakhurst* ☎ *559/683-6570* ⊕ *www.fresnoflatsmuseum.org.*

Yosemite Gateway Gallery Row. Find out what mountain art is all about at this enclave of five galleries representing dozens of painters, sculptors, and other artists. ⊠ *40982 Hwy. 41, 1¼ mile north of Hwy. 49, Oakhurst* ☎ *559/683-5551* ⊕ *www.yosemitegatewaygalleryrow. com* 🎫 *Free.*

FAMILY **Yosemite Mountain Sugar Pine Railroad.** Travel back to a time when powerful steam locomotives hauled massive log trains through the Sierra. This 4-mile, narrow-gauge railroad excursion takes you near Yosemite's south gate. There's a moonlight special ($58), with dinner and entertainment, and you can pan for gold ($10) and visit the free museum. ⊠ *56001 Hwy. 41, 8 miles south of Yosemite, Fish Camp* ☎ *559/683-7273* ⊕ *www.ymsprr.com* 🎫 *$22* 🕙 *Closed Nov.–Mar. Closed some weekdays Apr. and Oct.*

AREA ACTIVITIES

BOATING AND RAFTING

TOURS

Zephyr Whitewater Expeditions. This outfitter conducts half-day to three-day white-water trips on the Tuolumne, Merced, and American rivers for paddlers of all experience levels. ☎ *800/431-3636 reservations, 209/532-6249* ⊕ *www.zrafting.com* 🎫 *From $109.*

NIGHTLIFE

Queen's Inn Wine Bar & Beer Garden. A combination wine bar, tasting room, and small inn, this popular hangout on a bluff above the Fresno River serves about 100 wines by the glass or flight, plus microbrews and imported beers. At the tasting room, open from Wednesday through Sunday between 11 and 5, you can sample ($5 tasting fee) Tempranillo, Pinot Gris, and other limited-production wines. ⊠ *41139 Hwy. 41, Oakhurst* ☎ *559/683–4354* ⊕ *www.queensinn.com/wine-bar-beer-garden/* ⊘ *Closed Sun.–Tues.*

WHERE TO EAT

IN THE PARK

In addition to the dining options listed here, you'll find fast-food grills and cafeterias, plus temporary snack bars, hamburger stands, and pizza joints lining park roads in summer. Many dining facilities in the park are open summer only.

$$$
AMERICAN

✕ **Big Trees Lodge Dining Room.** Watch deer graze on the meadow while you dine in the romantic, candlelit dining room of the whitewashed Big Trees Lodge (formerly the Wawona Hotel), which dates from the late 1800s. The American-style cuisine favors fresh ingredients and flavors; trout and flatiron steaks are menu staples. $ *Average main: $28* ⊠ *8308 Wawona Rd., Wawona* ☎ *209/375–1425* ⊘ *Closed most of Dec., Jan., Feb., and Mar.*

$$$$
EUROPEAN
Fodor's Choice
★

✕ **The Majestic Yosemite Hotel Dining Room.** Formerly the Ahwahnee Hotel Dining Room, rave reviews about the dining room's appearance are fully justified—it features towering windows, a 34-foot-high ceiling with interlaced sugar-pine beams, and massive chandeliers. Although many continue to applaud the food, others have reported that they sense a dip in the quality both in the service and what is being served. $ *Average main: $39* ⊠ *The Majestic Yosemite Hotel, Ahwahnee Rd., about ¾ mile east of Yosemite Valley Visitor Center, Yosemite Village* ☎ *209/372–1489* ⊕ *www.travelyosemite.com.*

$$$
AMERICAN
Fodor's Choice
★

✕ **Mountain Room.** Though good, the food becomes secondary when you see Yosemite Falls through this dining room's wall of windows—almost every table has a view. The chef makes a point of using locally sourced, organic ingredients whenever possible, so you can be assured of fresh vegetables to accompany the hearty main courses, such as steaks and seafood, as well as vegetarian and even vegan options. $ *Average main: $28* ⊠ *Yosemite Valley Lodge, Northside Dr., about ¾ mile west of the visitor center, Yosemite Village* ☎ *209/372–1403* ⊕ *www.travelyosemite.com* ⊘ *No lunch except Sun. brunch.*

$$
FAST FOOD

✕ **Village Grill Deck.** If a burger joint is what you've been missing, head to this bustling eatery in Yosemite Village that serves veggie, salmon, and a few other burger varieties in addition to the usual beef patties. Order at the counter by 5 pm, then take your tray out to the deck and enjoy your meal under the trees. $ *Average main: $12* ⊠ *Yosemite Village* ⊹ *100 yards east of Yosemite Valley Visitor Center*

☎ *209/372–1207* ⊕ *www.travelyosemite.com* ⊗ *Closed Oct.–May. No dinner.*

PICNIC AREAS

Considering how large the park is and how many visitors come here—some 5 million people every year, most of them just for the day—it is somewhat surprising that Yosemite has few formal picnic areas, though in many places you can find a smooth rock to sit on and enjoy breathtaking views along with your lunch. The convenience stores all sell picnic supplies, and prepackaged sandwiches and salads are widely available. Those options can come in especially handy during the middle of the day, when you might not want to spend precious daylight hours in such a spectacular setting sitting in a restaurant for a formal meal. *None of the below options has drinking water available; most have some type of toilet.*

Cathedral Beach. You may have some solitude picnicking here, as this spot usually has fewer people than picnic areas at the eastern end of the valley. *Southside Dr. underneath spirelike Cathedral Rocks.*

Church Bowl. Tucked behind The Majestic Yosemite Hotel, this picnic area nearly abuts the granite walls below the Royal Arches. If you're walking from the village with your supplies, this is the shortest trek to a picnic area. *Behind The Majestic Yosemite Hotel, Yosemite Valley.*

El Capitan. Come here for great views that look straight up the giant granite wall above. *Northside Dr., at western end of valley.*

Sentinel Beach. Usually crowded in season, this area is right alongside a running creek and the Merced River. *Southside Dr., just south of Swinging Bridge.*

Swinging Bridge. This picnic area is just before the little wooden footbridge that crosses the Merced River, which babbles pleasantly by. *Southside Dr., east of Sentinel Beach.*

OUTSIDE THE PARK

10

$$$$
AMERICAN

✕ **Ducey's on the Lake/Ducey's Bar & Grill.** With elaborate chandeliers sculpted from deer antlers, the lodge-style restaurant at Ducey's attracts boaters, locals, and tourists with its lake views and standard lamb, beef, seafood, and pasta dishes. It's also open for breakfast: try the Bass Lake seafood omelet, huevos rancheros, or the Rice Krispies–crusted French toast. **Known for:** steaks and fresh fish; lake views. ⑤ *Average main: $31* ⊠ *Pines Resort, 54432 Rd. 432, Bass Lake* ☎ *559/642–3131* ⊕ *www.basslake.com.*

$$$$
EUROPEAN
Fodor's Choice
★

✕ **Erna's Elderberry House.** Erna Kubin-Clanin, the grande dame of Château du Sureau, created this culinary oasis, stunning for its understated elegance, gorgeous setting, and impeccable service. Earth-tone walls and wood beams accent the dining room's high ceilings, and arched windows reflect the glow of candles. **Known for:** elite waitstaff; romantic setting; seasonal prix-fixe and à la carte menus. ⑤ *Average main: $48* ⊠ *Château du Sureau, 48688 Victoria La., off Hwy. 41, Oakhurst* ☎ *559/683–6800* ⊕ *www.elderberryhouse.com* ⊗ *No lunch Mon.–Sat.*

$$ ✕ **South Gate Brewing Company.**
AMERICAN   Locals pack this family-friendly,
Fodor'sChoice   industrial-chic restaurant to social-
★   ize and savor small-lot beers,
crafted on-site, along with tasty
meals. The creative pub fare runs
a wide gamut, from shepherd's pie
Wellington and thin-crust brick-
oven pizzas to fish tacos, fish-and-
chips, vegan black-bean burgers,
and slow-roasted pulled-pork sand-
wiches. **Known for:** craft beer;
homemade desserts; live-music
calendar. $ *Average main: $14*
✉ *40233 Enterprise Dr., off Hwy.
49, north of Von's shopping center,
Oakhurst* ☎ *559/692–2739* ⊕ *southgatebrewco.com.*

> **LODGING TIP**
>
> Reserve your room or cabin in Yosemite as far in advance as possible. You can make a reservation up to a year before your arrival (within minutes after the reservation office makes a date available, The Majestic Yosemite Hotel, Yosemite Valley Lodge, and Big Trees Lodge often sell out their weekends, holiday periods, and all days between May and September).

WHERE TO STAY

At press time, a still-ongoing trademark dispute with a former park concessioner resulted in Yosemite National Park changing the names of several historic park lodges and properties, including the iconic Ahwahnee. This guide has changed the historic names, with some references to the former. The changes include: Yosemite Lodge at the Falls is Yosemite Valley Lodge, The Ahwahnee is The Majestic Yosemite Hotel, Curry Village is Half Dome Village, Wawona Hotel is Big Trees Lodge, and Badger Pass Ski Area is Yosemite Ski & Snowboard Area.

IN THE PARK

$$ 🏨 **Big Trees Lodge.** This 1879 National Historic Landmark at Yosemite's
HOTEL   southern end (formerly Wawona Hotel) is a Victorian-era mountain resort, with whitewashed buildings, wraparound verandas, and pleasant, no-frills rooms decorated with period pieces. **Pros:** lovely building; peaceful atmosphere. **Cons:** few modern amenities, such as phones and TVs; an hour's drive from Yosemite Valley; shared bathrooms in half the rooms. $ *Rooms from: $148* ✉ *8308 Wawona Rd., Wawona* ☎ *888/413–8869* ⊕ *www.travelyosemite.com* ⊘ *Closed Dec.–Mar., except mid-Dec.–Jan. 2* ⇆ *104 rooms, 50 with bath* ❏ *Breakfast.*

$$ 🏨 **Half Dome Village.** Opened in 1899 as a place for budget-conscious
HOTEL   travelers, Half Dome Village (formerly Curry Village) has plain accommodations: standard motel rooms, simple cabins with either private or shared baths, and tent cabins with shared baths. **Pros:** close to many activities; family-friendly atmosphere. **Cons:** not that economical after a recent price surge; can be crowded; sometimes a bit noisy. $ *Rooms from: $133* ✉ *South side of Southside Dr.* ☎ *888/413–8869, 602/278–8888 international* ⊕ *www.travelyosemite.com* ⇆ *583 rooms and cabins* ❏ *No meals.*

CAMPING IN BEAR COUNTRY

The national parks' campgrounds and some campgrounds outside the parks provide food-storage boxes that can keep bears from pilfering your edibles (portable canisters for backpackers can be rented in most park stores). It's imperative that you move all food, coolers, and items with a scent (including toiletries, toothpaste, chewing gum, and air fresheners) from your car (including the trunk) to the storage box at your campsite; day-trippers should lock food in bear boxes provided at parking lots. If you don't, a bear may break into your car by literally peeling off the door or ripping open the trunk, or ransack your tent. The familiar tactic of hanging your food from high tree limbs is not an effective deterrent, as bears easily can scale trees. In the southern Sierra, bear canisters are the only effective and proven method for preventing bears from getting human food.

$$$$ 🍽 **The Majestic Yosemite Hotel.** Formerly the Ahwahnee, this National
HOTEL Historic Landmark is constructed of sugar-pine logs and features Native
Fodor's Choice American design motifs; public spaces are enlivened with art deco flour-
★ ishes, Persian rugs, and elaborate iron- and woodwork. **Pros:** best lodge
in Yosemite; helpful concierge. **Cons:** expensive rates; some reports that
service has slipped in recent years. $ *Rooms from: $458 ⊠ Ahwahnee
Rd., about ¾ mile east of Yosemite Valley Visitor Center, Yosemite Village ☎ 801/559–4884 ⊕ www.travelyosemite.com ⇋ 125 rooms and
suites* ⦿ *No meals.*

$$ 🍽 **White Wolf Lodge.** Set in a subalpine meadow, the rustic accommoda-
HOTEL tions at White Wolf Lodge make it an excellent base camp for hiking
the backcountry. **Pros:** quiet location; near some of Yosemite's most
beautiful, less crowded hikes; good restaurant. **Cons:** far from the val-
ley. $ *Rooms from: $138 ⊠ Yosemite National Park ⊹ Off Tioga Rd.
(Rte. 120), 25 miles west of Tuolumne Meadows and 15 miles east of
Crane Flat ☎ 801/559–4884 ⊗ Closed mid-Sept.–mid-June ⇋ 24 tent
cabins, 4 cabins* ⦿ *No meals.*

$$$$ 🍽 **Yosemite Valley Lodge.** This 1915 lodge near Yosemite Falls (formerly
HOTEL Yosemite Lodge at the Falls) is a collection of numerous two-story,
glass-and-wood structures tucked beneath the trees. **Pros:** centrally
located; dependably clean rooms; lots of tours leave from out front.
Cons: can feel impersonal; prices recently skyrocketed. $ *Rooms from:
$247 ⊠ 9006 Yosemite Valley Lodge Dr., Yosemite Village ☎ 888/413–
8869 ⊕ www.travelyosemite.com/ ⇋ 245 rooms* ⦿ *No meals.*

OUTSIDE THE PARK

$$$ 🍽 **Best Western Plus Yosemite Gateway Inn.** Perched on 11 hillside acres,
HOTEL Oakhurst's best motel has carefully tended landscaping and rooms
FAMILY with stylish contemporary furnishings and hand-painted murals of
Yosemite. **Pros:** close to park's southern entrance; on-site restaurant;
indoor and outdoor swimming pools; frequent deer and wildlife
sightings. **Cons:** some rooms on the small side; Internet connection

10

CLOSE UP

Best Campgrounds in Yosemite

If you are going to concentrate solely on valley sites and activities, you should endeavor to stay in one of the "Pines" campgrounds, which are clustered near Half Dome Village and within an easy stroll from that busy complex's many facilities. For a more primitive and quiet experience, and to be near many backcountry hikes, try one of the Tioga Road campgrounds.

National Park Service Reservations Office. Reservations are required at many of Yosemite's campgrounds. You can book a site up to five months in advance, starting on the 15th of the month. Unless otherwise noted, book your site through the central National Park Service Reservations Office. If you don't have reservations when you arrive, many sites, especially those outside Yosemite Valley, are available on a first-come, first-served basis. ☎ *877/444–6777 reservations, 518/885–3639 international, 888/448–1474 customer service* ⊕ *www.recreation.gov.*

Bridalveil Creek. This campground sits among lodgepole pines at 7,200 feet, above the valley on Glacier Point Road. From here, you can easily drive to Glacier Point's magnificent valley views. ⊠ *From Rte. 41 in Wawona, go north to Glacier Point Rd. and turn right; entrance to campground is 25 miles ahead on right side.*

Camp 4. Formerly known as Sunnyside Walk-In, and extremely popular with rock climbers, who don't mind that a total of six are assigned to each campsite; no matter how many are in your group, this is the only valley campground available on a first-come, first-served basis. ⊠ *Base of Yosemite Falls Trail, just west of Yosemite Valley Lodge on Northside Dr., Yosemite Village.*

Housekeeping Camp. Composed of three concrete walls and covered with two layers of canvas, each unit has an open-ended fourth side that can be closed off with a heavy white canvas curtain. You can rent "bedpacks," consisting of blankets, sheets, and other comforts. ⊠ *Southside Dr., ½ mile west of Half Dome Village.*

Porcupine Flat. Sixteen miles west of Tuolumne Meadows, this campground sits at 8,100 feet. If you want to be in the high country, this is a good bet. ⊠ *Rte. 120, 16 miles west of Tuolumne Meadows.*

Tuolumne Meadows. In a wooded area at 8,600 feet, just south of its namesake meadow, this is one of the most spectacular and sought-after campgrounds in Yosemite. ⊠ *Rte. 120, 46 miles east of Big Oak Flat entrance station.*

Upper Pines. This is one of the valley's largest campgrounds and the closest one to the trailheads. Expect large crowds in the summer—and little privacy. ⊠ *At east end of valley, near Half Dome Village.*

Wawona. Near the Mariposa Grove, just downstream from a popular fishing spot, this year-round campground has larger, less densely packed sites than campgrounds in the valley. ⊠ *Rte. 41, 1 mile north of Wawona.*

White Wolf. Set in the beautiful high country at 8,000 feet, this is a prime spot for hikers from early July to mid-September. ⊠ *Tioga Rd., 15 miles east of Big Oak Flat entrance.*

can be slow. $\boxed{\$}$ *Rooms from: $160* $\boxtimes$ *40530 Hwy. 41, Oakhurst* $\textcircled{a}$ *559/683–2378* $\oplus$ *www.yosemitegatewayinn.com* $\looparrowright$ *149 rooms* $\lvert\bigcirc\rvert$ *No meals.*

$$$$
RESORT
Fodor's Choice
★

$\square$ **Château du Sureau.** The inn here is straight out of a children's book: every room is impeccably styled with European antiques, sumptuous fabrics, fresh-cut flowers, and oversize soaking tubs. **Pros:** luxurious; great views; sumptuous spa facility. **Cons:** expensive; cost might not seem worth it to guests not spa-oriented. $\boxed{\$}$ *Rooms from: $420* $\boxtimes$ *48688 Victoria La., Oakhurst* $\textcircled{a}$ *559/683–6860* $\oplus$ *www.chateausureau.com* $\looparrowright$ *10 rooms, 1 villa* $\lvert\bigcirc\rvert$ *Breakfast.*

$$$$
RESORT
FAMILY

$\square$ **Evergreen Lodge at Yosemite.** Amid the trees near Yosemite National Park's Hetch Hetchy entrance, this sprawling property is perfect for families. **Pros:** near the underrated Hetch Hetchy Valley; family atmosphere; clean cabins. **Cons:** not cheap; about an hour's drive to Yosemite Valley. $\boxed{\$}$ *Rooms from: $275* $\boxtimes$ *33160 Evergreen Rd., 33 miles north of El Portal, 30 miles east of town of Groveland, Groveland* $\textcircled{a}$ *209/379–2606* $\oplus$ *www.evergreenlodge.com* $\looparrowright$ *88 cabins.*

$$$
B&B/INN

$\square$ **Homestead Cottages.** Set on 160 acres of rolling hills that once held a Miwok village, these cottages (the largest sleeps six) have gas fireplaces, fully equipped kitchens, and queen-size beds. **Pros:** remote location; quiet setting; friendly owners. **Cons:** might be too quiet for some. $\boxed{\$}$ *Rooms from: $189* $\boxtimes$ *41110 Rd. 600, 2½ miles off Hwy. 49, Ahwahnee* $\textcircled{a}$ *559/683–0495* $\oplus$ *www.homesteadcottages.com* $\looparrowright$ *6 cottages* $\lvert\bigcirc\rvert$ *Breakfast.*

$$$$
B&B/INN

$\square$ **Narrow Gauge Inn.** The well-tended rooms at this family-owned property have balconies with views of the surrounding woods and mountains. **Pros:** close to Yosemite's south entrance; nicely appointed rooms; wonderful balconies. **Cons:** rooms can be a bit dark; dining options are limited, especially for vegetarians. $\boxed{\$}$ *Rooms from: $209* $\boxtimes$ *48571 Hwy. 41, Fish Camp* $\textcircled{a}$ *559/683–7720, 888/644–9050* $\oplus$ *www.narrowgaugeinn.com* $\looparrowright$ *26 rooms* $\lvert\bigcirc\rvert$ *Breakfast.*

$$$$
RESORT
FAMILY
Fodor's Choice
★

$\square$ **Rush Creek Lodge.** This sleek, nature-inspired complex occupies 20 acres on a wooded hillside and includes a pool and hot tubs, a restaurant and tavern with indoor/outdoor seating, a guided recreation program, an amphitheater, and a general store. **Pros:** close to Yosemite's Big Oak Flat entrance; YARTS bus stops here and connects with Yosemite Valley and Sonora. **Cons:** no TVs; pricey in high season; remote setting. $\boxed{\$}$ *Rooms from: $350* $\boxtimes$ *34001 Hwy. 120, Groveland* $\oplus$ *25 miles east of Groveland, 23 miles north of Yosemite Valley* $\textcircled{a}$ *209/379–2373* $\oplus$ *www.rushcreeklodge.com* $\looparrowright$ *143 rooms and suites* $\lvert\bigcirc\rvert$ *No meals.*

$$$$
HOTEL

$\square$ **Sierra Sky Ranch.** Off Highway 41 just 10 miles south of the Yosemite National Park, this 19th-century cattle ranch near a hidden grove of giant sequoia trees provides a restful, rustic retreat. **Pros:** peaceful setting; historic property; full hot breakfast. **Cons:** some rooms on the small side; not in town. $\boxed{\$}$ *Rooms from: $229* $\boxtimes$ *50552 Rd. 632, Oakhurst* $\textcircled{a}$ *559/683–8040* $\oplus$ *www.sierraskyranch.com* $\looparrowright$ *26 rooms* $\lvert\bigcirc\rvert$ *Breakfast.*

$$$
RESORT

$\square$ **Tamarack Lodge Resort.** Tucked away on the edge of the John Muir Wilderness Area, where cross-country ski trails loop through the woods, this 1924 lodge looks like something out of a snow globe.

10

Pros: rustic but not run-down; tons of nearby outdoor activities. **Cons:** thin walls; some shared bathrooms. $ *Rooms from: $169* ✉ *Lake Mary Rd., off Rte. 203, Mammoth Lakes* ☎ *760/934–2442, 800/237–6879* ⊕ *www.tamaracklodge.com* ⤵ *45 rooms and cabins* ⓞ *No meals.*

$$$$ 🛏 **Tenaya Lodge.** One of the region's largest hotels, Tenaya Lodge is ideal

RESORT   for people who enjoy wilderness treks by day but prefer creature com-

FAMILY   forts at night. **Pros:** rustic setting with modern comforts; exceptional

Fodor's Choice   spa and exercise facility; close to Yosemite; activities for all ages. **Cons:**

★   so big it can seem impersonal; pricey during summer. $ *Rooms from: $379* ✉ *1122 Hwy. 41, Fish Camp* ☎ *559/683–6555, 888/514–2167* ⊕ *www.tenayalodge.com* ⤵ *302 rooms* ⓞ *No meals.*

$$$$ 🛏 **Yosemite Lodging at Big Creek Inn.** A romantic bed-and-breakfast in a

B&B/INN   woodsy setting south of the park, the inn offers perks that place it ahead of the competition. **Pros:** friendly, knowledgeable innkeeper; hearty home-cooked breakfast; intimate setting. **Cons:** with only three rooms it books up quickly; no pets allowed. $ *Rooms from: $269* ✉ *1221 Hwy. 41, Fish Camp* ☎ *559/641–2828* ⊕ *www.yosemiteinn.com* ⤵ *3 rooms* ⓞ *Breakfast.*

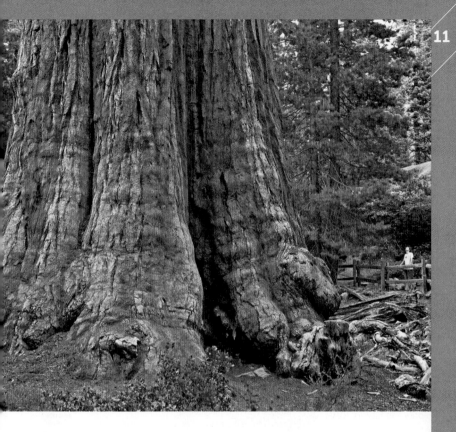

SEQUOIA AND KINGS CANYON NATIONAL PARKS

WELCOME TO SEQUOIA AND KINGS CANYON NATIONAL PARKS

TOP REASONS TO GO

★ **Gentle giants:** You'll feel small—in a good way—walking among some of the world's largest living things in Sequoia's Giant Forest and Kings Canyon's Grant Grove.

★ **Because it's there:** You can't even glimpse it from the main part of Sequoia, but the sight of majestic Mount Whitney is worth the trip to the eastern face of the High Sierra.

★ **Underground exploration:** Far older even than the giant sequoias, the gleaming limestone formations in Crystal Cave will draw you along dark, marble passages.

★ **A grander-than-Grand Canyon:** Drive the twisting Kings Canyon Scenic Byway down into the jagged, granite Kings River Canyon, deeper in parts than the Grand Canyon.

★ **Regal solitude:** To spend a day or two hiking in a subalpine world of your own, pick one of the many trailheads at Mineral King.

1 Giant Forest–Lodgepole Village. One of the most heavily visited areas of Sequoia contains major sights such as Giant Forest, General Sherman Tree, Crystal Cave, and Moro Rock.

2 Grant Grove Village–Redwood Canyon. The "thumb" of Kings Canyon National Park is its busiest section, where Grant Grove, General Grant Tree, Panoramic Point, and Big Stump are the main attractions.

3 Cedar Grove. The drive through the high-country portion of Kings Canyon National Park to Cedar Grove Village, on the canyon floor, reveals magnificent granite formations of varied hues. Rock meets river in breathtaking fashion at Zumwalt Meadow.

4 Mineral King. In the southeast section of Sequoia, the highest road-accessible part of the park is a good place to hike, camp, and soak up the unspoiled grandeur of the Sierra Nevada.

5 Mount Whitney. The highest peak in the Lower 48 stands on the eastern edge of Sequoia; to get there from Giant Forest you must either backpack eight days through the mountains or drive nearly 400 miles around the park to its other side.

CALIFORNIA

GETTING ORIENTED

The two parks comprise 865,964 acres (1,353 square miles), mostly on the western flank of the Sierra. A map of the adjacent parks looks vaguely like a mitten, with the palm of Sequoia National Park south of the north-pointing, skinny thumb and long fingers of Kings Canyon National Park. Between the western thumb and eastern fingers, north of Sequoia, lies part of Sequoia National Forest, which includes Giant Sequoia National Monument.

Updated by Cheryl Crabtree

Although *Sequoiadendron giganteum* is the formal name for the redwoods that grow here, everyone outside the classroom calls them sequoias, big trees, or Sierra redwoods. Their monstrously thick trunks and branches, remarkably shallow root systems, and neck-craning heights are almost impossible to believe, as is the fact they can live for more than 2,500 years. Many of these towering marvels are in the Giant Forest stretch of Generals Highway, which connects Sequoia and Kings Canyon national parks.

Next to or a few miles off the 46-mile Generals Highway are most of Sequoia National Park's main attractions and Grant Grove Village, the orientation hub for Kings Canyon National Park. The two parks share a boundary that runs from the Central Valley in the west, where the Sierra Nevada foothills begin, to the range's dramatic eastern ridges. Kings Canyon has two portions: the smaller is shaped like a bent finger and encompasses Grant Grove Village and Redwood Mountain Grove (two of the parks' largest concentration of sequoias), and the larger is home to stunning Kings River Canyon, whose vast, unspoiled peaks and valleys are a backpacker's dream. Sequoia is in one piece and includes Mount Whitney, the highest point in the lower 48 states (although it is impossible to see from the western part of the park and is a chore to ascend from either side).

PLANNING

WHEN TO GO

The best times to visit are late spring and early fall, when temperatures are moderate and crowds thin. Summertime can draw hordes of tourists to see the giant sequoias, and the few, narrow roads mean congestion at peak holiday times. If you must visit in summer, go during the week. By contrast, in wintertime you may feel as though you have the parks all to yourself. But because of heavy snows, sections of the main park roads can be closed without warning, and low-hanging clouds can move in and obscure mountains and valleys for days. From early October to late April, check road and weather conditions before venturing out. ■TIP→ Even in summer, you can escape hordes of people just walking ¼ to ½ mile off the beaten path on a less-used trail.

PLANNING YOUR TIME
SEQUOIA NATIONAL PARK IN ONE DAY

After spending the night in Visalia or Three Rivers—and provided your vehicle's length does not exceed 22 feet—shove off early on Route 198 to the **Sequoia National Park entrance.** Pull over at the **Hospital Rock** picnic area to gaze up at the imposing granite formation of Moro Rock, which you later will climb. Heed signs that advise "10 mph" around tight turns as you climb 3,500 feet on **Generals Highway** to the **Giant Forest Museum.** Spend a half hour here, then examine trees firsthand by circling the lovely **Round Meadow** on the **Big Trees Trail,** to which you must walk from the museum or from its parking lot across the road.

Get back in your car and continue a few miles north on Generals Highway to see the jaw-dropping **General Sherman Tree.** Then set off on the **Congress Trail** so that you can be further awed by the Senate and House big-tree clusters. Buy lunch at the **Lodgepole** complex, 2 miles to the north, and eat at the nearby **Pinewood** picnic area. Now you're ready for the day's big exercise, the mounting of **Moro Rock.**

You can drive there or, if it is summer, park at the museum lot and take the free shuttle. Count on spending at least an hour for the 350-step ascent and descent, with a pause on top to appreciate the 360-degree view. Get back in the car, or on the shuttle, and proceed past the **Tunnel Log** to **Crescent Meadow.** Spend a relaxing hour or two strolling on the trails that pass by, among other things, **Tharp's Log.** By now you've probably renewed your appetite; head to **Sequoia Barbequeat Wuksachi Lodge** (summer evenings only) or the restaurant at **Wuksachi Lodge.**

KINGS CANYON NATIONAL PARK IN ONE DAY

Enter the park via the **Kings Canyon Scenic Byway** (Route 180), having spent the night in Fresno or Visalia. Better yet, wake up already in **Grant Grove Village,** perhaps in the **John Muir Lodge.** Stock up for a picnic with takeout food from the **Grant Grove Restaurant,** or purchase prepackaged food from the nearby market. Drive east a mile to see the **General Grant Tree** and compact **Grant Grove's** other sequoias. If it's no later than midmorning, walk up the short trail at **Panoramic Point,** for a great view of Hume Lake and the High Sierra. Either way, return to Route 180 and continue east. Stop at Junction View to take in several noteworthy peaks that tower over Kings Canyon. From here, visit **Boyden Cavern** or continue to **Cedar Grove Village,** pausing along the way for a gander at **Grizzly Falls.** Eat at a table by the **South Fork of the Kings River,** or on the deck off the Cedar Grove Snack Bar. Now you are ready for the day's highlight, strolling **Zumwalt Meadow,** which lies a few miles past the village.

After you have enjoyed that short trail and the views it offers of **Grand Sentinel** and **North Dome,** you might as well go the extra mile to **Roads End,** where backpackers embark for the High Sierra wilderness. Make the return trip—with a quick stop at **Roaring River Falls**—past Grant Grove and briefly onto southbound **Generals Highway.** Pull over at the **Redwood Mountain Overlook** and use binoculars to look down upon the world's largest sequoia grove, then drive another couple of miles to the **Kings Canyon Overlook,** where you can survey some of what you have done today. If you've made reservations and have time, have a late dinner at **Wuksachi Lodge.**

GETTING HERE AND AROUND
AIR TRAVEL
The closest airport to Sequoia and Kings Canyon national parks is Fresno Yosemite International Airport (FAT).

Airport Contacts Fresno Yosemite International Airport *(FAT).* ⊠ *5175 E. Clinton Way, Fresno* ☎ *800/244–2359 automated info, 559/454–2052 terminal info desk* ⊕ *www.flyfresno.com.*

CAR TRAVEL
Sequoia is 36 miles east of Visalia on Route 198; Grant Grove Village in Kings Canyon is 56 miles east of Fresno on Route 180. There is no automobile entrance on the eastern side of the Sierra. Routes 180 and 198 are connected by Generals Highway, a paved two-lane road that sometimes sees delays at peak times due to ongoing improvements. The road is extremely narrow and steep from Route 198 to Giant Forest, so keep an eye on your engine temperature gauge, as the incline and congestion can cause vehicles to overheat; to avoid overheated brakes, use low gears on downgrades.

If you are traveling in an RV or with a trailer, study the restrictions on these vehicles. Do not travel beyond Potwisha Campground on Route 198 with an RV longer than 22 feet; take straighter, easier Route 180 instead. Maximum vehicle length on Generals Highway is 40 feet, or 50 feet combined length for vehicles with trailers.

Generals Highway between Lodgepole and Grant Grove is sometimes closed by snow. The Mineral King Road from Route 198 into southern Sequoia National Park is closed 2 miles below Atwell Mill either on November 1 or after the first heavy snow. The Buckeye Flat–Middle Fork Trailhead road is closed from mid-October to mid-April when the Buckeye Flat Campground closes. The lower Crystal Cave Road is closed when the cave closes (typically in November). Its upper 2 miles, as well as the Panoramic Point and Moro Rock–Crescent Meadow roads, close with the first heavy snow. Because of the danger of rockfall, the portion of Kings Canyon Scenic Byway east of Grant Grove closes in winter. For current road and weather conditions, call ☎ *559/565–3341.*

■ TIP➔ Snowstorms are common from late October through April. Unless you have a four-wheel-drive vehicle with snow tires, you should carry chains and know how to install them.

PARK ESSENTIALS
PARK FEES AND PERMITS
The admission fee is $30 per vehicle, $25 per motorcycle, and $15 per person for those who enter by bus, on foot, bicycle, horse, or any other mode of transportation; it is valid for seven days in both parks. U.S. residents over the age of 62 pay $10 for a lifetime pass, and permanently disabled U.S. residents are admitted free.

If you plan to camp in the backcountry, you need a permit, which costs $15 for hikers or $30 for stock users (e.g., horseback riders). One permit covers the group. Availability of permits depends upon trailhead quotas. Reservations are accepted by mail or email for a $15 processing fee, beginning March 1, and must be made at least 14 days in advance (☎ 559/565–3766). Without a reservation, you may still get a permit on a first-come, first-served basis starting at 1 pm the day before you plan to hike. For more information on backcountry camping or travel with pack animals (horses, mules, burros, or llamas), contact the Wilderness Permit Office (☎ 530/565–3766).

PARK HOURS
The parks are open 24/7 year-round. They are in the Pacific time zone.

EDUCATIONAL OFFERINGS
Educational programs at the parks include museum-style exhibits, ranger- and naturalist-led talks and walks, film and other programs, and sightseeing tours, most of them conducted by either the park service or the nonprofit Sequoia Natural History Association. Exhibits at the visitor centers and the Giant Forest Museum focus on different aspects of the park: its history, wildlife, geology, climate, and vegetation—most notably the giant sequoias. Weekly notices about programs are posted at the visitor centers and elsewhere.

Grant Grove Visitor Center at Kings Canyon National Park has maps of self-guided park tours. Ranger-led walks and programs take place throughout the year in Grant Grove. Cedar Grove and Forest Service campgrounds have activities from Memorial Day to Labor Day. Check bulletin boards or visitor centers for schedules.

EXHIBITS
Giant Forest Museum. Well-imagined and interactive displays at this worthwhile stop provide the basics about sequoias, of which there are 2,161 with diameters exceeding 10 feet in the approximately 2,000-acre Giant Forest. ⊠ *Sequoia National Park* ✛ *Generals Hwy., 4 miles south of Lodgepole Visitor Center* ☎ *559/565–4480* 🎟 *Free* 🚌 *Shuttle: Giant Forest or Moro Rock–Crescent Meadow.*

PROGRAMS AND SEMINARS
Evening Programs. The Sequoia Parks Conservancy presents films, hikes, and evening lectures during the summer and winter. From May through October the popular Wonders of the Night Sky programs celebrate the often stunning views of the heavens experienced at both parks. ⊠ *Sequoia National Park* ☎ *559/565–4251* 🌐 *www.exploresequoiakingscanyon.com.*

Free Nature Programs. Almost any summer day, ½-hour to 1½-hour ranger talks and walks explore subjects such as the life of the sequoia, the geology of the park, and the habits of bears. Giant Forest, Lodgepole Visitor Center, and Wuksachi Village are frequent starting points. Look for less frequent tours in the winter from Grant Grove. Check bulletin boards throughout the park for the week's offerings. ⊕ *www. exploresequoiakingscanyon.com.*

Seminars. Expert naturalists lead seminars on a range of topics, including birds, wildflowers, geology, botany, photography, park history, backpacking, and pathfinding. Reservations are required. Information about times and prices is available at the visitor centers or through the Sequoia Parks Conservancy. ⊠ *Sequoia National Park* ☎ *559/565–4251* ⊕ *www. exploresequoiakingscanyon.com.*

TOURS

Fodor's Choice **Sequoia Field Institute.** The Sequoia Parks Conservancy's highly regarded
★   educational division conducts single-day and multiday "EdVenture" tours that include backpacking hikes, natural-history walks, cross-country skiing, kayaking excursions, and motorcoach tours. ⊠ *47050 Generals Hwy., Unit 10, Three Rivers* ☎ *559/565–4251* ⊕ *www.exploresequoia-kingscanyon.com* ⊠ *From $275 for a ½-day guided tour.*

Sequoia Sightseeing Tours. This locally owned operator's friendly, knowledgeable guides conduct daily interpretive sightseeing tours in Sequoia and Kings Canyon. Reservations are essential. The company also offers private tours. ⊠ *Three Rivers* ☎ *559/561–4189* ⊕ *www. sequoiatours.com* ⊠ *From $69 tour of Sequoia; from $139 tour of Kings Canyon.*

RESTAURANTS

In Sequoia and Kings Canyon national parks, you can treat yourself (and the family) to a high-quality meal in a wonderful setting in the Peaks restaurant at Wuksachi Lodge, but otherwise you should keep your expectations modest. A good strategy is to embrace outdoor eating. You can grab bread, spreads, drinks, and fresh produce at one of several small grocery stores, or get take-out food from the Grant Grove Restaurant, the Cedar Grove snack bar, or one of the two small Lodgepole eateries. The summertime Sequoia Barbeque at Wuksachi Lodgeue is a hybrid experience between dining in and picnicking out. Between the parks and just off Generals Highway, the Montecito Sequoia Lodge has a year-round buffet. *Restaurant reviews have been shortened. For full information, visit Fodors.com.*

HOTELS

Hotel accommodations in Sequoia and Kings Canyon are limited, and—although they are clean and comfortable—tend to lack much in-room character. Keep in mind, however, that the extra money you spend on lodging here is offset by the time you'll save by being inside the parks. You won't be faced with a 60- to 90-minute commute from the less-expensive motels in Three Rivers (by far the most charming option), Visalia, and Fresno. Reserve as far in advance as you can, especially for summertime stays. *Hotel reviews have been shortened. For full information, visit Fodors.com.*

WHAT IT COSTS				
	$	**$$**	**$$$**	**$$$$**
Restaurants	under $12	$12–$20	$21–$30	over $30
Hotels	under $100	$100–$150	$151–$200	over $200

Restaurant prices in the reviews are the average cost of a main course at dinner, or if dinner is not served, at lunch. Hotel prices are the lowest cost of a standard double room in high season, excluding taxes and service charges.

VISITOR INFORMATION
National Park Service Sequoia and Kings Canyon National Parks. ⊠ *47050 Generals Hwy. (Rte. 198), Three Rivers* ☎ *559/565–3341* ⊕ *nps.gov/seki.*

SEQUOIA VISITOR CENTERS
Foothills Visitor Center. Exhibits here focus on the foothills and resource issues facing the parks. You can pick up books, maps, and a list of ranger-led walks, and get wilderness permits. ⊠ *47050 Generals Hwy., Rte. 198, 1 mile north of Ash Mountain entrance, Sequoia National Park* ☎ *559/565–3341.*

Lodgepole Visitor Center. Along with exhibits on the area's history, geology, and wildlife, the center screens an outstanding 22-minute film about bears. You can buy books, maps, and tickets to cave tours and the Wolverton barbecue here. ⊠ *Sequoia National Park* ✛ *Generals Hwy. (Rte. 198), 21 miles north of Ash Mountain entrance* ☎ *559/565–3341* ⊙ *Closed Oct.–Apr.* ☞ *Shuttle: Giant Forest or Wuksachi-Lodgepole-Dorst.*

KINGS CANYON VISITOR CENTERS
Cedar Grove Visitor Center. Off the main road and behind the Sentinel Campground, this small ranger station has books and maps, plus information about hikes and other activities. ⊠ *Kings Canyon National Park* ✛ *Kings Canyon Scenic Byway, 30 miles east of Rte. 180/198 junction* ☎ *559/565–3341* ⊙ *Closed mid-Sept.–mid-May.*

Kings Canyon Park Visitor Center. The center's 15-minute film and various exhibits provide an overview of the park's canyon, sequoias, and human history. Books, maps, and weather advice are dispensed here, as are (if available) free wilderness permits. ⊠ *Kings Canyon National Park* ✛ *Grant Grove Village, Generals Hwy. (Rte. 198), 3 miles northeast of Rte. 180, Big Stump entrance* ☎ *559/565–3341.*

SEQUOIA NATIONAL PARK

EXPLORING

SCENIC DRIVES
Fodor's Choice
★
Generals Highway. One of California's most scenic drives, this 46-mile road is the main asphalt artery between Sequoia and Kings Canyon national parks. Some portions are also signed as Route 180, others as Route 198. Named after the landmark Grant and Sherman trees that leave so many visitors awestruck, Generals Highway runs from

Sequoia's Foothills Visitor Center north to Kings Canyon's Grant Grove Village. Along the way, it passes the turnoff to Crystal Cave, the Giant Forest Museum, Lodgepole Village, and other popular attractions. The lower portion, from Hospital Rock to the Giant Forest, is especially steep and winding. If your vehicle is 22 feet or longer, avoid that stretch by entering the parks via Route 180 (from Fresno) rather than Route 198 (from Visalia or Three Rivers). Take your time on this road—there's a lot to see, and wildlife can scamper across at any time. ⊠ *Sequoia National Park.*

SCENIC STOPS

Sequoia National Park is all about the trees, and to understand the scale of these giants you must walk among them. If you do nothing else, get out of the car for a short stroll through one of the groves. But there is much more to the park than the trees. Try to access one of the vista points that provide a panoramic view over the forested mountains. Generals Highway (on Routes 198 and 180) will be your route to most of the park's sights. A few short spur roads lead from the highway to some sights, and Mineral King Road branches off Route 198 to enter the park at Lookout Point, winding east from there to the park's southernmost section.

Auto Log. Before its wood showed signs of severe rot, cars drove right on top of this giant fallen sequoia. Now it's a great place to pose for pictures or shoot a video. ⊠ *Sequoia National Park* ⊹ *Moro Rock–Crescent Meadow Rd., 1 mile south of Giant Forest.*

Crescent Meadow. A sea of ferns signals your arrival at what John Muir called the "gem of the Sierra." Walk around for an hour or two and you might decide that the Scotland-born naturalist was exaggerating a wee bit, but the verdant meadow is quite pleasant and you just might see a bear. Wildflowers bloom here throughout the summer. ⊠ *Sequoia National Park* ⊹ *End of Moro Rock–Crescent Meadow Rd., 2.6 miles east off Generals Hwy.* ☞ *Shuttle: Moro Rock–Crescent Meadow.*

Fodor's Choice **Crystal Cave.** One of more than 200 caves in Sequoia and Kings Canyon, ★ Crystal Cave is composed largely of marble, the result of limestone being hardened under heat and pressure. It contains several eye-popping formations. There used to be more, but some were damaged or obliterated by early-20th-century dynamite blasting. You can only see the cave on a tour. The Daily Tour ($16), a great overview, takes about 50 minutes. To immerse yourself in the cave experience—at times you'll be crawling on your belly—book the exhilarating Wild Cave Tour ($135). Purchase Daily Tour tickets at either the Foothills or Lodgepole visitor center; they're not sold at the cave itself. ⊠ *Crystal Cave Rd., off Generals Hwy.* ☎ *877/444–6777* ⊕ *www.explorecrystalcave.com* ⊠ *$16* ⊘ *Closed Oct.–late May.*

Fodor's Choice **General Sherman Tree.** The 274.9-foot-tall General Sherman is one of the ★ world's tallest and oldest sequoias, and it ranks No. 1 in volume, adding the equivalent of a 60-foot-tall tree every year to its approximately 52,500 cubic feet of mass. The tree doesn't grow taller, though—it's dead at the top. A short, wheelchair-accessible trail leads to the tree from Generals Highway, but the main trail (½ mile) winds down from a parking lot off Wolverton Road. The walk back up the main trail is steep, but benches along the way provide rest for the short of breath. ⊠ *Sequoia National Park* ✛ *Main trail Wolverton Rd. off Generals Hwy. (Rte. 198)* ☞ *Shuttle: Giant Forest or Wolverton–Sherman Tree.*

Mineral King Area. A subalpine valley of fir, pine, and sequoia trees, Mineral King sits at 7,500 feet at the end of a steep, winding road. This is the highest point to which you can drive in the park. It is open only from Memorial Day through late October. ⊠ *Sequoia National Park* ✛ *Mineral King Rd., 25 miles east of Generals Hwy. (Rte. 198)* ☾ *Closed late Oct.–May.*

Fodor's Choice **Moro Rock.** Sequoia National Park's best nontree attraction offers pan-
★ oramic views to those fit and determined enough to mount its 350 or so steps. In a case where the journey rivals the destination, Moro's stone stairway is so impressive in its twisty inventiveness that it's on the National Register of Historic Places. The rock's 6,725-foot summit overlooks the Middle Fork Canyon, sculpted by the Kaweah River and approaching the depth of Arizona's Grand Canyon, although smoggy, hazy air often compromises the view. ⊠ *Sequoia National Park* ✛ *Moro Rock–Crescent Meadow Rd., 2 miles east off Generals Hwy. (Rte. 198) to parking area* ☞ *Shuttle: Moro Rock–Crescent Meadow.*

Tunnel Log. This 275-foot tree fell in 1937, and soon a 17-foot-wide, 8-foot-high hole was cut through it for vehicular passage (not to mention the irresistible photograph) that continues today. Large vehicles take the nearby bypass. ⊠ *Sequoia National Park* ✛ *Moro Rock–Cres-cent Meadow Rd., 2 miles east of Generals Hwy. (Rte. 198)* ☞ *Shuttle: Moro Rock–Crescent Meadow.*

SPORTS AND THE OUTDOORS

The best way to see Sequoia is to take a hike. Unless you do so, you'll miss out on the up-close grandeur of mist wafting between deeply scored, red-orange tree trunks bigger than you've ever seen. If it's winter, put on some snowshoes or cross-country skis and plunge into the snow-swaddled woodland. There are not too many other outdoor options: no off-road driving is allowed in the parks, and no special provisions have been made for bicycles. Boating, rafting, and snowmobiling are also prohibited.

BIRD-WATCHING

More than 200 species of birds inhabit Sequoia and Kings Canyon national parks. Not seen in most parts of the United States, the white-headed woodpecker and the pileated woodpecker are common in most mid-elevation areas here. There are also many hawks and owls, including the renowned spotted owl. Species are diverse in both parks due to the changes in elevation, and range from warblers, kingbirds, thrushes, and sparrows in the foothills to goshawk, blue grouse, red-breasted nuthatch, and brown creeper at the highest elevations. The Sequoia Parks Conservancy (☎ *559/565–4251* ⊕ *www.sequoiaparksconservancy.org*) has information about bird-watching in the southern Sierra.

CROSS-COUNTRY SKIING

For a one-of-a-kind experience, cut through the groves of mammoth sequoias in Giant Forest. Some of the Crescent Meadow trails are suitable for skiing as well; none of the trails is groomed. You can park at Giant Forest. Note that roads can be precarious in bad weather. Some advanced trails begin at Wolverton.

Alta Market and Ski Shop. Rent cross-country skis and snowshoes here. Depending on snowfall amounts, instruction may also be available. Reservations are recommended. Marked trails cut through Giant Forest, about 5 miles south of Wuksachi Lodge. ⊠ *Sequoia National Park ✛ At Lodgepole, off Generals Hwy. (Rte. 198)* ☎ *559/565–3301* ⌕ *Shuttle: Wuksachi-Lodgepole-Dorst.*

FISHING

There's limited trout fishing in the creeks and rivers from late April to mid-November. The Kaweah River is a popular spot; check at visitor centers for open and closed waters. Some of the park's secluded backcountry lakes have good fishing. A California fishing license, required for persons 16 and older, costs about $15 for one day, $24 for two days, and $47 for 10 days (discounts are available for state residents and others). For park regulations, closures, and restrictions, call the parks at ☎ *559/565–3341* or stop at a visitor center. Licenses and fishing tackle are usually available at Hume Lake.

California Department of Fish and Game. The department supplies fishing licenses and provides a full listing of regulations. ☎ *916/928–5805* ⊕ *www.wildlife.ca.gov.*

HIKING

The best way to see the park is to hike it. The grandeur and majesty of the Sierra is best seen up close. Carry a hiking map and plenty of water. Visitor center gift shops sell maps and trail books and pamphlets. Check with rangers for current trail conditions, and be aware of rapidly changing weather. As a rule of thumb, plan on covering about a mile per hour.

EASY

Fodor's Choice ★ **Big Trees Trail.** This hike is a must, as it does not take long and the setting is spectacular: beautiful Round Meadow surrounded by many mature sequoias, with well-thought-out interpretive signs along the path that explain the ecology on display. The 0.7-mile Big Trees Trail is wheelchair accessible. Parking at the trailhead lot off Generals Highway is for cars with handicap placards only. The round-trip loop from the Giant Forest Museum is about a mile long. *Easy.* ⊠ *Sequoia National Park ✛ Trailhead: off Generals Hwy. (Rte. 198), near the Giant Forest Museum* ⌕ *Shuttle: Giant Forest.*

Fodor's Choice ★ **Congress Trail.** This 2-mile trail, arguably the best hike in the parks in terms of natural beauty, is a paved loop that begins near General Sherman Tree. You'll get close-up views of more big trees here than on any other Sequoia hike. Watch for the clusters known as the House and Senate. The President Tree, also on the trail, supplanted the General Grant Tree in 2012 as the world's second largest in volume (behind the General Sherman). An offshoot of the Congress Trail leads to Crescent Meadow, where in summer you can catch a free shuttle back to the Sherman parking lot. *Easy.* ⊠ *Sequoia National Park* ⊕ *Trailhead: off Generals Hwy. (Rte. 198), 2 miles north of Giant Forest* ↷ *Shuttle: Giant Forest.*

Crescent Meadow Trails. A 1-mile trail loops around lush Crescent Meadow to Tharp's Log, a cabin built from a fire-hollowed sequoia. From there you can embark on a 60-mile trek to Mount Whitney, if you're prepared and have the time. Brilliant wildflowers bloom here in midsummer. *Easy.* ⊠ *Sequoia National Park* ⊕ *Trailhead: the end of Moro Rock–Crescent Meadow Rd., 2.6 miles east off Generals Hwy. (Rte. 198)* ↷ *Shuttle: Moro Rock–Crescent Meadow.*

MODERATE

Tokopah Falls Trail. This trail with a 500-foot elevation gain follows the Marble Fork of the Kaweah River for 1.75 miles one-way and dead-ends below the impressive granite cliffs and cascading waterfall of Tokopah Canyon. The trail passes through a mixed-conifer forest. It takes 2½ to 4 hours to make the round-trip journey. *Moderate.* ⊠ *Sequoia National Park* ⊕ *Trailhead: off Generals Hwy. (Rte. 198), ¼ mile north of Lodgepole Campground* ↷ *Shuttle: Lodgepole-Wuksachi-Dorst.*

DIFFICULT

Mineral King Trails. Many trails to the high country begin at Mineral King. Two popular day hikes are Eagle Lake (6.8 miles round-trip) and Timber Gap (4.4 miles round-trip). At the Mineral King Ranger Station (559/565–3768) you can pick up maps and check about conditions from late May to late September. *Difficult.* ⊠ *Sequoia National Park* ⊕ *Trailheads: at end of Mineral King Rd., 25 miles east of Generals Hwy. (Rte. 198).*

HORSEBACK RIDING

Trips take you through forests and flowering meadows and up mountain slopes.

TOURS AND OUTFITTERS

Grant Grove Stables. Grant Grove Stables isn't too far from parts of Sequoia National Park, and is perfect for short rides from June to September. Reservations are recommended. ☎ *559/335–9292 summer, 559/799–7247 off-season* ⊕ *www.visitsequoia.com/grant-grove-stables. aspx* ⊠ *From $40.*

KINGS CANYON NATIONAL PARK

EXPLORING

SCENIC DRIVES

Fodor's Choice ★ **Kings Canyon Scenic Byway.** The 30-mile stretch of Route 180 between Grant Grove Village and Zumwalt Meadow delivers eye-popping scenery—granite cliffs, a roaring river, waterfalls, and Kings River Canyon itself—much of which you can experience at vista points or on easy walks. The canyon comes into view about 10 miles east of the village at **Junction View.** Five miles beyond, at **Yucca Point,** the canyon is thousands of feet deeper than the more famous Grand Canyon. **Canyon View,** a special spot 1 mile east of the Cedar Grove Village turnoff, showcases evidence of the area's glacial history. Here, perhaps more

than anywhere else, you'll understand why John Muir compared Kings Canyon vistas with those in Yosemite. Driving the byway takes about an hour each way without stops. ⊠ *Kings Canyon National Park ✛ Rte. 180 north and east of Grant Grove village.*

HISTORIC SITES

Fallen Monarch. This toppled sequoia's hollow base was used in the second half of the 19th century as a home for settlers, a saloon, and even to stable U.S. Cavalry horses. As you walk through it (assuming entry is permitted, which is not always possible), notice how little the wood has decayed, and imagine yourself tucked safely inside, sheltered from a storm or protected from the searing heat. ⊠ *Kings Canyon National Park ✛ Grant Grove Trail, 1 mile north of Kings Canyon Park Visitor Center.*

SCENIC STOPS

Kings Canyon National Park consists of two sections that adjoin the northern boundary of Sequoia National Park. The western portion, covered with sequoia and pine forest, contains the park's most visited sights, such as Grant Grove. The vast eastern portion is remote high country, slashed across half its southern breadth by the deep, rugged Kings River Canyon. Separating the two is Sequoia National Forest, which encompasses Giant Sequoia National Monument. The Kings Canyon Scenic Byway (Route 180) links the major sights within and between the park's two sections.

General Grant Tree. President Coolidge proclaimed this to be the "nation's Christmas tree," and 30 years later President Eisenhower designated it as a living shrine to all Americans who have died in wars. Bigger at its base than the General Sherman Tree, it tapers more quickly. It's estimated to be the world's third-largest sequoia by volume. A spur trail winds behind the tree, where scars from a long-ago fire remain visible. ⊠ *Kings Canyon National Park ✛ Trailhead: 1 mile north of Grant Grove Visitor Center.*

Redwood Mountain Sequoia Grove. One of the world's largest sequoia groves, Redwood contains within its 2,078 acres nearly 2,200 sequoias whose diameters exceed 10 feet. You can view the grove from afar at an overlook or hike 6 to 10 miles down into the richest regions, which include two of the world's 25 heaviest trees. ⊠ *Kings Canyon National Park ✛ Drive 6 miles south of Grant Grove on Generals Hwy. (Rte. 198), then turn right at Quail Flat; follow it 2 miles to the Redwood Canyon trailhead.*

SPORTS AND THE OUTDOORS

The siren song of beauty, challenge, and relative solitude (by national parks standards) draws hard-core outdoors enthusiasts to the Kings River Canyon and the backcountry of the park's eastern section. Backpacking, rock-climbing, and extreme-kayaking opportunities abound, but the park also has day hikes for all ability levels. Winter brings sledding, skiing, and snowshoeing fun. No off-road driving or bicycling is allowed in the park, and snowmobiling is also prohibited.

Kings Canyon's
Cedar Grove Area

Lewis Creek

Hotel Creek Trail

Lewis Creek Trail

Hotel Creek

Cedar Grove
Viewpoint

Cedar Grove
Village and Lodge

Sheep
Creek

Sentinel

Canyon
View

Moraine

Motor Nature Trail

South Fork Kings River

Don Cecil Trail

Canyon
Viewpoint

Roaring River
Falls

Roaring River

Granite Creek

North Dome
8,717 ft

Copper Creek Trail

Roads End

Grand Sentinel Viewpoint

Zumwalt Meadow

Zumwalt
Meadow
Trail

Grand Sentinel
8,508 ft

0 ___ 1 mi
0 ___ 1 km

CROSS-COUNTRY SKIING

Roads to Grant Grove are accessible even during heavy snowfall, making the trails here a good choice over Sequoia's Giant Forest when harsh weather hits.

HIKING

You can enjoy many of Kings Canyon's sights from your car, but the giant gorge of the Kings River Canyon and the sweeping vistas of some of the highest mountains in the United States are best seen on foot. Carry a hiking map—available at any visitor center—and plenty of water. Check with rangers for current trail conditions, and be aware of rapidly changing weather. Except for one trail to Mount Whitney, permits are not required for day hikes.

Roads End Permit Station. You can obtain wilderness permits, maps, and information about the backcountry at this station, where bear canisters, a must for campers, can be rented or purchased. When the station is closed (typically October–mid-May, complete a self-service permit form. ⊠ *Kings Canyon National Park* ✛ *Eastern end of Kings Canyon Scenic Byway, 6 miles east of Cedar Grove Visitor Center.*

Plants and Wildlife in Sequoia and Kings Canyon

The parks can be divided into three distinct zones. In the west (1,500–4,500 feet) are the rolling, lower-elevation foothills, covered with shrubby chaparral vegetation or golden grasslands dotted with oaks. Chamise, red-barked manzanita, and the occasional yucca plant grow here. Fields of white popcorn flower cover the hillsides in spring, and the yellow fiddleneck flourishes. In summer, intense heat and absence of rain cause the hills to turn golden brown. Wildlife includes the California ground squirrel, noisy blue-and-gray scrub jay, black bears, coyotes, skunks, and gray fox.

At middle elevation (5,000–9,000 feet), where the giant sequoia belt resides, rock formations mix with meadows and huge stands of evergreens—red and white fir, incense cedar, and ponderosa pines, to name a few. Wildflowers like yellow blazing star and red Indian paintbrush bloom in spring and summer. Mule deer, golden-mantled ground squirrels, Steller's jays, and black bears (most active in fall) inhabit the area, as does the chickaree.

The high alpine section of the parks is extremely rugged, with a string of rocky peaks reaching above 13,000 feet to Mount Whitney's 14,494 feet. Fierce weather and scarcity of soil make vegetation and wildlife sparse. Foxtail and whitebark pines have gnarled and twisted trunks, the result of high wind, heavy snowfall, and freezing temperatures. In summer you can see yellow-bellied marmots, pikas, weasels, mountain chickadees, and Clark's nutcrackers.

EASY

Big Stump Trail. From 1883 until 1890, logging was done here, complete with a mill. The 1-mile loop trail, whose unmarked beginning is a few yards west of the Big Stump entrance, passes by many enormous stumps. *Easy.* ⊠ *Kings Canyon National Park* ✢ *Trailhead: near Big Stump Entrance, Generals Hwy. (Rte. 180).*

Fodor's Choice ★ **Grant Grove Trail.** Grant Grove is only 128 acres, but it's a big deal. More than 120 sequoias here have a base diameter that exceeds 10 feet, and the **General Grant Tree** is the world's third-largest sequoia by volume. Nearby, the Confederacy is represented by the **Robert E. Lee Tree**, recognized as the world's 11th-largest sequoia. Also along the easy-to-walk trail are the **Fallen Monarch** and the **Gamlin Cabin,** built by 19th-century pioneers. *Easy.* ⊠ *Kings Canyon National Park* ✢ *Trailhead: off Generals Hwy. (Rte. 180), 1 mile north of Kings Canyon Park Visitor Center.*

Roaring River Falls Walk. Take a shady five-minute walk to this forceful waterfall that rushes through a narrow granite chute. The trail is paved and mostly accessible. *Easy.* ⊠ *Kings Canyon National Park* ✢ *Trailhead: 3 miles east of Cedar Grove Village turnoff from Kings Canyon Scenic Byway.*

Fodor's Choice
★

Zumwalt Meadow Trail. Rangers say this is the best (and most popular) day hike in the Cedar Grove area. Just 1.5 miles long, it offers three visual treats: the South Fork of the Kings River, the lush meadow, and the high granite walls above, including those of Grand Sentinel and North Dome. *Easy.* ⊠ *Kings Canyon National Park* ⊹ *Trailhead: 4½ miles east of Cedar Grove Village turnoff from Kings Canyon Scenic Byway.*

MODERATE

Big Baldy. This hike climbs 600 feet and 2 miles up to the 8,209-foot summit of Big Baldy. Your reward is the view of Redwood Canyon. Round-trip the hike is 4 miles. *Moderate.* ⊠ *Kings Canyon National Park* ⊹ *Trailhead: 8 miles south of Grant Grove on Generals Hwy. (Rte. 198).*

Redwood Canyon Trails. Two main trails lead into Redwood Canyon Grove, the world's largest sequoia grove. The 6.5-mile **Hart Tree and Fallen Goliath Loop** passes by a 19th-century logging site, pristine Hart Meadow, and the hollowed-out Tunnel Tree before accessing a side trail to the grove's largest sequoia, the 277.9-foot-tall Hart Tree. The 6.4-mile **Sugar Bowl Loop** provides views of Redwood Mountain and Big Baldy before winding down into its namesake, a thick grove of mature and young sequoias. *Moderate.* ⊠ *Kings Canyon National Park* ⊹ *Trailhead: off Quail Flat. Drive 5 miles south of Grant Grove on Generals Hwy. (Rte. 198), turn right at Quail Flat and proceed 1½ miles to trailhead.*

DIFFICULT

Hotel Creek Trail. For gorgeous canyon views, take this trail from Cedar Grove up a series of switchbacks until it splits. Follow the route left through chaparral to the forested ridge and rocky outcrop known as Cedar Grove Overlook, where you can see the Kings River Canyon stretching below. This strenuous 5-mile round-trip hike gains 1,200 feet and takes three to four hours to complete. *Difficult.* ⊠ *Kings Canyon National Park* ⊹ *Trailhead: at Cedar Grove Pack Station, 1 mile east of Cedar Grove Village.*

HORSEBACK RIDING

One-day destinations by horseback out of Cedar Grove include Mist Falls and Upper Bubb's Creek. In the backcountry, many equestrians head for Volcanic Lakes or Granite Basin, ascending trails that reach elevations of 10,000 feet. Costs per person range from $35 for a one-hour guided ride to around $250 per day for fully guided trips for which the packers do all the cooking and camp chores.

TOURS AND OUTFITTERS

Cedar Grove Pack Station. Take a day ride or plan a multiday adventure along the Kings River Canyon with Cedar Grove Pack Station. Popular routes include the Rae Lakes Loop and Monarch Divide. Closed early September–late May. ⊠ *Kings Canyon National Park* ⊹ *Kings Canyon Scenic Byway, 1 mile east of Cedar Grove Village* ☎ *559/565–3464* ⊕ *www.nps.gov/seki/planyourvisit/horseride.htm* 🖂 *From $40 per hr or $100 per day.*

CLOSE UP

Mount Whitney

At 14,494 feet, Mount Whitney is the highest point in the contiguous United States and the crown jewel of Sequoia National Park's wild eastern side. The peak looms high above the tiny, high-mountain desert community of Lone Pine, where numerous Hollywood Westerns have been filmed. The high mountain ranges, arid landscape, and scrubby brush of the eastern Sierra are beautiful in their vastness and austerity.

Despite the mountain's scale, you can't see it from the more traveled west side of the park because it is hidden behind the Great Western Divide. The only way to access Mount Whitney from the main part of the park is to circumnavigate the Sierra Nevada via a 10-hour, nearly 400-mile drive outside the park. No road ascends the peak; the best vantage point from which to catch a glimpse of the mountain is at the end of Whitney Portal Road. The 13

miles of winding road leads from U.S. 395 at Lone Pine to the trailhead for the hiking route to the top of the mountain. Whitney Portal Road is closed in winter.

Mt. Whitney Trail. The most popular route to the summit, the Mt. Whitney Trail can be conquered by very fit and experienced hikers. If there's snow on the mountain, this is a challenge for expert mountaineers only. All overnighters must have a permit, as must day hikers on the trail beyond Lone Pine Lake, about 2½ miles from the trailhead. From May through October, permits are distributed via a lottery run each February by Recreation.gov. The Eastern Sierra Interagency Visitor Center (*760/876–6222*), on Route 136 at U.S. 395 about a mile south of Lone Pine, is a good resource for information about permits and hiking. ⊠ *Kings Canyon National Park* ☎ *760/873–2483 trail reservations* ⊕ *www.fs.usda.gov/inyo.*

Grant Grove Stables. A one- or two-hour trip through Grant Grove leaving from the stables provides a taste of horseback riding in Kings Canyon. Closed October–early June. ⊠ *Kings Canyon National Park* ⊹ *Rte. 180, ½ mile north of Grant Grove Visitor Center* ☎ *559/335–9292 mid-June–Sept.* ⊕ *www.nps.gov/seki/planyourvisit/horseride. htm* ⬚ *From $45.*

SLEDDING AND SNOWSHOEING

In winter, Kings Canyon has a few great places to play in the snow. Sleds, inner tubes, and platters are allowed at both the Azalea Campground area on Grant Tree Road, ¼ mile north of Grant Grove Visitor Center, and at the Big Stump picnic area, 2 miles north of the lower Route 180 entrance to the park.

Snowshoeing is good around Grant Grove, where you can take occasional naturalist-guided snowshoe walks from mid-December through mid-March as conditions permit. Grant Grove Market rents sleds and snowshoes.

NEARBY TOWNS

Numerous towns and cities tout themselves as "gateways" to the parks, with some more deserving of the title than others. One that certainly merits the name is frisky **Three Rivers,** a Sierra foothills hamlet (population 2,200) along the Kaweah River. Close to Sequoia's Ash Mountain and Lookout Point entrances, Three Rivers is a good spot to find a room when park lodgings are full. Either because Three Rivers residents appreciate their idyllic setting or because they know that tourists are their bread and butter, you'll find them almost uniformly pleasant and eager to share tips about the best spots for "Sierra surfing" the Kaweah's smooth, moss-covered rocks or where to find the best cell-phone reception (it's off to the cemetery for Verizon customers).

Visalia, a Central Valley city of about 128,000 people, lies 58 miles southwest of Sequoia's Wuksachi Village and 56 miles southwest of the Kings Canyon Park Visitor Center. Its vibrant downtown contains several good restaurants. If you're into Victorian and other old houses, drop by the visitor center and pick up a free map of them. A clear day's view of the Sierra from Main Street is spectacular, and even Sunday night can find the streets bustling with pedestrians. Visalia provides easy access to grand Sequoia National Park and the serene Kaweah Oaks Preserve.

Closest to Kings Canyon's Big Stump entrance, **Fresno,** the main gateway to the southern Sierra region, is about 55 miles west of Kings Canyon and about 85 miles northwest of Wuksachi Village. This Central Valley city of nearly a half-million people is sprawling and unglamorous, but it has all the cultural and other amenities you'd expect of a major crossroads.

GETTING HERE AND AROUND

Sequoia Shuttle. In summer the Sequoia Shuttle connects Three Rivers to Visalia and Sequoia National Park. ☎ *877/287–4453* ⊕ *www.sequoiashuttle.com* ✉ *$15 round-trip.*

Visitor Information Fresno/Clovis Convention & Visitors Bureau. ✉ *1550 E. Shaw Ave., Suite 101, Fresno* ☎ *559/981–5500, 800/788–0836* ⊕ *www.playfresno.org.* **Sequoia Foothills Chamber of Commerce.** ✉ *42268 Sierra Dr., Three Rivers* ☎ *559/561–3300* ⊕ *www.threerivers.com.* **Visalia Convention & Visitors Bureau.** ✉ *Kiosk, 303 E. Acequia Ave., at S. Bridge St., Visalia* ☎ *559/334–0141, 800/524–0303* ⊕ *www.visitvisalia.org.*

NEARBY ATTRACTIONS

OFF THE
BEATEN
PATH

Exeter Murals. More than two dozen murals in the Central Valley city of Exeter's cute-as-a-button downtown make it worth a quick detour if you're traveling on Route 198. Several of the murals, which depict the area's agricultural and social history, are quite good. All adorn buildings within a few blocks of the intersection of Pine and E streets. If you're hungry, the **Wildflower Cafe,** at 121 South E Street, serves inventive salads and sandwiches. Shortly after entering Exeter head west on Pine Street (it's just before the water tower) to reach downtown. ✉ *Exeter* ⊹ *Rte. 65, 2 miles south of Rte. 198, about 11 miles east of Visalia* ⊕ *cityofexeter.com/about-8187/gallery/murals.*

OFF THE
BEATEN
PATH

Colonel Allensworth State Historic Park. It's worth the slight detour off Highway 99 to learn about and pay homage to the dream of Allen Allensworth and other black pioneers who in 1908 founded Allensworth, the only California town settled, governed, and financed by African Americans. At its height, the town prospered as a key railroad transfer point, but after cars and trucks reduced railroad traffic and water was diverted for Central Valley agriculture, the town declined and was eventually deserted. Today the restored and rebuilt schoolhouse, library, and other structures commemorate Allensworth's heyday, as do festivities that take place each October. ⊠ *4129 Palmer Ave., off Hwy. 43; from Hwy. 99 at Delano, take Garces Hwy. west to Hwy. 43 north; from Earlimart, take County Rd. J22 west to Hwy. 43 south, Allensworth* ☎ *661/849–3433* ⊕ *www.parks.ca.gov* ⊡ *$6 per car.*

FAMILY

Fodor's Choice

★

Forestiere Underground Gardens. Sicilian immigrant Baldassare Forestiere spent four decades (1906–46) carving out an odd, subterranean realm of rooms, tunnels, grottoes, alcoves, and arched passageways that once extended for more than 10 acres between Highway 99 and busy, mall-pocked Shaw Avenue. Though not an engineer, Forestiere called on his memories of the ancient Roman structures he saw as a youth and on techniques he learned digging subways in New York and Boston. Only a fraction of his prodigious output is on view, but you can tour his underground living quarters, including bedrooms (one with a fireplace), the kitchen, living room, and bath, as well as a fishpond and auto tunnel. Skylights allow exotic full-grown fruit trees to flourish more than 20 feet belowground. ⊠ *5021 W. Shaw Ave., 2 blocks east of Hwy. 99, Fresno* ☎ *559/271–0734* ⊕ *www. undergroundgardens.com* ⊡ *$17* ⊘ *Closed Dec.–Feb.*

Kaweah Oaks Preserve. Trails at this 344-acre wildlife sanctuary off the main road to Sequoia National Park lead past majestic valley oak, sycamore, cottonwood, and willow trees. Among the 134 bird species you might spot are hawks, hummingbirds, and great blue herons. Bobcats, lizards, coyotes, and cottontails also live here. The Sycamore Trail has digital signage with QR codes you can scan with your smartphone to access plant and animal information. ⊠ *Follow Hwy. 198 for 7 miles east of Visalia, turn north on Rd. 182, and proceed ½ mile to gate on left side, Visalia* ☎ *559/738–0211* ⊕ *www.sequoiariverlands.org* ⊡ *Free.*

Project Survival's Cat Haven. Take the rare opportunity to glimpse a Siberian lynx, a clouded leopard, a Bengal tiger, and other endangered wild cats at this conservation facility that shelters more than 30 big cats. A guided hour-long tour along a quarter mile of walkway leads to fenced habitat areas shaded by trees and overlooking the Central Valley. ⊠ *38257 E. Kings Canyon Rd. (Rte. 180), 15 miles west of Kings Canyon National Park, Dunlap* ☎ *559/338–3216* ⊕ *www.cathaven.com* ⊡ *$15.*

Sequoia National Forest and Giant Sequoia National Monument. Delicate spring wildflowers, cool summer campgrounds, and varied winter-sports opportunities—not to mention more than half of the world's giant sequoia groves—draw outdoorsy types year-round to this sprawling district surrounding the national parks. Together, the forest and monument cover nearly 1,700 square miles, south from the Kings River and east from the foothills along the San Joaquin Valley. The monument's groves are both north and south of Sequoia National Park. One of the most popular is the **Converse Basin Grove,** home of the Boole Tree, the forest's largest sequoia. The grove is accessible by car on an unpaved road.

The Hume Lake Forest Service District Office, at 35860 Kings Canyon Scenic Byway (Route 180), has information about the groves, along with details about recreational activities. In springtime, diversions include hiking among the wildflowers that brighten the foothills. The floral display rises with the heat as the mountain elevations warm up in summer, when hikers, campers, and picnickers become more plentiful. The abundant trout supply attracts anglers to area waters, including 87-acre **Hume Lake,** which is also ideal for swimming and nonmotorized boating. By fall the turning leaves provide the visual delights, particularly in the Western Divide, Indian Basin, and the Kern Plateau. Winter activities include downhill and cross-country skiing, snowshoeing, and snowmobiling. ⊠ *Sequoia National Park ✛ Northern Entrances: Generals Hwy. (Rte. 198), 7 miles southeast of Grant Grove; Hume Lake Rd. between Generals Hwy. (Rte. 198) and Kings Canyon Scenic Byway (Rte. 180); Kings Canyon Scenic Byway (Rte. 180) between Grant Grove and Cedar Grove. Southern Entrances: Rte. 190 east of Springville; Rte. 178 east of Bakersfield* ☎ *559/784–1500 forest and monument, 559/338–2251 Hume Lake* ⊕ *www.fs.usda.gov/sequoia.*

AREA ACTIVITIES

SPORTS AND THE OUTDOORS

BOATING AND RAFTING

Hume Lake. This reservoir, built by loggers in the early 1900s, is now the site of several church-affiliated camps, a gas station, and a public campground. Outside Kings Canyon's borders, Hume Lake offers intimate views of the mountains. Summer lodge room rentals start at $150. ⊠ *Hume Lake Rd., off Kings Canyon Hwy., 8 miles northeast of Grant Grove, 64144 Hume Lake Rd., Hume* ☎ *559/305-7770* ⊕ *www. humelake.org.*

Kaweah White Water Adventures. Kaweah's trips include a two-hour excursion (good for families) through Class III rapids, a longer paddle through Class IV rapids, and an extended trip (typically Class IV and V rapids). ⊠ *40443 Sierra Dr., Three Rivers* ☎ *559/740–8251* ⊕ *www. kaweah-whitewater.com* 💲 *$50–$120 per person.*

Kings River Expeditions. This outfit arranges one- and two-day white-water rafting trips on the Kings River. ⊠ *1840 W. Shaw Ave., Clovis* ☎ *559/233–4881, 800/846–3674* ⊕ *www.kingsriver.com* 💲 *From $145.*

HORSEBACK RIDING

Wood 'n' Horse Training Stables. For hourly horseback rides or riding lessons, contact this outfit. ⊠ *42846 N. Fork Dr., Three Rivers* ☎ *559/561–4268* ⊕ *www.wdnhorse.com.*

WHERE TO EAT

IN THE PARKS

SEQUOIA

$ CAFÉ   ✗ **Lodgepole Market, Deli, and Snack Bar.** The choices here run the gamut from simple to very simple, with the three counters only a few strides apart in a central eating complex. For hot food, including burgers, hot dogs, and pizzas, venture into the snack bar. **Known for:** quick and convenient dining; many healthful options. ⑤ *Average main: $10* ✉ *Next to Lodgepole Visitor Center, Sequoia National Park* ☎ *559/565–3301.*

$$$ MODERN AMERICAN   ✗ **The Peaks.** Huge windows run the length of the Wuksachi Lodge's high-ceilinged dining room, and a large fireplace on the far wall warms both body and soul. The diverse dinner menu—by far the best at both parks—reflects a commitment to locally sourced and sustainable products. ⑤ *Average main: $28* ✉ *Wuksachi Lodge, 64740 Wuksachi Way, Wuksachi Village* ☎ *559/565–4070* ⊕ *www.visitsequoia.com/ the-peaks-restaurant.aspx.*

$$$ BARBECUE   ✗ **Sequoia Barbeque at Wuksachi Lodge.** Weather permitting, diners congregate nightly for traditional Old West barbecue. After the meal, listen to a naturalist talk, join in an interactive living history presentation, and clear your throat for a campfire sing-along. ⑤ *Average main: $25* ✉ *Sequoia National Park* ✛ *Wolverton Rd., 1½ mile northeast off Generals Hwy. (Rte. 198)* ☎ *559/565–4070* ⊗ *No lunch. Closed early Sept.–mid-June.*

KINGS CANYON

$$ AMERICAN   ✗ **Cedar Grove Snack Bar.** The menu here is surprisingly extensive, with dinner entrées such as pasta, pork chops, trout, and steak. For breakfast, try the biscuits and gravy, French toast, pancakes, or cold cereal. ⑤ *Average main: $15* ✉ *Cedar Grove Village, Kings Canyon National Park* ☎ *559/565–0100* ⊗ *Closed Oct.–May.*

OUTSIDE THE PARKS

$ CAFÉ   ✗ **Antoinette's Coffee and Goodies.** For smoothies, well-crafted espresso drinks, breakfast bowls, and pumpkin chocolate-chip muffins and other homemade baked goods, stop for a spell at this convivial coffee shop. Antoinette's is known as the town's hub for vegan and gluten-free items. **Known for:** plentiful vegan and gluten-free items; Wi-Fi on site. ⑤ *Average main: $7* ✉ *41727 Sierra Dr., Three Rivers* ☎ *559/561–2253* ⊕ *www.antoinettescoffeeandgoodies.com* ⊗ *Closed Tues. No dinner.*

$$ AMERICAN   ✗ **Buckaroo Diner.** Set on a bluff overlooking the Kaweah River, the boho-chic Buckaroo serves fresh, house-made dishes made with seasonal organic ingredients. A local couple started the restaurant in 2014, first operating out of a food truck and later expanding into a building that housed the original 'ol Buckaroo restaurant for decades. **Known for:** lemon ricotta pancakes for brunch; fried organic chicken; daily specials. ⑤ *Average main: $14* ✉ *41695 Sierra Dr., Three Rivers* ☎ *559/465–5088* ⊕ *theolbuckaroo.com* ⊗ *No lunch weekdays. Closed Tues.–Weds.*

$$ ✕ **Café 225.** High ceilings and contemporary decor contribute to the
MODERN relaxed and sophisticated atmosphere at this popular downtown res-
AMERICAN taurant. Chef-owner Karl Merten can often be spotted at area markets
seeking out locally grown ingredients for his seasonally changing dishes.
Known for: wood-fired rotisserie menu items; fresh local ingredients;
sophisticated vibe. ⑤ *Average main: $19* ✉ *225 W. Main St., Visalia*
☎ *559/733–2967* ⊕ *www.cafe225.com* ☾ *Closed Sun.*

$$$ ✕ **Gateway Restaurant and Lodge.** The view's the draw at this roadhouse
AMERICAN that overlooks the Kaweah River as it plunges out of the high country.
The Gateway serves everything from osso buco and steaks to shrimp in
Thai chili sauce. **Known for:** scenic riverside setting; fine dining in oth-
erwise casual town; popular bar. ⑤ *Average main: $29* ✉ *45978 Sierra
Dr., Three Rivers* ☎ *559/561–4133* ⊕ *www.gateway-sequoia.com.*

$ ✕ **The Lunch Box.** A casual downtown café and bakery, the Lunch Box
AMERICAN serves healthful meals at reasonable prices. Choose from nearly 50
types of hot and cold sandwiches and wraps, more than 20 different salads, and soups such as chicken noodle and Tuscan tomato.
Known for: fresh, healthful local ingredients; quick service; many
menu option and combinations. ⑤ *Average main: $10* ✉ *112 N. Court
St., at Main St., Visalia* ☎ *559/635–8624* ⊕ *lunchboxcateringcom-
pany.com* ☾ *Closed Sun.*

$$$ ✕ **School House Restaurant & Tavern.** A Wine Country–style establish-
MODERN ment that sources ingredients from the on-site gardens and surround-
AMERICAN ing farms and orchards, this popular restaurant occupies a redbrick
1921 schoolhouse in the town of Sanger. Chef Ryan Jackson, who
grew up on local fruit farms, returned home after stints cooking at
prestigious Napa Valley restaurants to create seasonal menus from
the bounty of familiar backyards. **Known for:** fresh ingredients from
neighboring farms and orchards; historic country setting; convenient
stop between Kings Canyon and Fresno. ⑤ *Average main: $27* ✉ *1018
S. Frankwood Ave., at Hwy. 180 (King's Canyon Rd.), 20 miles east of
Fresno, Sanger* ☎ *559/787–3271* ⊕ *schoolhousesanger.com* ☾ *Closed
Mon. and Tues.*

$ ✕ **Sierra Subs and Salads.** This well-run sandwich joint satisfies car-
AMERICAN nivores and vegetarians alike with crispy-fresh ingredients prepared
with panache. Depending on your preference, the centerpiece of the
Bull's Eye sandwich, for instance, will be roast beef or a portobello
mushroom, but whichever you choose, the accompanying flavors—of
ciabatta bread, horseradish-and-garlic mayonnaise, roasted red pep-
pers, Havarti cheese, and spinach—will delight your palate. **Known
for:** many vegetarian, vegan, and gluten-free options; weekly specials.
⑤ *Average main: $8* ✉ *41717 Sierra Dr., Three Rivers* ☎ *559/561–4810*
⊕ *www.sierrasubsandsalads.com* ☾ *Closed Mon. No dinner.*

$$$$ ✕ **The Vintage Press.** Built in 1966, this is the best restaurant in the Cen-
EUROPEAN tral Valley. The California–Continental cuisine includes dishes such as
Fodor's Choice crispy veal sweetbreads with a port-wine sauce and filet mignon with
★ a cognac-mustard sauce. **Known for:** wine list with more than 900
selections; chocolate Grand Marnier cake and other homemade des-
serts and ice creams. ⑤ *Average main: $32* ✉ *216 N. Willis St., Visalia*
☎ *559/733–3033* ⊕ *www.thevintagepress.com.*

CLOSE UP

Best Campgrounds in Sequoia and Kings Canyon

Campgrounds in Sequoia and Kings Canyon occupy wonderful settings, with lots of shade and nearby hiking trails. Some campgrounds are open year-round, others only seasonally. Except for Bearpaw (around $350 a night including meals), fees at the campgrounds range from $12 to $35, depending on location and size. There are no RV hookups at any of the campgrounds; expect a table and a fire ring with a grill at standard sites. Only Bearpaw, Lodgepole, Dorst Creek, Potwisha, and Buckeye Flat accept reservations, and for all of these you'll need to book well ahead. The rest are first come, first served. Campgrounds around Lodgepole and Grant Grove get busy in summer with vacationing families. Keep in mind that this is black-bear country and carefully follow posted instructions about storing food. Bear-proof metal containers are provided at many campgrounds.

IN SEQUOIA
Atwell Mill Campground. At 6,650 feet, this peaceful, tent-only campground is just south of the Western Divide. ⊠ *Mineral King Rd., 20 miles east of Rte. 198* ☎ *559/565–3341.*

Bearpaw High Sierra Camp. Classy camping is the order of the day at this tent hotel and restaurant. Make reservations starting on January 2. ⊠ *High Sierra Trail, 11.5 miles from Lodgepole Village* ☎ *888/252–5757* ⊕ *www.visitsequoia.com.*

Dorst Creek Campground. Wildlife sightings are common at this large campground at elevation 6,700 feet. ⊠ *Generals Hwy., 8 miles north of*

Lodgepole Visitor Center ☎ *559/565–3341 or 877/444–6777.*

Lodgepole Campground. The largest Lodgepole-area campground is also the noisiest, though things quiet down at night. ⊠ *Off Generals Hwy. beyond Lodgepole Village* ☎ *559/565–3341 or 877/444–6777.*

Potwisha Campground. On the Marble Fork of the Kaweah River, this midsize campground, open year-round, at elevation 2,100 feet gets no snow in winter and can be hot in summer. ⊠ *Generals Hwy., 4 miles north of Foothills Visitor Center* ☎ *559/565–3341 or 877/444–6777.*

IN KINGS CANYON
Azalea Campground. Of the three campgrounds in the Grant Grove area, Azalea is the only one open year-round. It sits at 6,500 feet amid giant sequoias. ⊠ *Kings Canyon Scenic Byway, ¼ mile north of Grant Grove Village* ☎ *559/565–3341.*

Sentinel Campground. At 4,600 feet and within walking distance of Cedar Grove Village, Sentinel fills up fast in summer. ⊠ *Kings Canyon Scenic Byway, ¼ mile west of Cedar Grove Village* ☎ *559/565–3341.*

Sheep Creek Campground. Of the overflow campgrounds, this is one of the prettiest. ⊠ *Off Kings Canyon Scenic Byway, 1 mile west of Cedar Grove Village* ☎ *No phone.*

Sunset Campground. Many of the easiest trails through Grant Grove are adjacent to this large camp, near the giant sequoias at 6,500 feet. ⊠ *Off Generals Hwy., near Grant Grove Visitor Center* ☎ *No phone.*

WHERE TO STAY

11

IN THE PARKS

SEQUOIA

$$

RESORT

 Silver City Mountain Resort. High on Mineral King Road, this privately owned resort has rustic cabins and Swiss-style chalets, all with at least a stove, refrigerator, and sink. **Pros:** rustic setting; friendly staff; "off the grid" ambience. **Cons:** electricity (by generator) available only between noon and 10 pm. $ *Rooms from: $120* ⊠ *Sequoia National Park* ⚓ *Mineral King Rd., 21 miles southeast of Rte. 198* ☎ *559/561–3223* ⊕ *www.silvercityresort.com* ⊘ *Closed Nov.–late May* ⇨ *11 units, 6 with shared bath* ⦿ *No meals.*

$$$$

HOTEL

Fodor's Choice

★

Wuksachi Lodge. The striking cedar-and-stone main building is a fine example of how a structure can blend effectively with lovely mountain scenery. **Pros:** best place to stay in the parks; lots of wildlife. **Cons:** rooms can be small; main lodge is a few-minutes' walk from guest rooms; slow Wi-Fi. $ *Rooms from: $229* ⊠ *64740 Wuksachi Way, Wuksachi Village* ☎ *559/565–4070, 888/252–5757* ⊕ *www.visitsequoia.com/lodging.aspx* ⇨ *102 rooms* ⦿ *No meals.*

KINGS CANYON

$$

HOTEL

Cedar Grove Lodge. Backpackers like to stay here on the eve of long treks into the High Sierra wilderness, so bedtimes tend to be early. **Pros:** a definite step up from camping in terms of comfort. **Cons:** impersonal; not everybody agrees it's clean enough. $ *Rooms from: $141* ⊠ *Kings Canyon Scenic Byway, Kings Canyon National Park* ☎ *866/807–3598* ⊕ *www.visitsequoia.com/Cedar-Grove-Lodge.aspx* ⊘ *Closed mid-Oct.–mid-May* ⇨ *21 rooms* ⦿ *No meals.*

$

HOTEL

Grant Grove Cabins. Some of the wood-panel cabins here have heaters, electric lights, and private baths, but most have woodstoves, battery lamps, and shared baths. **Pros:** warm, woodsy feel; clean. **Cons:** can be difficult to walk up to if you're not in decent physical shape; costly for what you get. $ *Rooms from: $94* ⊠ *Kings Canyon Scenic Byway in Grant Grove Village, Kings Canyon National Park* ☎ *866/807–3598* ⊕ *www.visitsequoia.com/Grant-Grove-Cabins.aspx* ⇨ *33 cabins, 9 with bath; 17 tent cabins* ⦿ *No meals.*

$$$

HOTEL

John Muir Lodge. In a wooded area in the hills above Grant Grove Village, this modern, timber-sided lodge has rooms and suites with queen- or king-size beds and private baths. **Pros:** open year-round; common room stays warm; quiet. **Cons:** check-in is down in the village. $ *Rooms from: $200* ⊠ *Kings Canyon Scenic Byway, ¼ mile north of Grant Grove Village, 86728 Highway 180, Kings Canyon National Park* ☎ *866/807–3598* ⊕ *www.visitsequoia.com/john-muir-lodge.aspx* ⇨ *36 rooms* ⦿ *No meals.*

OUTSIDE THE PARKS

The only lodging immediately outside the parks is in Three Rivers. Options include inns, chain and mom-and-pop motels, and riverside cabins. Numerous chain properties operate in Visalia or Fresno (your favorite is likely represented in one or both cities), about an hour from the south and north entrances, respectively.

$$$
HOTEL
FAMILY
Montecito-Sequoia Lodge. Outdoor activities are what this year-round family resort is all about, including many that are geared toward teenagers and small children. **Pros:** friendly staff; great for kids; lots of fresh air and planned activities. **Cons:** can be noisy with all the activity; some complaints about cleanliness; not within national park. $ *Rooms from: $179 ⊠ 63410 Generals Hwy., 11 miles south of Grant Grove, Sequoia National Forest* ☎ *559/565–3388, 800/227–9900* ⊕ *www.montecitosequoia.com* ⊘ *Closed 1st 2 wks of Dec.* ⇗ *37 rooms, 13 cabins* ⊙ *All meals.*

$$
B&B/INN
Fodor's Choice
★
Rio Sierra Riverhouse. Guests at Rio Sierra come for the river views, the sandy beach, and the proximity to Sequoia National Park (6 miles away), but invariably end up raving equally about the warm, laid-back hospitality of proprietress Mars Roberts. **Pros:** seductive beach; winning hostess; river views from all rooms; contemporary ambience. **Cons:** books up quickly in summer; some road noise audible in rooms. $ *Rooms from: $185 ⊠ 41997 Sierra Dr., Hwy. 198, Three Rivers* ☎ *559/561–4720* ⊕ *www.rio-sierra.com* ⇗ *5 rooms* ⊙ *No meals* ⇗ *2-night min stay on summer weekends.*

$
B&B/INN
The Spalding House. This restored Colonial Revival inn is decked out with antiques, oriental rugs, handcrafted woodwork, and glass doors. **Pros:** warm feel; old-time atmosphere; great place for a twilight stroll. **Cons:** no TVs in rooms. $ *Rooms from: $95 ⊠ 631 N. Encina St., Visalia* ☎ *559/739–7877* ⊕ *www.thespaldinghouse.com* ⇗ *3 suites* ⊙ *Breakfast.*

SACRAMENTO AND THE GOLD COUNTRY

WELCOME TO SACRAMENTO AND THE GOLD COUNTRY

TOP REASONS TO GO

★ **Gold Rush:** Marshall Gold Discovery State Park is where it all started—it's a must-see—but there are historic and modern gems all along California Highway 49 from Nevada City to Mariposa.

★ **State Capital:** Easygoing Sacramento offers sights like the Capitol and historic Old Sacramento.

★ **Bon Appétit:** Sacramento has emerged as a foodie destination in the past decade, but its celebrations of food, drink, and culture date back to the gold-rush parade of immigrants.

★ **Wine Tasting:** With bucolic scenery and friendly tasting rooms, the Gold Country's Shenandoah Valley has become an acclaimed wine-making region, specializing in Zinfandel.

★ **Rivers, Sequoias, and Caverns:** Natural beauty here is rich (stream beds are still lined with gold), high (sequoias in Calaveras Big Trees State Park), and deep (Moaning Cavern's main chamber is big enough to hold the Statue of Liberty).

1 Sacramento and Nearby. The gateway to the Gold Country, the seat of state government, and an agricultural hub, Sacramento plays many important contemporary roles. About 2.5 million people live in the metropolitan area, which offers up more sunshine and lower prices than coastal California.

2 The Gold Country— South. South of its junction with U.S. 50, Highway 49 traces in asphalt the famed Mother Lode. The peppy former gold-rush towns strung along the road have for the most part been restored, many with money from a modern-day boom in vineyards and wineries.

3 The Gold Country— North. Highway 49 north of Placerville links the towns of Coloma, Auburn, Grass Valley, and Nevada City. Most are gentrified versions of once-rowdy mining camps, vestiges of which remain in roadside museums, old mining structures, and restored homes now serving as inns.

12

GETTING ORIENTED

The Gold Country is a largely rural destination popular with those seeking a reasonably priced escape from Southern California and the Bay Area. Sacramento and Davis are in an enormous valley just west of the Sierra Nevada range. Foothill communities Nevada City, Auburn, Placerville, and Sutter Creek were products of the gold rush, and remain popular stopovers with travelers en route to Lake Tahoe.

Updated by
Steve Pastorino

The Gold Country is one of California's less expensive and more sublime destinations, a region of the Sierra Nevada foothills that's filled with natural and cultural pleasures. Visitors come for the boomtowns and ghost towns; to explore art galleries and shop for antiques; to savor "farm-to-fork" restaurants and delicious wine at tasting rooms; and to rest at friendly, atmospheric inns. Spring brings wildflowers, and in fall the hills are colored by bright red berries and changing leaves. Because it offers plenty of outdoor diversions, the Gold Country is a great place to take kids.

Old Sacramento's museums provide a good introduction to the region's considerable history, but the Gold Country's heart lies along Highway 49, which winds the approximately 300-mile north–south length of the historic mining area. The highway—often a twisting, hilly, two-lane road—begs for a convertible with the top down.

A new era dawned for California when James Marshall turned up a gold nugget in the tailrace of a sawmill he was constructing along the American River. On January 24, 1848, Mexico and the United States were still wrestling for ownership of what would become the Golden State. Marshall's discovery helped compel the United States to tighten its grip on the region, and prospectors from all over the world soon came to seek their fortunes in the Mother Lode.

As gold fever seized the nation, California's population of 15,000 swelled to 265,000 within three years. The mostly young, male adventurers who arrived in search of gold—the '49ers—became part of a culture that discarded many of the button-down conventions of the eastern states. It was also a violent time. Yankee prospectors chased Mexican miners off their claims, and California's leaders initiated a plan to exterminate the local Native American population. Bounties were paid and private militias were hired to wipe out the Native Americans or sell them into slavery. California was to be dominated by the Anglo.

The gold-rush boom lasted scarcely 20 years, but it changed California forever, producing 546 mining towns, of which fewer than 250 remain. The hills of the Gold Country were alive, not only with prospecting and mining but also with business, the arts, gambling, and a fair share of crime. Opera houses went up alongside brothels, and the California State Capitol, in Sacramento, was built partly with the gold dug out of the hills.

The mild climate and rich soil in and around Sacramento Valley are responsible for the region's current riches: fresh and bountiful food and high-quality wines. Gold Country restaurants and wineries continue to earn national acclaim, and they're without the high prices of the Bay Area and Sonoma and Napa wine regions. There's a growing local craft-beer scene, too.

PLANNING

WHEN TO GO

The Gold Country is most pleasant in spring, when the wildflowers are in bloom, and in fall. Summers can be hot in the valley (temperatures of 100°F are fairly common), so head for the hills. Sacramento winters tend to be cool, with occasionally foggy or rainy days. Throughout the year Gold Country towns stage community and ethnic celebrations. In December many towns are decked out for Christmas.

GETTING HERE AND AROUND

AIR TRAVEL

Sacramento International Airport (SMF) is served by Aeromexico, Alaska, American, Delta, Hawaiian, JetBlue, Southwest, United, and Volaris. A taxi from the airport to Downtown Sacramento costs about $40, but services like Lyft and Uber often cost much less. The Super Shuttle fare starts at $13. Public buses *(Bus and Light-Rail Travel)* are also an option.

Contacts Sacramento International Airport. ⊠ *6900 Airport Blvd., 12 miles northwest of downtown off I–5, Sacramento* ☎ *916/929–5411* ⊕ *www.sacramento.aero/smf.* **Super Shuttle.** ☎ *800/258–3826* ⊕ *www.supershuttle.com.*

BUS AND LIGHT-RAIL TRAVEL

Greyhound serves Sacramento from San Francisco and Los Angeles. Sacramento Regional Transit serves the capital area with buses and light-rail vehicles. Yolobus public buses Nos. 42A and 42B connect SMF airport and Downtown Sacramento, West Sacramento, Davis, and Woodland.

Contacts Greyhound. ⊠ *420 Richards Blvd.* ☎ *916/444-6858* ⊕ *www.greyhound.com.* **Sacramento Regional Transit.** ☎ *916/321–2877* ⊕ *www.sacrt.com.* **Yolobus.** ☎ *530/666–2877, 916/371–2877* ⊕ *www.yolobus.com.*

CAR TRAVEL

Interstate 5 (north–south) and Interstate 80 (east–west) are the two main routes into and out of Sacramento. From Sacramento, three highways fan out toward the east, all intersecting with historic Highway 49: Interstate 80 heads northeast 34 miles to Auburn; U.S. 50 goes east

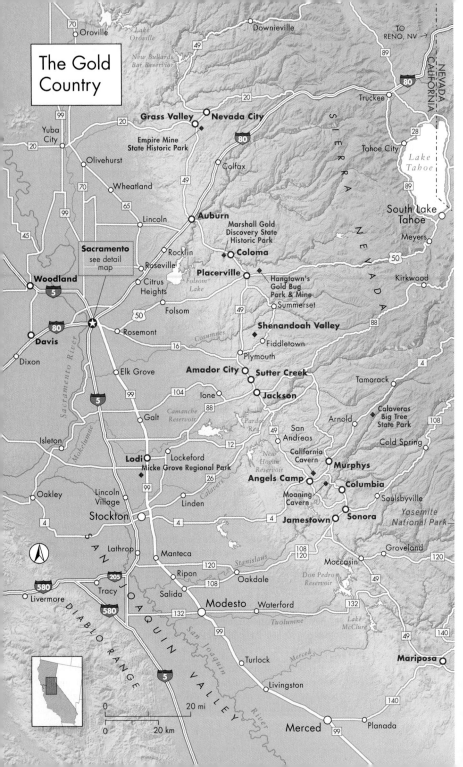

40 miles to Placerville; and Highway 16 angles southeast 45 miles to Plymouth. Highway 49, also called the Golden Chain highway, is one of America's great drives. It's an excellent two-lane road that winds and climbs through the foothills and valleys, linking the principal Gold Country towns. Traveling by car is the only practical way to explore the Gold Country.

TRAIN TRAVEL

One of the most authentic ways to relive the Old West is traveling via train. On the Amtrak *California Zephyr,* you can ride the same route traveled by prospectors in the late 1800s. Docents from the Sacramento Railroad Museum ride the route from Sacramento to Reno daily, and are available to answer questions. The route into the Sierra Nevadas is memorable, especially if you book a sleeper car. Amtrak trains serve Sacramento and Davis from San Jose, Oakland, and Emeryville (Amtrak buses transport passengers from San Francisco's Ferry Building to Emeryville). Amtrak also runs trains and connecting motor coaches from the Central Valley.

Contacts Amtrak. ⊠ *401 I St.* ☎ *800/872–7245* ⊕ *www.amtrak.com.*

RESTAURANTS

American, Italian, Chinese, and Mexican are common Gold Country fare, but chefs also prepare ambitious European, French, and contemporary regional cuisine that mixes California ingredients with cosmopolitan preparations. Grass Valley's meat- and vegetable-stuffed *pasties,* introduced by 19th-century gold miners from Cornwall, are one of the region's more unusual treats.

HOTELS

Sacramento has plenty of full-service hotels, budget motels, and small inns. Larger towns along Highway 49—among them Auburn, Grass Valley, and Jackson—have chain motels and inns. Many Gold Country bed-and-breakfasts occupy former mansions, miners' cabins, and other historic buildings. *Hotel reviews have been shortened. For full information, visit Fodors.com.*

Contacts Amador Council of Tourism. ⊠ *460 Sutter Hill Road, Suite D, Sutter Creek* ☎ *209/267–9249, 877/868–7262* ⊕ *www.touramador.com.* **California Association of Bed & Breakfast Inns.** ☎ *800/373–9251* ⊕ *www.cabbi.com/region/gold-country.*

VISITOR INFORMATION

Contacts Amador County Chamber of Commerce & Visitors Bureau. ⊠ *115 Main St., Jackson* ☎ *209/223–0350* ⊕ *amadorchamber.com.* **El Dorado County Visitors Authority.** ⊠ *542 Main St., Placerville* ☎ *530/621–5885, 800/457–6279* ⊕ *visit-eldorado.com.* **Grass Valley/Nevada County Chamber of Commerce.** ⊠ *128 E. Main St., Grass Valley* ☎ *530/273–4667* ⊕ *www.grassvalleychamber.com.* **Tuolumne County Visitors Bureau.** ⊠ *542 W. Stockton Rd., Sonora* ☎ *209/533–4420, 800/446–1333* ⊕ *www.yosemitegoldcountry.com.* **Yosemite/Mariposa County Tourism Bureau.** ⊠ *5158 Hwy. 140, Mariposa* ☎ *209/742–4567* ⊕ *www.yosemiteexperience.com.*

WHAT IT COSTS				
	$	$$	$$$	$$$$
Restaurants	under $16	$16–$22	$23–$30	over $30
Hotels	under $120	$120–$175	$176–$250	over $250

Restaurant prices are the average cost of a main course at dinner or, if dinner is not served, at lunch, excluding sales tax. Hotel prices are the lowest cost of a standard double room in high season, excluding taxes.

SACRAMENTO AND NEARBY

California's capital is an ethnically diverse city, with sizable Mexican, Hmong, and Ukrainian populations, among many others.

SACRAMENTO

87 miles northeast of San Francisco; 384 miles north of Los Angeles.

All around the Golden State's seat of government you'll experience echoes of the gold-rush days, most notably in Old Sacramento, whose wooden sidewalks and horse-drawn carriages on cobblestone streets lend the waterfront district a 19th-century feel. The California State Railroad Museum and other venues hold artifacts of state and national significance, and historic buildings house shops and restaurants. River cruises and train rides are fun family diversions for an hour or two.

Due east of Old Sacramento is Downtown, where landmarks include the Capitol building and the surrounding Capitol Park. Golden 1 Center, the new sports and concert venue, and the convention center are also here. The area is a little uneven economically, but revitalization is taking full effect.

Farther east, starting at about 15th Street, lies the city's most interesting neighborhood, Midtown, a mix of genteel Victorian edifices, ultramodern lofts, and innovative restaurants and cozy wine bars. The neighborhood springs to life on the second Saturday evening of the month, when art galleries hold open houses and the sidewalks are packed. A few intersections are jumping most evenings when the weather's good; they include the corner of 20th and L Streets in what's known as Lavender Heights, the center of the city's gay and lesbian community.

GETTING HERE AND AROUND

Most people drive to Sacramento and get around by car. Yellow Cab, Lyft, and Uber are reliable cab options.

BUS TRAVEL Sacramento Regional Transit buses and light-rail vehicles serve the area. The No. 30 DASH shuttle bus links Old Sacramento, Midtown, and Sutter's Fort.

CAR TRAVEL Assuming that traffic is not a factor (though it often is), Sacramento is a 90-minute drive from San Francisco and a seven-hour drive from Los Angeles. Parking garages serve Old Sacramento and other tourist spots; on-street parking in Downtown can be difficult to find.

ESSENTIALS

Transportation Contacts Sacramento Regional Transit. ☎ 916/321–2877 ⊕ www.sacrt.com. **Yellow Cab Co. of Sacramento.** ☎ 916/444–2222 ⊕ www. yellowcabsacramento.com.

Visitor Information Old Sacramento Visitor Information Center. ✉ 1002 2nd St. ☎ 916/442–7644 ⊕ www.oldsacramento.com. **Sacramento Convention and Visitors Bureau.** ✉ 1608 I St., Downtown ☎ 916/808–7777, ⊕ www. visitsacramento.com.

EXPLORING
TOP ATTRACTIONS

American River Bicycle Trail. The Jedediah Smith Memorial Trail, as it's formally called, runs for 32 miles from Old Sacramento to Beals Point in Folsom. Walk or ride a bit of it and you'll see why local cyclists and pedestrians adore its scenic lanes, if not always each other: confrontations do occur between humorless speeders and meandering gawkers. Enjoy great views of the American River and the bluffs overlooking it. ■TIP→ **Bring lunch or a snack. Pretty parks and picnic areas dot the trail.** ✉ *Old Sacramento* ⊕ *www.american-riverbiketrail.com.*

California Automobile Museum. More than 150 automobiles—from Model Ts, Hudsons, and Studebakers to modern-day electric-powered ones—are on display at this museum that pays tribute to automotive history and car culture. Check out a replica of Henry Ford's 1896 Quadracycle and a 1920s roadside café and garage exhibit. The docents are ready to explain everything you see. The museum is south of downtown and Old Sacramento, with ample free parking. ⊠ *2200 Front St., Downtown* 🕾 *916/442–6802* ⊕ *www.calautomuseum.org* 🎫 *$10* ⏾ *Closed Tues.*

FAMILY **California State Railroad Museum.** Near what was the terminus of the transcontinental and Sacramento Valley railroads, this 100,000-square-foot museum is a re-creation of the original train station and roundhouse. There are 19 steam locomotives and dozens of railroad cars on display along with a variety of other exhibits. You can walk through a post-office car and peer into cubbyholes and canvas mailbags, enter a sleeping car that simulates the swaying on the roadbed and the flashing lights of a passing town at night, or glimpse inside the first-class dining car. The room containing the gold "Last Spike," one of two cast in 1869 to commemorate the completion of the transcontinental railroad, is quietly compelling. Kids have lots of fun at this museum and can become Junior Engineers. ∎ TIP➡ You can visit an original roundhouse, not just a replica, at Railtown 1897 in Jamestown, near Sonora. ⊠ *125 I St., at 2nd St., Old Sacramento* 🕾 *916/323–9280* ⊕ *www.csrmf.org* 🎫 *$12.*

Fodor's Choice **Capitol.** Built in 1869 and entirely renovated (and seismologically ret-
★ rofitted) in 1982, the Capitol's 128-foot gilded dome encapsulates both a working museum and the active seat of California's government. Wander freely by reproductions of century-old state offices and into legislative chambers (in session from January to September) decorated in the style of the 1890s. Look for the abstract portrait of Gov. Edmund "Jerry" Brown, alongside the likes of Ronald Reagan and Arnold Schwarzenegger. Guides conduct tours of the building and the 40-acre Capitol Park, which contains a rose garden, a fragrant display of camellias (Sacramento's city flower), and California Veterans Memorials. ∎ TIP➡ Wander the Capitol's botanical grounds to glimpse the diverse collection of trees, shrubs, and flowers, including some 1,200 trees from around the world. The original deodar cedars on the west side date back to 1872. ⊠ *Capitol Mall and 10th St., Downtown* 🕾 *916/324–0333* ⊕ *capitolmuseum.ca.gov* 🎫 *Free.*

Fodor's Choice **Crocker Art Museum.** Established in 1885 with a collection first assembled
★ by California Supreme Court judge E.B. Crocker and his wife, Margaret, the Crocker contains a fine collection of Californian, American, and Asian art. A highlight is the magnificent *Great Canyon of the Sierra, Yosemite* (1871) by Thomas Hill. The museum has exceptional holdings of master drawings as well as an impressive collection of international ceramics and works from Europe, Asia, and Africa. A huge contemporary wing was added in 2010 and regularly hosts outstanding traveling exhibitions. Recent exhibitions have included works by Toulouse-Lautrec, Ansel Adams, Diego Rivera, and William S. Rice. ⊠ *216 O St., at 3rd St., Downtown* 🕾 *916/808–7000* ⊕ *www.crockerartmuseum.org* 🎫 *$10* ⏾ *Closed Mon.*

12

WORTH NOTING

FAMILY **California Museum.** California's authentic artifacts—from the State Constitution to surfing magazines—are on display at this unique celebration of the Golden State. Witness life behind the barbed wire of a WWII–era Japanese internment camp, visit a Chinese herb shop maintained by a holographic proprietor, or find familiar names inducted into the annually expanded California Hall of Fame. Steinbeck, Disney, and Earhart are among many you'll know just by their surname. ⊠ *1020 O St., at 11th St., Downtown* ☎ *916/653–7524* ⊕ *www.californiamuseum.org* 🖼 *$9* ⊙ *Closed Mon.*

FAMILY **Central Pacific Railroad Passenger Station.** At this reconstructed 1876 depot there's rolling stock to admire, a typical waiting room, and a small restaurant. Part of the year a train departs from the freight depot, south of the passenger station, making a 45-minute out-and-back trip that starts along the banks of the Sacramento River. ⊠ *930 Front St., at J St., Old Sacramento* ☎ *916/445–5995* ⊕ *www.csrmf.org* 🖼 *Train rides $12; first class $20* ⊙ *Closed Oct.–Mar.; call for hrs.*

Huntington, Hopkins & Co. Store. Picks, shovels, gold pans, and other paraphernalia used by gold-rush miners are on display at this re-creation of a 19th-century hardware store. Though it's named for two of the Big Four railroad barons, their store was far more elaborate. ⊠ *113 I St., at Front St., Old Sacramento* ☎ *916/323–7234* ⊕ *www.californiarailroad. museum* 🖼 *Free.*

State Indian Museum. Adjacent to Sutter's Fort, this small but engaging museum explores the lives and history of California's native peoples. Among the interesting displays is one about Ishi, the last Yahi Indian to emerge from the mountains, in 1911. Arts-and-crafts exhibits, a demonstration village, knowledgeable rangers, and an evocative video offer a fascinating portrait of the history and lifestyle of the state's earliest inhabitants. ⊠ *2618 K St., at 26th St., Midtown* ☎ *916/324–0971* ⊕ *www.parks.ca.gov* 🖼 *$5.*

FAMILY **Sutter's Fort.** German-born Swiss immigrant John Augustus Sutter founded Sacramento's earliest Euro-American settlement in 1839. Eight years later, assistance from Sutter's Fort helped save some members of the Donner Party. A self-guided tour includes a blacksmith's shop, bakery, prison, living quarters, and livestock areas. Costumed docents sometimes reenact fort life, demonstrating crafts, food preparation, and firearms maintenance. ⊠ *2701 L St., at 27th St., Midtown* ☎ *916/445–4422* ⊕ *www.suttersfort.org* 🖼 *$5 most days, $7 on interpretive program days.*

WHERE TO EAT

$$$ ✕ **Biba.** Since 1986, nationally recognized chef and owner Biba Caggiano has prepared northern Italian cuisine in her inviting restaurant near Sutter's Fort. The Capitol crowd flocks here for menus that change quarterly, with staples such as a 10-layer lasagne with Bolognese sauce, braised lamb shanks, and house-made gnocchi. **Known for:** celebrity chef; 10-layer lasagne; elegant but comfortable dining room. ⑤ *Average main: $28* ⊠ *2801 Capitol Ave., at 28th St., Midtown* ☎ *916/455–2422* ⊕ *www.biba-restaurant.com* ⊙ *Closed Sun. No lunch Mon. or Sat.*

NORTHERN
ITALIAN
Fodor's Choice
★

$$$$ ✕ **Ella.** With fresh white calla lilies on the tables, ivory linen curtains,
MODERN and distressed-wood shutters installed across the ceiling, this swank
AMERICAN restaurant and bar near the Capitol building is artfully designed and
thoroughly modern. Ella's decor matches the stellar California–French
farm-to-table cuisine served within. **Known for:** fresh, seasonal local
ingredients; classy dining room, cocktail selection, and wine list. $ *Average main: $38* ✉ *1131 K St., Downtown* ☎ *916/443–3772* ⊕ *www.
elladiningroomandbar.com* ⊗ *No lunch Sat. Closed Sun.*

$$$$ ✕ **The Firehouse.** The city's first brick firehouse has been restored with
AMERICAN elegant dining spaces that showcase Chef Jay Veregge's award-winning
Fodor's Choice contemporary menu. Creative dishes range from foie gras and carpaccio
★ to locally sourced specialty beef cuts. **Known for:** steaks and seafood;
sophisticated menu and setting; celeb clientele. $ *Average main: $41*
✉ *1112 2nd St., at L St., Old Sacramento* ☎ *916/442–4772* ⊕ *www.
firehouseoldsac.com* ⊗ *No lunch weekends.*

$$ ✕ **Hook & Ladder Manufacturing Company.** Youthful and interesting, with
MODERN found-art decorative elements and exposed vents, this historic former
AMERICAN fire station is a favorite stop for creative cocktails, craft beers, and deli-
cious farm-to-fork fare. Delectable salads and soups are enhanced by
the area's year-round farmers' markets. **Known for:** carefully sourced
ingredients; small bites; happy hour. $ *Average main: $22* ✉ *1630 S.
St., Midtown* ☎ *916/442–4885* ⊕ *www.hookandladder916.com.*

$$$ ✕ **Kru.** Owner and inventive sushi chef Billy Ngo has earned a reputation
JAPANESE for serving some of the freshest and most interesting sushi in Sacra-
FUSION mento at this hip and stylish mod-Japanese restaurant. Try the sunshine
roll, with spicy tuna, walu (escolar), and shrimp tempura and the surprising bite of green apples, lemon, and sweet chili. **Known for:** nearly
two dozen styles of rolls; creative sushi; impressive sake, wine, and
whisky offerings. $ *Average main: $25* ✉ *3135 Folsom St., Midtown*
☎ *916/551–1559* ⊕ *www.krurestaurant.com* ⊗ *No lunch weekends.*

$$$ ✕ **Magpie Cafe.** This hip Midtown eatery with a casual vibe takes its
AMERICAN food quite seriously: nearly all the produce is sourced locally, and menus
Fodor's Choice are printed each day, reflecting availability from local farms. The array
★ of small-batch farmstead cheeses, all from California, is mouthwater-
ing (especially the Point Reyes Blue, drizzled with honey). **Known for:**
California cheeses; new menus daily; homemade ice-cream sandwiches.
$ *Average main: $25* ✉ *1601 16th St., Midtown* ☎ *916/452–7594*
⊕ *www.magpiecafe.com* ⊗ *No dinner Sun.*

$$$ ✕ **The Waterboy.** Rural French cooking with locally sourced, seasonal,
EUROPEAN high-quality (often organic) ingredients is the hallmark of this upscale
Fodor's Choice Midtown restaurant that's as appealing for a casual meal with friends
★ as it is for a drawn-out romantic dinner for two. The artisanal-cheese
and antipasto plates are appealing starters for sharing, but you can't
go wrong with marinated olives or oysters (in season). **Known for:**
exceptional French cooking; quality local ingredients; welcoming
chef. $ *Average main: $28* ✉ *2000 Capitol Ave., at 20th St., Midtown* ☎ *916/498–9891* ⊕ *www.waterboyrestaurant.com* ⊗ *No lunch
weekends.*

WHERE TO STAY

$$$
B&B/INN
🖫 **Amber House Bed & Breakfast Inn.** Veer from the beaten path of traditional lodging at Amber House Inn's two historic homes—a 1905 Craftsman-style home and an 1895 Dutch colonial–revival home—just 1 mile from the Capitol. **Pros:** Midtown location; attentive service. **Cons:** freeway access isn't easy; not exactly kid-friendly. ⑤ *Rooms from: $199* ✉ *1315 22nd St., Midtown* 🕾 *916/444–8085,* ⊕ *www. amberhouse.com* 🖙 *10 rooms* ⑩ *Breakfast.*

$$$
HOTEL
Fodor's Choice
★
🖫 **The Citizen Hotel.** This boutique hotel built within the historic 1926 Cal Western Life building is dapper and refined, with marble stairs, striped wallpaper, and plush velvet chairs, lending the place a Roaring '20s charm. **Pros:** hip, sophisticated decor; smooth and solicitous service; terrific restaurant and bar. **Cons:** rooms near elevator can be noisy; rates vary widely depending on conventions, legislature, season. ⑤ *Rooms from: $208* ✉ *926 J St., Downtown* 🕾 *916/447–2700* ⊕ *www.thecitizenhotel.com* 🖙 *198 rooms* ⑩ *No meals.*

$$
HOTEL
🖫 **Delta King.** Wake up to the sound of geese taking flight along the river when you book a stay in one of Sacramento's most unusual and historic relics, a carefully restored riverboat hotel, permanently moored on Old Sacramento's waterfront. **Pros:** unique lodgings; steps from historic Old Town shopping and dining. **Cons:** slanted floors can feel a bit jarring; rooms are cramped. ⑤ *Rooms from: $156* ✉ *1000 Front St., Old Sacramento* ✛ *At the end of K St.* 🕾 *916/444–5464, 800/825–5464* ⊕ *www. deltaking.com* 🖙 *44 rooms* ⑩ *Breakfast.*

$$$
HOTEL
🖫 **Embassy Suites by Hilton Sacramento Riverfront.** Immediately adjacent to Sacramento's iconic Tower Bridge, this property has huge common areas, updated large rooms, locally commissioned public art, and a well-deserved reputation for exceptional customer service. **Pros:** best river view in town; proximity to Old Town and downtown. **Cons:** the atrium feels sterile. ⑤ *Rooms from: $219* ✉ *100 Capitol Mall, Downtown* 🕾 *916/326–5000* ⊕ *embassysuites3.hilton.com* 🖙 *242 suites* ⑩ *Breakfast.*

$$$
HOTEL
🖫 **Hyatt Regency Sacramento.** With a marble-and-glass lobby and luxurious rooms, this hotel across from the Capitol and adjacent to the convention center is one of Sacramento's finest. **Pros:** Capitol Park is across the street; some rooms have small balconies; excellent service. **Cons:** nearby streets can feel a little dodgy at night; somewhat impersonal. ⑤ *Rooms from: $239* ✉ *1209 L St., Downtown* 🕾 *916/443–1234, 800/633–7313* ⊕ *sacramento.regency.hyatt.com* 🖙 *505 rooms* ⑩ *No meals.*

NIGHTLIFE AND PERFORMING ARTS
NIGHTLIFE

Blue Cue. A billiard lounge with a bright blue door, the Blue Cue is upstairs from the popular Mexican restaurant Centro. Wednesday night's trivia contest is a spirited event. ✉ *1004 28th St., at J St., Midtown* 🕾 *916/441–6810* ⊕ *www.bluecue.com.*

Dive Bar. Live "mermaids" and "mermen" swim in a massive tank above the bar at this lively downtown nightspot known for its extensive list of craft cocktails and local beers. ✉ *1016 K St., Downtown* 🕾 *916/737–5999* ⊕ *divebarsacramento.com.*

Fox and Goose. This casual pub with live music serves fish-and-chips, Cornish pasties, and other traditional items—plus vegetarian and vegan fare—on weekdays until 9:30. Music and revelry go until 2 am on weekends. ⊠ *1001 R St., at 10th St., Downtown* ☎ *916/443–8825* ⊕ *www.foxandgoose.com.*

Harlow's. This sceney restaurant draws a youngish crowd to its art-deco bar-nightclub, inviting patio, and Sacramento's most diverse live-music lineup after 9 pm. ⊠ *2708 J St., at 27th St., Midtown* ☎ *916/441–4693* ⊕ *www.harlows.com.*

Streets Pub and Grub. A favorite among Anglophiles, Streets is open until 2 am nightly. Darts and TV soccer, anyone? ⊠ *1804 J St., at 18th St., Midtown* ☎ *916/498–1388* ⊕ *www.streetspubandgrub.com.*

PERFORMING ARTS

California Musical Theatre. This group presents Broadway shows at the Sacramento Community Center Theater and the summer Music Circus musicals (think *Oklahoma, Annie*) at the theater-in-the-round Wells Fargo Pavilion. ⊠ *1419 H St., at 14th St., Downtown* ☎ *916/557–1999* ⊕ *www.calmt.com.*

Crest Theatre. It's worth peeking inside the Crest even if you don't catch a show there, just to see the swirling and flamboyant art-deco design in the foyer, or to dine at the new Empress Tavern restaurant within. It's a beloved venue for classic and art-house films, along with concerts and other cultural events. ⊠ *1013 K St., at 10th St., Downtown* ☎ *916/476–3356* ⊕ *www.crestsacramento.com.*

SHOPPING

Greater Sacramento is filled with familiar shops. To try something new but maybe find something old, wander through Midtown, especially J, K, and L Streets between 16th and 26th Streets.

Westfield Galleria at Roseville. From Sears to Nordstrom to Tiffany & Co., this shopping complex is a sprawling, heavily trafficked collection of chain stores and restaurants. It's always jumping. ⊠ *1151 Galleria Blvd., north of Sacramento off I–80 Exit 105A, Roseville* ⊕ *www.westfield.com/galleriaatroseville.*

WOODLAND

20 miles northwest of Sacramento.

In its heyday, Woodland was among California's wealthiest cities. Established by gold seekers and entrepreneurs, it later became an agricultural gold mine. The legacy of the old land barons lives on in the restored Victorian and Craftsman architecture downtown; the best examples are south of Main Street on College, Elm, 1st, and 2nd Streets. The town's top attraction is the splendid California Agriculture Museum.

GETTING HERE AND AROUND

Yolobus (⊕ *www.yolobus.com*) serves downtown Woodland from Sacramento, but it's far more practical to drive here via Interstate 5.

ESSENTIALS

Visitor Information Woodland Chamber of Commerce. ✉ *307 1st St., at Dead Cat Alley* ☏ *530/662–7327* ⊕ *www.woodlandchamber.org.*

EXPLORING

FAMILY **California Agriculture Museum.** This gigantic space provides a marvelous overview of the entire history of motorized agricultural vehicles through dozens and dozens of threshers, harvesters, combines, tractors, and more. A separate wing surveys the evolution of the truck, with an emphasis on ones used for farm work. ✉ *1962 Hays La., off County Rd. 102* ☏ *530/666–9700* ⊕ *www.CaliforniaAgMuseum.org* ⊠ *$10* ⊘ *Closed Mon. and Tues.*

Woodland Opera House. On the U.S. National Register of Historic Places, this 1896 structure hosted minstrel shows, John Philip Sousa's marching band, and early vaudeville acts before closing for six decades. Now restored, it hosts plays, musicals, and concerts year-round. If the box office is open, ask for a backstage tour or a peek at the auditorium. ✉ *340 2nd St.* ☏ *530/666–9617* ⊕ *www.woodlandoperahouse.org.*

WHERE TO EAT

$$ ✕ **Kitchen428 and Mojo's Lounge.** Originally built in 1891 to house luxury
AMERICAN apartments, the Jackson building roared back to life in 2012 as Woodland's best restaurant, showcasing locally sourced California cuisine from filet mignon to cioppino. A friendly, stylish, and "green" place, Mojo's rewards like-minded customers; ride a bike here, and you'll receive 10% off your bill. **Known for:** local and sustainable menu; historic building; weekend brunch. ⑤ *Average main: $21* ✉ *428 1st St., off Main St.* ☏ *530/661–0428* ⊕ *www.mojoskitchen428.com.*

DAVIS

10 miles west of Sacramento.

Davis began as a rich agricultural area and remains one, but it doesn't feel like a cow town. It's home to the University of California at Davis, whose 35,000-plus students hang at downtown cafés, galleries, and bookstores (most of the action takes place between 1st and 4th and C and G Streets), lending the city a decidedly college-town feel.

GETTING HERE AND AROUND

Most people arrive here by car via Interstate 80. In a pinch, you can get here via Yolobus (⊕ *www.yolobus.com*) from Sacramento. Downtown is walkable. Touring by bicycle is also a popular option—Davis is very flat.

ESSENTIALS

Visitor Information Davis Chamber of Commerce. ✉ *640 3rd St.* ☏ *530/756–5160* ⊕ *www.davischamber.com.*

EXPLORING

University of California, Davis. A top research university, UC Davis educates many of the Wine Country's vintners and grape growers, in addition to farmers, veterinarians, and brewmasters, too. Campus tours depart from Buehler Alumni and Visitors Center. On a tour or not, worthy stops include the **Arboretum** (⊕ *arboretum.ucdavis.edu*), the **Manetti Shrem Museum of Art** (⊕ manettishremmuseum.ucdavis.edu), and the **Mondavi Center for the Performing Arts** (⊕ *mondaviarts.org*), a striking modern glass structure that presents top-tier artists. ⊠ *Visitor Center, 550 Alumni La.* ☎ *530/752–8111 for tour information* ⊕ *visit.ucdavis.edu.*

LODI

41 miles north of Modesto, 34 miles south of Sacramento.

With about 100,000 acres of mostly rich alluvial soils planted to more than six-dozen grape varieties—more types than in any other California viticultural area—Lodi is a major a wine-making grape hub, particularly for Zinfandel. Eighty or so wineries do business in Lodi and neighboring Acampo, Lockeford, and Woodbridge. Founded on agriculture, Lodi was once the watermelon capital of the country. Today it's surrounded by fields of asparagus, pumpkins, beans, safflowers, sunflowers, kiwis, melons, squashes, peaches, and cherries. Lodi itself retains an old rural charm. You can stroll downtown or visit a wildlife refuge, all the while benefiting from a Sacramento River delta breeze that keeps this micro-climate cooler in summer than anyplace else in the area.

GETTING HERE AND AROUND
Most of Lodi lies to the west of Highway 99, several miles east of Interstate 5. Buses and Amtrak trains stop here frequently. Although the GrapeLine bus (☎ 209/333–6806) can get you around town and to many of the wineries, you are better off with your own vehicle.

ESSENTIALS
Visitor Information Lodi Conference & Visitors Bureau. ⊠ *25 N. School St.* ☎ *209/365–1195, 800/798–1810* ⊕ *www.visitlodi.com.*

EXPLORING
TOP ATTRACTIONS
Lodi Wine & Visitor Center. A fine place to sample Lodi wines, the center has a tasting bar and viticultural exhibits. You can also buy wine and pick up a free winery map. The knowledgeable pourers can suggest wineries to explore. ⊠ *2545 W. Turner Rd., at Woodhaven La.* ☎ *209/365–0621* ⊕ *www.lodiwine.com* 🍷 *Tasting $7.*

Lucas Winery. David Lucas was one of the first local producers to start making serious wine, and today his Zinfandels are among Lodi's most sought-after vintages. In addition to fruity Zins, Lucas makes a light Chardonnay with subtle oaky flavors. The 90-minute tour and tasting will get you up to speed on the Lodi wine appellation. ⊠ *18196 N. Davis Rd., at W. Turner Rd.* ☎ *209/368–2006* ⊕ *www.lucaswinery.com* 🍷 *Tastings $10–$55, tour (includes tasting) $55* ⊗ *Closed Mon. and Tues.*

Fodor's Choice ★ **M2 Wines.** With its translucent polycarbonate panels, concrete floor, and metal framing, this winery's high-ceilinged tasting room strikes an iconoclastic, industrial-sleek pose along an otherwise relentlessly rural lane north of Lodi. The Soucie Vineyard old-vine Zinfandel and the Trio Red Wine blend are the flagships. ⊠ *2900 E. Peltier Rd., Acampo* ✛ *Near Lower Sacramento Rd.* ☎ *209/339–1071* ⊕ *www.m2wines.com* 🍷 *Tasting $10* ⊗ *Closed Tues. and Wed.*

Fodor'sChoice **Michael David Winery.** Fifth-generation farmers turned winery owners
★ Michael and David Phillips operate their tasting room at the rustic
roadside **Phillips Farms Fruit Stand,** where they also sell their family's gorgeous produce. Michael David is well known for Zinfandels, among
them 7 Deadly Zins. ■TIP→ Breakfast or lunch at the café here is a
treat. ⊠ *4580 W. Hwy. 12, at N. Ray Rd.* ☎ *209/368–7384* ⊕ *www.
michaeldavidwinery.com* ⊠ *Tastings $5–$10* ⊗ *No reserve tasting
Mon.–Thurs.*

WORTH NOTING

Berghold Estate Winery. The tasting room at Berghold recalls an earlier
wine era with its vintage Victorian interior, including restored, salvaged
mantlepieces, leaded glass, and a 26-foot-long bar. The wines—among
them Viognier, Cabernet Sauvignon, Merlot, Syrah, and Zinfandel—
pay homage to French winemaking styles. ⊠ *17343 N. Cherry Rd.,
off E. Victor Rd./Hwy. 12* ☎ *209/333–9291* ⊕ *bergholdvineyards.com*
⊠ *Tasting $10* ⊗ *Closed Mon.–Wed.*

FAMILY **Micke Grove Regional Park.** This 258-acre, oak-shaded park has a Japanese
tea garden, picnic tables, children's play areas, an agricultural museum,
a zoo, a golf course, and a water-play feature. **Fun Town at Micke Grove,**
a family-oriented amusement park, is geared toward younger children.
⊠ *11793 N. Micke Grove Rd., off Hwy. 99 Armstrong Rd. exit, 5 miles
south of downtown* ☎ *209/953–8800 park info, 209/369–7330 Fun
Town, 209/331–2010 zoo* ⊠ *Parking $5 weekdays, $6 weekends and
holidays; pets $1 (leash required); Fun Town ride prices vary; zoo $5.*

Van Ruiten Family Vineyards. For an affordable experience of what Lodi's
hardworking old Zinfandel vines can produce, sample the Van Ruiten
Old Vine Zin and the Reserve Sideways Lot 69 Old Vine Zin. Other
wines of note include the Chardonnays and the Cabernet-Shiraz blend.
⊠ *340 W. Hwy. 12* ☎ *209/334–5722* ⊕ *www.vrwinery.com* ⊠ *Tastings $10–$15.*

WHERE TO EAT

$$ ✕ **The Dancing Fox Winery and Bakery.** This is a good downtown stop for
AMERICAN coffee and fresh pastries, a granola parfait, or more filling breakfast
selections. The Dancing Fox also serves lunch and dinner and has
a tasting room for its eponymous wines. **Known for:** fresh organic
breads and pizzas; many dishes baked in Spanish wood-fired oven;
historic downtown setting. ⑤ *Average main: $19* ⊠ *203 S. School St.*
☎ *203/366–2634* ⊕ *www.dancingfoxwinery.com* ⊗ *Closed Mon. No
dinner Sun.*

$$$ ✕ **Pietro's Trattoria.** Lodi's go-to spot for Italian–American classics
ITALIAN wins fans for its quality ingredients, Tuscan-courtyard ambience, and
plant-filled outdoor patio (reservations essential on weekends). Expect
straightforward, well-executed renditions of chicken and veal piccata,
filling lasagna and fettucine Alfredo (with chicken or prawns), pizzas, and the like, all delivered with informal good cheer by the cadre
of servers. **Known for:** wine list focused on local vintages; Italian–
American classics; authentic Tuscan atmosphere. ⑤ *Average main:
$25* ⊠ *317 E. Kettleman La.* ☎ *209/368–0613* ⊕ *www.pietroslodi.
com* ⊗ *Closed Sun. No lunch Mon.*

$$$$
MODERN
AMERICAN
Fodor's Choice
★

✕ **Towne House Restaurant.** Lodi power breakfasts and lunches and special-occasion dinners often take place in the distinguished rooms of this former residence behind, and part of, the Wine and Roses hotel. Painted in rich, textured hues offset by wide white molding, the rooms exude a subtle sophistication matched by the cuisine of executive chef John Hitchcock. Jazz musicians perform nightly in the lounge, noteworthy for its specialty cocktails and selection of local wines by the glass. **Known for:** 70-plus local wines by the glass; nightly live music; fresh seasonal local ingredients. $ *Average main: $40* ⊠ *2505 W. Turner Rd., at Woodhaven La.* ☎ *209/371–6160* ⊕ *winerose.com/ towne-house-restaurant.*

WHERE TO STAY

$$
B&B/INN

🛏 **The Inn at Locke House.** Built between 1862 and 1882, the inn occupies a pioneer doctor's family home that rates a listing on the National Register of Historic Places. **Pros:** friendly; quiet; can be hard to find. $ *Rooms from: $149* ⊠ *19960 Elliott Rd., Lockeford* ☎ *209/727–5715* ⊕ *www.theinnatlockehouse.com* ⪡ *5 rooms* ⎮◎⎮ *Breakfast.*

$$$$
HOTEL

🛏 **Wine & Roses Hotel and Restaurant.** Set on 7 acres amid a tapestry of informal gardens, this hotel has cultivated a sense of refinement typically associated with Napa or Carmel. **Pros:** luxurious; relaxing; quiet. **Cons:** expensive; some guests mention that walls are thin. $ *Rooms from: $259* ⊠ *2505 W. Turner Rd.* ☎ *209/334–6988* ⊕ *www.winerose. com* ⪡ *66 rooms* ⎮◎⎮ *No meals.*

SPORTS AND THE OUTDOORS

Lodi Lake Park. Shaded by grand old elms and oaks, the lake's banks are much cooler in summer than other spots in town. You can swim, watch birds, picnic, and rent a kayak, canoe, or pedal boat here. ⊠ *1101 W. Turner Rd., at Mills Ave.* ☎ *209/333–6742* ⊕ *www.lodi.gov/prcs/lodi-lake.html* ⎯ *$5 vehicle entrance fee, $3 public swimming.*

THE GOLD COUNTRY—SOUTH

This hilly region has an old-timey vibe. It's rich with antiques shops, quaint coffee shops, and delightfully appointed Victorian B&Bs.

PLACERVILLE

44 miles east of Sacramento.

It's hard to imagine now, but in 1849 about 4,000 miners staked out every gully and hillside in Placerville, turning the town into a rip-roaring camp of log cabins, tents, and clapboard houses. The area was then known as Hangtown, a graphic allusion to the nature of frontier justice. It took on the name Placerville in 1854 and became an important supply center for the miners. (*Placer* is defined roughly as valuable minerals found in riverbeds or lakes.) Mark Hopkins, Philip Armour, and John Studebaker were among the industrialists who got their starts here. Today Placerville ranks among the hippest towns in the region, its Main Street abuzz with indie shops, coffeehouses, and wine bars, many of them inside rehabbed historic buildings.

12

GETTING HERE AND AROUND

You'll need a car to get to and around Placerville; it's a 45-minute drive from Sacramento via U.S. 50.

EXPLORING

FAMILY **Apple Hill.** During the fall harvest season (September through December), the members of the Apple Hill Growers Association open their orchards and vineyards for apple and berry picking, picnicking, and wine and cider tasting. Start your tour at High Hill Ranch, where there are fishing ponds for kids (they'll clean and pack the fish for you). Nibble on apple doughnuts or buy jewelry from local crafters. Stop at Larsen Apple Barn, a legacy farm. Family-favored Kid's Inc. serves apple pies and empanadas, and you can sample Cabernet and Bordeaux-style blends at Grace Patriot Wines and fresh-pressed juices at Barsotti. Stop at Wofford Acres Vineyard just to see a dramatic view of the American River canyon below. ■TIP→ Traffic on weekends is often backed up, so take the Camino exit or go during the week to avoid the crowds (although kid-centric events are on weekends). ✉ *About 5 miles east of Hwy. 49; take Camino exit from U.S. 50* ☎ *530/644–7692* ⊕ *www.applehill.com.*

FAMILY **Hangtown's Gold Bug Park & Mine.** Take a self-guided tour of this fully lighted mine shaft within a park owned by the City of Placerville. The worthwhile audio tour (included) makes clear what you're seeing. ■TIP→ A shaded stream runs through the park, and there are picnic facilities. ✉ *2635 Goldbug La., off Bedford Ave., 1 mile off U.S. 50* ☎ *530/642–5207* ⊕ *www.goldbugpark.org* ▭ *Park free; mine tour $7.*

WHERE TO EAT AND STAY

$ ✕**The Cozmic Cafe.** Crowds come for healthful wraps, burritos, sandVEGETARIAN wiches, salads, and the like, including vegan and vegetarian options. Portions are big, prices are low, and the ambience is distinctly communal and small town. **Known for:** healthy eats; live music. $ *Average main: $9* ✉ *594 Main St.* ☎ *530/642–8481* ⊕ *www.ourcoz.com* ☾ *Closed Mon.*

$$$$ **Eden Vale Inn.** Handcrafted by the owners, this lavish but rustic B&B
B&B/INN occupies a converted turn-of-the-20th-century hay barn, the center-
FAMILY piece of which is a 27-foot slate fireplace that rises to a sloping roof
Fodor's Choice of timber beams. **Pros:** rooms are exceptionally plush; the patio and
★ grounds are stunning; plenty of places outside for kids to run. **Cons:** expensive for the area, plus two-night minimum on weekends; book summer weekends well in advance. $ *Rooms from: $318* ✉ *1780 Springvale Rd.* ☎ *530/621–0901* ⊕ *www.edenvaleinn.com* ⤴ *7 rooms* ⦿ *Breakfast.*

$$ **Seasons Bed & Breakfast.** One of Placerville's oldest buildings, a gold
B&B/INN stamp mill that dates to 1859, has been transformed into a lovely and relaxing oasis with a main house, cottages, and gardens filled with paintings and sculptures. **Pros:** quiet setting; short walk to downtown; attentive hosts. **Cons:** better for romantics than business travelers. $ *Rooms from: $135* ✉ *2934 Bedford Ave.* ☎ *530/626–4420* ⊕ *www.theseasons.net* ⤴ *3 rooms, 1 cottage* ⦿ *Breakfast.*

SHENANDOAH VALLEY

20 miles south of Placerville.

The most concentrated Gold Country wine-touring area lies in the hills of the Shenandoah Valley, east of Plymouth. Robust Zinfandel is the primary grape grown here, but vineyards here produce plenty of other varietals, from Rhône blends to Italian Barberas and Sangioveses. Most wineries are open for tastings at least on weekend afternoons, and some of the top ones are open daily; several have shaded picnic areas. ■ TIP➜ **This region is gaining steam as a less-congested alternative to the Napa Valley.**

GETTING HERE AND AROUND
Reach the Shenandoah Valley by turning east on Fiddletown Road in Plymouth, between Placerville and Sutter Creek, and then north on Plymouth-Shenandoah Road. You will need a car to explore the valley and its vineyards.

EXPLORING

Shenandoah Vineyards. A plummy Barbera and an almost chocolaty Zinfandel top this winery's repertoire, but for a contrast you can also try a startlingly crisp Sauvignon Blanc. The Tempranillo is also good. An adjacent gallery sells contemporary art, pottery, photographs, and souvenirs. ■ TIP➜ **Shenandoah is affiliated with the nearby Sobon Estate Winery, which has an engaging on-site museum about the area.** ⊠ *12300 Steiner Rd., Plymouth* ☎ *209/245–4455* ⊕ *www.sobonwine. com* ☑ *Tasting $5.*

Terre Rouge and Easton Wines. The winery of Bill Easton and Jane O'Riordan has two labels with two different wine-making styles: Terre Rouge focuses on Rhône-style wines, while Easton covers old-vine Zinfandel and Barbera. The winery has had good results with inky, soft Syrahs and Enigma, a Rhône-style white blend of Marsanne, Viognier, and Roussane. ■ TIP➜ **You can picnic on the shaded patio here and there's a pétanque court nearby.** ⊠ *10801 Dickson Rd., Plymouth* ☎ *209/245–4277* ⊕ *www.terrerougewines.com* ☑ *Tasting $5* ☉ *Closed Tues. and Wed.*

Vino Noceto. Noceto draws raves for its Sangiovese wines which range from light and fruity to rich and heavy. Look for the Little Red Barn, where you'll find welcoming owners Suzy and Jim Gullett offering tastings and tours seven days a week. They also produce small lots of wines from other varietals. ⊠ *11011 Shenandoah Rd., at Dickson Rd., Plymouth* ☎ *209/245–6556* ⊕ *www.noceto.com* ☑ *Tasting free.*

WHERE TO EAT

$$$$
MODERN
AMERICAN
Fodor'sChoice
★

✕ **Taste.** A serendipitous find on the dusty streets of tiny Plymouth, Taste serves eclectic modern dishes made from fresh local fare. Phyllo-wrapped mushroom "cigars" are a small-plate staple, and quail, rack of lamb, and duck confit are examples of chef Mark Berkner's sustainably sourced, creative dishes. **Known for:** fine dining in tiny Plymouth; knowledgeable sommeliers. ⑤ *Average main: $33* ⊠ *9402 Main St., Plymouth* ☎ *209/245–3463* ⊕ *www.restauranttaste.com* ☉ *Closed Wed. No lunch weekdays.*

12

AMADOR CITY

6 miles south of Plymouth.

The history of tiny Amador City (population 200) mirrors the boom-bust-boom cycle of many Gold Country towns. With an output of $42 million in gold, its Keystone Mine was one of the most productive in the Mother Lode. After all the gold was extracted, the miners cleared out, and the area suffered. Amador City now derives its wealth from tourists, who come to browse through its antiques and specialty shops.

GETTING HERE AND AROUND

Park where you can along Old Highway 49 (a bypass diverts Highway 49 traffic around Sutter Creek and Amador City), and walk around.

WHERE TO STAY

$$
B&B/INN
Imperial Hotel. Located on the bend in this one-block town, the whimsically decorated mock-Victorian rooms at this 1879 hotel give a modern twist to the excesses of the Gold Rush. **Pros:** unique history-evoking stay; good restaurant and bar. **Cons:** the hotel and bar are the town nightlife. $ *Rooms from: $130* ⊠ *14202 Old Hwy. 49* ☎ *209/267–9172* ⊕ *www.imperialamador.com* ↪ *9 rooms* ⦿| *Breakfast.*

SUTTER CREEK

2 miles south of Amador City.

Sutter Creek is a charming conglomeration of balconied buildings, Victorian homes, and neo–New England structures. The stores on Main Street (formerly part of Highway 49, which was rerouted) are worth visiting for works by the many local artists and craftspeople.

GETTING HERE AND AROUND

Arrive here by car on Highway 49. There's no public transit, but downtown is walkable. The visitor center organizes walking tours.

ESSENTIALS

Information Sutter Creek Visitor Center. ⊠ *71A Main St.* ☎ *209/267–1344* ⊕ *www.suttercreek.org.*

EXPLORING

Monteverde Store Museum. This store, opened 1896, is a relic from the past: its final owner walked out more than four decades ago and never returned. These days you can peruse what he left behind, including typical wares from a century ago, an elaborate antique scale, and a chair-encircled potbellied stove. ⊠ *3 Randolph St.* ☎ *209/267–0493.*

WHERE TO STAY

$$
HOTEL
FAMILY
Days Inn Sutter Creek. Relative to the cost of boutique inns and bed-and-breakfast hotels in the region, the Days Inn offers a clean, updated place to stay in Gold Country at a reasonable price. **Pros:** easy, especially with families, pets and/or oversized vehicles; clean. **Cons:** you can walk to historic downtown, but sidewalks aren't great. $ *Rooms from: $155* ⊠ *271 Hanford St.* ☎ *209/267–9177* ⊕ *www.wyndhamhotels.com/days-inn/sutter-creek-california/days-inn-sutter-creek/overview* ↪ *52 rooms* ⦿| *Breakfast.*

CLOSE UP

California's Gold Rush

When James W. Marshall burst into John Sutter's Mill on January 24, 1848, carrying flecks of gold in his hat, the millwright unleashed the glittering California gold rush with these immortal words: "Boys, I believe I've found a gold mine!" Before it was over, drowsy San Francisco had become the boomtown of the Golden West, Columbia's mines alone yielded $87,000,000, and California's Mother Lode—a vein of gold-bearing quartz that stretched 150 miles across the Sierra Nevada foothills—had been nearly tapped dry. Even though the gold rush soon became the gold bust, today you can still strike it rich by visiting the historic sites where it all happened. Journey down the Gold Country Highway—a serpentine, nearly 300-milelong two-lane route appropriately numbered 49—to find pure vacation treasure: fascinating Mother Lode towns, rip-roaring mining camps, and historic strike sites. In fact, in Placerville—as the former Hangtown, this spot saw so much new money and crime that outlaws were hanged in pairs—you can still pan the streams.

BOOM TO BUST

From imagination springs adventure, and perhaps no event in the 19th century provoked more wild adventures than the California gold rush of 1848 to 1855. **January 24, 1848:** James W. Marshall spies specks of bright rock in the streambed at his sawmill's site. **May, 1848:** California's coastal communities empty out as prospectors flock to the hills to join the "forty-eighters." **August 19, 1848:** *The New York Herald* is the first East Coast newspaper to report a gold rush in California. **October 13, 1849:** California's state constitution is approved in Monterey. The state's new motto becomes "Eureka!" **1855:** The California gold rush effectively ends, as digging for the precious mineral becomes increasingly difficult, and large corporations monopolize mining operations.

HOW TO PAN FOR GOLD

Grab any non-Teflon-coated pan with sloping sides and head up to "them thar hills." Find a stream—preferably one containing black sand—you can stoop beside, and then scoop out sediment to fill your pan. Add water, then gently shake the pan sideways, back and forth. This allows any gold to settle at the bottom. Pick out and toss away any larger rocks. Keep adding water, keep shaking the pan, and slowly pour the loosened waste gravel over the rim of the pan, making sure not to upend the pan while doing so. If you're left with gold, yell "Eureka!" then put it in a glass container. Your findings may not make you rich, but will entitle you to bragging rights. If you'd rather go with a guide, plenty of attractions and museums in the Gold Country will let you try your hand at prospecting.

$$
B&B/INN
🏠 **Eureka Street Inn.** The lead- and stained-glass windows and the original redwood paneling, wainscoting, and beams—and, oh yes, those gas-log fireplaces in most rooms—lend the Eureka Street Inn a cozy feel. **Pros:** quiet location; lovely porch; engaging owners. **Cons:** two-night stay required at times. $ *Rooms from: $155* ✉ *55 Eureka St.* ☎ *209/267–5500, 800/399–2389* ⊕ *www.eurekastreetinn.com* ➴ *4 rooms* ⏐◯⏐ *Breakfast.*

$$$
B&B/INN
The Foxes Inn of Sutter Creek. The rooms in this 1857 yellow-clapboard house are handsome, with high ceilings, antique beds, and armoires; five have gas fireplaces. **Pros:** lovely inside and out; friendly owners. **Cons:** two-night minimum stay at times. $ *Rooms from: $199* ✉ *77 Main St.* ☎ *209/267–5882, 800/987–3344* ⊕ *www.foxesinn.com* ⇆ *7 rooms* ❍*Breakfast.*

$$$
B&B/INN
Grey Gables Inn. Charming if you like lace and frills, this inn—with rooms named after British poets—brings the English countryside to Gold Country. **Pros:** English-manor feel; tasteful interiors and grounds; complimentary bottle of wine in rooms. **Cons:** adjacent to busy main drag into town; two-night stay required at times. $ *Rooms from: $220* ✉ *161 Hanford St.* ☎ *209/267–1039, 800/473–9422* ⊕ *www.greygables.com* ⇆ *10 rooms* ❍*Breakfast.*

JACKSON

8 miles south of Sutter Creek.

Jackson wasn't the Gold Country's rowdiest town, but the party lasted longer here than most anywhere else: "girls' dormitories" (aka brothels) and nickel slot machines flourished until the mid-1950s. Jackson also had the world's deepest and richest gold mines, the Kennedy and the Argonaut, which together produced $70 million in gold. Most of the miners who worked the lode were of Serbian or Italian origin, and they gave the town a European character that persists to this day. Jackson has pioneer cemeteries whose headstones tell the stories of local Serbian and Italian families. The city's official website (⊕ *ci.jackson.ca.us*; *click on "Visitor Center"*) has great cemetery and walking-tour maps; there are some interesting shops downtown.

GETTING HERE AND AROUND

Arrive by car on Highway 49. You can walk to downtown sights but otherwise will need a car.

EXPLORING

Kennedy Gold Mine. On weekends, docents offer guided surface tours of one of the most prolific mines of the gold-rush era. Exhibits inside the remaining buildings illustrate how the mine used "skips" to lower miners and materials into the mile-long shaft, and to carry ore and tailings to the surface. Plan for 90 minutes to enjoy the guided tour. ✉ *Kennedy Mine Rd., at Argonaut La.* ✛ *½ mile east of Hwy. 49* ☎ *209/223–9542* ⊕ *www.kennedygoldmine.com* 🎫 *Free; guided tours $10.*

Preston Castle. History buffs and ghost hunters regularly make the trip to this fantastically creepy building that was built to house troubled youth in 1894. Having fallen into a state of disrepair, the building is slowly undergoing a full renovation. Tours are available by appointment and on certain Tuesdays and Saturdays (it's best to call ahead to confirm schedule). Ask about evening and overnight tours when tales of paranormal activity are truly spooky. The dramatic Romanesque Revival structure has appeared on TV's *Ghost Hunters,* and during tours of this 156-room building you'll learn all sorts of spine-tingling tales, including one about a student murdering a housekeeper and then

12

rolling her up in a carpet. ⊠ *909 Palm Dr., 12 miles west of Jackson via Hwys. 88 and 104, Ione* ☎ *209/256–3623* ⊕ *www.prestoncastle.com* ⊡ *$15* ☉ *Closed Sept.-Mar.*

WHERE TO EAT AND STAY

$ ✕ **Mel and Faye's Diner.** Since 1956, the Gillman family has been serving
AMERICAN up its famous "Moo Burger" with two patties and special sauce—so
FAMILY big it still makes cow sounds, presumably. Breakfast is available all day
at this homey diner. **Known for:** Moo burgers; milk shakes. ⑤ *Average main: $12* ⊠ *31 Highway 88* ☎ *209/223–0853* ⊕ *www.melandfayes. homestead.com.*

$ ☗ **Hotel Leger.** Dramatically remodeled in 2013 as part of a makeover
HOTEL television show ("Hotel Impossible"), this convivial old saloon and
hotel was a rowdy miners' haunt during the gold rush. **Pros:** rich in
history; friendly and accommodating proprietors. **Cons:** some might
not appreciate the creaky wood floors; rooms above the saloon can
be noisy. ⑤ *Rooms from: $115* ⊠ *8304 Main St., Mokelumme Hill* ☎ *209/286–1401* ⊕ *www.hotelleger.com* ⇥ *13 rooms* ⏇ *No meals.*

ANGELS CAMP

20 miles south of Jackson.

Angels Camp is famous chiefly for its May jumping-frog contest, based
on Mark Twain's short story "The Celebrated Jumping Frog of Calaveras County." The writer reputedly heard the story of the jumping frog
from Ross Coon, proprietor of Angels Hotel, which has been in operation since 1856. It's a favorite destination these days among outdoor
adventurers, who love exploring the subterranean caverns and fishing
for salmon, trout, and bass in the area's crystal clear rivers and lakes.

GETTING HERE AND AROUND

Angels Camp is at the intersection of Highway 49 and Highway 4.
You'll need a car to get here and around.

EXPLORING

FAMILY **Angels Camp Museum.** Learn about Mark Twain's "The Celebrated
Fodor's Choice Jumping Frog of Calaveras County" and check out mining equip-
★ ment and relics from the gold-rush era. The grounds include a carriage
house, little red schoolhouse, and mercantile store. ⊠ *753 S. Main St.* ☎ *209/736–2963* ⊕ *www.angelscampmuseumfoundation.org* ⊡ *$5.*

FAMILY **California Cavern.** A ½-mile subterranean trail winds through large chambers and past underground streams and lakes. There aren't many steps
to climb, but it's a strenuous walk with some narrow passageways and
steep spots. The caverns, at a constant 55°F, contain crystalline formations not found elsewhere, and the 80-minute guided tour explains
local history and geology. ⊠ *9565 Cave City Rd., 9 miles east of San Andreas on Mountain Ranch Rd., then about 3 miles on Cave City Rd., Mountain Ranch* ☎ *209/736–2708* ⊕ *www.caverntours.com* ⊡ *$17.50.*

FAMILY **Moaning Cavern.** For a different sort of underground jewel, wander into
Fodor's Choice an ancient limestone cave, where stalactites and stalagmites, not gold
★ and silver, await you. Take the 235-step spiral staircase built in 1922
into this vast cavern, or more intrepid explorers can rappel into the

chamber—ropes and instruction are provided. Outside there are three zip lines, starting at $45 per person, and a climbing tower. ⊠ *5350 Moaning Cave Rd., off Parrotts Ferry Rd., about 2 miles south of Vallecito, Vallecito* ☎ *209/736–2708* ⊕ *www.caverntours.com* ☜ *$17.50.*

MURPHYS

10 miles northeast of Angels Camp.

Murphys is the Gold Country's most compact, orderly town, with enough shops and restaurants to keep families busy for at least a half day, and more than 20 tasting rooms within walking distance. A well-preserved town of white-picket fences, Victorian houses, and interesting shops, it exhibits an upscale vibe. Horatio Alger and Ulysses S. Grant came through here, staying at what's now called the Murphys Historic Hotel & Lodge when they, along with many other 19th-century tourists, came to investigate the giant sequoia groves in nearby Calaveras Big Trees State Park.

GETTING HERE AND AROUND

Murphys is 10 miles northeast of Highway 49 on Highway 4. You'll need to drive here. Parking can be difficult on summer weekends.

EXPLORING

FAMILY

Fodor's Choice

★

Calaveras Big Tree State Park. The park protects hundreds of the largest and rarest living things on the planet—magnificent giant sequoia redwood trees. Some are 3,000 years old, 90 feet around at the base, and 250 feet tall. There are campgrounds, cabin rentals, and picnic areas; swimming, wading, fishing, and sunbathing on the Stanislaus River are popular in summer. Enjoy the "three senses" trail, designated for the blind, with interpretive signs in braille that guide visitors to touch the bark and encourage children to slow down and enjoy the forest in a more sensory way. ⊠ *Off Hwy. 4, 15 miles northeast of Murphys, 4 miles northeast of Arnold, Angels Camp* ☎ *209/795–2334* ⊕ *www. parks.ca.gov* ☜ *$10 per vehicle.*

Ironstone Vineyards. Tours here take in spectacular gardens and underground tunnels cooled by a waterfall, and include the automated performance of a restored silent-movie-era pipe organ. On display near the tasting room is a 44-pound specimen of crystalline gold. The winery, known for Merlot, Cabernet Sauvignon, and Cabernet Franc, hosts concerts and other events. Its deli has picnic items. ■TIP➜ **Ironstone is worth a visit even if you don't drink wine.** ⊠ *1894 6 Mile Rd.* ✛ *From Jones St. in town, head south on Scott St.* ☎ *209/728–1251* ⊕ *www. ironstonevineyards.com* ☜ *Tasting $5.*

WHERE TO EAT AND STAY

$$

AMERICAN

✕ **Grounds.** From risotto to rib eye, this bustling bistro and coffee shop has something for all palates. Lighter grilled vegetables, chicken, sandwiches, salads, and homemade soups always shine here. **Known for:** potato pancakes at breakfast; carefully curated wine list. ⑤ *Average main: $22* ⊠ *402 Main St.* ☎ *209/728–8663* ⊕ *www.groundsrestaurant. com* ⊙ *No dinner Mon. and Tues.*

12

$$ **Murphys Historic Hotel & Lodge.** This 1855 stone hotel, whose register
HOTEL claims to have seen the signatures of Mark Twain, John Wayne, Susan
B. Anthony, and Ulysses S. Grant is a 19th-century throwback in the
heart of Murphys. **Pros:** historic ambience; great bar; rumors suggest it's
haunted, if you're into that. **Cons:** original building lacks modern ame-
nities; newer building has motel feel; restaurant can be noisy. $ *Rooms
from: $140* ✉ *457 Main St.* ☎ *209/728–3444, 800/532–7684* ⊕ *www.
murphyshotel.com* 🛏 *29 rooms* ❄ *No meals.*

COLUMBIA

14 miles south of Angels Camp.

Columbia is the gateway for Columbia State Historic Park, one of the
Gold Country's most visited sites. The historic Fallon House Theater
is a great place for families to participate in living history activities like
candle dipping and soap making on weekends. There are several inviting
spots for a picnic in the area.

GETTING HERE AND AROUND

The only way to get here is by car, via either Highway 4 (the northern
route) or Highway 49 (the southern) from Angels Camp.

EXPLORING

FAMILY **Columbia State Historic Park.** Columbia is both a functioning community
Fodor's Choice and a historically preserved gold-rush town. Usually you can ride a
★ stagecoach, pan for gold, and watch a blacksmith working at an anvil.
Street musicians perform in summer. Restored or reconstructed build-
ings include a Wells Fargo Express office, a Masonic temple, an old-
fashioned candy store, saloons, a firehouse, churches, a school, and a
newspaper office. At times, all are staffed to simulate a working 1850s
town. The park also includes the must-stop **Historic Fallon House Theater,**
where Broadway-quality shows are performed Wednesday through Sun-
day—Mark Twain once performed in this gorgeous Victorian structure.
The town's two 19th-century historic lodgings, the Fallon Hotel ($) and
City Hotel ($–$$) perch you in the past; to reserve a hotel or cottage
go to *www.reserveamerica.com.* ✉ *11255 Jackson St.* ☎ *209/588–9128*
⊕ *www.parks.ca.gov/columbia* 🆓 *Free.*

SONORA

4 miles south of Columbia.

Miners from Mexico founded Sonora and made it the biggest town in
the Mother Lode. Following a period of racial and ethnic strife, the
Mexican settlers moved on, and Yankees built the commercial city visible today. Sonora's historic downtown section sits atop the Big Bonanza
Mine, one of the richest in the state. Another mine, on the site of nearby
Sonora High School, yielded 990 pounds of gold in a single week in
1879. Reminders of the gold rush are everywhere in Sonora, in prim
Victorian houses, typical Sierra-stone storefronts, and awning-shaded
sidewalks. Reality intrudes beyond the town's historic heart, with strip
malls, shopping centers, and modern motels.

GETTING HERE AND AROUND

Arrive in Sonora by car via Highway 49 (if coming from Columbia, drive south on Parrots Ferry Road). Parking can be difficult on the busy main drag, Washington Street (Highway 49).

EXPLORING

Tuolumne County Museum and History Centers. The small museum occupies a historic gold-rush-era building that served as a jail until 1960. Vintage firearms and paraphernalia, gold specimens, and Me-Wuk baskets are among the many artifacts on display. ⊠ *158 W. Bradford St.* ☎ *209/532–1317* ⊕ *www.tchistory.org* ☒ *Free* ⊗ *Closed Sun.*

WHERE TO EAT AND STAY

$ ✕ **Diamondback Grill and Wine Bar.** The bright decor and refined atmo-
AMERICAN sphere suggest more ambitious fare, but burgers are what this place is about. Locals crowd the tables, especially after 6 pm, for the ground-meat patties, beer-battered onion rings, veggie burgers, and fine wines. **Known for:** half-pound burgers and garlic fries; wine bar and wine club. ⑤ *Average main: $12* ⊠ *93 S. Washington St.* ☎ *209/532–6661* ⊕ *www. thediamondbackgrill.com.*

$$ ⌂ **Barretta Gardens Bed and Breakfast Inn.** Perfect for a romantic get-
B&B/INN away or peaceful escape, this inn's elegant Victorian rooms and three antiques-filled parlors are furnished with period pieces. **Pros:** lovely grounds; delicious breakfasts; great location. **Cons:** only seven rooms. ⑤ *Rooms from: $159* ⊠ *700 S. Barretta St.* ☎ *209/532–6039, 800/206–3333* ⊕ *www.barrettagardens.com* ⌁ *7 rooms* ⦿ *Breakfast.*

JAMESTOWN

4 miles south of Sonora.

Compact Jamestown supplies a touristy view of gold-rush-era life. Shops in brightly colored buildings along Main Street sell antiques and gift items. You can try your hand at panning for gold here or explore a bit of railroad history.

GETTING HERE AND AROUND

Jamestown lies at the intersection of north–south Highway 49 and east–west Highway 108. You'll need a car to tour here.

EXPLORING

FAMILY **Gold Prospecting Adventures.** You'll get a real feel (sort of) for the life of a prospector on the three-hour gold-panning excursions led by this outfit's congenial tour guides. You might even strike gold at the Jim-town Mine. Reservations recommended—call ahead to confirm hours and fees. ⊠ *18170 Main St.* ☎ *209/984–4653, 800/596–0009* ⊕ *www. goldprospecting.com.*

FAMILY **Railtown 1897.** A must for rail enthusiasts and families with kids, this
Fodor'sChoice is one of the most intact early roundhouses (maintenance facilities) in
★ North America. You can hop aboard a steam train for a 40-minute journey—bring along the family dog if you'd like. The docents entertain guests with tales about the history of locomotion. Listen to the original rotor and pulleys in the engine house and take in the smell of axle grease. Walk through a genteel passenger car with dusty-green

12

velvet seats and ornate metalwork, where Grace Kelly and Gary Cooper filmed a scene in the epic Western *High Noon.* You can also climb onto a historic train to see where the fireman once shoveled coal into the tender. ⊠ *18115 5th Ave.* ☎ *209/984–3953* ⊕ *www.railtown1897.org* 🎫 *Roundhouse tour $5; train ride $15.*

WHERE TO STAY

$

RESORT

🏨 **Black Oak Casino Resort.** About 12 miles east of Jamestown off Highway 108, this flashy, contemporary property appeals heavily to casino gamers, but it's also just a nice place to stay with well-outfitted rooms (comfy bedding, down pillows, and alarm clocks with MP3 players) and a central Gold Country location. **Pros:** clean and spacious rooms; plenty of diversions on hand for both kids and adults. **Cons:** must go through smoky casino to reach bowling alley and restaurants; there's nothing quaint or historic about this place. ⑤ *Rooms from: $99* ⊠ *19400 Tuolumne Rd. N, Tuolumne* ☎ *209/928–9300* ⊕ *www.blackoakcasino. com* 🛏 *148 rooms* ❌ *No meals.*

$$

B&B/INN

🏨 **McCaffrey House Bed and Breakfast Inn.** Surrounded by trees on the edge of the Stanislaus National Forest, McCaffrey's appeal lies in its remoteness. **Pros:** rooms outfitted with stoves and Amish quilts; wonderful nearby hiking; romantically remote. **Cons:** too remote for some. ⑤ *Rooms from: $169* ⊠ *23251 Hwy. 108, Twain Harte* ☎ *209/586–0757, 888/586–0757* ⊕ *www.mccaffreyhouse.com* 🛏 *9 rooms* ❌ *Breakfast.*

$$

B&B/INN

🏨 **National Hotel.** In business since 1859, the National has survived the gold rush, gambling, prostitution, at least two fires, a ghost named Flo, and Prohibition, and stands today a well-maintained property with all the authentic character and charm its storied past suggests. **Pros:** feels straight out of a Western movie; authentic character; great brunches. **Cons:** not much happens in town after dark. ⑤ *Rooms from: $140* ⊠ *18183 Main St.* ☎ *209/984–3446,* ⊕ *www.national-hotel.com* 🛏 *9 rooms* ❌ *Breakfast.*

MARIPOSA

50 miles south of Jamestown.

Mariposa marks the southern end of the Mother Lode. Much of the land in this area was part of a 44,000-acre land grant Colonel John C. Fremont acquired from Mexico before gold was discovered and California became a state. Many people stop here on the way to Yosemite National Park, about an hour's drive east on Highway 140.

GETTING HERE AND AROUND

If driving, take Highway 49 or Highway 140. YARTS (⊕ *www.yarts.com*), the regional transit system, can get you to Mariposa from the Central Valley town of Merced (where you can also transfer from Amtrak) or from Yosemite Valley. Otherwise, you'll need a car to get here and around.

EXPLORING

FAMILY

California State Mining and Mineral Museum. A California state park since 1999, the museum has displays on gold-rush history including a replica hard-rock mine shaft to walk through, a miniature stamp mill, and a 13-pound chunk of crystallized gold. ⊠ *5005 Fairground Rd., off Hwy. 49* ☎ *209/742–7625* ⊕ *www.parks.ca.gov* 🎫 *$4.*

Mariposa Museum and History Center. You'll leave this small museum feeling like you just found your own gold nugget. Detailed exhibits, both indoors and out, tell the history of Mariposa County. Visit a replica of a typical miner's cabin; see a working stamp mill; tour the blacksmith shop. Artifacts, photographs, and maps, along with the knowledgeable staff, will capture your imagination and transport you back to 1849. ⊠ *5119 Jessie St.* ☎ *209/966–2924* ⊕ *www.mariposa-museum.com* ☞ *$5.*

WHERE TO EAT

$$

AMERICAN

✕ **Savoury's.** Seafood, pasta, and portobello mushrooms are some of the savory treats that draw high praise from locals at the kind of refined and competent spot that you'd expect in an urban environment, not in mellow Mariposa. Vegetarians and vegans will find lots of options. **Known for:** well-prepared American food from seafood to steak; high-quality food and service. ⑤ *Average main: $20* ⊠ *5034 Hwy. 140* ☎ *209/966–7677* ☉ *Closed Wed. No lunch.*

THE GOLD COUNTRY—NORTH

Gold has had a significant presence along this northern stretch of Highway 49, whose highlights include the bucolic Empire State Historic Park and Coloma, where the discovery of a few nuggets triggered the gold rush.

COLOMA

On Highway 49 between Placerville (8 miles) and Auburn (18 miles).

The California gold rush started in Coloma. "My eye was caught with the glimpse of something shining in the bottom of the ditch," James Marshall recalled. Marshall himself never found any more "color," as gold came to be called.

GETTING HERE AND AROUND

A car is the only practical way to get to Coloma, via Highway 49. Once parked, you can walk to all the worthwhile sights.

EXPLORING

FAMILY

Fodor's Choice

★

Marshall Gold Discovery State Historic Park. Most of Coloma lies within the historic park along the banks of the south fork of the American River. Though crowded with tourists in summer, Coloma hardly resembles the mob scene it was in 1849, when 2,000 prospectors staked out claims along the streambed. The town's population grew to 4,000, supporting seven hotels, three banks, and many stores and businesses. But when reserves of the precious metal dwindled, prospectors left as quickly as they had come. A working reproduction of an 1840s mill lies near the spot where James Marshall first saw gold. Trails lead to the mill, remnants of buildings and mining equipment, and to a statue of Marshall with sublime views. ■TIP➔ **For $7 per person, rangers give gold-panning lessons on the hour, year-round.** ⊠ *310 Back St., off Hwy. 49* ☎ *530/622–3470* ⊕ *www.parks.ca.gov* ☞ *$8 per vehicle.*

AUBURN

18 miles northwest of Coloma; 34 miles northeast of Sacramento.

Located halfway between San Francisco and Reno on Interstate 80, Auburn is enjoying a renaissance buoyed by its central location to many gold-rush sites, outdoor recreation opportunities, and thriving farms and vineyards. The self-proclaimed "endurance capital of the world" is abuzz almost every summer weekend with running, cycling, rafting or kayaking, and equestrian events. Downtown Auburn has its own gold-rush charm with narrow climbing streets, cobblestone lanes, wooden sidewalks, and many original buildings. ■TIP➔ Fresh produce, flowers, baked goods, and gifts are for sale at the farmers' market, held on Saturday morning year-round.

GETTING HERE AND AROUND
Amtrak serves Auburn, though most visitors arrive by car on Highway 49 or Interstate 80. Once downtown, you can tour on foot.

EXPLORING

Bernhard Museum Complex. Party like it's 1889 at this space whose main structure opened in 1851 as the Traveler's Rest Hotel and for 100 years was the residence of the Bernhard family. The congenial docents, dressed in Victorian garb, describe the family's history and 19th-century life in Auburn. ⊠ *291 Auburn–Folsom Rd.* ☎ *530/889–6500* ⊕ *www.placer.ca.gov* ⊠ *Free.*

FAMILY **Gold Rush Museum.** You'll get a feel for life in the mines at this museum whose highlights include a re-created mine tunnel and an indoor gold-panning stream. ⊠ *601 Lincoln Way* ☎ *530/889–6506* ⊠ *Free.*

Placer County Courthouse. Visible from the highway and an easy detour on your drive to or from Lake Tahoe, Auburn's standout structure is the Placer County Courthouse. The classic gold-dome building houses the Placer County Museum, which documents the area's history—Native American, railroad, agricultural, and mining—from the early 1700s to 1900. Look for the Thomas Kinkade original painting and the wall safe housing gold nuggets valued at more than $300,000 today. ⊠ *101 Maple St.* ☎ *530/889–6500* ⊠ *Free.*

WHERE TO EAT AND STAY

$
AMERICAN
FAMILY
✕ **Auburn Alehouse.** This craft brewer serves up the best beer in Gold Country along with decent gastropub fare in this historic American Block building, the centerpiece of Auburn's old town since 1856. Gold Country Pilsner, Old Town Brown, and Hop Donkey Red Ale are all Great American Beer Festival award winners, and you can see them being brewed through glass walls behind the dining area. **Known for:** historic building; award-winning pilsner. $ *Average main: $12* ⊠ *289 Washington St.* ☎ *530/885–2537* ⊕ *www.auburnalehouse.com.*

$
AMERICAN
FAMILY
✕ **Awful Annie's.** One of Auburn's favorite old-time breakfast and lunch spots retains all its old charm in its new home at the north end of town. The breakfast menu is mouthwatering, from "awful" waffles to chili omelets, Bloody Marys, burgers, and sandwiches. **Known for:** best breakfast in the foothills; Grandma's bread pudding. $ *Average main: $10* ⊠ *13460 Lincoln Way* ☎ *530/888–9857* ⊕ *www.awfulannies.com* ☉ *No dinner.*

Almost 6 million ounces of gold were extracted from the Empire Mine.

$$$ ✕**Carpe Vino.** What started as a boutique wine retailer has become a
MODERN must-visit experience for foodies who appreciate chef Eric Alexander's
AMERICAN hearty and imaginative French-inspired dishes and this gem's charming
Fodor's Choice setting, tucked into an old downtown saloon and mine with a hand-
★ some old bar. The sophisticated fare is presented in a nonchalant,
almost effortless way, as if ingredients rolled right from the farm
basket onto your plate. **Known for:** 500 wines, one rock-star chef;
impeccable service; 21-plus only. ⑤ *Average main: $28* ✉ *1568 Lin-
coln Way* ☎ *530/823–0320* ⊕ *www.carpevinoauburn.com* ⊘ *Closed
Sun. and Mon.*

$$ ⌕**Holiday Inn Auburn Hotel.** Above the freeway across from Old Town,
HOTEL this hotel has a welcoming lobby and chain-standard but updated and
FAMILY nice rooms. **Pros:** Auburn's nicest hotel; great base for Gold Country exploring; on-site restaurant. **Cons:** can't walk to Old Town restaurants and shops. ⑤ *Rooms from: $165* ✉ *120 Grass Valley Hwy.*
☎ *530/887–8787, 800/814–8787* ⊕ *www.auburnhi.com* ⇆ *96 rooms*
⦶*No meals.*

GRASS VALLEY

24 miles north of Auburn.

More than half of California's total gold production was extracted from
mines around Grass Valley, including the Empire Mine, which, along
with the North Star Mining Museum, is among the Gold Country's
most fascinating attractions.

12

GETTING HERE AND AROUND

You'll need a car to get here. Take Highway 20 east from Interstate 5 or west from Interstate 80. Highway 49 is the north–south route into town. Gold Country Stage vehicles (☎ 530/477–0103 Weekdays 7–6) serve some attractions. Expect to wait, though.

EXPLORING

FAMILY
Fodor's Choice
★
Empire Mine State Historic Park. Starting with the "secret map" that mine management hid from miners, you can relive the days of gold, grit, and glory, when this mine was one of the biggest and most prosperous hard-rock gold mines in North America. Empire Mine yielded an estimated 5.8 million ounces of gold from 367 miles of underground passages. You can walk into a mine shaft and peer into dark, deep recesses, and almost imagine what it felt like to work this vast operation. Dressed-up docents portraying colorful characters who shaped Northern California's history share stories about the period. The grounds have the exquisite Bourn Cottage (call for tour times), picnic tables, and gentle trails—perfect for a family outing. ⊠ *10791 E. Empire St.* ☎ *530/273–8522* ⊕ *www. empiremine.org* ⊡ *$7.*

Holbrooke Hotel. This landmark hotel ($$) is a Main Street icon. Built in 1851, it hosted entertainer Lola Montez and writer Mark Twain as well as Ulysses S. Grant and other U.S. presidents. The hotel is best appreciated as a sight rather than a lodging option (it begs a renovation) but the restaurant-saloon ($$) is worth a visit as one of the oldest operating west of the Mississippi. ⊠ *212 W. Main St.* ☎ *530/273–1353, 800/933–7077* ⊕ *www.holbrooke.com.*

FAMILY
North Star Mining Museum. Housed in a former powerhouse, the museum displays the 32-foot-high Pelton Water Wheel, said to be the largest ever built. It was used to power mining operations and was a forerunner of the modern turbines that generate hydroelectricity. Hands-on displays are geared to children. You can picnic nearby. ⊠ *10933 Allison Ranch Rd.* ☎ *530/264–7569* ⊕ *www.nevadacountyhistory.org* ⊡ *Donation requested.*

WHERE TO EAT

$
MEXICAN
✕ **Maria's Mexican Restaurant.** The bright adobe walls and the colorful Talavera tile are as welcoming as the fragrance of owner Maria Ramos's fresh-cooked dishes with Mexican chilies, avocado, and garlic. Go for the beef *Chicana,* which includes peppers, tomatoes, and onions; the shredded and sautéed beef has a completely different flavor and texture than beef fajitas. **Known for:** house salsas and sauces; authentic Mexican food; 70 tequilas at the round cantina bar. ⑤ *Average main: $15* ⊠ *226 E. Main St.* ☎ *530/274–2040* ⊕ *www. mariasgrassvalley.com.*

NEVADA CITY

4 miles north of Grass Valley.

Nevada City, once known as the Queen City of the Northern Mines, is the most appealing of the northern Mother Lode towns. The iron-shutter brick buildings that line the narrow downtown streets contain antiques shops, galleries, boutiques, B&Bs, restaurants, and a winery. Horse-drawn-carriage tours add to the romance, as do gas street lamps. At one point in the 1850s, Nevada City had a population of nearly 10,000—enough to support much cultural activity. Today, about 3,000 people live here.

GETTING HERE AND AROUND

You'll need a car to get here. Take Highway 20 east from Interstate 5 or west from Interstate 80. Highway 49 is the north–south route into town. Gold Country Stage vehicles (☎ 530/477–0103 ⊘ *Weekdays 7–6*) serve some attractions.

ESSENTIALS

Visitor Information Nevada City Chamber of Commerce. ✉ *132 Main St.* ☎ *530/265–2692* ⊕ *www.nevadacitychamber.com.*

EXPLORING

Nevada City Winery. For an unassuming winery located in a garage, Nevada City Winery has earned a loyal following for its wine club, the tasting-room ambience, the service team's friendliness, and the quality of its reds—especially Syrah and Zinfandel. ✉ *Miners Foundry Garage, 321 Spring St., at Bridge St.* ☎ *530/265–9463, 800/203–9463* ⊕ *www.ncwinery.com* 🎫 *Tasting and tour free.*

WHERE TO EAT AND STAY

$$$ ✕ **Friar Tuck's.** Popular Friar Tuck's specializes in creative, interactive
EUROPEAN fondues and has an extensive menu of seafood, steaks, and pasta dishes, too. The sparkling interior has a late-19th-century ambience—it's one of Nevada City's best indoor spaces. **Known for:** cheese fondue; rebuilt in 14 months after burning to the ground in 2002; live music nightly. ⑤ *Average main: $27* ✉ *111 N. Pine St.* ☎ *530/265–9093* ⊕ *friartucks. com* ⊘ *No lunch.*

$ ✕ **South Pine Cafe.** Locals flock here for lobster Benedict, chorizo break-
AMERICAN fast tacos, and other dishes that are anything but your ordinary eggs and pancake fare. Imaginative burritos and burgers highlight the lunch menu, and there are plenty of vegan, gluten-free, and organic options, too. **Known for:** creative cooking; homemade muffins all day; vegan and gluten-free options. ⑤ *Average main: $13* ✉ *110 S. Pine St.* ☎ *530/265–0260* ⊕ *www.southpinecafe.com* ⊘ *No dinner.*

$ 🏨 **Outside Inn.** It looks like a typical one-story motel, but Outside Inn
HOTEL offers a variety of unique accommodations inspired by nature or activi-
FAMILY ties in nature (there's a climbing wall in the rock-climbing suite), in an ideal location to enjoy Northern California's four seasons. **Pros:** character and comfort; a fun reinvention of a motel; convenient to trails and hikes. **Cons:** rooms are on the smaller side; a half mile from town. ⑤ *Rooms from: $109* ✉ *575 E. Broad St.* ☎ *530/265–2233* ⊕ *www.outsideinn.com* 🛏 *15 rooms* 🍽 *No meals.*

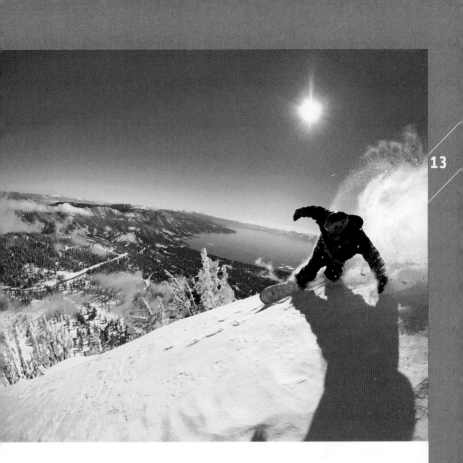

LAKE TAHOE

with Reno, Nevada

WELCOME TO LAKE TAHOE

TOP REASONS TO GO

★ **The lake:** Blue, deep, and alpine pure, Lake Tahoe is far and away the main reason to visit this High Sierra paradise.

★ **Skiing:** Daring black-diamond runs or baby-bunny bumps—whether you're an expert, a beginner, or somewhere in between, the numerous Tahoe-area ski parks abound with slopes to suit your skills.

★ **The great outdoors:** A ring of national forests and recreation areas linked by miles of trails makes Tahoe excellent for nature lovers.

★ **Dinner with a view:** You can picnic lakeside at state parks or dine in restaurants perched along the shore.

★ **A date with lady luck:** Whether you want to roll dice, play the slots, or hope the blackjack dealer goes bust before you do, you'll find round-the-clock gambling at the casinos on the Nevada side of the lake and in Reno.

1 California Side. With the exception of Stateline, Nevada—which, aside from its casino-hotel towers, seems almost indistinguishable from South Lake Tahoe, California—the California side is more developed than the Nevada side. Here you can find both commercial enterprises—restaurants, motels, lodges, ski resorts, residential subdivisions—and public-access facilities, such as historic sites, parks, campgrounds, marinas, and beaches.

2 Nevada Side. You don't need a highway sign to know when you've crossed from California into Nevada: the flashing lights and elaborate marquees of casinos announce legal gambling in garish hues. But you'll find more here than tables and slot machines. Reno, the Biggest Little City in the World, has a vibrant arts scene and a serene downtown Riverwalk. And when you really need to get away from the chip-toting crowds, you can hike through pristine wilderness at Lake Tahoe–Nevada State Park, or hit the slopes near Incline Village.

GETTING ORIENTED

In the northern section of the Sierra Nevada mountain range, the Lake Tahoe area covers portions of four national forests, several state parks, and rugged wilderness areas with names like Desolation and Granite Chief. Lake Tahoe, the star attraction, straddles California and Nevada and is one of the world's largest, clearest, and deepest alpine lakes. The region's proximity to the Bay Area and Sacramento to the west and Reno to the east draws thrill seekers during ski season and again in summer when water sports, camping, and hiking are the dominant activities.

13

TO SACRAMENTO AND
SAN FRANCISCO

80

80

TO
RENO

TO
RENO

Mt. Rose
Summit
8900 ft.

Tahoe
National Forest

Humboldt–
Toiyabe
National Forest

431

Rose
Knob

Donner
Lake

Sugar
Bowl
Ski Resort

Donner
Memorial
State Park

Truckee

267

89

Northstar
California

Washoe
Lake

I-580

395

Kings Beach
State Recreation
Area

Incline Village

2

Tahoe Vista

Carnelian Bay

Kings
Beach

Crystal
Bay

Cedar Flat

28

Crystal Bay

Brockway

Sand Harbor
Beach

Carnelian
Bay

Lake Tahoe
Nevada
State Park

Olympic
Valley

Village at
Squaw Valley

Squaw
Peak

High Camp

Tahoe City

River

Thunderbird
Lodge

Snow Valley
Peak
9,214 ft.

28

C
A
R
S
O
N

R
A
N
G
E

50

Twin
Peaks

89

1

Lake
Tahoe
el 6,229 ft.

C
A
L
I
F
O
R
N
I
A

N
E
V
A
D
A

Glenbrook

50

206

Tahoe Pines

Homewood

Tahoma

Cave Rock

Ed Z'berg
Sugar Pine Point
S.P.

Lakeridge

Genoa Peak
9,150 ft.

Meeks Bay

Skyland

Humboldt–
Toiyabe
National
Forest

Rubicon
Bay

Rubicon
River

Rubicon
Peak

89

D. L. Bliss
State Park

Zephyr
Cove

Genoa

Emerald Bay
State Park

Emerald Bay

Nevada
Beach

Kingsbury

207

South Lake
Tahoe

Stateline

Heavenly
Village/
Gondola

East Peak

207

El Dorado
National
Forest

Fallen Leaf
Lake

Jacks Peak

Pope-Baldwin
Recreation
Area

206

50

89

Meyers

0   5 mi

0   5 km

TO PLACERVILLE
AND SACRAMENTO

Updated by
Daniel Mangin

Whether you swim, fish, sail, or simply rest on its shores, you'll be wowed by the overwhelming beauty of Lake Tahoe, the largest alpine lake in North America. Famous for its cobalt-blue water and surrounding snowcapped peaks, Lake Tahoe straddles the state line between California and Nevada. The border gives this popular Sierra Nevada resort region a split personality. About half its visitors are intent on low-key sightseeing, hiking, camping, and boating. The rest head directly to the Nevada side, where bargain dining, big-name entertainment, and the lure of a jackpot draw them into the glittering casinos.

To explore the lake area and get a feel for its many differing communities, drive the 72-mile road that follows the shore through wooded flatlands and past beaches, climbing to vistas on the rugged southwest side of the lake and passing through busy commercial developments and casinos on its northeastern and southeastern edges. Another option is to actually go out *on* the 22-mile-long, 12-mile-wide lake on a sightseeing cruise or kayaking trip.

The lake, the communities around it, the state parks, national forests, and protected tracts of wilderness are the region's main draws, but other nearby destinations are gaining in popularity. Truckee, with an Old West feel and innovative restaurants, entices visitors looking for a relaxed pace and easy access to Tahoe's north shore and Olympic Valley ski parks. And today Reno, once known only for its casinos, attracts tourists with its buzzing arts scene, downtown riverfront, and campus events at the University of Nevada.

PLANNING

WHEN TO GO

A sapphire-blue lake shimmering deep in the center of an ice-white wonderland—that's Tahoe in winter. But those blankets of snow mean lots of storms that often close roads and force chain requirements on the interstate. In summer the roads are open, but the lake and lodgings are clogged with visitors seeking respite from valley heat. If you don't ski, the best times to visit are early fall—September and October—and late spring. The crowds thin, prices dip, and you can count on Tahoe being beautiful.

Most Lake Tahoe accommodations, restaurants, and even a handful of parks are open year-round, but many visitor centers, mansions, state parks, and beaches are closed from October through May. During those months, winter-sports enthusiasts swamp Tahoe's downhill resorts and cross-country centers, North America's largest concentration of skiing facilities. In summer it's cooler here than in the scorched Sierra Nevada foothills, the clean mountain air is bracingly crisp, and the surface temperature of Lake Tahoe is an invigorating 65°F to 70°F (compared with 40°F to 50°F in winter). This is also the time, however, when it may seem as if every tourist at the lake—100,000 on peak weekends—is in a car on the main road circling the shoreline (especially on Highway 89, just south of Tahoe City; on Highway 28, east of Tahoe City; and on U.S. 50 in South Lake Tahoe). Christmas week and July 4th are the busiest times, and prices go through the roof; plan accordingly.

GETTING HERE AND AROUND

AIR TRAVEL

The nearest airport to Lake Tahoe is Reno–Tahoe International Airport (RNO), in Reno, 50 miles northeast of the closest point on the lake. Airlines serving RNO include Alaska, Allegiant, American, Delta, JetBlue, Southwest, United, and Volaris. Except for Allegiant, these airlines plus Aeromexico and Hawaiian serve Sacramento International Airport (SMF), 112 miles from South Lake Tahoe. North Lake Tahoe Express runs buses ($49 each way) between RNO and towns on the lake's western and northern shores, plus Incline Village, Truckee, Squaw Valley, and Northstar. South Tahoe Airporter runs buses ($29.75 one-way, $53 round-trip) between Reno–Tahoe Airport and resort hotels in the South Lake Tahoe area.

Airport Contacts Reno Tahoe International Airport. ✉ *2001 E. Plumb La., off U.S. 395/I–580, at Reno-Tahoe International Airport Exit, Reno* ☎ *775/328–6400* ⊕ *www.renoairport.com.* **Sacramento International Airport.** ✉ *6900 Airport Blvd., 12 miles northwest of downtown off I–5, Sacramento* ☎ *916/929–5411* ⊕ *www.sacramento.aero/smf.*

Transfer Contacts North Lake Tahoe Express. ☎ *866/216–5222* ⊕ *www.northlaketahoeexpress.com.* **South Tahoe Airporter.** ☎ *775/325–8944, 866/898–2463* ⊕ *southtahoeairporter.com.*

13

BUS TRAVEL

Greyhound stops in San Francisco, Sacramento, Truckee, and Reno. BlueGO ($2 per ride) provides year-round local service in South Lake Tahoe. On the north shore, Tahoe Area Regional Transit (TART; $1.75) operates buses between Tahoma and Incline Village and runs shuttles to Truckee. RTC RIDE buses ($2) serve the Reno area. All local rides require exact change.

In winter, BlueGO provides free ski shuttle service from South Lake Tahoe hotels and resorts to various Heavenly Mountain ski lodge locations. Most of the major ski resorts offer shuttle service to nearby lodging.

Bus Contacts Greyhound. ☎ 800/231–2222 ⊕ www.greyhound.com. **BlueGO.** ☎ 530/541–7149 ⊕ www.tahoetransportation.org/transit/south-shore-services. **RTC RIDE.** ☎ 775/348–7433 ⊕ www.rtcwashoe.com. **Tahoe Area Regional Transit (TART).** ☎ 530/550–1212, 800/736–6365 ⊕ www.placer.ca.gov/departments/works/transit/tart.

CAR TRAVEL

Lake Tahoe is 198 miles northeast of San Francisco, a drive of less than four hours in good weather and light traffic—if possible avoid heavy weekend traffic, particularly leaving the San Francisco area for Tahoe on Friday afternoon and returning on Sunday afternoon. The major route is Interstate 80, which cuts through the Sierra Nevada about 14 miles north of the lake. From there Highway 89 and Highway 267 reach the west and north shores, respectively.

U.S. 50 is the more direct route to the south shore, a two-hour drive from Sacramento. From Reno you can get to the north shore by heading south on U.S. 395/Interstate 580 for 10 miles, then west on Highway 431 for 25 miles. For the south shore, head south on U.S. 395/Interstate 580 through Carson City, and then turn west on U.S. 50 (56 miles total).

The scenic 72-mile highway around the lake is marked Highway 89 on the southwest and west shores, Highway 28 on the north and northeast shores, and U.S. 50 on the east and southeast. Sections of Highway 89 sometimes close during snowy periods, usually at Emerald Bay because of avalanche danger, which makes it impossible to complete the circular drive around the lake. Interstate 80, U.S. 50, and U.S. 395/Interstate 580 are all-weather highways, but there may be delays while snow is cleared during major storms.

Interstate 80 is a four-lane freeway; much of U.S. 50 is only two lanes with no center divider. Carry tire chains from October through May, or rent a four-wheel-drive vehicle. Most rental agencies do not allow tire chains to be used on their vehicles; ask when you book.

Contacts California Highway Patrol. ☎ 530/577–1001 South Lake Tahoe ⊕ www.chp.ca.gov. **Caltrans Current Highway Conditions.** ☎ 800/427–7623 ⊕ www.dot.ca.gov. **Nevada Department of Transportation Road Information.** ☎ 877/687–6237 ⊕ nvroads.com. **Nevada Highway Patrol.** ☎ 775/687–5300 ⊕ nhp.nv.gov.

TRAIN TRAVEL

Amtrak's cross-country rail service makes stops in Truckee and Reno. Amtrak also operates several buses daily between Reno and Sacramento to connect with coastal train routes.

Train Contact Amtrak. ☎ *800/872–7245* ⊕ *www.amtrak.com.*

RESTAURANTS

On weekends and in high season, expect a long wait at the more popular restaurants. And expect to pay resort prices almost everywhere. During the "shoulder seasons" (from April to May and September to November), some places may close temporarily or limit their hours, so call ahead. Also, check local papers for deals and discounts during this time, especially two-for-one coupons. Many casinos use their restaurants to attract gamblers. Marquees often tout "$8.99 prime rib dinners" or "$4.99 breakfast specials." Some of these meals are downright lousy and they are usually available only in the coffee shops and buffets, but at those prices, it's hard to complain. The finer restaurants in casinos deliver pricier food, as well as reasonable service and a bit of atmosphere. Unless otherwise noted, even the most expensive area restaurants welcome customers in casual clothes. *Restaurant reviews have been shortened. For full information, visit Fodors.com.*

HOTELS

Quiet inns on the water, suburban-style strip motels, casino hotels, slope-side ski lodges, and house and condo rentals throughout the area constitute the lodging choices at Tahoe. The crowds come in summer and during ski season; reserve as far in advance as possible, especially for holiday periods when prices skyrocket. Spring and fall give you a little more leeway and lower—sometimes significantly lower, especially at casino hotels—rates. Check hotel websites for the best deals.

Head to South Lake Tahoe for the most activities and the widest range of lodging options. Heavenly Village in the heart of town has an ice rink, cinema, shops, fine-dining restaurants, and simple cafés, plus a gondola that will whisk you up to the ski park. Walk two blocks south from downtown, and you can hit the casinos.

Tahoe City, on the west shore, has a small-town atmosphere and is accessible to several nearby ski resorts. A few miles northwest of the lake, Squaw Valley USA has its own self-contained upscale village, an aerial tram to the slopes, and numerous outdoor activities once the snow melts.

Looking for a taste of Old Tahoe? The north shore with its woodsy backdrop is your best bet, with Carnelian Bay and Tahoe Vista on the California side. And across the Nevada border are casino resorts where Hollywood's glamour-stars once romped. *Hotel reviews have been shortened. For full information, visit Fodors.com.*

WHAT IT COSTS				
	$	$$	$$$	$$$$
Restaurants	under $16	$16–$22	$23–$30	over $30
Hotels	under $120	$120–$175	$176–$250	over $250

Restaurant prices are the average cost of a main course at dinner or, if dinner is not served, at lunch. Hotel prices are the lowest cost of a standard double room in high season.

OUTDOORS AND BACKCOUNTRY TIPS

If you're planning to spend any time outdoors around Lake Tahoe, whether hiking, climbing, skiing, or camping, be aware that weather conditions can change quickly in the Sierra. To avoid hypothermia, always bring a pocket-size, fold-up rain poncho (available in all sporting-goods stores) to keep you dry. Wear long pants and a hat. Carry plenty of water. Because you'll likely be walking on granite, wear sturdy, closed-toe hiking boots, with soles that grip rock. If you're going into the backcountry, bring a signaling device (such as a mirror), emergency whistle, compass, map, energy bars, and water purifier. When heading out alone, tell someone where you're going and when you expect to return.

If you plan to ski, be aware of resort elevations. In the event of a winter storm, determine the snow level before you choose the resort you'll ski. Often the level can be as high as 7,000 feet, which means rain at some resorts' base areas but snow at others.

BackCountry, in Truckee, operates an excellent website with current information about how and where to (and where not to) ski, mountain bike, and hike in the backcountry around Tahoe. The store also stocks everything from crampons to transceivers. For storm information, check the National Weather Service's website; for ski conditions, visit ⊕ *onthesnow.com*. For reservations at campgrounds in California state parks, contact Reserve California. If you plan to camp in the backcountry of the national forests, you'll need to purchase a wilderness permit, which you can pick up at the forest service office or at a ranger station at any forest entrance. If you plan to ski the backcountry, check the U.S. Forest Service's recorded information for conditions.

Contacts and Information BackCountry. ⊠ *11400 Donner Pass Rd., at Meadow Way, Truckee* ☎ *530/582–0909 Truckee* ⊕ *www.thebackcountry.net.* **National Weather Service.** ⊕ *www.wrh.noaa.gov/rev.* **OntheSnow.com.** ⊕ *www.onthesnow.com/california/skireport.html.* **Reserve California.** ⊕ *www. reservecalifornia.com.* **U.S. Forest Service.** ⊠ *Office, 35 College Dr., South Lake Tahoe* ☎ *530/543–2600 general backcountry information, 530/587–3558 backcountry information recording after office hours* ⊕ *www.fs.usda.gov/ltbmu.*

SKIING AND SNOWBOARDING

The mountains around Lake Tahoe are bombarded by blizzards throughout most winters and sometimes in fall and spring; 10- to 12-foot bases are common. Indeed, the Sierras often have the deepest snowpack on the continent, but because of the relatively mild temperatures over the Pacific, falling snow can be very heavy and wet—it's nicknamed "Sierra Cement" for a reason. The upside is that you can sometimes ski and board as late as May (snowboarding is permitted at all Tahoe ski areas). The major resorts get extremely crowded on weekends. If you're going to ski on a Saturday, arrive early and quit early. Avoid moving with the masses: eat at 11 am or 1:30 pm, not noon. Also consider visiting the ski areas with few high-speed lifts or limited lodging and real estate at their bases: Alpine Meadows, Sugar Bowl, Homewood, Mt. Rose, Sierra-at-Tahoe, Diamond Peak, and Kirkwood. And to find out the true ski conditions, talk to waiters and bartenders—most of them are ski bums.

The Lake Tahoe area is also a great destination for Nordic skiers. Cross-country skiing at the resorts can be costly, but you get the benefits of machine grooming and trail preparation. If it's bargain Nordic you're after, take advantage of thousands of acres of public forest and parkland trails.

TOURS

Lake Tahoe Balloons. Take a hot-air balloon flight over the lake from mid-May through mid-October with this company that launches and lands its balloons on a boat. The four-hour excursion begins shortly after sunrise and ends with a traditional champagne toast. ⊠ *Tahoe Keys Marina, at end of Venice Dr. East, South Lake Tahoe* ☎ *530/544–1221, 800/872–9294* ⊕ *www.laketahoeballoons.com* ✉ *From $295* ☞ *From $299.*

MS Dixie II. The 520-passenger *MS Dixie II*, a stern-wheeler, sails year-round from Zephyr Cove to Emerald Bay on sightseeing and dinner cruises. ⊠ *Zephyr Cove Marina, 760 U.S. Hwy. 50, near Church St., Zephyr Cove* ☎ *775/589–4906, 800/238–2463* ⊕ *www.zephyrcove.com/cruises* ✉ *From $51* ☞ *$59.*

North Lake Tahoe Ale Trail. The concept of these great self-guided tours is simple: bike or walk one of North Lake Tahoe's dozens of fantastic trails, then reward yourself with a craft brew (or two) at an ale house near the end of the trail you choose. A dedicated website has an interactive map, descriptions, and short videos pairing trails and drinking spots. There are also suggestions for paddleboarders and kayakers. ⊕ *www.gotahoenorth.com/things/north-lake-tahoe-ale-trail.*

Sierra Cloud. From May to September, the *Sierra Cloud*, a 41-passenger catamaran, departs from the Hyatt Regency beach at Incline Village and cruises the north and east shore areas. ⊠ *Hyatt Regency Lake Tahoe, 111 Country Club Dr., Incline Village* ☎ *775/831–4386* ⊕ *www.awsincline.com* ✉ *From $65* ☞ *$80.*

Tahoe Gal. Docked in Tahoe City this old-style 120-passenger paddlewheeler departs daily from June through September and on some days in May on brunch, lunch, happy hour, and sunset tours of Emerald Bay and Lake Tahoe's north and west shores. Specialty excursions include ones with live music or other entertainment. ⚠ **Closed October–April and some days in May.** ⊠ *Departures from Lighthouse Center, 952 N. Lake Blvd., Tahoe City* ☎ *800/218–2464* ⊕ *www.tahoegal.com* ✉ *From $28.*

Tahoe Boat Cruises. From mid-May to mid-October, this company offers barbecue lunch, happy-hour, sunset, and champagne cruises (from $50) aboard the *Safari Rose*, an 80-foot-long wooden motor yacht. Shuttle-bus pick-up service is available. ⊠ *Departures from Ski Run Marina, 900 Ski Run Blvd., South Lake Tahoe* ☎ 888/867–6394 ⊕ *www.tahoecruises.com* ✍ *From $34.*

Fodor'sChoice ★ **Thunderbird Lodge Cruise & Tour.** From mid-May to mid-October, the captain of the *Tahoe*, a classic wooden boat, takes passengers on an east shore cruise whose highlights are a walking tour and picnic lunch at the Thunderbird Lodge, a historic mansion. ⊠ *Departures from Zephyr Cove Pier, 760 U.S. 50, Zephyr Cove* ☎ 775/230–8907 ⊕ *www.cruise-tahoe.com/public-cruises* ✍ *$139.*

VISITOR INFORMATION

Contacts Go Tahoe North. ☎ *530/581–6900, 888/434–1262* ⊕ *www.gotahoenorth.com.* **Visit Lake Tahoe South.** ☎ *775/588–5900, 800/288–2463* ⊕ *tahoesouth.com.*

THE CALIFORNIA SIDE

The most hotels, restaurants, ski resorts, and state parks are on the California side of the lake, but you'll also encounter the most congestion and developed areas.

SOUTH LAKE TAHOE

60 miles south of Reno, 198 miles northeast of San Francisco.

The city of South Lake Tahoe's raison d'être is tourism: the casinos of adjacent Stateline, Nevada; the ski slopes at Heavenly Mountain; the beaches, docks, bike trails, and campgrounds all around the south shore; and the backcountry of Eldorado National Forest and Desolation Wilderness. Less appealing are the strip malls, old-school motels, and low-rise prefab buildings lining U.S. 50, the city's main drag. Although in recent years a few jazzed-up motels and new boutique hotels have joined a few longtime high-quality inns, many places provide little more than basic accommodation. The small city's saving grace is its convenient location, bevy of services, and gorgeous lake views.

GETTING HERE AND AROUND

The main route into and through South Lake Tahoe is U.S. 50; signs say "Lake Tahoe Boulevard" in town. Arrive by car or, if coming from Reno airport, take the South Tahoe Express bus. BlueGO operates daily bus service in the south shore area year-round, plus a ski shuttle from the large hotels to Heavenly Mountain Resort in the winter.

ESSENTIALS

Visitor Information Visit Lake Tahoe South. ⊠ *Visitor Center, 169 U.S. Hwy. 50, at Kingsbury Grade, Stateline* ☎ *775/588–5900, 800/288–2463* ⊕ *tahoe-south.com* ⊠ *Visitor Center, 3066 Lake Tahoe Blvd., at San Francisco Ave.* ☎ *530/541–5255* ⊕ *tahoesouth.com.*

13

EXPLORING

FAMILY
Fodor's Choice
★

Heavenly Gondola. Whether you ski or not, you'll appreciate the impressive view of Lake Tahoe from the Heavenly Gondola. Its eight-passenger cars travel from Heavenly Village 2.4 miles up the mountain in 15 minutes. When the weather's fine, you can take one of three hikes around the mountaintop and then have lunch at Tamarack Lodge. ⊠ *4080 Lake Tahoe Blvd.* ☎ *775/586–7000, 800/432–8365* ⊕ *www. skiheavenly.com* ⊠ *$52.*

Heavenly Village. This lively complex at the base of the Heavenly Gondola has good shopping, an arcade for kids, a cinema, a brewpub, a skating rink in winter, miniature golf in summer, and the Loft for magic shows and other live entertainment. Base Camp Pizza Co., Azul Latin Kitchen, and Kalani's for seafood stand out among the several restaurants. ⊠ *1001 Heavenly Village Way, at U.S. 50* ⊕ *www.theshopsatheavenly.com.*

WHERE TO EAT

$$
MEDITERRANEAN

✕ **Artemis Lakefront Cafe.** A festive marina restaurant with a heated outdoor patio, Artemis reveals its Greek influences in breakfast dishes like baklava French toast and gyros and egg pita wraps. All day, though, the menus encompass more familiar options (eggs Benedict in the morning, burgers and grilled mahi mahi later on). **Known for:** heated outdoor patio; many Greek-influenced menu items; festive atmosphere. ⑤ *Average main: $19* ⊠ *900 Ski Run Blvd.* ☎ *530/542–3332* ⊕ *www. artemislakefrontcafe.com.*

$$
ECLECTIC

✕ **Blue Angel Café.** A favorite of locals, who fill the dozen or so wooden tables, this cozy spot with Wi-Fi serves basic sandwiches and salads along with internationally inspired dishes like chipotle shrimp tacos and Thai curry. On cold days warm up with wine or an espresso in front of the stone fireplace. **Known for:** varied menu; locals' hangout; easy-going staff. ⑤ *Average main: $17* ⊠ *1132 Ski Run Blvd., at Larch Ave.* ☎ *530/544–6544* ⊕ *www.blueangelcafe.com.*

$$$$
ECLECTIC
Fodor's Choice
★

✕ **Evan's American Gourmet Cafe.** Its excellent service, world-class cuisine, and superb wine list make this intimate restaurant the top choice for high-end dining in South Lake. Inside a converted cabin, Evan's serves creative American cuisine that includes catch-of-the-day seafood offerings and meat dishes such as rack of lamb marinated with rosemary and garlic and served with raspberry demi-glace. **Known for:** intimate atmosphere; world-class cuisine; superb wine list. ⑤ *Average main: $33* ⊠ *536 Emerald Bay Rd., Hwy. 89, at 15th St.* ☎ *530/542–1990* ⊕ *evanstahoe.com* ☾ *No lunch.*

$$$$
ASIAN

✕ **Kalani's at Lake Tahoe.** Fresh-off-the-plane seafood gets delivered from the Honolulu fish market to Heavenly Village's sleekest (and priciest) restaurant. The white-tablecloth dining room is decked out with carved bamboo, a burnt-orange color palette, and a modern-glass sculpture, all of which complement contemporary Pacific Rim specialties such as melt-from-the-bone baby-back pork ribs with sesame-garlic soy sauce. **Known for:** fresh Hawaiian seafood; inventive and traditional sushi combinations; upscale setting. ⑤ *Average main: $36* ⊠ *1001 Heavenly Village Way, #26, at U.S. 50* ☎ *530/544–6100* ⊕ *www.kalanis.com.*

$ | **✕ My Thai Cuisine.** Fantastic flavors and gracious owners have earned
THAI | this humble roadside restaurant the loyalty of Tahoe residents and regular visitors. The aromatic dishes include crab pad Thai, basil lamb, sizzling shrimp, and numerous curries. **Known for:** many vegetarian options; lunch specials a steal; lively atmosphere. $ *Average main: $14* ⊠ *2108 Lake Tahoe Blvd., ¼-mile north of "Y" intersection of U.S. 50 and Hwy. 89* ☎ *530/544–3232* ⊕ *www.thairestaurant-southlaketahoe.com.*

$$$ | **✕ Nepheles Restaurant.** The mood is low-key but the California cuisine
AMERICAN | is outstanding at this small white-tablecloth restaurant inside an old cabin. Start with escargots or herb crab cakes with Thai chili aioli before moving on to one of several creative salads—perhaps the fruit and Gorgonzola on a mesclun mix—and an entrée like elk medallions, shrimp pasta, or grilled portobello stuffed with ratatouille. **Known for:** chef with a deft touch; house-baked breads; full bar, good wine list. $ *Average main: $25* ⊠ *1169 Ski Run Blvd.* ☎ *530/544–8130* ⊕ *www.nepheles.com.*

$$ | **✕ Scusa! Italian Ristorante** This longtime favorite turns out big plates of
ITALIAN | veal scallopine, chicken piccata, and garlicky linguine with clams—straightforward Italian-American food (and lots of it), served in an intimate dining room warmed by a crackling fire on many nights. There's an outdoor patio that's open in warm weather. **Known for:** intimate dining room; outdoor patio; classic Italian-American food. $ *Average main: $22* ⊠ *2543 Lake Tahoe Blvd., at Sierra Blvd.* ☎ *530/542–0100* ⊕ *www.scusalaketahoe.com* ⊘ *No lunch.*

$ | **✕ Sprouts Natural Foods Cafe.** If it's in between normal mealtimes and
AMERICAN | you're hungry for something healthful, head to this order-at-the-counter
Fodor's Choice | café for salads, overstuffed wraps, hot sandwiches, homemade vegan
★ | soups, all-day breakfasts, and the best smoothies in town. Dine at wooden tables in the cheery contemporary indoor space or out front on the patio, or just order food to go. **Known for:** fresh, healthy cuisine; vegan and vegetarian friendly; congenial staff. $ *Average main: $9* ⊠ *3123 Harrison Ave., U.S. 50 at Alameda Ave.* ☎ *530/541–6969* ⊕ *www.sproutscafetahoe.com* ▭ *No credit cards.*

WHERE TO STAY

$$ | **Base Camp South Lake Tahoe.** This spunky three-floor boutique hotel
HOTEL | near the Heavenly Gondola, Stateline casinos, and several good res-
Fodor's Choice | taurants provides solid value in a hip yet family-friendly setting. **Pros:**
★ | convenient location; great for groups; cool public spaces include rooftop hot tub with mountain views. **Cons:** communal dinners won't appeal to all travelers; near a busy area; not on the lake. $ *Rooms from: $169* ⊠ *4143 Cedar Ave., off U.S. 50* ☎ *530/208–0180* ⊕ *www.basecamptahoesouth.com* ⇗ *74 rooms* ⎮◎⎮ *Breakfast.*

$$$ | **Black Bear Lodge.** The rooms and cabins at this well-appointed inn fea-
B&B/INN | ture 19th-century American antiques, fine art, and fireplaces; cabins also
Fodor's Choice | have kitchenettes. **Pros:** near Heavenly skiing; within walking distance
★ | of good restaurants; good for groups. **Cons:** no room service; lacks big-hotel amenities; social types may find setting too sedate. $ *Rooms from: $199* ⊠ *1202 Ski Run Blvd.* ☎ *530/544–4451* ⊕ *www.tahoeblackbear.com* ⇗ *9 rooms* ⎮◎⎮ *Breakfast.*

$$$
HOTEL

🏨 **Hotel Azure.** Across the road from a beach, the former Inn by the Lake began 2017 totally revamped (to the tune of $3.5 million), as a high-end motel meets boutique hotel. **Pros:** clean, spacious rooms; good work spaces and tech amenities; short drive to Heavenly Mountain. **Cons:** on busy Lake Tahoe Boulevard; no bell or room service; some sound bleed-through from room to room. $ *Rooms from: $180* ✉ *3300 Lake Tahoe Blvd.* ☎ *530/542–0330, 800/877–1466* ⊕ *www.hotelazuretahoe.com* 🛏 *99 rooms* ❀ *No meals.*

$$$
RESORT

🏨 **Marriott's Grand Residence and Timber Lodge.** You can't beat the location of these two gigantic, modern condominium complexes right at the base of Heavenly Gondola, smack in the center of town. **Pros:** central location; great for families; near excellent restaurants. **Cons:** can be jam-packed on weekends; no room service; lacks serenity. $ *Rooms from: $200* ✉ *1001 Heavenly Village Way* ☎ *530/542–8400 Marriott's Grand Residence, 800/845–5279, 530/542–6600 Marriott's Timber Lodge* ⊕ *www.marriott.com* 🛏 *431 rooms* ❀ *No meals.*

$$
RESORT

🏨 **Sorensen's Resort.** Escape civilization by staying in a log cabin at this woodsy 165-acre resort within the Eldorado National Forest, 20 minutes south of town. **Pros:** gorgeous, rustic setting; on-site restaurant; outdoor activities. **Cons:** nearest nightlife is 20 miles away; lacks amenities of larger properties; basic furnishings. $ *Rooms from: $135* ✉ *14255 Hwy. 88, Hope Valley* ☎ *530/694–2203, 800/423–9949* ⊕ *www.sorensensresort.com* 🛏 *36 rooms* ❀ *No meals.*

NIGHTLIFE

Most of the area's nightlife is concentrated in the casinos over the border in Stateline. To avoid slot machines and blinking lights, try the California-side nightspots in and near Heavenly Village.

BARS

The Loft. Crowd-pleasing magic shows and other entertainment, DIY s'mores, and a casual-industrial setting keep patrons happy at this Heavenly Village bar and lounge where kids aren't out of place. The mood is upbeat, the specialty cocktails are potent, and if you're in the mood for dinner the kitchen turns out Italian fare more tasty than one might expect at such a venue. ✉ *1001 Heavenly Village Way* ☎ *530/523–8024* ⊕ *www.thelofttahoe.com.*

Mc P's Taphouse & Grill. You can hear live bands—rock, jazz, blues, alternative—on most nights at Mc P's while you sample a few of the 40 beers on draft. Lunch and dinner (pub grub) are served daily. ✉ *4125 Lake Tahoe Blvd., Ste A, near Friday Ave.* ☎ *530/542–4435.*

SPORTS AND THE OUTDOORS
FISHING

Tahoe Sport Fishing. One of the area's largest and oldest fishing-charter services offers morning and afternoon trips. Outings include all necessary gear and bait, and the crew cleans and packages your catch. ✉ *900 Ski Run Blvd., off U.S. 50* ☎ *530/541–5448, 800/696–7797 in CA* ⊕ *www.tahoesportfishing.com* 🎣 *From $110.*

13

HIKING

Desolation Wilderness. Trails within the 63,960-acre wilderness lead to gorgeous backcountry lakes and mountain peaks. It's called Desolation Wilderness for a reason, so bring a topographic map and compass, and carry water and food. You need a permit for overnight camping (877/444–6777). In summer you can access this area by boarding a boat taxi ($14 one-way) at **Echo Chalet** (*9900 Echo Lakes Rd., off U.S. 50, 530/659–7207, www.echochalet.com*) and crossing Echo Lake. The Pacific Crest Trail also traverses Desolation Wilderness. ⊠ *El Dorado National Forest Information Center* ☎ *530/644–2349* ⊕ *www.fs.usda.gov/eldorado.*

ICE-SKATING

FAMILY **Heavenly Village Outdoor Ice Rink.** If you're here in winter, practice your jumps and turns at this rink between the gondola and the cinema. ⊠ *1001 Heavenly Village Way* ☎ *530/542–4230* ⊕ *www.theshopsathe-eavenly.com* ⌨ *$22, includes skate rental.*

South Lake Tahoe Ice Arena. For year-round fun, head to this NHL regulation–size indoor rink where you can rent equipment and sign up for lessons. *Hrs vary; call or check website for public skate times.* ⊠ *1176 Rufus Allen Blvd.* ☎ *530/544–7465* ⊕ *tahoearena.com* ⌨ *$15; includes skate rental.*

KAYAKING

Kayak Tahoe. Sign up for lessons and excursions (to the south shore, Emerald Bay, and Sand Harbor), offered from May through September. You can also rent a kayak and paddle solo on the lake. ⊠ *Timber Cove Marina, 3411 Lake Tahoe Blvd., at Balbijou Rd.* ☎ *530/544–2011* ⊕ *www.kayaktahoe.com* ⌨ *From $40.*

MOUNTAIN BIKING

Tahoe Sports Ltd. You can rent road and mountain bikes and get tips on where to ride from the friendly staff at this full-service sports store. ⊠ *Tahoe Crescent V Shopping Center, 4000 Lake Tahoe Blvd., Suite 7* ☎ *530/542–4000* ⊕ *www.tahoesportsltd.com.*

SKIING

If you don't want to pay the high cost of rental equipment at the resorts, you'll find reasonable prices and expert advice at Tahoe Sports Ltd. *(Mountain Biking, above).*

Fodor's Choice **Heavenly Mountain Resort.** Straddling two states, vast Heavenly Moun-
★ tain Resort—composed of nine peaks, two valleys, and four base-lodge areas, along with the largest snowmaking system in the western United States—pairs terrain for every skier with exhilarating Tahoe Basin views. Beginners can choose wide, well-groomed trails, accessed from the California Lodge or the gondola from downtown South Lake Tahoe; kids have short and gentle runs in the Enchanted Forest area all to themselves. The Sky Express high-speed quad chair whisks intermediate and advanced skiers to the summit for wide cruisers or steep tree-skiing. Mott and Killebrew canyons draw experts to the Nevada side for steep chutes and thick-timber slopes. For snowboarders and tricksters, there are five different terrain parks.

The ski school is big and offers everything from learn-to-ski packages to canyon-adventure tours. Call about ski and boarding camps. Skiing lessons are available for children ages four and up; there's day care for infants older than six weeks. Summertime thrill seekers participate in Epic Discovery—fun for the whole family that includes a mountain coaster, zip lines, a climbing wall, ropes courses, hiking opportunities, and a learning center. **Facilities:** 97 trails; 4,800 acres; 3,427-foot vertical drop; 30 lifts ⌧ *Ski Run Blvd., off U.S. 50* ☎ *775/586–7000, 800/432–8365* ⊕ *www.skiheavenly.com* ✉ *Lift ticket $137.*

Hope Valley Outdoors. Operating from a yurt at Pickett's Junction, Hope Valley provides lessons and equipment rentals to prepare you for cross-country skiing and snowshoeing. The outfit has more than 60 miles of trails through Humboldt–Toiyabe National Forest, about 10 of which are groomed. ⌧ *Hwy. 88, at Hwy. 89, Hope Valley* ☎ *530/721–2015* ⊕ *www.hopevalleycrosscountry.com.*

Kirkwood Ski Resort. Thirty-six miles south of Lake Tahoe, Kirkwood is the hard-core skiers' and boarders' favorite south-shore mountain, known for its craggy gulp-and-go chutes, sweeping cornices, steep-aspect glade skiing, and high base elevation. But there's also fantastic terrain for newbies and intermediates down wide-open bowls, through wooded gullies, and along rolling tree-lined trails. Families often head to the Timber Creek area, a good spot to learn to ski or snowboard. Tricksters can show off in two terrain parks on jumps, wall rides, rails, and a half-pipe, all visible from the base area. The mountain normally gets hammered with more than 600 inches of snow annually, and often has the most in all of North America. If you're into out-of-bounds skiing, check out Expedition Kirkwood, a backcountry-skills program that teaches basic safety awareness. Kirkwood is also the only Tahoe resort to offer Cat-skiing. If you're into cross-country, the resort has 80 km (50 miles) of superb groomed-track skiing, with skating lanes, instruction, and rentals. Nonskiers can snowshoe, snow-skate, and go dogsledding or snow-tubing. The children's ski school has programs for ages 3 to 12. **Facilities:** 87 trails; 2,300 acres; 1,100-foot vertical drop; 15 lifts. ⌧ *1501 Kirkwood Meadows Dr., off Hwy. 88, 14 miles west of Hwy. 89, Kirkwood, Kirkwood* ☎ *800/967–7500 information, 209/258–7248 cross-country, 209/258–7293 lodging information, 209/258–7332 snow phone* ⊕ *www.kirkwood.com* ✉ *Lift ticket $107.*

Sierra-at-Tahoe. Wind-protected and meticulously groomed slopes, excellent tree-skiing, and gated backcountry skiing are among the draws at this low-key but worthy resort. Extremely popular with snowboarders, Sierra has several terrain parks, including Halfpipe, with 18-foot walls and a dedicated chairlift. For beginners, Sierra-at-Tahoe has more than 100 acres of learning terrain, and there's a snow-tubing hill. **Facilities:** 46 trails; 2,000 acres; 2,250-foot vertical drop; 14 lifts. ⌧ *1111 Sierra-at-Tahoe Rd., 12 miles from South Lake Tahoe off U.S. 50, past Echo Summit, Twin Bridges* ☎ *530/659–7453 information, 530/659–7475 snow phone* ⊕ *www.sierraattahoe.com* ✉ *Lift ticket $101.*

POPE-BALDWIN RECREATION AREA

5 miles west of South Lake Tahoe.

To the west of downtown South Lake Tahoe, U.S. 50 and Highway 89 come together, forming an intersection nicknamed "the Y." If you head northwest on Highway 89, also called Emerald Bay Road, and follow the lakefront, commercial development gives way to national forests and state parks. One of these is Pope-Baldwin Recreation Area.

GETTING HERE AND AROUND

The entrance to the Pope-Baldwin Recreation Area is on the east side of Emerald Bay Road. The area is closed to vehicles in winter, but you can cross-country ski here.

EXPLORING

Tallac Historic Site. At this site you can stroll or picnic lakeside year-round, and then in late spring and summer you can also explore three historic estates. The **Pope House** is the magnificently restored 1894 mansion of George S. Pope, who made his money in shipping and lumber and played host to the business and cultural elite of 1920s America. The **Baldwin Museum** is in the estate that once belonged to entrepreneur "Lucky" Baldwin; today it houses a collection of family memorabilia and Washoe Indian artifacts. The **Valhalla** (*valhallatahoe.com*), with a spectacular floor-to-ceiling stone fireplace, belonged to Walter Heller. Its Grand Hall and a lakeside boathouse, refurbished as a theater, host summertime concerts, plays, and cultural activities. Docents conduct tours of the Pope House in summer; call for tour times. ⊠ *Hwy. 89* ☎ *530/541–5227 late May–mid-Sept., 530/543–2600 year-round* ⊕ *tahoeheritage.org* 🎫 *Free, summer guided site walk $5, Pope House tour $10* ⊗ *House and museum closed late Sept.–late May.*

FAMILY **Taylor Creek Visitor Center.** At this center operated by the U.S. Forest Service you can visit the site of a Washoe Indian settlement; walk self-guided trails through meadow, marsh, and forest; and inspect the Stream Profile Chamber, an underground display with windows right into Taylor Creek. In fall you may see spawning kokanee salmon digging their nests. In summer Forest Service naturalists organize discovery walks and evening programs. ⊠ *Hwy. 89, 3 miles north of junction with U.S. 50* ☎ *530/543–2674 late May–Oct., 530/543–2600 year-round* ⊕ *www.fs.usda.gov/recarea/ltbmu/recarea/?recid=11785* 🎫 *Free.*

EMERALD BAY STATE PARK

4 miles west of Pope-Baldwin Recreation Area.

You can hike, bike, swim, camp, scuba dive, kayak, or tour a lookalike Viking castle at this state park. Or you can simply enjoy the most popular tourist stop on Lake Tahoe's circular drive: the high cliff overlooking Emerald Bay, famed for its jewel-like shape and color.

GETTING HERE AND AROUND

The entrance to Emerald Bay State Park is on the east side of a narrow, twisting section of Highway 89. Caution is the key word for both drivers and pedestrians. The park is closed to vehicles in winter.

Fjord-like Emerald Bay is possibly the most scenic part of Lake Tahoe.

EXPLORING

Fodor's Choice
★

Emerald Bay. A massive glacier millions of years ago carved this 3-mile-long and 1-mile-wide fjordlike inlet. Famed for its jewel-like shape and colors, the bay surrounds Fannette, Tahoe's only island. Highway 89 curves high above the lake through Emerald Bay State Park; from the Emerald Bay lookout, the centerpiece of the park, you can survey the whole scene. This is one of the don't-miss views of Lake Tahoe. The light is best in mid- to late morning, when the bay's colors really pop. ⊠ *Hwy. 89, 20 miles south of Tahoe City* ☎ *530/525–7232* ⊕ *www. parks.ca.gov* ✉ *$10 parking fee.*

Vikingsholm. This 38-room estate was completed in 1929 and built as a precise copy of a 1,200-year-old Viking castle, using materials native to the area. Its original owner, Lora Knight, furnished it with Scandinavian antiques and hired artisans to build period reproductions. The sod roof sprouts wildflowers each spring. There are picnic tables nearby and a gray-sand beach for strolling. A steep 1-mile-long trail from the Emerald Bay lookout leads down to Vikingsholm, and the hike back up is hard (especially if you're not yet acclimated to the elevation), although there are benches and stone culverts to rest on. At the 150-foot peak of Fannette Island are the ruins of a stone structure known as the Tea House, built in 1928 so that Knight's guests could have a place to enjoy afternoon refreshments after a motorboat ride. The island is off-limits from February through mid-June to protect nesting Canada geese. The rest of the year it's open for day use. ⊠ *Hwy. 89* ☎ *530/525–7232* ⊕ *www.vikingsholm.com* ✉ *Day-use parking fee $10; mansion tour $10* ☉ *Closed late Sept.–late May.*

SPORTS AND THE OUTDOORS
HIKING
Eagle Falls. To reach these falls, leave your car in the parking lot of the Eagle Falls picnic area (near Vikingsholm; arrive early for a good spot), and walk up the short but fairly steep canyon nearby. You'll have a brilliant panorama of Emerald Bay from this spot near the boundary of Desolation Wilderness. For a strenuous full-day hike, continue 5 miles, past Eagle Lake, to Upper and Middle Velma Lakes. Pick up trail maps at Taylor Creek Visitor Center in summer, or year-round at the main U.S. Forest Service Office in South Lake Tahoe, at 35 College Drive. ⊠ *Hwy. 89, South Lake Tahoe.*

D.L. BLISS STATE PARK

3 miles north of Emerald Bay State Park, 17 miles south of Tahoe City.

This park shares six miles of shoreline with adjacent Emerald Bay State Park, and has two white-sand beaches. Hike the Rubicon Trail for stunning views of the lake.

GETTING HERE AND AROUND
The entrance to D.L. Bliss State Park is on the east side of Highway 89 just north of Emerald Bay. No vehicles are allowed in when the park is closed for the season.

EXPLORING
D.L. Bliss State Park. This park takes its name from Duane LeRoy Bliss, a 19th-century lumber magnate. At one time Bliss owned nearly 75% of Tahoe's lakefront, along with local steamboats, railroads, and banks. The park shares 6 miles of shoreline with Emerald Bay State Park; combined the two parks cover 1,830 acres, 744 of which the Bliss family donated to the state. At the north end of Bliss is Rubicon Point, which overlooks one of the lake's deepest spots. Short trails lead to an old lighthouse and Balancing Rock, which weighs 250,000 pounds and balances on a fist of granite. The 4.5-mile Rubicon Trail—one of Tahoe's premier hikes—leads to Vikingsholm and provides stunning lake views. Two white-sand beaches front some of Tahoe's warmest water. ⊠ *Hwy. 89* ☎ *530/525–3345, 800/777–0369* ⊕ *www.parks.ca.gov* ⊠ *$10 per vehicle, day use.*

ED Z'BERG SUGAR PINE POINT STATE PARK

8 miles north of D. L. Bliss State Park, 10 miles south of Tahoe City.

Visitors love to hike, swim, and fish here in the summer, but this park is also popular in winter, when a small campground remains open. Eleven miles of cross-country ski and snowshoe trails allow beginners and experienced enthusiasts alike to whoosh through pine forests and glide past the lake.

GETTING HERE AND AROUND
The entrance to Sugar Pine Point is on the east side of Highway 89, about a mile south of Tahoma. A bike trail links Tahoe City to the park.

EXPLORING

Hellman-Ehrman Mansion. The main attraction at Sugar Pine Point State Park is Ehrman Mansion, a 1903 stone-and-shingle summer home furnished in period style. In its day it was the height of modernity, with electric lights and complete indoor plumbing. Also in the park are a trapper's log cabin from the mid-19th century, a nature preserve with wildlife exhibits, a lighthouse, the start of the 10-mile biking trail to Tahoe City, and an extensive system of hiking and cross-country skiing trails. If you're feeling less ambitious, you can relax on the sun-dappled lawn behind the mansion and gaze out at the lake. ⊠ *Hwy. 89* ☎ *530/525–7982 mansion in season, 530/525–7232 year-round* ⊕ *www.parks.ca.gov* ⌑ *$10 per vehicle, day use; mansion tour $10.*

Ed Z'Berg Sugar Pine Point State Park. Named for a state lawmaker who sponsored key conservation legislation, Lake Tahoe's largest state park has 2,000 acres of dense forests and nearly 2 miles of shore frontage. A popular spot during snow season, Sugar Pine provides 11 miles of cross-country trails and winter camping on a first-come, first-served basis. Rangers lead full-moon snowshoe tours from January to March. ⊠ *Hwy. 89, 1 mile south of Tahoma* ☎ *530/525–7982, 530/525–7232 year-round* ⊕ *www.parks.ca.gov* ⌑ *$10 per vehicle, day use.*

TAHOMA

1 mile north of Ed Z'berg Sugar Pine Point State Park, 23 miles south of Truckee.

With its rustic waterfront vacation cottages, Tahoma exemplifies life on the lake in its quiet early days before bright-lights casinos and huge crowds proliferated. In 1960 Tahoma was host of the Olympic Nordic-skiing competitions. Today there's little to do here except stroll by the lake and listen to the wind in the trees, making it a favorite home base for mellow families and nature buffs.

GETTING HERE AND AROUND

Approach Tahoma by car on Highway 89, called West Lake Boulevard in this section. From the northern and western communities, take a TART bus to Tahoma. A bike trail links Tahoe City to Tahoma.

WHERE TO STAY

$$$

B&B/INN

Tahoma Meadows B&B Cottages. With sixteen individually decorated little red cottages sitting beneath towering pine trees, it's hard to beat this serene property for atmosphere and woodsy charm. **Pros:** lovely setting; good choice for families; close to Homewood ski resort. **Cons:** far from the casinos; may be too serene for some guests; old-style decor. ⓢ *Rooms from: $199* ⊠ *6821 W. Lake Blvd.* ☎ *530/525–1553, 866/525–1553* ⊕ *www.tahomameadows.com* ⇄ *16 rooms* ⏐◎⏐ *Breakfast.*

SPORTS AND THE OUTDOORS

SKIING

Homewood Mountain Resort. Schuss down these slopes for fantastic views—the mountain rises across the road from the Tahoe shoreline. This small, usually uncrowded resort is the favorite area of locals on a snowy day, because you can find lots of untracked powder. It's also the most protected and least windy Tahoe ski area during a storm; when every other resort's lifts are on wind hold, you can almost always count on Homewood's to be open. There's only one high-speed chairlift, but there are rarely any lines, and the ticket prices are some of the cheapest around—kids 5 to 12 ski for $24, and those four and under are free. The resort may look small as you drive by, but most of it isn't visible from the road. **Facilities:** 64 trails; 2,010 acres; 1,625-foot vertical drop; 8 lifts. ⊠ *5145 W. Lake Blvd., Hwy. 89, 6 miles south of Tahoe City, Homewood* ☎ *530/525–2992 information, 530/525–2900 snow phone* ⊕ *www.skihomewood.com* ⬚ *Lift ticket $59.*

TAHOE CITY

9 miles north of Tahoma, 14 miles south of Truckee.

Tahoe City is the only lakeside town with a charming downtown area good for strolling and window-shopping. Stores and restaurants are all within walking distance of the Outlet Gates, where water is spilled into the Truckee River to control the surface level of the lake.

GETTING HERE AND AROUND
Tahoe City is at the junction of Highway 28, also called North Lake Boulevard, and Highway 89 where it turns northwest toward Squaw Valley and Truckee. TART buses serve the area.

ESSENTIALS
Visitor Information Go Tahoe North. ☎ *530/581–6900, 888/434–1262* ⊕ *www.gotahoenorth.com.*

EXPLORING
Gatekeeper's Museum. This museum preserves a little-known part of the region's history. Between 1910 and 1968 the gatekeeper who lived on this site was responsible for monitoring the level of the lake, using a winch system (still used today and visible just outside the museum) to keep the water at the correct level. Also here, the fantastic Marion Steinbach Indian Basket Museum displays intricate baskets from 85 tribes. ⊠ *130 W. Lake Blvd.* ☎ *530/583–1762* ⊕ *www.northtahoemuseums. org* ⬚ *$5* ☉ *Closed Mon.–Wed. early-Sept.–late May.*

WHERE TO EAT
$
ECLECTIC

✕ **Cafe Zenon.** Straightforward Vietnamese pho noodle soup is served all day at chef Suzanne Nguyen's restaurant at Tahoe City's public golf course, but she also prepares everything from poutine and kimchi hot dogs to pork and green beans. The Vietnamese French Dip, a local favorite, substitutes pho broth for the traditional beef. **Known for:** classic Vietnamese dishes; mushroom skillet with a fried egg for weekend breakfast; golf course setting (skating rink in winter). ⑤ *Average main: $11* ⊠ *251 N. Lake Blvd.* ☎ *530/583–1517* ⊕ *www.cafezenon. com* ☉ *Closed Mon.–Tues. No breakfast weekdays.*

$$$$
AMERICAN
Fodor's Choice
★

✕ **Christy Hill.** Huge windows reveal stellar lake views at this Euro–Cal restaurant serving seafood, beef, and vegetarian entrées, along with small plate offerings. The extensive wine list and exceptionally good desserts earn accolades, as do the gracious service and casual vibe. **Known for:** Euro–Cal menu; romantic choice; dinner on the deck.

$ *Average main: $31* ✉ *115 Grove St., at N. Lake Blvd.* ☎ *530/583–8551* ⊕ *www.christyhill.com* ⊗ *No lunch.*

$ ✕ **Fire Sign Café.** There's often a wait for breakfast and lunch at this great
AMERICAN little diner 2 miles south of Tahoe City, but it's worth it. The pastries
are made from scratch, the salmon is smoked in-house, the salsa is hand
cut, and there's real maple syrup for the many types of pancakes and
waffles. **Known for:** pastries from scratch; many pancakes and waffles;
fruit cobbler. $ *Average main: $11* ✉ *1785 W. Lake Blvd., at Fountain
Ave.* ☎ *530/583–0871* ⊕ *www.firesigncafe.com* ⊗ *No dinner.*

$$$$ ✕ **Wolfdale's.** Consistent, inspired cuisine makes Wolfdale's one of the
ECLECTIC top restaurants on the lake, albeit among the most expensive as well.
The imaginative entrées, many involving seafood, merge Asian and
European cooking, and everything from teriyaki glaze to smoked fish
is made in-house. **Known for:** imaginative entrées; lake view; elegantly
simple dining room. $ *Average main: $33* ✉ *640 N. Lake Blvd., near
Grove St.* ☎ *530/583–5700* ⊕ *www.wolfdales.com* ⊗ *Closed Tues.
No lunch.*

WHERE TO STAY

$$ 🛏 **Basecamp Tahoe City.** A downtown motel for the 21st century,
B&B/INN Basecamp charms its guests with a combination of industrial, retro,
FAMILY and rustic styles. **Pros:** lively public spaces; stylish rooms; passion-
Fodor's Choice ate staff. **Cons:** some road noise; lacks amenities of large properties;
★ 8-minute walk to local beach. $ *Rooms from: $149* ✉ *955 N. Lake
Blvd.* ☎ *530/580–8430* ⊕ *www.basecamptahoecity.com* ⟿ *24 rooms*
⦿| *Breakfast.*

$$ 🛏 **Cottage Inn.** Avoid the crowds by staying in one of these charm-
B&B/INN ing circa-1938 log cottages under the towering pines on the lake's
west shore. **Pros:** romantic, woodsy setting; each room has a fireplace; full breakfast. **Cons:** no kids under 12; weak Wi-Fi; old-school
decor. $ *Rooms from: $150* ✉ *1690 W. Lake Blvd.* ☎ *530/581–4073,
800/581–4073* ⊕ *www.thecottageinn.com* ⟿ *22 rooms* ⦿| *Breakfast.*

$$ 🛏 **Granlibakken Tahoe.** A condo community with its own snow-play
RESORT area in winter, this secluded 74-acre resort's name means "a hillside
sheltered by fir trees" in Norwegian. **Pros:** fitness and wellness orienta-
tion; secluded location; pool and spa treatments. **Cons:** some guests find
the location too secluded; more for families than romantic interludes;
conference activities and weddings. $ *Rooms from: $160* ✉ *725 Gran-
libakken Rd.* ☎ *530/583–4242 front desk, 800/543–3221 reservations*
⊕ *granlibakken.com* ⟿ *165 rooms* ⦿| *Breakfast.*

$$$ 🛏 **Sunnyside Steakhouse and Lodge.** The views are superb and the hos-
HOTEL pitality gracious at this lakeside lodge three miles south of Tahoe City.
Fodor's Choice **Pros:** complimentary Continental breakfast and afternoon tea; most
★ rooms have balconies overlooking the lake; lively bar and restaurant.
Cons: can be pricey for families; can be noisy in summer; pricey entrées
at steak house. $ *Rooms from: $200* ✉ *1850 W. Lake Blvd., Box 5969*
☎ *530/583–7200, 800/822–2754* ⊕ *www.sunnysideresort.com* ⟿ *23
rooms* ⦿| *Breakfast.*

SPORTS AND THE OUTDOORS

RAFTING

FAMILY **Truckee River Rafting.** In summer you can take a self-guided raft trip down a gentle 5-mile stretch of the Truckee River. This outfitter will shuttle you back to Tahoe City at the end of your two- to three-hour trip. On a warm day, this makes a great family outing. ✉ *175 River Rd., near W. Lake Blvd.* ☎ *530/583–1111* ⊕ *www.truckeeriverrafting.com* ⊠ *From $35.*

SKIING

Fodor'sChoice **Alpine Meadows Ski Area.** With an average 450 inches of snow annually,
★ Alpine has some of Tahoe's most reliable conditions. It's usually one of the first areas to open in November and one of the last to close in May or June. Alpine isn't the place for show-offs; instead, you'll find down-to-earth alpine fetishists. The two peaks here are well suited to intermediate skiers, with a number of runs for experts only. Snowboarders and hot-dog skiers will find a terrain park with a super-pipe, rails, and tabletops, as well as a boarder-cross course. Alpine is a great place to learn to ski and has a ski school that coaches those with physical and mental disabilities. On Saturday, because of the limited parking, there's more acreage per person than at other resorts. Lift tickets are good at neighboring Squaw Valley; a free shuttle runs all day between the two ski parks. **Facilities:** 100 trails; 2,400 acres, 1,802-foot vertical drop; 13 lifts. ✉ *2600 Alpine Meadows Rd., off Hwy. 89, 6 miles northwest of Tahoe City and 13 miles south of Truckee* ☎ *530/583–4232, 800/403–0206* ⊕ *www.squawalpine.com* ⊠ *Lift ticket $114.*

Tahoe Dave's Skis and Boards. You can rent skis, boards, and snowshoes at this shop, which has the area's best selection of downhill rental equipment. ✉ *590 N. Lake Blvd.* ☎ *530/583–6415* ⊕ *www.tahoedaves.com.*

OLYMPIC VALLEY

7 miles north of Tahoe City to Squaw Valley Road; 8½ miles south of Truckee.

Olympic Valley got its name in 1960, when Squaw Valley USA, the ski resort here, hosted the Winter Olympics. Snow sports remain the primary activity, but once summer comes, you can hike into the adjacent Granite Chief Wilderness, explore wildflower-studded alpine meadows, or lie by a swimming pool in one of the Sierra's prettiest valleys.

GETTING HERE AND AROUND

Squaw Valley Road, the only way into Olympic Valley, branches west off Highway 89 about 8 miles south of Truckee. TART connects the Squaw Valley ski area with the communities along the north and west shores, and Truckee, with year-round public transportation. Squaw Valley Ski Resort provides a free shuttle to many stops in those same areas.

EXPLORING

High Camp. You can ride the Squaw Valley Aerial Tram to this activity hub, which at 8,200 feet commands superb views of Lake Tahoe and the surrounding mountains. In summer, go for a hike, sit by the pool, or have a cocktail and watch the sunset. In winter you can ski, ice-skate, snow-tube, or go for a full-moon snowshoe hike. There's also a restaurant, a

Squaw Valley USA has runs for skiers of all ability levels, from beginner to expert trails.

lounge, and a small Olympic museum. Pick up trail maps at the tram building. ✉ *Aerial Tram Bldg., Squaw Valley* ☎ *800/403–0206* ⊕ *www. squawalpine.com/events-things-do/aerial-tram-rides* 🚠 *Aerial Tram, $44.*

FAMILY **Village at Squaw Valley.** The centerpiece of Olympic Valley is a pedestrian mall at the base of several four-story ersatz Bavarian stone-and-timber buildings, where you'll find restaurants, high-end condo rentals, boutiques, and cafés. ✉ *1750 Village East Rd.* ☎ *530/584–1000, 800/403–0206 information, 800/731–8021 condo reservations* ⊕ *www. squawalpine.com/explore/about/squaw-valley-village-map.*

WHERE TO EAT

$ ✕ **Fireside Pizza Company.** Adults might opt for the signature pear and
PIZZA Gorgonzola pizza at this modern Italian restaurant, but most kids
FAMILY clamor for the house favorite: an Italian-sausage-and-pepperoni combo with a bubbly blend of four cheeses. Salads and pasta dishes round out the menu at this family-friendly spot. **Known for:** inventive pizzas; good, inexpensive dining option in a pricey area; family friendly. $ *Average main: $15* ✉ *The Village at Squaw Valley, 1985 Squaw Valley Rd., #25* ☎ *530/584–6150* ⊕ *www.firesidepizza.com.*

$$$ ✕ **Graham's of Squaw Valley.** Sit by a floor-to-ceiling river-rock hearth
ECLECTIC under a knotty-pine peaked ceiling in this well-run restaurant's intimate dining room. The southern European–inspired menu changes often, but expect hearty entrées such as grilled beef tenderloin with wild mushroom sauce, along with lighter-fare small plates like quail with fig demi-glace or tasty crab salad. **Known for:** hearty entrées, small plates; highly regarded wine list; fireside bar for appetizers. $ *Average main: $30* ✉ *Christy Inn Lodge, 1650 Squaw Valley Rd.* ☎ *530/581–0454* ☉ *Closed Mon. and Tues. No lunch.*

$$$$ ✕ **PlumpJack Cafe.** The menu at this chic restaurant for serious foodies
AMERICAN changes seasonally, but look for rib-eye steak in a green peppercorn
Fodor'sChoice demi glace, seared diver scallops with toasted Israeli cous cous, and
★ inventive vegetarian dishes. Rather than complicated, heavy sauces,
the chef uses simple reductions to complement a dish. **Known for:** chic
setting; clean, dynamic flavors; varied, reasonably priced wines. $ *Average main: $39* ✉ *1920 Squaw Valley Rd.* ☎ *530/583–1578* ⊕ *www.
plumpjackcafe.com* ☽ *No lunch (except at bar).*

WHERE TO STAY

$$$ ⬚ **PlumpJack Squaw Valley Inn.** Stylish and luxurious, this two-story,
HOTEL cedar-sided inn has a snappy, sophisticated look and laid-back sensi-
Fodor'sChoice bility, perfect for the Bay Area cognoscenti who flock here on week-
★ ends. **Pros:** small and intimate; loaded with amenities; personable and
attentive service. **Cons:** not the best choice for families with small
children; not all rooms have tubs; laid-back sensibility may not work
for some guests. $ *Rooms from: $225* ✉ *1920 Squaw Valley Rd.*
☎ *530/583–1576, 800/323–7666* ⊕ *www.plumpjacksquawvalleyinn.
com* ⬅ *56 rooms* ⦿⊙ *Breakfast.*

$$$$ ⬚ **Resort at Squaw Creek.** This multi-facility Squaw Valley resort offers
RESORT a plethora of year-round activities. **Pros:** every conceivable amenity;
private chairlift to Squaw Valley USA for ski-in, ski-out; attractive fur-
nishings. **Cons:** so large it can feel impersonal; high in-season rates; a
lot of hubbub during ski season. $ *Rooms from: $279* ✉ *400 Squaw
Creek Rd.* ☎ *530/583–6300, 800/327–3353* ⊕ *www.squawcreek.com*
⬅ *405 rooms* ⦿⊙ *No meals.*

$$$ ⬚ **The Village at Squaw Valley USA.** Right at the base of the slopes, at
HOTEL the center point of Olympic Valley, the Village's condominiums (from
studio to three bedrooms) come complete with gas fireplaces, daily
maid service, and heated slate-tile bathroom and kitchen floors. **Pros:**
family-friendly; near Village restaurants and shops; at base of slopes.
Cons: claustrophobia-inducing crowds on weekends; nicely appointed
but not high style. $ *Rooms from: $199* ✉ *1750 Village East Rd.*
☎ *530/584–1000, 888/259–1428* ⊕ *www.squawalpine.com/lodging*
⬅ *198 rooms* ⦿⊙ *No meals.*

SPORTS AND THE OUTDOORS
GOLF
Resort at Squaw Creek Golf Course. For beautiful views of Squaw Valley's
surrounding peaks, play this narrow, challenging championship course
designed by Robert Trent Jones, Jr. The design emphasizes accuracy
over distance, especially on the front nine. All fees include a golf cart
plus valet parking; rates drop after noon and again after 3 pm. ✉ *400
Squaw Creek Rd.* ☎ *530/583–6300, 530/581–6637 pro shop* ⊕ *www.
destinationhotels.com/squawcreek/recreation* ⬚ *$89 weekdays; $99
weekends* ⸙ *18 holes, 6,931 yards, par 71.*

ICE-SKATING
FAMILY **Olympic Ice Pavilion.** Ice-skate here from late November to early March.
A ride up the mountain in the Aerial Tram costs $44, plus $14 for
skate rental and one hour of skate time. In summer the pavilion converts into a roller-skating rink. Year-round, you get fabulous views

of the lake and the Sierra Nevada. ⊠ *1960 Squaw Valley Rd., High Camp, Squaw Valley* ☎ *800/403–0206* ⊕ *www.squawalpine.com/ events-things-do/ice-skating.*

SKIING

Fodor's Choice
★
Squaw Valley USA. Known for some of the toughest skiing in the Tahoe area, this park was the centerpiece of the 1960 Winter Olympics. Today it's the definitive North Tahoe ski resort and among the top-three megaresorts in California (the other two are Heavenly and Mammoth). Although Squaw has changed significantly since the Olympics, the skiing is still world-class and extends across vast bowls stretched between six peaks. Experts often head directly to the untamed terrain of the infamous KT-22 face, which has bumps, cliffs, and gulp-and-go chutes, or to the nearly vertical Palisades, where many famous extreme-skiing films have been shot. Fret not, beginners and intermediates: you have plenty of wide-open, groomed trails at High Camp (which sits at the *top* of the mountain) and around the more challenging Snow King Peak. Snowboarders and show-off skiers can tear up the five fantastic terrain parks, which include a giant super-pipe. Ski passes are good at neighboring Alpine Meadows; free shuttles run all day between the two ski parks. **Facilities:** 170 trails; 3,600 acres; 2,850-foot vertical drop; 29 lifts. ⊠ *1960 Squaw Valley Rd., off Hwy. 89, 7 miles northwest of Tahoe City* ☎ *800/731–8021 lodging reservations, 530/452–4355 snow phone, 800/403–0206 information* ⊕ *www.squawalpine.com* ⊠ *Lift ticket $124.*

Tahoe Dave's Skis and Boards. If you don't want to pay resort prices, you can rent and tune downhill skis and snowboards at this shop. ⊠ *3039 Hwy. 89, at Squaw Valley Rd.* ☎ *530/583–5665* ⊕ *www.tahoedaves.com.*

TRUCKEE

13 miles northwest of Kings Beach, 14 miles north of Tahoe City.

Formerly a decrepit railroad town in the mountains, Truckee is now the trendy first stop for many Tahoe visitors. The town was officially established around 1863, and by 1868 it had gone from a stagecoach station to a major stopover for trains bound for the Pacific via the new transcontinental railroad. Every day, freight trains and Amtrak's *California Zephyr* still idle briefly at the depot in the middle of town. The visitor center inside the depot has a walking-tour map of historic Truckee.

Across from the station, where Old West facades line the main drag, you'll find galleries, gift shops, boutiques, a wine-tasting room, old-fashioned diners, and several good restaurants.

GETTING HERE AND AROUND
Truckee is off Interstate 80 between highways 89 and 267. Greyhound and Amtrak stop here, and TART buses serve the area.

ESSENTIALS
Visitor Information Truckee Donner Chamber of Commerce and the California Welcome Center. ⊠ *Amtrak depot, 10065 Donner Pass Rd., near Spring St.* ☎ *530/587–8808 chamber of commerce, 866/443–2027 welcome center* ⊕ *www.truckee.com.*

EXPLORING

Donner Memorial State Park and Emigrant Trail Museum. The park and museum commemorate the 89 members of the Donner Party, westward-bound pioneers who became trapped in the Sierra in the winter of 1846–47 in snow 22 feet deep. Barely more than half survived, some by resorting to cannibalism. The absorbing Emigrant Trail Museum in the visitor center contains exhibits about the Donner Party, regional Native Americans, and railroad and transportation development in the area. In the park, you can picnic, hike, camp, and go boating, fishing, and waterskiing in summer; winter brings cross-country skiing and snowshoeing on groomed trails. ✉ *12593 Donner Pass Rd., off I–80, 2 miles west of Truckee* ☎ *530/582–7892 museum* ⊕ *www.parks.ca.gov* 🚗 *$10 parking, day use ($5 in winter).*

WHERE TO EAT

$$$
ECLECTIC
Fodor'sChoice
★

✕ **Cottonwood Restaurant & Bar.** Perched above town on the site of North America's first chairlift, this local institution has a bar decked out with old wooden skis, sleds, skates, and photos of Truckee's early days. The ambitious menu includes grilled steak, baby-back short ribs with honey-chipotle barbecue sauce, and butternut-squash raviolis with sage brown butter—plus fresh-baked breads and desserts. **Known for:** local institution; ambitious menu; hilltop views. ⑤ *Average main: $26* ✉ *10142 Rue Hilltop Rd., off Brockway Rd., ¼ mile south of downtown* ☎ *530/587–5711* ⊕ *www.cottonwoodrestaurant.com* ☾ *No lunch.*

$$
AMERICAN

✕ **FiftyFifty Brewing Company.** In this Truckee brewpub the warm red tones and comfy booths, plus a pint of the Donner Party porter (or a shot of bourbon), will take the nip out of a cold day on the slopes. The menu includes salads, burgers, inventive pizzas, barbecued ribs, pan-seared salmon, and the house specialty, a pulled-pork sandwich. **Known for:** inventive pizzas; pulled-pork sandwich; après-ski action. ⑤ *Average main: $20* ✉ *11197 Brockway Rd., near Martis Valley Rd.* ☎ *530/587–2337* ⊕ *www.fiftyfiftybrewing.com.*

$
AMERICAN
Fodor'sChoice
★

✕ **Marty's Cafe.** You'd never know from this café's laid-back decor that the namesake owner-chef's resume includes stints at fancy restaurants from Beverly Hills to Kennebunkport. Marty's hearty breakfasts (like the house-made granola or the fried egg sandwich with bacon and Gruyère on toasted French bread) and lunches—burgers, hoagies, "char dogs," sloppy joes, and a winning chicken and avocado BLT—are served from opening until closing. **Known for:** hearty breakfasts and lunches served all day; daily specials and seasonal salads; ebullient hospitality. ⑤ *Average main: $14* ✉ *10115 Donner Pass Rd.* ☎ *530/550–8208* ⊕ *martyscafetruckee.com* ☾ *No dinner.*

$$$
ECLECTIC

✕ **Moody's Bistro, Bar & Beats.** Head here for contemporary-Cal cuisine in a sexy dining room with pumpkin-color walls, burgundy velvet banquettes, and art-deco fixtures. The earthy, sure-handed cooking features organically grown ingredients: look for ahi poke, snazzy pizzas bubbling-hot from a brick oven, braised lamb shanks, pan-roasted wild game, fresh seafood, and organic beef. **Known for:** lighter fare for lunch; summer alfresco dining; live music in bar some nights. ⑤ *Average main: $25* ✉ *10007 Bridge St., at Donner Pass Rd.* ☎ *530/587–8688* ⊕ *www.moodysbistro.com.*

$$$ ✕ **Pianeta Ristorante.** A town favorite for a decade-plus, Pianeta serves high-
ITALIAN style Italian cuisine in a warmly lit bilevel redbrick space on Truckee's
historic main drag. Start with a beef carpaccio antipasto plate or perhaps
house-made spicy-fennel and mild sausages, following up with a pasta
course of ravioli Bolognese (both pasta and sauce made in-house), an
entrée of ragout with spicy sausage and Mexican prawns—or both. **Known
for:** house-made sausages, pastas, and sauces; warmly lit redbrick space;
well-conceived wine list. ⑤ *Average main: $25* ✉ *10096 Donner Pass Rd.*
☎ *530/587–4694* ⊕ *www.pianetarestauranttruckee.com* ⊘ *No lunch.*

$ ✕ **Squeeze In.** Meet the locals at Truckee's top choice for breakfast,
AMERICAN thanks to the dozens of omelets and several variations on eggs Bene-
dict along with banana-walnut pancakes and French toast oozing with
cream cheese. At lunch savor homemade soups and sandwiches. **Known
for:** omelets and eggs Benedict; homemade soups. ⑤ *Average main: $13*
✉ *10060 Donner Pass Rd., near Bridge St.* ☎ *530/587–9814* ⊕ *www.
squeezein.com* ⊘ *No dinner.*

$$$ ✕ **Truckee Tavern & Grill.** The wood-fired grill in this downtown restaurant
AMERICAN turns out steaks, chicken, and chops along with buffalo tri-tip and other
house specialties. Non-carnivores enjoy pasta (linguine with ricotta and
vegetables) and fish (salmon with green-lentil ragout) entrées. **Known
for:** wood-fired meats; pasta and fish entrées; small-batch gin and whiskey. ⑤ *Average main: $26* ✉ *10118 Donner Pass Rd., near Spring St.*
☎ *530/587–3766* ⊕ *www.truckeetavern.com* ⊘ *No lunch.*

WHERE TO STAY

$$ ⊞ **Cedar House Sport Hotel.** The clean, spare lines of the Cedar House's
HOTEL wooden exterior evoke a modern European feel, while energy-saving
heating, cooling, and lighting systems emphasize the owners' commit-
ment to sustainability. **Pros:** environmentally friendly; hip yet com-
fortable; heated-tile bathroom floors. **Cons:** some bathrooms on the
small side; not all bathrooms have tubs; about a mile from historic
downtown Truckee. ⑤ *Rooms from: $170* ✉ *10918 Brockway Rd.*
☎ *530/582–5655, 866/582–5655* ⊕ *www.cedarhousesporthotel.com*
◄ *40 rooms* ⋈ *Breakfast.*

$$$ ⊞ **Northstar California Resort.** The area's most complete destination resort
RESORT entices families with its sports activities and concentration of restau-
rants, shops, and accommodations. **Pros:** array of lodging types; on-site
shuttle; several dining options in Northstar Village. **Cons:** family accommodations are very pricey; lacks intimacy; some units not as attractive
as others. ⑤ *Rooms from: $249* ✉ *100 Northstar Dr., off Hwy. 267, 6
miles southeast of Truckee* ☎ *530/562–1010, 800/466–6784* ⊕ *www.
northstarcalifornia.com* ◄ *250 rooms* ⋈ *No meals.*

$$$$ ⊞ **Ritz-Carlton Highlands Court, Lake Tahoe.** Nestled mid-mountain on the
RESORT Northstar ski resort, the plush accommodations of the four-story Ritz-
Fodor'sChoice Carlton have floor-to-ceiling windows for maximum views, along with
★ fireplaces, cozy robes, and down comforters. **Pros:** superb service; gorgeous setting; ski-in, ski out convenience. **Cons:** prices as breathtaking
as the views; resort fee and mandatory valet parking add to cost of stay;
must go off-site for golf and tennis. ⑤ *Rooms from: $362* ✉ *13031 Ritz-
Carlton Highlands Court* ☎ *530/562–3000, 800/241–3333* ⊕ *www.
ritzcarlton.com/laketahoe* ◄ *169 rooms* ⋈ *No meals.*

$$
B&B/INN
🛏 **River Street Inn.** On the banks of the Truckee River, this 1885 wood-and-stone inn has uncluttered, comfortable rooms that are simply deco-rated, with attractive, country-style wooden furniture and extras like flat-screen TVs. **Pros:** tidy rooms; good value; in historic downtown Truckee. **Cons:** parking is a half-block from inn; decor is simple; noise from on-site restaurant and bar and nearby trains. $ *Rooms from: $145* ⊠ *10009 E. River St.* ☎ *530/550–9290, 530/550–9222 restaurant* ⊕ *www.riverstreetinntruckee.com* ⤶ *7 rooms* ⦿ *Breakfast.*

SPORTS AND THE OUTDOORS
GOLF
Coyote Moon Golf Course. With towering pine trees lining the fairways and no houses to spoil the view, this course is as beautiful as it is challenging. Fees include a shared cart; the greens fee drops at 1 pm and dips again at 3. ⊠ *10685 Northwoods Blvd., off Donner Pass Rd.* ☎ *530/587–0886* ⊕ *www.coyotemoongolf.com* 🎫 *$175* ⛳ *18 holes, 7177 yards, par 72* ☉ *Closed late fall–late spring.*

Northstar California Golf. Robert Muir Graves designed this course that combines hilly terrain and open meadows. The front nine holes here are open-links style, while the challenging back nine move through tight, tree-lined fairways. Fees starting at $55 for nine holes include a shared cart, and twilight rates begin at 2 pm. ⊠ *168 Basque Dr., off Northstar Dr., west off Hwy. 267* ☎ *530/562–3290 pro-shop* ⊕ *www.northstarcalifornia.com/info/summer/golf.asp* 🎫 *$55 for 9 holes, $85 for 18 holes* ⛳ *18 holes, 6781 yards, par 72.*

Old Greenwood. Beautiful mountain and forest views add to the pleasure of a round played at north Lake Tahoe's only Jack Nicklaus Signature Golf Course. The regular fees are high, but there's a $75 twilight rate beginning at 4 pm. ⊠ *12915 Fairway Dr., off Overland Trail Rd., off I–80, Exit 190* ☎ *530/550–7010* ⊕ *www.golfintahoe.com/old-green-wood/course* 🎫 *$150–$200* ⛳ *18 holes, 7518 yards, par 72.*

MOUNTAIN BIKING
Cyclepaths Mountain Bike Adventures. This combination full-service bike shop and bike-adventure outfitter offers instruction in mountain biking, guided tours, tips for self-guided bike touring, bike repairs, and books and maps on the area. ⊠ *Pioneer Center, 10825 Pioneer Trail, Suite 105* ☎ *530/582–1890* ⊕ *www.cyclepaths.net.*

Northstar California Bike Park. In summer Northstar's ski slopes transform into a magnificent lift-served bike park with 100 miles of challeng-ing terrain, including the aptly named Livewire trail. Guided tours, multiday retreats, and downhill, cross-country, and endurance races are available for riders of all abilities. ⊠ *Northstar Dr., off Hwy. 267* ☎ *530/562–1010* ⊕ *www.northstarcalifornia.com/bike-and-hike/mtn-biking-rentals.aspx* 🎫 *Lift $59.*

SKIING
Boreal Mountain Resort. These slopes have 380 skiable acres and 500 verti-cal feet of terrain visible from the freeway. Lift-served snow-tubing and night skiing go until 9. ⊠ *19749 Boreal Ridge Rd., at I–80, Boreal/Castle Peak exit, Soda Springs* ☎ *530/426–3666* ⊕ *www.rideboreal.com.*

Donner Ski Ranch. This ski park has 505 acres and 750 vertical feet. A popular area with kids in this small, family-friendly park is the Tubing Hill. Riders whisk down the slope in a huge inflated inner tube and then go back to the top on a moving carpet. ⊠ *19320 Donner Pass Rd., Norden* ☎ *530/426–3635* ⊕ *www.donnerskiranch.com.*

Fodor'sChoice ★ **Northstar California.** Meticulous grooming and long cruisers make this resort a paradise for intermediate skiers and a fine choice for families. Although the majority of the trails are intermediate in difficulty, advanced skiers and riders have access to Lookout Mountain's more than two dozen expert trails and 347 acres of gated terrain and steeps. The diversity of terrain in proximity makes it easier for families and groups with varying skills to hang out with each other. As for terrain parks, the ones here are considered among North America's best, with features that include a 420-foot-long super-pipe, a half-pipe, rails and boxes, and lots of kickers. The Cross Country, Snowshoe and Telemark Center, located mid-mountain, is the starting point for a network of 35 km (22 miles) of groomed trails, including double-set tracks and skating lanes. The trails are also fat-bike friendly, so nonskiers can enjoy the park, too. The school has programs for skiers ages three and up, and on-site care is available for tots two and older. **Facilities:** 97 trails; 3,170 acres; 2,280-foot vertical drop; 20 lifts. ⊠ *5001 Northstar Dr.* ☎ *530/562–1010 information, 800/466–6784 lodging, 530/562–1330 snow phone* ⊕ *www.northstarcalifornia.com* 🎟 *Lift ticket $126.*

Royal Gorge. If you love to cross-country, don't miss Royal Gorge, which serves up 200 km (124 miles) of track for all abilities, eight trail systems on a whopping 6,000 acres, a ski school, and nine warming huts. Because the complex, affiliated with Sugar Bowl, sits right on the Sierra Crest, the views are drop-dead gorgeous. ⊠ *9411 Pahatsi Dr., off I–80, Soda Springs/Norden exit, Soda Springs* ☎ *530/426–3871, 800/500–3871* ⊕ *www.royalgorge.com.*

Sugar Bowl Ski Resort. Opened in 1939 by Walt Disney, this is the oldest—and one of the best—resorts at Tahoe. Atop Donner Summit, it receives an incredible 500 inches of snowfall annually. Four peaks are connected by 1,650 acres of skiable terrain, with everything from gentle groomed corduroy to wide-open bowls to vertical rocky chutes and outstanding tree skiing. Snowboarders can hit two terrain parks with numerous boxes, rails, and jumps. Because it's more compact than some of the area's megaresorts, there's a gentility here that distinguishes Sugar Bowl from its competitors, making this a great place for families and a low-pressure, low-key place to learn to ski. It's not huge, but there's some very challenging terrain (experts: head to the Palisades). There's limited lodging at the base area. Facilities: 102 trails; 1,650 acres; 1,500-foot vertical drop; 12 lifts. ⊠ *629 Sugar Bowl Rd., off Donner Pass Rd., 3 miles east of I–80 Soda Springs/Norden exit, 10 miles west of Truckee, Norden* ☎ *530/426–9000 information and lodging reservations, 530/426–1111 snow phone, 866/843–2695 lodging referral* ⊕ *www.sugarbowl.com* 🎟 *Lift ticket $115.*

Tahoe Dave's. You can save money by renting skis and boards at this shop, which has the area's best selection and also repairs and tunes equipment. ⊠ *10200 Donner Pass Rd., near Spring St.* ☎ *530/582–0900* ⊕ *www.tahoedaves.com.*

Tahoe Donner. Just north of Truckee, this park covers 120 acres and 600 vertical feet; the cross-country center includes 51 trails on 100 km (62 miles) of groomed tracks on 4,800 acres, with night skiing on Wednesday in January and February. ⊠ *11603 Snowpeak Way* ☎ *530/587–9444* ⊕ *www.tahoedonner.com.*

CARNELIAN BAY TO KINGS BEACH

5–10 miles northeast of Tahoe City.

The small lakeside commercial districts of Carnelian Bay and Tahoe Vista service the thousand or so locals who live in the area year-round and the thousands more who have summer residences or launch their boats here. Kings Beach, the last town heading east on Highway 28 before the Nevada border, is full of basic motels and rental condos, restaurants, and shops.

GETTING HERE AND AROUND

To reach Kings Beach and Carnelian Bay from the California side, take Highway 89 north to Highway 28 north and then east. From the Nevada side, follow Highway 28 north and then west. TART provides public transportation in this area.

BEACHES

FAMILY   **Kings Beach State Recreation Area.** The north shore's 28-acre Kings Beach State Recreation Area, one of the largest such areas on the lake, is open year-round. The 700-foot-long sandy beach gets crowded in summer with people swimming, sunbathing, Jet Skiing, riding in paddleboats, spiking volleyballs, and tossing Frisbees. If you're going to spend the day, come early to snag a table in the picnic area; there's also a good playground. **Amenities:** food and drink; parking (fee); toilets; water sports. **Best For:** sunrise; sunset; swimming; windsurfing. ⊠ *8318 N. Lake Blvd., Hwy. 28, Kings Beach* ☎ *530/546–7248* ⊕ *www.parks. ca.gov* 🖘 *$10 parking fee.*

WHERE TO EAT AND STAY

$$$$ ✕ **Gar Woods Grill and Pier.** The view's the thing at this lakeside stal-
ECLECTIC   wart, where you can watch the sun shimmer on the water through the dining room's plateglass windows or from the heated outdoor deck. Grilled steak and fish are menu mainstays, but be sure to try specialties like crab chilis rellenos and pomegranate braised pork ribs. **Known for:** lake views; grilled steak and fish; better bet price wise for lunch or weekend breakfast. ⑤ *Average main: $35* ⊠ *5000 N. Lake Blvd., Hwy. 28, Carnelian Bay* ☎ *530/546–3366* ⊕ *www. garwoods.com.*

$$$ ✕ **Soule Domain.** Rough-hewn wood beams, a vaulted wood ceiling,
ECLECTIC   and, in winter, a roaring fireplace lend high romance to this cozy 1927 pine-log cabin next to the Tahoe Biltmore casino. Chef-owner Charlie Soule's specialties include curried almond chicken, fresh sea

scallops poached in champagne with a kiwi and mango cream sauce, and a vegan sauté judiciously flavored with ginger, jalapeños, sesame seeds, and teriyaki sauce. **Known for:** cozy, romantic setting; skilfully prepared cuisine; suave service. ⑤ *Average main: $27* ✉ *9983 Cove St., ½ block up Stateline Rd. off Hwy. 28, Kings Beach* ✛ *Restaurant is just west of Tahoe Biltmore casino at California-Nevada border.* ☎ *530/546–7529* ⊕ *www.souledomain.com* ☉ *No lunch.*

$$$
AMERICAN

✕ **Spindleshanks American Bistro and Wine Bar.** A local favorite on the Old Brockway Golf Course, Spindleshanks serves mostly classic American cooking—ribs, steaks, and seafood updated with adventurous sauces—as well as house-made ravioli. Savor a drink from the full bar or choose a wine from the extensive list while you enjoy views of Lake Tahoe or the historic greens where Bing Crosby hosted his first golf tournament in 1934. **Known for:** classic American cooking; Lake Tahoe views; outdoor patio. ⑤ *Average main: $24* ✉ *400 Brassie Ave., at Hwy. 267 & N. Lake Tahoe Blvd., Kings Beach* ☎ *530/546–2191* ⊕ *www.spindleshankstahoe.com.*

$
HOTEL
FAMILY

🛏 **Ferrari's Crown Resort.** Great for families with kids, the family-owned and-operated Ferrari's has straightforward motel rooms in a resort setting. **Pros:** family-friendly; lakeside location; a few rooms value-priced. **Cons:** older facility; unappealing exterior; thin walls. ⑤ *Rooms from: $115* ✉ *8200 N. Lake Blvd., Kings Beach* ☎ *530/546–3388, 800/645–2260* ⊕ *www.tahoecrown.com* 🗘 *72 rooms* ⊗ *Breakfast.*

$$$$
B&B/INN

🛏 **Mourelatos Lakeshore Resort.** At first glance this family-run waterfront property looks like a slightly above-average two-story motel, but with a private beach, two hot tubs, ceaselessly alluring lake and mountain vistas, and summertime barbecuing, kayaking, and other extras it legitimately lays claim to the title of resort. **Pros:** private beach; some rooms have full kitchens; summertime barbecuing and kayaking. **Cons:** decor a tad dated; books up quickly for summer; some rooms lack sufficient heat in winter. ⑤ *Rooms from: $290* ✉ *6834 N. Lake Blvd., Tahoe Vista* ☎ *530/546–9500* ⊕ *www.mlrtahoe.com* 🗘 *32 rooms* ⊗ *Breakfast.*

$
HOTEL
FAMILY

🛏 **Rustic Cottages.** These charming clapboard cottages sit clustered beneath tall pine trees across the road from Lake Tahoe and a little beach. **Pros:** woodsy Old Tahoe feel; expanded Continental breakfast; good value. **Cons:** older facility; some rooms are very small; lacks big-hotel amenities. ⑤ *Rooms from: $109* ✉ *7449 N. Lake Blvd., Tahoe Vista* ☎ *530/546–3523, 888/778–7842* ⊕ *www.rusticcottages.com* 🗘 *20 rooms* ⊗ *Breakfast.*

THE NEVADA SIDE

The difference on the Nevada side of the lake from Crystal Bay south to Stateline, is, of course, gambling. Crystal Bay contains a few casinos whose glory has long faded, and Incline Village has a casino (at the Hyatt Lake Tahoe), but Stateline has the main gaming action. Top scenic stops along the shore include Sand Harbor, Zephyr Cove, and Nevada Beach.

INCLINE VILLAGE

3 miles east of Crystal Bay.

Incline Village dates to the early 1960s, when an Oklahoma developer bought 10,000 acres north of Lake Tahoe. His idea was to sketch out a plan for a town without a central commercial district, hoping to prevent congestion and to preserve the area's natural beauty. One-acre lakeshore lots originally fetched $12,000 to $15,000; today you couldn't buy the same land for less than several million.

GETTING HERE AND AROUND

From the California side, reach Incline Village via Highway 89 or 267 to Highway 28. From South Lake Tahoe, take U.S. 50 north to Highway 28 north. TART serves the communities along Lake Tahoe's north and west shores from Incline Village to Tahoma.

ESSENTIALS

Visitor Information Lake Tahoe Incline Village/Crystal Bay Visitors Bureau. ⊠ *969 Tahoe Blvd.* ☎ *775/832–1606, 800/468–2463* ⊕ *www.gotahoenorth.com.*

EXPLORING

Lakeshore Drive. Take this beautiful drive to see some of the most expensive real estate in Nevada. The route is discreetly marked: to find it, start at the Hyatt hotel and drive westward along the lake. ⊠ *Incline Village.*

Fodor'sChoice ★ **Thunderbird Lodge.** George Whittell, a San Francisco socialite who once owned 40,000 acres of property along the lake, began building this lodge in 1936, completing it in 1941. You can tour the mansion and the grounds by reservation only, and though it's pricey to do so, you'll be rewarded with a rare glimpse of a time when only the very wealthy had homes at Tahoe. The lodge is accessible via a bus from the Incline Village Visitors Bureau, a catamaran from the Hyatt in Incline Village ($120), or a 1950 wooden cruiser from Tahoe Keys Marina in South Lake Tahoe, which includes Continental breakfast and lunch ($139). ⊠ *5000 Hwy. 28* ☎ *775/832–8752 lodge info, 800/468–2463 reservations, bus tour, 775/588–1881, 888/867–6394 Tahoe Keys boat, 775/831–4386 Hyatt Incline catamaran* ⊕ *www.thunderbirdtahoe.org/ tours* 🖻 *$39 bus tour, $120 and $139 for boat tours.*

BEACHES

Lake Tahoe–Nevada State Park and Sand Harbor Beach. Protecting much of the lake's eastern shore from development, this park comprises several sections that stretch from Incline Village to Zephyr Cove. Beaches and trails provide access to a wilder side of the lake, whether you're into cross-country skiing, hiking, or just relaxing at a picnic. With a gently sloping beach for lounging, crystal-clear water for swimming and snorkeling, and a picnic area shaded by cedars and pines, **Sand Harbor Beach** is so popular that it sometimes fills to capacity by 11 am on summer weekends. Boaters have two launch ramps. A handicap-accessible nature trail has interpretive signs and beautiful lake views. Pets are not allowed. **Amenities:** food and drink; parking ($12 mid-Apr.–mid-Oct., $7 rest of the year); toilets; water sports. **Best For:** snorkeling; sunset; swimming; walking. ⊠ *Sand Harbor Beach, Hwy. 28, 3 miles south of Incline Village* ☎ *775/831–0494* ⊕ *parks.nv.gov/parks/sand-harbor.*

13

WHERE TO EAT AND STAY

$$$
ECLECTIC

✕ **Fredrick's Fusion Bistro.** Copper-top tables lend a chic look to the dining room at this intimate bistro. The menu consists of a mélange of European and Asian dishes—braised short ribs, roasted duck with caramel-pecan glaze, fresh sushi rolls—most of them prepared with organic produce and free-range meats. **Known for:** chic and intimate; organic, free-range meat in most dishes; fireside tables. Ⓢ *Average main: $24* ⊠ *907 Tahoe Blvd., at Village Blvd.* ☎ *775/832–3007* ⊕ *fredricksbistro. com* ☽ *Closed Sun. and Mon. No lunch.*

$$$$
FRENCH

✕ **Le Bistro.** Incline Village's hidden gem changed owners in late 2016 but is still going strong, serving French-country cuisine in a relaxed, romantic dining room. The five-course prix-fixe menu ($65) may include dishes like pâté de campagne, escargots, herb-crusted roast lamb, and fresh fish, paired with award-winning wines if you choose. **Known for:** romantic dining room; five-course prix-fixe meal with wine pairings; gracious, attentive service. Ⓢ *Average main: $65* ⊠ *120 Country Club Dr., #29, off Lakeshore Blvd.* ☎ *775/831–0800* ☽ *Closed Sun. and Mon. No lunch.*

$
AMERICAN
Fodor'sChoice
★

✕ **Mountain High Sandwich Company.** An all-natural deli serving breakfast and lunch, Mountain High may well be the only place in Tahoe to find coconut chia seed pudding and similar delicacies. More familiar fare—biscuits and sausage gravy for breakfast, house-smoked tri-tip sandwiches for lunch—is also on the menu, with many selections gluten-free and vegan or vegetarian friendly. **Known for:** casual atmosphere; inventive soups; sustainable practices. Ⓢ *Average main: $9* ⊠ *120 Country Club Dr., Suite 28* ☎ *775/298–2636* ⊕ *www.mountainhighsandwichco.com.*

$
SOUTHERN

✕ **T's Mesquite Rotisserie.** There's nothing fancy about T's (it looks like a small snack bar), but the mesquite-grilled chicken and tri-tip steaks are delicious and inexpensive—a rare combination in pricey Incline Village. It's mainly a take-out spot; seating is limited. **Known for:** chicken and tri-tip steaks; delicious and inexpensive; meals for take-out. Ⓢ *Average main: $9* ⊠ *901 Tahoe Blvd., at Village Blvd.* ☎ *775/831–2832* ▭ *No credit cards.*

$$$$
RESORT

🏨 **Hyatt Regency Lake Tahoe.** A full-service destination resort on 26 acres of prime lakefront property, the Hyatt has a range of luxurious accommodations, from tower-hotel rooms to lakeside cottages. **Pros:** incredible views; low-key casino; luxurious accommodations. **Cons:** pricey (especially for families); feels corporate; smallish beach. Ⓢ *Rooms from: $379* ⊠ *111 Country Club Dr.* ☎ *775/832–1234, 888/899–5019* ⊕ *www.laketahoe.hyatt.com* ⤢ *422 rooms* ⦿ *No meals.*

Get to Sand Harbor Beach in Lake Tahoe–Nevada State Park early; the park sometimes fills to capacity before lunchtime in summer.

SPORTS AND THE OUTDOORS

GOLF

Incline Championship. Robert Trent Jones Sr. designed this challenging course of tightly cut, tree-lined fairways laced with water hazards that demand accuracy as well as distance skills. Greens fee includes a cart, except for the 4:30 pm Super Twilight rate of $3 per hole (cart $25). ⊠ *955 Fairway Blvd., at Northwood Blvd., north off Hwy. 28* ☎ *866/925–4653 reservations, 775/832–1146 pro shop* ⊕ *www.yourtahoeplace.com/golf-incline* 🖃 *$170 weekdays, $190 weekends* 🏌 *18 holes, 7106 yards, par 72.*

Incline Mountain. Robert Trent Jones, Jr. designed this executive (shorter) course that requires accuracy more than distance skills. The greens fee includes a cart. ⊠ *690 Wilson Way, at Golfer's Pass, south off Hwy. 431* ☎ *866/925–4653 reservations, 775/832–1150 pro shop* ⊕ *www.yourtahoeplace.com/golf-incline* 🖃 *$65–$70* 🏌 *18 holes, 3527 yards, par 58.*

MOUNTAIN BIKING

Flume Trail Bikes. You can rent bikes and get helpful tips from this company, which also operates a bike shuttle to popular trailheads. ⊠ *1115 Tunnel Creek Rd., at Ponderosa Ranch Rd., off Hwy. 28* ☎ *775/298–2501* ⊕ *www.flumetrailtahoe.com* 🖃 *From $39.*

SKIING

Diamond Peak. A fun family mood prevails at Diamond Peak, which has affordable rates and many special programs. Snowmaking covers 75% of the mountain, and runs are groomed nightly. The ride up the 1-mile Crystal Express rewards you with fantastic views. Diamond Peak is less crowded than Tahoe's larger ski parks and provides free shuttles to nearby lodgings. A great place for beginners and interme-diates, it's appropriately priced for families. Though there are some steep-aspect black-diamond runs, advanced skiers may find the acre-age too limited. For snowboarders there's a small terrain park. **Facili-ties:** 30 trails; 655 acres; 1,840-foot vertical drop; 7 lifts. ⊠ *1210 Ski Way, off Country Club Dr.* ☎ *775/832–1177* ⊕ *www.diamondpeak. com* 🎫 *Lift ticket $79.*

Mt. Rose Ski Tahoe. At this park, ski some of Tahoe's highest slopes and take in bird's-eye views of Reno, the lake, and Carson Valley. Though more compact than the bigger Tahoe resorts, Mt. Rose has the area's highest base elevation and consequently the driest snow. The mountain has a wide variety of terrain. The most challenging is the Chutes, 200 acres of gulp-and-go advanced-to-expert vertical. Intermediates can choose steep groomers or mellow, wide-open boulevards. Beginners have their own corner of the mountain, with gentle, wide slopes. Boarders and tricksters have three terrain parks to choose from, on opposite sides of the mountain, allowing them to follow the sun as it tracks across the resort. The mountain gets hit hard in storms; check conditions before heading up during inclement weather or on a windy day. **Facilities:** 61 trails; 1,200 acres; 1,800-foot vertical drop; 8 lifts. ⊠ *22222 Mt. Rose Hwy., Hwy. 431, 11 miles north of Incline Village, Reno* ☎ *775/849–0704, 800/754–7673* ⊕ *www.skirose.com* 🎫 *Lift ticket $109.*

Tahoe Meadows Snowplay Area. This is the most popular area near the north shore for noncommercial cross-country skiing, sledding, tubing, snowshoeing, and snowmobiling. ⊠ *Off Hwy. 431, between Incline Village and Mt. Rose.*

ZEPHYR COVE

22 miles south of Incline Village.

The largest settlement between Incline Village and the Stateline area is Zephyr Cove, a tiny resort. It has a beach, marina, campground, picnic area, coffee shop in a log lodge, rustic cabins, and nearby riding stables.

GETTING HERE AND AROUND

From the north shore communities, reach Zephyr Cove by following Highway 28 along the eastern side of the lake. From South Lake Tahoe, take U.S. 50 north and then west. Public transportation isn't available in Zephyr Cove.

EXPLORING

Cave Rock. Near Zephyr Cove, this 75 feet of solid stone at the southern end of Lake Tahoe–Nevada State Park is the throat of an extinct vol-cano. The impressive outcropping towers over a parking lot, a lakefront picnic ground, and a boat launch. The views are some of the best on the lake; this is a good spot to stop and take a picture. However, this area is a sacred burial site for the Washoe Indians, and climbing up to the cave, or through it, is prohibited. ⊠ *U.S. 50, 4 miles north of Zephyr Cove* ☎ *775/831–0494* ⊕ *www.parks.nv.gov/parks/lake-tahoe-nevada-state-park-2* 🎫 *$10 mid-Apr.–mid-Oct.; $7 rest of yr.*

WHERE TO EAT AND STAY

$$$
ITALIAN
✕**Capisce?** The signature mushroom and tomato sauce is so thick it's called "gravy" at this handsome roadside restaurant whose menu emphasizes old favorites from the Italian-American side of the family that runs it. The mildly spicy concoction adds zest to cioppino—seafood stew, here served on risottolike white-wine rice—and to house-made raviolis that many diners order half slathered with it and the other half with a velvety butter and Parmesan cheese sauce. **Known for:** handsome high-ceilinged dining room; old family recipes; full bar patronized by many locals. ⑤ *Average main: $26* ⊠ *178 U.S. 50* ☎ *775/ 580–7500* ⊕ *www.capiscelaketahoe.com* ⊗ *Closed Mon. No lunch.*

$$$
RENTAL
FAMILY
🏠 **Zephyr Cove Resort.** Beneath towering pines at the lake's edge stand 28 cozy, modern vacation cabins with peaked knotty-pine ceilings. **Pros:** family-friendly; cozy cabins; old-school ambience. **Cons:** lodge rooms are basic; can be noisy in summer; not all cabins have fireplaces. ⑤ *Rooms from: $200* ⊠ *760 U.S. 50, 4 miles north of Stateline* ☎ *775/589–4906, 800/238–2463* ⊕ *www.zephyrcove.com* ↙ *32 rooms* ⦿ *No meals.*

STATELINE

5 miles south of Zephyr Cove.

Stateline is the archetypal Nevada border town. Its four high-rise casinos are as vertical and contained as the commercial district of South Lake Tahoe, on the California side, is horizontal and sprawling. And Stateline is as relentlessly indoors-oriented as the rest of the lake is focused on the outdoors. This small strip is where you'll find the most concentrated action at Lake Tahoe: restaurants (including typical casino buffets), showrooms with semi-famous headliners and razzle-dazzle revues, tower-hotel rooms and suites, and 24-hour casinos.

GETTING HERE AND AROUND

From South Lake Tahoe take U.S. 50 north across the Nevada border to reach Stateline and its casinos. If coming from Reno's airport, take U.S. 395/Interstate 580 south to Carson City, and then head west on U.S. 50 to the lake and head south. Or take the South Tahoe Express bus. BlueGO operates daily bus service.

BEACHES

Nevada Beach. Although less than a mile long, this is the widest beach on the lake and especially good for swimming (many Tahoe beaches are rocky). You can boat and fish here, and there are picnic tables, barbecue grills, and a campground beneath the pines. This is the best place to watch the July 4th or Labor Day fireworks, but most of the summer the subdued atmosphere attracts families and those seeking a less-touristy spot. **Amenities:** parking ($8 fee), water sports, toilets. **Best For:** sunrise, swimming, walking. ⊠ *Elk Point Rd., off U.S. 50, 3 miles north of Stateline* ☎ *530/543–2600, 877/444–6777 camping reservations* ⊕ *www.fs.usda.gov/detail/ltbmu/recreation/?cid=stelprdb5134175* ☞ *Dogs permitted on leash in picnic areas but not on beach.*

WHERE TO EAT AND STAY

$$
AMERICAN
Fodor'sChoice
★
✕**Brooks Bar & Deck.** Stateline's best spot for lunch or a casual dinner serves up clever takes on comfort cuisine—tacos, burgers, daily changing grilled-cheese panini, and a crispy-chicken sandwich with Sriracha aioli. Although this is the Edgewood Tahoe resort's golf-course restaurant, you needn't have finished 18 holes to enjoy the food and lake, forest, and golf course views from the high-ceilinged restaurant or stone-floored outdoor deck. **Known for:** casual comfort food; outdoor deck; eclectic clientele. ⑤ *Average main: $19* ⌧ *Edgewood Tahoe, 100 Lake Pkwy.* ☎ *775/588–6183* ⊕ *www.edgewoodtahoe.com.*

$
HOTEL
🏨**Harrah's Tahoe Hotel/Casino.** The hotel's major selling point is that every room has two full bathrooms, a boon if you're traveling with family. **Pros:** central location; great midweek values; two full bathrooms in every room. **Cons:** can get noisy; uneven housekeeping; lacks intimacy. ⑤ *Rooms from: $109* ⌧ *15 U.S. 50, at Stateline Ave.* ☎ *775/588–6611, 800/427–7247* ⊕ *www.caesars.com/harrahs-tahoe* ⇆ *512 rooms* ⦿*No meals.*

$
HOTEL
🏨**Harveys Resort Hotel/Casino.** This resort began as a cabin in 1944, and now it's Tahoe's largest casino-hotel; premium rooms have custom furnishings, oversize marble baths, minibars, and good lake views. **Pros:** hip entertainment; just a few blocks north of the Heavenly Gondola; good lake views. **Cons:** can get loud at night; high summer rates; large property. ⑤ *Rooms from: $119* ⌧ *18 U.S. 50, at Stateline Ave.* ☎ *775/588–2411, 800/648–3361* ⊕ *www.caesars.com/harveys-tahoe* ⇆ *742 rooms* ⦿*No meals.*

$
HOTEL
🏨**Lakeside Inn and Casino.** The smallest of the Stateline casinos, the property has good promotional room rates and simple, attractive accommodations in two-story motel-style buildings separate from the casino. **Pros:** daily dining specials; casino separate from accommodations; no resort or parking fee. **Cons:** some rooms are on the small side; some rooms are dark; motel-style buildings. ⑤ *Rooms from: $109* ⌧ *168 U.S. 50, at Kingsbury Grade* ☎ *775/588–7777, 800/624–7980* ⊕ *lakeside-inn.com* ⇆ *124 rooms* ⦿*No meals.*

$$$$
RESORT
Fodor'sChoice
★
🏨**The Lodge at Edgewood Tahoe.** The lodge, which debuted in mid-2017 on a prime lakefront parcel, makes a bold impression with its stone and walnut Great Hall, whose four-story wall of windows frames views across Lake Tahoe to grand Mt. Tallac. **Pros:** prime lakefront location; haute-rustic design; all rooms have balconies and fireplaces. **Cons:** high rates in-season; some rooms have no lake views; long walk to pool and hot tub from some rooms. ⑤ *Rooms from: $300* ⌧ *100 Lake Pkwy.* ☎ *775/588–2787, 888/881–8659* ⊕ *www.edgewoodtahoe.com/lodge* ⇆ *154 rooms.*

NIGHTLIFE

Each of the major casinos has its own showroom, featuring everything from comedy to magic acts to sexy floor shows to Broadway musicals.

LIVE MUSIC

Harveys Outdoor Summer Concert Series. Harveys Lake Tahoe books outdoor concerts on weekends in summer with headliners such as The Who, Paul Simon, and Lenny Kravitz. ⌧ *18 U.S. 50* ☎ *775/588–2411* ⊕ *www.caesars.com/harveys-tahoe/shows.html.*

South Shore Room. Classic acts like Robin Trower and the Yardbirds play Harrah's big showroom, along with comedians like Louie Anderson and the psychedelic Pink Floyd Laser Spectacular show. ✉ *Harrah's Lake Tahoe, 15 U.S. 50* ☎ *775/586–6244 tickets, 775/588–6611* ⊕ *www.caesars.com/harrahs-tahoe/shows.html.*

SPORTS AND THE OUTDOORS
GOLF
Edgewood Tahoe. Golfers of all skill levels enjoy this scenic lakeside course that has four sets of tees, offering a variety of course lengths. The greens fee includes an optional cart. ✉ *100 Lake Pkwy., at U.S. 50* ☎ *775/588–3566, 866/761–4653* ⊕ *www.edgewood-tahoe.com* ☑ *$140–$260 (varies throughout season)* 🏌 *18 holes, 7529 yards, par 72.*

RENO

32 miles east of Truckee, 38 miles northeast of Incline Village.

Established in 1859 as a trading station at a bridge over the Truckee River, Reno grew along with the silver mines of nearby Virginia City and the transcontinental railroad that chugged through town. Train officials named it in 1868, but gambling—legalized in 1931—put Reno on the map. This is still a gambling town, with most of the casinos crowded into five square blocks downtown, but a thriving university scene and outdoor activities also attract tourists.

Parts of downtown are sketchy, but things are changing. Reno now touts family-friendly activities like kayaking on the Truckee, museums, and a downtown climbing wall. With over 300 days of sunshine annually, temperatures year-round in this high-mountain-desert climate are warmer than at Tahoe, though rarely as hot as in Sacramento and the Central Valley, making strolling around town a pleasure.

GETTING HERE AND AROUND
Interstate 80 bisects Reno east–west, U.S. 395 north–south (south of town the road is signed U.S. 395/Interstate 580). Greyhound and Amtrak stop here, and several airlines fly into Reno-Tahoe International Airport. RTC Ride provides bus service.

ESSENTIALS
Bus Contact RTC Ride. ✉ *Transit Center, E. 4th and Lake Sts.* ☎ *775/348-7433* ⊕ *www.rtcwashoe.com.*

Visitor Information Reno Tahoe USA Visitor Center. ✉ *11 N. Sierra St.* ☎ *775/827-7650, 800/367-7366* ⊕ *www.visitrenotahoe.com.*

EXPLORING
TOP ATTRACTIONS
FAMILY

Fodor'sChoice

★

National Automobile Museum. Antique and classic automobiles, including an Elvis Presley Cadillac, a Mercury coupe driven by James Dean in the movie *Rebel Without a Cause*, and the experimental and still futuristic-looking 1938 Phantom Corsair, are all on display at this museum. ✉ *10 S. Lake St., at Mill St.* ☎ *775/333-9300* ⊕ *www.automuseum.org* ☑ *$12.*

Riverwalk District. The makeover of Reno's waterfront has transformed this formerly dilapidated area into the toast of the town. The Riverwalk itself is a half-mile promenade on the north side of the Truckee River, which flows around lovely Wingfield Park, where outdoor festivals and other events take place. On the third Saturday of each month, local merchants host a **Wine Walk** between 2 and 5. For $20 you receive a wine glass and can sample fine wines at participating shops, bars, restaurants, and galleries. In July, look for stellar outdoor art, opera, dance, and kids' performances as part of the monthlong **Artown festival** (*renoisartown.com*), presented mostly in Wingfield Park. Also at Wingfield is the **Truckee River Whitewater Park.** With activities for all skill levels, it's become a major attraction for water-sports enthusiasts. ✉ *Riverwalk, north side of Truckee River between Lake and Ralston Sts.* ⊕ *www.renoriver.org.*

13

WORTH NOTING

Nevada Museum of Art. A dramatic four-level structure designed by Will Bruder houses this splendid museum's collection, which focuses on themes such as the Sierra Nevada/Great Basin and altered-landscape photography. The building's exterior torqued walls are sided with a black zinc-based material that has been fabricated to resemble textures found in the Black Rock Desert. Inside the building, a staircase installed within the central atrium is lit by skylights and suspended by a single beam attached to the atrium ceiling. ✉ *160 W. Liberty St., and Hill St.* ☎ *775/329–3333* ⊕ *www.nevadaart.org* ▱ *$10* ⊘ *Closed Mon. and Tues.*

WHERE TO EAT

$$$ ✕ **Beaujolais Bistro.** Across from the Truckee River, this Reno favorite
FRENCH serves earthy, country-style French food with zero pretension. Expect
Fodor'sChoice classics like escargots, steak frites with red wine sauce, cassoulet, and
★ crisp sweetbreads with madeira, along with fish and vegetarian selections. **Known for:** country-style French; intimate atmosphere. $ *Average main: $29* ✉ *753 Riverside Dr., near Winter St.* ☎ *775/323–2227* ⊕ *www.beaujolaisbistro.com* ⊘ *No lunch. Closed Mon.*

$$$ ✕ **4th St. Bistro.** For deliciously simple, smart cooking, head to this
AMERICAN charming little bistro on the edge of town. The chef-owner uses organic
Fodor'sChoice produce and meats in her soulful preparation of dishes like grilled cobia
★ wrapped in Serrano ham or Moroccan spiced organic chicken breast with braised rainbow chard and couscous. **Known for:** soulful preparation; organic produce and meats; fireplace in winter, deck dining in summer. $ *Average main: $30* ✉ *3065 W. 4th St.* ☎ *775/323–3200* ⊕ *www.4thstbistro.com* ⊘ *Closed Sun. and Mon. No lunch.*

WHERE TO STAY

$ ⊞ **Eldorado Hotel Casino.** In the middle of glittering downtown, this
HOTEL resort's huge tower has rooms overlooking either the mountains or the lights of the city. **Pros:** fun; good food; amusingly kitschy decor. **Cons:** noisy. $ *Rooms from: $60* ✉ *345 N. Virginia St.* ☎ *775/786–5700, 800/879–8879* ⊕ *www.eldoradoreno.com* ⇆ *679 rooms, 137 suites* ⊘ *No meals.*

$ ▢ **Harrah's Reno.** Of the big-name casino hotels in downtown Reno,
HOTEL   double-towered Harrah's remains a reliable choice with its large guest
rooms, decorated in browns and pale gold tones, overlooking downtown and the entire mountain-ringed valley. **Pros:** good location; great
online midweek rates; large guest rooms. **Cons:** large property; impersonal service; some housekeeping lapses. $⑤$ *Rooms from: $70* ✉ *219
N. Center St., at E. 2nd St.* ☏ *775/786–3232, 800/427–7247* ⊕ *www.
harrahsreno.com* ↝ *928 rooms* ꙮ *No meals.*

$ ▢ **Peppermill Reno.** A few miles removed from downtown's flashy main
HOTEL   drag, this property set a high standard for luxury in Reno, especially in
the Tuscan Tower, whose 600 baroque suites have plush king-size beds,
marble bathrooms, and European soaking tubs. **Pros:** luxurious rooms;
casino decor; good coffee shop. **Cons:** deluge of neon may be off-putting
to some; enormous size; mostly expensive dining. $⑤$ *Rooms from: $109*
✉ *2707 S. Virginia St., at Peppermill La.* ☏ *775/826–2121, 866/821–
9996* ⊕ *www.peppermillreno.com* ↝ *1,623 rooms* ꙮ *No meals.*

NIGHTLIFE

CASINOS

Eldorado. Action packed, with lots of slots and popular bar-top video
poker, this casino also has good coffee-shop and food-court fare. Don't
miss the Fountain of Fortune with its massive Florentine-inspired sculptures. ✉ *345 N. Virginia St., at W. 4th St.* ☏ *775/786–5700, 800/879–
8879* ⊕ *www.eldoradoreno.com.*

Peppermill. A few miles from downtown, this casino is known for its
excellent restaurants and neon-bright gambling areas. The Fireside
cocktail lounge is a blast. ✉ *2707 S. Virginia St., at Peppermill La.*
☏ *775/826–2121, 866/821–9996* ⊕ *www.peppermillreno.com.*

Silver Legacy. A 120-foot-tall mining rig and video poker games draw
gamblers to this razzle-dazzle casino. ✉ *407 N. Virginia St., at W. 4th
St.* ☏ *775/325–7411, 800/215–7721* ⊕ *www.silverlegacyreno.com.*

THE FAR NORTH

with Lake Shasta, Mt. Shasta, and
Lassen Volcanic National Park

WELCOME TO THE FAR NORTH

TOP REASONS TO GO

★ **Mother Nature's wonders:** California's Far North has more rivers, streams, lakes, forests, and mountains than you'll ever have time to explore.

★ **Volcanoes:** With two volcanoes to view—Lassen and Shasta—you can learn firsthand what happens when a mountain blows its top.

★ **Fantastic fishing:** Whether you like casting from a riverbank or letting your line bob beside a boat, you'll find fabulous fishing in all the northern counties.

★ **Cool hops:** On a hot day there's nothing quite as inviting as a visit to Chico's world-famous Sierra Nevada Brewery. Take the tour, and then savor a chilled glass on tap at the adjacent brewpub.

★ **Shasta:** Wonderful in all its forms: lake, dam, river, mountain, forest, and town.

1 From Chico to Mt Shasta. The Far North is bisected, south to north, by Interstate 5, which passes through several historic towns and state parks, as well as miles of mountainous terrain. Halfway to the Oregon border is Lake Shasta, a favorite recreation destination, and farther north stands the spectacular snowy peak of Mt. Shasta.

2 The Backcountry. East of Interstate 5, the Far North's main corridor, dozens of scenic two-lane roads crisscross the wilderness, leading to dramatic mountain peaks and fascinating natural wonders. Small towns settled in the second half of the 19th century seem frozen in time, except that they are well equipped with tourist amenities.

GETTING ORIENTED

14

The Far North is a vast area that stretches from the upper reaches of the Sacramento Valley north to the Oregon border and east to Nevada. The region includes all or part of eight counties with sparsely populated rural farming and mountain communities, as well as thriving small cities in the valley. Much of the landscape was shaped by two volcanoes—Mt. Shasta and Mt. Lassen—that draw amateur geologists, weekend hikers, and avid mountain climbers to their rugged terrain. An intricate network of high-mountain watersheds feeds lakes large and small, plus streams and rivers that course through several forests.

OREGON

Dorris Tulelake

Goose Lake

Lava Beds National Monument ◆

Clear Lake

139

395

Canby Alturas

299

89

Adin

McArthur-Burney Falls Memorial State Park ◆

Burney

44 139 395

2

Old Station

Shingletown

Mt. Lassen ▲ Lassen Volcanic National Park ◆

Susanville

Chester 36 Honey Lake (Dry)

Westwood

Greenville

395

32 70

Quincy

70

Portola

Chico

Loyalton

SIERRA NEVADA

99 Oroville

Gridley

Reno

Live Oak

Nevada City

80 Truckee

70 20 Grass Valley

Yuba City Olivehurst 49 Colfax Lake Tahoe

70 Wheatland

65

Auburn

Woodland Rocklin

Citrus Heights

Sacramento 50

NEVADA

Updated by
Daniel Mangin

The Far North's soaring mountain peaks, trail-filled national forests, alpine lakes, and wild rivers teeming with trout make it the perfect destination for outdoor enthusiasts, including hikers, cyclists, kayakers, and bird-watchers. You won't find many hot nightspots or cultural enclaves in this region, but you will find crowd-free national and state parks, crystal-clear mountain streams, superlative hiking and fishing, plus small towns worth exploring. And the spectacular landscapes of Lassen Volcanic National Park and Mt. Shasta are sure to impress.

The wondrous landscape of California's northeastern corner is the product of volcanic activity. At the southern end of the Cascade Range, Lassen Volcanic National Park is the best place to witness the Far North's fascinating geology. Beyond the sulfur vents and bubbling mud pots, the park owes much of its beauty to 10,457-foot Mt. Lassen and 50 wilderness lakes.

The most enduring image of the region, though, is Mt. Shasta, whose 14,179-foot snowcapped peak beckons outdoor adventurers of all kinds. There are many versions of Shasta to enjoy—the mountain, the lake, the river, the town, the dam, and the forest—all named after the Native Americans known as the Shatasla, or Sastise, who once inhabited the region.

PLANNING

WHEN TO GO

Heat scorches the valley in summer. Temperatures above 110°F are common, but the mountains provide cool respite. Fall throughout the Far North is beautiful, rivaled only by spring, when wildflowers bloom and mountain creeks fed by the snowmelt splash through the forests. Winter is usually temperate in the valley, but cold and snowy in high country. Some tourist attractions are closed in winter.

GETTING HERE AND AROUND

AIR TRAVEL

For the cheapest fares, fly into Sacramento and then rent a car—you'll need one anyway—and drive north. Redding, which is served by PenAir and United, has a small airport. There's no shuttle service, but you can take a taxi for about $32 to downtown Redding.

Air Contacts Redding Municipal Airport. ✉ *6751 Woodrum Circle, off Airport Rd., Redding* 📞 *530/224–4320* ⊕ *www.cityofredding.org/departments/airports.*

Ground Transportation Anytime Taxi. 📞 *530/828–7962 for Chico transfers.* **Road Runner Taxi.** 📞 *530/241–7433 for Redding transfers* ⊕ *www.roadrunnertaxicab.com.*

BUS TRAVEL

Greyhound buses stop in Chico, Red Bluff, Redding, and Weed. TRAX buses serve Corning and Red Bluff. STAGE buses serve Dunsmuir and Mt. Shasta. Various other transit authorities provide local public transit *(see individual town listings for details).*

Bus Contacts Greyhound. 📞 *800/231–2222* ⊕ *www.greyhound.com.* **STAGE.** 📞 *530/842–8295* ⊕ *www.co.siskiyou.ca.us/content/transportation-division-stage.* **TRAX.** 📞 *530/385–2877* ⊕ *www.taketrax.com.*

CAR TRAVEL

Interstate 5 runs up the center of California through Red Bluff and Redding. Chico is east of Interstate 5 on Highway 32. Lassen Volcanic National Park can be reached by Highway 36 from Red Bluff or (except in winter) Highway 44 from Redding. Highway 299 connects Weaverville and Redding. Check weather reports and carry detailed maps, warm clothing, and tire chains whenever you head into mountainous terrain in winter.

Road Conditions Caltrans. 📞 *800/427–7623* ⊕ *www.dot.ca.gov.*

TRAIN TRAVEL

Amtrak serves Chico, Redding, and Dunsmuir.

Train Contact Amtrak. 📞 *800/872–7245* ⊕ *www.amtrak.com.*

RESTAURANTS

Redding, the urban center of the Far North, and college-town Chico have the greatest selection of restaurants. Cafés and simple eateries are the rule in the smaller towns. Dress is always informal. *Restaurant reviews have been shortened. For full information, visit Fodors.com.*

HOTELS

Chain hotels and motels predominate in this region, with the occasional small rustic or Victorian inn. Wilderness resorts close in fall and reopen after the snow season ends in May. For summer holiday weekends in towns such as Mt. Shasta, Dunsmuir, and Chester, and at camping sites within state or national parks, make lodging reservations well in advance. *Hotel reviews have been shortened. For full information, visit Fodors.com.*

B&B Info California Association of Boutique & Breakfast Inns. 📞 *800/373–9251* ⊕ *www.cabbi.com/region/Mount-Shasta.*

WHAT IT COSTS			
$	**$$**	**$$$**	**$$$$**
Restaurants	under $16	$16–$22	$23–$30	over $30
Hotels	under $120	$120–$175	$176–$250	over $250

Restaurant prices are the average cost of a main course at dinner or, if dinner is not served, at lunch. Hotel prices are the lowest cost of a standard double room in high season.

VISITOR INFORMATION

Contacts Shasta Cascade Wonderland Association. ✉ *Shasta Outlets, 1699 Hwy. 273, off I–5, Exit 667, Anderson* ☎ *530/365–7500, 800/474–2782* ⊕ *www. shastacascade.com.* **Trinity County Chamber of Commerce.** ✉ *509 Main St., Weaverville* ☎ *530/623–6101* ⊕ *www.trinitycounty.com.* **Visit Siskiyou.** ☎ *530/926–3696 Mt. Shasta Chamber of Commerce* ⊕ *visitsiskiyou.org.*

FROM CHICO TO MT. SHASTA

From blooming almond orchards in the fertile Sacramento River valley to forested mountains and the dominating peak of a dormant volcano, this section of the Far North entices tourists in all seasons.

CHICO

86 miles north of Sacramento.

The Sacramento Valley town of Chico (Spanish for "small") offers a welcome break from the monotony of Interstate 5. The Chico campus of California State University, the scores of local artisans, and the area's agriculture (primarily almond orchards) all influence the culture here. Chico's claim to fame, however, is the Sierra Nevada Brewery, which keeps beer drinkers across the country happy with its distinctive brews.

GETTING HERE AND AROUND

Highway 99, off Interstate 5 from the north or south, and Highway 32 east off the interstate, intersect Chico. Amtrak and Greyhound stop here, and Butte Regional Transit's B-Line buses serve the area. Chico's downtown neighborhoods are great for walking.

ESSENTIALS

Bus Contact B-Line. ☎ *530/342–0221* ⊕ *www.blinetransit.com.*

Visitor Information Chico Chamber of Commerce. ✉ *441 Main St., Suite 150, near E. 5th St.* ☎ *530/891–5556, 800/852–8570* ⊕ *www.chicochamber.com.*

TOURS

Sacramento River Eco Tours. Wildlife biologist Henry Lomeli guides boat tours down the Sacramento River to explore its diverse fish, fowl, and plant life. ✉ *Chico* ☎ *530/864–8594* ⊕ *www.sacramentoriverecotours. com* 🛥 *From $85.*

EXPLORING

Bidwell Mansion State Historic Park. Built between 1865 and 1868 by General John Bidwell, the founder of Chico, this mansion was designed by Henry W. Cleaveland, a San Francisco architect. Bidwell and his wife welcomed many distinguished guests to their pink Italianate home, including President Rutherford B. Hayes, naturalist John Muir, suffragist Susan B. Anthony, and General William T. Sherman. A one-hour tour takes you through most of the mansion's 26 rooms. ⊠ *525 The Esplanade, at Memorial Way* ☎ *530/895–6144* ⊕ *www.parks.ca.gov/ parkindex* ⊠ *$6* ⊘ *Closed Tues.–Fri.*

Bidwell Park. The sprawling 3,670-acre Bidwell Park is a community green space straddling Big Chico Creek, where scenes from *Gone With the Wind* and the 1938 version of *Robin Hood* (starring Errol Flynn) were filmed. The region's recreational hub, it includes a golf course, swimming areas, and biking, hiking, horseback riding, and in-line skating trails. Chico Creek Nature Center serves as the official information site for Bidwell Park. ⊠ *1968 E. 8th St., off Hwy. 99* ☎ *530/891–4671* ⊕ *www.bidwellpark.org* ⊠ *Park free, nature center $4* ⊘ *Nature center closed Sun.–Tues.*

Fodor'sChoice
★ **Sierra Nevada Brewing Company.** This pioneer of the microbrewery movement still has a hands-on approach to beer making. Tour the brew house and see how the beer is produced—from the sorting of hops through fermentation and bottling, and concluding with a complimentary tasting. You can also enjoy lunch or dinner in the taproom. ■TIP➔ **Tours fill up fast; call or sign up online before you visit.** ⊠ *1075 E. 20th St., at Sierra Nevada St.* ☎ *530/345–2739 taproom, 530/899–4776 tours* ⊕ *www.sierranevada.com* ⊠ *Free.*

WHERE TO EAT AND STAY

$$$
STEAKHOUSE
Fodor'sChoice
★ ✕ **5th Street Steakhouse.** Hand-cut steak is the star in this refurbished early 1900s building, the place to come when you're craving red meat, a huge baked potato, or some fresh seafood. Exposed redbrick walls warm the dining rooms, and a long mahogany bar catches the overflow crowds that jam the place on weekends. **Known for:** weekday happy hour 4:30–6; weekend crowds; prime cuts of beef with white tablecloth service. ⑤ *Average main: $30* ⊠ *345 W. 5th St., at Normal Ave.* ☎ *530/891–6328* ⊕ *www.5thstreetsteakhouse.com* ⊘ *No lunch Sat.–Thurs.*

$
AMERICAN ✕ **Madison Bear Garden.** This downtown favorite inside a historic structure lies two blocks south of the Chico State campus. It's a great spot for checking out the college scene while enjoying a burger and a brew. **Known for:** beer selection; curly fries; lengthy weekday happy hours. ⑤ *Average main: $8* ⊠ *316 W. 2nd St., at Salem St.* ☎ *530/891–1639* ⊕ *www.madisonbeargarden.com.*

$$
HOTEL 🏨 **Hotel Diamond.** Crystal chandeliers and gleaming century-old wood floors and banisters welcome guests into the foyer of this restored 1904 gem near Chico State University. **Pros:** great downtown location; refined rooms, some with bay windows and fireplaces; one of the town's best restaurants. **Cons:** street scene can be noisy on weekends; some rooms are small; some rooms lack tubs. ⑤ *Rooms from: $132* ⊠ *220 W. 4th St., near Broadway* ☎ *530/893–3100, 866/993–3100* ⊕ *www.hoteldiamondchico.com* ⇆ *43 rooms* ❙❘❙ *Breakfast.*

CORNING

29 miles northwest of Chico, 50 miles south of Redding.

Signs along Highway 99 and Interstate 5 beckon travelers to Corning, whose favorable soil and plentiful sunshine have made the town a center of olive cultivation and olive oil manufacturing. At several tasting rooms you can sample olives, olive oil, and other products.

GETTING HERE AND AROUND

Corning lies just off Interstate 5 at Exit 631. From Chico take Highway 99 for 17½ miles and follow signs west to Corning. TRAX provides weekday bus service from Red Bluff.

EXPLORING

Fodor's Choice ★ **Lucero Olive Oil.** As a brand Lucero dates back to the mid-2000s, but the family that started the company began farming olives in the Corning area in 1947. Lucero's Extra Virgin olive oils have won countless awards in California and abroad. In the tasting room adjacent to the mill you can taste oils like Ascalona and Koroneiki and ones infused with lemon, chili, and other flavors, sometimes paired with excellent balsamic vinegars. ⌧ *2120 Loleta Ave., off Hwy. 99 W, 1 mile south of Solano St.* ☎ *530/824–2190* ⊕ *www.lucerooliveoil.com* ✉ *Free.*

FAMILY **Olive Pit.** Three generations of the Craig family run this combination café, store, and tasting room where you can learn all about California olive production and sample olive products, craft beers and small-lot wines, and other artisanal foods. Sandwich selections at the café include muffulettas (of course) and olive burgers. Wash your choice down with a balsamic shake in flavors that include peach, coconut, strawberry, and French prune. ■TIP➔ The Olive Pit opens at 7 am and closes at 8 pm. ⌧ *2156 Solano St., off I–5, Exit 631 (Corning Rd.)* ☎ *530/824–4667, 800/654–8374* ⊕ *www.olivepit.com* ✉ *Tastings free for olive oil, $5 for beer and wine.*

RED BLUFF

41 miles north of Chico.

Red Bluff is a gateway to Lassen Volcanic National Park. Established in the mid-19th century as a shipping center on the Sacramento River, and named for the color of its soil, the town, filled with dozens of restored Victorians, makes a good base for outdoor adventures in the area. The Tehama Country Visitor Center has information about wine tasting and other activities.

GETTING HERE AND AROUND

Access Red Bluff via exits off Interstate 5, or by driving north on Highway 99. Highway 36 travels east–west through town; east of the freeway it's called Antelope Boulevard, west of it Oak Street. Greyhound buses stop in Red Bluff and provide connecting service to Amtrak. TRAX (Tehama Rural Area Express) provides bus service on weekdays.

ESSENTIALS

Visitor Information Tehama Country Visitor Center. ⌧ *250 Antelope Blvd., ¼-mile east of I–5* ☎ *530/529–0133* ⊕ *www.visittehamacountry.com.*

EXPLORING

Fodor'sChoice ★ **Gaumer's Jewelry.** The Gaumer family has been making and selling jewelry in Red Bluff since the 1960s, and has been collecting rocks, gems, and minerals for even longer. When the jewelry shop is open, you can tour its fascinating museum, whose displays include crystals, gemstone carvings, fossils, and fluorescent minerals. ✉ 78 *Belle Mill Rd. ⊹ From I–5, Exit 649, head west on Hwy. 36 (Antelope Blvd.); make a right on Center Ave. and immediately make another right onto Belle Mill* ☎ *530/527–6166* ⊕ *www.gaumers.com* 🔊 *Free* ☉ *Closed weekends.*

RED BLUFF ROUND-UP

Check out old-time rodeo at its best during the Red Bluff Round-Up. Held the third weekend of April, this annual event attracts some of the best cowboys in the country. For more information, visit ⊕ *redbluffroundup.com.*

14

Tuscan Ridge Estate Winery. Depending on the day, this crowd-pleasing winery with a vineyard-view tasting room serves pizzas or antipasti to accompany some of the nearly two dozen reds and whites made here. Most of the grapes for them come from the Sierra foothills; the Zinfandel and Syrah in particular are worth seeking out. ■**TIP**➜ **The winery opens in the late afternoon on Thursday and Friday.** ✉ *19260 Ridge Rd.* ☎ *530/527–7393* ⊕ *www.tuscanridgeestate.com* 🔊 *Tasting $10* ☉ *Closed Mon.–Wed.*

WHERE TO EAT AND STAY

$$ ✕ **Green Barn Steakhouse.** You're likely to find cowboys sporting Stetsons
STEAKHOUSE and spurs feasting on beef medallions, baby back ribs, and prime rib at "the Barn," Red Bluff's premier steak house. For lighter fare, try the fish or pasta entrées, but whatever you choose don't miss the bread pudding with rum sauce for dessert. **Known for:** top-quality beef; old-style Western steakhouse decor; bread pudding with rum sauce. Ⓢ *Average main: $22* ✉ *5 Chestnut Ave., at Antelope Blvd.* ☎ *530/527–3161* ⊕ *www.greenbarnsteakhouse.com* ☉ *Closed Sun.; no lunch Sat.*

$ 🏨 **Hampton Inn & Suites Red Bluff.** In a town filled with budget chain prop-
HOTEL erties, this three-story hotel with clean, spacious rooms and a high-ceilinged lobby qualifies as the grande dame. **Pros:** clean, spacious rooms; Wi-Fi works well; pool and business and fitness centers. **Cons:** pricey for the area; on the north end of town away from most attractions; lacks personality. Ⓢ *Rooms from: $119* ✉ *520 Adobe Rd.* ☎ *530/529–4178* ⊕ *www.hamptoninn3.hilton.com* ↩ *97 rooms* ⦿❙ *Breakfast.*

REDDING

32 miles north of Red Bluff on I–5.

As the largest city in the Far North and a gateway to Lassen Volcanic National Park's northern entrance, Redding is an ideal headquarters for exploring the surrounding countryside.

GETTING HERE AND AROUND

Interstate 5 is the major north–south route into Redding. Highway 299 bisects the city east–west, and Highway 44 connects Redding and Lassen Park's north entrance. Amtrak and Greyhound stop here.

ESSENTIALS

Bus Information Redding Area Bus Authority. ☎ 530/241–2877 ⊕ www.rabaride.com.

Visitor Information Redding Convention and Visitors Bureau. ✉ Visitor center, 844 Sundial Bridge Dr. ☎ 530/225–4100, 800/874–7562 ⊕ www.visitredding.com.

EXPLORING

Moseley Family Cellars. Although its street name conjures up pastoral images, this winery whose grapes come from Napa, Sonoma, Lodi, and some local vineyards is actually in an industrial park. It's still worth a visit, not only for its wines—two Chardonnays and a Grenache, Syrah, Mourvèdre red blend are among the stars—but also the hospitality of co-owner Mimi Moseley (husband Marty makes the wines), who's happy to help you plan other area winery stops. ✉ 4712 Mountain Lakes Blvd., Suite 300 ☎ 530/229–9463 ⊕ www.moseleyfamilycellars.com ⬚ Tasting $10 ⊗ Closed Mon.–Wed. (except by appointment).

Shasta State Historic Park. Six miles west of downtown lies the former town of Shasta City, which thrived in the mid- to late 1800s. The park's 19 acres of half-ruined brick buildings and overgrown graveyards, accessed via trails, are a reminder of the glory days of the California gold rush. The former county courthouse building, jail, and gallows have been restored to their 1860s appearance. The Litsch General Store, in operation from 1850 to 1950, is now a museum, with displays of many items once sold here. ✉ 15312 Hwy. 299 ☎ 530/243–8194 ⊕ www.parks.ca.gov/?page_id=456 ⬚ Free to park, $3 Courthouse Museum ⊗ Courthouse Museum closed Mon.–Wed.

FAMILY
Fodor's Choice
★

Turtle Bay Exploration Park. This park has walking trails, an aquarium, an arboretum and botanical gardens, and many interactive exhibits for kids. The main draw is the stunning **Sundial Bridge,** a metal and translucent glass pedestrian walkway, suspended by cables from a single tower, spanning a broad bend in the Sacramento River. On sunny days the tower lives up to the bridge's name, casting a shadow on the ground below to mark time. Access to the bridge and arboretum is free, but there's a fee for the museum and gardens. ✉ 844 Sundial Bridge Dr. ☎ 530/243–8850, 800/887–8532 ⊕ www.turtlebay.org ⬚ Museum $16 ⊗ Museum closed Mon. and Tues. early Sept.–mid-Mar.

WHERE TO EAT AND STAY

$$$$
AMERICAN

✕ **Clearie's Restaurant and Lounge.** The granddaughter of "Doc" Clearie, who ran a popular Redding restaurant long ago, returned the family name to fine-dining prominence with this white-tablecloth lounge and restaurant. Many guests begin with the signature blackberry lavender lemon drop "martini," bubbling like a cauldron courtesy of dry ice, and perhaps a baked Brie appetizer before, depending on the season, a main course like short-rib beef Stroganoff or pan-seared ahi tuna. **Known for:** white-tablecloth ambience; well-executed cuisine; decent wine list. Ⓢ Average main: $32 ✉ 1325 Eureka Way ☎ 530/241–4535 ⊕ www.cleariesrestaurant.com ⊗ Closed Sun.

$ ✗**From the Hearth Artisan Bakery & Café.** A homegrown variation on the
AMERICAN Panera theme, this extremely popular operation (as in expect a wait at
peak dining hours) serves pastries, eggs and other hot dishes, and good
coffee drinks, juices, and smoothies for breakfast, adding a diverse selection of wraps, panini, sandwiches, burgers, rice bowls, and soups the rest
of the day. Some sandwiches are made with a bread that FTH bills as
"Redding's original sourdough." There are two other locations in Redding (one downtown) and another in Red Bluff. **Known for:** baked goods;
breakfast until noon on weekends; diverse selection. $ *Average main:*
$11 ✉ *2650 Churn Creek Rd.* ☎ *530/646–4315* ⊕ *www.fthcafe.com.*

$$$ ✗**Jack's Grill.** The original Jack opened his grill (and an upstairs brothel)
STEAKHOUSE in 1938—tamer these days but often jam-packed and noisy, this place
is famous for its 16-ounce steaks and deep-fried shrimp and chicken
dishes. What Jack's lacks in culinary finesse it more than makes up for
in atmosphere. **Known for:** 1930s atmosphere; great martinis; thick slabs
of beef. $ *Average main: $24* ✉ *1743 California St., near Sacramento St.*
☎ *530/241–9705* ⊕ *www.jacksgrillredding.com* ⊗ *Closed Sun. No lunch.*

$$ ✗**Moonstone Bistro.** About a mile and a half southwest of downtown this
AMERICAN light-filled restaurant in a strip mall prides itself on its use of seasonal
organic produce, free-range meats, sustainable line-caught fish, and
cage-free eggs. All day you can dine on fish tacos, a large mixed-greens
salad, or burgers (standard, veggie, or teriyaki mushroom Swiss), with
fish, chicken, and pasta dishes available at lunch, and heavier pork
and beef dishes added for dinner. **Known for:** organic produce; all-day
bistro menu; Sunday brunch. $ *Average main: $21* ✉ *3425 Placer St.,*
near Buenaventura Blvd. ☎ *530/241–3663* ⊕ *www.moonstonebistro.*
com ⊗ *Closed Mon. No dinner Sun.*

$$$ ✗**View 202.** The view at this glass-walled hilltop restaurant is of the
MODERN Sacramento River below the wide outdoor patio and well beyond the
AMERICAN waterway to snowcapped mountains. The New American menu empha-
sizes grilled meats and fish from noted California purveyors but also
includes bouillabaisse and house-made ravioli. **Known for:** Sacramento
River and mountain views; specialty cocktails; wine list among the
North State's best. $ *Average main: $30* ✉ *202 Hemsted Dr., off E.*
Cypress Ave. ☎ *530/226–8439* ⊕ *www.view202redding.com.*

$ ⌂**Bridgehouse Bed & Breakfast.** In a residential area a block from the
B&B/INN Sacramento River and a half-mile from downtown Redding, this inn
Fodor'sChoice contains six rooms in two side-by-side homes. **Pros:** easy hospitality;
★ proximity to downtown and Turtle Bay; freshly baked scones at full
breakfast. **Cons:** lacks pool, fitness center, and other standard hotel
amenities; the two least expensive rooms are small; books up well ahead
in summer. $ *Rooms from: $119* ✉ *1455 Riverside Dr.* ☎ *530/247–*
7177 ⊕ *www.bridgehousebb.com* ⟿ *6 rooms* ⦿ *Breakfast.*

$$ ⌂**Fairfield Inn & Suites Redding.** The three-story Fairfield's clean rooms,
HOTEL amiable service, 24-hour business center, mountain views from some
FAMILY rooms, and bright, chipper public areas make it the best choice among
Redding's many chain properties. **Pros:** clean rooms; amiable service;
many amenities. **Cons:** prices often higher than competitors; corporate
feel; some rooms are small. $ *Rooms from: $146* ✉ *164 Caterpillar*
Rd. ☎ *530/243–3200* ⊕ *www.marriott.com/hotels/travel/rddre* ⟿ *75*
rooms ⦿ *Breakfast.*

14

NIGHTLIFE

Final Draft Brewing Company. This spacious brick-walled brewpub opened in 2017 to high acclaim for its accessible ales and above-average pub grub. Try the beer-battered fish and chips with swirly fries instead of regular ones. While they're cooking, order a sampler flight to decide which of the brews to wash them down with. ⊠ *1600 California St., at Placer St.* ☎ *530/338–1198* ⊕ *www.finaldraftbrewingcompany.com.*

Wildcard Brewing Tied House. At the mellow outpost of this brewery founded in 2012 you can sample an adventurous lineup that includes a pilsner, a red ale, several IPAs, and an almost chewy oatmeal porter. The flagship North State IPA's citrus notes are amped up to good effect in the Ruby Red Grapefruit, worth checking out if on tap when you visit. ⊠ *1321 Butte St., at Pine St.* ☎ *530/255–8582* ⊕ *www.wildcardbrewingco.com.*

Woody's Brewing Company. A fun downtown hangout with a partylike vibe, Woody's has built a loyal following for its pierogi, special-recipe tater tots, and range of beers from a pilsner and fruited wheat ales to a double Belgian white IPA and the Shasta Street stout. The reasonably priced sampler flights provide a good introduction. ⊠ *1257 Oregon St., at Shasta St.* ☎ *530/768–1034* ⊕ *www.woodysbrewing.biz.*

WEAVERVILLE

46 miles west of Redding on Hwy. 299.

Chinese miners erected the 1874 Joss House that anchors Weaverville's impressive downtown historic district. The town, population about 3,600, is also a popular headquarters for family vacations and hiking, fishing, and gold-panning excursions.

GETTING HERE AND AROUND

Highway 299, east from the Pacific Coast or west from Redding, becomes Main Street in central Weaverville. Highway 36 from Red Bluff to Highway 3 heading north leads to Weaverville. Trinity Transit provides bus service.

ESSENTIALS

Visitor Information Trinity County Visitors Bureau. ⊠ *509 Main St.* ☎ *530/623–6101* ⊕ *www.visittrinity.com.*

EXPLORING

Trinity County Hal Goodyear Historical Park. For a vivid sense of Weaverville's past, visit this park, especially its **Jake Jackson Memorial Museum.** A blacksmith shop and a stamp mill (where ore is crushed) from the 1890s are still in use during certain community events. Also here are the Trinity County Courthouse's original jail cells. ⊠ *780 Main St., at Bartlett La.* ☎ *530/623–5211* ⊕ *www.trinitymuseum.org* ⊙ *Museum closed various days Jan.–Apr. and Oct.–Dec.*

Fodor's Choice ★ **Weaverville Joss House State Historic Park.** Weaverville's main attraction is the Joss House, a Taoist temple built in 1874 and called Won Lim Miao ("the temple of the forest beneath the clouds") by Chinese miners. The oldest continuously used Chinese temple in California, it attracts worshippers from around the world. With its golden altar, antique weaponry, and carved wooden canopies, the Joss House is a piece of California history that can best be appreciated on a guided 30-minute tour. ⊠ *630 Main St., at Oregon St.* ☎ *530/623–5284* ⊕ *www.parks.ca.gov/?page_id=457* ✉ *Museum free; guided tour $4* ⊙ *Closed Mon.–Wed.*

WHERE TO EAT AND STAY

$$
AMERICAN
✕ **La Grange Café.** In 2016 new owners revived this locals'-fave restaurant and bar inside two 1854 brick buildings that rank among Weaverville's oldest structures. For lunch are salads, a few pastas, burgers, and sandwiches that include a nicely executed Monte Cristo, with most of the same repeating for dinner, supplemented by nightly specials, Angus steaks (topped with bourbon or herb butter), roasted half chicken, a pork chop, and spicy-good jambalaya. **Known for:** Angus steaks; spicy jambalaya; salads and pastas. $ *Average main: $20* ⊠ *520 Main St.* ☎ *530/623–5325* ⊙ *Closed Sun. and Mon.*

$
AMERICAN
✕ **Mamma Llama Eatery & Cafe.** Tap into the spirit of 21st-century Weaverville at this mellow café that serves breakfast (all day) and lunch and in winter specializes in hot soups to warm body and soul. Expect all the usual suspects at breakfast along with Country Cheesy Potatoes (topped with green chili) and sausage between two biscuits topped with homemade sausage gravy; a spicy club wrap and several vegetarian sandwiches are among the lunch offerings. **Known for:** mellow vibe; good soups; espresso drinks. $ *Average main: $9* ⊠ *490 Main St.* ☎ *530/623–6363* ⊕ *www.mammallama.com.*

$$
HOTEL
🛏 **Weaverville Hotel.** Originally built during the gold rush, this beautifully restored hotel is filled with antiques and period furniture. **Pros:** gracious on-site owners; in heart of town's historic district; beautifully restored. **Cons:** no breakfast on-site; children under 12 not permitted; only one room has a TV. $ *Rooms from: $140* ⊠ *481 Main St., near Court St.* ☎ *530/623–2222, 800/750–8853* ⊕ *www.weavervillehotel. com* ⚡ *7 rooms* ⍾ *No meals.*

$
B&B/INN
Fodor's Choice
★
🛏 **Whitmore Inn.** Amid Weaverville's historic district and shaded by black locust trees, this Victorian inn near shops and restaurants has five rooms, some with a shared bath. **Pros:** Victorian style with modern touches; convenient historic district location; innkeeper generous with sightseeing tips. **Cons:** some rooms share a bath; Victorian style in most rooms not for everyone; young children not permitted. $ *Rooms from: $100* ⊠ *761 Main St.* ☎ *530/623–2509* ⊕ *www.whitmoreinn.com* ⚡ *5 rooms* ⍾ *Breakfast.*

SPORTS AND THE OUTDOORS

Weaverville Ranger Station. Check here for maps, free wilderness and campfire permits, and information about local fishing and the 600 miles of hiking trails in the 500,000-acre Trinity Alps Wilderness. ⊠ *360 Main St.* ☎ *530/623–2121.*

14

LAKE SHASTA AREA

12 miles north of Redding.

When you think of the Lake Shasta Area, picture water, wilderness, dazzling stalagmites—and a fabulous man-made project, Shasta Dam, in the midst of it all.

GETTING HERE AND AROUND

Interstate 5 north of Redding is the main link to the Lake Shasta area. Get to the dam by passing through the tiny city of Shasta Lake. There is no local bus service.

EXPLORING

Lake Shasta. Numerous types of fish inhabit the lake, including rainbow trout, salmon, bass, brown trout, and catfish. The lake region also has California's largest nesting population of bald eagles. You can rent fishing boats, ski boats, sailboats, canoes, paddleboats, Jet Skis, and windsurfing boards at marinas and resorts along the 370-mile shoreline. ⊠ *Shasta Lake* ⊕ *www.shastacascade.com.*

Fodor's Choice **Lake Shasta Caverns National Natural Landmark.** Stalagmites, stalactites,
★ flowstone deposits, and crystals entice visitors to the Lake Shasta Caverns. To see this impressive spectacle, you must take the two-hour tour, which includes a catamaran ride across the McCloud arm of Lake Shasta and a bus ride up North Grey Rocks Mountain to the cavern entrance. The temperature in the caverns is 58°F year-round, making them a cool retreat on a hot summer day. The most awe-inspiring of the limestone rock formations is the glistening Cathedral Room, which appears to be gilded. ⊠ *20359 Shasta Caverns Rd., Exit 695 off I–5, 17 miles north of Redding, Lakehead* ☎ *530/238–2341, 800/795–2283* ⊕ *www.lakeshastacaverns.com* ⊒ *$26.*

Shasta Dam. This is the second-largest concrete dam in the United States (only Grand Coulee in Washington is bigger). The visitor center has computerized photographic tours of the dam construction, video presentations, fact sheets, and historical displays. Hour-long guided tours inside the dam and its powerhouse leave from the center. ⊠ *16349 Shasta Dam Blvd., off Lake Blvd., Shasta Lake* ☎ *530/275–4463* ⊕ *www.usbr.gov/mp/ncao/shasta* ⊒ *Free.*

SPORTS AND THE OUTDOORS

FISHING

The Fishen Hole. A couple of miles from the lake, this bait-and-tackle shop sells fishing licenses and provides information about conditions. ⊠ *3844 Shasta Dam Blvd., at Red Ave., Shasta Lake* ☎ *530/275–4123.*

HOUSEBOATING

Houseboats come in all sizes except small. As a rule, rentals are outfitted with cooking utensils, dishes, and most of the equipment you'll need—you supply the food and linens. When you rent a houseboat, you receive a short course in how to maneuver your launch before you set out. You can fish, swim, sunbathe on the flat roof, or sit on the deck and watch the world go by. Expect to spend at least $400 a day (two- or three-night minimum) for a craft that sleeps six. Bridge Bay Resort and Shasta Marina at Packers Bay are two reliable outfits.

Bridge Bay Resort. This resort offers modest lakeside lodging, a restaurant, boat and Jet Ski rentals, and a full-service marina. Houseboats for rent sleep from 8 to 13 people. ✉ *10300 Bridge Bay Rd., off I–5, Exit 690, Redding* ☎ *800/752–9669, 530/275–3021* ⊕ *www.bridgebay-houseboats.com* ✉ *From $550 per night in summer, 2-night minimum.*

FAMILY
Fodor'sChoice
★
Shasta Marina at Packers Bay. Packed with amenities, well-maintained, and clean, this highly regarded operator's deluxe houseboats sleep from 14 to 16 people. Some even have a hot tub onboard. ✉ *16814 Packers Bay Rd., west from I–5, Exit 693, Lakehead* ☎ *800/959–3359* ⊕ *shastalake.net* ✉ *From $1200 per night in summer, 3-night minimum.*

DUNSMUIR

14

10 miles south of Mt. Shasta.

Surrounded by towering forests and boasting world-class fly-fishing in the Upper Sacramento River, tiny Dunsmuir was named for a 19th-century Scottish coal baron who offered to build a fountain if the town was renamed in his honor. You can spend the night in restored cabooses at the fun Railroad Park Resort.

GETTING HERE AND AROUND

Reach Dunsmuir via exits off Interstate 5 at the north and south ends of town. Amtrak stops here; Greyhound stops in Weed, 20 miles north. On weekdays, STAGE buses serve Dunsmuir.

ESSENTIALS

Visitor Information Dunsmuir Chamber of Commerce. ✉ *5915 Dunsmuir Ave., Suite 100* ☎ *530/235–2177* ⊕ *dunsmuir.com.*

EXPLORING

Fodor'sChoice
★
Castle Crags State Park. Named for its 6,000-foot glacier-polished crags, which were formed by volcanic activity centuries ago, this park offers fishing on the upper Sacramento River, hiking in the backcountry, and a view of Mt. Shasta. The crags draw climbers and hikers from around the world. The 4,350-acre park has 28 miles of hiking trails, including a 2¾-mile access trail to **Castle Crags Wilderness,** part of the **Shasta-Trinity National Forest.** There are excellent trails at lower altitudes, too, including the 1-mile Indian Creek Nature Loop Trail (near the entrance), whose theme is the local water cycle. ✉ *6 miles south of Dunsmuir, Castella/Castle Crags exit off I–5, 20022 Castle Creek Rd., Castella* ☎ *530/235–2684* ⊕ *www.parks.ca.gov/parkindex* ✉ *$8 per vehicle, day use.*

WHERE TO EAT AND STAY

$$$
MEDITERRANEAN
✕ **Café Maddalena.** The chef here gained experience working in top San Francisco restaurants before moving north to prepare adventurous Mediterranean fare with a French influence. Selections change seasonally but always feature a vegetarian dish, along with fish, beef, and chicken entrées. **Known for:** Euro-centric wine list; daily prix-fixe menu; outdoor dining under grape arbor. $ *Average main: $26* ✉ *5801 Sacramento Ave.* ☎ *530/235–2725* ⊕ *www.cafemaddalena.com* ⊙ *Closed Mon.–Wed. and Jan.–mid-Feb. No lunch.*

$$ ✕ **Yaks on the 5.** Renowned for bacon-
AMERICAN jalapeño and many other grass-fed
burgers, Yaks has gotten so much
social-media lovin' the crowds can
be huge in-season, but this festive
joint wins most diners' hearts with its
house-made ingredients (even buns),
dozens of beers, and upbeat decor
and staffers. You'll pay more than
expected but will likely leave feeling

> **FINE FISHING**
>
> The upper Sacramento River near
> Dunsmuir is consistently rated
> one of the best fishing spots
> in the country. Check with the
> chamber of commerce for local
> fishing guides.

you got your money's worth. **Known for:** garlic, duck-chili, barbecue, and
other burgers; many beers on tap; upbeat decor and staffer. $ *Average
main: $17* ✉ *4917 Dunsmuir Ave.* ☎ *530/678–3517* ⊕ *www.yaks.com.*

$$ ☕ **Railroad Park Resort.** The antique cabooses here were collected over
HOTEL more than three decades and have been converted into 23 cozy motel
FAMILY rooms in honor of Dunsmuir's railroad legacy (there are also four cabins). **Pros:** gorgeous setting; unique accommodations; kitschy fun. **Cons:**
cabooses can feel cramped; must drive to Dunsmuir restaurants; some
guests find location too remote. $ *Rooms from: $135* ✉ *100 Railroad
Park Rd.* ☎ *530/235–4440* ⊕ *www.rrpark.com* ⤳ *27 rooms* ⦿ *No meals.*

MT. SHASTA

34 miles north of Lake Shasta.

While a snow-covered dormant volcano is the area's dazzling draw,
the town of Mt. Shasta charms visitors with its small shops, friendly
residents, and beautiful scenery in all seasons.

GETTING HERE AND AROUND

Three exits off Interstate 5 lead to the town of Mt. Shasta. When snow
hasn't closed the route, you can take Highway 89 from the Lassen Park
area toward Burney then northeast to Mt. Shasta. The ski park is off
Highway 89. Greyhound stops at Weed, 10 miles north; Amtrak stops
at Dunsmuir, 10 miles south. STAGE provides bus service.

ESSENTIALS

**Visitor Information Mt. Shasta Chamber of Commerce and Visitors
Bureau.** ✉ *300 Pine St., at W. Lake St.* ☎ *530/926–4865, 800/926–4865*
⊕ *www.mtshastachamber.com.*

EXPLORING

Fodor's Choice **Mt. Shasta.** The crown jewel of the 2.5-million-acre Shasta-Trinity
★ National Forest, Mt. Shasta, a 14,179-foot-high dormant volcano, is
a mecca for day hikers. It's especially enticing in spring, when fragrant
Shasta lilies and other flowers adorn the rocky slopes. A paved road,
the Everitt Memorial Highway, reaches only as far as the timberline; the
final 6,000 feet are a tough climb of rubble, ice, and snow (the summit is
perpetually ice-packed). Hiking enthusiasts include this trek with those
to the peaks of Kilimanjaro and Mount Fuji in lists of iconic must-do
mountain hikes. ■ TIP➔ **Always check weather predictions; sudden
storms have trapped climbers with snow and freezing temperatures.**
✉ *Mt. Shasta* ⊕ *www.mtshastachamber.com.*

WHERE TO EAT AND STAY

$$$ ✕ **Lilys.** This restaurant in a white-clapboard home, framed by a picket
ECLECTIC fence and arched trellis, offers an eclectic menu, starting with bourbon-
glazed French toast for breakfast. Lunch and dinner selections vary
seasonally but often include roasted beet salad, herb-stuffed fresh trout,
a walnut garbanzo veggie burger, and marinated pork chops with can-
nellini beans. **Known for:** eclectic menu; flavorful vegetarian options;
weekend brunch. $ *Average main: $25* ⊠ *1013 S. Mt. Shasta Blvd., at
Holly St.* ☎ *530/926–3372* ⊕ *www.lilysrestaurant.com.*

$ ✕ **Poncho & Lefkowitz.** The cuisine is Mexican and American at this small
MEXICAN stand popular with locals and visitors for its burritos, quesadillas, fish
tacos, tamales, sausages, and hot dogs. Order at the window and enjoy
your meal at outdoor picnic tables with Mt. Shasta views. **Known for:**
fish tacos; house-made strawberry lemonade; outdoor picnic tables
with Mt. Shasta views. $ *Average main: $8* ⊠ *401 S. Mt. Shasta Blvd.*
☎ *530/926–1505* ⊘ *Closed Sun. and Mon.*

$ ✕ **Seven Suns Coffee and Cafe.** A favorite gathering spot for locals, this
CAFÉ small coffee shop serves specialty wraps for breakfast and lunch, plus
soups and salad. Pastries, made daily, include muffins, cookies, and
scones (great blackberry ones in season). **Known for:** pastries made
daily; outside patio; blackberry scones in season. $ *Average main: $9*
⊠ *1011 S. Mt. Shasta Blvd., at Holly St.* ☎ *530/926–9701* ⊕ *www.
mtshastacoffee.com* ⊘ *No dinner.*

$$$ ⌂ **Best Western Tree House Motor Inn.** The clean, standard rooms at this
HOTEL motel less than a mile from downtown Mt. Shasta are decorated with
natural-wood furnishings. **Pros:** close to ski park; indoor pool; lobby's
roaring fireplace is a big plus on winter days. **Cons:** not all lodging
buildings have elevators; pricier than other chain properties (though it
delivers more); no free breakfast, though discount voucher provided.
$ *Rooms from: $179* ⊠ *111 Morgan Way* ☎ *530/926–3101, 800/545–
7164* ⊕ *www.bestwesterncalifornia.com/hotels/best-western-plus-tree-
house* ⤳ *98 rooms* ⦿ *Breakfast.*

$ ⌂ **Mount Shasta Inn & Suites.** Although its rooms are sparsely decorated
HOTEL with unremarkable furnishings, this two-story motel conveniently
located on Mt. Shasta's main drag wins points for cleanliness and
competitive rates. **Pros:** clean, spacious rooms; competitive rates; convenient location. **Cons:** no style; few amenities; front desk not staffed
24/7. $ *Rooms from: $80* ⊠ *710 S. Mt. Shasta Blvd.* ☎ *530/918–9292*
⊕ *www.mtshastainn.com* ⤳ *30 rooms* ⦿ *No meals.*

$$$ ⌂ **Mount Shasta Resort.** Private chalets are nestled among tall pine trees
RENTAL along the shore of Lake Siskiyou, all with gas-log fireplaces and full
kitchens. **Pros:** incredible views; romantic woodsy setting; some pet-
friendly rooms for extra fee. **Cons:** kids may get bored; must drive to
Mt. Shasta restaurants; some hospitality lapses. $ *Rooms from: $179*
⊠ *1000 Siskiyou Lake Blvd.* ☎ *530/926–3030, 800/958–3363* ⊕ *www.
mountshastaresort.com* ⤳ *65 rooms* ⦿ *No meals.*

14

SPORTS AND THE OUTDOORS
HIKING
Mt. Shasta Forest Service Ranger Station. Check in here for current trail conditions and avalanche reports. ✉ *204 W. Alma St., at Pine St.* ☎ *530/926–4511, 530/926–9613 avalanche conditions.*

MOUNTAIN CLIMBING
Fifth Season Mountaineering Shop. This shop rents bicycles and skiing and climbing equipment, and operates a recorded 24-hour climber-skier report. ✉ *300 N. Mt. Shasta Blvd.* ☎ *530/926–3606, 530/926–5555 ski phone* ⊕ *www.thefifthseason.com.*

Shasta Mountain Guides. These guides lead hiking, climbing, and skiing tours to Mt. Shasta's summit. ✉ *Mt. Shasta* ☎ *530/926–3117* ⊕ *shastaguides.com.*

SKIING
FAMILY **Mt. Shasta Board & Ski Park.** Three-quarters of the trails at this ski park on Mt. Shasta's southeast flank are for beginning or intermediate skiers. A package for beginners, available through the ski school, includes a lift ticket, ski rental, and a lesson. There's night skiing for those who want to see the moon rise as they schuss. The base lodge has a simple café, a ski shop, and a ski-snowboard rental shop. Facilities: 32 trails; 425 skiable acres; 1,435-foot vertical drop; 5 lifts. ✉ *Hwy. 89 exit east from I–5, south of Mt. Shasta* ☎ *530/926–8610, 800/754–7427,* ⊕ *www. skipark.com* 🎫 *Lift ticket $64.*

THE BACKCOUNTRY
The Far North's primitive, rugged backcountry is arguably full of more natural wonders than any other region in California.

MCARTHUR–BURNEY FALLS MEMORIAL STATE PARK
52 miles southeast of Mt. Shasta, 41 miles north of Lassen Volcanic National Park.

One of the most spectacular sights in the Far North is Burney Falls, where countless ribbonlike streams pour from moss-covered crevices. You have to travel forested back roads to reach this gem, but the park's beauty is well worth the trek.

GETTING HERE AND AROUND
To get to the falls, head east off Interstate 5 on Highway 89 at Mt. Shasta. From Redding, head east on Highway 299 to Highway 89; follow signs 6 miles to the park.

EXPLORING
FAMILY **McArthur–Burney Falls Memorial State Park.** Just inside this park's southern boundary, Burney Creek wells up from the ground and divides
Fodor's Choice into two falls that cascade over a 129-foot cliff into a pool below. ★ Countless ribbonlike streams pour from hidden moss-covered crevices; resident bald eagles are frequently seen soaring overhead. You can walk a self-guided nature trail that descends to the foot of the falls, which Theodore Roosevelt—according to legend—called "the

eighth wonder of the world." On warm days, swim at Lake Britton; lounge on the beach; rent motorboats, paddleboats, and canoes; or relax at one of the campsites or picnic areas. ⌧ *24898 Hwy. 89, 6 miles north of Hwy. 299, Burney* ☎ *530/335–2777* ⊕ *www.parks. ca.gov/?page_id=455* ⌧ *$8 per vehicle, day use.*

OFF THE BEATEN PATH

Lava Beds National Monument. Thousands of years of volcanic activity created this rugged landscape, which is distinguished by cinder cones, lava flows, spatter cones, pit craters, and more than 400 underground lava tube caves. During the Modoc War (1872–73), Modoc Indians under the leadership of their chief "Captain Jack" Kientopoos took refuge in a natural lava fortress now known as Captain Jack's Stronghold. They managed to hold off U.S. Army forces, which outnumbered them 20 to 1, for five months. When exploring this area, be sure to wear hard-soled boots and a bump hat. Bring a flashlight with you, although some are available for borrowing at the Indian Well Visitor Center, at the park's southern end. This is where summer activities such as guided walks, cave tours, and campfire programs depart from. ■TIP→ About 78 miles from McArthur-Burney Memorial State Park (85 miles from Mt. Shasta City), Lava Beds is extremely remote; see website for detailed driving instructions. ⌧ *1 Indian Well, Tulelake* ✛ *From McArthur-Burney state park, take Hwy. 89 south to Hwy. 299 east to Bieber-Lookout Rd. and Hwy. 139 north to Forest Service Rte. 97 west and follow signs; from Mt. Shasta City, take Hwy. 89 to Forest Service Rtes. 97 and 10* ☎ *530/667–2282* ⊕ *www.nps.gov/labe* ⌧ *$15 per vehicle; $10 on foot, bicycle, or motorcycle.*

LASSEN VOLCANIC NATIONAL PARK

45 miles east of Redding, 48 miles east of Red Bluff.

Fissures and fumaroles burble and belch as reminders of Lassen Peak's dramatic eruption a century ago. Four different types of volcanoes form part of this park's fascinating geothermal landscape.

GETTING HERE AND AROUND

Whether coming from the west or the east, reach the park's southern entrance via Highway 36E, and turn onto Highway 89 for a short drive to the park. The northwest entrance is reached via Highway 44 from Redding and Susanville. No buses serve the area.

EXPLORING

Fodor'sChoice ★ **Volcanic Legacy Scenic Byway.** This 185-mile scenic drive begins in Chester and loops through the forests, volcanic peaks, hydrothermal springs, and lava fields of Lassen National Forest and Lassen Volcanic National Park, providing an all-day excursion into dramatic wilderness. From Chester, take Highway 36 west to Highway 89 north, which within the park is called Lassen Volcanic National Park Highway, or Lassen Park Highway. Upon exiting the park at the north, follow Highway 44 east and then south to Highway 36, on which you can head back west to Chester. Parts of this route are inaccessible in winter and spring. ⌧ *Lassen Volcanic National Park* ☎ *800/427–7623 CA Highway info service, 530/595–4480 Lassen Park visitor center.*

Lassen Volcanic
National Park

1/2 mi
1/2 km

TO CHESTER
AND SUSANVILLE →

↑ TO BURNEY AND MT. SHASTA

TO BURNEY AND MT. SHASTA

89

44

89

↓ TO
REDDING

89

TO RED BLUFF
AND CHICO →

Prospect Peak
8,338 ft.

Butte Lake ◆

44

Cinder Cone

PAINTED DUNES

FANTASTIC LAVA BEDS

Ash Butte

Snag
Lake

Juniper
Lake

Fairfield
Peak

Crater Butte

Horseshoe
Lake

GRASSY SWALE

Pacific Crest Trail

Warner Valley ◆

CORRAL MEADOW

Hat Mt.

DERSCH MEADOWS

Summit Lake North

Summit Lake South

Devil's Kitchen

DEVASTATED AREA

READING PEAK

TWIN MEADOWS

CHAOS CRAGS

Lassen Peak
10,457 ft.

Bumpass Hell

89

Kings Creek ◆

Entrance Station

Ranger Station

Manzanita Lake ◆

Sulphur Works

Kohm Yah-mah-nee
Visitor Center

Entrance Station

BLUE LAKE CANYON

Fodor'sChoice **Lassen Volcanic National Park.** A dormant plug dome, Lassen Peak is the
★ main focus of Lassen Volcanic National Park, but this 165-square-mile
tract of dense forests and alpine meadows also abounds with memorable opportunities for hiking, camping, and wildlife photography. The
famed peak began erupting in May 1914, sending pumice, rock, and
snow thundering down the mountain and gas and hot ash billowing into
the atmosphere. Lassen's most spectacular outburst occurred in 1915,
when it blew a cloud of ash almost 6 miles high. The resulting mudflow
destroyed vegetation for miles; the evidence is still visible today, especially in the Devastated Area. The volcano finally came to rest in 1921.
Today fumaroles, mud pots, lakes, and bubbling hot springs create a
fascinating but dangerous landscape that can be viewed throughout the
park, especially via a hiked descent into Bumpass Hell. Because of its
significance as a volcanic landscape, Lassen became a national park in
1916. Several volcanoes—the largest of which is now Lassen Peak—
have been active in the area for roughly 600,000 years. Lassen Park
Road (the continuation of Highway 89 within the park) and 150 miles
of hiking trails provide access to many of these wonders. ⚠ **Heed signs
warning visitors to stay on the trails and railed boardwalks to avoid falling into boiling water or through thin-crusted areas.** ✉ *Mineral* ⊕ *www.
nps.gov/lavo* 🎫 *$20 per car, $15 per motorcycle, $10 per person if not
in motor vehicle* ⊗ *Main (Kohm Yah-mah-nee) visitor center closed
Mon. and Tues. Nov.–Mar.*

FAMILY **Sulphur Works Thermal Area.** Proof of Lassen Peak's volatility becomes
evident shortly after you enter the park at the southwest entrance. Sidewalks skirt boiling springs and sulfur-emitting steam vents. This area is
usually the last site to close because of snow. ✉ *Lassen Park Hwy., 1 mile
from southwest entrance ranger station, Lassen Volcanic National Park.*

WHERE TO EAT AND STAY

$$$ ✕ **Highlands Ranch Restaurant and Bar.** Dining at the Highlands Ranch
AMERICAN Resort's contemporary roadhouse restaurant is in a stained-wood,
high-ceilinged room indoors, or out on the deck, which has views of a
broad serene meadow and the hillside beyond. Among the few sophis-
ticated eating options within Lassen Volcanic National Park's orbit,
the restaurant serves regional American dishes like blackened ahi with
carrot-cucumber slaw and balsamic-marinated duck with blackber-
ries and wild mushrooms. **Known for:** striking views inside and out;
small plates and burgers in the bar; inventive sauces and preparations.
⑤ *Average main: $20* ✉ *Highlands Ranch Resort, 41515 Hwy. 36 E*
☎ *530/595–3388* ⊕ *highlandsranchresort.com/artisans-view-restaurant*
⊗ *Hrs vary seasonally; check website or call.*

$$$$ 🏨 **Drakesbad Guest Ranch.** With propane furnaces and kerosene lamps,
B&B/INN everything about this century-old property in the park's remote and
Fodor'sChoice beautiful southeastern corner harks back to a simpler time. **Pros:** back-
★ to-nature experience; great for family adventures; only full-service
lodging inside the park. **Cons:** accessible only via a partially paved
road leading out of Chester; rustic, with few in-room frills; not open
year-round. ⑤ *Rooms from: $354* ✉ *1 Warner Valley Rd., Chester*
☎ *866/999–0914* ⊕ *www.drakesbad.com* ⊗ *Closed mid-Oct.–early
June* 🛏 *19 rooms* ⦿❘ *All meals.*

$$$
B&B/INN
Fodor's Choice
★
Highlands Ranch Resort. On a gorgeous 175-acre alpine meadow 10 miles from Lassen National Park's southwest entrance, this cluster of smartly designed upscale bungalows is peaceful and luxurious. **Pros:** stunning views; most luxurious accommodations near the park; friendly and helpful staff. **Cons:** pricey for the area (but you get a lot for what you pay); party types may find location too remote; books up months ahead for summer stays. $⑤Rooms from: $239 ⊠ 41515 Hwy. 36 E ☎ 530/595–3388 ⊕ www.highlandsranchresort.com ⊗ Closed some Mon. and Tues. from fall to spring depending on weather; check website or call ⤳ 7 cottages ⦿ Breakfast.$

SPORTS AND THE OUTDOORS
HIKING
Fodor's Choice
★
Bumpass Hell Trail. Boiling springs, steam vents, and mud pots are the highlights of this 3-mile round-trip hike. Expect the loop to take about two hours. During the first mile there's a gradual climb of 500 feet before a steep 300-foot descent to the basin. You'll encounter rocky patches, so wear hiking boots. Stay on trails and boardwalks near the thermal areas, as what appears to be firm ground may be only a thin crust over scalding mud. *Moderate.* ⊠ *Lassen Volcanic National Park ✛ Trailhead: at end of paved parking area off Lassen Park Hwy., 6 miles from southwest entrance ranger station.*

Fodor's Choice
★
Lassen Peak Hike. This trail winds 2½ miles to the mountaintop. It's a tough climb—2,000 feet uphill on a steady, steep grade—but the reward is a spectacular view. At the peak you can see into the rim and view the entire park (and much of California's far north). Bring sunscreen, water, snacks, a first-aid kit, and, because it can be windy and cold at the summit, a jacket. ⊠ *Lassen Volcanic National Park ✛ Trailhead: at parking area off Lassen Park Hwy., 7 miles north of southwest entrance ranger station* ☎ *530/595–4480.*

CHESTER

71 miles east of Red Bluff.

The population of this small town on Lake Almanor swells from 2,500 to nearly 5,000 in summer as tourists come to visit. Chester serves as a gateway to Lassen Volcanic National Park.

GETTING HERE AND AROUND
Chester is on Highway 36E, the main route from Red Bluff. When snow doesn't close Highway 89 in Lassen Park, visitors can take Highway 44 from Redding to Highway 89 through the park and to Highway 36E and onto Chester and Lake Almanor. Plumas County Transit provides local bus service.

ESSENTIALS
Bus Information Plumas County Transit. ☎ *530/283–2538* ⊕ *www.plumastransit.com.*

Visitor Information Lake Almanor Area Chamber of Commerce and Visitors Bureau. ⊠ *328 #6 Main St., near Reynolds Rd.* ☎ *530/258–2426* ⊕ *www.lakealmanorarea.com.*

14

EXPLORING

Lake Almanor. This lake's 52 miles of forested shoreline are popular with campers, swimmers, waterskiers, and anglers. At an elevation of 4,500 feet, the lake warms to above 70°F for about eight weeks in summer. ⊠ *Off Hwys. 89 and 36* ☎ *530/258–2426* ⊕ *www.lakealmanorarea.com.*

WHERE TO EAT AND STAY

$
AMERICAN
Fodor'sChoice
★
✕ **Cravings Cafe Espresso Bar & Bakery.** This breakfast and lunch place with vegetarian-friendly options not only satisfies diners' cravings, but with dishes like homemade slow-cooked corned-beef hash topped with two eggs and accompanied by a slice of sourdough bread it also creates them. You can get breakfast and excellent pastries all day, with soups, salads, sandwiches, and burgers on the menu for lunch. **Known for:** breakfast all day; corn-beef hash; excellent pastries. ⑤ *Average main: $10* ⊠ *278 Main St.* ☎ *530/258–2229* ⊘ *Closed Tues. and Wed.*

$$
HOTEL
🏨 **Best Western Rose Quartz Inn.** Down the road from Lake Almanor and close to Lassen Volcanic National Park, this small-town chain property is basically a motel, but the helpful staff (especially with touring plans) and amenities like good Wi-Fi and spacious breakfast area make it a good choice for a short stay. **Pros:** within easy walking distance of town's restaurants; convenient to Lassen Volcanic National Park; good Wi-Fi and other amenities. **Cons:** a little pricey; cookie-cutter decor; noise audible between rooms. ⑤ *Rooms from: $149* ⊠ *306 Main St.* ☎ *530/258–2002* ⊕ *www.bestwestern.com* ⤴ *50 rooms* ⦿ *Breakfast.*

$$
B&B/INN
Fodor'sChoice
★
🏨 **Bidwell House.** Some guest rooms at this 1901 ranch house have wood-burning stoves, claw-foot tubs, and antique furnishings; a separate cottage with a kitchen sleeps six. **Pros:** unique decor in each room; beautiful wooded setting; near Lake Almanor. **Cons:** not ideal for kids; may be too remote for some guests; lacks some big-hotel amenities. ⑤ *Rooms from: $125* ⊠ *1 Main St.* ☎ *530/258–3338* ⊕ *www.bidwellhouse.com* ⤴ *14 rooms* ⦿ *Breakfast.*

TRAVEL SMART
NORTHERN
CALIFORNIA

GETTING HERE AND AROUND

▮ AIR TRAVEL

Flying time to California is about 6½ hours from New York and 4¾ hours from Chicago. Travel from London to either Los Angeles or San Francisco is 11 hours and from Sydney approximately 15. Flying between San Francisco and Los Angeles takes about 90 minutes.

AIRPORTS

Northern California Sacramento International Airport. ☎ *916/929-5411* ⊕ *www.sacramento.aero/smf.* **San Francisco International Airport.** ☎ *650/821-8211, 800/435-9736* ⊕ *www.flysfo.com.* **San Jose International Airport.** ☎ *408/392-3600* ⊕ *www.flysanjose.com.*

FROM SAN FRANCISCO TO:	BY AIR	BY CAR
San Jose	No flights	1 hr
Monterey	45 mins	2 hrs
Los Angeles	1 hr 30 mins	5 hrs 40 mins
Portland, OR	1 hr 50 mins	10 hrs
Mendocino	No flights	3 hrs
Yosemite NP/ Fresno	1 hr	4 hrs
Lake Tahoe/ Reno	1 hr	3 hrs 30 mins

▮ BUS TRAVEL

Greyhound is the major bus carrier in California. Regional bus service is available in metropolitan areas.

Bus Information Greyhound. ☎ *800/231-2222* ⊕ *www.greyhound.com.*

▮ CAR TRAVEL

Two main north–south routes run through California: Interstate 5 through the middle of the state, and U.S. 101, a parallel route closer to the coast. Slower but more scenic is Highway 1, which winds along much of the coast.

From north to south, the state's main east–west routes are Interstate 80, Interstate 15, Interstate 10, and Interstate 8. Much of California is mountainous, and you may encounter winding roads and steep mountain grades.

FROM SAN FRANCISCO TO:	ROUTE	DISTANCE
San Jose	U.S. 101	50 miles
Monterey	U.S. 101 to Hwy. 156 to Hwy. 1	120 miles
Los Angeles	U.S. 101 to Hwy. 156 to I-5	382 miles
Portland, OR	I-80 to I-505 to I-5	635 miles
Mendocino	Hwy. 1	174 miles
Yosemite NP	I-80 to I-580 to I-205 to Hwy. 120 east	184 miles
Lake Tahoe/ Reno	I-80	220 miles

GASOLINE

Gas stations are plentiful throughout the state. Many stay open late, except in rural areas, where Sunday hours are limited and where you may drive long stretches without a chance to refuel.

ROAD CONDITIONS

Rainy weather can make driving along the coast or in the mountains treacherous. Some smaller routes over mountain ranges and in the deserts are prone to flash flooding. When the weather is particularly bad, Highway 1 may be closed due to mud and rock slides.

Many smaller roads over the Sierra Nevada are closed in winter, and if it's snowing, tire chains may be required on routes that are open. ▮TIP→ It's less expensive to purchase chains before you get to the mountains. Chains or cables generally cost $30–$75, depending on tire size; cables are easier to attach than chains, but chains are more durable. Most rental-car companies prohibit chain installation on their vehicles. If you choose to disregard this rule, your insurance likely will not cover any chains-related damage.

In Northern California uniformed chain installers on Interstate 80 and U.S. 50 will apply chains for about $30 and take them off for half that. Chain installers are independent businesspeople, not highway employees. They are not allowed to sell or rent chains. On smaller roads, you're on your own.

Always carry extra clothing, blankets, water, and food when driving to the mountains in the winter, and keep your gas tank full to prevent the fuel line from freezing.

Road Conditions Caltrans Current Highway Conditions. ☎ 800/427-7623 ⊕ www.dot. ca.gov.

Weather Conditions National Weather Service. ☎ 707/443-6484 northernmost California, 831/656-1710 San Francisco Bay area and central California, 775/673-8100 Reno, Lake Tahoe, and northern Sierra, 805/988-6615 Los Angeles area, 858/675-8700 San Diego area, 916/979-3041 Sacramento area ⊕ www.weather.gov.

ROADSIDE EMERGENCIES
Dial 911 to report accidents and to reach the police, the California Highway Patrol (CHP), or the fire department. On some rural highways and on most interstates, look for emergency phones on the side of the road.

RULES OF THE ROAD
All passengers must wear a seat belt at all times. A child must be secured in a federally approved child passenger restraint system and ride in the back seat until at least eight years of age or until the child is at least 4 feet 9 inches tall. Children

who are eight but don't meet the height requirement must ride in a booster seat or a car seat. It is illegal to leave a child six years of age or younger unattended in a motor vehicle. Unless indicated, right turns are allowed at red lights after you've come to a full stop. Left turns between two one-way streets are allowed at red lights after you've come to a full stop. Drivers with a blood-alcohol level higher than 0.08 who are stopped by police are subject to arrest.

The speed limit on some interstate highways is 70 mph; unlimited-access roads are usually 55 mph. In cities, freeway speed limits are between 55 mph and 65 mph. Many city routes have commuter lanes during rush hour.

You must turn on your headlights whenever weather conditions require the use of windshield wipers. Texting on a wireless device is illegal for all drivers. If using a mobile phone while driving it must be hands-free and mounted (i.e., it's not legal having it loose on the seat or your lap). For more driving rules, refer to the Department of Motor Vehicles driver's handbook at ⊕ www.dmv.ca.gov.

CAR RENTAL
When you reserve a car, ask about cancellation penalties, taxes, drop-off charges (if you're planning to pick up the car in one city and leave it in another), and surcharges (for being under or over a certain age, for additional drivers, or for driving across state or country borders or beyond a specific distance from your point of rental). All these things can add substantially to your costs. Request car seats and extras such as GPS when you book.

Rates are sometimes—but not always—better if you book in advance or reserve through a rental agency's website. There are other reasons to book ahead, though: for popular destinations, during busy times of the year, or to ensure that you get certain types of cars (vans, SUVs, exotic sports cars).

■TIP➜ Make sure that a confirmed reservation guarantees you a car. Agencies sometimes overbook, particularly for busy weekends and holiday periods.

A car is essential in most parts of California. In compact San Francisco it's better to use public transportation, taxis, or ride-sharing services to avoid parking headaches.

Rates statewide for the least expensive vehicle begin as low as $30 a day, usually on weekends, and less than $200 a week. This does not include additional fees or the tax on car rentals (8%–10%). Be sure to shop around—you can get a decent deal by shopping the major car-rental companies' websites. A few companies rent specialty cars such as convertibles or sport-utility vehicles.

In California you must have a valid driver's license and be 21 to rent a car; rates may be higher if you're under 25. Some agencies will not rent to those under 25; check when you book. Non-U.S. residents must have a license, valid for the entire rental period, with text in the Roman alphabet that clearly identifies it as a driver's license. In addition, most companies also require an international license; check in advance.

Specialty Car Agencies Beverly Hills Rent a Car. ☎ *310/923–7833* ⊕ *www.bhrenta-car.com.* **Enterprise Exotic Car Rentals.** ☎ *866/458–9227* ⊕ *exoticcars.enterprise.com.* **MCar** (*Midway Car Rental*). ☎ *866/717–6802* ⊕ *www.midwaycarrental.com.*

▌ TRAIN TRAVEL

Amtrak provides rail service within California. On some trips—to Yosemite National Park, for example—passengers board motor coaches part of the way. The rail service's scenic *Coast Starlight* trip begins in Los Angeles and hugs the Pacific Coast to San Luis Obispo before it turns inland for the rest of its journey to Portland and Seattle.

Information Amtrak. ☎ *800/872–7245* ⊕ *www.amtrak.com.*

ESSENTIALS

ACCOMMODATIONS

The lodgings we review are the top choices in each price category. *For an expanded review of each property, please see www. fodors.com.* We don't specify whether the facilities cost extra; when pricing accommodations, ask what's included and what costs extra. *For price information, see the planner in each chapter.*

Be sure you understand the hotel's cancellation policy. Some places allow you to cancel without any kind of penalty—even if you prepaid to secure a discounted rate—if you cancel at least 24 hours in advance. Others require you to cancel a week in advance or penalize you the cost of one night. Small inns and B&Bs are most likely to require you to cancel far in advance. Most hotels allow children under a certain age to stay in their parents' room at no extra charge, but others charge for them as extra adults; find out the cutoff age for discounts.

BED-AND-BREAKFASTS

California has more than 1,000 bed-and-breakfasts. You'll find everything from simple homestays to lavish luxury lodgings, many in historic hotels and homes. The California Association of Boutique and Breakfast Inns has about 300 member properties that you can locate and book through its website.

Reservation Services **California Association of Boutique and Breakfast Inns.** ☎ *800/373–9251* ⊕ *www.cabbi.com.*

COMMUNICATIONS

INTERNET

Internet access is widely available in urban areas, but it can be difficult to get online in rural communities. Most hotels offer some kind of connection—usually broadband or Wi-Fi. Many hotels charge a daily fee ($10–$15) for Internet access. Cafés with free Wi-Fi are common throughout California.

EATING OUT

California has led the pack in bringing natural and organic foods to the forefront of American dining. Though rooted in European cuisine, California cooking sometimes has strong Asian and Latin influences. Wherever you go, you're likely to find that dishes are made with fresh produce and other local ingredients.

The restaurants we list are the cream of the crop in each price category. *For price information, see the planner in each chapter.*

CUTTING COSTS

The better grocery and specialty-food stores have grab-and-go sections, with prepared foods on a par with restaurant cooking, perfect for picnicking (remember, it infrequently rains between May and October). At resort areas in the off-season you can often find two-for-one dinner specials at upper-end restaurants; check coupon apps or local papers or with visitor bureaus.

RESERVATIONS AND DRESS

Regardless of where you are, it's a good idea to make a reservation if you can. For popular restaurants, book as far ahead as you can (often 30 days), and reconfirm as soon as you arrive in California. (Large parties should always call ahead to check the reservations policy.)

Online reservation services make it easy to book a table. OpenTable covers many California cities.

Contacts **OpenTable.** ⊕ *www.opentable.com.*

HEALTH

Smoking is illegal in all California bars and restaurants, including on outdoor dining patios in some cities. If you have an existing medical condition that may require emergency treatment, be aware that many rural and mountain communities have only daytime clinics, not hospitals with 24-hour emergency rooms.

Outdoor sports are a huge draw in California's moderate climate, but caution, especially in unfamiliar areas, is key. Drownings occur each year because beach lovers don't heed warnings about high surfs with their deadly rogue waves. Do not fly within 24 hours of scuba diving.

If you're spending time in the national parks or forests, be sure to follow posted instructions that outline how to avoid encounters with bears (e.g., store your food in bear lockers) and how to prevent exposure to hantavirus, carried in deer mouse droppings in remote areas.

▌ HOURS OF OPERATION

Banks in California are typically open weekdays 9–6; most are open on Saturday but close on Sunday and most holidays. Smaller shops usually operate 10 or 11–6, with larger stores remaining open until 8 or later. Hours vary for museums, historical sites, and state parks, and many are closed one or more days a week, or for extended periods during off-season months.

▌ MONEY

San Francisco is an expensive city to visit, and rates at coastal resorts are also high. Hotel rates average $150 to $250 a night (though you can find cheaper places), and dinners at even moderately priced restaurants often cost $20 to $40 per person. Costs in the Gold Country and the Far North are considerably less—many fine Gold Country bed-and-breakfasts charge around $125 a night, and some motels in the Far North charge less than $100.

CREDIT CARDS

It's a good idea to inform your credit-card company before you travel. Otherwise, unusual activity might prompt the company to put a hold on your card. Record all your credit-card numbers—as well as the phone numbers to call if your cards are lost or stolen—so you're prepared should something go wrong.

▌ SAFETY

California is a safe place to visit, as long as you take the usual precautions. In large cities ask the concierge or desk clerk to point out areas on your map that you should avoid. Lock valuables in a hotel safe when you're not using them. Keep an eye on your handbag when you're out in public. Security is high (but mostly invisible) at theme parks and resorts.

When hiking, stay on trails—rangers say that the majority of hikers needing to be rescued have gone off trail—and heed signs at trailheads about dangerous situations such as cliffs with loose rocks and how to react if you encounter predatory animals that live in the area. Bring plenty of water, hike with a companion if possible, and learn to identify and avoid contact with poison oak, a ubiquitous plant in California that causes a severe rash.

▌ TAXES

Sales tax in the state of California is 7.25%, but local taxes vary and may be as much as an additional 2.5%. Sales tax applies to all purchases except for food bought in a grocery store; food consumed in a restaurant is taxed, but takeout food is not. Hotel taxes vary widely by region, from about 8% to 16.5%.

▌ TIME

California is in the Pacific time zone. Pacific daylight time (PDT) is in effect from mid-March through early November; the rest of the year the clock is set to Pacific standard time (PST).

TIPPING

TIPPING GUIDELINES FOR CALIFORNIA	
Bartender	$1–$3 per drink, or 15%–20% per round
Bellhop	$2–$3 per bag, depending on the level of the hotel
Hotel Concierge	$5–$10 for advice and reservations, more for difficult tasks
Hotel Doorman	$2–$3 for hailing a cab
Valet Parking Attendant	$3–$5 when you get your car
Hotel Maid	$3–$5 per day; more in high-end hotels
Waiter	18%–22% (20%–25% is standard in upscale restaurants); nothing additional if a service charge is added to the bill
Skycap at Airport	$1–$2 per bag
Hotel Room-Service Waiter	15%–20% per delivery, even if a service charge was added since that fee goes to the hotel, not the waiter
Taxi Driver	15%–20%, but round up the fare to the next dollar amount
Tour Guide	15% of the cost of the tour, more depending on quality

TOURS

Guided tours are a good option when you don't want to do it all yourself. You travel along with a group (sometimes large, sometimes small), stay in prebooked hotels, eat with your fellow travelers (the cost of meals is sometimes included in the price of your tour, sometimes not), and follow a schedule.

But not all guided tours are an if-it's-Tuesday-this-must-be-Yosemite experience. A knowledgeable guide can take you places that you might never discover on your own, and you may be pushed to see more than you would have otherwise. Tours aren't for

everyone, but they can be just the thing for trips to places where making travel arrangements is difficult or time-consuming.

Whenever you book a guided tour, find out what's included and what isn't. A "land-only" tour includes all your travel (by bus, in most cases) in the destination, but not necessarily your flights to and from or even within it. Also, in most cases prices in tour brochures don't include fees and taxes. And remember that you'll be expected to tip your guide (in cash) at the end of the tour.

GENERAL TOURS

Trafalgar. A dependable tour operator whose guides know California well, Trafalgar conducts nearly a dozen excursions around the state. One takes in San Francisco, Monterey, Big Sur, Yosemite, and Lake Tahoe, and another surveys the Northern California Wine Country. ☎ 866/513–1995 ⊕ www.trafalgar.com/usa ⊠ From $1695.

SPECIAL-INTEREST TOURS
BIKING

Biking is a popular way to see the California countryside, and commercial tours are available throughout the state. Most three- to five-day trips are all-inclusive—you'll stay in delightful country inns, dine at good regional restaurants, and follow experienced guides. When booking, ask about level of difficulty, as nearly every trip will involve some hill work. Tours fill up early, so book well in advance. ■ TIP→ **Most airlines accommodate bikes as luggage, provided they're dismantled and boxed.**

The Northern California Wine Country, with its flat valley roads, is one of the most popular destinations.

Napa and Sonoma Valley Bike Tours. Single-day bike tours through beautiful Napa and Sonoma Wine Country offer a casual pace and frequent winery stops. ⊠ 6500 Washington St., Yountville ☎ 707/251–8687 Napa tours, 707/996–2453 Sonoma tours ⊕ www.napavalleybiketours.com ⊠ From $108.

MULTISPORT TOURS

Backroads. Based in Northern California, Backroads arranges guided tours that may include biking, hiking, or gentler walking, camping, or all of these. Tours might take in the state's national parks, beaches, and forests, or wine-growing regions, with overnight stays in accommodations that range from campgrounds to deluxe small inns. ☎ *800/462–2848, 510/527–1555* ⊕ *www.backroads.com* ✉ *From $1998.*

▌VISITOR INFORMATION

The California Travel and Tourism Commission's website takes you to each region of California, with digital visitor guides in multiple languages, driving tours, maps, welcome center locations, information on local tours, links to bed-and-breakfasts, and a complete booking center. It also links you—via the Destinations menu—to the websites of city and regional tourism offices and attractions. *For the numbers and websites of regional and city visitor bureaus and chambers of commerce, see the Planning section in each chapter.*

Contacts California Travel and Tourism Commission. ☎ *800/462–2543* ⊕ *www.visitcalifornia.com.*

INDEX

PHOTO CREDITS

Front cover: Josh Miller Photography /Aurora Photos/Offset [Description: Half Dome and Merced River, Yosemite National Park, California]. 1, Yuen Kwan, Fodors.com member. 2, Gordon Swanson/ Shutterstock. **Chapter 1: Experience Northern California:** 8-9, Jay Anderson, Fodors.com member. 18 (left), Aaron Kohr/iStockphoto. 18 (top right), Corbis. 18 (bottom right), Warren H. White. 19 (top left), Alan A. Tobey/iStockphoto. 19 (bottom left), Gary C. Tognoni / Shutterstock. 19 (right), Lorcel / Shutterstock. **Chapter 2: Northern California's Best Road Trips:** 21, Paul Giamou/iStockphoto. **Chapter 3: The Monterey Bay Area:** 33, mellifluous, Fodors.com member. 35, vittorio sciosia/ age fotostock. 36, Brent Reeves/Shutterstock. 43, Nadezhdasarkisian | Dreamstime.com. 51, Holger Mette/iStockphoto. 58, Wolterk | Dreamstime.com. **Chapter 4: San Francisco:** 79, Prisma Bildagentur AG / Alamy. 82, Robert Schlie / Shutterstock. 88, San Francisco Travel Association/Scott Chernis. 93, Charlie Manz/Artistic Visuals Photography. 94 (top), Arnold Genthe. 94 (bottom), Library of Congress Prints and Photographs Division. 95 (left), Sandor Balatoni/SFCVB. 95 (right), Library of Congress. 96, Brett Shoaf/Artistic Visuals Photography. 103, travelstock44/Alamy. 105, Brett Shoaf/ Artistic Visuals Photography. 106, San Francisco Municipal Railway Historical Archives. 111, Andresr | Dreamstime.com. 119, Robert Holmes. 125, aprillilacs, Fodors.com member. 129, Rafael Ramirez Lee/iStockphoto. 134, San Francisco Travel Association/Scott Chernis. 135 (top), Walleyelj | Dreamstime.com. 135 (bottom), T photography / Shutterstock. **Chapter 5: The Bay Area:** 159, Gary Crabbe / Alamy. 161, Jyeshern Cheng/iStockphoto. 162, Brett Shoaf/Artistic Visuals Photography. 168, California Travel and Tourism Commission / Bongo. 170, Nancy Hoyt Belcher / Alamy. 189, Robert Holmes. 195, S. Greg Panosian/iStockphoto. **Chapter 6: Napa and Sonoma:** 199, Andrew Zarivny / Shutterstock. 202, Warren H. White. 208, Robert Holmes. 209 (top), kevin miller/iStockphoto. 209 (bottom), Far Niente+Dolce+Nickel & Nickel. 210 (top and bottom) Robert Holmes. 211 (top) Domaine Carneros. 211 (bottom), star5112/Flickr. 212 (top left), Rubicon Estate. 212 (top right and bottom), and 213 (top and bottom), Robert Holmes. 214 (top), Philippe Roy/Alamy. 214 (center), Agence Images/Alamy. 214 (bottom), Cephas Picture Library/Alamy. 215 (top), Napa Valley Conference Bureau. 215 (second and third from top), Wild Horse Winery (Forrest L. Doud). 215 (fourth from top), Napa Valley Conference Bureau. 215 (fifth from top), Panther Creek Cellars (Ron Kaplan). 215 (sixth from top), Clos du Val (Marvin Collins). 215 (seventh from top), Panther Creek Cellars (Ron Kaplan). 215 (bottom), Warren H. White. 216, courtesy of the di Rosa Collection. 227, Terry Joanis/Frog's Leap. 234, Castello di Amorosa. 244, Robert Holmes. **Chapter 7: The North Coast:** 247, Thomas Barrat/Shutterstock. 249 (top), Russ Bishop/age fotostock. 249 (bottom), Robert Holmes. 250, Janet Fullwood. 256, 262, and 265, Robert Holmes. **Chapter 8: Redwood National Park:** 273, iStockphoto. 274, Michael Schweppe/wikipedia.org. 276, WellyWelly/Shutterstock. **Chapter 9: Eastern Sierra:** 283, Clicktrick | Dreamstime.com. 285, David T Gomez/iStockphoto. 286, christinea78, Fodors.com member. 294, moonjazz/Flickr. 305, Douglas Atmore/iStockphoto. **Chapter 10: Yosemite National Park:** 307, Sarah P. Corley, Fodors.com member. 308, Greg Epperson/age fotostock. 309, Andy Z./Shutterstock. 310, Doug Lemke/Shutterstock. 318, Jane Rix / Shutterstock. 323, Nathan Jaskowiak/Shutterstock. **Chapter 11: Sequoia and Kings Canyon National Parks:** 335, Robert Holmes. 337, Greg Epperson/age fotostock. 338, Robert Holmes. 349, urosr/Shutterstock. **Chapter 12: Sacramento and the Gold Country:** 363 and 365 (top and bottom), Robert Holmes. 366, Andy Z./Shutterstock. 385, Ambient Images Inc./Alamy. 394, RickC/Flickr. **Chapter 13: Lake Tahoe:** 397, Tom Zikas/North Lake Tahoe. 398, Rafael Ramirez Lee/iStockphoto. 399, Janet Fullwood. 400, Jay Spooner/iStockphoto. 413, Mblach | Dreamstime.com. 419, Hank de Vre/Squaw Valley Alpine Meadows. 430, Christopher Russell/iStockphoto. **Chapter 14: The Far North:** 437, NPS. 439 (top), Andy Z./Shutterstock. 439 (bottom), NPS. 440, ThreadedThoughts/Flickr. 455, kathycsus/Flickr. **Back cover, from left to right:** Celso Diniz/Shutterstock; Dan Harmeson/iStockphoto; Mblach | Dreamstime. com. **Spine:** S. Greg Panosian/iStockphoto. **About Our Writers:** All photos are courtesy of the writers except for the following: Cheryl Crabtree, courtesy of Bryn Berg; Denise Leto, courtesy of Kevin Finney; Daniel Mangin, courtesy of J. Rodby; Christine Vovakes, courtesy of Michael Vovakes.

ABOUT OUR WRITERS

Native Californian **Cheryl Crabtree** has worked as a freelance writer since 1987 and regularly travels up, down, and around California for work and fun. She has contributed to *Fodor's California* since 2003 and also contributes to the *Fodor's National Parks of the West* guide. Cheryl is editor of *Montecito Magazine* and co-authors *The California Directory of Fine Wineries* book series, Central Coast and Napa, Sonoma, Mendocino editions. Her articles have appeared in many regional and national magazines. Cheryl updated the Monterey Bay Area, Eastern Sierra, Yosemite National Park, and Sequoia & Kings Canyon National Park chapters this edition.

Daniel Mangin returned to California, where he's maintained a home for three decades, after two stints at the Fodor's editorial offices in New York City, the second one as the editorial director of Fodors.com and the Compass American Guides. With several-dozen wineries less than a half-hour's drive from home, he often finds himself transported as if by magic to a tasting room bar, communing with a sophisticated Cabernet or savoring the finish of a smooth Pinot Noir. For this edition, Daniel, the writer of *Fodor's Napa & Sonoma,* updated the Napa and Sonoma, North Coast, Redwood National Park, Far North, Lake Tahoe, and Travel Smart chapters.

Steve Pastorino has visited nearly a dozen national parks on behalf of Fodor's and has favorite spots in all of them. In the summer, the longtime sports marketer and his family of five are often found at baseball diamonds. He updated the Sacramento and the Gold Country chapter.

A veteran traveler, **Claire Deeks van der Lee** feels lucky to call San Diego home. Claire loves road-tripping around her adopted state of California, so it was a perfect fit for her to work on the Experience and Northern California's Best Road Trips chapters of this book. Claire has traveled to more than 40 countries, and has contributed to *Everywhere* magazine and several Fodor's guides.

Updating our San Francisco chapter was a team of writers from Fodor's San Francisco: **Amanda Kuehn Carroll, Denise M. Leto, Daniel Mangin, Andrea Powell, Rebecca Flint Marx,** and **Jerry James Stone.**